# William Blake

S Foster Damon

# William Blake

## ESSAYS FOR S. FOSTER DAMON

*Edited by Alvin H. Rosenfeld*

BROWN UNIVERSITY PRESS

*Providence · 1969*

"S. FOSTER DAMON: THE NEW ENGLAND VOICE"
BY MALCOLM COWLEY
IS REPRINTED BY PERMISSION OF THE AUTHOR
(COPYRIGHT © 1968 BY MALCOLM COWLEY).
A SLIGHTLY SHORTER VERSION APPEARED IN
*THE SOUTHERN REVIEW*
(NEW SERIES, VOL. IV, NO. 1 [JANUARY 1968]).

"THE VISIONARY CINEMA OF ROMANTIC POETRY"
BY HAROLD BLOOM
WHICH APPEARED IN SUBSTANTIALLY THE SAME FORM IN
*PARTISAN REVIEW* (VOL. XXXV, NO. 4 [FALL 1968]),
IS ALSO REPRINTED BY PERMISSION OF THE AUTHOR
(COPYRIGHT © 1968 BY HAROLD BLOOM).

PRINTED IN THE UNITED STATES OF AMERICA
TEXT BY THE CRIMSON PRINTING COMPANY
ON WARREN'S UNIVERSITY TEXT
PLATES BY THE MERIDEN GRAVURE COMPANY ON SN TEXT
BOUND BY THE STANHOPE BINDERY
DESIGNED BY RICHARD HENDEL

# Contents

# CONTENTS

# Illustrations

ILLUSTRATIONS

# ILLUSTRATIONS

# Preface

In a letter to me, Malcolm Cowley, a long-time friend of S. Foster Damon, referred to what he called Damon's "genius for concealing his genius from the public." The phrase seemed exactly right at the time and still does. For while it is true that Professor Damon's work on Blake has not gone unnoticed or unappreciated—indeed, he has been called "the father of modern Blake studies"—it is also true that he has neither sought nor gained a wide popularity.

S. Foster Damon's accomplishments over the years have been great, but he has worked quietly and never called attention to himself. His merits as a literary person are rare and will seldom be equaled, but through his own choosing he has not become one of our literary personalities and has never opted for his share of literary fame. Many who have and who have won it owe a debt to S. Foster Damon. A few have acknowledged this debt, but for the most part he remains a man still too little known.

This volume, offered to S. Foster Damon for his seventy-fifth birthday, publicly honors a man many of us have honored only privately until now. The twenty-two essays on Blake collected here have been written for the occasion by former students, friends, colleagues, and admirers from all over the world, and stand as both testimony and tribute to the influence he has had on so many of us. In "S. Foster Damon: The New England Voice" Mr. Cowley expands on the extent of this influence, revealing something of Damon's genius to the larger audience it deserves.

The rationale behind making this chiefly a Blake book is not difficult to explain. With the publication of his pioneering *William Blake, His Philosophy and Symbols* in 1924, Professor Damon took his place in the forefront of American literary scholars and established his reputation as one of the world's leading Blakists. His book is one of those that have stayed relevant for a long time, and it is still capable of teaching us a good deal about the poetry and thought of

William Blake. In addition, there have been important articles on Blake, and more recently, three additional books—*Blake's Grave* (1963), the monumental *A Blake Dictionary* (1965), and *Blake's "Job"* (1966)—testify to Professor Damon's continuing interest in Blake and the remarkable vigor and imagination that he displays in dealing with some of Blake's most difficult works. The signs are that S. Foster Damon has not yet completed his life's work on Blake.

At this point it is fitting to note that he has been writing about a good deal more than Blake all along, as a glance at the bibliography that precedes the text will show. Although Professor Damon's most illustrious work has been done on Blake, his range has been enormous. Joyce and Melville, Marie de France and Amy Lowell, Thomas Holley Chivers, Punch and Judy, the history of square dancing, and "Yankee Doodle"—Damon has written definitively on all of these. There have been articles on alchemy and the occult, on genealogy and gastronomy, on Schönberg and Stravinsky, on Scandinavian and Japanese literature, on popular music, Santa Claus, and the detective story. The author of major books on William Blake is also the author of an introduction to the *Annisquam Village Cook Book*, a Japanese Noh drama (*Kiri no Meijiyama*), and a children's Christmas book (*The Day after Christmas*).

Prolific and eminent as Professor Damon has been as a scholar, he has also written in a wide range of creative genres. His love for literature has always been matched by his love for music, and he has written dozens of musical compositions over the years. He has also written interestingly both as poet and as playwright. His *Witch of Dogtown* won a Russel Crouse award for drama in 1955, and his poetry has been published in numerous periodicals and collected in four volumes—all, unfortunately, hard to come by. *The Moulton Tragedy*, a long epic poem that he calls his "Yankee Faust," has been brewing over the last forty years and was finally completed in the summer of 1967.

Countless students at Harvard and Brown have found him a superb teacher. He has won the admiration and loyalty of hundreds, among them many who have gone on to win distinction as teachers and writers. Over the years Professor Damon has also been acknowledged as a musicologist, music collector, bibliophile, librarian, and book-collector. For some forty years he guided and helped build the Harris Collection of American Poetry and Plays at Brown University. The collection is recognized today as the best of its kind in the world.

This volume of essays on Blake celebrates that area of S. Foster Damon's work that rightfully has been the most acclaimed. This is as it should be, but it should not be forgotten that he is one of America's accomplished men of letters and, always and to all who have known him, a ready and generous friend.

A. H. R.

*Indiana University*

# S. Foster Damon:
# The New England Voice

At the end of a letter written the day after Thanksgiving, 1966, I asked Foster Damon a question. "Did you introduce me to Laforgue," I said, "or was I already Laforguing when I used to come out to Newton and drink tea in your room, in the spring of 1918? I remember your copy of *Tender Buttons*, but there is so much I forget." Foster waited a month, then answered frugally on a New Year's card. "Mal—" he said, using a nickname that everyone else has forgotten. "Yes, I remember showing you the poems of Jules Laforgue. We went over them together. Happy New Year to you both!"

So Laforgue was one more of my debts to Foster.

Since then I have been trying to make a list of the others. They include the early works of Ezra Pound, especially *Ripostes*, the poems of Stephen Crane, and the prose of Herman Melville, who as late as 1918 was an unknown writer in this country; I don't know where Foster had found his copy of *Moby Dick*. He was a specialist in hard-to-find books by forgotten authors. Blake, of course, was not forgotten; almost everyone had read *Songs of Innocence* and *Songs of Experience;* but Foster introduced me to the poems in the Rossetti and Pickering Manuscripts and to *The Marriage of Heaven and Hell.* He couldn't persuade me to follow him into the later Prophetic Books, and there were other gifts he offered that I was unwilling to accept: Gertrude Stein and Thomas Holley Chivers, for example, whom I always placed in the same category of might-be-interesting-to-others. His gift to me of Amy Lowell was not of her poems, on which I reserved judgment, but of her vivid and overwhelming personality; it was Foster who had her invite me to Sevenels, her big house in Brookline. I forget how many times we went there together to read our poems aloud and then to be praised and scolded by Miss Lowell as we puffed away at her Manila cigars.

Many others have owed the same sort of debts to Foster, who was "inveterately an opener of doors," as the composer Virgil Thomson remarks in his autobiography. The remark comes after some memories that greatly resemble my own. Thomson says:

I came to know S. Foster Damon, slender, pale poet with a blond mustache, at that time [1921] instructing in English A while preparing privately, since Harvard would have none of it, the book that was to open up the language of William Blake. Foster was a composer as well as a poet and a scholar—also a close associate of Amy Lowell, whose biographer he became in the 1930s. I do not remember how I first knew him; but I do remember long walks and talks; and I remember his bringing me music and books that he thought I ought to know. Some of these, such as the critical writings of T. S. Eliot and the Irish tales of James Stephens, I found merely informative or charming. Others changed my life. Among these last were the piano works of Erik Satie, a pile of them four inches high, and a thin small volume called *Tender Buttons*, by Gertrude Stein. I returned these favors by introducing him to peyote, which we would take together, sometimes with another poet and English A instructor, Robert Hillyer. Foster has often re-appeared in my life and almost always with gifts in hand. . . .

Among those who have acknowledged the gifts was E. E. Cummings, a close friend of Foster's when both were undergraduates. We read in his *i: six nonlectures* that "S. Foster Damon . . . opened my eyes and ears not merely to Domenico Theotocopuli [El Greco] and William Blake, but to all ultra (at that moment) modern music and poetry and painting." Cummings told his biographer, Charles Norman, "Practically everything I know about painting and poetry came to me through Damon." I wonder how many other poets might have ground for making a similar acknowledgment. Also I wonder, after fifty years, how it was that Foster opened so many doors for others while inveterately standing in the shadows to let them pass.

Poets abounded at Harvard, and would-be poets, when I went there in the fall of 1915. Foster was the ancient among them, for he belonged to the class of '14 and was starting his second year as a graduate student. I saw him for the first time at a meeting of the Harvard Poetry Society, which had just been organized. The poets were seated round a huge table in the dimly lighted sanctum of *The Harvard Monthly*. Pale in the lamplight, with straight ryestraw-colored hair, Foster read some poems that were chaste in form, but rather less chaste in sentiment. The reading was almost apologetic, with a notable lack of drama. When Foster came to a line that was shocking, for those days, his flat New England Seaboard voice would become even flatter and more noncommittal. Still there were a few gasps of indignation. I don't remember whether I spoke to him after the meeting—that would have been a presumptuous act for a fresh-man—or whether we were introduced on some later occasion. But it seems to me, as I go poking among my memories, that more than once in the following year we went into Boston together to drink seidels of dark beer at Jake Wirth's German saloon. One of my literary friends warned me against Foster's pernicious influence.

It was in 1918 that I saw more of him than in any other year. In February I had come back to Harvard after six months as assistant driver of a munitions truck for the French army, and another month with my Pittsburgh friends who had moved on to Greenwich Village. Foster, after trying to enlist in the American army, was continuing his graduate studies. Many times he appeared at my door with a green baize bag full of books. He would open the bag, select a book, and read aloud a passage that had struck his fancy; then we would talk about the usually forgotten or disparaged author. Once he had me visit the big family house in Newton for the weekend, and once or twice he took me to the rooms above the Western Club where he lived with Philip Hillyer Smith, now my neighbor in Connecticut, and a crowd of noisy seniors. Smith tells me that he used to prowl up and down the study, smoking a long-stemmed German porcelain pipe, then dart to the table and write either a line of verse or a bar of music—or perhaps a sentence about Blake's Prophetic Books; one could never be sure which it would be.

At that time his poetry was better known than his scholarship, as a result of his appearance the previous year in *Eight Harvard Poets*, a volume that included the best of his early work along with that of Cummings, Dos Passos, and Robert Hillyer, among others. I don't know what he saw in an awkward and acne'd boy of nineteen with country manners; it must have been our interest in poetry that brought us together. We were both enlisted in another war that raged simultaneously with the war in Europe: this one between the Ancients and the Moderns in poetry. Of course we were on the Modern side, and I ridiculed the Ancients for believing—or so I said—that poetry should express the daydreams of twelve-year-old girls in words of one syllable. Foster attacked them for artlessness and timidity.

In April of that year I was, to my amazement, elected president of *The Harvard Advocate*. It was not a tribute to my brilliance, as I thought for a dizzy moment, but simply a recognition of the fact that most of my colleagues on the editorial board were about to go into the army. To keep the paper alive in their absence, I enlisted the help of such friends as Foster and John Brooks Wheelwright, that tall, quizzical, High Church Anglican poet, whose sister Louise was later to become Foster's wife. Also I struck a blow for the Moderns by inviting Amy Lowell to read her new poems at an *Advocate* smoker on May 2. In his biography of Miss Lowell, Foster quotes her as saying, "I was, as usual, smuggled into an upper chamber, and kept quiet with cigars"—which I had been careful to provide—"while they heckled me in true undergraduate fashion." Miss Lowell, wreathed in smoke, crushed the hecklers as if with bolts from a thundercloud. But she made no answer of record to Jack Wheelwright's quite earnest question: "What do you do when you want to write a poem and haven't anything to write about?"

In June, Foster and I took a walking trip that ended in a shack on a hilltop near the village of Candor, New York. A Greenwich Village friend had told me about the shack, for which we paid in advance a month's rent of three dollars. On our first evening there, over a supper of trout and wild strawberries (with bread and milk from a farm in the valley), we began talking about the *Spectra* hoax. It had lately been a front-page story in several newspapers: "Poet Unmasks Huge Joke on World of Art." The joke was a widely reviewed book called *Spectra* that presented the work of a new literary school purportedly founded by two Pittsburgh poets: Emanuel Morgan, just home from Paris, and a tempestuous Hungarian beauty, Anne Knish. In reality Morgan was Witter Bynner, who at last revealed the imposture, and Knish was his friend Arthur Davison Ficke, another lyric poet of moderate skill and immense conservatism. Foster and I agreed that the joke was not only a good one but also a victory for the Ancients. It was time, we told each other, for the Moderns to stage a counterattack. Why couldn't we hoax the hoaxers?

On the following day, June 15, we produced almost the entire *opus poeticum* of Earl Roppel, later to be known as the "the plowboy poet of Tioga County" and "the bard of the rushing Catatonk." We also composed a letter to Bynner that served to introduce the poems. We said in part, or had Earl Roppel say, "I got your book out of the free library at Owego and read it all through that night and I like it very much though I do not understand it all. It gives you such a picture of life. Now, Mr. Bynner, what I want to say is this: I write some and I feel I write different from most. . . . And now I am drafted and have to leave next week. This seems to cut off all that my life has been. Before I go I would like to have the opinion of someone I feel knows what poetry is on my poems which enclosed please find."

I had supplied the name Earl Roppel and most of his country background. In writing his poems we tried as a general rule to adumbrate the utterly inane, but our particular purpose was to burlesque what we thought was the mindlessness and false innocence of lyric poets like Bynner. We each wrote about half of the poems, by count, though I have to admit that Foster's were better than mine; he showed a gift for mischievous parody that he should have cultivated in his later career.[1] A good example of his work was the precious quatrain "Moon Light," to which he appended a note for Bynner: "This one I wrote after reading your book."

> Last night when I was in our surrey,
>   Driving home with my best girl,
> I saw the moon run down the fence-row
>   Like a fat squirrel.

Soon after the birth of our plowboy poet, Kenneth Burke arrived at the hilltop shack with a stubbornly chaste young woman from Ohio (later she went to Paris and became a successful photographer). We saw a sample of her handwriting and thought it had exactly the unformed, ingenuous look that Earl Roppel's might have had. After providing ourselves with a ruled school tablet, we persuaded her to copy out the poems and the letter to Bynner. Then, thinking that the joke was too good to drop after a week—and forgetting our primary purpose of striking a blow for the Moderns—we made a few changes in the letter and had her copy it for Amy Lowell (with an additional poem that Foster had written as a pastiche of Miss Lowell's style). Revised once again, the letter and the poems were also copied for my friend Conrad Aiken, but then we had to stop; the young woman from Ohio was complaining that she had no time to enjoy the countryside. I was enjoying it hugely; every morning I set out with a can of worms and every afternoon I came back with a string of trout. Foster would match them with a sonnet and a lard bucket half full of wild strawberries. In the evening we argued about God knows what, Kenneth and I laughing boisterously, Foster chuckling, while our amanuensis toiled away at the only table, under the only lamp.

A few days later we scattered from the shack on a hilltop: I was taking a summer course in Military Science (mostly sham battles and bayonet drill), Foster had an assignment from the Red Cross, and Kenneth was going to work in a shipyard. We left word with the postmaster in Candor that letters for Earl Roppel should be forwarded to Kenneth's address in Greenwich Village. The letters were slow in reaching us. First to arrive by that roundabout course was the one from Conrad Aiken; it expressed a measured appreciation of young Roppel's poetic gift and advised him to read Keats and Tennyson. Aiken also sent him an inscribed copy of Palgrave's *Golden Treasury*, which I have kept to this day. Amy Lowell was less restrained in her enthusiasm. She offered to submit some of Roppel's verse to *Poetry* and felt sure that it would be printed. "He has the modern spirit," she told Foster when he next came out to dinner at Sevenels. "I don't know where he got it, but he has it."

No letter arrived from Bynner, and for a long time we thought that our joke had missed its principal target. Two years later, however, I wrote a short article about the plowboy poet, and Bynner, when he read it, was sporting enough to tell me the whole story. He had been teaching at the University of California when he received Earl Roppel's little sheaf of verses. He had shown them to his colleagues in the English Department at Berkeley, who had agreed with him that even Robert Burns might have admired their simplicity and freshness.

Of course he had written to Roppel—more than once, as a matter of fact—and he had offered to help him publish a volume of poems, but the letters had been returned from an address in New York City (Kenneth had moved) with a note on the envelopes: "No such person." At Berkeley Professor Arthur Farwell of the Music Department had seized upon one of the poems (Foster's masterpiece of parody) and had set it to a stirring tune. It was sung before a huge audience in San Francisco by a chorus of three thousand trained voices. Professor Farwell told the newspapers that "Sunset" (as Foster had entitled it) was the best patriotic song-poem in America:

> Flag of our country, strong and true,
>  The sky is rosy with your bars;
> But as they fade it turns to blue
>  And radiant with your stars.

> And as I watch the setting sun,
>  I call to God apart,
> "Give me the soul of Washington,
>  And give me Lincoln's heart!"

Meanwhile Bynner had written a letter of inquiry to the public library at Owego, ten miles from Candor. The librarian answered that nobody named Earl Roppel had ever been there to borrow books. Bynner began to suspect that someone had duped him: "Could it be Edna Millay?" he asked his friends. Others in the Bay Area maintained their faith in the plowboy poet. In his amusing book *The Spectra Hoax*, William Jay Smith quotes from an article that appeared after the Armistice in the San Francisco *Bulletin*. The author was Zoë Burns, and she said: "Ever since I read the story and some of the work of Witter Bynner's lost poet, I've been wondering about the lad who had such a freshly interesting outlook on life from the narrow confines of a little New York hamlet and to whom the great dreams came thronging while he plowed the fields. . . . And I'm wondering if the war took that fresh fine almost-girlish sweetness out of him and made him bitter as it has so many of our youths." Foster and I had worked hard to parody that twelve-year-old-girlish tone. "Was the heart of him smitten by the thunder of war?" Miss Burns continued. "And the melody of his spirit silenced by its horrors? Was perchance his very life blown out like a candle in the blast?" Of course she was correct in her surmise that Earl Roppel had been a wartime casualty; he died because his only begetters had been separated by military service. Still, he had enjoyed his moment of glory, which might have been Foster's moment too, if he could have been there to accept the applause. In the next fifty years S. Foster Damon was to receive many honors—if not a tithe of those he rightly earned—but nothing he signed with his own name was ever to be sung by a chorus of three thousand trained voices.

Thinking back on Foster's bogus anthem and how it was glorified as the work of another poet, I felt that it might have served as a portent of his career. Always he has displayed (or concealed) a talent for being unrecognized and, in relation to the public taste, untimely. In that age of celebrities, the 1920's, he remained the obscure and usually unacknowledged background of celebrities. His first scholarly work, *William Blake, His Philosophy and Symbols*, was an illustration of that singular gift. It was written too soon and it opened too many doors, with the result that official Harvard showed no interest in it. Foster did not even submit it "in partial fulfillment," as the phrase used to run, "of the requirements for the degree of doctor of philosophy." After its publication in 1924, it was to inspire many doctoral dissertations. All the subsequent Blake scholars have made use of it; some have written successful books that depended on it; but meanwhile Foster's book, which had appeared in an edition of only a thousand copies, was to remain out of print for twenty years or more.

That early example of his talent for anonymity was to be followed by others. He next wrote what is still the only extended study of Thomas Holley Chivers (1809–58). The book appeared in 1930 and, so far as I remember, attracted no attention whatever. In that first year of the Depression, nobody was interested in the question whether Poe had copied Chivers in some of his poems—or had it been Chivers who copied Poe? The Depression continued year after year, always breeding new crises, and Foster continued to stand aloof from the issues it raised. His new undertaking was a biography of

Amy Lowell, an authoritative record of all the picturesque, pathetic, or illuminating episodes in her Napoleonic career. In 1935, when the book was published, the literary world had turned away from Miss Lowell and everything she stood for.

Foster's next published work was for once more timely; it was a facsimile collection, with editorial notes, of fifty American popular songs from the years before the Civil War. It appeared in 1936, at a moment when American history was becoming a popular subject even in Hollywood, and composers were to use Foster's book as a source of the background music for some highly successful motion pictures. But the book itself had a limited sale, and again Foster received little credit as a pioneer. He was busy for several years with other projects, though they did not lead to published works. In 1952, after having breakfast with the Damons at their house in Providence, I sent him a perturbed letter:

DEAR FOSTER:

I'm addressing the letter to you because, in addition to its serving as a bread-and-butter, or buttered-toast, letter to you and Louise, it also has to touch on the great question of your unpublished manuscripts. They worry me. I don't know any writer of our time who has had so little recognition for what he has done. . . . On the other hand, I hesitate to say, "Send them all to me," because my time is so taken up now with editorial chores that there is little of it left for reading. . . .

The letter continued with what I hoped were some practical suggestions, but they had no practical results. Foster told me at the time—or was it a little later?—that he had set to work on a complete edition of Chivers' prose and poetry. "Chivers, Chivers," I said to myself in despair. Only the first of three projected volumes was published (1957), in the midst of a silence that shattered one's ears.

But Foster's masterpiece of anonymity was his last book of poems, *Nightmare Cemetery* (1964). He had published two much earlier collections, and they had earned him some of the usual honors, including, in his case, the presidency of the New England Poetry Society and its Golden Rose. *Astrolabe* (1927) was the more impressive of the early volumes, by virtue of two rather long mystical poems, both with the same title: "Apocalypse"; they seemed to

promise further visions and experiments. The promise was not fulfilled by the poems in *Tilted Moons* (1929), which were mostly
decorative and indebted to Foster's reading, with pervasive echoes
of Verlaine and Laforgue. I doubt whether he wrote many poems in
the next twenty or thirty years. In his late sixties, however, he struck
a new vein and worked on it until he had completed *Nightmare
Cemetery*, a double sequence of seventy-three sonnets that is, among
other things, a remarkable technical achievement.

That is not its principal claim to being remembered, but still the
virtuosity should not be overlooked. The work includes examples,
and good ones, of orthodox Petrarchan and Shakespearean sonnets,
with other examples of almost every possible variation, new and old,
from those two basic patterns. Foster does omit a few. Thus, he gives
us a sonnet in hexameter, but none in tetrameter or trimeter, none in
"sprung rhythm," and none in syllabic verse. Those metrical experiments, however, are hardly missed in the diversity of stanzaic forms
he offers. To list a few, there are sonnets in which the conventional
octave and sestet are replaced by two seven-line stanzas. There are
two double sonnets. There is one sonnet in rhyming couplets, one in
rhyming tercets, and one in *terza rima*. There is a sonnet in five
stanzas of two, three, four, three, and two lines respectively; of course
they add up to fourteen. All but two of the sonnets are of that conventional length, but there are also a thirteen-line sonnet with a
complicated rhyme scheme and an extended sonnet in which one
line, the twelfth, bursts indignantly into five lines, all rhyming in
"-ation." In still another sonnet, the word "myself" replaces the
rhyme in each of eight lines:

> Yes, even the scenery (not too bad): myself.
> And you, the disgusted audience,—myself.

It is a statement of philosophical idealism carried to the point of
solipsism, as with many New England poets of the last century. In
Foster's case, however, the dependence of the outer cosmos on the
inner cosmos is expressed not only in a variety of measures, but also
in a candid, self-deprecatory fashion (the world is a play written by
"myself," he says, but badly written) and in a tone of voice sustained
from the first sonnet to the last. He must have felt, and rightly, that

the book was immensely better than anything he had written in his early years.

And what did he do to bring *Nightmare Cemetery* to public attention? Did he submit the separate poems to a hierarchy of magazines, beginning with most prestigious and running down the scale (but not too far, since printing them in the littler magazines would be a tactical error)? Did he read them for radio programs or make those personal appearances on the poetry circuit that are now so easy to arrange? After those preliminary steps, did he keep sending the manuscript to big trade publishers until he found an editor with taste enough to admire it and authority enough to get it accepted? And then did he write to famous colleagues who might be persuaded to review the book or at least to furnish a few adulatory words for the jacket? Those are the usual shifts to which poets are driven by their thirst for glory and their recognition that poetry is not a popular art. I doubt whether they even occurred to Foster, burdened as he was with New England shyness and seventy years of accumulated ignorance about the technique of becoming a famous poet. Perhaps "incapacity" would be a better word. In 1918 he had known what steps to take in order to create the reputation of Earl Roppel, but neither then nor later had he been able to regard his own reputation in the same impersonal way, as a problem in literary mechanics. At any rate, he chose the most effective means of not recapturing an audience. He had the book printed by a friend at the Rhode Island School of Design, in an edition of two hundred numbered and expensive copies. Then, having sent out a few dozen copies for review and some others as gifts to friends, he simply waited for recognition.

Two years later he was still waiting. He said in a mildly querulous letter (October 13, 1966), "*Not one* of the copies of my *Cemetery* sent to *Poetry* and other literary magazines so much as got listed in 'Books Received.' And of course no reviews. I guess that one peek showed my poems to be sonnets, and sonnets are not worth noticing any more."

Sonnets are out of fashion, but there was another reason for the universal oversight. Foster had presented *Nightmare Cemetery* under a pseudonym—Samuel Nomad—and with a prefatory note that read:

"All the characters in this book are entirely imaginary including the author." He must have regarded the pseudonym and the note as a transparent literary device, since, as he explained in another letter, the author's identity is revealed in the thirteenth line of the sonnet on page ten: "the clumsy letters of my name reversed." Samuel Nomad and S. (for Samuel) Foster Damon: any reader could see the connection. But where were the readers? Foster did not realize that hardly anyone, these days, would even open a book by a pseudonymous author half-published in a small edition by a school of design. Hardly anyone, that is, took the peek that would have shown the poems to be sonnets, let alone reading as far as the thirteenth line of the sonnet on page ten. In the glut and gurry of contemporary writing, there are too many nominated poets wailing for attention. Hardly any editor thinks of assigning a completely unknown book for review.

Or did the author realize all this and was he obeying his instinct for self-obliteration?

What *Nightmare Cemetery* needed and still needs is the sort of adventurous reader that Foster was in his Harvard years. But is there such a reader today?—I mean with Foster's knight-errantry in riding to the rescue of neglected books as if they were maidens immured in a donjon keep. Some of those books had languished so long unread that they had become the equivalent of maiden great-aunts before he freed them from dusty shelves and displayed them to his friends. "Look at this, Estlin (or Jack, or Virgil)," he would say a little proudly, as if he had returned from a knightly quest with Sleeping Beauty riding on his crupper. But who will go questing after *Nightmare Cemetery?*

If Samuel Nomad were a person and if his book had been written fifty years ago—as in some ways it might have been, for it does not propose to be timely—I can imagine what Foster might have said about it, after producing it from that enormous green baize bag. "Look at this, Mal," he would have begun in his flat voice, but with an edge of excitement; "here's something I found today. The author calls it a Hallowe'en frolic, but it's a grisly and labored one, a double sequence of sonnets about death. Is it great poetry? No, it doesn't even try to be, and yet it belongs in a great line: Emerson, Jones

Very, Emily Dickinson, all the New England metaphysicals. Yes, and let's add Edward Rowland Sill and E. A. Robinson for a touch of pessimism. Here's why it impresses me: it's at the very end of the line."

I would open the book and read a sonnet. "This one doesn't sound like Emerson," I would say.

"Oh, you mean the one where Nomad compares his own death to pulling the chain and going down the toilet? That sonnet will prove my point as well as another. It's pure New England in its self-absorption—the wrong word: it makes me think of toilet paper—and in its identification of the self with the universe. But it's Emerson upside down, Emerson turned pessimist and raging cynic, Emerson's great tides of universal Being transformed into 'the gulp of the celestial watercloset.' I tell you, it's the end of the line."

Foster would snatch the book from my hand and go pacing up and down the room. "This Nomad fellow," he would say, "is evidently an old man telling what he thinks is the shameful truth about himself. He isn't a celebrity, he isn't popular and outgoing, and he faces what he calls 'the time when I am slowly, horribly, killed.' His dim hope of an afterlife depends on finding readers for his poems, yet some deep compulsion makes him insult them and drive them away. He can make jokes about his shameful truths or dress them in Hallowe'en masks from a children's party, but he hasn't time left to be bothered with telling lies. He hasn't time to be decorative in his language or to grope for figures of speech; one metaphor set forth in simple words, sometimes in slang, is all he finds room for in one sonnet. Listen:

> Life is the big neighborhood party, me lad,
> to which you weren't invited. And so what.
>
> . . . . . . . . . . . . . . . .
>
> walk in as though you owned the place—be brash
> and grab the prettiest girl and make her dance.
>
> (This is one party that you cannot crash.)
> —So, go home; climb into bed and try to sleep.
> (The cold, deep bed and your long, long last sleep.)

"He writes for the ear, not the eye," Foster would comment, "and his ear demands all sorts of variations from the familiar metrical pattern. He delights in asperities and rugosities. His iambic pentameters are sprinkled with trochees; there are two in the first line I read, besides one anapest, and the line about the cold, deep bed has three spondees. Reading such lines makes me think of New Hampshire fields that are strewn with boulders. The soil runs thin as the blood runs thin; Nomad is the last of a great line. Sometimes his voice wheezes like the hand-pumped organ in an old meetinghouse; it is the voice of New England, and yet his own voice unmistakably. Because of it his book exists in itself when so many books are the mere facsimiles of others. Listen for a last time."

Foster would page through the book and, in his own unmistakable voice, would read me six lines of "Epitaph":

> I tried to write my name: that much seemed needed.
> And I have failed if it has found a place
> only beneath the title. But I succeeded
> if in this verbal wilderness and valley
> sometimes you hear a voice you cannot place
> that speaks your own name softly, authentically.

It seems to me that Samuel Nomad, or rather S. Foster Damon in his latest book of poems, has succeeded in that self-absorbed but self-effaced and wholly authentic fashion.

ERNEST D. COSTA and ELIZABETH C. WESCOTT

# S. Foster Damon:
# A Bibliography

## · BOOKS AND PAMPHLETS ·

(Trans., with Robert Silliman Hillyer.) *A Book of Danish Verse.* New York: American-Scandinavian Foundation; London: Oxford University Press, Humphrey Milford, 1922.

(Ed., with Robert Hillyer.) *Eight More Harvard Poets.* New York: Brentano's, 1923.

*William Blake, His Philosophy and Symbols.* Boston and New York: Houghton Mifflin Co., 1924.

———. Reprinted. New York: Peter Smith, 1947.

———. Reprinted. Gloucester, Mass.: Peter Smith, 1958.

*A Note on the Discovery of a New Page of Poetry in William Blake's Milton.* Boston: Club of Odd Volumes, 1925.

*Astrolabe: Infinitudes and Hypocrisies.* New York and London: Harper & Bros., 1927.

*Tilted Moons.* New York and London: Harper & Bros., 1929.

*The Day After Christmas.* New York: Albert & Charles Boni, 1930.

*Thomas Holley Chivers, Friend of Poe.* New York and London: Harper & Bros., 1930.

*Amy Lowell, a Chronicle.* Boston and New York: Houghton Mifflin Co., Riverside Press, 1935.

———. Reprinted. Hamden, Conn.: Archon Books, 1966.

(Ed.) *Series of Old American Songs, Reproduced in Facsimile from Original or Early Editions in the Harris Collection of Early American Poetry and Plays, Brown University.* Providence: Brown University Library, 1936. (Distributed by the Brown University Press.)

(Ed.) *Colonial Poets, 1609–1760: A Selection from the Harris Col-*

*lection of American Poetry and Plays.* Providence: Friends of
the Library of Brown University, 1947.

*Yankee Doodle.* [Meriden, Conn.: Meriden Gravure Co., 1959].

(Ed.) *Blake's Grave: A Prophetic Book, Being William Blake's Illustrations for Robert Blair's "The Grave," Arranged as Blake
Directed.* Providence: Brown University Press, 1963.

*Nightmare Cemetery, A Hallowe'en Frolic,* by Samuel Nomad
[pseud.]. Providence: [By the author], 1964.

*A Blake Dictionary: The Ideas and Symbols of William Blake.*
Providence: Brown University Press, 1965.

————. 2d printing, 1967.

(Ed.) *Blake's "Job": William Blake's "Illustrations of the Book of
Job."* Providence: Brown University Press, 1966.

————. 2d printing, 1967.

*The Fig Tree: A Fragment.* Newport: Third & Elm Press, 1966.


## · ARTICLES AND CONTRIBUTIONS ·


"Oh! the Women," *Newton High School Review,* XXVII, No. 4
(January 1909), 12–13.

"A Flash from the Abyss," by Alphonse Dawdey [pseud.], *ibid.,*
No. 8 (May 1909), p. 9.

"Cherries," *ibid.,* No. 9 (June 1909), p. 34.

"When Aunt Martha Came," *ibid.,* XXVIII, No. 2 (November 1909),
11–13.

"The Saving of Bâle," *ibid.,* No. 5 (February 1910), pp. 8–9.

"Das Ewig Weibliche Zieht Uns Hinan," *ibid.,* No. 7 (April 1910),
pp. 3–4.

"Modern Popular Music," *Harvard Musical Review,* I, No. 2
(November 1912), [17]–19.

"Guiseppe Verdi—an Appreciation," *ibid.,* II, No. 1 (October 1913),
3–8, 26.

"Sibelius's Fourth," *ibid.,* No. 2 (November 1913), pp. 16–17.

"The Unwritten Music of a Great Man," *ibid.,* No. 3 (December
1913), pp. 3–8, 28–29.

"Eric Satie," *ibid.*, No. 6 (March 1914), pp. 18–20.

"Opera and the City," *ibid.*, pp. 3–6.

"Schönberg, Strindberg and Sibelius," *ibid.*, III, No. 6 (March 1915), 9–11.

"The Cerebralists," *The Harvard Advocate*, CIII, No. 10 (30 August 1917), [92]–97.

"American Influence on Modern French Music," *The Dial*, LXV, No. 771 (15 August 1918), [93]–95.

"Li Po," *Youth: Poetry of Today*, I, No. 1 (October 1918), 16–20.

"Thirty Years of Harvard Aesthetes," by Dorian Abbott, '15 [pseud.], *The Harvard Advocate*, CV, No. 1 (November 1918), 37–42.

"As One Would Not," *The Little Review*, V, No. 8 (December 1918), 22–25.

"Dolcezza e Luce in Boston," by Dorian Abbott, '15 [pseud.], *The Harvard Advocate*, CV, No. 2 (January 1919), 56–62.

"The New Work of Puccini," *The Dial*, LXVI, No. 781 (11 January 1919), 25–26.

"Altiplatitudes," by M. B. B., '18, and D. A., '15 [pseuds.], *The Harvard Advocate*, CV, No. 6 (June 1919), 267–69.

"The New Pessimism," *ibid.*, pp. 270–76.

"Exhibition of Blake's Books," *Harvard Alumni Bulletin*, XXII, No. 16 (15 January 1920), [360]–62.

"Blake's Illuminated Books now on Exhibition at Fogg," *The Harvard Crimson*, LXXVI, No. 93 [i.e., 94] (23 January 1920), 7.

"Thomas Vaughn," *The Little Review*, VI, No. 11 (April 1920), 39.

"The First Matter," *The Occult Review*, XXXV, No. 2 (January 1922), 104–10.

"The Roger Bacon Ms.," *ibid.*, No. 5 (May 1922), p. 302.

"Repast and Repose," *Broom*, II, No. 4 (July 1922), 339–40.

"The Symbols of Alchemy," *The Occult Review*, XXXVI (August 1922), 141–49.

"William Blake," *The Freeman*, VI, No. 151 (31 January 1923), 491–92.

"The Evidence for Literal Transmutation," *The Occult Review*, XXXVI (February 1923), 177–84.

"The Philosopher's Stone, to the Editor of the *Occult Review*," *ibid.*, XXXVII (March 1923), 190–92.

"Scepticism and Alchemy," *The Harvard Advocate,* CIX, No. 7 (7 April 1923), 275–78.

"Chaucer and Alchemy," *PMLA,* XXXIX, No. 4 (December 1924), 782–88.

"Three Generations of One Line," *MLN,* XL, No. 7 (November 1925), 441.

"Blake: Psychologist," *The Saturday Review of Literature,* III, No. 19 (4 December 1926), 357–58.

"Milton and Marston," *PMLA,* XLII, No. 4 (December 1927), 873–74.

"Cumming's 'Him,' " *The Saturday Review of Literature,* IV, No. 25 (14 January 1928), 522.

"Pierre the Ambiguous," *The Hound & Horn,* II, No. 2 (January–March 1929), 107–18.

"The Odyssey in Dublin," *ibid.,* III, No. 1 (October–December 1929), 7–[44].

———, *with a postscript, 1947.* In *James Joyce: Two Decades of Criticism,* edited by Seon Givens. New York: Vanguard Press, 1963, pp. 203–42.

"Marie de France: Psychologist of Courtly Love," *PMLA,* XLIV, No. 4 (December 1929), 968–96.

"A Portrait of Albertus Magnus," *Speculum,* V, No. 1 (January 1930), 102–3.

"Ashes Helped Daniel Turn Sleuth, an Array at the John Hay Library Shows Books That Have Figured in the History of the Mystery Story and the Thriller.—Some Rare Items," *Providence Journal,* 2 April 1930, p. 15.

"Some American References to Blake before 1863," *MLN,* XLV, No. 6 (June 1930), [365]–70.

"Why Ishmael Went to Sea," *American Literature,* II, No. 3 (November 1930), [281]–83.

"Mickey Mouse," *The Adelphi,* I, No. 5 (February 1931), 426.

"Tradition in American Painting," *The Hound & Horn,* V, No. 4 (July–September 1932), 668–70.

"No Longer an Orphan Is 'Jack's Daedal Mansion,' " *Providence Sunday Journal,* 29 January 1933, Sec. E, p. 3.

"Early Brown Poets and Playwrights," *Brown Alumni Monthly,* XXXIV, No. 2 (July 1933), 36–39.

"The Negro in Early American Songsters," *Bibliographical Society of America. Papers*, XXVIII, Pt. 2 (1934), 132–63.

"Francis Daniel Pastorius," *Poetry: A Magazine of Verse*, XLIV, No. 1 (April 1934), 37–40.

"The Genesis of Boston," *The Atlantic Monthly*, CLVI (October 1935), 487–91.

"Poetry," *Evening Bulletin* (Providence), 21 April 1936, p. 10.

"The Harris Collection of American Poetry and Plays," *Books at Brown*, II, No. 4 (June 1940), [1–4].

"Providence Theatricals in 1773," *Rhode Island History*, IV, No. 2 (April 1945), 55–58.

"Varnum's 'Ministerial Oppression,' a Revolutionary Drama," *Proceedings of the American Antiquarian Society*, LV (October 1945), [287]–98.

"Springfield Mountain," *Journal of American Folklore*, LIX, No. 234 (October–December 1946), 530–31.

["The Doctrine of Job"]. In *Job, Invented & Engraved by William Blake*. New York: United Book Guild, 1947. (Pp. 225–36 of *William Blake, His Philosophy and Symbols*, reprinted almost verbatim.)

———. In *Illustrations of the Book of Job, Invented & Engraved by William Blake*. New York: United Book Guild, 1950.

"The Harris Collection Sheet Music," *Books at Brown*, XIII, No. 1 (March 1951), [1]–4.

"The History of Square-dancing," *Proceedings of the American Antiquarian Society*, LXII (April 1952), [63]–98.

———. Reprinted. Barre, Mass.: Barre Gazette, 1957.

"Given New Account of British Raid," *Gloucester* (Mass.) *Daily Times*, 19 September 1952.

"High Art in Robert Frost's Simplicity," *ibid.*, 23 July 1953.

"How I Came to Discover Blake," *Faith and Freedom*, IX (Summer 1956), [137]–44.

"Blake and Milton." In *The Divine Vision: Studies in the Poetry and Art of William Blake*, edited by Vivian de Sola Pinto. London: V. Gollancz, 1957, pp. 91–96.

In "Comments," *Wagner Literary Magazine* (Spring 1959), pp. 25-26.

"Cummings as I Knew Him," *Brown Daily Herald Supplement*, VII, No. 2 (16 October 1962), p. 9.

(With Roger E. Stoddard.) "The Harris Collection of American Poetry and Plays; Report of Acquisitions for 1962–63," *Books at Brown*, XX (1965), 111–[30].

"How I Discovered Blake," *Blake Newsletter*, No. 3 (15 December 1967), pp. 2–3.

· REVIEWS ·

*Beethoven: Biographie Critique*, by Vincent d'Indy. *Harvard Musical Review*, I, No. 1 (October 1912), [22]–23.

*Style in Musical Art*, by Sir Charles Hubert Hastings Parry. *Ibid.*, pp. 24–25.

*Twelve Songs*, by Claude Debussy, edited by C. Fonteyn Manney. *Ibid.*, No. 7 (April 1913), p. 26.

*Preludes pour Piano* (2ᵉ Livre), by Claude Debussy. *Ibid.*, No. 8 (22 May 1913), pp. 24–25.

*Lyric Diction for Singers, Actors and Public Speakers*, by Dora Duty Jones. *Ibid.*, p. 25.

*Harvard Festival March, Introducing the Commencement Hymn of Professor John Knowles Paine*, by Percy Lee Atherton. *Ibid.*, No. 10 (July 1913), pp. 24–25.

*The Pathos of Distance*, by James Huneker. *Ibid.*, II, No. 1 (October 1913), 23–24.

*Colour-Music, the Art of Mobile Colour*, by Alexander Wallace Rimington. *Ibid.*, pp. 24–26.

*La Boîte à Joujoux*, by Claude Debussy; scenario by André Hellé. *Ibid.*, No. 5 (February 1914), pp. 20–21.

*Album of Ten Songs; by Russian Composers*, English version by Nathan Haskel[l] Dole, edited by Henry Clough-Leighter. *Ibid.*, No. 8 (May 1914), pp. 34–35.

*Dodecameron: a Lyric Cycle of Twelve Days*, by Virginia Kline, set for voice and piano by John H. Densmore. *Ibid.*, p. 36.

*A Study of Modern Harmony*, by René Lenormand. *Ibid.*, III, No. 5 (February 1915), 19.

*Berceuse Héroïque, pour Rendre Hommage à Sa Majesté le Roi Albert 1ᵉʳ de Belgique et à ses Soldats*, by Claude Debussy, in

*King Albert's Book; A tribute to the Belgian King and People from representative men and women throughout the world,* pp. 147–49. *Ibid.,* No. 6 (March 1915), p. 19.

*Japanese Prints,* by John Gould Fletcher. "In the Mode of Japan," *The New Republic,* XVI, No. 203 (21 September 1918), 235, 238.

*Reminiscences of Lafcadio Hearn,* by Setsu (Koizumi) Hearn (Mrs. Lafcadio Hearn), translated from the Japanese by Paul Kiyoshi Hisada and Frederick Johnson. "The Twain Shall Meet," *The Harvard Advocate,* CV, No. 2 (January 1919), 53–54.

*Teton Sioux Music,* by Frances Densmore. *The Dial,* LXVI, No. 790 (17 May 1919), 518.

*War and Love (1915–1918),* by Richard Aldington. *Youth: Poetry of Today,* I, No. 6 (August 1919), 115–17.

*Samurai Trails,* by Lucian Swift Kirtland. *The Dial,* LXVII, No. 797 (23 August 1919), 164.

*A Hundred and Seventy Chinese Poems,* translated by Arthur Waley; *Chinese Lyrics from The Book of Jade,* translated by Mme. Judith Gautier, translated from the French by James Whitall; *Sweden's Laureate: Selected Poems of Verner Von Heidenstam,* translated from the Swedish by Charles Wharton Stock. "Poetry in Translation," *The Harvard Advocate,* CVI, No. 2 (30 October 1919), 64.

*The Moon of the Caribbees, and Six Other Plays of the Sea,* by Eugene G. O'Neill. "A Playwright of the Seven Seas," *ibid.,* No. 4 (18 December 1919, i.e., January 1920), p. 142.

*Pictures of the Floating World,* by Amy Lowell. "The Two Realisms," *ibid.,* No. 6 (1 March 1920), pp. 221–22.

*The Five Books of Youth,* by Robert Hillyer. *The Harvard Crimson,* LXVII, No. 72 (8 May 1920), 3, 5–6.

*Pluriverse: an Essay in the Philosophy of Pluralism,* by Benjamin Paul Blood. "Aesthetic Anaesthesia," *The Harvard Advocate,* CVI, No. 9 (30 May 1920), 330.

*A History of Magic and Experimental Science, during the First Thirteen Centuries of Our Era,* by Lynn Thorndike. "Light on the Dark Ages," *The Dial,* LXXVI (January 1924), [75]–78.

*William Blake in This World,* by Harold Lawton Bruce; *Blake's Vision of the Book of Job,* by Joseph H. Wicksteed; *Blake and*

*Milton,* by Denis Saurat. "The Battle over Blake," *The New Republic,* XLIV, No. 565, Pt. I (30 September 1925), 2–4.

*The Halt in the Garden,* by Robert Hillyer. *The Crimson Bookshelf, the Monthly Literary Supplement of The Harvard Crimson,* II, No. 1 (3 October 1925), [1].

*The History of Witchcraft and Demonology,* by Montague Summers. "The Dark Ages Revived," *The Saturday Review of Literature,* III, No. 30 (19 February 1927), 594.

*East Wind,* by Amy Lowell; *Selected Poems of Carl Sandburg,* edited by Rebecca West; *The Candle in the Cabin,* by Vachel Lindsay; *Scarlet and Mellow,* by Alfred Kreymborg; *Dark of the Moon,* by Sara Teasdale; *Those Not Elect,* by Leonie Adams; *Troy Park,* by Edith Sitwell; *Humoresque,* by Humbert Wolfe. "East Wind: West Wind," *The Yale Review,* N.S. XVI, No. 3 (April 1927), 587–91.

*The Secret Tradition in Alchemy: Its Development and Records,* by Arthur Edward Waite. "Chemistry or Deity?" *The Dial,* LXXXIII (July 1927), [66–69].

*Demoniality,* by Ludovico Maria Sinistrari, Friar Minor, translated from the Latin by Montague Summers; *The Geography of Witchcraft,* by Montague Summers. "Civilization à Rebours," *The Saturday Review of Literature,* IV, No. 3 (13 August 1927), 36.

*The Engraved Designs of William Blake,* by Laurence Binyon; *Songs of Innocence,* by William Blake, reproduced from a copy in the British Museum; *Poetical Sketches,* by William Blake (London, 1926); *The Poems and Prophecies of William Blake* (New York, 1927); *An Introduction to the Study of Blake,* by Max Plowman; *The Mysticism of William Blake,* by Helen C. White. "Blake a Century Later," *ibid.,* No. 34 (17 March 1928), p. 680.

*Astrology: Your Place in the Sun,* by Evangeline Adams; *The Mysteries and Secrets of Magic,* by C. J. S. Thompson; *The Way of Power: Studies in the Occult,* by Lily Adams Beck; *A Mirror for Witches,* by Esther Forbes. "Red Spirits and Grey," *ibid.,* No. 43 (19 May 1928), p. 881.

*Blake's Innocence and Experience: A Study of the Songs and Manu-*

*scripts*, by Joseph H. Wicksteed. *Ibid.*, V, No. 36 (30 March 1929), 834.

*The Complete Works of Thomas Lovell Beddoes*, edited by Sir Edmund Gosse; *Thomas Lovell Beddoes, Eccentric & Poet*, by Royall H. Snow. *The Hound & Horn*, II, No. 3 (April–June 1929), 293–96.

*Witchcraft in Old and New England*, by George Lyman Kittredge; *Sibyls and Seers: A Survey of Some Ancient Theories of Revelation and Inspiration*, by Edwyn Bevan; *The History of the Devil: The Horned God of the West*, by R. Lowe Thompson; *The Story of Superstition*, by Philip F. Waterman. "The Devil Dies Hard," *The Saturday Review of Literature*, V, No. 39 (20 April 1929), 904–5.

*The Ordinall of Alchimy by Thomas Norton of Bristoll . . .* , edited by E. J. Holmyard. *Speculum*, IV, No. 3 (July 1929), 352–53.

*James Joyce's "Ulysses": A Study*, by Stuart Gilbert; *Anna Livia Plurabelle*, by James Joyce. "On Explaining Joyce," *The Adelphi*, N.S. I, No. 1 (October 1930), 79–82.

*Witchcraft, Magic and Alchemy*, by Grillot de Givry, translated by J. Courtenay Locke. *Providence Sunday Journal Magazine*, 1 November 1931, p. 18.

*Eimi*, by E. E. Cummings. *Providence Sunday Journal*, 23 April 1933, Sec. E, p. 4.

*Blake*, by Alan Clutton-Brock. "A Reworked Theory That William Blake Fled Reality," *ibid.*, 3 September 1933, Sec. E, p. 4.

*Katie Fox, an Epochmaking Medium and the Making of the Fox-Taylor Record*, by W. G. Langworthy Taylor. *Ibid.*, 22 October 1933, Sec. E, p. 4.

*The Poetical Works of Edward Taylor*, edited by Thomas H. Johnson. *New England Quarterly*, XII, No. 4 (December 1939), 777–80.

*Blake: Prophet against Empire*, by David V. Erdman. "The Facts behind the Vision," *The Saturday Review of Literature*, XXXVII, No. 18 (1 May 1954), 29.

*Elias Boudinot's Journey to Boston in 1809*, edited by Milton Halsey Thomas. *Rhode Island History*, XV, No. 3 (July 1956), 88–89.

*Letters of William Blake,* edited by Geoffrey Keynes. *Brunonia,* XII, No. 3 (Spring 1957), 30–31.

### · INTRODUCTIONS ·

*Leaving the Hermitage,* by Rohan Kōda, translated from the Japanese by Jirō Nagura. London: George Allen & Unwin, [1925], pp. 9–12.

*On the Minor Prophecies of William Blake,* by Emily S. Hamblen. London and Toronto: J. M. Dent & Sons; New York: E. P. Dutton & Co., 1930, pp. vii–x.

*Fire Testament,* by Willard Maas. New York: Alcestis Press, 1935, pp. 11–[12].

*The Poems of Maria Lowell, with Unpublished Letters,* edited by Hope Jillson Vernon. Providence: Brown University, 1936, pp. vii–[ix].

*Sam Lovel's Boy, with Forest & Stream Fables,* by Rowland E. Robinson. Rutland, Vt.: Chas. E. Tuttle Co., 1936, pp. [9]–14.

*Annisquam Village Cook Book,* compiled by Annisquam Sewing Circle [Annisquam, Mass., 1940], pp. [i–iv]. (With seven recipes by S. Foster Damon.)

*Water Colours by William Blake for Bunyan's The Pilgrim's Progress.* Loan exhibition 21 October to 8 November 1941 at the Galleries of M. Knoedler and Company, 14 East 57 Street, New York. [New York: Spiral Press, 1941], pp. [5–7].

*The Correspondence of Thomas Holley Chivers, 1838–1858,* edited by Emma Lester Chase and Lois Ferry Parks (Vol. I, *The Complete Works of Thomas Holley Chivers,* S. Foster Damon and Charles H. Watts II, general editors). Providence: Brown University Press, 1957, pp. xiii–xv.

" 'The Roll of Fame': A Poem by Thomas Holley Chivers," edited by Alvin H. Rosenfeld, *Books at Brown,* XIX (May 1963), 177–80.

### · ADDRESSES ·

"Music in Colonial New England." University Lecture, Brown University, 15 March 1939.

"Shakespeare Today." Address given in Central Park, New York, 23
April 1942 at the National Shakespeare Federation celebration of
the 378th birthday of William Shakespeare.
"Saint Nicholas in the Harris Collection." Radio script, performed
23 December 1951.
"Styles in Santa Claus." Television script, performed on "An Evening
on College Hill," series 3, program 4, 14 December 1954.
————. Performed on "From College Hill," series 4, program 10, 18
December 1955.

## · POEMS ·

"Alpha, Mu and Omega," *Newton High School Review*, XXVII,
No. 7 (April 1909), 10–11.
"Sunset," *The Harvard Monthly*, LX, No. 5 (July 1915), 142.
"A December Episode," *ibid.*, LXI, No. 4 (January 1916), 104–5.
"Calm Day, with Rollers." In *Eight Harvard Poets*, with E. Estlin
Cummings, J. R. Dos Passos, Robert Hillyer, R. S. Mitchell,
William A. Norris, Dudley Poore, and Cuthbert Wright. New
York: Laurence J. Gomme, 1917, p. 21.
"Decoration." *Ibid.*, p. 24.
"Incessu Patuit Deus." *Ibid.*, pp. 13–14.
"New MacAber." *Ibid.*, pp. 18–19.
————. In *Tilted Moons*, 1929, p. 19. (Retitled "The Modern Ma-
caber.")
"Phonograph-Tango." In *Eight Harvard Poets*, 1917, pp. 22–23.
"Threnody." *Ibid.*, p. 25.
"To War." *Ibid.*, p. 20.
"Venice." *Ibid.*, pp. 16–17.
["You Thought I Had Forgotten"]. *Ibid.*, p. 15.
"Midnight," *The Harvard Advocate*, CIII, No. 2 (14 March 1917),
21.
"Beauty," *ibid.*, No. 3 (28 March 1917), p. 37.
"Passion," *ibid.*, p. [40].
————. In *Tilted Moons*, 1929, p. 4.
"To ———— Reported Dead in France," *The Harvard Advocate*,
CIII, No. 5 (14 May 1917), 74.

"Sleep," *ibid.*, No. 6 (28 May 1917), p. 88.

"Haikai," *ibid.*, No. 7 (11 June 1917), p. 62.

"On the Cape," *ibid.*, No. 9 (21 June 1917), p. 82.

"Tanka," *ibid.*, p. [83].

"With Their Guns, a French Song for Americans Fighting in France," Boston: Oliver Ditson Co.; New York: Chas. H. Ditson & Co.; Chicago: Lyon & Healy, 1917. (A free translation from "Avec Leurs Fusils . . . ," written for the Harvard Regiment by Lt.-Col. Paul Azan; French air adapted by Chalmers Clifton.)

"Forsitan et Haec," *The Harvard Advocate*, CIII, No. 10 (30 August 1917), [89].

"Penumbra," *ibid.*, p. 91.

———. In *Tilted Moons*, 1929, p. 23.

["Dark Eyes Made Heavy . . ."], *The Harvard Advocate*, CIII, No. 10 (30 August 1917), [89].

"The Geisha Dawn," *ibid.*, CIV, No. 1 (19 October 1917), 45.

"Sonnet," *ibid.*, p. 41.

"Noon Fall-Out," *The Independent*, XCIV, No. 3624 (18 May 1918), 272.

"Sonnet from 'Le Parnasse Satyrique,' 1622," *The Little Review*, VI, No. 2 (June 1918), 30.

"Idyll," *The Century*, XCVI, No. 3 (July 1918), 422.

———. In *Tilted Moons*, 1929, p. 11.

" 'A Little, Called Pauline,' " *The Century*, XCVI, No. 4 (August 1918), 576.

———. In *Tilted Moons*, 1929, p. 63.

"Apparition: From Mallarmé," *The Touchstone*, III, No. 5 (August 1918), 437.

"Carnival," *Youth: Poetry of Today*, I, No. 1 (October 1918), 8.

"He Likens Her to a Star of Heaven," *ibid.*, pp. 8–9.

"Triolet," *ibid.*, p. 9.

"After the War," *The Century*, XCVI, No. 6 (October 1918), 812.

"Bayonet Drill," *The Harvard Advocate*, CV, No. 1 (November 1918), 18.

"Billy Sunday in Boston," *ibid.*, p. 31.

"Panel," *Youth: Poetry of Today*, I, No. 2 (December 1918), 34.

"A Ballade of Fair Ladies," *The Century*, XCVII, No. 3 (January 1919), [432].

"Anticipations I. Early Advent," *The Harvard Advocate*, CV, No. 2 (January 1919), 36.

"To Musette (1830) (From Henry Murger's 'Scènes de la Vie de Bohème')," *ibid.*, pp. 54–55, 36.

"Episode," *The Independent*, XCVII, No. 3666 (15 March 1919), 376.

———. In *Tilted Moons*, 1929, pp. 61–62.

"Night-Piece," *Youth: Poetry of Today*, I, No. 6 (August 1919), 112–14.

———. In *Tilted Moons*, 1929, pp. 36–39.

"An Aesthete of the Eighteen-Thirties," *The Harvard Advocate*, CVI, No. 3 (22 November 1919), 92–93.

"A Thought After Taps," *The North American Review*, CCXII (October 1920), [547].

———. In *Tilted Moons*, 1929, p. 32.

"Alexander," *St. Nicholas Magazine*, XLVIII, No. 4 (February 1921), 358–59.

"An Arabesque," from the Danish of J. P. Jacobsen, *American-Scandinavian Review*, IX, No. 6 (June 1921), 375–76.

———. In *A Book of Danish Verse*, 1922, pp. 118–20.

———, *Golden Book*, VII, No. 40 (April 1928), 520.

"Denmark's Consolation," *American-Scandinavian Review*, XXX, No. 3 (September 1942), 228. (Reprinted from *A Book of Danish Verse*, 1922.)

"Song to Mad Kit." In *Fellowship Anthology of the New England Poetry Club*. Natick, Mass.: Suburban Press, 1922.

———. In *Astrolabe*, 1927, pp. 19–20.

"Epilogue," *The Bookman*, LIV, No. 5 (January 1922), 453.

———. In *Astrolabe*, 1927, p. 80.

"The Holy Gilde," *The Dial*, LXXII (February 1922), [178]–82.

"Conversations," *Broom*, II, No. 3 (June 1922), 236.

———. In *Astrolabe*, 1927, p. 8. (Retitled "Conversation.")

"Voyage," *Broom*, II, No. 3 (June 1922), 237.

———. In *Astrolabe*, 1927, p. 30.

"Fête," *The New Republic*, XXXIII, No. 425 (24 January 1923), 223.

———, *The Bookman*, LVII, No. 2 (April 1923), 188.

———. In *Tilted Moons*, 1929, p. 13.

"The Zen Buddhist," *The Harvard Advocate*, CIX, No. 7 (7 April 1923), 273.

———. In *Astrolabe*, 1927, pp. 37–38.

———. In *Two Centuries of Brown Verse, 1764–1964*, edited by Sharon Brown. Providence: Brown University Bicentennial Publications Committee, 1965, pp. 219–20.

"Fantasia in a Restaurant," *Secession*, VI, No. 5 (September 1923), 20–24.

———. In *Astrolabe*, 1927, pp. 45–50.

"Bound Wings," *Poetry: A Magazine of Verse*, XXIV, No. 1 (April 1924), 7–9.

"Recrudescence," *The Harvard Advocate*, CX, No. 9 (1 June 1924), 376.

———. In *Tilted Moons*, 1929, p. 72.

"Eighteen," *The Harvard Advocate*, CX, No. 9 (1 June 1924), 380.

———. In *Tilted Moons*, 1929, p. 17.

"Rock of Ages," *The Saturday Review of Literature*, I, No. 31 (28 February 1925), 553.

———. In *Astrolabe*, 1927, p. 16. (Retitled "Rock of Sages.")

———, *The Saturday Review of Literature*, XXVIII, No. 48 (1 December 1945), 95. (Retitled "Rock of Sages.")

"Protest," *The Bookman*, LXI, No. 3 (May 1925), 266.

———. In *Tilted Moons*, 1929, p. 49.

"Persephone in Eden," *The Dial*, LXXVIII (June 1925), [445]–64.

"Dusk," *The Nation*, CXXI, No. 3130 (1 July 1925), 12.

———. In *Tilted Moons*, 1929, p. 53.

"Dialogue," *Forum*, LXXIV, No. 4 (October 1925), 604.

———. In *Astrolabe*, 1927, p. 10.

"Dusk: N. Y. C.," *The Saturday Review of Literature*, II, No. 14 (31 October 1925), [253].

———. In *Astrolabe*, 1927, p. 32.

"Tamora," *The Bookman*, LXII, No. 4 (December 1925), 470.

———. In *Tilted Moons*, 1929, p. 67.

"Symphony Hall," *Our Boston*, I, No. 5 (April 1926), 16.

"Epitaph Upon a Young Soldier," *Harper's Magazine*, CLII (May 1926), 695.

———. In *Gentlemen, Scholars and Scoundrels,* edited by Horace Knowles. New York: Harper & Bros., 1959, p. 385. (Retitled "Epitaph on a Young Soldier.")

———. In *Astrolabe,* 1927, p. 55. (Retitled "Epitaph on a Young Soldier.")

———. In *Two Centuries of Brown Verse,* 1965, p. 216. (Retitled "Epitaph on a Young Soldier.")

"To Lieut. E. S. C. (Killed February 5, 1918)," *The Saturday Review of Literature,* II, No. 47 (19 June 1926), [865].

———, *Literary Digest,* XC, No. 2 (10 July 1926), 34.

———. In *Astrolabe,* 1927, p. 64. (Retitled "To Lieutenant Edward S. Couch, Killed February 5, 1918.")

"Hotel Lobby," *The Commonweal,* IV, No. 7 (23 June 1926), 187.

———. In *Astrolabe,* 1927, p. 15.

"Moment," *The Saturday Review of Literature,* III, No. 3 (14 August 1926), [33].

———. In *Astrolabe,* 1927, p. 3.

"Epitaph," *The Nation,* CXXIII, No. 3194 (22 September 1926), [274].

———. In *Astrolabe,* 1927, p. 63.

"Epitaph in a Garden," *The Nation,* CXXIII, No. 3194 (22 September 1926), [274].

———. In *Astrolabe,* 1927, p. 59.

"Epitaph Upon a Philosopher," *The Nation,* CXXIII, No. 3194 (22 September 1926), [274].

———. In *Astrolabe,* 1927, p. 62. (Retitled "Epitaph On a Philosopher.")

"Commentary, on John X, 34," *The Nation,* CXXIII, No. 3208 (29 December 1926), 693.

———. In *Astrolabe,* 1927, p. 76. (Retitled "Commentary on John X, 34.")

"A Woman." In *The Copeland Reader, An Anthology of Poetry and Prose,* edited by Charles Townsend Copeland and Thurman Losson Hood. New York, Boston, Chicago: Charles Scribner's Sons, 1927 [Vol. 2], p. 1653.

———. In *Tilted Moons,* 1929, p. 69. (Retitled "A Neighbor.")

"Physics at the Piano," *The Bookman,* LXIV, No. 6 (February 1927), 692.

————. In *Astrolabe*, 1927, p. 5.

"Sweet-Peas Address the Ladies," *The Dial*, LXXXII (February 1927), 144.

————. In *Astrolabe*, 1927, p. 66.

"Beethoven: An Ode, March 26, 1927," *The Independent*, CXVIII, No. 4009 (2 April 1927), 365.

————. In *Tilted Moons*, 1929, pp. 77–80.

"Summer Lawn-Party," *Scribner's Magazine*, LXXXII (July 1927), 54.

————, *Literary Digest*, XCIV, No. 7 (13 August 1927), 33.

————. In *Tilted Moons*, 1929, p. 45.

"Image and After-Image," *The Dial*, LXXXV (July 1928), [43]–44.

————. In *Tilted Moons*, 1929, pp. 24–26.

"Epitaph upon an Invalid," *The Saturday Review of Literature*, V, No. 7 (8 September 1928), [97]. (Reprinted from *Astrolabe*, 1927.)

"Epitaph upon a Virgin," *ibid.* (Reprinted from Astrolabe, 1927.)

"Apparition," *Harper's Magazine*, CLVIII (February 1929), 311.

————. In *Tilted Moons*, 1929, p. 51.

————, *Literary Digest*, CIII, No. 5 (2 November 1929), 26.

"Family Portrait," *The Atlantic Monthly*, CXLIII (June 1929), [757]–58.

————. In *Tilted Moons*, 1929, pp. 59–60.

————. In *Rhode Island in Verse*, compiled by Mary Louise Brown. [Providence: Roger Williams Press], 1936, pp. 52–54.

————, *Museum Notes* (Rhode Island School of Design, Museum of Art), III, No. 3 (March 1945), [3].

————. In *Two Centuries of Brown Verse*, 1965, pp. 214–15.

"The Great Experiment," *The Hound & Horn*, II, No. 4 (July–September 1929), 351–60.

"Accident," *The Atlantic Monthly*, CXLIV (August 1929), [197].

————. In *Tilted Moons*, 1929, p. 54.

————. In *Two Centuries of Brown Verse*, 1965, p. 216.

"In the Late Sixteen Hundreds," *The Atlantic Monthly*, CXLIV (August 1929), [196].

————. In *Tilted Moons*, 1929, p. 66.

"Mistake," *The Atlantic Monthly*, CXLIV (August 1929), [197].

————. In *Tilted Moons*, 1929, p. 43.

"The Mad Huntsman," *Smoke*, I, No. 1 (May 1931), [3–4].
———. In *Two Centuries of Brown Verse*, 1965, pp. 221–22.
"Last Parting," *Smoke*, I, No. 3 (October 1931), [3].
"At the Edge," *ibid.*, II, No. 3 (October 1932), [3–4].
"Seelig's Confession," *ibid.*, No. 4 (December 1933), pp. [5]–12.
"Mt. Auburn," *The Harvard Advocate*, CXX, No. 4 (February 1934), 31.
"Hermit's End," *Rhode Island Review*, 3 February 1934, p. 19.
"Another Dinner Song," *Poetry: A Magazine of Verse*, XLIII, No. 6 (March 1934), 327.
———, *Literary Digest*, CXVII, No. 5 (14 April 1934), 33. (Retitled "Dinner Song.")
"Dawn Song to His First Born," *Poetry: A Magazine of Verse*, XLIII, No. 6 (March 1934), 324–25.
"Sung at a Private Dinner," *ibid.*, pp. 325–26.
"Prologue to a Puritan Epic," *American Poetry Journal*, April 1934, pp. 3–11.
"The Indian Girl Serenades Jonathan," *Alcestis*, I, No. 1 (October 1934).
"Little Josiah's Song," *The New Republic*, LXXXIV, No. 1080 (14 August 1935), 14.
"Atlantic Garden." In *Rhode Island in Verse*, compiled by Mary Louise Brown. [Providence: Roger Williams Press], 1936, p. 209. (Reprinted from *Astrolabe*, 1927.)
"Lilies of the Valley." *Ibid.*, p. 187. (Reprinted from *Tilted Moons*, 1929.)
"September." *Ibid.*, p. 194.
———, *Autumn Program.* Rhode Island Field Naturalists Club, 1936, p. [4].
"Join Us Here in Harvard Yard," *The Nineteen-Fourteen Jubilee*, Christmas issue, [1938], p. 12.
"Jonathan's Lullaby," *The Lyric*, XIX, No. 4 (Winter 1940), 44–46.
———. In *Anthology of Magazine Verse for 1938–1942*, edited by Alan F. Pater. New York: Paebar Co., 1942, pp. 107–8.
"From 'The Moulton Tragedy,' " *Poetry: A Magazine of Verse*, LX, No. 3 (June 1942), 115–22.
"Pastorius," *The American-German Review*, XVIII, No. 2 (December 1951), 30–31.

"Moon Light." In *The Spectra Hoax,* by William Jay Smith. Middletown, Conn.: Wesleyan University Press, 1961, p. 48.
"Memories." *Ibid.,* p. 49.
"Sunset." *Ibid.,* p. 50.
"Apocalypse." In *Two Centuries of Brown Verse,* 1965, pp. 218–19. (Reprinted from *Astrolabe,* 1927.)
"Greeks." *Ibid.,* p. 213. (Reprinted from *Astrolabe,* 1927.)
"Heat Lightning." *Ibid.,* pp. 217–18. (Reprinted from *Tilted Moons,* 1929.)
"Book Case," *Bulletin of the New York Public Library,* LXIX, No. 5 (May 1965), 280–81. (Reprinted from *Nightmare Cemetery,* 1964.)
"Sambo Psychopompos," *The New England Poetry Club WRIT,* 26 December 1965, pp. 6–7. (Reprinted from *Nightmare Cemetery,* 1964.)
——, *Pembroke Alumna,* XLII, No. 1 (January 1967), 14.
"Melville," *ibid.* (Reprinted from *Nightmare Cemetery,* 1964.)


· PLAYS ·


"The Flame," *The Newton High School Annual,* 1910, pp. 10–15.
"Kiri No Meijiyama: A Noh-drama in Japanese Syllabics," *The Dial,* LXVIII (February 1920), 205–[13]. Performed at Westhampton College, Richmond, Va., April 29–30, 1920.
*Punch & Judy as Presented Annually at the Annisquam Village Fair, Cape Ann, Massachusetts.* Barre, Mass.: Barre Gazette, 1957. (With introduction and bibliography.)
"Witch of Dogtown, a Drama in Three Acts." Typescript. First performed at Gloucester, Mass., 2–4 Sept. 1954.

# Literary Kinships

# Blake and the Postmodern

## · I ·

Blake's intimate relationship to literary modernism is now generally recognized and made much of by students of literature, mainly because several major writers of the early twentieth century display his influence. My purpose here is briefly to review this relationship, which was not always as clear as it is now, and then to step beyond it in order to discuss Blake's relation to "postmodernism" in literary theory, where his influence has been most recently felt.

Denis Saurat's *Blake and Modern Thought* (1929) precedes me and provides a way to chart the landscape, even though his definition of "modern" takes in more than literature and more than the twentieth century. For Saurat "modern" includes all that followed upon the vast upheaval—political, moral, social, in a word, philosophical—of the eighteenth century. "Blake stands at the moment of the change," which included the developments of liberalism, nationalism, and idealism. These may be characterized, respectively, as "rebellion against the Old Testament God, against moral law, against abstract intellect"; "the idealization of our own race to an entirely extravagant extent"; "replacing God by Man as a Creator, or identifying Man with God." Saurat goes on to compare Blake with Nietzsche and Proust— with Nietzsche because both were subverters of moral values, with Proust because both had the idea of "Eternal Man," spectre and emanation, etc. He indicates, however, that Blake refused to make the distinction Nietzsche made between superior and inferior beings and that he had a greater sense of synthesis than either Nietzsche or Proust. Blake's final value to modern thought is "his power of synthesis, or at least his desire for synthesis. He blends together perhaps more elements than any other modern writer." [1] Synthesis is what modern life lacks, and Blake senses its crucial needs. Although he is liberal, nationalistic, and idealistic, he attacks the divisiveness and analytical tendencies of modern life. He is a modern who thinks otherwise. Saurat constructs a book aimed to demonstrate how Blake goes about his synthesis, calling together various traditional, occult symbolisms. Some of these symbolisms are those of Gnosticism, druidism, the kabbalah, and Hinduism.

Writing in 1929, Saurat gave no attention to the influence Blake had already exercised upon modern writers. It was not easy at that time to recognize Blake as a major influence, nor was one likely to imagine that Blake would be a major influence on critics of the postforties and would influence, through some of them, our reading of Romantic poetry. For when Saurat wrote, Blake was still considered a sort of original. In 1920, T. S. Eliot had sought to alter that common image by writing in his well-known essay, "If one follows Blake's mind through the several stages of his poetic development, it is impossible to regard him as naïf, a wild man, a wild pet for the superculti-vated." [2] Eliot insisted that his peculiarity was the peculiarity of all great poetry, a "peculiar honesty." But the hint was not taken in the academy. Even now there are vestiges of the academic convention which allowed professors of the Romantic period to call Blake "eighteenth-century" and professors of the eighteenth century to call him "Romantic," with the result that in neither period was it necessary to teach him. His lyrics were either simple or eccentric, his Prophetic Books obscure, and he, perhaps, insane. The whole matter gives poets sanction for their traditional complaint about academic timidity.

Through the nineteenth century, by and large, it was a few poets and painters who kept Blake's work alive. These men were not, in-cidentally, the so-called major poets and artists. Coleridge knew of Blake and remarked on his *Songs*,[3] but apparently he was very little known to other well-known writers of the time. Those later poets who did find Blake interesting seem inevitably to have been influ-enced by him. The Pre-Raphaelites, including Rossetti, were among them, of course. They were interested in his remarks on style and in allegorical painting generally. Swinburne, who exercised his consid-erable critical powers on Blake, was perhaps the only writer until Yeats to take Blake's Prophetic Books seriously. His interest is im-portant, standing in relation, as it does, to his interest in French

poetry and the tradition of Symbolism in that country. In Arthur
Symons' literary interests there is a similar connection. Symons'
*William Blake* (1907) followed upon his better known *The Symbolist Movement in Literature* (1899). The latter is dedicated as
follows to W. B. Yeats:

> May I dedicate to you this book on the Symbolist movement in literature,
> both as an expression of a deep personal friendship and because you, more
> than any one else, will sympathize with what I say in it, being yourself the
> chief representative of that movement in our country? . . . Your own
> Irish literary movement is one of its expressions; your own poetry and
> A. E.'s poetry belong to it in the most intimate sense.

The Irish literary movement, whatever it was, had little in common
with French *symbolisme*. Against Nerval, Rimbaud, Verlaine,
Laforgue, and Mallarmé the ephemeral verse of A. E. is as uninteresting as second-rate German Romantic painting. But Yeats is a
different matter. Through his father Yeats developed an early attach-
ment to Pre-Raphaelitism and to Blake. In 1893 he brought out, in
collaboration with an occultist named Edwin J. Ellis, who apparently
knew both Blake and Blavatsky by heart, a three-volume edition of
Blake's work with copious notes and commentary. The best essay in
these volumes is Yeats's "The Necessity of Symbolism." Blake's
influence on Yeats is direct, pervasive, and lasting, though its nature
changes through Yeats's career.[4] The Blakean mythology attracted
Yeats from his youth onward, but the early work is Blakean via the
Pre-Raphaelites, while the later work seems more directly in touch
with the dialectic of *The Marriage of Heaven and Hell*. I shall
return to this matter shortly, for it is in Blake's strong sense of
dialectic that we discover the element in him that most influences
postmodern literary theory. I only suggest at this point that Yeats, as
a man of his time, helped to make Blake a man of our time.

Yeats was not, of course, alone in this matter. A very interesting
essay by Northrop Frye points out the major parallels between the
structure of *Finnegans Wake* and Blake's Prophetic Books.[5] The essay
establishes in particular the relationship of Joyce's ironic endless
cycle presided over by a Blakean female will to Blake's "Mental
Traveller." In his own lecture on Blake, Joyce didn't get very far

toward illuminating Blake's relation to his own work; the date of the lecture was, after all, 1912. But it is clear to the reader of *Finnegans Wake* that Joyce was strongly influenced by Blake, probably through the Yeats-Ellis edition, and that an understanding of Blake is probably as useful as any other single thing to an understanding of Joyce's epic.

Other writers have seen a different Blake or found useful different elements in him. In D. H. Lawrence it is the sexual ethic and the revolt against reason, but they are sentimentalized. Absent in Lawrence is the rationality with which Blake attacked reason. In Dylan Thomas, it is the bardic voice, the rhetorical element plus the symbolism of descent and cycle. The beat poets of the fifties were attracted to Blake's "simplicity" but did not understand its deceptiveness. They insisted on the same innocent wildness in Blake that Eliot attempted to put down. This was an unfortunate distortion indeed, since it reveals so clearly the limitations of these poets.

Blake's contemporaneity with all these writers and his modernism in relation to his own contemporaries is strange in at least one respect. If we look at the matter a certain way it is possible to conclude that the Blakean voice is a reactionary one. Between Wordsworth and Blake, for example, one would have to choose Wordsworth as the self-conscious rebel against tradition and Blake as the preserver. The cult of "originality" is Wordsworth's. Much of the "originality" of Blake lies in an illusion created by those who refused to take seriously his own insistent statements about the tradition in which he worked. In Blake we have a very traditional poet accused of obscurity because, in the growth of cant about romantic originality and irrationality as the soul of poetry, a sense of the traditions of symbolic patterns in literature became lost, emerging toward the end of the century in the apparently exotic interest of literary people in the occult. The reason for this is that in occultism various traditions of symbolic utterance were imperfectly and to some extent accidentally preserved in a culturally surreptitious way—preserved against the onslaughts of the misguided pseudoscientific theories of naturalism and realism.

In his own traditionalism Eliot rejected the whole occultist element and sought pattern in orthodox Christianity. He did not appreciate Blake's traditionalism, associated as it must have been in his mind with his own Madame Sosostris. But whether he liked it or not Eliot's demand for tradition as well as individual talent parallels in certain ways Yeats's and Joyce's Blakeanism, which in turn looks to Milton, Spenser, Dante, and the Bible.

The Blakean tradition springing alive in the twentieth century paralleled, of course, the well-known literary appropriation of developments in depth psychology and in anthropology, from analysis of the ritual elements of Greek tragedy to Freudian and Jungian patterns. Blake himself has been interpreted naïvely as a Jungian in a small book by W. P. Witcutt.[6] Perhaps the better tack would have been to interpret Jung as fundamentally Blakean, on the assumption that idea follows icon or that Jung's occultism is a nonliterary offshoot of an essentially literary mode of imagination. I assert this with hesitation, for some readers may wrongly consider it an attempt to make the Blakean tradition the one uncompromising monolith.

· II ·

This brings us to a consideration of the more precise relation of Blake to postmodern critical theory. Like most theory, postmodernism is the child of its immediate artistic forebears. It is a criticism that seeks to answer the demands of modern art. Modernism includes Eliot, Yeats, Joyce, Lawrence, and Thomas, and therefore, as I have suggested, Blake. Just as literary modernism has called on Blake, so has postmodern literary theory. The principal immediate source of postmodernism has been the Blakean critical theorizing of Northrop Frye. His work has recently been examined at some length,[7] and I shall try to pass beyond him here to the general characteristics of the criticism that has followed. I call it "postmodern" to avoid the appellations, derogatory or otherwise, recently given to it by various commentators—"apocalyptic," "Promethean," or whatever suits the attitude to be conveyed.

Fundamentally, it is a criticism that exploits dialectic of a Blakean sort, but it is also influenced variously by Husserl's phenomenology and by existentialism. It may exhibit in some versions the weaknesses of the old romantic expressivism; it may return to modes of discussion which care little for the medium and problems of technique and everything for philosophical content or a certain commitment. In extreme and, I think, irresponsible forms it is ready to praise a poet if only he seems to associate himself with a certain sort of political radicalism. Nevertheless, I believe these weaknesses or excesses, or wrong turns, are not inevitable to postmodern critical theory, though perhaps inevitable to certain minds attracted to it.

In a recent essay, which is an attack on an aspect of postmodernism, W. K. Wimsatt provides a brief historical survey of critical schools leading to the present situation.[8] Though his analysis is interesting, it draws lines too sharply between various movements. He begins by differentiating two schools of Romanticism, the first running from Kantian disinterest, formality, and beauty through French academic criticism and early Parnassian and Symbolist aesthetics to art for art's sake and Croce's systematic theory of expression. The second begins in the Romantic theories of imagination and "symbol," Coleridge, Poe, and Heine, through Baudelaire, to Mallarmé, Wagner, and *symbolisme* generally.[9]

In a later wave comes affective psychologism out of Hegel and Nietzsche on the one hand and out of utilitarian ethics through Santayana's hedonism to I. A. Richards' harmony of impulses on the other. To the side of all this Wimsatt observes T. E. Hulme, T. S. Eliot, Ezra Pound, *et al* emphasizing impersonality, craftsmanship, objectivity, irony, drama, ambiguity, etc.; in other words, the New Criticism.

Wimsatt observes more recently three movements: first, a new mode of historicism; second, a so-called neo-Aristotelianism with attention to plot and other bulkier elements of the literary object; and finally the supreme *bête noire* of the three, myth and ritual criticism. All of these movements Wimsatt regards as allied in their orientation toward a collective audience and therefore attractive in a collective age. The satanic "archmythopoeist" of the myth and ritual critics is, of course, Northrop Frye, who spins webs of metaphysical speculation from his citadel somewhere in the Mordor land of Canada. Myth and ritual criticism Wimsatt sees descending from Hegel and Schelling to Ernst Cassirer with help from Lucien Lévy-Bruhl, James G. Frazer, and the Cambridge anthropologists. But in the background is William Blake. Clearly Frye's system is Blakean; it is also related to Cassirer and the Neo-Kantian tradition Wimsatt mentions, so much so that when Frye reviewed the English translation of Cassirer's *Philosophy of Symbolic Forms* his point seems to have been that the translation had come too late, Cassirer had already been assimilated.[10] This was true, especially for Frye. Postmodernism feeds upon both strands of Romanticism isolated by Wimsatt (indeed, it is questionable whether the two strands are really separate) and appropriates as well the interests of the New Criticism and myth and ritual studies, both of which have Romantic affinities. Cassirer's anthropological and Neo-Kantian philosophical interests tend to synthesize these strands.

Kant, of course, tried to resolve the subject-object split as it was left to philosophy by Locke and Berkeley. As we know, Berkeley argued that the so-called objective and primary world was an abstraction from our experience and thus a fiction, while Locke had preceded him by arguing that the subjective world was an abstraction from objective measurable experience and therefore not the route to reality. Kant proposed the manifold of sensation organized by the creative power of the sensibility. We cannot know things in themselves; but through the forms of time and space and the categories of the understanding we can construct a workable reality. As a result science is possible.

Now the real contribution of Cassirer is that he refused to limit ways of knowing to the understanding and proposed the existence of additional ways of "constituting" reality. In so doing, he took the Kantian concept, transformed it, and raised the whole matter onto the level of language, so that it became the systems of language or symbolic forms which practically "constitute" reality. He, therefore, was part of the movement toward analytic philosophy and toward an analytic mode of literary theory. In this vein, Philip Wheelwright and other critics made linguistic distinctions between literature and other modes of language.[11] The philosophical objects which began to interest us were the structures which we create and which in turn make our thought possible.

Through his sense of contrariety, Blake influences postmodern critical thought along related lines. In his allegory he seems to anticipate (with a little extension by me) the sort of distinction between steno and depth language that we see in Wheelwright. Most important, he seems to sense the desirability of making the distinction a dialectical opposition suggesting that ultimately every individual must balance the claims of the steno language of his mythical figure Urizen (with all its Lockean implications) against the claims of the literary language of his heroic artist Los. Without this contrariety the world falls. Without it all the knowledge gained by a single symbolic form in isolation is self-defeating. Cassirer's concept of verbal symbolic forms or universes of discourse and Blake's sense of the dialectical relation of scientific to literary imagination seem to be combined in postmodern criticism. I do not deny that Cassirer sees a dialectical relationship among his symbolic forms, but he does not press very far into the heart of that dialectic. This Blake does. The conjunction of Blake and Cassirer enables postmodern criticism to reconstitute or broaden the modernist critical ideas of paradox, tension, drama, and irony. Literary language is naturally paradoxical from the point of view of its contrary.

In respect to this matter, Yeats, as a follower of Blake, is the most subtle modernist exponent of that "contrariety" characteristic of literature as a symbolic form. Attached to Blake, he saw beyond Cassirer without having had to see Cassirer. He became a thoroughgoing antinomialist; for him man lives always between complete primary being—dominated by the spirit of Platonic or scientific modes of abstraction—and complete antithetical being—dominated by the spirit of artistic abstraction. The direction of scientific and Platonic abstractions is toward the general. The direction of antithetical modes of abstraction is toward constituting the particular. Therefore, Yeats, as did Blake before him, associates art and its intellectual sensuosity with the here, the now, the experiential, the body, but not "matter." Primary abstraction creates the fiction of "matter," which cannot be experienced, and is thus related to the soul. Blake insisted that the currently received body-soul distinction with its ascription of primary matter to body and secondary experience to soul was a false or "cloven fiction," totally backward, created by "Bacon, Newton, Locke." Its result is to force upon us the modern sort of intellectual confusion which relegates art to the area of bodiless subjectivity, and leads to the "Platonic" sort of poetry attacked by John Crowe Ransom and Allen Tate. To this extent at the very least, Blake and Yeats are in the same camp as these New Critics.

What we talk *in* are linguistic worlds each with its own form of objectivity. Cassirer's concept of symbolic forms can be joined to the Blakean dialectic taken over by Yeats; and a new significance, always latent in the words, can be given to Blake's assertion that there is war and hunting in heaven. The point is that even the place of ultimate resolution is characterized by the intellectual and linguistic rather than the material strife of reason and art.

And they conversed together in Visionary forms dramatic which bright
Redounded from their Tongues in thunderous majesty, in Visions
In new Expanses, creating exemplars of Memory and of Intellect,
Creating Space, Creating Time, according to the wonders Divine
Of Human Imagination throughout all the Three Regions immense
Of Childhood, Manhood & Old Age; and the all tremendous unfathom-
    able Non Ens
Of Death was seen in regenerations terrific or complacent, varying
According to the subject of discourse; & every Word & Every Character
Was Human . . .                        (*J* 98:28-36, *K* 746)

· III ·

A number of critics have reservations about a criticism based upon Blakean dialectic. The most violent utterance of complaint has come from Wimsatt. In the essay to which I have already referred, he attacks "A generation of critics today, especially in America—the younger evangelists of Blake and of Yeats," who are "not likely to suffer from absentmindedness regarding the lovely colors of combustion, the fiery permanent discontent which may be generated by contemplating the gospel of contraries." [12] It is true that Blake has always had his evangelists. Indeed, in the past they were necessary if Blake was to obtain a hearing. But now, in the postmodern age, the tide has clearly turned. In much recent criticism of the Romantic poets, the tendency has been to read other poets from a Blakean vantage. Wimsatt's evangelical critic seems to suggest that as long as a Blakean critical language can be profitably employed the poet under question is worthy of keeping our interest. This can be carried too far, but so can all good things.

But I wonder whether a criticism based upon a Blakean dialectic must be quite so outrageous as Wimsatt makes it out. I cannot resist taking up one challenge Wimsatt tosses forth, mainly because it leads to the heart of the matter. I quote at some length:

The following collocation of materials has been arranged by me with the special design of provoking the Prometheans. Of course they will cry "unfair." It must be unfair. But if any Promethean will make the effort to explain why it is unfair, much, very much may be explained.

> James Brown, 45 years old, of Devon, was sentenced to life in prison today for the strangling of a high school girl last October. . . . A confession read to the jury during the trial told how Brown became aroused as he watched the girl knitting during a committee meeting at the Devon County Grange last October 20. . . . Brown followed the girl in his car after the meeting. . . .
>                         —From a New England newspaper during the spring of a
>                         recent year (names and dates adapted).

> He who desires but acts not, breeds pestilence. Sooner murder an infant in its cradle than nurse unacted desires.
>                         —William Blake again, *The Marriage of Heaven and Hell.*

There are two alternatives to *nursing* an unacted desire. One is to suppress the desire; the other is to act it.[13]

I do not like to think of myself as Promethean, nor do I claim to see apocalypse, but let me try an answer: First, these "Proverbs of Hell" are typically representative of one side of the dialectic between reason and energy. Martin K. Nurmi in his study of *The Marriage of Heaven and Hell*[14] argues that they are meant as a prolific contrary to, say, the Book of Proverbs, which develops the idea of moral virtue. In language the truth must be approached by sustaining a dialectic. We can sharpen the issue but never quite get it stated univocally. This is the reason from the postmodern point of view why poems are necessary. They can speak paradoxically. They can parade their irony. Like them, Blake's proverbs cannot be taken literally; their contraries must be imagined as present even as they are spoken.

This leads to the second point, which, I believe, helps clarify implications of the first: Blake's point within one side of the contrary must be understood. Blake would hold that Brown's perverse act is a perfect example of the result of someone's having suppressed or nursed Brown's "unacted desires." Just as Urizen's law suppresses the child Orc and results in violent revolution, so does perverse tyranny lead to the outburst of *perverted* desire. Blake's point is that we should not allow the situation of Brown to arise. From this point of view the suppression and "nursing" of desire just doesn't work very well; some other means of preventing Brown's act must be found. The irony of "Sooner murder an infant in its cradle than nurse unacted desires" is that the infant you don't murder in its cradle may, if you *nurse* his unacted desires, become a Brown.

I mention the matter of Brown not because of the ethical problem it brings up, but because it is the sort of ground on which Wimsatt wishes to argue a theoretical issue. For Wimsatt, there is something heretical about the Blakean dialectic as illustrated above. It has dangerous moral implications. Wimsatt's fundamental complaint against a criticism friendly to Blakean contrariety—a complaint at the basis of all his remarks—is that he cannot accept a constitutive epistemological principle, limited and defined as it is in the idea of symbolic forms. He is an epistemological realist. He is caught between his own friendliness to New Critical principles and an epistemology which conflicts with their Neo-Kantianism. Epistemologically post-modern Blakeanism has more affinity to the New Criticism than does Wimsatt. He writes of Blake's idea of the contraries: ". . . this doctrine lends itself peculiarly to a certain grand obscurity about the relation of poetics and poetry to the life of actuality." [15] Yes, that is true, but only because the precise relation of any symbolism to any blithely assumed actuality is indeed obscure, and we should not pretend that it isn't. The remark, which is that of a naïve realist, implies that actuality is a lot more easily locatable than it is.

I see no reason for despair in this matter. An acceptable conclusion might be that there is an irony or contrariety implicit in the very nature of our symbolisms. Once the whole question of knowledge and imagination is raised to a question about language or systems of symbols—once this has occurred—these symbols become our reality: worlds of ideas or worlds of objects, worlds of scientific or "Platonic" abstraction or worlds of particular experience. In another theory the former would be characterized as scientific reality, the latter as artistic "imitation." But the view suggested here is that there is nothing clear enough in the manifold of sensation for us to "imitate." There is the manifold itself to shape, or "constitute," as Los shapes the body of Urizen and builds Golgonooza. We can only "create" symbolic worlds. These are the only worlds, and we can only make a world with a language, indeed *in* a language. Imagination of the sort Coleridge had in mind can operate only in a symbolic form or *as* a symbolic form. There is nothing imaginable independent of a medium to imagine *in*.

The irony I have mentioned is completed by the admission that there is also something ultimately incompetent about our languages. We can never encompass in a single system what we want to encompass; we can never create all that we want to create. Every system provides its own limits and thus demands its own contradiction: "Without contraries is no progression," says Blake (*MHH* 3, *K* 149). On some ultimate level the very existence of literature is an allegory of this problem, constantly implying, as Blake does in his central myth, the danger of naïve commitment to only one of our incompetences, to "Single vision & Newton's sleep" (*K* 818).

· IV ·

One of the more penetrating criticisms of Frye, Wheelwright, and others, and one touching upon the issue here, has been made by Murray Krieger in his book, *A Window to Criticism*.[16] Generally he accuses them of returning to "mimetic" theories, foregoing the contextualism won by the moderns, and thus abandoning the idea of the poem as "constitutive." This is particularly interesting because their sort of criticism rejects the more conventional idea of imitation, that is, the idea of literature as a copy of an assumed outer reality. Krieger's point is that these critics shift the object of "mimesis" to a sort of Platonic body of literary conventions. They accept, he argues, the existence of a total order of literature, which is autonomous and contains the archetypes that each single work copies. According to Krieger there is nothing or very little left in this criticism of the idea of meaning found *in* the work instead of *through* it.

Whether or not the critical practice of these particular writers implies simply a new theory of imitation I cannot deal with here.

What I do want to insist is that a Blakean criticism need not suggest there is some system of symbols that individual works copy. The criticism I see as properly emerging from what Blake gives us should hold that literary works are bound together by means not of conventions and genres or other aspects of content but by the forms and categories of linguistic action. Of course, these forms and categories lead to the appearance of what we may call conventions, and we usually talk about the forms and categories in terms of the conventions they seem to generate. These we think of as concrete results of the way literary language works. In the process we often indulge ourselves in the illusion that the conventions are somehow pre-existent to the poems which contain them. But only the *way* of symbolizing can really be said to pre-exist. The conventions are not "Platonic" existences to be "imitated."

The categories of literary language can be characterized only imperfectly because as critics we must work within the contrary categories of discursive language to analyze them. It is best to begin discussion with the forms of space and time as literary linguistic action tends from the point of view of steno language to "distort" them. Blake's Prophetic Books suggest that all space is reducible to a single point which is everywhere and all time is reducible to a single moment which is all history. It is clear that such reductions are very strange from the point of view of a language tending always to spatialize and thus measure. It means that Blake's language is inclined to paradoxes, to testing its limits as discourse, to driving itself beyond those limits in order to chart a world unchartable in the categories that lead, apparently inevitably, to spatialization and finally measurement as their ends. When Blake denies the historical Jesus and makes of him the Antichrist, he speaks in behalf of literary constructions against spatializing historical ones. Jesus *comes* in the Bible; it is not that he *came*. His being is not tied to some abstractly constructed spatialized past temporal order but is always present in the presence of the Bible itself. This is a literary principle of total application. We speak of plots in the present tense, not in the past. Literary narratives are *here*, not *there;* their whole point is somehow to bring those events *here* that in all other linguistic forms are distanced from us.

The form of linguistic imagination stretching time on a tape—

logical analysis which organizes by measurement and therefore by spatializing time—is properly the contrary of this literary principle. Its attractiveness to culture is its own commonsensical straightforwardness. The apparent logic of language is on its side. Literary language must operate with the same spatializing materials but against their innate spatializing, measuring, and therefore reductive tendencies. Literary language must build reality by internal struggle which it organizes into paradox. Spatializing, linear language distances things. It abstracts toward the general principle rather than toward the concretely experienced moment, and it insists on the actuality, even the reality of its abstractions—as most of us accept the "objective reality" of history, though we can find it only in our constructions of history. Its danger, as the phenomenologists have felt, is its tendency to tyrannize over our imagination and dehumanize our experience, fictionalize it in the old Lockean way. For it drives a wedge, they claim, between what we actually experience and the way we symbolically construct things historically or scientifically. With the spirit of this phenomenological return to concrete actuality Blake would be in sympathy. But Blake believed that the real world was the world man makes, and therefore all that is worth calling real or actual lies in the products of the arts of man, not in what art is somehow construed to talk *about.* A criticism which discusses content separated from technique Blake would not have accepted; for it implies a formed, pre-existent actuality that the work of art is referring to, copying, or embellishing—something *about which* art talks. To talk *about* something is to distance it again, to lose its actuality.

Further, Blake would refuse to reduce reality to any *single* actuality, no matter how full of paradox or conventions it might happen to be. Although he propagandizes for art and literature, and insists on the reality of their vision, he does not negate the imaginative power of the rationalistic Urizen, who is, after all, the prince of light. When the heroic builder and artist, Los, is confronted with the vague, undifferentiated nature of Urizen, he must build Urizen, not destroy him. He must, for his own sake and culture's, help his enemy. Just as Blake wishes his Urizenic friend Hayley to "be my Enemy for Friendship's sake" (*K* 545), so might the converse be true: Los must be Urizen's friend in order that their enmity may be prolific. Los is the icon to Urizen's idea. Art is particularity to history's generality.

So there is contrariety both inside and outside the construction which literary imagination makes. For Blake, languages, and not the sheer unmediated experience of the phenomenologists, build actuality. Actuality and reality lie only in creations out of the primal chaos. The poem makes a world according to its own mode of statement, which is designed to constitute immediacy in its own form of abstraction. The world exists *in* the statement. But, of course, the poem, because it operates as it does, is clearly a poem and therefore, when subjected to logical analysis, like other similarly operating things. What these things have fundamentally in common are the forms and categories of literary imagination, a particular linguistic nature, not a pre-existing content or collection of devices, genres, images, verse forms, or whatever. Poems are fundamentally related to each other neither by content nor by what form commonly means but by a common mode of linguistic action.

Blake's spatial and temporal paradoxes imply the principle Krieger wants to preserve, the idea that primarily a poem means by its own coherence, for there is nothing else but coherence by which to judge. This coherence can be said finally to reach out and in some way have referential meaning as well, but this is a crude and unsatisfactory way of talking. In referential meaning we mean not that the poem "copies" an outer reality but that it has something to do with reality. It makes reality by drawing the world into its categorical troughs.

But also it doesn't quite make reality. Its world depends upon an opposite world. No symbolic form operating independently is quite enough, and that is illustrated by the failure of the language used in this essay to close the circle. No poem alone quite closes the circle either. The most viable Blakean criticism insists that poetry and the mode of science stand contrary, that neither can quite afford the luxury of the autonomy it must nevertheless insistently profess, that neither can quite devour its opposite. To sustain a proper intellectual struggle between these forms of knowing is to provide ourselves with what cultural and spiritual harmony we can, as symbolizing animals, achieve. Thus Blake wrote: "Los built the stubborn structure of the Language, acting against / Albion's melancholy, who must else have been a Dumb despair" (*J* 40:59–60, *K* 668).

HAROLD BLOOM

# The Visionary Cinema of Romantic Poetry

The inventor of my subject in this essay is, unsurprisingly, Eisenstein, who wrote with insight on the cinematic elements in Milton and Shelley. I want to deviate from Eisenstein's concern a little, and I choose my motto from a poem of Wallace Stevens, *The Creations of Sound*. Speaking of one X, a poet I take to have been Eliot, Stevens says of his poems, in courteous but firm disapproval: "They do not make the visible a little hard to see." [1] Blake, Wordsworth, and Shelley meant somewhat different things by vision, and their intentions in this matter were certainly not identical, but they all of them, in their poems, do tend to make the visible a little hard to see.

Critics have noted, during these last decades, the apparent conflict between theory and performance in this regard in these poets, particularly in Wordsworth. Blake seems just as odd when one starts to know him well. "General Knowledge," he insisted, "is Remote Knowledge it is in Particulars that Wisdom consists & Happiness too. Both in Art & in Life General Masses are as Much Art as a Pasteboard Man is Human" (*LJ* 82, *E* 550).

An experienced reader of Blake's major poems, his epics, learns to set aside the very early impression that there is anything cloudy or indefinite about the figures or actions in those poems. Yet there is a subtler problem in visualization that presents itself everywhere in Blake's poetry at its most characteristic; Blake invites the reader's ocular powers to the enjoyment of a dangerous freedom, dangerous I think not to Blake as a poet, but certainly to Blake as a visual artist and critically somewhat dangerous to the reader. I read one of the most eloquent descriptive passages in the language; I stare, disbelievingly, at an inadequate engraved illumination, and then I try, too strenuously, to isolate an image that Blake, as a poet, knew better than to isolate. Blake, I think, like his master Milton (as Eisenstein hinted) wants his reader to be more of a film-script reader or even a director than a film-viewer. He wants us to hear the fierce arguments between his Giant Forms, and he wants how we hear those disputes to waver depending upon our own states of being. And he wants us to see the transformations in his ruined worlds, but how we see and even at times what we see will depend upon the self-purging of our own eyes. Blake suggests a principle that I have seen applied only at scattered moments in a handful of films, one that might be called both auditory and visual counterpoint. The Urizen in us is meant to see one thing, the suffering Tharmas another, and so on down that sorrowing cast of internalized Titans.

There is an equivalent or parallel counterpoint in Wordsworth, a cinematic dialectic in which natural sight and sound reach their horizon and blend into a seeing and hearing of processes that cannot, in mere nature, be seen and heard. To Blake, Wordsworth's visionary cinema seemed not a counterpoint but a movingly fragmented single voice, the voice of Tharmas, a splintered but still visual, still instinctual unity, quaveringly seeking his harmony again in a context that could never afford him such harmony. But Wordsworth makes his blendings work, and invents the modern crisis poem by doing so. That a strictly controlled synesthesia should have been the mark, not of disaster, but of salvation in the Coleridge-Wordsworth crisis poem, is of peculiar importance in understanding how the Romantics suggest a more imaginative cinema than we can see in our theaters.

Shelley is the crucial case, and no originality is possible here, because of the brilliant commentary by Eisenstein on visual detail in Shelley's lyricism. Shelley, as always, is an imaginative extremist and does not deal in visual or auditory counterpoint as do Blake and Wordsworth. His desire is to make the visible almost impossible to see, and his cinema is too visionary for any techniques devised in our time to encompass. The sight or sound too keen for more than a flash of apprehension is the staple of his imagination, and seems to suggest the art of the lighting expert or of the sound-effects specialist more than that of the film creator. But, at his greatest moments, Shelley earns his assignment to Phase 17 of Yeats's *A Vision*, as one of the *daimonic* men whose Body of Fate is "Loss." Where Blake struggles to *see* an imaginative gain, and Wordsworth to *hear* the conversion of experiential loss into such gain, Shelley sees, hears, and describes imaginative loss. The dissolving of sight is given us, by him, as a presage of a greater fading of integrity, a yielding of every natural particular to what he ironically terms the Triumph of Life.

Keats is not primarily the creator of a visionary cinema, though *Endymion* acts itself out before us as a dissolving series of visions, and *The Fall of Hyperion* stations its scene and figures with a monumental sense of visual possibility that transcends what is ordinarily visible. A feeling for the weight of things, and a deliberate pacing, too slow for the impatience of the eye, combine to render Keats a maker poised before things-in-their-greeting, even as Blake, Wordsworth, and Shelley, in different ways, deal with things-in-their-farewell. Keats is nevertheless more than a naturalistic artist, however heroically we conceive his naturalism; like the other major Romantics, though to a lesser extent, he was, despite his yearnings, a Miltonic poet, and the central principle that organizes his art is not a particularly dramatic one. *To Autumn*, rightly accounted his masterpiece, presents us with a scenario of, first, an enacted process too slow for the eye to see; second, a sight so ambiguously blended that we cannot know for sure whether we love landscape or woman; third, a series of sounds, of autumnal music, that inevitably betoken death by their gentle tentativeness. Blake would have had no quarrel with the ode *To Autumn;* it gives firm outline, but spiritual as opposed to corporeal form.

I propose in what follows to sketch the rough outlines of a visionary cinema in Blake, Wordsworth, and Shelley, not in order to cast illumination upon the nature of any mere pragmatic cinema we already know, and not much in the hope that a study of poetry will ever make any particular cinematic artist any more gifted in his work.

The burden of Romantic poetry is absolute freedom, including freedom from the tyranny of the bodily eye, and this freedom appears to have resulted in part from the specifically Protestant influencing that made modern poetry possible. When Wordsworth seeks the middle passage between the sensual, sleeping the sleep of death in their vacancy and vanity, and the ascetics, studying their nostalgias and insisting that all earthly paradises have been lost, he is presumably not immediately conscious that he seeks what radical Protestantism so frequently sought, a renewal of the biblical program of hallowing the commonplace. It takes a while to realize that this Wordsworthian hallowing is not enacted through the eye. Wordsworth would rouse us from sleep by words, he says, that speak of nothing more than what we *are*, rather than of nothing more than what we *see*. Who could have thought, Stevens asks, in one of his more explicitly humanist declarations—who could have thought to make, out of what one sees and what one hears, so many separate selves. Wordsworth was too aware that his freedom was precarious to make so trusting a statement. In him the Christian Liberty of Milton had become what it nearly became in Coleridge, the power of the mind over a universe of death.

Christian Liberty, as a doctrine, led to Milton's conception of a sect of one (Abdiel), a church of one (himself). He appealed to the holy light to shine inward, and created English Romanticism by doing so. The implicit distrust of the visible in Blake and Wordsworth, in particular, has some relation to Milton's blindness, for Milton is the greatest visionary poet in the English language, as Isabel McCaffrey remarks. He yearns, most movingly, for the visible, but he does not need it, and its absence became one of the greatest of his astonishing panoply of strengths.

There is, I think, a profound sense in which poetry *is* antithetical to cinema, an opinion expressed rather strongly by Valéry. My concern here is not to say anything about the nature of cinema, but to apply the principle of Borges, that artists create their own precursors, and force us to read the precursors differently. Art forms do the same, and the consciousness of films compels us to read past poetry differently. That this difference is sometimes loss is beyond dispute; *Paradise Lost* has yielded some of its primary excitement to our cinematic experiences. But, if controlled, the difference becomes gain, becomes indeed another working of Wordsworth's compensatory imagination. I want, in this investigation, to bring a critical eye conditioned by cinema freshly to bear upon Blake's visionary procedure and Wordsworth's and Shelley's. Somewhere along the roads that led from the major Romantics to our poets who matter most—to Stevens and Hart Crane particularly—the distrust of the merely visible dissipated. One so much wishes Tennyson had freed his inner eye, had yielded himself to the phantasmagoria that was his truest mode. Browning, particularly in the greatest of his lyrics, *Childe Roland to the Dark Tower Came*, does yield momentously to vision, and renews something of the Romantic freedom. Stevens hestitates, endlessly, at the verge of that freedom. But, to this day, for a full-scale emancipation from a mere appearance of objects, we need to go back to the founders of modern poetry, to Blake and to Wordsworth.

If I ask myself what I remember most vividly, at all times, about Blake's three long poems, *The Four Zoas, Milton,* and *Jerusalem,* the answer is always argument—passionate, beautiful argument between mutually tormented consciousnesses—and never actions or sights as such. But Blake does more than make us hear these arguments; he stations the disputants in a context informed by conceptual images, images that either poise themselves just within the visible, or compel a new kind of visibility to appear. From their beginnings, his long poems refuse to seek the visually remembered world. Even Wordsworth, of course, is found not by the visually remembered world, but by that world taken up into the mind, and seen again by the eye of the mind, as Geoffrey Hartman insists. Blake shatters this blending with a single insistence; as he does not behold the outward creation, so he can affirm for himself that his Giant Forms are stationed in no remembered landscape, but only in the visionary finding of his own pulsation of an artery, that moment in each day that Satan's Watch-Fiends cannot find.

At the end of Night the Fourth of *The Four Zoas,* the Giant Form named Los, who will at last compel an imaginative salvation, wearies of the terrible task of hammering the falling Urizen into some kind of definite shape. Himself a malformed Imagination, Los, the affrighted Titan, at this point cannot bear the consequences of his own necessary labor. Instead of the heroic stance of the artificer before his own free creation, we are given the wavering of an enforced illusionist who "became what he beheld / He became what he was doing he was himself transformd." The final lines of Night IV read:

> The bones of Urizen hurtle on the wind the bones of Los
> Twinge & his iron sinews bend like lead & fold
> Into unusual forms dancing & howling stamping the Abyss.
>
> *(E* 331)

This vehement grotesquerie seems, at first, only an instance of what Blake's friend Fuseli charmingly called "Meester Blake's emancipated anatomy," prompting those Blakean manuscript sketches that impress our skepticism as being only so many flying geeks. But the rhetoric this vision emancipates in Blake at the very start of the next book, Night the Fifth, is monumentally impressive by any standards. This is the *Totentanz* of Los:

> Infected Mad he dancd on his mountains high & dark as heaven
> Now fixd into one stedfast bulk his features stonify
> From his mouth curses & from his eyes sparks of blighting
> Beside the anvil cold he dancd with the hammer of Urthona
> Terrific pale. Enitharmon stretchd on the dreary Earth
> Felt her immortal limbs freeze stiffning pale inflexible
> His feet shrunk withring from the deep shrinking & withering
> And Enitharmon shrunk up all their fibres withring beneath
> As plants witherd by winter leaves & stems & roots decaying
> Melt into thin air while the seed drivn by the furious wind
> Rests on the distant Mountains top. So Los & Enitharmon
> Shrunk into fixed space stood trembling on a Rocky cliff
> Yet mighty bulk & majesty & beauty remain but unexpansive
> As far as highest Zenith from the lowest Nadir. So far shrunk
> Los from the furnaces a Space immense & left the cold
> Prince of Light bound in chains of intellect among the furnaces
> But all the furnaces were out & the bellows had ceast to blow
>
> He stood trembling & Enitharmon clung around his knees
> Their senses unexpansive in one stedfast bulk remain
> The night blew cold & Enitharmon shriekd on the dismal wind
>
> Her pale hands cling around her husband & over her weak head
> Shadows of Eternal Death sit in the leaden air
>
> But the soft pipe the flute the viol organ harp & cymbal

And the sweet sound of silver voices calm the weary couch
Of Enitharmon but her groans drown the immortal harps
Loud & more loud the living music floats upon the air
Faint & more faint the daylight wanes. The wheels of turning darkness
Began in solemn revolutions. Earth convulsd with rending pangs
Rockd to & fro & cried sore at the groans of Enitharmon
Still the faint harps & silver voices calm the weary couch
But from the caves of deepest night ascending in clouds of mist
The winter spread his wide black wings across from pole to pole
Grim frost beneath & terrible snow linkd in a marriage chain
Began a dismal dance. The winds around on pointed rocks
Settled like bats innumerable ready to fly abroad          (*FZ* v, *E* 332)

If Wordsworth's method, as Pottle remarked, was one of transfiguration, then Blake's, in this terrific passage, seems to be poised between the phantasmagoria of the surrealists, and the massive and detailed visionary realism of Milton. The matter of common perception is wholly absent here; no descriptive detail awaits transfiguration. Yet the greatness of the passage does not dwell only in its carrying-over of the Miltonic sublime into a conceptualized nightworld. Like every major passage in Blake, it is polemical, and it fights not only the technologists and materialists of Blake's own time, but also the servants of Urizen who abound in our own technological dreariness. To explore the dens of Urizen is to come to terms with a fallen world, but to see the irrelevance of that world to the imagination, as Blake does in the passage just cited, is to see what an intellectual fighter must see if he believes, as Blake did, that the Eternal Great Humanity Divine can tear Himself free from any local, timebound accidents of context, whether the context be provided by nature or by the technological extensions of nature. For Blake, as for Wordsworth and Shelley, there are no extensions of man; there are only more humanized or less humanized men. Explorations that are not apocalyptic are, to Blake, exploitations; they lead to religions of concealment. The passage from Blake quoted above is about the completion of the Fall of man, which is made final when the imagination accepts unnecessary limitations. The terror felt by Los is founded on his stupidity; he cannot see that the hammering of error into definite shape, however repugnant, will lead to salvation. The great description of the dance of Los founds its irony on visionary counterpoint; the imagination is accepting a naturalization that is wholly unnecessary; it is yielding itself to the context of space. But it is recalcitrant to that context, and the landscape cannot hold it. With an eye made active by an awareness of cinema, we see what Blake gives us in his passage, a series of shifting views that are not in continuity with one another, and whose juxtapositions suggest an intolerable confusion between an inward world rolling outward, and an outward world that stands apart and is objectified as a mockery of our visual powers. Los is "Infected" because he is becoming what he beheld in the changes of Urizen; he is "Mad" because he cannot bear such transformations in himself. He dances "on his mountains," which are truly his, for they are forsaken elements of his own self. In the earth of Eden, before the Fall, the Imagination dwelt in underground caves, which were the auricular nerves of man, and identical with the apocalyptic sense of hearing. In Blake, the Fall turns everything inside out; the stonified ears have become the mountains on which the deafened Los dances. We see, in succession, but again without continuity, the following images: a mad Titan dancing on mountains as high and dark as an inhuman heaven; then a stedfast bulk, a horror of natural sculpture, with stony features, a cursing mouth, and eyes from which sparks of blighting come at us. Next we see the dancer again, but he is pale, and dances beside a cold anvil, ironically brandishing the now useless hammer of Urthona, his name in Eternity. The next shot shows us his female, emanative portion, Enitharmon, stretched on a denuded earth, and freezing and stiffening into that ground of unbeing. In the eye of vision we suddenly see both figures shrinking and withering from the feet up, and immediately the next frame shows us two plants withered by winter, uprooted, decaying, and then dissolving in a furious wind that carries the unseen seeds to a distant mountain top. We see the two more-than-human figures again, still mighty in bulk and majesty and beauty but curiously confined-looking, and then a shot of the cold furnaces and unused bellows is given us. The two figures tremble on a cliff at the edge of an abyss, the female clinging round Los's knees. The wind blows, and we hear her shriek; there is a chorus of soft instruments and silvery voices, but she shrieks louder to drown it out as the daylight wanes. The darkness comes in the shapes of the turning wheels of giant mills, as though industrial spectres were planted in the skies, and the earth responds to the dread revolutions of those dark wheels by rocking to and fro, convulsed in the rending pangs of an enormous childbirth. As Enitharmon groans again, the music of comfort attempts to return:

> But from the caves of deepest night ascending in clouds of mist
> The winter spread his wide black wings across from pole to pole
> Grim frost beneath & terrible snow linkd in a marriage chain
> Began a dismal dance. The winds around on pointed rocks
> Settled like bats innumerable ready to fly abroad

I have requoted these last five lines because their visionary power is so intense. Here, the winter wind is an enormous bat flying over the frozen chain of Jealousy that symbolizes all fallen marriage for Blake, and the dance of the weather completes Los's dance of death. Beneath the black bat and the white chain there now comes rending forth, out of the earth, the crimson form of natural man in revolt, the hellish figure of Orc, Rousseau's dream of man become a nightmare of revolt and unrestrained violence. A ghastly decomposition in layers of black, white, and red ends a scene that began with a maddened but still titanically heroic figure dancing itself on, through a frenzy of incomprehension, into its own destruction. The ear has heard a blowing wind, a silvery music too soft to endure, and a female howling in pangs of childbirth. The eye has seen human forms vacillating between stony masses and ruined vegetation, and eye and ear together end with a vision of a howling red child, menacing all of the senses it seeks to release; a vision of natural existence so violent that it can give vision no field in which to continue the labors of salvation.

What Blake has compelled us to see and to hear is not the redemption of physical reality, which Kracauer states as the central thesis of his theory of film, but rather the ocular and aural demonstration that physical reality cannot be redeemed by the arts of the eye and the ear. Uneasily but inevitably, the passage, like every major passage in Blake's mature poetry, makes us confront the abyss of the five senses, makes us realize, in Stevensian terms, the necessity for a violence from within to overcome this violence from without. In the war between the sky and the mind, Blake fights on the mind's side always, and he will resort to no external image for its own sake, but only as yet another index to our Fall. We cannot be saved by images, in Blake, and yet the emblem of salvation for Blake remains a central image, the Human Form Divine, a perfect human body stationed in no context but itself, seen against no background but the artifacts it itself has made, but artifacts poised against the created world. What Blake finally wants us to see breaks the confines of a possible cinema—a greater human form, male and female together, containing the world *within* it, from the caves of middle-earth to the starry wheels above. To visualize a poem, and a visionary poem at that, is to see what cannot be seen. In the closing lines of *Jerusalem* Blake speaks of what Stevens terms a seeing and unseeing in the eye, as an *identifying* of all human forms. He asks for too much, and perhaps at last we will be condemned to judge him as he judged Milton, a true poet when he wrote of visual torment, but a fettered bard of the absolute when he asked us to go beyond the abyss of the eye. Yet his eternal appeal is in his demand that we must and can do so.

With Wordsworth, we move to a more overt defeat of the eye, though the consequences of the defeat are deliberately mitigated by the poet, in contrast to Blake's grim delight in our apprehension of the defeat of sight by vision. Though Blake might have seen our movie theaters as so many more temples of Urizen, he would have found them demonically relevant, mills of the mind in retreat from the work of creation that might burn up *the* creation. But to Wordsworth, they would have been merely irrelevant to the inward eye of solitude, which is the eye of his song. As I have chosen what Blake himself termed one of his more "terrific" passages, I take, for contrast, Wordsworth in his eerie, his preternatural *quietness*, showing a strength of being perhaps more primordial, in its effect, than that of any other poet whatsoever. *The Ruined Cottage*, the tragic tale of Margaret, supplies the passages. Where, with Blake, we are rhetorically compelled to know that we are in the presence of a poet's prophetic *power*, here in Wordsworth the rhetoric makes us know the strength of a prophetic *endurance* that only an extraordinarily exalted poet possesses. Blake moves us by a counterpoint that turns on the irony of unnecessary limitations; Wordsworth moves us, possibly more deeply, by a counterpoint that turns on the anti-ironic, on the necessity of a suffering so permanent, obscure, and dark that it overcomes its own status as limitation, and shares the nature of infinitude. Blake shows us vision collapsing into space and time; Wordsworth shows a spot of time or moment of space that holds vision precariously open to further experience. For Blake the mind is always lord and master, even if the mastery belongs, at times, to Urizen, the writer of the great poem of winter. For Wordsworth, there is always a precise extent and a *howness*, to the mind's mastery, and always therefore an abiding recalcitrance in which outward sense is not just the servant of the mind's will, but has an unsuspended and dangerous will of its own. The tyranny of the eye, that most despotic of our senses, is only the most celebrated aspect of this recalcitrance. The tyranny of the ear, which Wordsworth would never acknowledge, subtly imposes itself by the compulsive repetition of the sound of universal waters far inland. Deep in his journey to the interior, Wordsworth is obsessed by the oceanic sense, the waters of judgment rushing all about his ears. It takes a while for the constant reader of Wordsworth to be disheartened by the excessive recurrence of this auricular image, but disheartened one can become. Yet compulsion in Wordsworth *is* strength, whatever it may be in the rest of us, and perhaps it is even, finally, an aesthetic strength.

That ruin should come out of the more than natural, the apocalyptic strength of hope and love, is the awful meaning of the Tale of Margaret, as harrowing a poem as any of us have read, a warning against the destructive power of the imagination. All through the old man's discourse that is the poem, the eye of the narrative pauses, with a racking slowness, on the outward signs of Margaret's inner self-destruction, and in a way that avoids the tyranny of the camera eye. I quote, in progression, three such passages, taken from context but forming a unit among them:

> The sun was sinking in the west, and now
> I sate with sad impatience. From within
> Her solitary infant cried aloud;
> The spot though fair seemed very desolate
> The longer I remained more desolate.

And looking round I saw the corner stones
Till then unmarked, on either side the door
With dull red stains discoloured, and stuck o'er
With tufts and hairs of wool as if the sheep
That feed upon the commons thither came
As to a couching-place and rubbed their sides
Even at her threshold. The church-clock struck eight,
I turned and saw her distant a few steps.
Her face was pale and thin, her figure too
Was changed. As she unlocked the door she said
"It grieves me you have waited here so long
But in good truth I've wandered much of late." [2]

A step further on and we are given this:

I turned towards the garden gate, and saw
More plainly still that poverty and grief
Were now come nearer to her; the earth was hard
With weeds defaced and knots of withered grass;
No ridges there appeared of clear black mould,
No winter greenness. Of her herbs and flowers
It seemed the better part were gnawed away
Or trampled on the earth; a chain of straw
Which had been twisted round the tender stem
Of a young apple-tree lay at its root,
The bark was nibbled round by truant sheep.
Margaret stood near, her infant in her arms
And seeing that my eye was on the tree
She said, "I fear it will be dead and gone
Ere Robert come again." [3]

And finally, the end, abrupt, and arousing in us that brother's love in
which we bless her in the impotence of grief:

Meanwhile her poor hut
Sank to decay, for he was gone, whose hand
At the first nippings of October frost
Closed up each chink, and with fresh bands of straw
Chequered the green-grown thatch. And so she lived
Through the long winter, reckless and alone;
Till this reft house, by frost, and thaw, and rain
Was sapped, and, when she slept, the nightly damps
Did chill her breast, and in the stormy day

Her tattered clothes were ruffled by the wind
Even at the side of her own fire. Yet still
She loved this wretched spot, nor would for worlds
Have parted hence, and still that length of road
And this rude bench one torturing hope endeared,
Fast rooted at her heart; and here, my friend,
In sickness she remained, and here she died,
Last human tenant of these ruined walls.[4]

Three visions of a spot made progressively more wretched by the yearning strength of a hope too willing to be fed, and yet three visions in which the visible is either very hard to see indeed, or else does not yield up to the eye the full purchase it has made upon reality. In the first, the aged narrator sits against a sunset, hears the cry of a solitary infant, and stares at the corner stones on either side the door. He sees a pastoral emblem, but one that shows a falling-away; the discolored stones, with their dull red stains, their tufts and hairs of wool, subtly tell of a collapse from cultivation back to the wild. The red-stained stone is itself a sunset, and the infant's cry of loneliness is another sunset, the three together betokening the twilight figure of Margaret, that lingering sunset whose slow self-destruction is the process that the poem enacts. In the second passage, the old man scrutinizes Margaret's ruined garden, and sees again a series of tokens that only the eye of the mind can link together. Where fixities and definites in the first passage dissolve into the sad unity of the pastoral sunset, here they dissolve into the image of a pastoral hunger shared both by the earth and by the wintry sheep. Again the hand of the human is missing, and the wild claims its own—the earth is hard, the withered grass is knotted, the herbs and flowers gnawed away and trampled, and the young apple tree gradually dies into its longest winter, its bark nibbled round by the hungry sheep. What the scene speaks of is at the borders of the visible, for the abandonment does not indicate despair, but grimly once again tells of the destructive strength of outrageously sustained hope. It is an instance where Valéry is proved correct, for here the poem is antithetical to its own cinema; what camera eye could gaze upon this scene, and tell us, mutely, that the voice that will rise from this solitude and wilderness will be the voice of a woman transfigured by an infinite hope, and not by a despair?

In the third passage, ending the poem, the torturing hope attains its visionary climax. Nature has been abandoned to apocalyptic yearnings, and it replies as it must, in the killing image of winter. The cottage and the woman fuse together, and both reach the borders of the visible, for the artifact and the human alike slide over into a blending where they are merely vegetal and animal, exposed remnants of nature yielding to natural entropy. The cottage is reft and sapped by frost and thaw and rain, and Margaret is chilled, asleep, by nightly damps and, awake, by a wind that blows by her own fireside. The last *more-than-visual* image is one of dreadful naturalization, even of a Blakean sort; the endearing but torturing hope holds her to the wretched and now deathly spot, "fast rooted at her heart." The final image is purely *visual*—the ruined walls of the cottage, but visual presentation has little to do with the Wordsworthian power of this final image. It is a complex of emotions that falls apart in this abandoned spot, and the falling-apart is truly one of the credences of winter.

We need not puzzle as to why Blake distrusted the merely visual, and insisted on the visionary in its place. But, despite the great line of Wordsworthian critics, from Bradley and Abercrombie through Wilson Knight and Hartman—that alternative convention that has insisted against Arnold that Wordsworth was *not* the poet of nature—despite that splendid array the Wordsworthian distrust of the eye remains a partial mystery. Wordsworth, at his very greatest, feared both the outward eye of nature and the inward eye of vision, though the fears never kept him from his courageous assaults upon both modes of seeing. Hartman suggests the influence of Burke on Wordsworth, quoting Burke's notion that the business of poetry "is, to affect rather by sympathy than imitation; to display rather the effect of things on the mind of the speaker, or of others, than to present a clear idea of the things themselves." [5] Pottle cites Wordsworth's letter to Landor, where what moves Wordsworth most in poetry is spoken of as that point of vision "where things are lost in each other, and limits vanish, and aspirations are raised." [6] The strength of hope, in Wordsworth as in Margaret, is more-than-natural, and perhaps the clue to his distrust of the bodily eye is to be found in the apocalyptic power of his hope. His sense of possible sublimity is always with him, and his poetry holds us, ultimately, by our own sense that it will reveal "something evermore about to be." The visible has been, and is, and even its actual sublimity is always a betrayal of its possible grandeur. The spirit of the unvisited haunts Wordsworth, and the unvisited resists even the counterpoint of the visual and the visionary.

Blake lived in apocalyptic hope also, but his response to that hope was unequivocal; the expanding eyes of Man would *see*, and in that revelation the deeps would shrink to their foundations. The blending or dual element in Wordsworth refuses a clarified sight as the gift of revelation; either common sight must suffice or, since it does not, a synesthetic blend of seeing-hearing must return, as once it existed for the young child. And, when this return is doubted or modified, the synesthetic phenomenon, the sober coloring that is also a still, sad music, must yield to hearing alone, as nothing in nature will satisfy the eye that quests for evidences of the mind's excursive power. The things not seen provide the substance of hope, and Wordsworth at last approximates Milton in practicing an art of the eye's abyss, in taking us down to that inward depth where no modern prophet of the eye has followed. An art so deep is a lasting reproof to our cinema, and to ourselves.

My epilogue is in Shelley, who went on until he had stopped eye and ear together. As I have used such melancholy passages of Blake and Wordsworth, I am happy to quote Shelley at his most loving. Here is one of the dazzling passages of his *Epipsychidion*, where he describes, or rather does not describe, the beauty of Emilia Viviani, that soul out of his soul:

> The glory of her being, issuing thence,
> Stains the dead, blank, cold air with a warm shade
> Of unentangled intermixture, made
> By Love, of light and motion: one intense
> Diffusion, one serene Omnipresence,
> Whose flowing outlines mingle in their flowing,
> Around her cheeks and utmost fingers glowing
> With the unintermitted blood, which there
> Quivers, (as in a fleece of snow-like air
> The crimson pulse of living morn may quiver,)
> Continuously prolonged, and ending never
> Till they are lost, and in that Beauty furled

Which penetrates and clasps and fills the world;
Scarce visible from extreme loveliness.
Warm fragrance seems to fall from her light dress
And her loose hair; and where some heavy tress
The air of her own speed has disentwined,
The sweetness seems to satiate the faint wind;
And in the soul a wild odour is felt,
Beyond the sense . . .[7]

I do not recall that any actual cinema I have seen does much to make the beauty of a woman a little hard to see. Shelley, unlike Milton, Blake, and Wordsworth, both liked and desired women; the three older prophet-poets desired women, but evaded the full portrayal of the total or spiritual form of that desire. Shelley was, intellectually, a ruthless skeptic, as tough-minded as you are, whoever you are. Rhetorically, he was, all critical misrepresentation to the contrary, an urbane ironist, but emotionally he was, to his eternal credit but personal sorrow, a passionate idealist. As an intellectual skeptic, he knows, too well, the narrow limits of both poetry and love; as an ironist he is too cultivated to indulge in the vulgarity of constantly showing us that he knows those limits. As an idealist, he merely keeps falling in love. Put together the skepticism, the urbanity, and the idealism, and you leave little reason for any visible appearance to move this poet. Intellectually he doubts that he can know its reality; rhetorically he doubts that it can be expressed with any decorum; and emotionally he doubts that it can satisfy a desire that will not settle for any outermost form whatsoever. Set him the task of describing the visual beauty of his beloved, and you get the extravagant and magnificent passage I have quoted, not so much a description of a human female as a fireworks display of what Stevens called "lights astral and Shelleyan." [8]

Yet a close inspection of the passage makes us dissatisfied, not with it, but with the ways we ordinarily describe a woman's beauty, and even more, with the grossness of the motion picture camera, or its manipulator, when an attempt is made to show us such beauty. "See where she stands!" Shelley cries in exultation, and we try to see. But the glory of her being is not visible in any ordinary sense. We cannot *see* a warmth compounded of light and motion, nor can we see the aura of love surrounding this beauty. And yet, as Shelley's poem knows and shows us, phenomenologically just *this* is given to us in the privileged moments of our lives. The problem is to describe a secularized epiphany that cannot be described, but Shelley was a specialist in the indescribable. I do not know the critical technique that would permit *us* to describe accurately just *what* happens in this passage that confronts the idealized Emilia. Confrontation takes place in the second person; all analysis or description takes place in the third. The Intellectual Beauty, a gleam just beyond the range of our senses to apprehend it, gets into this passage, but phenomenologically what counts most is what Shelley beautifully calls "the air of her own speed." The miracle of Shelley's art is in its continual impression of speed. Like the Psalmist, when his soul is uplifted, Shelley in moments of glory moves with a speed that reproves the slow dullness of the ordinarily visible. His nuances are subtler than Blake's or Wordsworth's; too subtle for the outward eye to apprehend, but not too subtle for the awakened spirit seeking, as Yeats said of Shelley, more in this world than any can understand.

The final use of Romantic poetry, or of poetry written in that tradition down to Yeats, Lawrence, Stevens, and Crane, is to teach us that we do not know either what our senses, just as they are, can reveal to us, or what can be revealed to us, perfectly naturalistically, and yet seemingly just beyond the range of our senses. All actual cinema that I know, including the rubbish that currently passes for experimental or "new" cinema but seems designed merely to bring on a saving myopia—all cinema yet made has failed in imagination, has absurdly fallen short of the whole aesthetic need of the awakened consciousness of man. One does not ask a film to be a poem; films-as-literature bore, and will go on boring. But one waits for an artist, and an art, to go beyond the relative crudity of what one has been offered. The burden of Romantic poetry, and the true though frequently evaded burden of post-Romantic poetry, is either to offer an apocalypse of the order of physical reality, as in Blake or Shelley or Yeats, or to move us towards that adventure in humanity in which, at last, we would be a race completely physical in a physical world, the dream of Keats and of the colder Stevens after him. Between these fierce alternatives there is the blending vision of Wordsworth, seeking the difficult rightness of a nature "first and last and midst and without end," in which the Characters of the Great Apocalypse could be read in every countenance and on every blossom. No medium has inherent limitations so great that the Imagination cannot overcome them, and no medium is its own message. Films will either become more imaginative, will either achieve their own apocalyptic form, whatever that may be, or they will die, leaving us again with those astral and Shelleyan lights that our poetic tradition throws upon us, adding nothing to our reality but themselves, and yet re-imagining our lives in that addition. Wallace Stevens, commenting in a letter on one of his own poems, concludes the matter as I would have it concluded. He writes: "The astral and Shelleyan lights are not going to alter the structure of nature. Apples will always be apples, and whoever is a ploughman hereafter will be what the ploughman has always been. For all that, the astral and the Shelleyan will have transformed the world." [9]

## HAROLD FISCH

# Blake's Miltonic Moment

Blake's deep and permanent interest in Milton, culminating in the mystic union between himself and the spirit of the dead poet which in 1804 he celebrates in a full-length epic-prophecy entitled simply *Milton*, can hardly be studied in isolation. The Miltonic obsessions of Blake are not exactly of a piece with the Miltonisms of Wordsworth and Keats, but they point to needs and paradoxes which are located at the heart of the Romantic movement as a whole. If they were in revolt against the Miltonic artificialities of the eighteenth century, the Romantic poets were also seeking to recover the voice of the prophet and visionary of a former age, an age of faith. Mr. Harold Bloom finds in the kinship with Milton one of the unifying factors in Romanticism: what links Collins, Keats, Blake, and Wordsworth, he says, "is one of the great traditions of English poetry, the prophetic and Protestant line of Spenser and Milton, which reaches its radical limits in the generation after Wordsworth." [1] It is this inspiration which accounts for the religious, apocalyptic quality of their poetry. They abandoned the Christian myth of Milton, replacing it with a mythology of their own. But if I understand Mr. Bloom correctly, he is claiming not only that they are in the same poetic tradition as Milton, but that this tradition attained its fullness specifically in the Romantic age, in the work of Blake, Wordsworth, and the rest.

In this article I shall endeavor to define rather more narrowly than has been customary hitherto the nature of the affinity between Blake and Milton. At the same time I hope to show that in spite of the depth and force of this affinity, Blake's poetry belongs in the last analysis to a tradition essentially different from Milton's. But first a brief glance at Wordsworth.[2]

· I ·

Two years before Blake began to engrave *Milton*, Wordsworth had also made his gesture of summoning the dead poet to life: "Milton! thou shouldst be living at this hour." Herbert Read reminds us[3] of how strikingly similar were the physical features of Wordsworth and Milton, a circumstance which might encourage those inclined to the occult to speculate on theories of metempsychosis and the rest. But leaving such tantalizing speculations aside, let us ask what it was in Milton that Wordsworth felt it necessary to attach to himself, what particular spiritual possession or faculty?

The answer, as most critics would agree, is to be found in his most Miltonic poem, *The Prelude*. Apart from the characteristic Miltonic nimbus of eloquence, there is the unmistakable note of lyrical egocentricity. Like Milton, Wordsworth is "called," singled out for greatness:

> Ye Presences of Nature in the sky
> ... can I think
> A vulgar hope was yours when ye employed
> Such ministry.[4]

Inevitably there is the same dream of immortal fame, the

> daring thought that I might leave
> Some monument behind me which pure hearts
> Should reverence[5]

—echoing the very words of Milton in *The Reason of Church Government*.[6] Wordsworth, like Milton, is a prophet whose lips have been touched with holy fire; he is the vessel of a messianic deliverance. There is an inward fire of inspiration, but it does not remain confined to the inner spirit: it seeks confirmation and expression in history and politics. It is this conjunction which constitutes Wordsworth's Miltonic moment. With Wordsworth, as with Milton, the spirit who visits him nightly is the same spirit which imparts to history its portentous meaning. The poet brings together in one fiery node the microcosmic world of personal fate and the macrocosmic order of universal purposes. This has naturally something to do with the Puritan tendency to sense a universal drama in the individual wayfarer's oscillations between grace and spiritual unrest. In Milton it had taken the form of an intense concern with history and its meaning; the elect poet carried upon him the burden of that history. He was one of "the select heralds of peace, and dispensers of treasure inestimable." If the nation of England had been chosen to be "the trumpet of Reformation to all Europe," [7] then he, the inspired poet, was chosen to be the trumpeter.

In this sense the Miltonic climax of *The Prelude* is reached when Wordsworth's destiny as prophet-poet is momentarily fused with that of France as he beholds her "standing on the top of golden hours." The biblical imagery with which he describes his meeting with the newly emancipated citizens—"Guests welcome almost as the angels were / To Abraham of old"—is itself mediated through *Paradise Lost* as is the reference to Robespierre and his "Atheist crew" [8] later on. The epic drama played out in France is in an important sense the private dream of the visionary prophet-poet, and yet his private world of meditative ecstasy projects itself through "daring sympathies with power" upon the wide arena of universal history in its revolutionary phase. He will in his dreams pronounce "long orations before unjust tribunals" and, with the spirit of prophecy upon him, see "Glimpses of retribution terrible / And in the order of sublime behests." [9] This is the historical orientation of Milton again, the feeling for a purpose revealing itself in world history and yet rooted in the personal life of the poet. Wordsworth's crossing the Alps has a revelational character as intense as the storming of the Bastille, and perhaps the one is the echo and accompaniment of the other.

But if we consider *The Prelude* in relation to its Miltonic inspiration, we shall see that it shows us Wordsworth just as clearly abandoning Milton and the specific mode of experience which he represented. *The Prelude* shows us Wordsworth rejecting History for Nature. The poet will depart for Racedown with his sister, leaving the Revolution to take care of itself. Indeed it is only through Wordsworth's remarkable power of recreative memory that we are at all enabled in *The Prelude* to recover the vibrations of his early tremendous ardors. For by the time the poem comes to be written the Revolution has already shrunk to an incident in the "Growth of a Poet's Mind," and the poet is primarily no longer the herald of change, but the guardian of his own inspiration. And we should add that this inspiration flows not from time but from the timeless. The tension of the time-bound man subject to the stress of great decisions in an era of change yields to a passive acceptance of a static, cyclical order of things. He is rolled round in earth's diurnal course; he is laid asleep in spirit; he is made one with Nature.[10]

Milton had been different to the end. For all his disappointments, he had never really abandoned the historical mode. He was always committed, grappling with the problem of what God wanted with England, and how that purpose would be furthered by John Milton. *Samson Agonistes* at the end of a lifetime of unrelaxed struggle for such meanings is, once again, an unmitigated theodicy—an attempt to peer into the mysteries of Providence in its dealings with the chosen one: "Why am I thus bereav'd thy prime decree?"[11] Wordsworth no longer asks such questions, nor does he any longer dream of pronouncing orations before unjust tribunals. What is left of the twofold focus of Milton is the one side only, the lyrical egocentricity. The electric spark which joins that inwardness of concern with the outwardness of concern for a world in travail has gone.

## · II ·

Blake's poetry reveals a movement curiously similar to Wordsworth's and at the same time curiously different. The first thing that may be said is that from the beginning, Blake's intuition of the historical events through which he lived was more detailed and intense than that of Wordsworth. His first major poems, *The French Revolution* and *America*, are primarily poems celebrating the revolutionary idea. Nor is Milton here the chief inspiration. Blake's first great soul-stirrings as a poet of history are evidently the direct effect of the American Revolution and the Gordon riots of 1780 when he had personally witnessed the burning of Newgate and other terrific sights. These remained with him, as Mr. Erdman has shown,[12] as poetic symbols. Moreover, it is important to note that the challenge of history directly opened up for Blake the world of prophetic or epic poetry. He does not abandon poetry for a dozen years as Milton had done in order to exercise his left hand in political debate: his inner poetic fire fuses at once with the burning vision already displayed around him in London, America, and France. This is the Orc phase of Blake's poetry, and it lasts longer than does the revolutionary excitement of either Wordsworth or Coleridge. Undismayed by Robespierre and the Terror, Blake holds fast to the cause of the French Revolution when his fellow poets have given it up. And even after the Lambeth period, the revolutionary fires continue to burn beneath in "a furnace of dire flames" (*FZ* vi:265, *K* 318). The Revolution as such is not abandoned, but there is a change in its form and direction. And Milton has something to do with Blake's successful recasting of the revolutionary principle after 1800.

But before we speak of Milton, there is one other important, non-Miltonic influence which helps to explain the early and later poems and their grasp of history. In a letter to John Flaxman, dated September 12, 1800 (*K* 799), Blake tells us of his early debt to Milton and Isaiah, but he adds also that "Paracelsus & Behmen appear'd to me." This latter "kabbalistic" influence—of which little is found in Milton[13]—provided Blake with a dialectical apparatus which could be applied to the squalid disappointments and failures of history. The realm of Providence is neither simple nor serene, but a realm of complex antagonisms out of which redemption is born.[14] The divine order which ultimately presides over Time and History is no simple static, hierarchical order—as it is perhaps for Milton—but a system of unalleviated tensions within which Mercy and Judgment—the right and left hand of the kabbalistic system of divinity—struggle for mastery, in which outbreaks of violent punishment testify no less than do hymns of praise to a divine movement forward. Only in some messianic climax will the tiger lie down with the lamb: in the meantime, it is necessary for the poet to seize both principles in all their fierce and unrelieved opposition, attaching himself to them both.[15] Rousseau and Voltaire, Newton and Bacon, for all Blake's awareness of their ominous and catastrophic power for evil, never cease to be positive imaginative entities. They will reappear in Heaven at the end of *Jerusalem* among "the innumerable Chariots of the Almighty" (*J* 98:8, *K* 745). Blake shows here a capacity for detachment which makes him markedly different from his fellow Romantics. Shelley never forgives Lord Eldon and Castlereagh; but Blake's dialectic ultimately overcomes even his obsessive feelings about Hayley and Scholfield. They are certainly identified with the Devil, but then even the Devil ultimately belongs to the poets' party without knowing it.

There is another "kabbalistic" aspect of his thinking[16] which helps to explain the tenacity of Blake's apprehension of history in his early and later poetry. For Blake, the poet is a kind of adept who, through the exercise of his art, actually promotes and controls the historical process. Here is something quite different from Wordsworth dreaming of addressing unjust tribunals, or Shelley calling upon the West Wind to scatter his thoughts about the world like dead leaves to quicken a new birth. In Shelley the poetic Word is disseminated in a "normal" fashion: it affects the course of history through its influence over the minds of people who read the poem in a book or find it floating in a bottle on the ocean. But here in Blake the release of poetic energy in art constitutes itself historical action. There is no need for the poet to move outside the realm of poetry, for history is made in poetry *itself*. The poet it is who builds Golgonooza, and he does so without having to persuade practical people of the value of his insights. Blake's standpoint here does not belong strictly to prophecy, but to magic! There is an occult sympathy between the deeds and thoughts of the adept (in Blake's case the poetical adept) on the one hand, and the macrocosmic, metaphysical order which governs history on the other. After Los enters his soul in Plate 22 of *Milton*, Los-Blake can declare "both Time & Space obey my will" (22:17).

This will explain why Blake never felt it necessary to leave poetry in order to employ the weapons of political debate as Milton had done. It was not because he was less politically conscious than Milton, but because he felt that in his poetry he could be more directly engaged in the revolutionary struggle than even Milton could have been while acting as Cromwell's Latin secretary. Los, the god of Time, is also the god of Poetry. There is a total integration of these two realms, the realm of private imaginative intensity, and the realm of cosmic revolution. The two meet in one orgasm, in one throb of spiritual activity. The poet is the Atlas who himself holds up the Revolution singlehanded. Were he to cease from mental fight there would be no redemption for the fallen principles of Orc and Urizen: America would be overwhelmed by the Atlantic and all would be lost. The poet is like the alchemist who, through his spagyric operations, governs the creative forces of the world, or like the kabbalistic "Masters of the Name" who, through contemplative ecstasies, prayers, and manipulations of words, raise up the fallen "husks" of divinity out of the profound abyss in which they have sunk.[17] Blake in his poetry claims to be doing just that—raising up the fallen fragments of divine life; and by doing so he makes it possible for them to be restored ultimately to the wholeness of existence. And so it is he who, through his poetry, directly ushers in the foreordained climax of time.

### · III ·

It should be obvious that such a position could not be long maintained while the poet-magician remained mystically harnessed to the actual revolutionary movements of his time. Los demands the apocalyptic: Pitt, Napoleon, and George III manifestly do not provide it. Even a magician has to show results. Blake was bound to feel, as Milton and Wordsworth had felt before him, and in spite of his greater "kabbalistic" nimbleness of mind, that politics were not heading in quite the direction required by his inspired poetry. History and Poetry were clearly not advancing toward a simultaneous accomplishment of their joint purposes. The sense of defeat and frustration for Blake came evidently after Napoleon had revealed the full extent of his onslaught on French liberties, that is, at the time of Blake's removal to Felpham in 1800.[18] This is the degeneration of Orc-Luvah lamented in the seventh Night of *The Four Zoas,* and rendered more cryptically in *The Mental Traveller:*

> The stars, sun, Moon, all shrink away,
> A desart vast without a bound,
> And nothing left to eat or drink,
> And a dark desart all around. (ll. 65–69, K 426)

Orc reveals himself as a burning babe, who is born, grows old, unites with Vala, the shadowy Female, principle of Nature and of the sterile Intellect, and finally degenerates into Luvah. There is an eternal cycle of repetition as in some nature myth; and the reader of *The Mental Traveller,* however troubled he may be with the precise interpretation of the symbols, cannot fail to sense the weariness with which the poet-prophet contemplates the eternal sameness of this monotonously repeated cycle. Instead of moving forward toward the vision of a world redeemed, we are caught in the vicious circle of revolution and counterrevolution, world without end. This is the threatened pre-emption of History by Nature to which Wordsworth had resigned himself when he gave up moral questions in despair. Orc, beginning as a Time-god, ends up as a Nature-god, his ritual birth, copulation, and death suggesting the monotony of a world-order which knows neither salvation nor change, but only the sameness of eternal forms, as in the Greek cosmos. In such a world genuine progress is impossible.

It is hardly an exaggeration to say that here we have the central issue of the Prophetic Books as a whole. There is a strong pull in the direction of a cyclical nature-mythology and an equally strong resistance to it. The tension between the two, the cyclical and the historical modes of experience, explains the mutations which Blake's major mythological figures undergo. Orc, Los, and Urthona are all different formulations of the reality of time as it is experienced by the prophet-poet, and each of them, while initially conceived as a setting-forth of the six-thousand-year span from Adam to doomsday, tends to lapse into the region of the timeless and the repetitive. It is the struggle between the Greek and the Hebrew spirits, the latter committed to History, the former to Nature. But Blake does not give up; he looks round for a means of salvaging his "Hebraic" commitment to History and its revolutionary, redemptive promise.

It is here, in fact, precisely at the point where Wordsworth abandoned the Miltonic mode, that Blake found Milton of most service. It is here that Blake's Miltonic moment occurred. It is Milton who enabled Blake to achieve a new adaptation to contemporary events while remaining committed to Revolution and Apocalypse. This moment can be located clearly in Blake's mythology: it occurs when Los takes over from Orc as the god of Time and Prophecy. The arrival of Los as Blake's motor-spirit suggests a new interiorization of the idea of Revolution, and also an increase in its religious depth. Orc, the leading principle of *America* and *The French Revolution*, was a secular phenomenon, a god of war and blood, rather than of the religious spirit. His direct progenitors are not Milton, but Rousseau, Voltaire, and Tom Paine. He is a "naked babe," bereft of all the beauty of traditional religion. Los, by contrast, is the spirit of that prophecy which spoke through Elijah and Ezekiel; and if with him the biblical dimension is introduced in its fullness into Blake's poetry, it should be added that it is Milton who presides over this transformation. Milton is the inspired biblical poet of an age of faith who had wedded poetry to the inspiration of the Bible. And so Los becomes the spirit of biblical poetry: with his arrival Eden and Jerusalem become major symbols. The new phase of Blake's poetry beginning with the later additions to *The Four Zoas* and reaching its fullness in *Milton* and *Jerusalem* is thus in a most particular degree biblical, and the agent of this transformation is Milton. We can watch the actual dynamics of the process. Los, busy creating the world and governing it through time to its predestined conclusion, looks around for some means of redeeming the enchained Orc (that is, the stifled spirit of Revolution). In Plate 20 of *Milton* that means is discovered:

> He recollected an old Prophecy in Eden recorded
> And often sung to the loud harp at the immortal feasts:
> That Milton of the Land of Albion should up ascend

Forwards from Ulro from the Vale of Felpham, and set free
Orc from his Chain of Jealousy. . . .           (ll. 57–61, K 503)

Here the epiphany is precisely located and its nature defined.
Milton is a prophet of England-Albion, but his arrival is prophesied
in Eden; that is, it is biblically motivated and directed. The transforming moment occurs, we are told, in the Vale of Felpham,
that is, between 1800 and 1803, and its outcome will be the freeing
of Orc from his Chain, that is to say, the giving of a new direction
to the perverted spirit of Revolution now disclosed in the ugliness
of the Napoleonic era in France and the parallel manifestations in the
England of Pitt and George III.

The fundamental value of Milton's spiritual achievement to Blake
then was that he enabled him to relate the temporal, political
reality to the biblical. In particular it was he who had welded together the matter of England and Israel and formed them into
one undifferentiated divine history. It is the England-Israel analogy
which lies at the heart of both *Milton* and *Jerusalem:*

I will not cease from Mental Fight,
Nor shall my Sword sleep in my hand
Till we have built Jerusalem
In England's green & pleasant Land.
                              (*Mil* 1:13–16, K 481)

The ground and warrant of this analogy is found throughout Milton's writings but nowhere more clearly perhaps than in the *Areopagitica,* the work to which Mr. Northrop Frye rightly directs us
as Blake's immediate inspiration for the poem *Milton.*[19] The key
passage in the *Areopagitica* therefore deserves to be carefully noted:

Yet that which is above all this, the favour and the love of heav'n, we have
great argument to think in a peculiar manner propitious and propending
towards us. Why else was this Nation chos'n before any other, *that out of
her as out of Sion* should be proclam'd and sounded forth the first tidings
and trumpet of Reformation to all Europ?[20]

The emphasis in Blake's later poems on Albion, the ideal form of
England, as the true fountain of revolutionary inspiration and the

eternal partner of Jerusalem, is here displayed in its genesis. At this moment in Blake's intellectual development, France and America (the Orc phase of the Revolution) recede, and the true source of historical renewal is found in England-Albion. The continuation of the above-quoted paragraph from the *Areopagitica* provides the exact prototype of Blake's change of direction:

And had it not bin the obstinat perversnes of our Prelats against the divine and admirable spirit of *Wicklef*, to suppresse him as a schismatic and *innovator*, perhaps neither the *Bohemian Husse* and *Jerom*, no nor the name of *Luther*, or of *Calvin* had bin ever known: the glory of reforming all our neighbours had bin compleatly ours.

Milton was reaching back from the shortcomings of the seventeenth-century revolutions sponsored by the spirit of Luther and Calvin to the Reformation as found in its purest form in the England of the fourteenth century. Blake adopts this precise strategy in his own reading of the history of revolutions. Turning away from the "Grecian worship" of Napoleon and George Washington,[21] he reaches back to the seventeenth century, the century of Milton, in the conviction that when the genuine taproot of Revolution is discovered it will prove to be a pure English root, and "the glory of reforming all our neighbours" will be "compleatly ours." The revolutionaries of his time in France and America represent the Urizenic distortion of history, while Los, the true spirit of prophetic idealism, identifiable with Blake's own poetic genius, reveals himself also as the genius of the English spiritual revolution of the seventeenth century, personified above all in the biblical poet, Milton.

· IV ·

It is one of the notable achievements of S. Foster Damon in his commentary on *Milton* and other poems to have shown how close Blake felt to the literary and intellectual world of the seventeenth century, in particular as we see it manifested in the writings of Browne, More, and the mystical Thomas Vaughan. Here in seventeenth-century England, Blake found the fundamental source for later history as well as the prefiguration of the warfare dramatized in his mythology. The scientific spirit of Bacon and Newton at war with the spiritual imagination of the Age of Elizabeth[22] provides the concrete historical reference point for the separation of Los and Urizen, Albion and Jerusalem.[23] Moreover, it is through Blake's historical intuitions—his enrooting of the divisive tendencies of his day in the spiritual conflicts of the seventeenth century—that he is enabled to affirm his confidence in the apocalyptic transformations which will yet occur. The betrayal of Liberty, Fraternity, and Equality is not a new calamity belonging to the age of Napoleon and Pitt: it has its origins in an earlier century, and if one can only trace it to its source one has the means also of meeting and overcoming it. For the poet-magician not only controls current history; he can also change the past. And the main object for such corrective action is no other than the poet Milton. He represented the continuation and climax of the creative spirit of the Elizabethan Age, and yet he had gone tragically wrong in surrendering himself to the Urizenic world of Bacon and the Puritans, the embodiment of the reasoning and repressive spirit. Milton walks toward the eternal universe of Los and Enitharmon, "but Urizen oppos'd his path" (*Mil* 19:25, 26; *K* 500). He comes, bringing with him "Jerusalem with songs on the Grecian Lyre" (19:46, *K* 501)—Greece in this context standing as the negative, betraying spirit, the enemy of true biblical poetry. As Blake says in the *Preface* to this same poem: "We do not want either Greek or Roman Models if we are but just & true to our own Imaginations" (*K* 480). These are the aspects of Milton which must be corrected.

Here we may pause to ask ourselves whether Blake is doing full justice to Milton at this point. Had Milton surrendered to the Urizenic world? If we return to the above-quoted passage from the *Areopagitica* we shall see that Milton is actually disassociating himself from the Puritan narrowness of the Presbyterians. He gently reminds his fellow Roundheads that not Calvin and Luther but the liberal, British reforming spirit of Wycliffe should be their guide. Urging the governors of England to turn away from all dogmatic narrowness, he asks them to consider what kind of a nation the English were—

a Nation not slow and dull, but of a quick, ingenious, and piercing spirit, acute to invent, subtle and sinewy to discours, not beneath the reach of any point the highest that human capacity can soar to.[24]

They must be given freedom for such infinite invention and such high discourse. The city of London is "a mansion-house of liberty," and its inhabitants should therefore not be controlled by the captious spirit of some blear-eyed, illiberal licenser of the press. There is no doubt that Milton here has his finger on that self-same narrow, dogmatic Urizenic spirit that Blake discerned in seventeenth-century Puritanism; and far from participating in it, he is actually condemning it. But Blake does not give Milton credit for this. On the contrary, he makes him a worshiper of Satan under the unutterable Name. Before the history of six thousand years can be consummated, Milton must be cured of his Puritan proclivities: he must be reunited with the virgin Ololon, representing the more occult side of seventeenth-century Hebraism,[25] and made to understand free love. Milton's praise of wedded love, it seems, shows his fundamental suspicion of free sexuality! He therefore becomes the ancestor of Gibbon and Voltaire and the deists; in short, of the spiritual attrition of the eighteenth century.

There is evidently some confusion here which may be worth discussion, for it may be claimed that at his best Milton had sought and found a balance between Law and Liberty, between the spirit of the Renaissance and that of the Reformation, and that this balance is what gives strength to his best poetry. He was not intoxicated by the spirit of freedom to the exclusion of any understanding of order or control, but at the same time he was never under the constraint of Puritan dogmatism to the extent of ignoring the call of the free imagination. It was the broad midday beam he sought, not the candle within doors. If there is confusion and error, therefore, we may conclude that it is not all Milton's but also partially Blake's own error and Blake's confusion. Not that the critical errors made by one poet in relation to another are necessarily of great interest in themselves, but in this case Blake's misrepresentation of Milton may help us to define some of the specific characteristics of Blake's own genius.

One simple way of explaining Blake's error would be to say that Blake, for all his enthusiasm for the Protestant seventeenth century, had no genuine appreciation of the *practical* piety of that age, which reveals itself for instance in the community of Little Gidding, in George Herbert's quiet application to his pastoral duties, and in Joseph Hall's qualified praise of the practical righteousness of the Pharisees. Caroline divinity (as distinct from Puritanism) had in it much of the this-worldly spirit of Hebraism. Coleridge knew and appreciated this, but on the whole his fellow poets did not. Blake certainly was not temperamentally fitted to weigh the virtues of the quiet unecstatic religion of the mid-seventeenth-century divines on the right or left wing of the Church, the religion that united Milton and Jeremy Taylor. His own Hebraism was of a more kabbalistic variety: his inclination was more to antinomianism than to the Law of Sinai, and in this he had with him the more anarchic spirits of the time. But this antinomianism of Blake's—if that is the right name for it—is no more than the outward symptom of some deeper and more complex antagonism to the religious world of the seventeenth century, an antagonism no less radical for being bound up paradoxically with a vast appreciation of the spiritual treasures of that age.

· V ·

One can seize this underlying difference between Blake and Milton by considering once again the apprehension of time in Blake's mythology as presented in the personality of Los. In a justly celebrated passage in *Milton*, Blake envisions the Sons of Los at work building "Moments & Minutes & Hours / And Days & Months & Years & Ages & Periods, wondrous buildings" (*Mil* 28:44–45, K 516). He proceeds to develop a sense of the vast constructions of history. "And every Age is Moated deep with Bridges of silver & gold." Minutes, hours, days, months, and years all have their intrinsic significance defined by the architectural imagery of tents, gates, walls, terraces, and towers (28:50–56). Time mounts upwards like a turreted building, unique, balanced, majestic, every part supporting the rest. A creative and purposeful structure, the six thousand years' span of human history is the supreme achievement of Los. Time-extension here is given solidity by the imagery of spatial extension. Moreover, it is an inhabited structure; it is built for the children of men, and "The Guard are Angels of Providence on duty evermore" (28:61). Providence oversees the building, ensuring that its purposes are fulfilled. But then, in his dialectical fashion, Blake seems to abolish the whole vision. Like Prospero he reveals the cloud-capp'd towers, the whole universe of space and time, as a fairy structure, an illusion. Truth is embodied not in the slow vast plan of Providence unfolding itself in history, but in "a Moment, a Pulsation of the Artery."

> For in this Period the Poet's Work is Done, and all the Great
> Events of Time start forth & are conciev'd in such a Period,
> Within a Moment, a Pulsation of the Artery.   (*Mil* 29:1-3, K 516)

T. S. Eliot in *The Four Quartets* struggled in his drier fashion to define "the intersection of the timeless moment." [26] He was likewise impressed by the sense of a historical tradition rooted in the Middle Ages and in the seventeenth century with their stable moral and social values, but he too finally turned his back on the prophetic vision of history with its pattern of irreversible moral choices made in time, and adopted a more Hellenic view of existence as a timeless continuum. "History," says Eliot, "is a pattern of timeless moments." [27] Significance is found at the still point of the turning wheel (the Hellenic image of the circle is notable here), not in the Gothic accumulation of vast piles soaring heavenwards. The key word for Eliot is not time but eternity, a word which in fact did not exist in the vocabulary of the Hebrew prophets.

Now here is also Blake's fundamental deviation from Milton, from the Hebraic spirit of the seventeenth-century religious poets and divines generally, and from the spirit of biblical prophecy. He expresses it in a richer, more pictorial manner than Eliot does, but the implication is the same:

> For every Space larger than a red Globule of Man's blood

Is visionary, and is created by the Hammer of Los:
And every Space smaller than a Globule of Man's blood opens
Into Eternity, of which this vegetable Earth is but a shadow.

(*Mil* 29:19–22, *K* 516–17)

Time and space as we know them are shadowy and unreal. Space ultimately resolves itself into the invisible blood-corpuscle (note once again the image of the circle or globule), time into the infinitesimal moment of poetic inspiration, "a Pulsation of the Artery." The Platonic formulation of the nature of eternity ("Eternity, of which this vegetable Earth is but a shadow") underlines the Greek character of these insights. As for Shelley, so for Blake, life is the colored dome which stains the white radiance of eternity. Keats in his earlier poetry had sought to portray the gigantic ages of history in its progressive evolution, but his final poetry reveals him too as abdicating this aim. The Grecian urn begins by being the "foster-child of silence and slow time," but in the end it teases us "out of thought / As doth eternity." The urn represents a transcendent moment of love, a transcendent chord of music, and a transcendent moment of devotion. Here in Blake, Shelley, and Keats we have the Greek spirit (it is a *Greek* urn, we should note) successfully overthrowing the historical earth-bound categories of biblical Hebraism.

The work of these poets reveals that they despaired of building up a significant imaginative structure in terms of contemporary reality, its churches, its revolutions, its institutions, its achievements in science, industry, and the rest. Their disenchantment expresses itself in a poetry of transcendence, in a lyrical affirmation of the reality of eternity and the emptiness of time. But it should be added that in the poetry itself, it is historical disenchantment which results in maximal lyrical enchantment. It is, as S. Foster Damon expresses it, "The Moment *versus* Puritanism," except that instead of "Puritanism" we should perhaps read, "the Hebraic spirit of the Reformation as a whole, and the middle-class confidence in the possibility of this-worldly salvation through human efforts in time." It is against this that Blake raises his voice in a superb, ecstatic affirmation of a more transcendent aim, and a more transcendent reality. Here is the source of his special lyrical power, but the irony of the situation should not be ignored.

Blake, in *Milton*, has written an epic to end all epics. He proclaims that the epic, which would seem to be the poet's attempt to give shape and meaning to history and its processes, is really a lyric, conceived and bodied forth in an ecstatic moment of vision:

> For in this Period the Poet's Work is Done, and all the Great
> Events of Time start forth & are conciev'd in such a Period,
> Within a Moment, a Pulsation of the Artery.

Wordsworth's *Prelude* likewise, while at one level it builds up a sense of biographical movement forward in which the poet is being trained and tested, at another level undermines the very existential possibility of such an epic conception of time and progress. Intersecting the whole are "spots of time," as Wordsworth calls them in Book XII, which have a reality beyond growth and change. It is these which give the poem its vertical depth—and that is a strength—but they also raise a question about the worth and significance of the historico-biographical frame in which the poet's experiences in this poem are disposed. Eliot, by disposing his experiences in *The Four Quartets* in a musical rather than a historical frame, has been truer to the timeless character of the experience which he is seeking to communicate to us.

· VI ·

Here then is Blake's deviation from Milton and the age of Milton, and it occurs interestingly at the moment of his affirmation of maximum kinship with Milton. He joins with him to divide. Mr. Bloom, though he has displayed so well the connection between the two poets, has failed to do justice to the ambiguity of this connection.[28] He urges us to consider *Milton* as a poem in the same tradition as *Paradise Lost, Paradise Regained,* and the Book of Job. Its theme is suffering and evil, and the justification of the ways of God to Man. Attempting to link up Blake's poem with the two poems of Milton, Mr. Bloom declares: "All three works centre on the dual theme of theodicy and self-recognition, God's justice and man's realization of that justice in his relation to God." [29]

Now it seems to me that a theodicy is precisely what Blake's poem is not. In spite of the claim made in the epigraph, Blake is not, in *Milton*, seeking to understand divine justice in its dealings with men. Such an attempt implies a need to explain the reverses and achievements of history, a need which in the last analysis Blake denies. Los is the god of history, but he is also paradoxically the god of that poetic inspiration which in a timeless moment renders all history nugatory. Blake assumes the mantle of the prophet,[30] but here is his radical departure from the mode of biblical prophecy. There is no need to arbitrate between Los and the poet, for they do not stand over against one another in the challenging posture of dialogue as do Samson and his God. Blake never challenges Los to explain "Why am I thus bereav'd thy prime decree?" On the contrary, there is a blending of their identities. Los and Blake fuse into one: he is Blake's own inspiration raising him above the flux of time and its frustrations. This may be kabbalistic, but it is not biblical: there is no biblical covenant-drama in Blake's poem, and Mr. Bloom is, I think, mistaken in employing the category of *dialogue* in his discussion both of this poem and of *Jerusalem*.[31] There is really no dialogue, but rather a thrilling and continuing monologue. Los, Blake, Milton, Jesus, Albion, and Ololon all blend and fuse. There is an eternal self-communion in which the tensions of real dialogue no longer exist. Blake's early Prophetic Books, especially *The French Revolution*, contain a measurable degree of dramatic confrontation, manifested in character, episode, and dramatic dialogue, but the spoken word as found in the later poems emerges more and more as an all-embracing lyrical voice. We do not have Ololon *addressing* Milton; we have a kind of antiphonal lyrical utterance, a certain high rhetoric culminating in a mystical union of the two "characters." What we have finally is the abolition of separateness, God and Man not standing dramatically confronting one another as in Milton's poetry and as in the Book of Job, but an indistinguishable God-Man incarnation which may be termed Jesus, Los, or Albion. It does not really matter from which verbal direction you approach this central mythic entity. Like the *mundus* of the Stoics, it is ultimately destined to swallow up all distinctions of form, shape, and existence that ever were, and reveal itself as the utterly complete and all-inclusive divine humanity. It is a motion and a spirit that rolls through all things. The sexes too will be abolished, and Man and God return to their hermaphroditic one-ness. Viewed in this way, Blake's poetry is the very antithesis of the dialogic; its voice is the lyric rather than the dramatic voice.

The fundamental image whereby the poem itself defines the na-ture of this single, passionately aspiring voice of the poet sounding out in a world devoid of any other presence, is the image of the mounting Lark. It occurs on three distinct and important occa-sions; the first, at the descent of Ololon at the beginning of Book II (31:29, K 520); the second, at the instant of revelation when the virgin Ololon appears in the poet's garden (36:1–10, K 526–27); and the third, at the very end of the poem when the poet awakens from his vision (42:29, K 534). On all three occasions it is asso-ciated with the symbol of "the wild Thyme"—a prophetic pun as Erdman calls it,[32] suggesting the dimension of Time, but "wild," that is, transcended and liberated from its bondage to the clock and the historical process:

> nor time nor space was
> To the perception of the Virgin Ololon, but as the
> Flash of lightning. (*Mil* 36:17–19, K 527)

But there is a third important symbol linked with the Lark and the wild Thyme. On its first occurrence the Lark is heralded by that most romantic of birds, the Nightingale:

> Thou hearest the Nightingale begin the Song of Spring.
> The Lark sitting upon his earthy bed, just as the morn
> Appears, listens silent; then springing from the waving Cornfield, loud
> He leads the Choir of Day: trill, trill, trill, trill,
> Mounting upon the wings of light into the Great Expanse,
> Reecchoing against the lovely blue & shining heavenly Shell,
> His little throat labours with inspiration; every feather
> On throat & breast & wings vibrates with the effluence Divine.
> (*Mil* 31:28–35, K 520)

Mr. Bloom is surely right in detecting in the Nightingale a tribute to the blind poet Milton,[33] who had, in a famous passage in Book III of *Paradise Lost,* compared himself to "the wakeful bird" which "Sings darkling, and in shadiest Covert hid / Tunes her nocturnal Note."

It is easy to see which side of Milton's poetry the Nightingale symbolizes. Milton's name for her was Urania, the spirit of sacred song who, as he tells us in the opening of Book VII of *Paradise Lost,* visited his slumbers nightly. She represents that privacy of inspiration, that religious inwardness, which Blake had found so serviceable after 1800. But though the Nightingale is "in shadiest Covert hid," it is also correctly associated by Blake with the "wild Thyme," with the revolutionary theme still powerfully present in Blake's later, Miltonically inspired poetry. For it was Milton as we have seen who provided Blake with the means of liberating the enchained spirit of Orc after the frustrations of the Napoleonic era. And so it comes about that the Nightingale's Song of Spring provides the signal, the cue for Blake's own song, that of the Lark. The Lark too comes from Milton, from a well-known passage in *L'Allegro,* but the Lark is not content with the earth-bound character of the Nightingale, with "sitting upon his earthy bed." He takes a higher flight: he feels the surge of transcendence! He springs up, mounting, and "His little throat labours with inspiration." Moreover, the Lark calls for no answer: unlike Milton's poetry it does not address, nor is it addressed by, God, but it "vibrates with the effluence Divine." [34] It does not engage in dialogue, but rather in a superb and unmitigated monologue, like Keats's Nightingale, like Shelley's Skylark, like Wordsworth's Solitary Reaper. In fact, Wordsworth has a lark too who functions in *The Prelude* in a way similar to Blake's Lark here. At the very end of his poem, in Book XIV, Wordsworth sums up the whole of his poetic journey, viewing it from the position of transcendence. He has retired now to the countryside, and can no longer quite affirm the substantial reality of his earlier pilgrimage through time and space ("I said unto the life which I had lived, / Where art thou"). It is then that he defines his poetic voice in terms of the song of the lark:

> Anon I rose
> As if on wings, and saw beneath me stretched

> Vast prospect of the world which I had been
> And was; and hence this Song, which like a lark
> I have protracted, in the unwearied heavens
> Singing . . .[35]

The loneliness of the lark, the sense of its transcendence, of its unwearied monologue which carries it beyond the bounds of time and space, these render it the peculiar symbol of the poet himself. Blake's Lark first "listens silent" to the voice of Milton's Nightingale, and after meditating deeply on that, it takes a higher flight out of darkness into light, and sings out wild and unconstrained in a universe from which all other reality has been banished, and its triumphant song can alone be heard.

GEOFFREY H. HARTMAN

# Blake and the "Progress of Poesy"

Blake's poems on the seasons, in *Poetical Sketches,* have not lacked recent commentators. The forceful inquiry that has made his other lyrics both richer and more problematic is now being devoted to them.[1] I would like to propose a point of view which would ground these earliest poems in Blake's sense of poetical vocation.

We feel at once their intensely vocative nature; that the prophetic or "speaking out," and the invocational or "calling upon," are more important than the conventional subject. Their mood is never purely descriptive but always optative or imperative: what description enters is ritual in character. It evokes an epiphany so strongly as to carry the poet toward it. "The hills tell each other, and the list'ning / Vallies hear; all our longing eyes are turned / Up to thy bright pavillions. . . ." This paraphrases Psalm 19 with its feeling for "open vision," or prophecy in Blake's sense.

To grant the primacy of invocation, of thou-saying, of the prophetic impulse, is less to interpret than to raise the question on which interpretation should turn: what is being invoked? What presence or epiphany? If voice as voice has an exceptional place, it should still be brought together with a person and a situation. Who is calling, to whom, for what?

Now each of the lyrics is a formal ode that contains a clearly stated petition. A season is invoked; it is asked to visit, or stay in, the speaker's land; in "To Winter" it is asked to stay away. On the literal level, therefore, it is the "voice of the bard" which adjures the seasons. This answer, however, makes little sense outside the charmed realm of convention. A natural force is asked to do what comes naturally; or is asked not to do it and does it anyway ("To Winter"). In this light Blake's cycle is no more than a brilliant, condensed imitation of Thomson's *Seasons* with its pseudoritual invitations.

Blake's relation to Thomson will be discussed later. The comparison cannot be direct because Blake's are not long poems, like *The Seasons*, nor of a descriptive-didactic nature. These differences of genre put the emphasis back on Blake's condensed lyricism. Everything within this lyric space is food for a style of invocation. If calling the seasons is a gratuitous or ritual act, this but helps to move into the foreground the lyric pathos, the *ore rotundo*, of their style. Here voice calls upon itself, calls up images of its previous power. Blake indulges in a continuous reminiscence of that power, by offering us a splendid pastiche of echoes and themes from the Bible, the classics, and even the high odic tradition of the eighteenth century. It is all poetic diction, but poetic diction in search of its truth—which is the identity, now lost, of the poetical and the prophetic spirit.

Even the measure of the poems is a reminiscence of a larger conception of poetry. Their blank verse is unusual, not only for its personality (the free enjambments, the energetic beat) but also for its very presence in short poems. Not until the 1790's will Southey, Coleridge, and Wordsworth experiment with *lyrics* in blank verse. With certain important exceptions, unrhymed lyrics before Blake were obvious imitations of the classics[2] or paraphrases of the Psalms, so that Blake's choice of verse may signify an "ancient liberty recover'd" and evoke the prophetic portions of both traditions.[3]

The thought that Blake's season poems are about poetry—that they recall poetry's higher destiny, its link to energy, liberty, and the prophetic spirit—is encouraged by a simple progression within the first three odes. The progression moves the theme of poetry into the center. "To Spring" can be viewed as invoking a new energy or springtide of verse, anticipated by its exotic style. But what is on the level of style in "To Spring" appears in the last stanza of "To Summer" as theme, then carries the greater part of "To Autumn" as song, as a poem within a poem. Our unifying hypothesis remains, however, unsatisfying on certain points. These are the relation of the apparent subject (the seasons) to the real subject (poetry); what to do with "To Winter"; and whether a modernist interpretation, that the poems are about poetry, respects the situation of a young poet writing in the England of the 1770's.

I do not propose to deal with these problems one at a time but to reformulate the thesis in historical terms and then to apply it to the entire cycle. To say they are "poems about poetry" does not mean Blake is primarily concerned with poetry as artifact or with the poet as specialist: he is concerned with the *poetical spirit* (Gray's "Poetic Genius," Collins' "Poetical Character")—with its future in England and the West, with the relation of poetry to the spirit of the age and human destiny. One of the few genuinely visionary themes of the eighteenth century was that of the "Progress of Poesy," and it is in relation to this theme that Blake writes poems about poetry. His cycle is a visionary anticipation of the progress, or migration, of the poetical spirit to England, "our western isle." The primacy of the invocational-prophetic mode suggests that this progress is linked to the very energy of anticipation, to a poetry that can envision what it calls for.

The reader may recall the reverse epiphany concluding Pope's *Dunciad,* or Shelley's description of the "Triumph" of life. These are among the great examples (and both ironical) of the Progress theme in an era desperately believing in progress. The Progress is always envisioned as a procession, apparently a triumphal one; yet the triumph can be heavily qualified. The Progress of Poesy, in particular, is represented less as a melioration than as a migration: like Astraea, poetry is forced into exile, though it remains on earth wandering from one civilization to another. Blake's little poem "To the Muses" alludes to this exile of the poetical genius, to the Muses who may be wandering about on earth, in heaven, under the sea— they are somewhere, but they are clearly not in eighteenth-century England.

The vision of a Progress of Poesy expresses an epoch with a self-conscious interest in literary history; and it offers us a specific myth about that history. Blake could have found this myth in Thomson, Gray, Collins, or Thomas Warton. They see a displacement of the poetical genius from East to West or South to North: from *Morgenland* to *Abendland.* This Westering of the Spirit is often explained by a supposed connection between liberty and letters: as liberty dies out in Greece (or prophecy in the Holy Land), poetry and learning depart and arrive finally in their new home, the "western isle." So Thomson in "Rule Britannia" (1740): "The Muses still with freedom found / Shall to thy happy coast repair." [4]

Yet only here and there is the conception of this Progress purely optimistic, and a simple aggrandizement of national ambitions in the realm of letters. The hope was fading, by the middle of the century, that the greatness of English poetry might be sustained. Dryden and Pope had kept alive a spark of the hope kindled by the Renaissance; but Warton's *History of English Poetry* (1774–81), published while Blake was composing *Poetical Sketches*, qualifies it significantly. Warton doubts that the poetical spirit, at least in its original fervor, in its true Oriental splendor, can make its permanent home in the West. Even the Nordic imagination (revealed, primarily, through Mallet's *Northern Antiquities*), is supposed to owe its vigor to an Oriental source via the migrations of Odin. For Warton the Elizabethan was the golden age of English poetry because the Eastern influence had not yet receded before the light of Western civilization. "Reason suffered a few demons still to linger, which she chose to retain . . . under the guidance of poetry," as he said elegantly.[5] Not Superstition but Enlightenment dooms the poetical genius. In his curiously honest scheme the growth of reason and the decline of imagination are linked.

We possess only one influential Progress of Poesy poem, that of Gray. Its pessimistic ending is well known. But the theme is everywhere, and can be the implicit background to an entire body of writings. Collins, for example, touches on the theme explicitly in the *Verses to Sir Thomas Hamner* (also fleetingly in the Preface to *Persian Eclogues*), and it is the hopeful or melancholy inspiration of almost every one of his odes. Thus, in the "Ode to Fear," he regrets his distance from the wilder and more terrible genius of Shakespeare and tries to recover something of the archaic force of personification; in the "Ode on the Poetical Character," he withdraws from his pursuit of Spenser and Milton, but not before leaving in the epode a proof of the mythopoeic power still in him;

and in the posthumously published "On the Superstitions of the Highlands," seeking a more "genial" country for the imagination, he turns to the northernmost part of England. And though the balance in Collins is toward defeat, toward a necessary sacrifice of the poetical spirit to the spirit of his age, one poem remains exceptionally hopeful. In the "Ode to Evening" he invokes directly the Westering of the Spirit, and anticipates a new *Hesperidean* poetry —not only in hope but also in fact, for his ode is an unusual blend of archaic and sophisticated elements, of ancient superstition and modern sentiment.

Blake's "To Spring" also heralds a Westering of the Spirit. Its salient difference from the "Ode to Evening," that it is a dawn and not a dusk poem, should not obscure the fact that it draws on the same mythology of history. The emphasis falls on *our* (western) isle, *our* clime, *our* land. Blake's England awaits a dawning or second birth of that fervid—Oriental, biblical, Miltonic—imagination which his luxurious style once more evokes. There is no need to dwell on echoes from the Bible or on the great Oriental themes of coronation and sacred marriage. But a subtler echo, from Milton, should be mentioned, because it reveals how Blake already modifies the elder poet. He invites the poetical spirit to England in words that echo Milton's address, in *Lycidas,* to his "Genius of the shore." Is not Blake's "turn / Thine angel eyes upon our western isle" his version of "Look homeward, Angel, now"? [6]

In *Lycidas* Milton is also concerned with the destiny of the poetical spirit, its relation to the classics and the Bible, and with the role of an English poet in that destiny. It is he who linked the themes of liberty and poetry; and it is also he, in *Lycidas* as elsewhere, who associated poetry and the spirit of prophecy. His career, inspired by the desire to have poetry "look homeward" as well as toward the Ancients, anticipates that of Blake at every turn.

Yet Milton, perhaps, did not look home sufficiently. Blake repeats Milton's invocation as if everything were to be done again. Though his point of departure is the same, the poetry he foresees is different. Blake separates from Milton, as from Collins, on the matter of the role of the classics in the Progress of the poetical spirit. The aim of *Lycidas* is a native poetry of prophetic scope, yet the possibility of an English or Western poetry was not conceivable for Milton without Virgil's guidance. Virgil was the great literary mediator who showed (together with Horace) that poetry could be written even at a distance from the source: at a distance from the archaic, the naïve, the directly prophetic. Virgil, in fact, introduced the theme of Evening into poetry.[7] He was often considered the first significant way-station in the Westering of the Poetical Spirit: it might almost be said that through him the idea of a Progress of Poesy became possible. For his hero is an émigré, and his idea of nationality is visionary enough to encompass the local gods of both Greece and Latium. What poets imitate, therefore, is not Virgil's style as such, but a method of mediation, the self-conscious acceptance of a secondary, a "translating" function. The "come hither" motif, the ritual invitation so important in Milton and Collins, stylizes this concept of poetry as translation. When Milton asks the Sicilian Muse to "call the Vales, and bid them hither cast / Their Bells and Flowrets of a thousand hues" —where "hither" is English poetry as well as the resting place of Lycidas—he adapts the opening passages of Books I and II of the *Georgics*:

> Et vos, agrestum praesentia numina, Fauni
> Ferte simul Faunique pedem Dryadesque puellae:
> munera vestra cano. (I. 10–13)

> huc, pater o Lenaee, veni nudataque musto
> tinge novo mecum dereptis crura coturnis. (II. 7–8)

It is precisely a Progress of Poesy based on cultural translation which Blake refuses to acknowledge. His parody of the second quotation, Virgil's address to Bacchus, is quite overt.[8] He insists on immediacy, on a directness to the source which Virgil's example, and the body of classical tradition, impede. Theirs is an insufficient, even perverted, "reception of the Poetic Genius." Not that Blake, in *Poetical Sketches*, rejects classical style: on the contrary, he tries to restore its pristine vigor by bringing it closer to the poetical parts of the Bible. It is a lapsed Orientalism, whose sparks have to be fanned into a new and open flame.[9] We said that Blake's "To Spring" heralds a Westering of the Spirit: we should have said a new "Eastering." His are dawn and not evening poems. So much so, that "To the Evening Star," which competes with Collins on classical ground, becomes almost a poem about dawn. It depicts the evening star as another sun, a dawn risen upon evening:

> Thou fair-hair'd angel of the evening,
> Now, whilst the sun rests on the mountains, light
> Thy bright torch of love; thy radiant crown
> Put on . . .[10]

The imperious vocatives, as in "To Spring," are no Collinsian, ritual supplications, but seek to "awake the dawn" (Ps. 57:8) of which they speak.

It is not sufficient to conclude from this that Blake chooses the Asiatic over the Attic mode. He is not a formalist deciding between stylistic options. What is attacked is the very basis of Atticism, the ideological source of its power over the Augustans and even Milton. Blake rejects the idea of a consciously Hesperidean Muse, a muzzled Orientalism, an accommodated prophetic vision. He rejects Virgil's exemplary mediation, the conception of style as a compromise, and the position of classical literature as an important station in the Westering of the Poetical Spirit. There is no Westering; there is only an Eastering, an immediacy to the source renewed by each great poet. If, in *Poetical Sketches*, the style is aggressively Oriental, this is not because Blake believed in the East as the exclusive source of poetical inspiration, but because Hebrew poetry, in its unmediated, prophetic vigor, is the right orientation. "Look homeward, Angel, now": Blake is not, like Virgil, the poet of a migration, of a man having to resettle his gods, his goods, his destiny, in a foreign land; he is the prophet of a spiritual homecoming, of a miraculous inner turn and restoration. In Blake the restoration is that of the poetical genius to England. The East is wherever poetry is.

It is time to look from "To Spring" to the entire cycle. The first three poems are clearly in the context of a Progress of Poesy. The "come hither" motif entices the seasons to England with one main suggestion: it is, or could be, the poetical country. If in the first poem the style itself must carry that suggestion, in the second the theme is explicitly stated:

> Our bards are fam'd who strike the silver wire:
> Our youths are bolder than the southern swains;
> Our maidens fairer in the sprightly dance:
> We lack not songs, nor instruments of joy

and in the third we actually hear a song, sung by Autumn to the poet's pipe, which recapitulates the three seasons, and evokes a momentary impression of the perfection of all in all—of poetry as part of the harvest, as a song that seasons the season. Autumn's "round" does not flow, like Thomson's recapitulative *Hymn* of 1730, into a transcendent theme: it transcends only the previous invocations, or the spiritual state they reflect. The land is no longer lovesick, unmated, desiring ardently its regeneration; nor aggressively admiring, countervirile, as in the presence of Summer. It is the poetic land, a fulfilled and human landscape.

"To Winter" is, of course, on the horizon; but this temporary climax of the cycle in "To Autumn" suggests the equal if not higher dignity of the Western Muse. Here Blake is English Blake; yet to ascribe to him a nationalistic or even hemispheric conception is a partial truth at best. He is not Wordsworth, for whom being an English poet is achieved through being a nature poet. Though "To Autumn" does anticipate both Wordsworth and Keats, the progress Blake has in mind is not linked, ultimately, to a geopolitical march of the spirit. That conception survives as a frame of the whole because Blake is engaged in transforming a nationalistic mythology of history into a universal topography of the imagination. He understands the Progress of Poesy as a spiritual rather than place-conditioned fact: there is progress whenever mankind recognizes that the human, the divine, and the poetical genius are one and the same. Hence the double, and perhaps confusing, scheme of Blake's cycle: in borrowing the historical frame of the Westering of the Spirit, and culminating in "To Autumn," the scheme is recognizably English; yet the progression is also universal because each poem expresses a different station in the resurgence of the poetical spirit anywhere. In this drama of three acts, the spirit of prophecy so conspicuous in the first poem, and the spirit of liberty in the second, advance toward their ripest epiphany as the poetical spirit of the third, its "golden load" of song.

Yet what of "To Winter"? It stands out from the sequence for several reasons. It reverses the "come hither" motif; it also reverses a second formula, for the stanza beginning "He hears me not, but o'er the yawning deep / Rides heavy . . ." portrays an epiphany based on the god's not-hearing, on his overriding the formal petition. It reverses, indeed, the entire direction of the cycle, since Winter is obviously a force which man cannot humanize. The poet assumes a Jobean humility ("I dare not lift mine eyes") and imagines a mariner-figure, homeless in this daemonic landscape.

Through the addition of "To Winter" Blake's quarrel with the traditional Progress is, if anything, put into clearer perspective. He seems to say to Winter, "Thou hast thy music too," meaning: There exists a genuine poetry of the North.[11] The poetical spirit is now seen to blow from all corners of the globe: from East ("To Spring"), South ("To Summer"), West ("To Autumn"), and North ("To Winter"). Blake will not localize the poetic genius: indeed, he considers the attempt to restrict it to one class or nation as a major cause for the dying out of prophecy and the birth of Priestly Religion. Whatever Holy Land the poetical spirit seems to come from, "The true Man is the source, he being the Poetic Genius."

"To Winter" is, moreover, a perfect second climax to the cycle. As always in Blake, strength dies into strength: in "To Autumn" there was no dying music except at the very end. Keats's Autumn ode contains within its final stanza an Ode to Evening, but here only the slightest hint of autumn as "fall." The processional image of Winter riding heavy in its "iron car" over the "yawning deep" rivals that of Summer's "fervid car" riding "o'er the deep of heaven." Winter really winters, even at the price of a retreat from the humanism of "To Autumn."

We can now face the delayed question of Thomson's influence. *The Seasons* is by origin a poem of the Scottish border, and began naturally enough with a *Winter*. Thomson gives the Northern imagination full scope: not in the form of locodescriptive detail (there is little) but in the form of a poetry expressing the *genius loci* of an entire sphere. Part of his subject is the Genius of the North, perhaps because it was constantly put in question.[12] There were two sharply conflicting opinions about the frozen North, and both were linked to rival Progress theories. One exalted Eastern (classical or biblical) origins, postulated a Westering of the Spirit, and viewed the North as a region intrinsically passive and barbarous. But in Thomson's age an opposite theory was in the ascendant, one which postulated a movement from North to South, and exalted Celts, Goths, and Germani (not always discriminated) as the womb of nations and home of the spirit of freedom. This alternate Progress practically reversed the assumptions of the first. The North is now what the East was: the cradle of liberty and of imagination.[13]

In "To Winter" Blake seems to change to a Progress moving along a North-South axis. Is this a confused, if high-spirited, play with *topoi?* A youthful confusion cannot be ruled out. In the 1770's Blake was at the center of intersecting visions of historical progress. Mallet's *Northern Antiquities*, translated in 1770 by Percy, also showed uncertainty about what was Eastern and what Northern in origin. The trouble is that Blake's confusion, if it exists, is permanent rather than youthful: the later Blake also indulges in it. Like Rudbeck the Elder, who identified Scandinavia with Plato's Atlantis, he identifies Albion with Jerusalem. A more likely interpretation of "To Winter" is that Blake, by shifting from one historical scheme to another, puts in doubt the historicity of either Progress, and so reinforces his thought that poetry is coterminous with man and not with a region. It is only the "Genius" in the *genius loci* that interests him.

If the confusion is purposeful, foreshadowing the "dialectical" Blake, then we understand better his decision to represent the poetical spirit as a season. He corrects Thomson as he will later seek to correct Milton. Blake's seasons are comparable to Thomsonian genii which determine, or represent synoptically, the dominant character of a region. Yet they are also quite different. The concept of *genii loci* helped Thomson to a peculiar kind of visionary history, which set man totally in the frame of nature, in the frame of migrations that are a Newtonian blend of spiritual force and cosmic determinism. *The Seasons* is a visionary history without a hero: the hero being Providence working through the forces of Nature. For Blake, however, the hero of any visionary history is the power of vision itself, the human and poetical genius, and Thomson's pseudoregional identification of this genius with a *genius loci* only narrowed it down, in his eyes, to druidism, deism, and nationalism. Blake is certainly right with respect to Thomson: *The Seasons*, which has a genuine visionary flair, was followed by *Liberty*, which had the right theme but little else.

The aim of Blake vis-à-vis Thomson is to view "Genius" as the only *genius loci*, the only true guardian of one's country. An England that has lost the poetical spirit has lost its identity. That is why Albion must call Jerusalem back; and why the land, in this cycle, invokes something that is really an inalienable part of itself. Genius calls unto Genius.

The exception is, again, "To Winter," where the poet is a mere figure in the landscape, who vainly seeks to hold back, instead of inviting, the Genius of the North. Even if the latter is identified as the spirit of liberty moving relentlessly toward the South, it is a tyrannous power as well. Try as we may, "To Winter" will not settle down to any one interpretation. It comes at the end of the cycle like a satyr play calling all sacred themes into question. It is a confusing poem, perhaps a confused one; yet a strong impression of reversal remains. The poem even ends with an absurd plot-reversal that is an inspired period cliché ("till heaven smiles," that is, Spring appears, and Winter, for all his bombast, turns tail). Thus "To Winter" moves close to absolute parody, and if we do not finally take it as such, it is because the other odes are not sufficiently different in style, and because the thought of "young Blake experimenting" comes to mind.

Granted, of course, that it is precarious to base too much on near-juvenilia, yet granted also that any thesis gains its strength from an understanding of Blake's total "spiritual form," we must ask whether this early penchant for parody (to the point of self-parody) does not foretell Blake's later and radical illusionism.[14]

The great show to come—the apocalyptic opera of the Prophetic Books—serves only to expand us back to ourselves, to the knowledge that "all deities reside in the human breast." The contrast in Blake's poetry between divine magic and apodictic humanism is such that one is tempted to see him as a Prospero, and this pageant of the seasons as his earliest revel. A sense of masquerade hovers over it, with the Orientalism of "To Spring" as much a mask as the Northern sublimity of "To Winter."

I would like to end with a view of Blake as *homo ludens*. Are not his maskings a gay science, an applied humanistic magic, part of those "enjoyments of Genius" which to the "Angels" look like "torment and insanity" (*MHH* 6)? To the Angels still among us, Blake's competitiveness with the prophets must indeed appear wanton, if not mad. Yet the poetical spirit, to return to itself, to its former and natural greatness, had to put on the prophetic style once more. In Blake it is religion that is unmasked, but poetry gaily puts on the mask. For religion without its mask, religion de-mystified, is the Poetic Genius; and in that knowledge Blake moves poetry toward a happier consciousness of itself.

DANIEL HUGHES

# Blake and Shelley:
# Beyond the Uroboros

· I ·

The Bard of Oxford, who is urged by Bath to cheer the stricken
Albion on Plate 45 of *Jerusalem*, is probably *not* Shelley, but the
poetaster Edward Garrad Marsh.[1] One appreciates Professor Damon's strong Blakean impulse to link the poets directly. Bath, speaking in "soft gentle tears," urges the Bard:

> "Oxford, take thou these leaves of the Tree of Life; with eloquence
> "That thy immortal tongue inspires, present them to Albion:
> "Perhaps he may recieve them, offer'd from thy loved hands."
>
> (ll. 30–32, K 675)

And Oxford's subsequent speech to Albion does have a possibly
Shelleyan ring, not in the mood of the apocalyptist of the *Ode to
the West Wind* or *Prometheus Unbound,* but in accents reminiscent
of the poet of *Alastor* or the narrator of *Epipsychidion* who seeks
a repose akin to the state Blake understood as Beulah. Oxford addresses Albion but fails to stir him:

> "Thou art in Error, Albion, the Land of Ulro.
> "One Error not remov'd will destroy a human Soul.
> "Repose in Beulah's night till the Error is remov'd.
> "Reason not on both sides. Repose upon our bosoms
> "Till the Plow of Jehovah and the Harrow of Shaddai
> "Have passed over the Dead to awake the Dead to Judgment."
> But Albion turn'd away refusing comfort.     (*J* 46:10–16, K 676)

That is, repose in a recovered innocence until the Last Judgment
has occurred. One assents poetically, looking *through* the eye, to
Professor Damon's asseveration: "Certainly, this forgotten poet

hardly deserved the tribute in *Jerusalem*," [2] while, at the same time, realizing there is no Urizenic or proper scholarly evidence that Blake could literally have had Percy Bysshe Shelley in mind. Indeed, a question remains whether the passage in *Jerusalem* is a tribute in the first place. The swooning Bard of Oxford may be contained in places in Shelley's work, but the great apocalyptic visionary of the *Ode* and Act IV of *Prometheus* would not have swooned, would not have urged a Beulah comfort upon Albion. It is, of course, a thrilling prospect that Blake might have known Shelley's work, but actual history is seldom so kind. The two great poet-prophets of the Romantic period *should* have known each other, but probably did not. Professor Damon, without whom there could be no Blake studies in the first place, has adopted a Blakean history which makes artistic, if not literal, sense. The desire to link Blake and Shelley is overpowering and proceeds apace, but before still another point of comparison is suggested, as it will be in this paper, the pitfalls in such a juxtaposition should be indicated.

Blake's poetic career seems so epically developed and raised to an intensity so Joycean in its scope that it becomes a great temptation to read his Romantic successors back into his work; the gloriously truncated poetic histories of Wordsworth and Coleridge, of Shelley and Keats, that fill us with pity and fear might, if we care to "complete" them, find a resolution in the work of Blake. Shelley is particularly tempting to have "contained" in Blake; the limits reached in Blake's only genuinely tragic poem, *The Mental Traveller*, might seem a paradigm of Shelley's life and career, with the pessimistic *Triumph of Life* demonstrating the truth of Blake's tragic vision of a merely cyclic existence. The reader is then stirred to "correct" or "extend" Shelley's work via Blake as Blake corrected and extended Milton's. But this impulse must be resisted. Shelley's early death and Blake's apparently rounded *œuvre* do not, by themselves, constitute a significant point of contrast—*The Triumph of Life* is surely a mournful climax to Shelley's work beyond which he could not have gone. More importantly, Shelley's genius was essentially lyrical, while Blake's sought and found extension in epic. There is nothing in Shelley's work, not even in *Prometheus Unbound*, which suggests that he would have written poems like the Prophetic Books. (I think he would have become a radical member of Parliament.) We make a great error in collapsing the work of one poet into another, thus robbing the work of each poet of its "selving" uniqueness. Any critical comparison between two poets, especially poets of the range of Blake and Shelley, should proceed, not strictly as criticism, perhaps, but as a fantasia, a suggestive juxtaposition that doth tease us out of thought, in the manner, for example, of Geoffrey Hartman's gently assumed comparison of Blake and Wordsworth in a quarreling Spirit Dialogue.[3] We are, after all, like the poets. We are making metaphors that we may better understand our experience.

I do not intend in this paper to explore the poems of Blake and Shelley as wholes. Rather, I wish to explore certain aspects of a single image in their work—the snake with its tail in its mouth—and by such exploration to show how these two great myth-makers can be discovered working towards similar, yet subtly distinctive, even conflicting, poetic and philosophical ends.

· II ·

*Europe*, dated 1794, is a harsh, obscure poem, the most coded and indirect of Blake's historical prophecies, a work that for all its notable passages and convincing surge seems without either historical or artistic resolution. The passage on Plate 10 describing the reactionary King who withdraws his wounded forces to the serpent-temple is the center of our interest:

In thoughts perturb'd they rose from the bright ruins, silent following
The fiery King, who sought his ancient temple, serpent-form'd,
That stretches out its shady length along the Island white.
Round him roll'd his clouds of war; silent the Angel went
Along the infinite shores of Thames to golden Verulam.
There stand the venerable porches that high-towering rear
Their oak-surrounded pillars, form'd of massy stones, uncut
With tool, stones precious, such eternal in the heavens,
Of colours twelve, few known on earth, give light in the opake,
Plac'd in the order of the stars, when the five senses whelm'd
In deluge o'er the earth-born man; then turn'd the fluxile eyes
Into two stationary orbs, concentrating all things:

The ever-varying spiral ascents to the heavens of heavens
Were bended downward, and the nostrils' golden gates shut,
Turn'd outward, barr'd and petrify'd against the infinite. (ll. 1–15, K 241)

This passage has occasioned much comment,[4] but I am not attempting to add to the explication which Professor Bloom has accomplished well. It is important to my argument to recognize that the serpent-temple, whose pillars are formed in the shape of the Zodiac, represents the fallen consciousness of man, the inhuman parallel of the remote and Urizenic stars. The stones are "uncut / With tool," not crafted by the human imagination, and their colors, "few known on earth," give light in the "opake" density of the temple, but not in the consciousness of man. The "fluxile" eyes, that is, eyes once capable of movement, range, expansion, are turned to "stationary orbs" and vision is lost, turned down to the fallen, merely natural world. The subject of Plate 10 of *Europe* is restricted mind and the search for an image adequate to that restriction which Blake finds in the circular snake, an image of the dull mechanic round of unliberated existence and the repeated natural cycle, "a mind-forged manacle" of its own devising. The next lines indicate a fuller meaning:

> Thought chang'd the infinite to a serpent, that which pitieth
> To a devouring flame; and man fled from its face and hid
> In forests of night: then all the eternal forests were divided
> Into earths rolling in circles of space, that like an ocean rush'd
> And overwhelmed all except this finite wall of flesh.
> Then was the serpent temple form'd, image of infinite
> Shut up in finite revolutions, and man became an Angel,
> Heaven a mighty circle turning, God a tyrant crown'd. (ll. 16–23)

"Thought," of course, takes place here in its fallen condition, unable to break into the open; "that which pitieth," syntactically equivalent to the "infinite," and akin to the pity of the *Songs of Innocence*, must be, as Bloom suggests, the pity of "unfallen human brotherhood," [5] changed to a reactionary flame of tyranny and oppression. The serpent-temple shuts the infinite into finite revolutions and makes man the conventional Angel of *The Marriage of Heaven and Hell*, imprisoned in a consciousness cut off from

Imagination. In the subsequent lines, Albion's Angel, "the ancient Guardian," arrives at the southern porch to find the human skull, here identified with the Stone of Night, now "o'erhung / With purple flowers and berries red, image of that sweet south / Once open to the heavens, and elevated on the human neck, / Now overgrown with hair and cover'd with a stony roof." The North, the realm of Imagination, cannot function; a "raging whirlpool," another image of meaningless circles, which stands opposed to the ascending spiral ascents to the heavens of heavens, draws the "dizzy enquirer," the mind that would be liberated, to his grave. The temple points directly to the end of inquiry and the end of art.

That the snake-temple of *Europe* can be usefully identified with the traditional uroboros, the archetype of eternity, and that through such identification Blake and Shelley can be connected, is what I intend to show. The snake of *Europe* does not literally have its tail in its mouth, but this image concentrates crucial meanings in both poets, and, for Blake as for Shelley, manifests itself as a malign node of meaning. Professor Frye's explanation of the symbol in Blake is applicable to Shelley's "mythy mind" as well: "The serpent with its tail in its mouth is a perfect emblem of the Selfhood: an earthbound, cold-blooded and often venomous form of life imprisoned in its own cycle of death and rebirth." [6]

In *The Daemon of the World*, the revision of *Queen Mab* which Shelley executed in 1815, we find a stanza (I:96–101) not in or suggested by the original. Ianthe, who must become the poetic witness and mediatrix of the vision in the poem, is urged by the Daemon to become a fully capable prophetess:

> Therefore from nature's inner shrine
> Where gods and fiends in worship bend,
> Majestic spirit, be it thine
> The flame to seize, the veil to rend
> Where the vast snake Eternity
> In charmèd sleep doth ever lie.

Both Professors Rogers and Notopoulous have identified this snake with the uroboros and examined those sources from which Shelley may have taken the emblem. [7] I am interested in its function in the poetry and the association between this archetype and the need to stir the revolutionary consciousness *beyond* it. Ianthe, the inchoate precursor of Cythna and Asia, should stir the snake awake, should, as D. H. Lawrence irreverently, but seriously, insisted, "give that serpent of eternity another dummy to suck." [8] Shelley's early poetry seeks the means by which the enclosing serpent of Eternity may be overcome. In *The Revolt of Islam* (1817), that still-locked treasure house of Shelleyan symbology, the snake of the first canto, an image of revolutionary force and its necessary chthonic power, is defeated in sky-combat by the eagle, the emblem of repression and tyrannic, imposed consciousness. Not until the concluding stanzas of the first canto, where the snake imagery is rescued and transmuted into the shape of the mysterious Figure who will bear witness to the story of Laon and Cythna, does Shelley find a means of moving his poem. The strange description of snake-eyes, gliding along the floor of the Temple of the Spirit to become a planet which will reveal the form of liberated man, can certainly be compared with those "fluxile eyes" that Blake saw man surrendering in *Europe*. In stanza 56 Shelley's narrator reports:

> Then first, two glittering lights were seen to glide
> In circles on the amethystine floor,
> Small serpent eyes trailing from side to side,
> Like meteors on a river's grassy shore,
> They round each other rolled, dilating more
> And more—then rose, commingling into one,
> One clear and mighty planet hanging o'er
> A cloud of deepest shadow, which was thrown
> Athwart the glowing steps and the crystalline throne.

The cloud is cleft to reveal the Form who will sit on a throne and listen, with the poet-narrator, to the "tale of human power" that Laon and Cythna now appear to tell. This tale, of course, is *The Revolt of Islam* itself, but not even the most devoted Shelleyan would believe that this poem, for all its incidental interest, is the poem toward which the snake imagery has been pointing. The elaborate, overwrought, and confusing narrative does not find its source nor exhibit its strength. We are tempted to answer Laon's question in the fourth canto in the negative: "did my spirit wake / From sleep as many-coloured as the snake / That girds eternity?" Shelley, at this point in his development, remains uncertain about his subject and his audience. A year later, he has discovered both.

By the time of *Prometheus Unbound,* the waking to a transfigured consciousness and the activation of the spirit are directly, almost deliberately, linked with the descent to and the uncoiling of the uroboros. This is the role assigned to Ianthe's successor, Asia, a wholly successful focus of symbol-charged activity. Shelley is careful not to identify Demogorgon with a concrete image, but there can be little doubt that this mysterious and crucial figure in the poem shares the character of the uroboros of *The Daemon of the World* and *The Revolt of Islam.* In the final stanza of the third scene of Act II of *Prometheus,* as Asia and Panthea make their descent to Demogorgon's cave, the Song of the Spirits predicts the uncoiling of the serpent:

> Resist not the weakness,
> Such strength is in meekness
> That the Eternal, the Immortal,
> Must unloose through life's portal
> The snake-like Doom coiled underneath his throne
> By that alone.

The Eternal, Demogorgon, will uncoil the snake, part of himself, through the "meekness," the surrender of self, which the Oceanides have manifested in their descent to his cave. We cannot know Demogorgon, but we can start to feel his force as the poem moves from the "imageless" description of Act II to the sculpturesque imagery of Act III. In the fourth scene of Act II, Demogorgon can be felt, but not identified:

> PANTHEA. What veilèd form sits on that ebon throne?
> ASIA. The veil has fallen.
> PANTHEA. I see a mighty darkness
> Filling the seat of power, and rays of gloom
> Dart round, as light from the meridian sun.
> —Ungazed upon and shapeless; neither limb,

> Nor form, nor outline; yet we feel it is
> A living Spirit.

In the fourth scene of Act III, when Jupiter has fallen and the major actors of the drama are imaged permanently in the temple of art, we encounter not the coiled uroboros but the twin-headed amphisbaena, the snake with a head at either end of its length, a crucial emblem for Shelley's millennium, a figure of sustained and perpetual consciousness. The Spirit of the Hour describes the final disposition of the chariot and the horses that have taken him on his wonderful rounds through the liberated world. His horses will pasture on vegetable fire and his moonlike car will stand within

> A temple, gazed upon by Phidian forms
> Of thee, and Asia, and the Earth, and me,
> And you fair nymphs looking the love we feel,—
> In memory of the tidings it has borne,—
> Beneath a dome fretted with graven flowers,
> Poised on twelve columns of resplendent stone,
> And open to the bright and liquid sky.
> Yoked to it by an amphisbaenic snake
> The likeness of those winged steeds will mock
> The flight from which they find repose.

It is obvious that a high point of the Shelleyan beatitude has been reached. This temple, surmounted by the familiar Shelleyan dome, is the Palace of Art where the Phidian forms of the dramatis personae attain sculptured permanence. The chariot has yoked to it (I take "it" to refer to moonlike car rather than to temple or dome) representations of the horses which are bound to the car by a yoke in the shape of a two-headed snake. Presumably, if we are to visualize this (and there is no reason to suppose that Shelley did, or should have), we should see this yoke as consisting of two rings (the heads of the snake) connected by a crossbeam (the snake's body), which is fastened to the necks of the sculptured horses, the yoke joined to the chariot by a pole, in the manner of the classical war chariot. This is a fascinating symbol for the totally conscious control of the mental universe, Plato's divine chariot brought into perfect order, *Prometheus Unbound* itself brought into sustained and continuous creation. Shelley's literary sources for the amphisbaena in Lucan, Dante, and Milton do not use it in any functional or resonant way; it merely appears on a list of horrid reptiles and has no place in the symbolic development of the *Pharsalia*, the *Divine Comedy*, or *Paradise Lost*. But here at a crucial moment in the poem, welling from conscious and unconscious sources, it appears to the poet as the necessary image, one of those sudden, intricate formings from the flux that are so characteristic of Shelley and so often hypostatize two of his most cherished wishes: permanence in life and art and a consciousness that sustains them forever, the mind freed for Blake's "ever-varying spiral ascents to the heavens of heavens."

But *Prometheus Unbound* does not end in full amphisbaenic openness. Demogorgon's concluding speech, in which he speaks of the future and the means by which the vision can be sustained, warns against the return of the uroboros:

> Gentleness, Virtue, Wisdom, and Endurance,
> These are the seals of that most firm assurance
>     Which bars the pit over Destruction's strength;
> And if, with infirm hand, Eternity,
> Mother of many acts and hours, should free
>     The serpent that would clasp her with his length;
> These are the spells by which to reassume
> An empire o'er the disentangled doom.     (IV:562–69)

We have seen this serpent before in Act II when potency becomes act and the snakelike Doom is uncoiled to pull Jupiter from his throne in Act III. But, now, at the apocalyptic, not millennial, resolution of the poem, if the snake were freed to embrace Eternity, thus restoring the condition of the maternal uroboros, a lapse into unconsciousness would set the whole historical cycle in motion again and wreck the vision and the poem. If the serpent were to encircle Eternity, the mind would again be subject to temporal processes and the poetic vision would be caught in tragic repetition. Shelley's Eternity in *Prometheus Unbound* is not symbolized by the snake biting its tail, but by the liberated demonic serpent which does not describe a circle, the tail not returned to the head, a figure unenclosed, two-headed, consciousness sustained and sustaining.

### · III ·

Blake's serpent symbolism remains consistently malign until the climax of his vision. In *Jerusalem*, Los, remembering the fallen world shortly before the stirring of Brittannia and the resuscitation of Albion, speaks of the area

> "around Jerusalem
> "Where the Druids rear'd their Rocky Circles to make permanent Remembrance
> "Of Sin, & the Tree of Good & Evil sprang from the Rocky Circle & Snake
> "Of the Druid, along the Valley of Rephaim from Camberwell to Golgotha,
> "And framed the Mundane Shell Cavernous in Length, Bredth & Highth."
> (*J* 92:23–27, *K* 740)

This is a recapitulation of the passage we have examined in *Europe*, and the Druid Snake that appears on the title page and in the border of Plate 10 of that poem is the same evil serpent alluded to here. But in the seventh Night of *The Four Zoas*, written between *Europe* and *Jerusalem*, Blake had deepened our understanding of his symbol by suggesting that it had its sources in a kind of cosmic character-armor, in a willed and defensive "choice." The imprisoned Orc, the rebel hero of Blake's historical prophecies, puts on a serpent body in response to the ironic blandishments of Urizen:

> And Orc began to organize a Serpent body,
> Despising Urizen's light & turning it into flaming fire,
> Recieving as a poison'd cup Recieves the heavenly wine,
> And turning affection into fury & thought into abstraction,
> A Self consuming dark devourer rising into the heavens.
> (*FZ* vii:152–56, *K* 324)

Urizen, appalled at the transformation of Orc, forces the snake up the Tree of Mystery: "He suffer'd him to climb that he might draw all human forms / Into submission to his will, nor knew the dread result" (ll. 164–65). Just as Urizen's repressive law is a protective exclusion, denying the minute particulars of human existence, so Orc's reaction creates the Druid Snake, the same dull round in which Orc and Urizen will repeatedly become each other. That Orc, hung on the Tree, recalls the Crucified and can be identified as Luvah, the Zoa of the passions, as Urizen suspects, does not, by itself, redeem the serpent symbol. It is essential to understand that the snake cannot be lifted up, "identified," until the whole creation comes to the Last Judgment.

Just as Asia's self-surrender, her "meekness" in descending to Demogorgon's cave, released the uroboros, so the sacrifice of the Man Albion for his friend Jesus on Plate 96 of *Jerusalem* brings a sudden glimpse of life utterly transformed. When Albion throws himself into the Furnaces of affliction, and the Zoas (his scattered parts) rise into his bosom, only then does the snake, together with the whole of existence, human and nonhuman, attain redemption. The Jehovah whom Blake hears now is not the tyrant of the Old Testament, but the God of inspiration and mercy who came into being after the death of Jesus.[9] At the Identifying Climax of *Jerusalem*, the poet hears and sees the loving Father:

> And I heard Jehovah speak
> Terrific from his Holy Place, & saw the Words of the Mutual Covenant
>     Divine
> On Chariots of gold & jewels, with Living Creatures, starry & flaming
> With every Colour, Lion, Tyger, Horse, Elephant, Eagle, Dove, Fly,
>     Worm
> And the all wondrous Serpent clothed in gems & rich array, Humanize
> In the Forgiveness of Sins according to thy Covenant, Jehovah.
>
>                                        (*J* 98:40–45, *K* 746)

The wondrous Serpent bears the same accouterments as elsewhere in Blake (cf. "I saw a chapel all of gold"), but these too have been transformed, and the "rich array" signifies not tyrannic pride, but the splendors of the apocalyptic clarification in which *Jerusalem* and Blake's literary career conclude. It is important to note that the humanized snake is the climactic image in this list of creatures, and that the "Worm" stands before the serpent in this listing. As Northrop Frye has pointed out,[10] there are *two* serpents in Blake: the fallen worm alluded to in *Europe*, a creature "of sixty winters / In an allegorical abode where existence hath never come" (5:6–7, *K* 240), and the demonic serpent, associated with the archetypal dragon which represents the druid culture that preceded Adam, the tail-biting reptile I have been examining in this paper. Both serpents share in the apocalyptic transformations.

The contrasting fates of the uroboros in Blake and Shelley point up precisely the subtle differences in their poetic methods and resolutions. The Blake of the Prophetic Books is an epic poet, working from a deeply Christian base to a purpose at once cosmic and national in character; the Shelley of *Prometheus Unbound* is a lyric poet, essentially agnostic in his poetic and philosophical solutions, working toward aesthetic stasis. Blake's Prophetic Books instruct, strain beyond art; *Prometheus Unbound* floats an image of renewed man, folded back on its own dialectic in the mind. *Blake would redeem the demonic serpent; Shelley seeks to release and maintain it.* The transformation of uroboros to amphisbaena, and those "spells" by which the tail-biter will be prevented from re-forming himself, are aesthetically-oriented means of maintaining a continuous consciousness, masquerading as ethical imperatives. Blake would influence behavior; Shelley yearns beyond it.

## · IV ·

The rediscovery and refurbishing of literary and psychic archetypes in the Romantic period is a familiar episode of literary history, but it is important to distinguish the use and meaning of these emblems as exactly as possible. The uroboros, as a fructifying and complex example of such images, plays a crucial role in the resonant mind of that poet who most resembled Blake and Shelley but whose development and poetic objectives were so ultimately different. The tail-biting reptile in Coleridge's dazzlingly rich imagination represented his completest dream: that unitive ground all his desires sought, whether he was describing the unity of a poem or the just orderliness of God's creation. In a letter to Joseph

Cottle in 1815, while commenting on a poem the latter had sent him, he wrote:

The common end of all *narrative*, nay, of *all*, Poems is to convert a *series* into a *Whole:* to make those events, which in real or imagined History move on in a *strait* line, assume to our Understandings a *circular* motion—the snake with it's [sic] Tail in its mouth. Hence indeed the almost flattering and yet appropriate Term, Poesy—i.e. poiesis-*making*. Doubtless, to his eye, which alone comprehends all Past and all Future in one eternal Present, what to our short sight appears strait is but part of the great Cycle—just as the calm Sea to us *appears* level, tho' it indeed [be] only a part of a *globe*. Now what the Globe is in Geography, *miniaturing* in order to *manifest* the Truth, such is a Poem to that Image of God, which we were created with, and which still seeks that Unity or Revelation of the *One* in and by the *Many*, which reminds it, that tho' in order to be an individual Being it must go forth *from* God, yet as the *receding* from *him* is to *proceed* towards Nothingness and Privation, it must still at every step turn back toward him in order to *be* at all—Now, a straight Line, continuously retracted forms of necessity a circular orbit. Now God's Will and Word *cannot* be frustrated. His aweful Fiat was with ineffable awefulness applied to Man, when all things and all living Things, himself (as a mere animal included,) were called forth by the Universal—*Let there be*—.[11]

This fine passage, written two years before the publication of the *Biographia Literaria* in 1817, contains at the same time a theory of poetry and a theodicy of which the poetics are a part. It is the nature of the poetic universe, *"miniaturing* in order to *manifest* the truth,"* to be an analogue of the creation of the Godhead as the poet is akin to God the Creator, a long-standing idea in poetic theory and expressed most succinctly for Shelley in the famous assertion attributed to Tasso: *Non merita nome di creatore, se non Iddio ed il Poeta.* But we must notice carefully the essentially mediated character of Coleridge's conception. The God of this letter with his "aweful Fiat" is nearer to Blake's Nobodaddy and Shelley's Jupiter than he is to a beneficent father or humanized Creator. Later in this letter, Coleridge assures his correspondent that death *cannot* be nothing because of that medium between nothing and true Being "which Scripture and inmost reason present"; and we understand then that his tail-biter needs neither redemption nor release. Like Job, Coleridge is overcome; a tenor of submission is strong in his attitude. It is only in the most Blakean-Shelleyan of his poems, *Kubla Khan*, in the Los-like, potentially Promethean poet who would build a dome in air, finer than Kubla's, that we catch accents of deep poetic transformations, a coming to consciousness not through Scripture or the guilt that so dogged Coleridge's genius, but through the beginning of mythic order and recovery in the self and in the poem. The causes of Coleridge's poetic decline, his manifold unfinished projects, the glorious fragment that both his life and work seem to be, remain mysterious. I am only suggesting a further image of his decline in his unpoetic acceptance of the uroboros which he did not master or recreate in his poetry. The contrast with Blake and Shelley is instructive.

The uroboros has been in cultural history and in individual psychology a universal image of both the beginning and the consummation of development. In the *Origins and History of Consciousness*, Erich Neumann writes of this emblem:

The uroboros, traceable in all epochs and cultures, then appears as the latest symbol of individual psychic development, signifying the roundedness of the psyche, life's wholeness, and perfection regained. It is the place of transfiguration and illumination of finality, as well as the place of mythological origination.[12]

But this is the *end* of process, the uroboros reclaiming and reclaimed, a biologically determined and historically conditioned symbol which revolutionary poets like Blake and Shelley could not simply accept. The stages of consciousness, as Neumann discusses them, involve growth *away* from uroboric imagery into an ego-consciousness which must not be confused with what Blake and Shelley understood as the limiting Selfhood. The work of both poets, to a degree greater than in the poetry of the other Romantics, concerns itself precisely with the "place of mythological origination," a cleansing, a redeeming of that place. The progress into consciousness involves the breaking of the circle formed by the snake because "consciousness equals deliverance: that is the watchword inscribed above all man's efforts to deliver himself from the embrace of the primordial dragon." [13] It is true that the transformation of the serpent in Blake from the demonic to the apocalyptic creature seems a fuller development than the mere release of the demonic serpent in Shelley, but both poets find the "place of transfiguration and illumination" in their poems, Blake in his last major work, Shelley in his first. We do not compare Homer and Catullus and find the latter lacking in Homeric virtues. We read Blake and Shelley because they show us that Demogorgon, after all, was wrong. The deep truth is *not* imageless.

VIVIAN DE SOLA PINTO

# William Blake and
# D. H. Lawrence

It was recognized very early that there was an affinity between Blake and Lawrence. F. R. Leavis, one of Lawrence's earliest and most perceptive critics, wrote of Lawrence that he had "Blake's gift of knowing what he was interested in, the same power of distinguishing his own feelings and emotions from conventional sentiment, the same 'terrifying honesty.' " [1] Aldous Huxley compared what he called Lawrence's "polytheism" with Blake's doctrine of "the independence of states of being." [2] More recently Constantine N. Stavrou in an interesting article on "William Blake and D. H. Lawrence," contributed to the *University of Kansas City Review* (Spring, 1956), has pointed to a number of similarities between the thought of the two writers, stressing particularly the agreement of their ideas on space, time, and eternity and their insistence on the value of "spontaneity born of instinct," [3] while Eugene Goodheart in his suggestive study, *The Utopian Vision of D. H. Lawrence*, has emphasized Lawrence's affinity both to Blake and to Nietzsche as "tablet-breakers" and artists who "managed to see and judge the quality of life (its norms and perversities) from a vantage point outside civilization." [4]

The present essay is a tentative and fragmentary attempt to develop some of the hints thrown out by these critics and to make some further exploration of the points of contact between these two major English writers. I am not going to try to estimate the precise extent to which Lawrence was directly influenced by Blake; generalizations about literary "influences" are seldom very profitable. Artists are always stimulated by the study of the work of other artists, and all that we can say definitely is that Blake was one of the artists whose work, both as a poet and as a painter, attracted and stimulated Lawrence.

It may, however, be of interest at the outset to notice some of Lawrence's recorded reactions to Blake. He certainly knew some of Blake's poetry at an early stage in his career. Jessie Chambers gave him a copy of the *Songs of Innocence and of Experience* when he was very young, and she tells us that he "talked to me in his rapt way about Blake, telling me what a wonderful man he was, quite poor, who taught himself everything he knew. How he made pictures and wrote poems that were interdependent, and did the printing and engraving himself, in fact producing the book entirely by his own hands. He told me Blake's wife was a poor girl whom he taught to read, and also to print and engrave, and what a marvellous helpmate she was to him. . . . For a little while," Jessie adds, "we lived with Blake and his wife." [5]

Several of Lawrence's early poems contain echoes of *Songs of Innocence and of Experience*, and he seems to have planned a series of "Baby Songs," perhaps in emulation of *Songs of Innocence*. Later, however, certain aspects of Blake's work seem to have exasperated him. It was quite normal with Lawrence to criticize severely the work of writers who meant a great deal to him. Dostoevski and Whitman, two writers whom he certainly admired, receive even more severe treatment than Blake. Lawrence's adverse criticisms of Blake may also have been partly due to his friend and antagonist, Middleton Murry. Murry made a profound study of Blake's longer poems and his metaphysic and wrote an excellent book on this subject. Lawrence disliked abstract metaphysical discussions, and it is possible that Murry bored him with talk about Blake's philosophy. We hear a note of exasperation in a passage in Lawrence's essay on Poe in which he quotes Poe's poem on "The Conquering Worm." This poem Lawrence rather strangely calls "the American equivalent for a William Blake poem," and adds, "For Blake, too, was one of those ghastly obscene 'Knowers.'" The "Knowers," according to Lawrence in this essay, are the lovers who want to know the woman whom they love with their minds and are not content with knowing her "darkly, in the blood." "Man," he writes, "does so horribly want to master the secret of life and individuality with his mind." This kind of knowledge is "the temptation of the vampire fiend." [6] It is curious that Lawrence should bring this accusation against Blake who is never tired of denouncing the sort of cold, intellectual probing described by Lawrence as "knowing with the mind." This is the kind of knowledge symbolized by Blake as the "Spectre": "a Negation," the "idiot Questioner who is always questioning, / But never capable of answering" (*Mil* 41:12–13, *E* 141). I think it likely that in this passage Lawrence is attacking not so much Blake as Blake interpreted by Murry. Perhaps a clue may also be found in a remark in a letter to his friends Earl and Achsah Brewster, the American Buddhists. They had sent him a poem called *The White Stallion,* and he replied that he was disappointed with it, adding, "I am never very fond of abstract poetry, not even Blake." [7] The words "not even Blake" are significant. They show that he felt the attraction of Blake's poetry but disliked what seemed to him the abstract quality of much of its subject matter. Up to a point Blake himself would have agreed. In one of his letters to Thomas Butts he notes and deplores the tendency of his poetry to become abstract: "I labour incessantly & accomplish not one half of what I intend, because my Abstract folly hurries me often away while I am at work, carrying me over Mountains & Valleys which are not Real, in a Land of Abstraction where Spectres of the Dead wander" (11 Sept. 1801, *E* 685).

Lawrence certainly knew and admired Blake's painting, and he pays a very notable and discerning tribute to it in his essay called "Introduction to These Paintings": "Blake is the only painter of imaginative pictures apart from landscape that England has produced. And unfortunately there is so little Blake, and even in that little the symbolism is artificially imposed. Nevertheless, Blake paints with real intuitional awareness and solid instinctive feeling. He dares handle the human body, even if he sometimes makes it a mere ideograph. And no other Englishman has dared to handle it with live imagination." [8] This seems to be about the best short criticism of Blake's painting ever written, but it is time we turned to the main theme of this paper, which is not Lawrence's reactions to Blake but the fundamental spiritual kinship between the two men.

There is certainly a resemblance in the pattern of their lives. Both sprang from what I call "the Other England," the England of Bunyan, Defoe, and Cobbett, which was outside the pale of the governing class with its wealth and leisure and university and public school education.

Lawrence's father was a Nottinghamshire coal miner, and Blake's was a little London shopkeeper, and in both their families the religious tradition was that of the Puritan dissenters, not the Anglican church. This meant that both of them were steeped at an early age in the rhythms and imagery of the King James version of the Bible. Both were remarkably gifted boys who fought successfully to avoid being sucked into the dreary business of earning a living by mechanical toil. Blake wrote:

> Thank God I never was sent to school
> To be Flogd into following the Style of a Fool.  (*E* 502)

And Lawrence wrote:

In my generation the boys I went to school with, colliers now, have all been beaten down, what with the din-din-dinning of Board Schools, books, cinemas, clergymen, the whole national and human consciousness, hammering on the fact of material prosperity above all things.[9]

Blake was more fortunate than Lawrence. In his time the industrial society was still in its infancy; there was no compulsory education, and the individual craftsman still played an important part in the economy. Blake had the great good luck to learn thoroughly at an early age a craft which was also an art. He could practice that craft in his own home, and it was sufficient to support him and his wife, if not in affluence, at any rate in decent poverty, while it also enabled him to produce those illuminated books in which he succeeded so brilliantly in combining his gifts as poet, painter, designer, and craftsman. Lawrence, in his early days, when he talked about Blake to Jessie Chambers, must have looked enviously at the man who "taught himself everything he knew" and who was able to make pictures and poems that were "interdependent," and produce books "entirely by his own hands." Lawrence's lot was a much harder one. For a collier's son with literary gifts in the English Midlands at the opening of the twentieth century, the only avenue of escape from the industrial machine was to enter the teaching profession, and the only way to break out of the grind of teaching in the national schools was to write successful fiction. The immense labor involved in emancipating himself by these methods put a very heavy strain on Lawrence's frail constitution. Blake, the craftsman, living in obscurity and dignified poverty in early nineteenth-century London, died at the age of seventy. Lawrence, the famous novelist and wanderer through four continents, died, worn out in self-imposed exile, at the age of forty-five.

Both Blake and Lawrence were "taken up" for a time by representatives of the upper-class literary and artistic intelligentsia. Both reacted violently against this sort of patronage. Blake's denunciations of Sir Joshua Reynolds and the bigwigs of the Royal Academy can be compared with Lawrence's denunciations of the Cambridge-Bloomsbury set, with which he had a brief association. (It is curious that he actually calls his caricature of Bertrand Russell in *Women in Love* "Sir Joshua.")[10] In both their lifetimes England was engaged in a major war, and both were out of sympathy with the prevalent jingoistic mood of their fellow countrymen, while their attitudes were completely misunderstood by contemporary officialdom. Blake was absurdly tried for sedition on the evidence of a drunken soldier, and Lawrence was equally absurdly expelled from Cornwall as a spy by blundering official busybodies, because he had a German wife. Yet both were patriots in a far deeper sense than that of the contemporary war-hawks. Blake called himself "English Blake" and looked forward to the building of Jerusalem in "England's green and pleasant land," while Lawrence declared that he was "English in the teeth of all the world, even in the teeth of England." [11]

Lawrence in his "Study of Thomas Hardy" wrote of Hardy that "his feeling, his instinct, his sensuous understanding, is, however, apart from his metaphysic, very great and deep, deeper perhaps than that of any other English novelist." [12] This passage can be applied to a fundamental resemblance between Blake and Lawrence apart from any similarity in their thought. In both these writers there is a profound "sensuous understanding," a deep, instinctive, religious apprehension of the wonder of creative vitality. This is what Blake in his most Lawrentian work, *The Marriage of Heaven and Hell,* calls "The Prolific":

The pride of the peacock is the glory of God.
The lust of the goat is the bounty of God.
The wrath of the lion is the wisdom of God.
. . . . . . . . . . . . . . . .
Joys impregnate. Sorrows bring forth.
. . . . . . . . . . . . . . .
The cistern contains: the fountain overflows
. . . . . . . . . . . . . . .
The soul of sweet delight, can never be defil'd,
. . . . . . . . . . . . .
To create a little flower is the labour of ages.
(*MHH* 8:22–24, 29, 35; 9:54, 57. *E* 36–37)

Beside these aphorisms of Blake we can place these sentences from Lawrence's wonderful neglected essay, "Reflections on the Death of a Porcupine":

Vitality depends upon the clue of the Holy Ghost inside a creature, a man, a nation, a race. When the clue goes, the vitality goes. And the Holy Ghost seeks for ever a new incarnation, and subordinates the old to the new. . . . No man, or creature, or race can have vivid vitality unless it be moving towards a blossoming: and the most powerful is that which moves towards the as-yet-unknown blossom.

Blossoming means the establishing of a pure, *new* relationship with all the cosmos. This is the state of heaven. And it is the state of a flower, a cobra, a jenny-wren in spring, a man when he knows himself royal and crowned with the sun, with his feet gripping the core of the earth! [13]

Along with this profound sensuous apprehension of creative vitality, Blake and Lawrence are both deeply conscious of the tragic split in human consciousness caused by the excessive development of the analytic intellect at the expense of the imaginative and sensual life. This is what Blake calls the separation of the Spectre from the Emanation, typified by the "dark Satanic Mills" of Locke and Newton, the abstract thinkers whose work is associated by Blake with the Industrial Revolution:

> cruel Works
> Of many Wheels I view, wheel without wheel, cogs tyrannic
> Moving by compulsion each other: not as those in Eden: which
> Wheel within Wheel in freedom revolve in harmony & peace.
> (*J* 15:17–20, *E* 157)

Both writers stress the dehumanization of society caused by abstract thought and mechanical organization. Blake sees it in the London of the early stages of the Industrial Revolution as Lawrence sees it in the Derbyshire of the nineteen twenties:

> I wander thro' each charter'd street,
> Near where the charter'd Thames does flow.
> And mark in every face I meet
> Marks of weakness, marks of woe.
>
> In every cry of every Man,
> In every Infants cry of fear,
> In every voice: in every ban,
> The mind-forg'd manacles I hear . . .   ("London," *E* 26–27)

The car ploughed uphill through the long squalid straggle of Tevershall, the blackened brick dwellings, the black slate roofs glistening with their sharp edges, the mud black with coal dust, the pavements wet and black. It was as if dismalness had soaked through and through everything. The utter negation of natural beauty, the utter negation of the gladness of life, the utter absence of the instinct of shapely beauty which every bird and beast has, the utter death of the human intuitive faculty was appalling. . . .

Tevershall! That was Tevershall! Merrie England! Shakespeare's England! No, but the England of today, as Connie had realised since she came to live in it. It was producing a new race of mankind, over-conscious in the money and social and political side, on the spontaneous, intuitive side dead,—but dead! Half-corpses, all of them: but with a terrible insistent consciousness in the other half.[14]

Both Blake and Lawrence associate the dehumanization of so-

ciety with the poisoning of sex through repression and the identification of sex with "sin." In a defiant quatrain Blake writes:

> Abstinence sows sand all over
> The ruddy limbs & flaming hair
> But Desire Gratified
> Plants fruits of life & beauty there.     (*E* 465)

And in the terrible lament of Oothoon in *Visions of the Daughters
of Albion* he foreshadows Freud and the depth-psychologists of
the twentieth century:

The moment of desire! the moment of desire! the virgin
That pines for man; shall awaken her womb to enormous joys
In the secret shadows of her chamber; the youth shut up from
The lustful joy. shall forget to generate. & create an amorous image
In the shadows of his curtains and in the folds of his silent pillow.
Are not these the places of religion? the rewards of continence?
The self enjoyings of self denial? Why dost thou seek religion?
Is it because acts are not lovely, that thou seekest solitude,
Where the horrible darkness is impressed with reflections of desire.

Father of Jealousy. be thou accursed from the earth!
Why hast thou taught my Theotormon this accursed thing?
Till beauty fades from off my shoulders darken'd and cast out,
A solitary shadow wailing on the margin of non-entity.

I cry, Love! Love! Love! happy happy Love! free as the mountain wind!
(*VDA* 7:3–16, *E* 49)

Similarly Lawrence in his essay on "Sex versus Loveliness" writes:

Science has a mysterious hatred of beauty, because it doesn't fit in with
the cause-and-effect chain. And society has a mysterious hatred of sex,
because it perpetually interferes with the nice money making schemes
of social man. So the two hatreds made a combine, and sex and beauty are
mere propagation appetite. . . .
    Sex and beauty are inseparable, like life and consciousness. And the
intelligence which goes with sex and beauty, and arises out of sex and
beauty, is intuition. The great disaster of our civilization is the morbid
hatred of sex.[15]

The following passage from Lawrence's essay "The State of Funk" is a prosaic counterpart to the lament of Oothoon in Blake's poem:

> I know, when I was a lad of eighteen, I used to remember with shame and rage in the morning the sexual thoughts and desires I had had in the night before. Shame, and rage, and terror lest anybody else should have to know. And I *hated* the self I had been, the night before.
> Most boys are like that, and it is, of course, utterly wrong. The boy that had excited sexual thoughts and feelings was the living, warm-hearted passionate me. The boy that in the morning remembered these feelings with such fear, shame and rage was the social mental me: perhaps a little priggish, and certainly in a state of funk, but the two were divided against one another. A boy divided against himself; a girl divided against herself; a people divided against itself; it is a disastrous condition.
> . . . . . . . . . . . . . . . . . . . . . . . . . . . . . .
> Accept the sexual, physical being of yourself, and of every other creature. . . . Conquer the fear of sex and restore the natural flow.[16]

The divided condition of modern man described by Lawrence in this passage is pithily summarized by Blake in a single quatrain:

> My Spectre around me night & day
> Like a Wild beast guards my way
> My Emanation far within
> Weeps incessantly for my Sin.     (ll. 1-4, *E* 467)

Blake and Lawrence were both prophetic artists, and to communicate their prophecies they both needed the framework of a myth in symbolism and a literary form. Blake made various preliminary experiments: in the short lyric, in prose, even once in the novel form. But his fragment of a novel, *An Island in the Moon,* is a satiric fantasy in the manner of Swift and Sterne, too frail a thing to bear the weight of his serious thought. The novel in his time had not yet developed an adequate form for the embodiment of prophetic poetry. He solved the problem by constructing his own mythology and developing a new type of symbolic epic in the Prophetic Books with the help of the Old Testament, Milton, and Ossian. This form suited his peculiar kind of genius, because he was naturally a visionary and a mythological thinker, something very rare in the modern world.

Between Blake and Lawrence there was a century of development of the Western novelistic tradition: Scott, Jane Austen, Balzac, Tolstoi, Dostoevski, Dickens, the Brontës, Flaubert, Hawthorne, Melville, George Eliot, Meredith, Henry James, and Hardy. By the early twentieth century the novel had come of age in western Europe and America and indeed was now the only large-scale literary form that had any real vitality. Moreover, just as Blake was naturally a visionary, so Lawrence's genius was that of a keen-eyed observer of human life, and this is, perhaps, the chief difference between the two men:

> Now I a fourfold vision see
> And a fourfold vision is given to me
> Tis fourfold in my supreme delight
> And three fold in soft Beulah's night
> And twofold Always. May God us keep
> From Single vision & Newtons sleep
> (To Thomas Butts, 22 Nov. 1802, *E* 693)

Blake would doubtless have suspected that Lawrence (except, perhaps, in the final phase of his work) was a man of the twofold and threefold vision—the vision of the material world illuminated by the moon of "soft Beulah's night," the poetry of the purified senses. But this is not the whole truth. Lawrence, though no visionary, like Blake was essentially a prophetic and symbolic poet, not only in his poetry and his poetic essays but in his novels—I should say especially in his novels. Of course, Lawrence's novels can be appreciated in the way that Dr. Leavis has taught us to read and appreciate them, as works in the great realistic tradition of the English novel. But any sensitive reader can perceive that there is something in them that is very different from anything to be found in the novels of Dickens or George Eliot or Thomas Hardy. It is the quality which Professor Angelo Bertucci in his valuable essay on "Symbolism in *Women in Love*" has called "religious vision." [17] I would even suggest that Lawrence's fiction can be read as a cycle of religious vision bearing a close resemblance to the cycle of Blake's poetry. *The White Peacock* and *Sons and Lovers* would correspond respectively to *Songs of Innocence* and *Songs of Experience*. Then Lawrence, like Blake, planned a huge symbolic epic which he never completed. Lawrence's *The Sisters or the Marriage Ring* can be compared with Blake's *Vala, or the Four Zoas*, and just as Blake's two great symbolic epics, *Milton* and *Jerusalem*, were quarried, as it were, from the great mass of the unfinished *Vala*, so Lawrence's two major prophetic novels, *The Rainbow* and *Women in Love*, seem to have emerged from the vast design of that ghost epic novel *The Sisters*. Here, however, we can notice a curious divergence between the two patterns of artistic development. Blake and Lawrence, like most major artists, went through a period of *Sturm und Drang*, a difficult period of agonized groping and experiment. Blake's "difficult" period is that of the so-called Lambeth books, the books of *Urizen, Los,* and *Ahania* and *The Song of Los*. It preceded the achievement of his major symbolic epics. Lawrence, however, seems to have passed straight from the splendid but limited success of his early novels to the great plan of his major work which finally crystallized in *The Rainbow* and *Women in Love*. It is only after the publication of these works that we find Lawrence's phase of "agony and experiment" in those rather unsatisfactory novels, *Aaron's Rod, Kangaroo,* and *The Plumed Serpent*. The final phase of spiritual illumination, found in such stories as *St Mawr* and *The Man Who Died* and in *Etruscan Places* and the wonderful *Last Poems,* can be compared with that of Blake's last work, *The Everlasting Gospel* and *Illustrations of the Book of Job*.

It has often been observed that the characters in Lawrence's major novels are unlike those belonging to the realistic tradition. Lawrence himself in a famous and often-quoted letter warned Edward Garnett that his characters were not of the traditional kind:

You mustn't look in my novel for the old stable *ego*—of the character. There is another *ego*, according to whose action the individual is unrecognisable, and passes through, as it were, allotropic states which it needs a deeper sense than any we've been used to exercise, to discover . . . states of the same single radically unchanged element. (Like as diamond and coal are the same pure single element of carbon. . . .[18]

Lawrence's "pure single element of carbon" is what Blake calls

"The Divine Humanity," and the characters in his novels can be compared with the characters in Blake's epics representing faculties of the Divine Humanity (Blake's "Albion") which have become separated and fallen into a condition of conflict. It is true that Lawrence, in the Foreword to *The Fantasia of the Unconscious*, warns us that his "pseudo-philosophy" is "deduced from the novels and poems, not the reverse" and that "the novels and poems are pure passionate experience. These 'pollyanalytics' are inferences made afterwards, from the experience." [19] However, as H. M. Daleski has acutely pointed out, this is not quite the whole truth.[20] We must, indeed, regard Blake and Lawrence as imaginative writers, not as "pseudo-philosophers," but it is also true that their imaginative creations have a profound philosophic meaning. This meaning, however, is the product of thinking in terms of symbol and myth, not in the discursive terms of abstract reasoning. They were both "mythical thinkers" of the kind described by Ernst Cassirer in his *Essay on Man:* they interpret life and the universe in mythological terms, making use of what Cassirer calls "the deepest stratum of perception." [21] This fact is partly obscured in Lawrence's work by his use of the realistic setting of the novelistic tradition.

I am not, of course, suggesting that their works are allegories. Both Blake and Lawrence distinguish sharply and in remarkably similar terms between allegory and symbolism (or "vision" as Blake calls it). "Symbols," wrote Lawrence, "are organic units of consciousness with a life of their own, and you can never explain them away, because their value is dynamic, emotional, belonging to the sense-consciousness of the body and soul, not merely mental. An allegorical image has a *meaning*, Mr Facing-both-ways has a meaning. But I defy you to lay your finger on the full meaning of Janus, who is a symbol." [22] Similarly Blake tells us that "Fable or Allegory are a totally distinct & inferior kind of Poetry. Vision or Imagination is a Representation of what Eternally Exists. Really & Unchangeably" and he advises the spectator of his pictures to "Enter into these Images in his Imagination" and "make a Friend & Companion of one of these Images of Wonder" (*LJ* 68, 82; *E* 544, 550).

The fundamental theme of both Blake and Lawrence may be

described as unity in diversity or the tension between opposites. It is the theme crystallized by Blake in memorable words in *The Marriage of Heaven and Hell:* "Without Contraries is no progression. Attraction and Repulsion, Reason and Energy, Love and Hate, are necessary to Human existence" (*MHH* 3, *E* 34). Similarly Lawrence tells us that the Lion and the Unicorn "would both cease to be, if either of them really won" in the fight for the Crown "which is their sole reason for existing"[23] and "Homer was wrong in saying, 'Would that strife might pass away from among gods and men!' He did not see that he was praying for the destruction of the universe;—for in the tension of opposites all things have their being."[24] In both Blake and Lawrence the essential conflict is seen at first in fairly simple terms. In Blake it is the conflict between the Tyger and the Lamb, Innocence and Experience, the spirit of Earth and the Father of Jealousy. In Lawrence it is the conflict between Mr. and Mrs. Morel and between the dehumanized life of the industrial Midlands and Paul Morel's eager, questing spirit. Both Blake and Lawrence, however, came to see the conflict in terms of greater complexity and subtlety. This complexity is symbolized by Blake in his great myth of the Four Zoas: Los, or the Imagination; Urizen, or the Intellect; Tharmas, who is the Body; and Luvah, the spirit of passionate Love. There is a further elaboration representing the polarity of the sexes. Each Zoa has an "Emanation" or female counterpart, Enitharmon for Los, Ahania for Urizen, Enion for Tharmas, and Vala for Luvah. Like the ancient gods, the Zoas are individuals as well as symbols, and Los in particular is not only the Imagination but Blake himself, while Enitharmon is his wife Catherine. The Emanations, too, are women as well as symbols, and they are all aspiring to the condition of Jerusalem or the perfect womanhood, while in their fallen state they tend to lapse into the condition of Rahab, the eternal harlot, or Tirzah, the eternal prude. It seems to me that this archetypal symbolism of Blake provides a valuable guide to the inner meaning of Lawrence's fiction. Paul Morel in *Sons and Lovers* is not only Lawrence himself but Los seeking for his true Emanation and finding her neither in his mother nor in Miriam and Clara, who may be equated respectively to Enion, Ahania, and Vala. In *The Rainbow* we have a whole series of imperfect "spectral" Zoas searching for their Emanations, and, with still greater emphasis, Emanations searching for their Zoas. Ursula Brangwen in the latter part of the novel prefigures one of the great themes of Lawrence's later fiction which may be described as Enitharmon striving towards the state of Jerusalem.

But *Women in Love* is the work of Lawrence to which Blake's mythology provides the most effective illustration. I called *The Marriage of Heaven and Hell* Blake's most Lawrentian work; *Women in Love* seems to me Lawrence's most Blakean, as well as, perhaps, his greatest work. It is highly significant that Blake is mentioned at a crucial point in the novel, and I cannot help thinking that Lawrence had Blake in mind when he wrote it; some of the parallels (even verbal parallels) seem to me to be too striking to be accidental. It is in this novel that we find Lawrence's clearest and most impressive handling of the theme of tension between contraries. Underlying Blake's elaborate scheme is the fundamental opposition between Los, the spirit of Imagination, and Urizen, the analytic Intellect, the representative of mechanism as opposed to organism, the law as opposed to the gospel. This opposition is adumbrated in Lawrence's earlier work as the opposition between the pastoralism of the old English countryside and the mechanized industrialism which was spreading over the face of the Midlands in the early twentieth century. His hatred of the mechanized, industrial world receives striking expression in the description of Wiggiston and Ursula's uncle Tom Brangwen, the colliery manager in chapter xii of *The Rainbow:*

A meaningless squalour of ash-pits and closets and irregular rows of backs of houses, each with its small activity made sordid by barren cohesion with the rest of the small activities . . . the whole place was unreal, just unreal . . . it was like some gruesome dream, some ugly amorphous mood become concrete.

Wiggiston and Uncle Tom are seen in purely negative terms, a universe of death, without a redeeming feature. In *Women in Love,* however, Gerald Crich, the dynamic mine-owner, is an attractive, even a heroic figure. Lawrence had developed in much the same way that Blake developed between *Songs of Innocence* and *Vala, or the Four Zoas*. Middleton Murry has shown how Blake became more and more sympathetic to Urizen, the Zoa representing the analytic intellect and the will.[25] Like Milton before him and Lawrence after him, and, indeed, as he himself pointed out, like all true artists, he tended to be of the Devil's party (*MHH* 6, *E* 35). Urizen in *Visions of the Daughters of Albion* is simply the "Father of Jealousy," the spirit of inhibition, "accursed from the earth" (7:12, *E* 49); but in *The Book of Urizen* he is humanized, a great, if mistaken, demiurge, curiously co-operating with Los, his opponent, with whom he was once united, while in *Vala, or the Four Zoas* he becomes the Prince of Light, a mighty tragic hero. Similarly in Lawrence's early work the spirit of industrialism is seen simply as a negation, but in *Women in Love* it is embodied in the handsome Gerald Crich, the soldier–explorer–mine-owner, a mistaken, unhappy man, indeed, but a great dynamic intellect, a radiant human being, and a prince among lovers. As Urizen is perhaps Blake's finest mythological creation, so Gerald Crich is perhaps the most powerfully drawn male figure in Lawrence's fiction. The closeness of the resemblance between Gerald and Urizen is indeed remarkable. In *Vala, or the Four Zoas*, Urizen is called an "obscure Demon of destruction" and a "Cold Demon" (vi: p. 68, l. 25; p. 69, l. 6. *E* 339). Rupert Birkin describes Gerald as "one of those strange white wonderful demons from the North, fulfilled in the destructive frost mystery." The term "demon" is applied several times to Gerald, and like Urizen, he is constantly associated with the North and with frost.[26] Both Urizen and Gerald are great builders and organizers. Urizen with immense toil builds the mathematical Newtonian Universe:

> He dug mountains & hills in vast strength,
> He piled them in incessant labour,
> In howlings & pangs & fierce madness
> . . . . . . . . . . . .
> And a roof, vast petrific around,
> On all sides He fram'd: like a womb;
> Where thousands of rivers in veins
> Of blood pour down the mountains to cool

The eternal fires . . .
             . . . & like a black globe
    . . . . . . . . . . . . . . . .
The vast world of Urizen appear'd.
                    (*Ur* 5: 22–24, 28–33, 37; *E* 72)

This "world of Urizen" is also the world of the early industrial revolution.

Then siezd the Lions of Urizen their work, & heated in the forge
Roar the bright masses, thund'ring beat the hammers, many a pyramid
Is form'd & thrown down thund'ring into the deeps of Non Entity
Heated red hot they hizzing rend their way down many a league
Till resting. each his [center] finds; suspended there they stand
Casting their sparkles dire abroad into the dismal deep
For measurd out in orderd spaces the Sons of Urizen
With compasses divide the deep; they the strong scales erect
That Luvah rent from the faint Heart of the Fallen Man
And weigh the massy Cubes, then fix them in their awful stations.
                    (*FZ* ii: p. 28, ll. 25–32; p. 29, ll. 1–2. *E* 312)

Urizen proclaims himself god and believes that he is bringing peace and harmony to the world:

           One command, one joy, one desire,
           One curse, one weight, one measure
           One King, one God, one Law.    (*Ur* 4:38–40, *E* 71)

Similarly Gerald Crich, when he takes over the management of his father's mines, reorganizes the business on purely inhuman principles. He creates, we are told, "a new order, strict, terrible, inhuman": Like Urizen's, his ideal is harmony, and, like Urizen, he feels himself to be at once a high priest and a god (these terms are applied to both of them) overcoming and organizing the world of matter:

Immediately he *saw* the firm, he realised what he could do. He had a fight to fight with Matter, with the earth and the coal it enclosed. This was the sole idea, to turn upon the inanimate matter of the underground, and reduce it to his will. And for this fight with matter, one must have perfect instruments in perfect organization, a mechanism so subtle and harmonious in its workings that it represents the single mind of man, and by its relentless repetition of given movement, will accomplish a purpose irresistibly, inhumanly. It was this inhuman principle in the mechanism he wanted to construct that inspired Gerald with an almost religious exaltation. He, the man, could interpose a perfect, changeless, godlike medium between himself and the Matter he had to subjugate. There were two opposites, his will and the resistant Matter of the earth. And between these he could establish the very expression of his will, the incarnation of his power, a great and perfect machine, a system, an activity of pure order, pure mechanical repetition, repetition *ad infinitum*, hence eternal and infinite. He found his eternal and his infinite in the pure machine-principle of perfect co-ordination with one pure complex, infinitely repeated motion, like the spinning of a wheel, but a productive spinning, as the revolving of the universe may be called a productive spinning, a productive repetition through eternity, to infinity. And this is the God-motion, this productive repetition *ad infinitum*. And Gerald was the God of the Machine, *Deus ex Machina*. And the whole productive will of Man was the Godhead.[27]

We can notice that the wheel is the symbol of Gerald's world as it is the symbol of Urizen's. Blake tells us that the Sons of Urizen

> intricate wheels invented, wheel without wheel:
> To perplex youth in their outgoings, & to bind to labours in Albion
> Of day & night the myriads of eternity that they may grind
> And polish brass & iron hour after hour laborious Task!
> Kept ignorant of its use, that they might spend the days of wisdom
> In sorrowful drudgery . . .                    (*J* 65:21–26, *E* 214)

Gudrun in her final disillusionment concerning Gerald in chapter xxx of *Women in Love* sees his life as a "terrifying complex" of wheels from the one "humble wheel" of the wheelbarrow to the hundred thousand little wheels of the General Manager and finally the million wheels of Gerald himself: "poor Gerald, such a lot of little wheels to his make-up! He was more intricate than a chronometer watch. But oh heavens, what weariness! . . . so many wheels to count and consider and calculate!"[28]

Urizen's immense labors only bring him frustration and misery. He cries: "Can I not leave this world of Cumbrous wheels / Circle oer Circle . . . / . . . O thou poor ruind world / Thou horrible ruin . . ." And he feels himself falling "into a Void where air / Is not down falling thro immensity ever & ever" (*FZ* vi: p. 72, ll. 22–23, 35–36; p. 73, ll. 6–7. *E* 342–43). So Gerald Crich in spite of all his triumphs as a captain of industry, feels a terrible inner emptiness, "a mortal dry fear." He is afraid that his blue eyes might be "false blue bubbles that would burst in a moment and leave clear annihilation" and that "one day he would break down and be a purely meaningless babble lapping round a darkness." [29] Blake shows us Urizen wandering hopelessly through the cold dark dens of Urthona; Lawrence shows us Gerald Crich going to his death amid the snows and cold black rocks of the Tyrolese mountains.

Over against Urizen in Blake's myth is Los, the spirit of Imagination, the archetypal artist who is Blake himself. Los, it may be remembered, was once united with Urizen, and there is a curious love-hate relationship between them. Rupert Birkin, the artistic and philosophic school inspector in *Women in Love*, corresponds to Blake's Los, and as Los is also Blake, so Birkin is also Lawrence. The title of *Women in Love* is somewhat misleading. The central theme is not so much the relationships between Rupert Birkin and Ursula Brangwen and Gerald Crich and Gudrun as that between Rupert and Gerald. Throughout the novel there is a curious tension, a mixture of attraction and repulsion, between these two very different men. Gerald enjoys Rupert's conversation but does not take him very seriously, regarding him as an impractical theorist; yet he feels that he needs him. Rupert admires Gerald's beauty and strength but dislikes his conventional opinions. Very significantly we are told that he saw in Gerald "a sort of fatal halfness." [30] Gerald, in fact, for all his physical magnificence, was only half of a complete man, and Rupert was the other half just as in that terrible design in Blake's *Book of Urizen* we see the division of the complete man into the skeleton Urizen and the fully fleshed yet agonized Los with a great wall of flame between them. For a moment in the amazing wrestling scene in chapter xx of *Women in Love* Rupert and Gerald are united. The wrestling is the symbol of the creative tension, unity in diversity, which is the ideal condition for the imagination and the intellect. But Lawrence is telling us that in the modern world this can only happen in a moment of play—a piece of make-believe. In the end Gerald goes to his death alone, separated from his friend, and, when his body is found and brought back, Rupert looks at it with dismay, remembering "how once Gerald had clutched his hand with a warm, momentaneous grip of final love." [31]

The two sisters, Ursula and Gudrun, in Blake's terminology are the "Emanations" of Rupert and Gerald. It is significant that Ursula and Rupert (Enitharmon and Los) are united at the end of the novel, whereas, before his death, Gerald has quarreled violently with Gudrun and is separated from her just as Blake's Urizen is separated from Ahania,[32] who is the spirit of pleasure as Enitharmon is the spirit of pity.

Besides Los and Urizen the other two Zoas can be found in *Women in Love*. Tharmas, or the animal nature, is only faintly sketched in the beautiful Arab mare which Gerald cruelly forces to stay by the level crossing in chapter ix in spite of her deadly fear of the noise of the train. The passage is a terrible symbol of the animal nature of man tortured by the masterful will and intellect. Much more striking is the appearance of Luvah, the Zoa of Love, in the novel. His incarnation is old Mr. Thomas Crich, Gerald's father, the old-fashioned industrial magnate who tries to conduct his business and his relationship with his employees on purely Christian principles: "He had been so constant to his lights, so constant to charity and to his love for his neighbour. Perhaps he had loved his neighbour even better than himself—which is going one better than the commandment." He believed that "in Christ he was one with his workmen." [33] Yet all his idealism, powerless against the strong current of industrial development and the masterful will of his son Gerald, only results in a vague, indiscriminate charity, humiliating alike to the giver and the recipient. He dies a lingering, painful death, after seeing all his hopes for a truly Christian community crumble before Gerald's triumphant aggressive materialism. His death is a symbol of the death of the old Christian England. In Blake's epic, Luvah, the Prince of Love, also dies, cast by Urizen into "the Furnaces of affliction" (*FZ* ii: p. 25, l. 40; *E* 310), but he is an immortal like all the Zoas and cannot be wholly killed. He rises again in the shape of Orc, the spirit of Revolution who is seen to be one with Jesus. In the apocalypse at the end of the poem Urizen himself at length awakens from his "slumbers of . . . cold abstraction" and regains his pristine brightness (*FZ* ix: pp. 120–21; *E* 374–76). No such apocalypse was possible for Lawrence in the nineteen twenties: the hope of a glorious, renovating revolution which had inspired the men of the Romantic age has faded in the disillusion that followed the First World War.

One other character in *Women in Love* can be interpreted in terms of Blake's mythology. This is the little German sculptor Loerke, whom the English party meet at the *Gasthaus* in the Tyrolese mountains. If Gerald is a mighty Contrary, Loerke is what Blake calls a "Negation." Birkin actually calls him "a gnawing little negation, gnawing at the roots of life." [34] He is an artist or pseudo artist and wants to make art an expression of modern industrialism, but his art is dehumanized like the mechanized industrialism which he admires. Lawrence describes him as "a chatterer, a magpie, a maker of mischievous word-jokes that were sometimes very clever, but which often were not." [35] He is Blake's "idiot Questioner who is always questioning, / But never capable of answering" (*Mil* 41:12, 13; *E* 141). Gerald compares him to a flea, "a hopping flea with a proboscis," and, as he says these words, Gudrun is significantly reminded of "Blake's representation of the soul of a flea." [36] This is the allusion to which I have already referred as showing that Lawrence was thinking of Blake when he wrote *Women in Love*. Blake's grotesque drawing of "The Ghost of a Flea" (see PLATE 1) is a vision of a completely dehumanized man, a man with the soul of an insect, a face of "pure brutish evil, cold and insect-like," to quote a phrase of Lawrence from *The Plumed Serpent*.[37]

A major theme of Lawrence's later writings, as I have already suggested, can be described as Enitharmon striving towards the condition of Jerusalem. This is the theme of the three great short fictions: *The Virgin and the Gipsy*, *The Woman Who Rode Away*, and *St Mawr*, and also of the last great novel, *Lady Chatterley's Lover*. In terms of Jung's psychology, it is the theme of the anima striving to free itself from the disintegrating influences of the modern world. In terms of Blake's mythology it is Enitharmon striving to escape from the states of Rahab and Tirzah and achieve the state of Jerusalem. Blake calls that state "pity" and Lawrence "tenderness." The motto which could be suitably prefixed to all these later fictions of Lawrence is to be found in Blake's lines in *Milton:*

All that can be annihilated must be annihilated
. . . . . . . . . . . . . . . . .
The Negation must be destroyed to redeem the Contraries.

(*Mil* 40:30, 33; *E* 141)

It is remarkable that both men at the end of their careers were preoccupied with the character of Jesus and that both tried to produce a picture of Jesus which would include the spirit of Eros as well as that of agape. Lawrence's *The Man Who Died* is a remarkable prose counterpart to Blake's *The Everlasting Gospel.*

Blake believed in his youth in a Jacobin revolution, and Lawrence, for a time, flirted with a near-fascist conception of leadership. Blake, however, came to see that the French Revolution, which he had once hailed as the herald of an apocalypse, only produced a new tyranny; in terms of his own myth, it was only one more recurrence of the endless cycle of struggles between Orc and Urizen. His final description of it is equally applicable to the Russian Revolution:

The hand of Vengeance found the Bed
To which the Purple Tyrant fled
The iron hand crushed the Tyrants head
And became a Tyrant in his stead.

("The Grey Monk," ll. 33–36; *E* 481)

And in his *Public Address* he declared, "I am really sorry to see my Countrymen trouble themselves about Politics. If Men were Wise the Most arbitrary Princes could not hurt them If they are not Wise the Freest Government is compelld to be a Tyranny [.] Princes appear to me to be Fools Houses of Commons & Houses of Lords appear to me to be fools they seem to me to be something Else besides Human Life" (p. 18, *E* 569). In one of his poems Lawrence is saying much the same thing:

the robots sit on the thrones of the world

in all the high places, and they are masters of industry
and rulers of millions of robots, being robots themselves.[38]

And in his essay on "Democracy" he describes politics as "Just
another extra-large, commercial wrangle over buying and selling," [39]
while in a significant letter, dated March 13, 1928, he rejects the
idea of leadership: ". . . the hero is obsolete and the leader of men
is a back number. After all at the back of the hero is the militant
ideal; and the militant ideal or the ideal militant, seems to me
also a cold egg.[40]

The final testament of both writers is that a solution is only to
be found in the individual soul. The minority, the "reprobate" in
Blake's inverted Calvinist terminology, must go on fighting, not
with physical weapons, not, as Lawrence puts it, in the old " 'O
Glory!' sort of way," [41] but with the weapons of the spirit, a fight
for the restoration of the Whole Man, the true unity based on the
healthy tension between Contraries. "What's to be done?" Lawrence
writes in *St Mawr*.

Generally speaking, nothing. The dead will have to bury their dead,
while the earth stinks of corpses. The individual can but depart from the
mass, and try to cleanse himself. Try to hold fast to the living thing,
which destroys as it goes, but remains sweet. And in his soul fight, fight,
fight to preserve that which is life in him from the ghastly kisses and
poison-bites of the myriad evil ones. Retreat to the desert, and fight. But
in his soul adhere to that which is life itself, creatively destroying as it
goes: destroying the stiff old thing to let the new bud come through. The
one passionate principle of creative being, which recognizes the natural
good, and has a sword for the swarms of evil. Fights, fights, fights to
protect itself. But with itself is strong and at peace.[42]

Blake is saying the same thing in his most famous poem with all
the magnificent afflatus of romantic lyricism:

> Bring me my Bow of burning gold:
> Bring me my Arrows of desire:
> Bring me my Spear: O clouds unfold!
> Bring me my Chariot of fire!
>
> I will not cease from Mental Fight,

Nor shall my Sword sleep in my hand:
Till we have built Jerusalem,
In Englands green & pleasant Land.   (*Mil* 1:9–16, *E* 95)

Blake and Lawrence are the two major prophets of the Other England: iconoclasts, yet makers of splendid images; revolutionary, yet religious; earthy and irreverent, yet spiritual and apocalyptic. There is, I am convinced, a real link between them, more subtle than any direct "influence." "Every true artist," Lawrence wrote, "is the salvation of every other." [43] There is a special sense, I believe, in which Blake was part of Lawrence's salvation.

# The Graphic Artist

MARTIN BUTLIN

# The Evolution of Blake's Large Color Prints of 1795

Blake's large color prints of 1795 have a good claim to be his greatest works.[1] "Elohim creating Adam" (see PLATE II), "Nebuchadnezzar" and "Newton" are probably the most striking of all his designs, both visually and in their iconographic significance. The recent discovery that the so-called "Elijah in the Chariot of Fire" is really the long-lost "God judging Adam" merely confirms the awe-inspiring severity of its composition (see PLATE III).[2] "Pity" (PLATE IV) is one of the most inspired of all "literal" illustrations of a text in the history of art. In "The House of Death" (PLATE V) Blake rivals the sublime horror of his friend Fuseli. "The Good and Evil Angels" has an epic quality apparent even to the beholder ignorant of its complex relationship to Blake's writings.[3] "Naomi entreating Ruth" is an outstanding example of Blake's more fluid type of composition in its sense of turning movement. And so one could continue through the whole series of twelve designs.

This achievement is heralded scarcely at all in Blake's previous independent pictures. Comparison with the closely related watercolor versions of "God judging Adam" and "The Good and Evil Angels" only serves to demonstrate the sudden maturing of Blake's style.[4] Significantly there are also earlier versions of "The Good and Evil Angels" and "Nebuchadnezzar" among Blake's illustrations to his illuminated books, but they again lack the impact and sense of scale of the large prints.[5] Nor do these precursors have the culminative effect of the complete series of prints, in which the dogmatic purpose that alone for Blake justified his art is fulfilled through each design expressing, in a way that has not yet been fully unraveled, an aspect of his fundamental beliefs about the dilemma of man in the created world.[6] Both in the degree to which, in this sense, Blake's art is a literary one, and in the way the prints represent the culmination of tendencies and techniques developed in the illuminated books, the large color prints of 1795 mark the point at which Blake's primary and most successful means of expression ceased to be poetry and its illustration and became purely visual.

A vital factor in the impact of the large color prints is their technique. This consisted of printing in heavy opaque pigment from a plate, probably of millboard, and finishing in pen and water color. The opaque pigment was probably akin to the form of tempera, made with carpenters' glue, used by Blake in all but his latest tempera paintings; he sometimes called this medium "fresco." [7] This technique produced the extraordinarily rich and subtle textures that characterize, for instance, the Tate Gallery's copies of "Newton" and "Nebuchadnezzar." Although most of the prints exist in more than one copy, usually three, the thick colors seem to have been applied to the plate only once: successive pulls were then taken while the pigment was still wet, each print receiving less pigment than the one before and consequently requiring more finishing in pen, for the outlines, and water color.[8] Thus, paradoxically, those least finished by hand were closest to Blake's original intentions.

To the extent that the prints were created by a reproductive process, while at the same time differing in details of line and color, they were conditioned by Blake's experience as a printer and engraver and more especially, in just this very particular of variation within a set design, by the technique of his illuminated books. In these, from the *Songs of Innocence* of 1789 onwards, the initial etching of the copper plates established, in relief, both the text and the main lines of the illustrations, but each copy was colored by hand, the order of pages was often altered, and even the text itself was sometimes modified. Each copy was usually prepared at the time it was sold; as a result it is possible to trace much of Blake's evolution as a colorist in his books alone. The years 1789 to 1795 were vital in the development of Blake's illuminated books, in their coloring, in their technique, and in the relationship of text and illustration, and this development was indissolubly linked with the evolution of Blake's thought. The independent color prints of 1795, in their absence of supporting texts, paradoxically marked both the culmination of this development and the virtual extinction for about ten years of Blake's production of illuminated books. *The First Book of Urizen* of 1794, itself succeeded by no completing volume or volumes, was followed the next year by *The Song of Los, The Book of Ahania* and *The Book of Los,* scrappy and relatively insignificant and never repeated after the initial copies; the last two are represented by only one complete copy each. There followed nearly ten years of abortive work on the manuscript of *Vala, or the Four Zoas,* and only with *Milton* and *Jerusalem,* begun in 1804, did Blake resume his production of illuminated books.

The evolution of Blake's thought between 1789 and 1795 has often been summarized, as have the general lines of the development of the illustrations in the illuminated books, from the tender and decorative to the sombre and powerful: the classic comparison of the *Songs of Innocence* with the *Songs of Experience* displays this clearly. In *Songs of Innocence* the illustrations, however delightful in themselves and however important as a complement to the imagery of the poems, are pictorially merely a decorative supplement to the printed word, but over the next five years the illustrations became more and more visually important as they came to convey in themselves alone more and more of Blake's expressive intentions.

This development embodied two main trends. The first was merely the enlargement in scale of the page as a whole. From the approximately 2 x 1½-inch platemarks of *There is No Natural Religion* and *All Religions are One* of ca. 1788,[9] by way of the 4¼ x 2¾ inches of *Songs of Innocence,* Blake evolved a more or less standard 6¼ x 4¼-inch size of *The Book of Thel* of the same year, 1789. This he used in *Visions of the Daughters of Albion, The Marriage of Heaven and Hell, Urizen, The Book of Ahania* and *The Book of Los.* But in 1793, in *America,* he increased this to 9½ x 6¾ inches, retaining this larger format for *Europe,* 1794, and *The Song of Los,* 1795. On most of the pages of these larger books Blake adhered to the decorative treatment of *Songs of Innocence,* with irregularly shaped designs spilling over into the text, tendrils and small motives festooning and sometimes punctuating the printed words. But a few full-page designs, such as the famous "Ancient of Days," frontispiece to *Europe*, together with its counterparts in the other two books, and in particular the two additional full-page designs in *The Song of Los*, reflect a radically different attitude to illustration which had already begun to develop in other books.

The first signs of this new attitude can be seen in *Visions of the Daughters of Albion*, 1793. In the late copy in the British Museum there are areas of irregular printing that make it clear that Blake originally etched his plates (as usual in relief, so as to print from the raised rather than from the sunken portions of the plates) with the intention of producing a much more decorative scheme than that eventually printed; in particular there are signs that Blake intended decorative borders on at least three of the pages.[10] Earlier copies, such as the two in the British Museum and that belonging to Lord Cunliffe, all colored about 1793–94,[11] show much fainter traces of the same features, and on some pages Blake printed from a still more restricted area of the raised, unetched plate, presumably by masking the plate or by inking only those areas he wanted to print. The result of this selective printing is that the illustrations are less integrated with the writing and more self-sufficient as designs in their own right; those on the last two pages in particular convey a new power and sense of doom appropriate to the text. Even the printing of the actual writing is sober in comparison with the exuberance of the earlier books, for instance *The Marriage of Heaven and Hell* (dated 1790 in one copy and by allusion to Swedenborg, though probably not completed until 1793).[12]

In *Songs of Experience*, added to *Songs of Innocence* in 1794, Blake was restricted to the size and general pattern of the earlier book. These limitations only serve to emphasize the way in which his use of more sombre color and rectilinear rather than curvilinear compositions tended both to detach the illustrations from the text and to endow them with a gravity that adds to the pessimism of the book as a whole. In *Urizen* of the same year the evolution is complete. Not only is nearly a third of the book devoted to full-page illustrations but over half of the remaining plates are occupied by designs filling half or more of the page. The internal scale of the designs is also larger, dwarfing the text, and even the title page, usually the most decorative part of Blake's illuminated books, shows the heavier, more oppressive form of composition first found in *Songs of Experience.*

But the most important contribution to the revolutionary character of the illustrations to *Urizen* was the use of color printing instead of water color. In *Urizen* this technique was used from the beginning; only in the late copy in the Rosenwald Collection did Blake use water color in the rich and elaborate manner, with some use of gold, that characterizes his late illuminations.[13] So too the earliest copies of *Europe,* also of 1794, seem to have been color-printed, though in a less heavy and consistent manner.[14] Copies of *Visions of the Daughters of Albion, The Marriage of Heaven and Hell* and *Songs of Experience,* which had all previously been colored in water color, were also color-printed, likewise, there is good reason to believe, in about 1794 or 1795. This development had been anticipated by the increasing heaviness of Blake's coloring, as in the first copy of *America* in 1793[15] and certain books in which the opaque pigment may have been applied by hand rather than by printing.[16]

The technique of color printing in the books was close to that already described in connection with the large color prints of 1795, but in the books the opaque pigment seems generally to have been printed from the same etched plate following the monochrome printing of text and outlines common to all copies of the books. The uneven surface of the plate sometimes added effects of its own to the texture produced by the color printing, as on pages 11, 14, 19 and 27 of the British Museum's copy of *Urizen.*[17] The similar effects in the sole example of the separate color print of "Lucifer and the Pope in Hell" in the Huntington Library made it clear, long before the recent discovery of the monochrome print now in the British Museum,[18] that this was printed from an etched plate, and the same can be said of "Joseph of Arimathea preaching to the Inhabitants of Britain," [19] of which no monochrome print is yet known.

The sustained power of the color-printed illustrations to *Urizen* is unparalleled in Blake's books. It is no coincidence that they accompany Blake's most concise, and most negatively pessimistic, expression of his views on man's creation and fall. The internal logic of Blake's evolution as a philosopher, together with external forces such as the failure of his earlier hopes in practical politics as one of the group of Radicals that also included Joseph Johnson, Tom Paine, Joseph Priestley, William Godwin and Mary Wollstonecraft, seems to have made this period, the mid 1790's, the most gloomy of his life, when the apparently insuperable problem of evil led him to a form of Manichaeism.

The despairing, agonized protagonists of *Urizen* almost break out of the bounds of the page, and the next step was literally that—the production of some of the illustrations from the books as separate color-printed designs without text. Some were bound up to form the so-called "Large" and "Small" Books of Designs; the latter incorporate the title page of *Urizen*, retaining its original date 1794 in one copy but with this altered to 1796 in the other.[20] One set of these designs, produced for Ozias Humphry (who went blind in 1797), was later described by Blake in a letter of June 9, 1818, as "a selection from the different Books of such as could be Printed without the Writing, tho' to the Loss of some of the best things. For they when Printed perfect accompany Poetical Personifications & Acts, without which Poems they never could have been Executed" (K 867). It was the special virtue of the large prints of 1795 that, at least for Blake, they were self-sufficient from the beginning.

The Books of Designs include illustrations from *Urizen* (by far the greatest number), *The Book of Thel, The Marriage of Heaven and Hell, Visions of the Daughters of Albion* and *America*. In addition the "Large Book of Designs" contains three designs not from books, "The Dance of Albion," "The Accusers of Theft, Adultery and Murder" and "Joseph of Arimathea preaching to the Inhabitants of Britain," while "Lucifer and the Pope in Hell" seems to date from the same time and, like a number of extra color-printed designs from the books unlisted by Keynes and Wolf, [21] can be associated with this production of separate designs.

The largest of these designs, "The Dance of Albion," does not exceed 10¾ x 8 inches, whereas the large prints of 1795 are in the region of 18 x 24 inches. The color printing of separate prints of existing book illustrations or engravings seems to have led on naturally to the completely self-sufficient larger works. The slightly under half-size version, 7¾ x 10¹³⁄₁₆ inches, of "Pity" in the British Museum is far less accomplished but in its broad areas of a few simple colors it may well show Blake experimenting with the feature that distinguished the technique of the large prints from that of his previous experience of color printing, the use of a plain plate instead of an already etched one and the consequent absence of printed outlines.

Even this difference was anticipated or at least paralleled in the illuminated books produced by Blake in 1795. He seems to have realized that, if the designs were to be heavily color-printed, there was no point in etching even the outlines on the plate. In *The Song of Los* the full-page designs and even the title page, including the writing, were executed entirely by color printing, while in *Ahania* and *The Book of Los* Blake abandoned his usual process of etching the plates in relief, which had enabled him to etch text and designs together, for the simpler process of etching the text alone in intaglio; the illustrations were then added by color printing in spaces left for them.

The color printing in these books is again more assured than that of the half-size version of "Pity," but a small detail suggests that they may have pointed the way towards an important feature of the large color prints. A comparison of the title pages of the two copies of *The Song of Los* in the British Museum[22] shows that, as in the other color-printed books, the plate was freshly colored before printing each copy: not only the colors but the actual forms of the written words differ. Blake must have painted fairly freely over what traces were left by the previous printing. But in the second, Butts-Palgrave, copy one can still see traces of the red bird that appears in the first, enough of the pigment having remained on the plate to leave a slight imprint when printed again. This and similar accidents may have suggested the practice in the large color prints of printing more than one copy from a single coloring of the plate.

The very weight of the color-printed pages in *The Song of Los* may have given further impetus to the production of separate designs: on the flexible page they must always have seemed vulnerable to cracking, though another failing, the tendency for some oily substance in the pigment to stain the adjacent pages, may only have revealed itself after a considerable passage of time. Certainly, when Blake resumed his production of new illuminated books with *Milton* and *Jerusalem* he returned to water color, and his coloring of the earlier books also seems to have reverted to water color by the late 1790's or early 1800's.

Meanwhile the large color prints of 1795 had been followed by a prodigious output of other designs. Some, the over five hundred illustrations to Young's *Night Thoughts* and the hundred or so to the poems of Gray, were still in book form, but Blake approached the problem of illustrating the poems of other writers in a way totally different from the illuminated books. Already in the *Night Thoughts* designs of 1796–97, Blake had returned to water color, but his technique of color printing must have suggested the medium of his next important series of independent pictures, the temperas of biblical subjects of 1799–1800. When Blake exhibited a group of slightly later temperas in 1809 he used the same word, "fresco," to describe their medium as he had on some of the large color prints.[23] The discoveries made by Blake in his illuminated books in the earlier 1790's thus affected much of his later practice as a painter. The large color prints of 1795 mark the point of transfer from one field of activity to the other; they are also the point at which the fundamental unity of all aspects of Blake's art is most clearly demonstrated.

ANNE T. KOSTELANETZ

# Blake's 1795 Color Prints: An Interpretation

Blake's most famous paintings, the large color prints sold to Thomas Butts in 1805 and now (with three exceptions) residing in the Tate Gallery, reveal a radical tension between style and meaning. By 1795, the date Blake assigned to this series, Blake had developed and consistently used a non-illusionistic, linear, geometrical style which affirmed form and the human form in particular as the vehicle of primal vision.[1] But the poetry Blake wrote in 1793–95 strongly condemns the human form and form in general as an imposition of Urizenic limitations upon divine energy. Blake tried to resolve this contradiction between aesthetically necessary and intellectually destructive form by developing a personal iconography in his illuminated books and color prints of 1789–95, an iconography which distinguishes between the closed, limiting, evil forms of Urizen and the open, energy-releasing, good forms of Poetic Genius. But since Blake uses the same style and medium to depict both closed and open forms, his normative attitude toward form often blurs: he paints the fallen human form with the same precision, linear rhythm, and beauty as the divine human form. Inevitably, as we shall see in the Tate Gallery color prints, a tension arises between content and style in Blake's art: his iconographic condemnation of the human form as fallen and corrupt conflicts with his aesthetic celebration of the ideal human form.

· BLAKE'S ICONOGRAPHY ·

Although Blake often drew on traditional sources for both his visual ideas and his iconography,[2] the meaning of his designs for his own illuminated books often depends on the accompanying text and in fact on occasion contradicts the actual tradition from which it derived. Milton's golden compasses, for instance, with which God the Creator imposed "number, weight and measure" upon the universe, the compasses which often appear in medieval manuscripts and Renaissance paintings as the instrument of the omnipotent, benevolent creator, become for Blake the tool of the demiurge, the Ancient of Days, who restricts pure energy to arbitrary and stultifying forms. To understand the meaning of Blake's designs, then, we must study both the development of his visual symbolism in his own works and the context of these symbols in his poetic texts.

Blake's two most important visual symbols represent the two sides of what he saw to be the primary division of the human psyche and of human society: the essential energy or divine poetic genius of man which expresses itself socially as candid sexuality, political liberty, and artistic creation on the one hand; and, on the other, the abstracting reason which subordinates the particular to the general and human variety to a single rule, and which attempts to construct a society based on law, moral codes, and political repression governed by a tyrant or oligarchy. Politically, the opposition is between what Karl Popper calls an open society (based on democracy and "piecemeal engineering") and its enemies, the advocates of a closed totalitarian society based on oligarchy and "Utopian engineering" which justifies the cruelty of its means by its ends.[3] As we shall see, Blake develops a visual personification for each of these two states of mind: the open mind is depicted finally as a naked youth in flames, often running or standing with open arms or carrying a hammer; the closed mind is depicted as an old, often blind, white-haired and bearded man, usually clothed in a white robe and seated in a crouching position over a scroll or decalogue.

We first see the old man in Blake's *All Religions are One* (1788–90), where he appears on Plate 3 as the creating God, his arms spread open above the clouds. Here he personifies the Poetic Genius and is obviously based on traditional representations of the Hebraic prophets; in fact, Blake uses this figure again in this conventional way in the illustration for "The Voice of the Bard" in *Songs of*

*Experience* where the white-haired and bearded old man holding the harp represents the bard of the Welsh Triads (as in similar depictions of the Welsh Bard by Fuseli, Barry, and John Martin). In the designs for Blake's *Tiriel* (1790), however, the old bearded man is associated both with Har, the holy father who has preserved the divine vision of innocence, and, significantly, with Tiriel himself, the cursing demagogue of oppressive law. This confusion of iconographic meaning is finally clarified on Plate 11 of *The Marriage of Heaven and Hell* (1790–93) where Blake traces the history both of religious thought and of his own image: the original personifications of "the ancient Poets" who saw living deities in every natural phenomenon became in time abstracted from their objects and formulated into a system by the "Priesthood." Thus the old man as a personification of the divine father, the poetic genius, became corrupted into an image of the Father as Law-Giver. The true poetic personifications at the top of Plate 11—where the sun rises as a shrieking woman with flaming hair; the sea is a stately, tender woman dressed in blue who gently nurses the shore, shown as a helpless baby; and most important, the barren tree on the shore is depicted as the white-haired and bearded old man—have degenerated into abstract images at the bottom of the page. The single, rationalizing vision of the Priesthood has abstracted the white-haired, bearded old man from the tree and established him as the tyrant-God who now rules alone, his arms spread over dark clouds, storms, and night, cruelly tormenting the prostrate woman beside him. Blake further links this image in *The Marriage of Heaven and Hell* illustrations with the tyrant Nebuchadnezzar on Plate 24, where the white-haired and bearded man crowned with golden spikes crawls on the ground and looks back in abject terror.

In *Visions of the Daughters of Albion* (1793), the white-haired, bearded man appears both as Bromion, the slave-driving tyrant who affirms "one law for the lion and the ox" and who is seen chained in his cave of political oppression and social misery in the frontispiece, and as Theotormon, the impotent lover who submits to the rules of reason and empirical sense data and is thus confined in a crouching position to a tiny island in the sea (Pl. 4) or to the margins of Bromion's cave (frontispiece). The most specific linking of this image to a closed mind in Blake's work before 1794 is in the illustration for "The Human Abstract" of *Songs of Experience*. The poem describes a mental state of cruelty, selfishness, and abstract, oppressive modes of thought, and the illustration is Blake's visual personification of that state of mind. We see a white-haired and bearded old man, dressed in white, crouching beneath a net of heavy ropes. His face grimaces with hatred and tears of anger flow from his eyes. He kneels upon a small, sandy island, enclosed (like Theotormon) by dark waves, and heavy serpentine reeds arch over the background. The design is thus a precise depiction of the text:

> Then Cruelty knits a snare,
> And spreads his baits with care.
>
> He sits down with holy fears,
> And waters the ground with tears:
> Then Humility takes its root
> Underneath his foot. (E 27)

After 1793, this image occurs frequently in Blake's illuminated books and is always an emblem of an oppressive, tyrannical mode of thought or political program. The old, crippled man in the design for "London" depicts the "Marks of weakness, marks of woe" left by "mind-forg'd manacles"; the old man with legal scroll and spear (Pl. 4) and the old cripple entering Death's Door (Pl. 12) in the designs for *America* (1793) present the moral, political, and social oppressions and murders of Albion's Angel, George III; and the compass-wielding Ancient of Days (frontispiece), gluttonous Pope (Pl. 10), and crowned, scaly warrior with spear (Pl. 14) represent the religious and political tyranny denounced in *Europe* (1794). This image receives its most thorough treatment, of course, in the designs for *The Book of Urizen* (1794), where the old, bearded man *is* Urizen, the creator of the abstract void and of divided, limited man enclosed in the human form.

By studying Blake's various presentations of Urizen as old, bearded man, we can compile a fairly consistent list of the objects or situations usually associated with Urizen and thus emblematic of the enclosed mind. Such a list, garnered from both Blake's poetry and his art, would include: (1) nets, chains, briars, and spider webs; (2) all such severely rectilinear forms as tombs or horizontal corpses, closed doors, pyramids, and cradles; (3) all enclosed circular forms, such as caves, islands, crowns, embryos, and circles; (4) all limited human forms, such as the skeleton or the partially formed body; (5) water, sea, and rain in their traditional association with materialism; (6) such conventionally malevolent animals as the serpent, vulture, dragon, and bat; and finally, (7) such traditional accoutrements of a rationalistic and oppressive tyrant as a compass, book, scroll or decalogue, and spear.[4] Throughout this list, we notice Blake's tendency to link geometrical, closed forms—the circle, square, and triangle—with the closed mind and bounded human form of Urizen.

In opposition to Urizen as old man, Blake develops an iconology for the open, intuitive mind of poetic energy. Blake's first image for this idea occurs in 1780 in the drawing later known as "Glad Day." Here we see a naked youth standing upon a hill, his arms spread open, and at his feet a butterfly just emerging from a cocoon. Both the open arms and the newborn butterfly imply the energy and delight with which Innocence greets the world. Similarly open-armed children and adolescents figure prominently in the illustrations for *Songs of Innocence:* the child floating upon a cloud who inspires the piper in the frontispiece spreads his arms in blessing; the child upon its mother's lap in the first design for "Spring" reaches out towards the horizon; one of the *putti* on the flame in the "Blossom" design dances with open arms; and the leader of the "Laughing Song" opens his arms, in a backwards version of the Glad Day figure, in joy and delight. This open-armed, joyful acceptance of all experience as "holy" is seen again on Plate 4 of *The Book of Thel* where Thel welcomes her responsibility to be "the food of worms" with arms spread in delight over the tiny infant resting on the ground. This gesture of open-armed, often floating delight is explicitly linked with sexual delight in *The Book of Thel* where both the cloud (seen as a handsome youth flying over Thel's head with open arms on Plate 4) and the dew (pictured as a young maiden very like Thel who, with open arms, accepts the embrace of the cloud-youth on the title page) appear with arms spread. This open acceptance of experience is also represented in *Visions of the Daughters of Albion* by Oothoon, who appears first in the cruciform position prostrated beneath the attacks of the ravaging vulture (on Pl. 6) and then chained by the left ankle in a flamelike wave, with her arms reaching out to the island-bound Theotormon on Plate 7. At the end of the poem, Oothoon appears in flames over the daughters of Albion as they crouch upon the rocky shore, her arms spread open in blessing. Here she represents that open mind of Innocence which looks upon all life as holy, which loves every object for its unique and infinite capacities.

This figure of open-armed youth is explicitly linked to energy and poetic creation in *The Marriage of Heaven and Hell*. A running, open-armed maiden in flames is identified with "the Eternal Hell," "the active springing from Energy," on Plate 3. On the following plate, the maiden becomes a handsome youth, chained by the ankle in flames over the sea (as Oothoon was), who reaches out towards the fiercely struggling, open-armed child in the restraining arms of another youth. In this early version of Blake's famous color-print tempera, "The Good and Evil Angels Struggling for a Child," it is interesting to note that the chained youth and the child assume similar positions: legs spread and arms open. Here the chains of the adolescent youth and the arms of the parent are both aspects of the Urizenic attempt to repress energy. This youth as emblem of energy appears again in *The Marriage of Heaven and Hell* as the blue devil from "Hell" on Plate 10 and as the triumphant speaker who sits in the rising sun on Plate 21; and, in female guise, as the "cherub with flaming sword" who bends in flames over the corpse on Plate 14. This figure of energy is explicitly identified with Orc, the personification of repressed and violent energy, in *America* where the child Orc is chained to the ground in the cruciform, Glad Day position on Plate 1; with the triumphant vanquisher of Urizen who appears on Plate 10, the youth kneeling in flames with arms spread open in a gesture which parodies that of the blessing God the Father of Plate 8; and, finally, with the artistic imagination on Plate 15, where the youth again appears, standing in flames, with the smith's hammer in hand.

The youth as poet-creator is explicitly identified as a personification of Los, the poetic imagination incarnate, in *The Book of Los* where he is shown on the final plate as a naked youth in flames, hammer in hand, and in *The Book of Urizen* where Urizen's antagonist, Los, is pictured consistently as an open-armed figure racing through flames (Pls. 3, 18, 20) or as the fallen, crouching youth who, though still surrounded by the flames of energy, has begun to shrink into a limited, Urizenic body (as on Pls. 9 and 14).

Associated with this emblem of the open mind of Innocence-Energy are such objects as (1) flames, often in an S-shaped design, much like Hogarth's line of beauty, and flamelike foliage or waves; (2) vines, especially those bearing bunches of grapes; (3) brightly-colored, nonpredatory birds; (4) the radiant dawn or rainbow, both traditional emblems of newborn hope and a covenant with God; (5) the tools of artistic creation, such as anvil and hammer; and, above all, (6) all figures in open-armed, running, flying, or embracing positions.[5] These images become Blake's visual shorthand for his notions of the Prolific, of energy, of sensual and mental delight and freedom, of the completely open mind.

## · TATE GALLERY COLOR PRINTS ·

With this fairly consistent iconography and iconology in mind, we can perhaps offer a reading of the famous Tate Gallery color prints which Blake sold to Butts in 1805. Blake himself listed eight of these large color prints in his debtor-creditor correspondence with Thomas Butts on July 5 and September 7, 1805, thus: "4 Prints Viz 1 Good & Evil Angel 2 House of Death 3 God Judging Adam 4 Lamech" and "4 Prints Viz 1 Nebuchadnezzar 2 Newton 3 God Creating Adam 4 Christ appearing." [6] In addition to these eight prints, the Tate Gallery possesses two others, "Hecate" and "Pity"; and two more, similar to these in style and color, size, and date, are the "Satan exulting over Eve" (in the collections of Gregory Bateson and John Craxton) and the "Naomi entreating Ruth" (in the Victoria and Albert Museum and the collection of Geoffrey Keynes). All these color prints are dated 1795 (which may refer to the time when they were conceived rather than the date of execution) and thus demand to be read in conjunction with Blake's illuminated poetry of that period. Although Blake chose his subjects from literary works as diverse as the Bible, Milton, Shakespeare, and his own poetry, all the prints illustrate themes which he discussed and interpreted in his own work of this period.

As Sir Anthony Blunt has suggested, these prints can be seen in the light of Blake's conception of the creation as an evil act which reduces man "from the life of infinity to the restricted and finite life of this world." [7] They are thus a pictorial equivalent to Blake's Bible of Hell, *The Book of Urizen*, where Urizen as demiurge forms man into a limited, fallen body and confines him to the abstract void of reason, tyranny, and death. Stylistically, however, as we shall see, these prints depend upon severely linear, geometrical patterns; their great power and control comes primarily from Blake's use of planar, two-dimensional, and clearly outlined forms.

In the "Elohim creating Adam" (or "God creating Adam," to use Blake's simpler title; see PLATE II), the Elohim is clearly similar to Blake's depictions of Urizen in *The Book of Urizen*. Here, God has the same white hair and beard, the same white robe and muscular body as Urizen; and his creation, like Urizen's, is molded from a "clod of clay" into a human body (Adam's head and right arm have not yet been fully formed). That this creation is a fall from Eternity is evidenced by the serpent that winds its binding, restricting coils around Adam's body (it is, of course, the serpent specifically associated with the enclosing world of Experience in *America* and *Europe*). This fall into a mathematical, limited form is emphasized by the composition of the print, a series of geometrically straight horizontals (God's body and wings and Adam's torso) counterpointed against the right-left diagonals of God's and Adam's arms and placed against a background of a half-circle, the rising (or setting) sun. That this Creation is indeed a Fall is demonstrated by the next print in the series, "Satan exulting over Eve." The repetition of the winged figure over the prostrate body wrapped round by a serpent encourages an identification of God with Satan and Adam with Eve: God-Urizen's molding of the human body is equivalent to Eve's eating of the forbidden fruit—both are an expulsion from paradise. The presence of Satan's shield, spear, and green bat-wings further underlines his association with the militant, tyrannical Urizen. The expulsion itself occurs in the next print, "God judging Adam" (the print formerly called "Elijah" but retitled by Martin Butlin in 1965;[8] see PLATE III), where Adam's fall is seen both in his willingness to obey Urizen (before whom he stands with bowed head) and in his physical assimilation to Urizen—both figures have identical beards, white hair, and physique. (Blake often used this pictorial device of repeated features and positions to reveal the spiritual identity of two seemingly separate characters, as Joseph Wicksteed has pointed out in his discussion of Job's relation to God in Blake's illustrations for the Book of Job.)[9] Adam's limited vision which cannot see beyond Urizen or his abstracted world is emphasized by the strict repetition of line, form, and color in the print: the vertical lines of Adam's right leg and torso are repeated in the horse's left foreleg and in God's back and legs; the horizontal line of God's knees and thighs, accentuated by the stone book upon his lap, are repeated in the horse's back; the single left-right diagonal of the horse's upper rein runs directly through God's extended, judging arm and sceptre; and the entire scene is flatly placed against the circle of flames of God's chariot on the right. The colors too are limited to the yellow/reds of the horse and flames and the contrasting white of God's figure and Adam's hair.

The results of this Urizenic creation, this fall from eternity into a limited human form and mind, are depicted in the next six prints. Adam is confined within a mental and physical world ruled by Urizen, a world of political tyranny, rationalism, superstition, a total restraint of energy, sickness, and death. "Nebuchadnezzar" represents the oppressive policies of the tyrant who, like Bromion in *Visions of the Daughters of Albion*, imposes "one law for the lion and ox" (as the caption under the Nebuchadnezzar on Plate 24 of *The Marriage of Heaven and Hell* makes clear) and is thus associated with the Urizen who rules with

> One command, one joy, one desire,
> One curse, one weight, one measure,
> One King, one God, one Law.     (*Ur* 4:38–40, *E* 71)

The design itself is appropriately confined to a central rectangle (bounded by Nebuchadnezzar's back, right arm, palm, knee, and right thigh) placed against a large triangle formed by two intersecting wheat sheaves. "Newton," the companion piece to the "Nebuchadnezzar," represents the limited, rationalistic philosophy which is based solely on the empirical sense data of the five senses as stated in *The Song of Los:*

> Thus the terrible race of Los & Enitharmon gave
> Laws & Religions to the sons of Har binding them more
> And more to Earth: closing and restraining:
> Till a Philosophy of Five Senses was complete
> Urizen wept & gave it into the hands of Newton & Locke.
>
> (*SoL* 4:14–17, *E* 66)

The limited vision of Newton is further emphasized by the fact that he looks *downward* rather than up to heaven, by his use of compass and geometric diagram (linked to the Urizenic creation of the "Ancient of Days" frontispiece to *Europe*), and by his environment which is probably under water. The deep blue-green coloring and the curious plant life (possibly anemones) indicate a seascape and thus link Newton to the figure of Urizen under water on Plate 6 of *The Book of Urizen*. Like Newton's mind, the composition itself is severely limited; here, to a series of intersecting triangles: the hill on the left, the figure of Newton in which his head forms the apex, the calves of Newton's legs, the compasses, and the triangle actually drawn on the scroll.

The threefold figure of Hecate is a traditional emblem of witchcraft, superstition, and mystery, as in Shakespeare's *Macbeth* where her brew includes many of Blake's Hecate's companions:

> Eye of newt and toe of frog,
> Wool of bat and tongue of dog,
> Adder's fork and blind-worm's sting,
> Lizard's leg and howlet's wing . . .     (IV, i, 14–17)

and again in Puck's description of Hecate in *Midsummer Night's Dream:*

Now the hungry lion roars,
And the wolf behowls the moon:
Whilst the weary ploughman snores,
All with weary task fordone.
Now the wasted brands do glow,
Whilst the screech-owl, screeching loud,
Puts the wretch that lies in woe
In remembrance of a shroud.
Now it is the time of night
That the graves all gaping wide,
Every one lets forth his sprite,
In the church-way paths to glide:
And we fairies, that do run
By the triple-Hecate's team,
From the presence of the sun,
Following darkness like a dream,
Now do frolic . . .                    (V, i, 378–94)

In Blake's "Hecate," Hecate is specifically linked with Urizen's rule of one religion and one mystery by her crouching position over a book of indecipherable hieroglyphs (the position assumed by Urizen on the title page of *The Book of Urizen*) and by the bat-winged monster above her head. The fact that Blake chose a female witch to illustrate this theme may anticipate his later emphasis on the Female Will as both cause and result of the Fall. All three themes—political oppression, rational thought, and superstition—are summarized in the more general statement of "The Good & Evil Angels Struggling for a Child" which seems to represent the restraint of all energy, both of the child and of the adult. The youth in flames, Blake's familiar image for the poetic imagination, has been blinded and chained down by the dictates of empirical reason, as were both Oothoon in the *Visions of the Daughters of Albion*, Plate 4, and a similar figure of energy in an early version of this print in *Marriage of Heaven and Hell*, Plate 4. But here, energy has been perverted into evil; like Los in *The Book of Urizen*, the creative impulse has been distorted into a blind fury which jealously attacks the very child (Orc?) it should protect. And this newborn child, like Orc, struggles with open arms and kicking legs to be free; but he, too, is pinioned in the arms of the well-intentioned "Good Angel," who, like the protective nurses and mothers of *Songs of Experience* or Enitharmon in *The Book of Urizen*, tries to temper the child's exuberance into socially acceptable behavior.

The physical results of the Fall are depicted in the next two prints, "The Lazar House" and "Lamech and his Two Wives." "The Lazar House" or "House of Death" (see PLATE V) is based on Milton's famous description in *Paradise Lost* (II, 477–99) of "maladies of ghastly Spasm, or racking Torture" over which "triumphant Death his Dart / Shook but delaid to strike, though oft invok't / With vows, as their chief good, and final hope." The horizontal corpses upon the ground, the vertical figure of Pestilence or Death with dagger in hand (later used for the traitor Hand in "Jerusalem and Hand," *J* 25,) at the right, and the ironically blessing arms of a blind Urizen-God spread horizontally above the scene and raining down spears—all reveal the physical disease and suffering brought down upon man by Urizen's imprisonment of his spirit in a mortal, bodily form. The other immediate result of the Fall, of course, was murder and death; and Blake returns to the Bible, not to the too-well-known tale of Cain and Abel but to the Genesis 4 account of Lamech's murder of a man, to illustrate this theme in "Lamech and his Two Wives," in a composition whose severely vertical lines of the bodies and horizontal line of the corpse are relieved only by the slight curves in the robes of Lamech and his wives.

The cause of man's Fall, of the imagination's submission to the restrictive, closed rule of reason, was the natural pity of one man for another. As Blake explained in *The Book of Urizen*, Los fell because he took pity upon Urizen shut up in the void:

> He saw Urizen deadly black,
> In his chains bound, & Pity began,
>
> In anguish dividing & dividing
> For pity divides the soul . . .    (*Ur* 13:48–51, *E* 76)

Blake illustrates this natural pity in the print of "Naomi entreating Ruth" where Ruth is shown clinging sympathetically to Naomi while Orpah abandons her mother-in-law. The evil implications of this act are suggested in the more complex print "Pity" (see PLATE IV), however, which is based on Shakespeare's description in *Macbeth:*

> And pity, like a naked new-born babe,
> Striding the blast, or heaven's cherubim, hors'd
> Upon the sightless couriers of the air,
> Shall blow the horrid deed in every eye,
> That tears shall drown the wind.          (I, vii, 21–26)

Here, the newborn child, who assumes the same posture as the newborn Orc who appears in flames on Plate 20 of *The Book of Urizen,* leaves behind a dying or dead mother; the division of mother and child, the result of "man begetting his likeness, / On his own divided image" (*Ur* 19:15–16, *E* 78), brings death and separation into the world. In this sense, then, the print includes a reference to Macbeth's "horrid deed," the murder of Duncan, the breaking of all familial ties and social bonds.

The final print of the series, which may have been added after 1795 during the time when Blake was illustrating the Bible for Butts in 1801–5, the "Christ appearing to the Apostles after the Resurrection" (now in the Yale University Art Gallery), anticipates Blake's final solution to the problem of the Fall into a limited human body. As defined in "To Tirzah," an 1805 addition to *Songs of Experience,* the fallen mortal body must be "raised a spiritual body." Christ's resurrected body, then, is both natural—he appears in his anthropomorphic, traditional guise—and spiritual. This return to a Christian resolution is the pattern of the many visions and revisions of Blake's complicated manuscript, *Vala, or the Four Zoas,* undertaken between 1796 and 1807. Here Blake specifically wrestles with the problem posed by the Tate Gallery color prints: if form, especially the human form, is a sign of man's fall from Eternity into the limited, closed world of Urizenic Experience, and if, contradictorily, the severely formalist style based on abstract geometric patterns, strong linear rhythms, and clear outlines which Blake used so effectively in the color-print series is the most authentic articulation of antique, divinely inspired images (as Cumberland,

Flaxman, and Fuseli had taught Blake to believe), then Blake is at the same time rejecting and affirming form, and especially the human form. His finest designs both denounce the fall into the human form as an unmitigated evil and portray that same human form as an ideally beautiful, heroic, Michelangelesque figure. The human form cannot at one and the same time be the destructive prison of man's innate divinity and a powerful aesthetic image of beauty, strength, and grace. Blake was therefore forced to seek a new conception of the human form which would allow for both its manifest natural beauty and its possible perversion into a closed system. His initial solution, articulated both in *Vala* and here, in "Christ appearing to the Apostles after the Resurrection," was an affirmation of the traditional Christian concept of the resurrection of the spiritual body. After death, the fallen, vegetating, mortal body of man is cast off; and man is raised a "spiritual body," in the "human form divine" of Christ himself.

MORTON D. PALEY

# Blake's *Night Thoughts:* An Exploration of the Fallen World

In 1795 William Blake embarked on what was to be the largest project of his artistic career, the illustrating of Edward Young's *The Complaint, or, Night Thoughts on Life, Death and Immortality.* He produced for this series 537 water colors and engraved forty-three of them for the folio edition of the first four Nights which Richard Edwards published in 1797.[1] The project was no doubt prompted by the extraordinary interest in illustrated editions of poets in the late eighteenth century, the most ambitious of all these being John Boydell's Shakespeare. Engravers had been busy since 1791 on the work of reproducing the paintings in Boydell's Shakespeare Gallery; when the edition was finally completed in 1803, its Advertisement declared "One Hundred and Sixty-three Historical Pictures, many of them of a large size, have been painted by BRITISH ARTISTS, on purpose to adorn this work." [2] There were also in the last decade of the eighteenth century a Poet's Gallery, a Bible Gallery, and two Milton Galleries, one of the latter by Fuseli.[3] Even in appealing to popular taste, however, Blake used a method characteristically his own: "The engravings," as Edwards' prospectus states, "are in a perfectly new style of decoration, surrounding the text which they are designed to elucidate." [4] This was, of course, the way in which Blake arranged the pages of his own illuminated works. Now he extended the method to another author but without abandoning his own themes, symbols, and subject matter.

Young's works were popular and Blake's engraving was, in 1795, being talked of; the venture should have succeeded. Unfortunately, the market for illustrated books and for engravings, which had flourished before the war with France, became depressed after several years of it. John Boydell, who in 1787 could leave £500 on Sir Joshua Reynolds' table as an unsolicited down payment toward one picture for the Shakespeare Gallery, was ruined by the war; and the collection which had cost £300,000 for the engraved plates alone was in 1804 put to public lottery.[5] The *Night Thoughts*, a modest scheme by comparison, was discontinued with five Nights unpublished. In 1799 Blake wrote bitterly to his friend George Cumberland: "For as to Engraving, in which art I cannot reproach myself with any neglect, yet I am laid by in a corner as if I did not Exist, & Since my Young's Night Thoughts have been publish'd, Even Johnson & Fuseli have discarded my Graver" (*K* 795). The water colors passed into the possession of Richard Edwards' brother Thomas, in whom they found a great admirer. Thomas Edwards offered them for sale at the then incredible price of £300 in 1821, and described them in his auction catalogue of 1826 in terms as rapturous as Blake could have wished:

It would be difficult, if not impossible, to convey to those at a distance and who had not seen this magnificent work, an adequate or even a faint idea of the singular nature of these most extraordinary and sublime conceptions of our artist; but those who have seen his truly original designs for Blair's Grave, may form some faint idea of the style and manner of treating this equally eccentric and original Poem; to embody which and give it a visible form and reality, required the skill of a great artist, and the poetic feeling of the original author combined. How far he has succeeded, the present beautiful and sublime Commentary upon his Author, bears ample and delightful evidence; and it may truly be averred that a more extraordinary, original, and sublime production of Art has seldom, if ever, been witnessed since the days of the celebrated Mich. Angelo, whose grandeur and elevation of design it greatly resembles, and this, ALONE, if he had left no other work of merit, would be sufficient to immortalize his name, and transmit it to posterity, as that of an Artist of the very highest order.[6]

The pictures did not find a buyer and were again offered for sale after Thomas Edwards' death in 1828, but passed unsold into the hands of his heirs. They remained in Halifax until 1874, when they were brought to London and bought by a bookseller named James Bain, who later sold them to an American collector, William Augustus White. In 1928 Mr. White's daughter, Mrs. Frances White Emerson, presented them to the British Museum. They have remained the least known as well as the largest of Blake's sets of designs, and no detailed consideration of their symbolism, thematic structure, and meaning has yet been published.[7]

It is difficult for us today to understand Blake's interest in Young, a poet whose religion is, as George Eliot said, "egoism turned heavenward," [8] and whose rhetoric is often as uninteresting as the truisms it expounds. Yet Blake read *Night Thoughts* at least several years before Edwards engaged him to do the illustrations, and read it with enough care to echo it in several of his own works. In, for example, *For the Sexes: The Gates of Paradise,* the famous "Truly, My Satan, thou art but a Dunce" (Epilogue, l. 1; *K* 771) alludes to Young's line, "*Satan,* thy master, I dare call a dunce." [9] The sixth emblem of *The Gates,* with its inscription "At length for hatching ripe he breaks the shell," was probably suggested by Young's "Embryos we must be, till we burst the shell, / Yon ambient azure shell, and spring to life" (i, 16). In the water color Blake did for this page a naked female form escapes from a bright blue eggshell, while a caterpillar is seen on a leaf as in the frontispiece to *The Gates.* The winged infant who emerges from the shell in emblem 6 reappears in *NT* 15. Some other affinities between *The Gates* and the illustrations to Young have been noted by Professor Damon, including the repetition of the design "The Traveller hasteth in the Evening," emblem 14, in *NT* 113.[10] All these correspondences indicate that although the edition of *Night Thoughts* owned by Blake was that of 1796,[11] he had read the poem by 1793, when the emblems of *The Gates* were engraved (with their titles but without the accompanying poem). Blake also alludes to or echoes Young in *An Island in the Moon, The Book of Thel, The Marriage of Heaven and Hell,* and *Songs of Experience.* The allusions in *An Island* are comic: Steelyard the Lawgiver, though "taking extracts from . . . Young's Night thoughts" (*K*

52), quotes as Young's "The wreck of matter & the crush of worlds," a line from Addison's *Cato*.[12] In *Thel*, "where the fibrous roots / Of every heart on earth infixes deep its restless twists" (6:3–4, *K* 130) is either directly or indirectly derived from Young's "O the soft Commerce! O the tender Tyes, / Close-twisted with the Fibres of the Heart!" (v, 60).[13] Blake's vivid metaphor for the senses in *The Marriage* is, with one significant difference, very close to Young's:

If the doors of perception were cleansed every thing would appear to man as it is, infinite.
For man has closed himself up, till he sees all things thro' narrow chinks of his cavern. (*MHH* 14, *K* 154)

> Thro' Chinks, styl'd Organs, dim *Life* peeps at light;
> *Death* bursts th'Involving Cloud, and all is Day:
> All Eye, all Ear, the disembody'd Power. (iii, 30)

Young gives to death what Blake gives to life, but both agree not only in their use of an image but also in their view of spirituality as a heightening of sensory perception.

Another interesting comparison can be made with respect to "The Sick Rose" of *Experience* and a passage in *Night Thoughts:*

> O Rose, thou art sick!
> The invisible worm
> That flies in the night,
> In the howling storm,
>
> Has found out thy bed
> Of crimson joy:
> And his dark secret love
> Does thy life destroy. (*K* 213)

> Death's subtle seed within,
> (Sly, treacherous Miner!) working in the Dark,
> Smil'd at thy well-concerted scheme, and beckon'd
> The Worm to riot on that Rose so red,
> Unfaded e'er it fell; one moment's Prey! (i, 4)

Of course Blake needed no source for the image of the worm in the flower, but the connection between secrecy and pleasure in both texts ("working in the Dark," "That flies in the night"; "riot on that Rose so red," "thy bed / Of crimson joy") gives additional support to Professor Damon's suggestion that "Blake disentangled Young's decidedly mixed metaphor, and made it into a poem as well as a picture." [14] The contrast is at least as interesting as the similarity. Young's is a conventional trope: decay is present in Beauty although we cannot see it. Blake uses the same image to make a subtle symbolic statement: the Rose is sick because her desire is secret, unacknowledged, perhaps unacknowledged even to herself; therefore the phallic worm, the desire that can be hidden or perhaps repressed but not destroyed, comes as an intruder which she can neither admit nor deny, destroying the wholeness of her life. Young's personification becomes Blake's symbol. This is precisely the relationship between some of the *NT* pictures and the texts which they supposedly illustrate. Here we see something of the way in which Blake read Young—not as a poet to be admired and cherished as, for example, he did Cowper, but as a storehouse of familiar sentiments, expressions, and attitudes which suited Blake's purposes. Young, too, was a defender of faith against skepticism, a professed seeker of the infinite, and a votary of genius and inspiration. His *Conjectures on Original Composition,* for example, contains many passages which Blake could have echoed with enthusiasm:

*Blank* is a term of diminution; what we mean by blank verse, is verse unfallen, uncurst; verse reclaim'd, reinthron'd in the true *language of the Gods* ...

*Dryden* had a great, but a general capacity; and as for a general Genius, there is no such thing in nature: A Genius implies the rays of the mind concenter'd, and determined to some particular point ...[15]

Young's style, containing as it does a superabundance of similes and personifications, is also suited to Blake's purposes. As Jean Hagstrum suggests, Blake probably read Young's verses "as the regnant aesthetics dictated they should be read—with a keen eye for their animation and with the ability to translate even their vaguest visual suggestion into full-blown pictorial allegory." [16] Yet Blake pictorialized his subject in a unique way: he assimilated it into the mythological system that he was creating in his own prophetic works. Neither his own contemporaries nor his Victorian rediscoverers perceived this, and so the meaning of the pictures was not understood, and the series failed to find the appreciation it deserved.

We first find the *Night Thoughts* project mentioned in Joseph Farington's diary for June 24, 1796, where a charge is made that we shall hear again. "Fuseli has known him several years and thinks He has a great deal of invention, but that 'fancy is the end and not a means in his designs.' He does not employ it to give novelty and decoration to regular conceptions but the whole of his aim is to produce singular shapes & odd combinations." [17] It is, in most cases, a particular facet of Blake's fantasy that is condemned, as in these remarks of Henry Crabb Robinson:

They are of very unequal merit; sometimes the inventions of the artist rival those of the poet, but often they are only preposterous translations of them, by reason of the unfortunate idea peculiar to Blake, that whatsoever the fancy of the spiritual eye may discern must also be as clearly penetrable to the bodily eye. So Young is literally translated, and his thought turned into a picture. Thus for example the artist represents in a drawing Death treading crowns under foot, the sun reaching down his hand, and the like. Yet these drawings are frequently exquisite.[18]

In *The Library Companion*, published in 1824, Thomas Frognall Dibdin praised the imaginative power of the engravings but in such a way as to deprive them of any possible meaning:

Wherefore is it, that I love to read that portion of the poem, published in a folio form, with bizarre but original and impressive ornaments by BLAKE? At times, the pencil of the artist attains the sublimity of the poet: and it is amidst the wild uproar of the wintry elements—when piping winds are howling for entrance round every corner of the turretted chamber, and the drifted snow works its way into the window casement, however closely fastened—it is in moments LIKE THESE that I love to open that portion of the text of Young which has been embellished by the pencil of Blake. My friends will laugh . . peradventure deride . . but let us all be endured in these venial moments of hallucination. The soul of poetry itself (we are told) is fiction: and I would feign happiness at such moments.[19]

Blake's literalism was again condemned by Edward Bulwer-Lytton in 1830:

I saw, a few days ago, a copy of the "Night Thoughts," which he had illustrated in a manner at once so grotesque, so sublime—now by so literal an interpretation, now by so vague and disconnected a train of invention, that the whole makes one of the most astonishing and curious productions which ever balanced between the conception of genius and the raving of positive insanity.[20]

Allan Cunningham remarked that "he illustrated Young's Night Thoughts with naked groupes, which startled the serious." [21] Swinburne, who considered Young's "dead and rotten" text merely a peg to hang the pictures on, found the designs had "less of . . . Blake's great qualities and more of his faults or errors than usual." [22] More recently, the poet Philippe Soupault has argued that Blake shared "the fallacy of the age" in believing that "it was the function of engravings to complete the text," even believing that "they might add to and extend it." [23] These critics would no doubt have endorsed Yeats's remark that Blake was "a too literal realist of imagination, as others are of nature." [24] Yet none of them perceive the *direction* of his supposed literalism. It is true that at times Blake does merely turn a trope into a picture, but frequently he only appears to be doing this. What neither Robinson nor Bulwer-Lytton nor the others realize is that for Blake the pictorialized trope is often a means of making a symbolic statement which depends for its meaning not on Young's text but on the myth developed in the Lambeth books and in *Vala*. In pictures such as these, Blake adapts, ignores, or even subverts Young's meaning in order to develop his own.

We can see with what freedom Blake treated his subject in certain pictures which actually satirize either the passages they are supposed to illustrate or their author. For example, in *NT* 7 the poet is shown falling asleep, pen in hand, while two figures carry his opening scroll down the left margin toward the lower right, where an old man sits writing under a black, leafless tree. Someone unfamiliar with Blake's symbolism would have no clue to the meaning here, but we can connect it with Blake's description of Urizen writing his books of Law:

> For Urizen fix'd in envy sat brooding & cover'd with snow;
> His book of iron on his knees, he trac'd the dreadful letters
>
> . . . . . . . . . . . . . . . . . . . . . .
>
> Age after Age, till underneath his heel a deadly root
> Struck thro' the rock, the root of Mystery accursed shooting up
> Branches into the heaven of Los.       (*FZ* vii:28–33, *K* 321) [25]

Where Young writes "Oft bursts my song beyond the bounds of life," Blake shows us a leaping figure whose right foot is securely chained to the earth (33, *Edw* 16), having previously shown him lying on the ground with a book in his hand, overgrown with briars and oblivious to the fairy figures around him. ("Indeed," as George Eliot wrote, "we remember no mind in poetic literature that seems to have absorbed less of the beauty and the healthy breath of the common landscape than Young's.") [26] In *NT* 492, Blake provides his own answer to Young's rhetorical question "Has Matter *more* than Motion? Has it Thought, / Judgment, and Genius?" "If so," Young goes on, "how each *sage* Atom laughs at *me*, / Who think a *Clod* inferior to a *Man?*" Blake, we remember, had asked a fairy "What is the material world, and is it dead?" and had been shown "all alive / The world, when every particle of dust breathes forth its joy" (*Eur* iii:13, 17, 18; *K* 237).[27] Therefore Blake inverted Young's meaning by illustrating his ironical conclusion as if it were literal, showing a tiny family in a green leaf pointing up in laughter at the poet.

Our examples so far have been very simple, but Blake was also able to make statements of some complexity, using Young's lines only as a starting point for his own symbolism. This may be seen in two very interesting pictures which present themes that recur throughout the series. One of these is *NT* 26, *Edw* 12 (see PLATE VI). According to the anonymous "Explanation" of the engravings, the subject is "The frailty of the blessings of this life demonstrated, by a representation in which the happiness of a little family is suddenly destroyed by the accident of the husband's death from the bite of a serpent." [28] If Fuseli was indeed the author of these remarks, he must have understood Blake's method less than is often assumed. The figure of a man entwined by a serpent, his arms thrown cruciform against a rock, is a Blakean emblem of the Fall: Man, stung by the knowledge of Good and Evil, lies against the Rock of the Decalogue, a sacrifice to Law. In the painting "Elohim creating Adam," man is created in such a state, and in *The Four Zoas*

> "The Eternal Man sleeps in the Earth, nor feels the vig'rous sun
> "Nor silent moon, nor all the hosts of heaven move in his body.
> "His fiery halls are dark, & round his limbs the Serpent Orc
> "Fold without fold encompasses him . . .
>
> . . . . . . . . . . . . . . . . . . . . . . . .
>                                    . . . leaning his faded head
> "Upon the Oozy rock inwrapped with the weeds of death."
>                          (*FZ* viii:507–10, 513–14; *K* 354)

The meaning of the rest of the family group is emblematic as well. The mother who holds her child back from reaching toward a brightly colored bird is the female principle of the Lambeth books and *The Four Zoas*, Enitharmon. She gives birth to the child Orc, who incarnates energy and desire, but she also limits his awareness to the plane of things-as-they-are. The same figures, a mother restraining a child who reaches after a bird, appear in *There is No Natural Religion*, first series, illustrating the proposition that "Man by his reasoning power can only compare & judge of what he has already perciev'd." This proposition, like the others in the first series, is undermined in the second series, its contrary being "Reason, or the ratio of all we have already known, is not the same that it shall be when we know more" (II, *K* 97). The bird is what we shall know, as in *The Marriage* (6–7, *K* 150), "an immense world of delight, clos'd by your senses five." The message of the picture then becomes clear: in a world tainted by the conviction of sin, human consciousness is prevented from pursuing the infinite through the finite. This is part of a process of education, the next phase of which is depicted in *NT* 64, *Edw* 46. This picture is described in the "Explanation" as showing "A parent communicating instruction to his family." The parent is the white-bearded Urizen. He sits on a bat-winged chair, as does the pope in *Europe*. He also resembles the "Aged Ignorance" of *The Gates*, a plate which bears the motto "Perceptive Organs closed, their Objects close" (*K* 767). He is teaching counting—the wisdom of number, weight, and measure. At the right is a figure we shall frequently encounter: an old woman wearing a veil and a loose gown. Another manifestation of the Female Will, she is the *maya*, the illusion of an absolutely material reality. She has enfolded one child in her skirts, supplementing the work of Urizen, just as in Wordsworth's Immortality Ode "Earth," "the homely Nurse"

> doth all she can
> To make her Foster-child, her Inmate Man,
> Forget the glories he hath known,
> And that imperial palace whence he came.

These two pictures have a topic in common, as do the others we have discussed so far—the nature of life in a "fallen" world, a world in which man becomes the victim of limiting and brutalizing forces in nature, in society, and, worst of all, in himself. This is also a major theme, together with humanity's struggle toward unity, culminating in apocalypse, in the Lambeth books and in *Vala*. As Northrop Frye has said, Blake's central myth is bounded by "creation, fall, redemption, and apocalypse";[29] this is no less true of the *NT* series than of the prophetic works. Of these four "boundaries," however, two are chiefly of importance here, for in this phase of Blake's thought—as in *The Book of Urizen*, for example—the creation is viewed pessimistically as part of the fall; while redemption, though the subject of quite a few *NT* pictures, is not presented with great conviction or power. (By 1795 Blake had abandoned the view that the French Revolution would revivify society,[30] but had not yet found a new personal source of redemptive expectation in visionary Christianity.) Most, though by no means all, of Blake's *Night Thoughts* is concerned with an exploration of the fallen world up to its apocalyptic termination.

In the Lambeth books and in *Vala,* Blake created a mythology in which eight figures, which he eventually called the four Zoas and their Emanations, were most important. Of these eight, at least five appear in the *NT* series. The most unmistakable is perhaps Urizen, whom we have already encountered. He appears most often as Death, armed with either the traditional dart, which becomes a spear in *Vala,* or with the black bow of morality, which Blake elsewhere assigns to Satan-Jehovah. Among his many appearances, we find him pulling down the sun (20, *Edw* 8), descending with his dart upon a mother and child (31, *Edw* 13), and triumphing over past empires (425). In *NT* 183 he becomes Charon. The same white-bearded father-figure is Wealth ("a cruel Taskmaster!") in *NT* 247 and Fate, enthroned in a cloud with a huge gear-wheel behind him, in *NT* 473. He is also "brute *Matter's* restive Lump," his huge head and wings supported by grotesquely tiny legs as he squats on a cloud in the night sky (491). Below even this is Chaos, and in *NT* 314 there is a transition to it: a group of grotesque stonified figures, one with Urizen's weeping face, "All gone to rot in *Chaos;* or, to make / Their happy Transit into Blocks, or *Brutes.*" Finally (514 and 515) he represents Chaos itself.

Blake was not so weak of invention that he had to use the same figure for these diverse meanings as an economy measure. There is an equation being made here, one which has its source in Blake's myth. To make the same figure represent several meanings is to say that they are all aspects of one meaning. Urizen is the setter of limits—blighter of joy, killer of the body, schoolmaster and workmaster—and behind all his activities is a vision of the universe as a material chaos. The gear-wheel of *NT* 473 is an indication of this, ironically illustrating Young's "*Mathematic* Glories of the Skies: / In Number, Weight, and Measure All ordain'd." It is half of a contrast made in *Jerusalem* 15:17–20 (*K* 636):

> ... cruel Works
> Of many Wheels I view, wheel without wheel, with cogs tyrannic
> Moving by compulsion each other, not as those in Eden, which,
> Wheel within Wheel, in freedom revolve in harmony & peace.

It was part of the greatness of Blake to pierce through external attitudes to the realities behind them. Behind the apparent love of order of the Urizenic mind, he saw the conviction of chaos; behind its zeal for legislating values, its inability to realize them. He starts with the figures in Young's text but makes them a vehicle for his own statement. We begin with imagery but end in myth.

The same method may be seen at work in a number of designs featuring another ruler of the fallen world, the female figure whom Blake elsewhere calls Vala. She is the natural world seen as an end in itself, veiling the essence of reality. Blake portrays her, as in the *Four Zoas* manuscript, as a young woman, often nude, sometimes wearing the spiked crown of dominion. As H. M. Margoliouth notes, she has a variety of roles.[31] As Fate (22) she is enthroned with a crozier in her right hand and a chain descending from her left. Below, men labor in a mine, and on the top margin of the picture Blake has drawn a cardinal's hat and a bishop's miter. Thus the conventional personification of Fate is turned into an emblem of social and spiritual constraint. This Vala-figure also plays the role of "Life" (105), a term which Young uses in much the sense that Shelley later did. "Is not the mighty *Mind*, that Son of Heaven! / By Tyrant *Life* dethron'd, imprison'd, pain'd?" We see a powerful male figure, his hands and feet chained, sprawling in a prison cell. Outside sits the triumphant Vala. The apertures of the cell bars are the senses, "narrow chinks of his prison," for this is the page on which occurs the line "Thro' Chinks, styl'd Organs, dim *Life* peeps at light." (Blake marked this last line as well as the two quoted above.) After the fall, man becomes subject to the forces of "Life," to "the blind world-rulers of this life," to use the words which Blake quoted from Paul on the title page of *Vala*. Yet another name for these forces is Fortune, and Vala appears as Fortune in no less than seven *NT* pictures. Her favors are, as traditionally, both indiscriminate and dangerous. She flings coins and a crown through the air in *NT* 210, in *NT* 208 her own child. Wearing a scarlet robe, she foments war, pouring gold coins and armed men out of a cornucopia (212). She lies on the globe of the earth (405) and offers a crown to a youth who refuses, but a less circumspect youth accepts "Earth's inchanted Cup" from a crowned, bare-breasted Vala (185). (Vala's cup, as Professor Damon points out, is "the Cup of Mystery, the Whore of Babylon," as in Revelation 17.[32]) "The man of *Reason*" scorns her bag of gold (249), but a Lorenzo who "still affects *the World*" Sisyphus-like pushes a rock up a hill at her command (347). "The Goddess Fortune," Blake wrote in contradiction to Dante, "is the devil's servant, ready to Kiss any one's Arse" (Notes on . . . Dante, 16; *K* 785).

We can easily see the connections between Fate, "Life," and Fortune. All involve a surrender of the will in helpless passivity, a projection outward of responsibility. Some other manifestations of Vala are not as immediately obvious in meaning. In *NT* 162, for example, this delusive goddess is the inspiration of a certain kind of love poetry. She regards herself in a mirror while the poet, crowned with laurel but chained to a golden chair, plays a musical instrument. A cupid rests one knee on Vala's thigh as he draws his bow. Young's text condemns what he considers to be obscenity:

> the Muse
> Has often blusht at her degenerate Sons,
> Retain'd by *Sense* to plead her filthy Cause.

Blake, however, condemns not the gratification of the senses but the enslavement of the senses by a world of false appearances. His picture satirizes the poetry of the Petrarchan tradition, the sado-masochistic celebration of passion as sung by Enitharmon:

> "The joy of woman is the death of her most best beloved
> "Who dies for Love of her
> "In torments of fierce jealousy & pangs of adoration."
> (*FZ* ii:349-51, *K* 289)

As in the case of Urizen, Blake uses Vala as a means of creating a meaning by bringing together different aspects of an underlying reality, and what first seems a mere reiteration of imagery is actually a mythical statement. In this instance, the equation includes the conventional ideas of reason and virtue. *NT* 151 (*Edw* 92) is supposed to illustrate the lines "*Reason* the Root, fair Faith

is but the Flow'r . . . When *Faith* is Virtue, *Reason* makes it so."
Blake shows Faith looking up to Virtue, who holds in her right
hand the scales of justice. She also wears the spiked crown of
Vala. It is as if Blake were saying through these pictures, "What
you praise as Virtue is as arbitrary and as external as what you
condemn as Fortune, and a Reason that can only weigh quantities
is merely a function of sense." In seeming to illustrate Young's
commonplaces, he actually strikes through them.

A third tutelary deity of the fallen world is Enitharmon, one
manifestation of whom we have seen (26). More often she is
shown as an old crone wearing a veil, as in the "education scene,"
(64). Her function in either guise is to bind her victims to the
limitations of the fallen world. In Blake's illustrations to Gray,
probably executed a few years after the *NT* series, she appears
as "Malignant Fate," cutting the thread of the unfortunate Favourite
Cat's life and throwing her into the Tub of Gold Fishes.[33] Similarly,
as Destiny in *NT* 197, she cuts the poet's own "thread of life,"
which in the picture is shown as a rope which he climbs. As
"cruel Fate" (226), she breaks, once again, the black thread of
life—but the golden thread of immortality hangs out of her reach.
Spinning at her wheel, she becomes "Virtue, kept alive by Care,
and Toil" (294); she is also Austerity (375), brandishing two clusters of birch switches. Her most striking appearance is as Lot's
wife[34] in the title page for Night V (158), a beautiful picture
in which we see a walled city in flames with a domed building
visible above its battlements, and the Enitharmon figure, colored
bluish gray and wearing a filmy dress, seeming to regard the inset
title page in tears. Once again, we have a thematic equation here.
The spinning wheel is associated with other images of the cycle
of nature which we shall soon discuss; the goldfish bowl into which
the cat-nymph is thrown is a miniature Sea of Time and Space
(cf. *Job*, Illustration 15), and she a soul descending into the material world. Repressive virtue is as deathly a conception as pre-
determined Fate. Finally, the title of Night V is *The Relapse*. The
example of Lot's wife is appropriate for obvious reasons, and she
is a form of Enitharmon because she looks back from the path to
human identity—back to a world of mere nature, appetency, and

pain. Becoming mineral, she is a *reductio ad absurdum* of the world-view that she represents.

Another of the major figures of Blake's *Night Thoughts,* Los, takes three different and in this case unrelated forms. He is Time, the charioteer of the sun, and father of the child Orc. As Time he appears as a gigantic old man with the conventional white beard and scythe; he is bald, except for the traditional forelock by which alone Time can be plucked. Sometimes he wears a chaplet of roses, and in *NT* 182 Blake gives him a lantern to carry as Los does in the frontispiece to *Jerusalem.* It must be said that the effect is not on the whole successful, and perhaps the reason for this is that Blake is portraying not his own conception of Time but what he regards as a common *mis*conception:

> Los is by mortals nam'd Time, Enitharmon is nam'd Space:
> But they depict him bald & aged who is in eternal youth
> All powerful and his locks flourish like the brows of morning.
> (*Mil* 24:68–70, *K* 509)

Particularly grotesque is *NT* 434, where Los-Time literally falls on his own scythe. Here the charge of overliteral translation would certainly be correct. Much more successful are three pictures in which Los is god of the sun—*NT* 87 (*Edw* 49), 125, and 339, the last of these illustrating "A *Christian* dwells, like URIEL, in the sun." The intensity of coloration and the powerful simplicity of design in these pictures place them among the most successful of the *NT* series. The muscular, radiant figure which they show in the disc of the sun was again seen by Blake's inward eye at Felpham:

> Then Los appear'd in all his power:
> In the Sun he appear'd, descending before
> My face in fierce flames; in my double sight
> 'Twas outward a Sun: inward Los in his might.
> (To Thomas Butts, 22 Nov. 1802, ll. 55–56; K 818)

In his third aspect, as husband of Enitharmon and father of Orc, Los is seen in his fallen state, as in 26, which we discussed earlier.

The family group reappears in *NT* 44 (*Edw* 23; see PLATE VII). Here the father is shown measuring the infant with the span of his hand. In the Edwards edition an asterisk marks the lines "We censure nature for a span too short; / That span too short, we tax as tedious too." Bulwer-Lytton found Blake's picture "literal to ridicule," and so it would be if we accepted the view of the "Explanation" that its meaning is merely "in allusion to the shortness of life." [35] However, the word "span" has another dimension of meaning for Blake. It is an extension of the use of the term in the Authorized Version, as in "Who hath measured the waters in the hollow of his hand, and meted out heaven with the span . . ." (Isa. 40:12). Blake thinks of this version of the creation as both limiting and limited. To measure by spanning is in Blake's terms to reduce possibilities. Vala, material Nature, "became a little weeping Infant a span long" (*FZ* ii:92, *K* 282); this in turn echoes "children of a span long" in Lamentations 2:20. We should keep in mind another, related meaning of the word as, by an inevitable metaphorical extension, the length of human life: "Lord, what a nothing is this little span, / We call a Man!" [36] If we examine the *NT* page in Blake's original, we find that, as in a number of other instances, the lines Blake marked are not the ones marked in Edwards. The lines Blake did mark include "Who murders Time, He crushes in the Birth / A Pow'r Ethereal, only *not* Ador'd" (ii, 116–17). The meaning of the picture now becomes clearer. The child is the divine Orc, who in *The Book of Urizen* is made subject to limits by Los, his father. "In his hands he siez'd the infant, / He bathed him in springs of sorrow . . ." (*Ur* 20:3–4, *K* 233). Similarly, the child of "Infant Sorrow" (*K* 217) is "Struggling in my father's hands, / Striving against my swadling bands . . ." The father lays hands on the child to hold, baptize, or measure, initiating him into a constricted reality. An infant, as Blake well knew, cannot be measured by the span of a man's hand. Blake's pictorial statements, as well as his verbal ones, are capable of irony.

One more major personification of the Prophetic Books appears in Blake's *Night Thoughts*, but not as prominently as the others we have mentioned. He is Luvah, the incarnation of passion, seen as a Dionysiac reveler in *NT* 380. Reclining beneath vines bearing clusters of grapes, he holds a glass of wine in which there is a little serpent ("A thousand Daemons lurk within the Lee"). His wine vats are shown in *NT* 409 ("A Dance of Spirits, a mere Froth of Joy") in a delightful picture which resembles the scene described in *Vala:*

> How red the sons & daughters of Luvah! how they tread the Grapes!
> Laughing & shouting, drunk with odors, many fall o'erwearied:
> Drown'd in the wine is many a youth & maiden . . .
>
> (*FZ* ix:743-45, *K* 377)

*NT* 409 depicts a ring of tiny figures dancing around a bowl of wine, others dancing around goblets, and still others carrying and spilling jugs and goblets. At the top is a bat-winged creature reminiscent of Bosch; another extends his wings in the right margin. *NT* 410 follows with the collapse after the orgy—the wine bowl shattered, the face of the demon at the top now revealed. Only once, in *NT* 331, does Luvah take on some of the political significance Blake gives him in *The Four Zoas.* Here he is shown chained and drunken as an example of "Boasters of Liberty, fast-bound in Chains!" This foreshadows the parallel Blake will make between the cycle of nature and the cycle of revolution, where the process of making wine becomes an analogy of the destructive aspects of passion and energy, culminating in an intoxication with destruction:

> They dance around the dying & they drink the howl & groan;
> They catch the shrieks in cups of gold; they hand them to one another.
> These are the sports of love & these the sweet delights of amorous play:
> Tears of the grape, the death sweat of the Cluster, the last sigh
> Of the mild youth who listens to the luring songs of Luvah.
>
> (*FZ* ix:767-71, *K* 377)

The meaning of Luvah is not, however, further extended in the *NT* series, and the three other important figures of *The Four Zoas,* Tharmas, Enion, and Ahania, do not appear in it in recognizable form.

The fallen world which these gods preside over is described by means of a number of thematic images which are equally familiar in Blake's other works. One group of such images involves forms of debased or undeveloped life—fibers, roots, webs, larvae—suggestive of passivity and entrapment. In *NT* 258, for example, we see a striking dryadic figure whose arms sprout into branches and whose legs become a network of roots. "Here, dormant Matter, waits a call to Life; / Half-life, half-death join There; Here, Life and Sense." Young praises Nature's gradation, but Blake embodies a state of consciousness, underlining his meaning by drawing a youth with a worm coiled about his body. Marie Antoinette, in Blake's Notebook poem about LaFayette, is represented in just such a state:

> But our good Queen quite grows to the ground,
> [There is just such a tree at Java found. *del.*]
> And a great many suckers grow all around.
>
> (60, 24–26; *K* 185)

Another failure to become a truly human being is portrayed in *NT* 17, where a creature with a green caterpillar body and a human head regards himself in a mirror. He is suspended in a gray-black cocoon, "wrapt round and round / In silken thought, which reptile *Fancy* spun. . . ." At the right, his horrified Emanation looks on. Tendrils entwine the text of *NT* 32, where we see an old man wearing a fool's cap and lying in a sort of vegetative sleeping bag, "For ever on the brink of being born." Love itself, if it excludes the rest of the human community, can produce such a vegetated state, as Blake indicates in *NT* 215: a naked couple interlace in a hollow part of a tree trunk, branches twisting about their bodies. This illustrates the lines which Blake directly or indirectly echoed in *Thel:* "O the soft Commerce! O the tender Tyes, / Close-twisted with the Fibres of the Heart!"

Blake uses certain mythical beings, "dishumaniz'd men" as he elsewhere calls them, to represent some other inner states. One of these is Nebuchadnezzar, used both by Young and by Blake as an emblem of the self which turns away from the divinity of man and, failing to become human, becomes bestial, "With low, terrestrial Appetite, to graze / On trash, on Toys, dethron'd from high Desire" (vii, 27). This illustration (299) is similar to Blake's treatment of the same subject in *The Marriage* and in the color print of 1795—Nebuchadnezzar is shown covered with fur, his toes talons, eating grass. Another degenerate self, Nimrod, is used in connection with Young's "Till *Death*, that mighty Hunter, earths them all." He is a demonic figure with a spear and terrible hounds, one of which leaps at the throat of a naked male figure (117).[37] As in *Jerusalem* 22, where he is associated with Skofield, Nimrod represents the savagery of power, the will to dominate and destroy others. Another mythological being, Cerberus (334), is one of a number of triple figures in Blake's works—others are Satan, Hand, and the accusers of Socrates—who are willful destroyers of what others create.

In the fallen world, love is transformed into perverse and cruel delight, teasing and yearning. Blake represents this condition as the pursuit by the Spectre of his Emanation.

> A Fathomless & boundless deep,
> There we wander, there we weep;
> On the hungry craving wind
> My Spectre follows thee behind.
> ("My Spectre . . . ," 23-26; *K* 415)

In *NT* 351, Blake seizes an opportunity to portray this situation, taking off from Young's lines "How frail, Men, Things? How momentary, Both? / Fantastic Chace, of Shadows hunting Shades!" We see a male and a female figure in ghostly white outline against a cloudy gray background. The Spectre lunges toward the Emanation, who flies upward toward the right, looking back at him with an expression of hatred and horror.

> "Thro' the Heaven & Earth & Hell
> "Thou shalt never never quell:
> "I will fly & thou pursue,
> "Night & Morn the flight renew."
> ("My Spectre . . . ," 55-58; *K* 416)

Such love, or "Jealousy," as Blake frequently calls it, compounded of irrational passion, fear, and possessiveness, is the subject of *NT*

88. Again, the text provides only the merest suggestion for the picture:

> Lean not on Earth; 'twill pierce thee to the Heart;
> A broken Reed, at best; but, oft, a spear:
> On its sharp point Peace bleeds, and Hope expires.

A nude male figure stands buried to the waist beside a huge briar plant, looking away from his Emanation, who is impaled on one of the briars. A black bird hovers in the background. The briars suggest, as in "The Garden of Love," sexual constraint "binding with briars my joys & desires" (*K* 215), and the scene as a whole recalls Theotormon's guilt-obsessed rejection of the love of Oothoon in *Visions of the Daughters of Albion*. Another Emanation comes to grief in *NT* 81 (*Edw* 46; see PLATE VIII), which is supposed to illustrate "Where *Sense* runs Savage, broke from *Reason's* chain, / And sings false Peace, till smother'd by the Pall." From above the naked joyful girl descends Urizen with his cloak. The effect is much enhanced by intense coloration, as in the copy of Edwards which belonged to Sir John Soane: Urizen's hair and hands are chalky white, as is the underside of his cloak, the upper side of which is jet black; all in sharp contrast to the Emanation, whose skin is a healthy flesh color and whose breasts are tipped in rose. This picture, which subverts its text, was regarded by Bulwer-Lytton as very literal.[38]

Two more thematic images familiar to readers of Blake are the chain and the compasses, representing constricting and circumscribing forces. "The chains are the cunning of weak and tame minds which have power to resist energy" (*MHH* 16, *K* 155). The worst chains are those which are internalized so that no external constraint is necessary in order to enforce repression. This is what happens to Orc in Night V of *The Four Zoas*, as the spirit of revolution is assimilated by the world of things-as-they-are.

> Lo, the young limbs had strucken root into the rock, & strong
> Fibres had from the Chain of Jealousy inwove themselves
> In a swift vegetation round the rock & round the Cave
> And over the immortal limbs of the terrible fiery boy.
>
> (*FZ* v:156–59, *K* 309)

Such a chain appears in *NT* 307, where we see a naked male figure "chain'd down to Pangs, and Death," enfolded in the coils of a serpent with open crocodile-jaws. Another such figure, representing the result of not hoping in Eternity, is in *NT* 287 manacled and chained in a yellow sphere. Once the chain is itself the central subject (322), where Young praises the *"Chain of Ages,"* but Blake shows it as sinisterly dwarfing the tiny figures who clamber onto it from a lake of fire. Here Blake is intentionally rejecting the central analogy of his century, "the great chain, that draws all to agree," as Pope calls it in the *Essay on Man,* with its implications of conservative pessimism and acceptance of social inequality.[39] Blake wanted not the hierarchy of Degree but something more like D. H. Lawrence's "democracy of touch." Consequently at the Last Judgment Urizen asks "What Chain encompasses?" and is answered when "riv'n link from link, the bursting Universe explodes" (*FZ* ix:226, 230; *K* 363).[40]

The compasses, a related symbol of limitation, are perhaps best known from the frontispiece to *Europe,* also extant as a separate plate, "The Ancient of Days." This design is an ironical version of Milton's description, itself derived from Proverbs 8:27, of the creation:

> He took the golden Compasses, prepar'd
> In Gods Eternal store, to circumscribe
> This Universe, and all created things.[41]

The demiurge creates the material world but in so doing he limits it; his compasses indicate the circumscribed nature of his activity. (Cf. Blake's epigram "To God," *K* 557: "If you have form'd a Circle to go into, / Go into it yourself & see how you would do.") Newton, in the great color print, is both creator and victim of the same limits, and so his magnificent torso bends over his compasses in a posture approaching that of Nebuchadnezzar. Blake shows one of Young's "Newtonian Angels" in this same posture (509), and he ironically illustrates the lines "To rise in Science, as in Bliss / Insatiate in the secret of the Skies" with a figure whose hand stretches upward with compasses, the points of which approach the stars (227). The education motif reappears in *NT* 360: a man with enormous compasses points to the ground, where he has drawn a triangle; a child stands on his knees before it. "Alas! the World's a Tutor more severe" is the line marked in Edwards, but here again we find that on this page Blake marked a different passage, one of greater thematic importance:

> Ah! what avails his Innocence? The Task
> Injoined must discipline his early Pow'rs;
> He learns to sigh, ere he has known to sin;
> Guiltless, and sad! A Wretch before the Fall!     (viii, 14)

A parallel situation is shown in one of Blake's pictures for Gray's "Ode to Adversity": Virtue sits in the lap of Adversity, her "stern rugged nurse," writing in a book; Adversity is Enitharmon in her crone form, and holds a huge pair of compasses.

The circle drawn by the stiff twin compasses is one of a number of models or diagrams of the shape of human experience in Blake's *Night Thoughts*. Others include the gear-wheel of *NT* 473 and, in *NT* 353, Fortune's Wheel on which the Daughters of Time spin our hours. The most important of these symbols is the serpent, whose folds, becoming the "Churches" of history in *The Four Zoas*, indicate man's seeming imprisonment in cyclical recurrence. Of the numerous serpents drawn for this series, by far the most striking is the one in *NT* 78, the title page of Night III (see PLATE IX). Above this huge resplendent serpent's head stands Young's Narcissa on a crescent moon. Her arms reach upward with a sweep reinforced by the lines of the rest of her body. In contrast to the multicolored serpent, she is white; radiance streams from her figure. The "Explanation" suggests that she is being admitted to "an eternity of glory," and that "eternity is represented by its usual emblem—a serpent with its extremities united." This ignores, however, the two kinds of eternity represented in the picture. The serpent's is one of infinite recurrence —the same dull round of a universe conceived as going on without end. It is in Blake's view man's specifically human ability to transcend this cycle of devouring and devoured. In *Jerusalem*, after naming the "Twenty-seven Heavens & their Churches," he writes "But Jesus, breaking thro' the Central Zones of Death & Hell, / Opens Eternity in Time & Space, triumphant in Mercy" (76:21–22, *K* 716). Narcissa's aspiring figure beautifully embodies this second alternative. Young himself elaborates this same theme in Night VI, page 36:

> As in a wheel, All sinks, to reascend.
> Emblems of man, who passes, not expires.
> With this minute distinction, Emblems just,
> *Nature* revolves, but Man *advances;* Both
> Eternal, *that* a Circle, *this* a Line.

As Blake found Young's imagery very close to his own here, he could follow it rather closely. He painted another serpent, its tail in its mouth and the circle it encloses darkened to indicate the "dark world," as Böhme calls it, of nature separated from its divine source. On the serpent's back stands a male form ready to spring upwards (257). As in the Narcissa frontispiece, man leaves the cycle of nature to realize his identity in brotherhood and love. On the verso of the frontispiece, *NT* 79, Blake showed the alternative to this: a horrified female figure chained inside a circle formed by another crested serpent—a self-enclosed existence, trapped in a world of money, law, and violence, overcome by cosmic despair. The cycle of nature may thus be perceived either optimistically or pessimistically, depending on the perspective from which man views it. It can even become an argument for immortality, as in *NT* 256, one of the most beautiful pictures in the series, showing the four seasons in a magnificent design which brings to mind a line from *Jerusalem:* "O holy Generation, Image of regeneration" (7:65, *K* 626).

The opposition between cyclical recurrence and transcendence is resolved in *NT* 474 (ix, 56), which shows the eyed wheels of Ezekiel's vision:

> Orb above Orb ascending without End!
> Circle in Circle, without End, inclos'd!
> Wheel within Wheel, EZEKIEL! like to Thine!

This is a visual presentation of the conception which Blake later elaborated as the Eyes of God.[42] When viewed from "below," from the perspective of the fallen world, as in "The Mental Traveller," human life is seen as subject to the agonies of eternal recurrence. But when viewed from the perspective of Eternity, what seemed to be a circle becomes an ever-expanding spiral, each arc of which brings man closer to a casting-out of error and the recognition of truth. Both in the *NT* series and in the later prophetic works Blake presents a model of human experience by which we may move from imprisonment in the cycle of history to apocalyptic freedom.

> Thus are the Heavens form'd by Los within the Mundane Shell.
> And where Luther ends Adam begins again in Eternal Circle
> To awake the Prisoners of Death, to bring Albion again
> With Luvah into light eternal in his eternal day.
>
> (*J* 76:23–26, *K* 716)

In Blake's *Night Thoughts,* as in *The Four Zoas,* apocalyptic elements become predominant in Nights VIII and IX. Having described the nature of the fallen world, Blake turns in both cases to its destruction. The first step must be the identification of evil, which is the subject of *NT* 345, the title page of Young's Night VIII (see PLATE X). Sir Geoffrey Keynes rightly calls this one of the finest paintings Blake ever did, commenting that "The accumulated force of his imagination is challenging the things that stand in opposition to it."[43] The subject is that of Revelation 17—the seven-headed beast with the Mother of Harlots whom John calls Babylon and Blake Rahab, "the false church of this world, the opponent of Jerusalem, and the crucifier of Jesus."[44] As in Revelation, she has Mystery written on her forehead and holds in her hand a cup full of her abominations. She is seated on the back of the seven-headed monster. The situation is that of *The Four Zoas,* Night VIII, where "Orc augmented swift / In fury, a Serpent wondrous among the Constellations of Urizen," and "the dark Shadowy female . . . spread herself thro' all the branches in the power of Orc" (ll. 67–68, 80, 85; *K* 342, 343). (The little patches of white in the background, which Keynes thinks are flakes of snow, are almost certainly the stars of Urizen.) This configuration was suggested by, but goes far beyond, the title it surrounds:

VIRTUE'*s* APOLOGY
OR,
*The* MAN *of the* WORLD *Answer'd*

In which are Considered
*The* LOVE *of* This LIFE;
*The* AMBITION *and* PLEASURE, *with the* WIT
*and* WISDOM *of the* WORLD.

Blake plunges beneath Young's dead abstractions to create a figural situation in which the dead church and secular power combine forces in a dehumanized society. Ironically, Virtue becomes part of "The World," or "Life," in the sense we have already seen Blake impart to such terms. Rahab is one aspect of Vala—in this painting she wears Vala's spiked crown, and in *The Four Zoas,* Night VIII:

Vala, drawn down into a Vegetated body, now triumphant.
The Synagogue of Satan Clothed her with Scarlet robes & Gems,
And on her forehead was her name written in blood, "Mystery."
(ll. 280–82, *K* 348)

Later in this passage we are told "She is named Rahab." The beast which she rides, representing the State and its Church, has seven wonderfully grotesque heads. The one on the lower right is a judge, scaly, fanged, and red-eyed. Somewhat resembling Blake's later painting of the Ghost of a Flea, this representative of Law has a single horn and wears a judicial wig. Next comes the armored head of a warrior, then a crowned head with ram's horns. The fourth head has goat's horns and the papal tiara, the fifth the crown of a king. The next two wear, respectively, a bishop's miter and a priest's black biretta. The picture as a whole epitomizes the institutions of the fallen world revealed in their true monstrous nature as "Religion hid in War, a Dragon red and hidden Harlot" (*J* 89:53, *K* 735).

Another manifestation of the promised end is the Leviathan of
*NT* 349, in Young's text merely a simile.

> Lorenzo! since *Eternal* is at hand,
> To swallow Time's Ambitions; as the vast
> *Leviathan*, the bubbles vain, that ride
> High on the foaming Billow . . .

Blake supplies a scaly green merman, crowned with the papal
tiara, who rides the monster's back and directs its course. This
figure, wielding a red crozier, reminds us of the scaly Rintrah of
*Europe* (Pl. 5), who represents Pitt in his role as leader of the war
against France.[45] He also resembles the scaly-genitaled Satan of
the sixth *Job* design and the Nelson of Blake's spiritual portrait,
*"guiding Leviathan, in whose wreathings are infolded the Nations
of the Earth"* (*DesC*, No. 1; *K* 564). Blake's Leviathan, of which
the crested and bejeweled Orc of *The Four Zoas*, Night VIII, is
yet another version, brings together the biblical meaning of the
symbol with that of Hobbes, ironically inverting the latter: it is
the warfare state stripped of its jargon. The appearance of Leviathan in the fallen world, like that of the Whore and the Beast,
is part of that process of definition which immediately precedes
the Day of Judgment, itself the subject of a number of later pictures in the series. Number 427 illustrates "Final Ruin fiercely
guides / Her Ploughshare o'er Creation," lines in which Young
uses an apocalyptic symbol which Blake himself employs in *The
Four Zoas*, Night IX.[46] The sleeper in *NT* 429 awakes to the
flames of the Last Day, a theme enlarged on by the holocaust
scenes of *NT* 430 and 432. In *NT* 463 "this Manuscript of Heav'n"
—another apocalyptic symbol used by both Young and Blake[47]—burns
"like a Parchment-Scroll, shrunk up by Flames"; stars fall, and men
and animals are consumed. Time and Death are destroyed (434);
choiring angels (437) hail the reign of Eternity.

Twelve years after the publication of his engravings in the Edwards edition, Blake stated, in his *Descriptive Catalogue*, his doctrine of the relation of art to myth:

Visions of these eternal principles or characters of human life appear to poets, in all ages; the Grecian gods were the ancient Cherubim of Phoenicia; but the Greeks, and since them the Moderns, have neglected to subdue the gods of Priam. These gods are visions of the eternal attributes, or divine names, which, when erected into gods, become destructive to humanity. They ought to be the servants, and not the masters of man, or of society. They ought to be made to sacrifice to Man, and not man compelled to sacrifice to them; for when separated from man or humanity, who is Jesus the Saviour, the vine of eternity, they are thieves and rebels, they are destroyers. (No. 3, *K* 571)

These remarks are as applicable to Blake's *Night Thoughts* as they are to his Canterbury pilgrims; they remind us that the great personifications of Blake's works were not abstractions into which the subject was translated. They were parts of a mythical reality, a way of structuring human experience and at the same time a way of communicating his perception of it to others. As Laurence Binyon has perceptively remarked of Blake's art in general: "The energies and movements which underlie and cause the phenomena of life were his pictorial themes; and these he personified, as the primitive imagination of mankind has personified the forces that it saw or divined around it."[48] In the *Night Thoughts* series, these are mainly the forces of a fallen world, a world whose gods have become masters of society, and whose metaphorical terrain is littered with the wrecks of man's divided existence. The series as a whole, despite lapses of taste and of interest, builds up an accumulated impression of power and pathos. It deserves to be known more widely and to be made available, as a group of Blake scholars has proposed, in facsimile reproduction. "If"—to let William Blake have the last word—"the Spectator could Enter into these Images in his Imagination, approaching them on the Fiery Chariot of his Contemplative Thought . . . then would he meet the Lord in the Air & then he would be happy" (*LJ* 82, *K* 611).

ALBERT S. ROE

# "The Thunder of Egypt"

*Israel deliver'd from Egypt, is Art deliver'd*
*from Nature & Imitation.*[1]

· INTRODUCTION ·

In one of the most creatively imaginative and, at the same time, most frustratingly unfinished works of his career, William Blake summed up in an extremely subtle and personal sketch his final comment upon Dante's *Divine Comedy*. Entitled "The Queen of Heaven in Glory" (see PLATE XI), this pencil drawing, lightly touched with ink and colored wash, is the final one of his ninety-nine illustrations to Dante's poem and the tenth based upon the *Paradiso*.[2] In a remarkable paraphrase of Dante's vision of the Celestial Rose, which brings the *Divine Comedy* to a conclusion, the Virgin is revealed naked, seated not upon a rose but upon a sunflower.[3] Thus does Blake express his conviction that Dante, a poet whom as visionary and as literary artist he regarded with "the highest admiration," [4] had none the less fallen into the ultimate error of confusing the Religion of Christ with the Religion of This World. Blake sets forth graphically at this point what he had jotted down in a pencil notation on his sketch for the seventh illustration of the *Inferno:* "Every thing in Dante's Comedia shews That for Tyrannical Purposes he has made This World the Foundation of All, & the Goddess Nature Mistress; Nature is his Inspirer & not the Holy Ghost." [5]

Close to the upper rim of the sunflower, on either side of the principal figure, are placed two groups, each depicting the closed book of the Bible bound around with a chain and surmounted by a crouching form. It was S. Foster Damon who first suggested that these were intended to represent sphinxes.[6] While the drawing is so sketchy as to make identification uncertain, it would seem that, in terms of Blake's symbolism, such an explanation is indeed highly probable. The following pages will be devoted to a study of the theme of Egypt as it is introduced in Blake's writings and in his works in various visual media. From such an examination, it will become evident that Egypt and things Egyptian are subject to consistent interpretation as symbols for Blake of the Fallen World of materialism and spiritual annihilation.

## · BLAKE AND ERASMUS DARWIN ·

The manner in which the concept of Egypt is employed in the Dante designs furnishes a striking example of the consistency with which Blake utilized certain symbolic themes over a period of many years. The illustrations to the *Divine Comedy* are the last works of Blake's life, the series having been begun late in 1824 and left far from completion at the time of his death in August, 1827. It is of interest, therefore, to compare another design from this group based upon an early episode of the *Inferno*, "The Mission of Virgil" (PLATE XII), with an engraving of many years before when Blake was actively employed in supplying plates for the publishing trade. The work in question, entitled "Fertilization of Egypt" (PLATE XIII), appeared in 1791 in the first edition of Erasmus Darwin's poem, *The Botanic Garden.*[7]

The most significant feature of this illustration, which links it with the Dante drawing, is the bearded figure with outspread arms and wings that hovers dimly in the background, poised above a waterfall representing a cataract of the Nile. This apparition, appearing here for the first time, was destined to become important in Blake's symbolic repertoire, and reappears not only on other occasions in much the same form, but also in a number of easily recognizable variants. In short, the personification of Darwin's "dark Monsoon" became the archetype of Jehovah-Urizen whose many appearances figure in striking passages of Blake's prophetic poems, and in numerous major examples of his art. Among the latter is the Dante illustration just referred to. As Dante and Virgil set forth upon their journey and reach the gate of the Fallen World—that same gate which leads to Blake's and our own World of Generation as well as to Dante's Hell—the figure which originated many years before as the Nile God towers once more at the head of the page. So that there may be no mistaking his identity, Blake has written above him "The Angry God of this World." Of particular significance for our theme, however, is a second inscription, too faint to discern in reproduction, but quite apparent in the original. Beside the forks of lightning issuing from the hands Blake has penciled the words "The Thunder of Egypt."

*The Botanic Garden* is a poem in two parts, of which the second, subtitled *The Loves of the Plants,* was actually published some years before the first, *The Economy of Vegetation.* "Fertilization of Egypt" is an illustration to the third canto of *The Economy of Vegetation,* and the particular passage which called it into being (ll. 129–34) is introduced by a footnote referring to the testimony of recent travelers who "have ascribed the rise of the Nile to the monsoons which deluge Nubia and Abyssinia with rain."

> Sailing in air, when dark Monsoon inshrouds
> His tropic mountains in a night of clouds;
> Or drawn by whirlwinds from the Line returns,
> And showers o'er Afric all his thousand urns;
> High o'er his head the beams of Sirius glow,
> And, Dog of Nile, Anubis barks below.

In the original form of the Darwin design, which appeared in the three editions of the folio issued from 1791 to 1795, the plate is inscribed "H. Fuseli, R. A. inv. W. Blake sc." Notwithstanding this ascription to Henry Fuseli, Sir Geoffrey Keynes pointed out some time ago that the hovering figure described previously is "a characteristic product of Blake's mind." We can in the present author's opinion go further and, in spite of the contrary evidence of the caption and also of the preparatory drawing by Fuseli in the Print Room of the British Museum,[8] justifiably infer that the basic inspiration for the design may well have been suggested by Blake.[9] Indeed, if we consider the engraved version of the "Fertilization of Egypt" from a stylistic point of view, it is not strongly reminiscent of Fuseli,[10] while the frontispiece of the same volume of *The Botanic Garden,* engraved by Anker Smith after Fuseli, reveals the latter's characteristic mannerisms in striking fashion.

Taken by itself this contrast would be flimsy evidence, but there is a much more significant indication that Blake had an important part in the formative phases of the design and was not involved solely in the passive role of engraver, as the caption would indicate.

In the continuation of the passage just quoted, Darwin proceeds to extol at considerable length the beneficent qualities of water. When one turns to the illustration, however, not only is the winged genius of the river recognizable as Blake's personification of "The Angry God of this World," but taken as a whole the design fits in remarkably with Blake's developed symbolism and can be interpreted, in a manner so typical of Blake, as a critical commentary upon the text, containing as it does many of the attributes of the Fallen World which are familiar in Blake's symbolic vocabulary. Water is here not life-giving and this is no River of Paradise, but rather the stream which feeds the Lake of Udan-Adan and the Sea of Ulro. Its topography is that of the barren land which lies beyond the boundaries of Golgonooza—the City of Art which, in his Divine mercy, God caused to be built as a refuge for Man so that he might be saved from total annihilation after the Fall.

> Around Golgonooza lies the land of death eternal, a Land
> Of pain and misery and despair and ever brooding melancholy.
> . . . . . . . . . . . . . . . . . . . . . .
> The Land of earthquakes, and the land of woven labyrinths:
> The land of snares & traps & wheels & pit-falls & dire mills:
> The Voids, the Solids, & the land of clouds & regions of waters
> . . . . . . . . . . . . . . . . . . . . .
> . . . Los walks round the walls night and day.
> He views the City of Golgonooza & its smaller Cities,
> The Looms & Mills & Prisons & Work-houses of Og & Anak,
> The Amalekite, the Canaanite, the Moabite, the *Egyptian*,
> And all that has existed in the space of six thousand years.
> (J 13:30–31, 48–50, 55–59; K 633–34)[11]

This then is the bleak land of the illustration, the land which is forever barren and dominated since time out of name by its monuments of death, the land where Israel was held captive, the great prototype of "the Kingdoms of the World & all their glory that grew on Desolation." All of the symbols of Blake's wasteland are united in this design: the "pyramids of pride," which are themselves "the ruin of a Part of Nimrod's tower, which I conjecture to have spread over many Countries"; the desert shore flanking the river of oblivion, the waters of which are rained down amidst lightning by "the Angry God of this World," above whose figure tower up great banks of clouds—always emblematic for Blake of the impenetrable wall which cuts off man in the Fallen World from the Light of Eternity. In the center of all is Fallen Man, making obeisance to rational law in the person of Jehovah-Urizen, beneath the light not of the Spiritual Sun, but of the *six*-pointed star of the old dispensation, an indication that he is governed by the cruelties of Moral Law and not by the true Gospel, which is "Forgiveness of Sins." [12] It will be noted too that Man turns his back upon a musical instrument, which lies by the side in the foreground. As so often with Blake, we can interpret this detail from two points of view and as such we are led to reflect upon the contrary aspects of human experience. The instrument is the sistrum, which is regularly associated with the worship of Isis.[13] As such it would suggest the subjugation of the creative arts to the Female Will in the Fallen World, for "These are not the Works Of *Egypt* nor Babylon, Whose Gods are the Powers Of this World, Goddess Nature, Who first spoil & then destroy Imaginative Art" (*Laoc*, K 776–77). At the same time, however, we are led to reflect that the arts remain potentially man's binding tie with his divine nature. For "Poetry, Painting, & Music are the three Powers in Man of conversing with Paradise, which the flood did not Sweep away" (*LJ* 81, *K* 609),[14] and it is in song that Jerusalem, the Emanation of Fallen Man, speaks to him in moments of inspiration:

Turkey & Grecia saw my instruments of music; they arose,
They siez'd the harp, the flute, the mellow horn of Jerusalem's joy;
They sounded thanksgivings in my courts. *Egypt* & Lybia heard,
The swarthy sons of Ethiopia stood round the Lamb of God
Enquiring for Jerusalem . . .                    (*J* 79:48–52, *K* 721)

For the moment, however, Man is at the nadir of the Fall, even to the point of having lost his divine likeness and, in the guise of the dog-headed Anubis, being altogether reduced to a bestial state. This is the figure of Tharmas, Blake's Zoa representative of the purely physical and brutish aspect of man's nature. It is his Emanation, Enion, who laments: "I have chosen the serpent for a councellor, & the *dog* / For a schoolmaster to my children." This is man in the "state" when he has lost all sight of the Divine Humanity, and bows to the worship of "those Fiends, the Egyptian Gods." [15] His obeisance is thus to be construed not as an act of tribute to the life-giving waters of the Nile and to the star which signifies the commencement of its annual rise, but as homage to Urizen, the God of the Fallen World, which for Blake is the world beneath the stars.

> . . . their children wept, & built
> Tombs in the desolate places,
> And form'd laws of prudence, and call'd them
> The eternal laws of God.
>
> And the thirty cities remain'd,
> Surrounded by salt floods, now call'd
> Africa: its name was then *Egypt*.
>
> The remaining sons of Urizen
> Beheld their brethren shrink together
> Beneath the Net of Urizen.
> . . . . . . . . .
> And they left the pendulous earth.
> They called it *Egypt*, & left it.
> ( *Ur* 28:4–13, 21–22; *K* 236–37) [16]

It may be objected that in thus interpreting this engraving in terms of Blake's developed mythology we are not only drawing conclusions which ignore the evidence of the caption which gives the design to Fuseli, but are attempting to support this theory with quotations which were, in most cases, not written until well after the plate was published. However, as has been pointed out earlier, once Blake attached symbolic meaning to a certain image, he tended to employ it consistently thereafter, often over a period of many years. By the time Blake came to execute the plates for Darwin's *Botanic Garden*, his period of apprenticeship was long past and he was in his early thirties, the period of the first full flowering of his genius. Already *Songs of Innocence* and the *Book of Thel* had been published, utilizing the original method of relief etching which he had developed (both are dated 1789), and *The Marriage of Heaven and Hell* was in active process of creation. The last of these works represents the most revealing statement of Blake's ideas up to this time, and dates from precisely the period of the Darwin engraving. Within the next three or four years all of the shorter prophecies were to be etched and published. Hence, the main lines of Blake's personal mythology were already formed and the symbolic significance of the principal characters who were to figure in all of his later cosmic dramas was well advanced. Thus in this design we can expect to find an early instance of Blake's later practice of employing the dramatis personae of his own symbolism as actors in the illustrations which he provided for the works of others.

We may now return to the passage of *Jerusalem* of which a portion was previously quoted, and examine further Blake's description of the City of Golgonooza, man's imaginative refuge in the Fallen World:

> ... the Four Points are thus beheld in Great Eternity:
> West, the Circumference: South, the Zenith: North,
> The Nadir: East, the Center, unapproachable for ever.
> . . . . . . . . . . . . . . . . . .
> And the North Gate of Golgonooza, toward Generation
> Has four sculptur'd Bulls, terrible, before the Gate of iron,
> And iron the Bulls; and that which looks toward Ulro,
> Clay bak'd & enamel'd, eternal glowing as four furnaces.
> (*J* 12:54–56, 61–64; *K* 632)

May we now perhaps go further and infer that the cataract of the Nile, as shown in the design, should be taken to represent the North Gate? As the text informs us, this faces toward Generation, Blake's term for the Fallen World of man's present life which in Great Eternity is beheld as the Nadir. The fact that in geographical reality the apparent direction would be south does not pose any problem, since Fallen Man, the dog-headed Anubis, though quite unaware of his predicament, is to be thought of as in an upside-down position, and hence sees above him the six-pointed star of the Nadir, the realm of the God of this World, and not the sun of the Divine Imagination.

The description of the Gates of Golgonooza continues:

> And sixty-four thousand Genii guard the Eastern Gate,
> And sixty-four thousand Gnomes guard the Northern Gate,
> And sixty-four thousand Nymphs guard the Western Gate,
> And sixty-four thousand Fairies guard the Southern Gate.
>
> (*J* 13:26–29, *K* 633)

This passage confirms that Blake must have read Darwin's poem and that it left a lasting impression upon him. *The Economy of Vegetation*, the first of the two parts of *The Botanic Garden*, is divided into four cantos, of which the "Fertilization of Egypt" serves as an illustration to the third. The poem opens with a passage in which "The Genius of the Place" invokes the "Botanic Goddess," who appears at once accompanied by a train of Gnomes, Sylphs, and Nymphs. For the remainder of the poem it is the Goddess who speaks, and in each canto she addresses her various attendants in turn, calling first upon the "Nymphs of Primeval Fire" and then upon the Gnomes, the "Aquatic Nymphs," and finally in the fourth canto the Sylphs.

A decade and more was to elapse between the time Blake engraved his plate for Darwin's poem and the commencement of the composition of *Jerusalem*, and yet, as indicated above, some of Darwin's imagery is embodied in the description of the City of Art. At first glance, this might seem to suggest that Blake shared Fuseli's views concerning Darwin's stature as a poet, Joseph Farington having recorded that "Fuseli thinks Cowper the best of all the Poets of his period above Hayley &c. and *even Darwin*." [17] Fuseli had, of course, reasons for gratitude to Darwin. In *The Loves of the Plants* which, while designated as Part II of *The Botanic Garden*, actually was published first (1789), Fuseli's "Nightmare" is described as the creation of a "poetic eye; / Whose daring tints, with Shakespeare's happiest grace, / Gave to the airy phantom form and place." [18] When the first issue of the combined poem appeared, not only was this passage retained, but in a later edition it was accompanied by an engraving of the painting.

While such recognition of his friend's art, which some years later he was vigorously to defend in print,[19] would have pleased Blake, there is further evidence that he was favorably impressed by some of Darwin's views. Of especial interest is a footnote to be found in the first canto of *The Economy of Vegetation* which is so suggestive with reference to Blake, as well as so indicative of the character of Darwin's work, as to be quoted here:[20]

*The holy Halo. l. 358.* I believe it is not known with certainty at what time the painters first introduced the luminous circle round the head to import a Saint or holy person. It is now become a symbolic language of painting, and it is much to be wished that this kind of hieroglyphic character was more frequent in that art; as it is much wanted to render historic pictures both more intelligible, and more sublime; and *why should not painting as well as poetry express itself in a metaphor, or in indistinct allegory?* [italics supplied] A truly great modern painter lately endeavored to enlarge the sphere of pictorial language, by putting a demon behind the pillow of a wicked man on his death bed. Which unfortunately the cold criticism of the present day has depreciated; and thus barred perhaps the only road to further improvement in this science.[21]

In this note Darwin advocates an approach to art of which Blake would most heartily have approved. It is striking to observe how closely the wording anticipates that of a well-known passage from the "Descriptive Catalogue" which Blake issued in connection with his ill-fated exhibition of 1809: ". . . shall Painting be confined to the sordid drudgery of fac-simile representations of merely mortal and perishing substances, and not be as poetry and music are, elevated into its own proper sphere of invention and visionary conception? No, it shall not be so! Painting, as well as poetry and music, exists and exults in immortal thoughts" (*K* 576).[22]

However, in spite of such instances of the influence of Darwin's poem upon him as have been demonstrated above, there can be little doubt that the work as a whole would have seemed to Blake not only vapid poetically but fundamentally vicious in its philosophy. In fact, he would not have had to read very far before finding one of his most cherished convictions disputed. Early in the first

canto of *The Economy of Vegetation* (ll. 101–12) immediately
after the appearance of the Goddess, she addresses the Fiery Nymphs
and relates to them the Creation of the Universe:

> When Love Divine, with brooding wings unfurl'd,
> Call'd from the rude abyss the living world.
> —"Let there be Light!" proclaim'd the Almighty Lord,
> Astonish'd *Chaos* heard the potent word;
> Through all his realms the kindling Ether runs,
> And the mass starts into a million suns;
> Earths round each sun with quick explosions burst,
> And second planets issue from the first;
> Bend, as they journey with projectile force,
> In bright elipses their reluctant course;
> Orbs wheel in orbs, round centres centres roll,
> And form, self-balanced, one revolving Whole.[23]

It is in the context of such a passage as this that we must surmise Blake's considered attitude to the poem. Some twenty years
later he wrote: "Many suppose that before the Creation All was
Solitude & Chaos. This is the most pernicious Idea that can enter
the Mind, as it takes away all sublimity from the Bible & Limits
All Existence to Creation & to Chaos, To the Time & Space fixed
by the Corporeal Vegetative Eye" (*LJ* 91–92, *K* 614). Thus in
Blake's view, "the Jehovah of the Bible [is] no other than he
who dwells in flaming fire" (*MHH* 6, *K* 150), and his creation
is "Satan's Labyrinth," ruled over by the Female Will. All of this
reads like a refutation of Darwin, whose amorphous "Genius of
the Place" summons the "Botanic Goddess" to describe the creation of the Vegetated Universe with its Newtonian bodies which
follow Urizen's Laws and move "along their order'd ways / In
right lined paths outmeasur'd by proportions of number, weight
/ And measure, mathematic motion wondrous along the deep, /
In fiery *pyramid* or Cube" (*FZ* ii:272–75, *K* 287). The design of
the "Fertilization of Egypt" considered in this context could well
be interpreted as Blake's comment on Darwin's account of creation,
for the Urizenic River God, whom Fallen Man bows before, is
indeed a true God of Egypt, one of those to whom Blake refers
as a "Mathematical Diagram." Doubtless, therefore, Blake's final

assessment of Darwin's poem would have been expressed in similar terms to those in which, as we have seen, he summed up his opinions concerning Dante's epic: "Nature is his Inspirer & not the Holy Ghost."

As before, it may be objected that we are anticipating Blake's ideas of many years later and even suggesting that Blake did not distinguish the artistic quality of the masterpiece of perhaps the greatest of poets from the work of one of the most pedestrian. To Blake, who years before he engraved this plate for *The Botanic Garden* had written the "Mad Song," who at this very time was composing such lyrics as "The Tyger," and who some years later in the preface to the first chapter of *Jerusalem* would speak of even Milton and Shakespeare as users of "a Monotonous Cadence . . . derived from the modern bondage of Rhyming," Darwin's qualities as a versifier could scarcely have been impressive.

Nevertheless, as we have shown, Darwin's poem did remain in Blake's memory in a remarkable way, as is most strikingly attested by the unexpected appearance of the Botanic Goddess's train of Nymphs, Gnomes, and Sylphs in one of the most significant and "terrific parts" of *Jerusalem*. In this connection a comparison of Darwin's footnote, which introduces them on their first appearance in *The Economy of Vegetation*, with further lines from the same important passage of *Jerusalem* will prove most illuminating.

*Pleased Gnomes. l. 73.* The Rosicrucian doctrine of Gnomes, Sylphs, Nymphs, and *Salamanders,* [italics added] affords proper machinery for a philosophic poem; as it is probable that they were originally the names of the hieroglyphic figures of the Elements, or of Genii presiding over their operations. The Fairies of more modern day seem to have been derived from them, and to have inherited their powers.

These, then, in the form of the Genii, Gnomes, Nymphs, and Fairies are the guardians of the Gates of the City of Golgonooza, the barriers which separate the Fallen World from Eternity, the symbols of that false art which forever excludes Fallen Man from Los's City of the Divine Imagination.

There is the Cave, the Rock, the Tree, the Lake of Udan Adan,
The Forest and the Marsh and the Pits of bitumen deadly,

The Rocks of solid fire, the Ice valleys, the Plains
Of burning sand, the rivers, cataract & Lakes of Fire,
The Islands of the fiery Lakes, the Tree of Malice, Revenge
And black Anxiety, and the Cities of the *Salamandrine* men.
(J 13:38–43, K 634)<sup>24</sup>

Milton was in error, and in his prophetic poem *Milton* Blake set out to expose that error, just as he was later to comment visually upon Dante's error. Thus in choosing to employ Darwin's symbolism at this point, Blake is no doubt suggesting, among all the other overtones of *Jerusalem*, that Darwin's vision is partial and that it is a portion, however small, of Blake's task to expose that error. "Los reads the Stars of Albion, the Spectre Reads the Voids / Between the Stars" (*J* 91:37–38, *K* 738). The Gates of Golgonooza are indeed "all clos'd up till the last day, when the graves shall yield their dead" (*J* 13:11, *K* 633). But we must recall that "Whenever any Individual Rejects Error & Embraces Truth, a Last Judgment passes upon that Individual" (*LJ* 82–84, *K* 613). Blake, the servant of the Divine Imagination, knows that it is his supreme mission, ordained for him as for all men of creative vision, to expose error and to set men free that the Gates of Golgonooza may then be opened to them.

I rest not from my great task!
To open the Eternal Worlds, to open the immortal Eyes
Of Man inwards into the Worlds of Thought, into Eternity
Ever expanding in the Bosom of God, the Human Imagination.
(J 5:17–20, K 623)

### · BLAKE AND JACOB BRYANT ·

The quotation from *The Book of Urizen* given in the previous section represents the earliest instance of the appearance of Egypt as a symbol of the Fallen World in Blake's writings, having been published in 1794. In one of Blake's earliest works, "Then she bore Pale desire," dating from 1777 or earlier, Egypt does not figure in a passage which lists many countries and cities of the ancient world. However, as has been demonstrated in the preceding section, by 1791 when the engraving "Fertilization of Egypt" was published, Egypt had already acquired special significance as a symbol of the Fallen World.

Is it possible to identify the probable origin of the particular association which Blake came to apply to Egypt? The clue is to be found in Jacob Bryant's *A New System, or An Analysis of Ancient Mythology*.[25] Published in three volumes from 1774 to 1776, the illustrative plates for this work were engraved in the shop of James Basire during the years when Blake served his apprenticeship there. On a number of previous occasions convincing relationships have been established which link certain of these plates with various of Blake's original designs.[26] That Blake knew Bryant's text well and remembered it is indeed attested by his reference to it in the discussion of his painting "The Ancient Britons" which appeared in the Descriptive Catalogue issued in connection with his exhibition of 1809. "The Antiquities of every Nation under Heaven, is no less sacred than that of the Jews. They are the same thing, as Jacob Bryant and all antiquaries have proved" (*K* 578).[27] In the following pages, more connections with Bryant's text will be developed than have previously been noted, and instances will be discussed which will demonstrate that not only some of Blake's designs but also the germs of a number of his important and consistent symbols originated in his reading of Bryant's *Ancient Mythology*. Egypt is a case in point, for references to Egypt abound in Bryant's text, which contains a very considerable section entitled "Of Egypt and Its first Inhabitants and of Its Kings, and Dynasties." [28]

In the preceding study of Blake and Erasmus Darwin, the passage and accompanying footnote from *The Economy of Vegetation* were quoted which served as the basis for the illustration "Fertilization of Egypt." When Blake read these verses and the note, he could well have been put in mind of Bryant's passage relating to the monsoon: "The fable of the Mundane Egg, and of Typhon, is I imagine, of the same original and purport: for Typhon signified a Deluge. The overflowing of the Nile was called by the Egyptians Typhon." [29] In these two sentences we find the germs of two of Blake's most enduring symbols, the waters of Ulro or annihilation, and the Mundane Shell ordained by God as "a Creation of mercy

& love from the Satanic Void" (*J* 13:45, *K* 634). The Mundane Shell developed into one of Blake's most subtle images, signifying on the one hand the created universe as exemplified by "whatever is visible to the Generated Man" (*J* 13:44), and also representative of the individuality of Fallen Man, the meeting point of the Zoas, and the focus of the endless struggle of good and evil. The familiar and suggestive diagram of Plate 33 of *Milton* did indeed evolve from an idea which had its origin in Blake's reading of Bryant's text, and represents a transformation of one of the accompanying engravings. At the top of Plate IV of the second volume of *A New System,* the Mundane Egg appears twice, once surmounted by a crescent moon and in the other instance entwined within the coils of a serpent.[30]

The serpent of the Fallen World became, of course, one of the most familiar of Blake's images and figures in many designs, among the most striking of which are the title page of *Europe* and the Temptation of Eve in the series of water-color illustrations for *Paradise Lost.* In the latter, the serpent coils itself about the human form at the instant when the masculine form of the Imagination turns its back and the feminine aspect of the soul eagerly accepts the serpent's material gift which precipitates the Fall.

While less familiar than the symbolism of the serpent, the suggestion supplied by the engraving of the Mundane Egg surmounted by the crescent can be traced in a whole series of designs made by Blake many years later in illustration of several of his major creative works. In Bryant's work also, the same concept is much more artistically and expressively embodied in an engraving which has for a long time been convincingly attributed to Blake, the vignette on the last page of the third volume.[31] In this the ark is shown in the form of a crescent with the dove hovering above it. Blake states explicitly as early as 1788 in an annotation to Lavater's *Aphorisms on Man,* "Man is the ark of God" (*K* 82), and this moon-shaped vessel represents for him the salvation of man, through the mercy of God, from annihilation beneath the waters of Ulro. The depiction of a boat in the shape of a crescent moon is found on a number of later occasions, most notably in the third of his illustrations for Dante's *Purgatorio,* "The Angelic

Boat Wafting Over the Souls for Purgation" (PLATE XIV).[32] When we turn to Bryant's text, we shall find the source which links together the ark and the crescent moon, and once more the trail will lead us back to Egypt.

Bryant's basic thesis is that "All the mysteries of the Gentile world seem to have been memorials of the Deluge." [33] In support of this theory he draws upon an extraordinary conglomeration of Grecian, Persian, Egyptian, and other sources, and seeks to demonstrate the universal scope of epic traditions: "The same mythology and the same hieroglyphics were carried as far as China and Japan; where they are to be found to this day." [34] We have already, in connection with the illustration to Darwin's poem, quoted Bryant in reference to the overflowing of the Nile. In the same passage, he continues as follows:

Typhon . . . signified a high altar of the Deity. There were several such in Egypt; upon which they offered human sacrifices . . . But there was another Typhon, who was very different from the former . . . By this was signified a mighty whirlwind, and innundation: and it oftentimes denoted the ocean; and particularly the ocean in ferment. . . . The history of Typhon was taken from hieroglyphical descriptions. In these the dove, Oinas, was represented as hovering over the mundane egg . . . For an egg, containing in it the elements of life, was thought no improper emblem of the Ark, in which were preserved the rudiments of the future world. . . . The Ark was represented under the figure of a ship, *whose extremities were alike.* It was a kind of crescent, such as is exhibited by the new moon; which in consequence of it was made a type of the Ark. . . . For the Moon and the Ark were synonymous terms. Analogous to the above we are informed by Plutarch, that the chief concern of the Egyptians was shewn *at the disappearing of Osiris* . . . which they stiled the interment of the Deity. At this season they constructed by way of memorial a remarkable machine, . . . *an Ark in the shape of a crescent or new moon.*[35]

In addition to this passage, Bryant had already described the Egyptian crescent boat in connection with a discussion of the rites of Amon in the first volume of his work, and both there and in the second volume, from which we have just quoted, there are plates giving no fewer than three views of such a vessel; these are based directly, as indicated in the text and the caption of one of the plates, upon an engraving in the first great illustrated work by an English traveler in Egypt, Richard Pococke's *Description of the East*.[36]

Blake, as Basire's apprentice, was of course familiar with these plates, and from the connections suggested above and his reference to Bryant in his *Descriptive Catalogue* it is now evident that he read the text as well. Indeed, it is tempting to speculate that as he was engraving the small vignette which comes at the end of Volume III he was already thinking in terms which would evolve into his fully developed symbolic vocabulary. When, some forty years later, he came to illustrate the landing of the souls at the base of the Mountain of Purgatory, he again showed the boat in the form of a crescent moon, and indeed the figure of the angel standing within the vessel is strongly reminiscent of another of the plates in the second volume of Bryant's *New System* (see PLATE XV).[37]

Bryant's *New System* thus had an enduring influence upon Blake, supplying him with ideas and suggesting images that were to remain with him throughout his life. It will be recalled that Blake was without formal schooling. It is, therefore, not surprising that the impact of Bryant's work upon a youth of his gifts during the most impressionable years should have been profound. We can imagine him between the ages of seventeen and nineteen engaged in the task of engraving plates for these volumes, the text of which abounds with every sort of reference to classical and to more exotic literary sources—the whole directed toward the end of establishing the truth of the biblical account of the origin of the world and of the early years of human history. With all of its strangeness to a more sophisticated age and to those of wider educational background than young Blake, Bryant's text teems with suggestions for poetic imagery. Blake at this time had no ability to acquaint himself in the original with the classical writers and other sources drawn upon by Bryant. He could, however, and in later years he did, weave the images suggested by Bryant's work into the rich fabric of his own symbolic language, transmuting it in the process with that rare subtlety and poetic insight which were peculiar to his individual and very exceptional genius. The Mundane Egg, the moon-shaped boat, the ark adrift upon raging waters, the barren desert of Egypt with its earliest civilization, its monumental architecture devoted to a funeral cult, its political and theocratic tyranny—such is indeed Blake's World of Generation. The Fall of Los began in "Coldness, darkness, obstruction, a Solid / Without fluctuation, hard as adamant, / Black as marble of *Egypt*" (*BoL* 4:4–6, K 257).[38] The concept of Egypt thus came to serve Blake as a perfect symbol of the Fallen World, and of the state of darkness that comes before enlightenment.

> I also stood in Satan's bosom & beheld its desolations:
> A ruin'd Man, a ruin'd building of God, not made with hands:
> Its plains of burning sand, its mountains of marble terrible:
> Its pits & declivities flowing with molten ore & fountains
> Of pitch & nitre: its ruin'd palaces & cities & mighty works:
> Its furnaces of affliction, in which his Angels & Emanations
> Labour with blacken'd visages among its stupendous ruins,
> Arches & *pyramids* & porches, colonnades & domes,
> In which dwells Mystery . . .      (*Mil* 38:15–23, K 529)

Yet in spite of its seemingly soul-destroying topography and tyrannical laws, the evil of the Fallen World will ultimately become so apparent that man, even in his fallen state, will recognize error and cast it off, thus rendering possible his redemption, which is the miraculous pledge of God's infinite mercy.

> Yet why despair? I saw the finger of God go forth
> Upon my Furnaces from within the Wheels of Albion's Sons,
> Fixing their systems permanent, by mathematic power
> Giving a body to Falsehood that it may be cast off for ever,
> . . . . . . . . . . . . . . . . . . . .
> God is within & without: he is even in the depths of Hell!
>      (*J* 12:10–13, 15; K 631)

Egypt then is a land of bondage—but it is also the land where Moses was miraculously delivered from the waters and saved to lead his people forth to the Promised Land, and it was in Egypt that the Holy Family took refuge when the powers of darkness of this world sought to destroy the Infant Lord. Egypt is, in other words, the meeting place of Contraries, the natural symbol of the World of Generation—barren, filled with the ruined monuments of gigantic human tyrannies but, as is the Fallen World, at the same time a creation of mercy to keep man from falling into the abyss. These then are the implications which Egypt suggests when it figures in Blake's prophetic poems and in the various designs in which the theme of Egypt is introduced.

#### · BLAKE'S DESIGNS BASED ON EGYPTIAN THEMES ·

It has already been established that Egypt became a significant symbol of the Fallen World in Blake's mind during his early years, and continued to have this connotation in the imagery of his later works. In the following pages a number of notable instances will be discussed in which an understanding of the special significance of this concept will contribute to the elucidation of the symbolism underlying a number of Blake's works in various visual media. These will fall into two classes. In one the subject itself, as in the case of various illustrations to the Bible, is specifically connected with Egypt. There is another series of works, however, in which allusion to Egypt and things Egyptian is introduced without dependence upon a direct textual source. Instances of the latter category have already been noted in the case of the two illustrations to Dante, one with its penciled reference to "The Thunder of Egypt," and the other in which sphinxlike figures squat upon closed books. To this class belong also the pencil drawings entitled "The Man Who Built the Pyramids" and "The Egyptian Taskmaster." [39] Both of these are among the series of Visionary Heads sketched for John Varley, and in company with the most notable of this group, "The Ghost of a Flea" (PLATE I), are clearly intended as archetypes of humanity debased by servitude to the tyrannical systems of the Fallen World.

A particularly fascinating and puzzling example of the class lacking any apparent literary source is a relief etching of which but two impressions are known, both in the Lessing J. Rosenwald Collection of the National Gallery of Art, Washington (PLATE XVI).[40] This design has no caption and, unlike the many enigmatic illustrative pages of the Prophetic Books, there is no associated text to provide a clue. Is it a plate which relates to one of the

Prophetic Books but which was never issued with it? A. G. B. Russell in his important catalogue of Blake's engravings, published in 1912, took notice of the similarity of the pose of the figure to that in the design at the top of Plate 6 of *America* and on this basis hazarded a title based upon the text of that page: "Let Him Look Up into the Heavens & Laugh in the Bright Air." [41] Russell also compared the figure with that above the tomb in the well-known "Death's Door," one of the designs made by Blake for an edition of Robert Blair's *The Grave*, first published in 1808.

In many respects, however, the most apt comparison in the present connection is with the design at the head of Plate 21 of *The Marriage of Heaven and Hell*, in which the figure of a nude youth in a very similar pose sits upon desert sand with a skull beneath his left knee. Of particular interest is the fact, noted by Keynes and Wolf, that in some copies a pyramid is visible behind the figure, and in one copy, which there is reason to believe was completed at least by 1794, two pyramids have been painted in the background. [42] This then provides another instance of Blake's association of the theme of Egypt with the Fallen World at an early stage in his career. Stylistically, however, the relief etching relates to Blake's later technique, being closely related to the plates of *Jerusalem*, [43] and also to Blake's own engraving of "Death's Door," the unique impression of which had not yet come to light when Russell published his catalogue. [44]

With regard to the relief etching under discussion, it would seem that for the present, lacking further information, it would be most logical to classify it with a small group of works which Blake issued somewhere between 1818 and 1822. These include *The Ghost of Abel* (dedicated "To Lord Byron in the Wilderness," and dated in the latter year), "On Homer's Poetry" and "On Virgil," and the comments which accompany Blake's engraving of the Laocoön. [45] It is of interest to note that two of these works, the Laocoön plate and "On Virgil," have reference to Egypt in the sense we have come to associate with it as representing Blake's view of the Fallen World.

Israel deliver'd from Egypt, is Art deliver'd from Nature & Imitation.

The Gods of Greece & Egypt were Mathematical Diagrams.

The Spoilers say, "Where are his Works That he did in the Wilderness?
Lo, what are these? Whence came they?" These are not the Works Of
Egypt nor Babylon, Whose Gods are the Powers Of this World, Goddess
Nature, Who first spoil & then destroy Imaginative Art; For their Glory
is War and Dominion. 　　　　　　　　　　　　(*Laoc*, K 776–77)

Sacred Truth has pronounced that Greece & Rome, as Babylon & Egypt,
so far from being parents of Arts & Sciences as they pretend, were destroyers of all Art. 　　　　　　　　　　　　　("On Virgil," K 778)

A reference to Egypt in Berkeley's *Siris*, Blake's copy of which
must have been annotated at about this time according to Keynes
(*K* 923), also produces a remark in similar vein. When Berkeley
observes that "the Aegyptians considered God and nature as making one whole, or all things together as making one universe,"
Blake comments: "They also considered God as abstracted or distinct from the Imaginative World, but Jesus, as also Abraham &
David, consider'd God as a Man in the Spiritual or Imaginative
Vision" (p. 212, *K* 774).

Turning back to the enigmatic print under discussion, it would
seem that the clue must lie in the band of cryptic signs which
divides the plate in the middle. Can we perhaps speculate that
Blake's intention is to portray Fallen Man in the Old Dispensation
and in the New? In the lower section, one sees beside him the heads
of his brutalized Spectre and of his Emanation buried to their
chins in the earth, much in the manner of Egyptian statues buried
in the sand. Man seems to be struggling upwards, but his head
is cut off by a band of hieroglyphs, the "Mathematical Diagrams,"
a schematic representation of rationalism unenlightened by imagination. Among the hieroglyphs we may observe the pyramid,
both in section and in plan, and an arc suggestive not of the
Spiritual Sun of Imagination, but of that other sun which appears
to the rational eye as no more than a round disk of burning gas,
and which Blake described to Henry Crabb Robinson. "I have
conversed with the Spiritual Sun—I saw him on Primrose-hill. He
said, 'Do you take me for the Greek Apollo?' 'No,' I said, pointing
to the sky with my stick, 'that is the Greek Apollo. He is Satan!' " [46]

Turning to the upper portion of the plate, we see Man "deliver'd from Egypt," which is beneath him. While still in his Fallen State, and thus bereft of the distinguishing mark of his Divine Likeness, he has passed beyond the nadir of his Fall. The Spectre beside him has taken on the catlike (or "Tyger"-like) aspect of man's physical violence, and the Emanation in agony "Groans to be deliver'd" (*LJ* 92, *K* 616). However, they are no longer passive, but writhe with tension as they strive to free themselves from the earth. Most promising of all, on Fallen Man's right, or spiritual, side the "rustling bird of dawn" is arising in anticipation of Albion's redemption and awakening.

In closing our discussion of this design, it would seem appropriate to substitute another title for the work to replace "Let Him Look Up into the Heavens." Sir Geoffrey Keynes made the suggestion a few years ago that the familiar design known as "Glad Day" should be renamed "Albion's Awakening." Surely the symbolic meaning of these two works is related, and our divided plate represents two stages of Man in his Fallen State. Prior to his awakening, we see here "The Sleep of Albion."

By contrast to such a work as that just discussed, the theme of Egypt is inherent in a number of biblical episodes which Blake illustrated, and in connection with representations of the stories of Joseph and Moses and the infancy of Christ the introduction of Egyptian references is to be expected. While in certain instances, as in the case of the two pyramids introduced in the background of the water color "Joseph and Potiphar's Wife," [47] such elements apparently serve no other purpose than to suggest the locale, in others one must expect to find overtones of meaning which derive from the symbolism which it has been the purpose of this paper to establish. Some significant instances of this will now be considered in detail.

To take an example from the Old Testament first, we may cite one of Blake's most notable and dramatic water colors, "Pestilence: The Death of the First-Born." [48] The scaled satanic figure which dominates this design is Blake's ultimate realization of the Angry God of This World. As in the engraving for Darwin's *Botanic Garden*, his arms are outspread and from them fire streams down like a torrent while lurid flames surround the figure and reflect upon the billowing cloud of smoke above. In the background on either side of the demon great pyramids loom—emblems of that "ruin of a Part of Nimrod's tower, which I conjecture to have spread over many Countries; for he ought to be reckon'd of the Giant brood" (To Thomas Butts, 6 July 1803, K 824).[49] It is significant to observe, however, that even in this most frightful vision of the Fallen World—for it is evident that the implications of this design go far beyond the mere representation of Egypt in a more literal sense—Blake has introduced the small figure of an angel, who stands in the background within a niche placed between the legs of the monster, quietly surveying the scene.[50] It is thus Blake reminds us that, no matter how monstrous the evil of this world may appear, man must not despair, for God has not forsaken him: "he is even in the depths of Hell!" (J 12:15, K 631).

The commencement of Man's journey through the Fallen World of Generation forms the subject of the next work to be considered, which is "The Hiding of Moses," in the collection of the Huntington Library and Art Gallery, San Marino, California (PLATE XVII).[51] This beautiful water color provides a particularly happy instance of Blake's ability to fuse his own ideas so perfectly with the theme which he is illustrating that one can take the greatest pleasure in the finished design as a work of art without appreciating that, beneath the surface of an apparently literal representation of a text, there resides a wealth of symbolism which is very personally Blake's own.[52]

In reflecting upon this drawing, we should first call to mind the design at the top of Plate 37 of *Jerusalem*, in which the Saviour is shown supporting the form of the sleeping Albion beneath a palm tree, much in the manner in which the mother of Moses is here supported by her husband. The child in the ark among the bulrushes is, of course, representative of every soul as it sets out upon the winding voyage along the river of the Generated World at the instant of its Fall from Eternity.[53] At this moment the palm serves as a reminder of the branches that were strewn before the Lord as He rode into Jerusalem to lay down His life in order that mankind might be redeemed.

Behind the foreground group is a parapet with four steps; these are emblematic of the four stages of the Circle of Destiny. The top step, touched by the branches of the palm of salvation, is Eden. Upon the next step of Beulah stands the Emanation looking back over her shoulder to the Eternal World. The third step represents Generation; over it bends the bulrush, symbol of the Vegetated World. Upon the lowest step squats the Sphinx, bestialized embodiment of the Female Will, gazing down the river towards the Sea of Ulro.[54]

On the far shore of the river we see the material structures of the Fallen World, dominated by the pyramids. These towering monuments loom above the mid-course of the stream, for it is in this stage of man's journey that the forces of materialism become overpowering. Innocence has long since given way to Experience and to the realities of mid-life when "souls are bak'd / In bricks to build the pyramids" (J 31:11–12, K 657).[55] Such was the labor of the Israelites from which, however, it was to be the destiny of Moses to free them, and in the far distance beyond the pyramids one may descry the spires of the heavenly city. Already the far-off hills are faintly illuminated by the first gleams of dawn, the promise that God in His grace will guide man safely through the vale of error to salvation.

A companion to the work just described is "The Compassion of Pharaoh's Daughter: or the Finding of Moses," in the Victoria and Albert Museum.[56] The cradle has reached the bank and the child, who in the previous drawing was asleep, now raises his arms joyously toward the kneeling form of his mother, who offers him her breast. Pharaoh's daughter watches intently, accompanied by two children and two attendant maids. Here again, while the episode as recounted in Exodus is literally rendered in a design of great beauty, one must also interpret it in the context of Blake's particular terminology. This is the beginning of life in the World of Generation, which is "a Creation of mercy & love from the Satanic Void" (J 13:45, K 634). The child is born into the material world in a state of Innocence; he reaches up to embrace the love that will sustain him as a child and in his mature years, for by God's mercy "The daughters of Beulah follow sleepers in all their

Dreams, / Creating spaces, lest they fall into Eternal Death" (*FZ* i:99–100, *K* 267). The Fallen World, just as Egypt, has its threatening monuments of death, but through imagination and love it can become as here a setting of tranquillity and beauty. Once more the palm trees serve as reminders of the love of Christ; to emphasize this connection a very prominent place is given in the foreground to the ibis feeding her young, clearly an association to the traditional pelican as emblematic of the Saviour. For the infant prophet, as it will be for the Infant Lord, Egypt is a place of refuge—so the Fallen World becomes for all men who reject the errors of selfhood and materialism and embrace truth through the power of the Divine Imagination.

> Sweet babe, in thy face
> Holy image I can trace.
> Sweet babe, once like thee,
> Thy maker lay and wept for me,
>
> Wept for me, for thee, for all,
> When he was an infant small.
> Thou his image ever see,
> Heavenly face that smiles on thee,
>
> Smiles on thee, on me, on all;
> Who became an infant small.
> Infant smiles are his own smiles;
> Heaven & earth to peace beguiles.
>                  ("A Cradle Song," 21–32, *SoI; K* 120) [57]

The relationship of the Moses theme with that of the infancy of Christ is best exemplified by a comparison of "The Hiding of Moses" with the water color "The Holy Family in Egypt" in the Metropolitan Museum of Art (PLATE XVIII).[58] It will be noted that in both paintings the palm tree frames the right side of the design and the male figure is placed beside it. Joseph stands with hands clasped in prayer as he worships the nursing child; the branches of the tree form a protecting arch above. The animate created world, represented as at Christ's Nativity by the ass, bows its head before Him. The river again winds away into the distance, but it is further removed. The pyramids in particular no longer dominate the background, but are seen only in the far distance. The dark sky of "The Hiding of Moses," with just the faintest trace of light along the horizon, has now become suffused with the brilliant light of dawn, as the disk of the sun rises over the hill. It is the moment of sunrise and of salvation—the moment when, in Blake's words, "I see an Innumerable company of the Heavenly host crying 'Holy, Holy, Holy is the Lord God Almighty!'" (*LJ* 95, *K* 617).

In Christ's Incarnation the Fallen World of the old Egypt is indeed delivered from bondage. Such is the theme of the Metropolitan Museum's water color. The tempera painting in the Victoria and Albert Museum, "The Virgin and Child in Egypt," [59] presents us with the vision of the Infant Saviour enthroned as Lord of the World of Generation. The palm of salvation serves as the emblem of God's supreme act of mercy in the redemption of the Material World—here symbolized as before by the pyramids, sphinx, and obelisk. The final act, the freeing of the individual soul from the bonds of the Fallen World and its return to its true home in Eternity, is depicted by Blake in a little-known water color in the Royal Library, Windsor Castle, "The Assumption of the Virgin." [60] At either side of an open sarcophagus, which bears a design of palms, three bearded figures kneel in prayer. In the center the Virgin floats upwards, restored at the supreme moment to the radiance of her youthful form. She raises her arms to the celestial vision of her Infant Son and Saviour who hovers above, giving the gesture of blessing and framed within the disk of the radiant sun of Divine Love and Imagination. Behind the figure of the Virgin we find striking confirmation of Blake's association of Egypt with the Fallen World, for her form is silhouetted against a massive hovering pyramid, shown with its point *downward*. By the supreme act of mercy the Material World is completely overthrown at the instant of the redemption of each individual soul. "Whenever any Individual Rejects Error & Embraces Truth, a Last Judgment passes upon that Individual" (*LJ* 84, *K* 613).[61]

The final work to be discussed here is the tempera version of "The Flight into Egypt" (PLATE XIX).[62] This drawing is both the counterpart and the antithesis of perhaps the most impressive of all the Dante series, "Beatrice Addressing Dante from the Car" (PLATE XX), which must therefore be briefly summarized at this point.[63] The episode represented is the first appearance of Beatrice to Dante in the heavenly procession in the garden at the summit of the Mount of Purgatory. In this design Beatrice is enthroned upon a chariot drawn by a monstrous gryphon and surrounded by the fallen forms of the Four Zoas. Three female attendants surround her car. They represent for Dante Faith, Hope, and Charity, but Blake equates them not with the Daughters of Beulah, or Inspiration, but with the Daughters of Memory. One of them is accompanied by five small figures which have the likeness of children, but somehow strangely blended with vegetable forms; they represent the five senses of Fallen Man. Dante to the right bows in submission to Beatrice, who is here to be equated with the Female Will, as made apparent by the wheel of the chariot, which is no ordinary wheel but a vortex emblematic of the Fall into Ulro.

By contrast "The Flight into Egypt" shows the Zoas in their true relationship, when they cease their submissiveness to the Fallen Goddess of the Material World and find salvation in the harmony of the Divine Humanity. In the place of the proud and richly dressed Beatrice upon the chariot, we find the figure of the Virgin riding upon the humble ass. Her Divine Infant is cradled in her arms, His head surrounded by radiant light. Again as in the Dante illustration, two figures go before and two bring up the rear. The six "infant loves" which float beside the Madonna are the counterparts of the vegetated forms in the design to the *Divine Comedy*, but now together with the Holy Infant they serve to remind us of the Seven Eyes of God which watch over Man in his Fall. The angel and Joseph who lead the way are to be thought of as the Zoas of Imagination (Los) and Intellect (the redeemed Urizen appearing as Joseph); they look back at the Divine Vision. The Zoas of Love (Luvah, an angel with wings outspread) and of the Physical Aspect of Man in the Generated World (Tharmas) guard the rear. In the mysterious darkness of the Fallen World, Man goes forward peacefully into the unknown, illumined by the divine grace within him. The depths of Hell are dark no longer, for God not only is without, He is within.

The Four Living Creatures, Chariots of Humanity Divine Incomprehen-
sible,
In beautiful Paradises expand. These are the Four Rivers of Paradise
And the Four Faces of Humanity, fronting the Four Cardinal Points
Of Heaven, going forward, forward irresistible from Eternity to Eternity.

$(J\ 98{:}24{-}27, K\ 745)$

## · BLAKE AND EGYPTIAN ART ·

From classical times the western world has been fascinated by the
remote and alien character of Egyptian culture and art, by its
seemingly timeless antiquity and by the massive scale of its monuments. The Greeks and Romans had come to invest the concept
of Egypt with an aura of mystery which persisted through the
Middle Ages, and which expanded enormously at the time of the
Renaissance, with its love of the emblematic and allegorical. Obe-
lisks which had been brought from Egypt in ancient times were
re-erected and if their hieroglyphs had been obliterated, they were
redecorated with devices outwardly resembling them. Other motifs
relating to Egypt, notably the sphinx, became part of the Renaissance design vocabulary. Side by side there grew up a whole
tradition of mythical writings, linked with astrology and alchemy,
in which things Egyptian were invested with special mystical
significance.[64] We have already seen how Blake was introduced
to Egypt by the writings of Jacob Bryant, whose speculative
mythology grew out of a movement which forms one of the
branches of this tradition. We have also observed the manner in
which Blake absorbed Egypt into his individual allegoric language
and visual symbolism, and on this basis it has been possible to suggest new interpretations of a number of his designs.

By the time of Blake's youth, however, considerable knowledge
of Egypt and its art was already available, both from the published accounts of travelers and through the fruits of systematic
scholarship. Of outstanding significance in the latter class is the
monumental work of Bernard de Montfaucon, *L'Antiquité expli-
quée et representée en figures*, published in five volumes between
1719 and 1724. Important sections of the text are devoted to the
religion of the Egyptians, and there are many plates illustrating

Egyptian sculpture and other antiquities; these were based with varying degrees of fidelity upon original objects in numerous European collections.[65]

Before the middle of the seventeenth century a number of accounts of English travelers in Egypt had appeared, of which the most important are those of George Sandys and John Greaves. The former contains an engraving of the Pyramids and Sphinx which for the first time shows them in accurate relationship. Greaves, the predecessor of Christopher Wren as Professor of Astronomy at Oxford, made highly exact measurements of the Great Pyramid; his account is illustrated by a number of cuts, which include a section showing the interior passageways with surprising accuracy.

A new advance was marked, however, with the publication in 1743 of Richard Pococke's *Description of the East*. This work contains numerous plates and, although the quality and accuracy of these varies considerably, the volume devoted to Egypt presents by far the most complete body of illustrative material available in a work in English at the time. As has already been noted, the three views showing the sacred boat of Egypt which appear in Bryant's *New System* were re-engraved from a plate in Pococke.[66] Even if only an unbound impression was available in Basire's shop to engrave from, the caption beneath the plate in Bryant and references to it in his text would have served to call Blake's attention to Pococke; however, he may well have had the opportunity to examine the complete volume, and from it he could certainly have formed a reasonably valid overall impression of the general character of Egyptian art.

In 1737 and 1738, at the same time as Pococke, though not in his company, Captain Norden of the Danish Navy traveled up the Nile Valley. His *Travels in Egypt and Nubia* was published in London in 1757, the year of Blake's birth, with the assurance of the editor in his preface that "no pains nor cost have been spared to render the English edition as pompous as the original." [67] The work is indeed handsomely and copiously illustrated and, while the majority of the plates are topographical, a significant number are devoted to antiquities.

By the time of Blake's apprenticeship Egyptian motifs had also been adopted into the decorative vocabulary of the designer, and had become part of the same movement of exotic revivalism which gave birth to the vogue for the Gothic and the Chinese. In 1760 Piranesi had introduced the style with his decoration of the Caffè Inglese in Rome, and numerous further designs of amazing richness and inventiveness in this vein are included among the magnificent plates of his *Diverse maniere d'adornare i cammini*, published in 1769. In the *"ragionamento apologetico in defesa dell'architettura egizia"* which introduces this work, Piranesi writes: "What I pretend by the present designs is to show what use an able architect may make of the ancient monuments by properly adapting them to our own manners and customs." Whereas, however, as we have seen, for Blake Egypt was to become suggestive of symbolical connotations, Piranesi utilized Egyptian motifs to purely decorative ends. In fact, in his introduction he is at pains to discourage the prevailing tendency to attribute occult significance to all Egyptian ornament. In speaking of the motifs decorating an Egyptian pillar, he makes this clear. "Now from whence could such a disposition of things . . . take its rise? from the artist's intention of representing a mystery, or of delighting the eye with ornaments? . . . These in my opinion were certainly not Symbols, but in fact the meer [*sic*] ornaments of those stones, which rather belong to architecture than to anything else. Neither ought we to attribute to mystery certain forms of utensils executed with taste, and adorned with flutings, twisting meanders, roses, triglyphs, tetraglyphs interspersed with pateras, or something like them. These are not mysteries, but caprices of the Egyptian artists." [68]

We have dealt so far with sources published prior to Blake's formative years, and from which he might have formed a visual concept of Egyptian art. We must also raise and examine a number of other points: Was Blake ever in contact with anyone who had visited Egypt? To what extent was he familiar with the events, expeditions, and resultant publications which, during the middle and later years of his life, were to advance the knowledge of Egypt so tremendously, and to lay the foundations of Egyptology? What works of Egyptian art could he have known in the original, and is there any evidence that they did in fact influence his own descriptions and manner of representing things Egyptian?

To turn to the first of these questions, it is of especial interest to take note of an exchange of letters between Willey Reveley and Blake. Dating from October, 1791, the year of the publication of the engravings to Darwin's *Botanic Garden*, this ranks as the earliest of Blake's correspondence which has been preserved. The tone both of Reveley's letter and of Blake's reply (*K* 790) is formal. Reveley was at this time engaged in preparing for publication the third volume of Stuart and Revett's *Antiquities of Athens*, and his letter contains an offer of employment in the task of engraving certain of William Pars's drawings for the forthcoming work. Blake at the age of ten had attended a drawing school kept by Pars's brother, Henry; in his reply he accepts the offer, and did in fact execute four plates, published in 1792.[69]

Reveley was an architect and in the capacity of draftsman had visited Egypt in the company of Sir Richard Worsley during the latter's travels in the eastern Mediterranean between 1785 and 1787. Some years later during the nineties, Worsley issued privately a sumptuous publication concerning his travels and collection under the title *Museum Worsleyanum*. In the introduction he speaks of the "drawings made on the spot, with great accuracy, by that ingenious artist, Mr. Reveley." Among the numerous plates in the work, there is a fine view of the Sphinx and the Pyramids bearing the caption "G.[uglielmo] Reveley del."[70] It is indeed possible that the correspondence referred to above may have led to personal contact, and that Blake would thus have had the opportunity of conversing with a fellow artist who had visited and made drawings of major monuments of Egyptian art.

From the days of Pococke and Norden to the end of the century, there were no further significant illustrated publications devoted to Egypt and Egyptian antiquities. During the last thirty years of Blake's life, however, Egypt came to make an impact upon the western European world unparalleled before. The dramatic events of the Napoleonic invasion of 1798, followed swiftly by Nelson's great victory at Abukir Bay, focused the attention of the European and British worlds upon the Nile Valley, and at the same time gave rise to conditions which permitted the recording and study of the monuments of ancient civilization on an unprecedented scale. No longer was knowledge of Egypt confined to what could be derived from the accounts of occasional travelers or the publication of engravings of Egyptian objects which had been in European collections in most cases since early times. The scholars who accompanied the French army and staffed the Institut d'Egypte set up by Bonaparte established the new era of systematic exploration and scientific publication which has ever since characterized modern Egyptology. This was but the beginning of a long series of expeditions of many nations which for the first time gave to the western world a comprehensive knowledge of ancient Egypt. During the first quarter of the century publications appeared containing handsome engravings far exceeding in number and accuracy any pictorial record of Egyptian art previously available. Also in these years many original objects were transported to Europe and the great national collections were instituted. Of the publications, the most spectacular and influential was the official *Description de l'Egypte*, of which the first edition in twenty volumes appeared between 1809 and 1822 (2nd ed., 26 vols., 1812–29). The work has a learned text and nearly nine hundred engravings of high quality, issued in elephant folios. Five of the eleven volumes of plates are devoted to antiquities, and present a magnificent record of all of the major monuments then known from Philae to Alexandria.

The first illustrated publication, however, to appear following the Nile campaign was Vivant Denon's *Voyage dans la basse et la haute Egypte,* issued in 1802. The production of this enormous handsomely designed work, which consists of a volume each of text and engravings, within such a short space of time ranks as a remarkable achievement.[71] The intense interest awakened by the availability of reliable contemporary views of Egyptian topography, life, and antique monuments can be judged by the fact that two independent translations were made into English in the same year. In 1802 and 1803 a number of editions were published in England in a variety of formats, and in the latter year an edition was issued in New York. All of these are illustrated with a copious selection of views re-engraved on smaller scale from those of the original publication.

An intriguing puzzle suggests itself when one examines the list of subscribers, which is given at the end of the text volume of the Paris edition. Headed by the name of the Emperor, it includes numerous ministers of state, crowned heads, princes, and other nobility, as well as ambassadors among whom is listed *"Rufus-King, ministre plénipotentiaire des Etats-Unis de l'Amérique."* The long list that follows contains the names of a number of additional Americans (including Joel Barlow), and quite a few English subscribers are also identifiable. These include nobility, as well as several booksellers specified as *"libraire à Londres,"* and private citizens. Among the latter one is not surprised to find Bekfort [*sic!*]. The name Edwards is also there, otherwise unidentified, as subscriber to one copy on regular paper, and also listed, as subscriber to a similar single copy, is "Blake (W.)."

Could this indeed be William Blake? The idea at first seems preposterous, even more so as we are informed in the advertisement of the English octavo of 1803 that the London price of the original edition was twenty-one guineas. However, a number of further questions suggest themselves. Edwards was in all likelihood James Edwards, the bookseller of Pall Mall, elder brother of Richard Edwards of Bond Street. The latter had been the publisher in 1797 of the unsuccessful edition of Young's *Night Thoughts*, for which Blake had provided the designs. Richard Edwards withdrew from the publishing business in 1799, so he cannot be the "Mr. Edwards" referred to in a number of Blake's letters to William Hayley dating from October, 1803, to the end of 1804.[72] In 1802, the year of the publication of Denon's work, Blake was still at Felpham under the patronage of William Hayley. Hayley had a fine library, and was an ardent collector of books and a student of Romance languages.[73] He might well have sought to acquire such a volume, perhaps using James Edwards as his agent, as the letters cited above show that he was again to do in 1804 when he desired to correspond with Lady Hamilton in Naples in connection with his projected *Life of Romney*. Hayley's name does not appear, however, among those listed in Denon's work. Could his subscription for some reason have been made in Blake's name?

The largest English subscription, in fact exceeded only by that of Bonaparte himself, was by T. Payne, a London bookseller. Payne also had contacts with Hayley, and was the publisher of his *Life of Romney*. Of much greater interest, however, is the fact that the 1803 octavo edition of Arthur Aikin's translation of Denon's work was published by Richard Phillips as a joint venture with Longman and Rees. While Phillips' name does not appear as a subscriber to the French edition, he was to employ Blake as an engraver on a number of occasions, and most notably to figure as the publisher of the 1805 edition of Hayley's *Ballads* with engravings by Blake from his own designs. Blake knew Phillips well and mentions him in a number of letters to Hayley in 1804–5. "Mr. Phillips is a man of vast spirit & enterprize with a solidity of character which few have; . . . he is spiritually adjoin'd with us" (7 Apr. 1804, K 841).[74] Even, therefore, if "Blake (W.)" was in fact another, there is a high degree of possibility that Blake was familiar with Denon, if not in the original at least through Phillips' edition.

In the latter half of the eighteenth century, British explorers, of whom the most important were James Bruce and William George Browne, had continued to contribute to knowledge of the Nile Valley. As was to be expected, this activity increased markedly in the aftermath of the Nile campaign. In the years between the turn of the century and the end of Blake's life, numerous accounts of the area were published in London. For the most part, however, these were the journals of travelers intent primarily upon further exploration of Central Africa. Such information as they provide concerning ancient monuments is thus haphazard and they are of negligible value as sources of illustrative material. Only one work by an Englishman in these years could in any sense be considered a guide to antiquities, William Richard Hamilton's *Aegyptiaca*, which appeared in 1809. A separate atlas volume was published in conjunction with it; however, the plates it contains are few in number and of little interest. For a pictorial record of Egyptian art, England produced nothing during these years even remotely comparable to the French publications.

The arrival of the Rosetta stone in London, where it was placed on display in the British Museum in 1802, marked the beginning of intensive efforts to decipher hieroglyphs. In this task Dr. Thomas Young played a significant role from 1814, which contributed to Champollion's success in 1822. Attention was thus focused upon original objects of Egyptian antiquity, and systematic collecting of them was begun. By 1819 the catalogue of the British Museum listed fifty-six objects in the room devoted to Egyptian sculpture, and the nucleus of this great collection had been formed.[75]

Perhaps the most remarkable episode of English Egyptology during these years was provided by the exploits of a Paduan, Giovanni Battista Belzoni, a man of gigantic strength and stature. Coming to England in 1803, he made a career as a strongman in pantomime and the circus for ten years or so before finding his way to Egypt in 1815, ostensibly as a self-proclaimed expert on irrigation. In Cairo he became friendly with the Swiss-born explorer, John Lewis Burckhardt, who awakened his interest in Egyptian antiquities and provided information which directed the course of his travels. During 1816 and 1817, encouraged at least originally by the British Consul General, Henry Salt, Belzoni organized the transportation of the colossal head of a fallen statue from the Rameseum to the banks of the Nile, from whence it was shipped down the river and eventually reached the British Museum. Belzoni then continued upstream to Abu Simbel, where he directed the clearing of the sand from the façade of the Great Temple and first revealed its interior. On his return journey, he turned aside to explore the Valley of the Kings, where within a short time he uncovered a number of tombs and made his greatest discovery, that of the Tomb of Seti I.[76]

Leaving Egypt in 1819, Belzoni returned to England in 1820. In that year he published his *Narrative of the Operations and Recent Discoveries within the Pyramids, Temples, Tombs and Excavations in Egypt and Nubia,* with an added publication of forty-four plates in the same year, followed by six more in 1822. What brought Belzoni particularly before the London public, however, was the exhibition of his collection at Bullock's Egyptian Hall in Piccadilly. A striking example of the new wave of Egyptianism in architecture and the decorative arts which followed in the wake of the Napoleonic invasion, this building with its pylonlike façade was, of course, highly appropriate for the purpose. Belzoni's exhibition included original objects collected and excavated by him, but its principal feature was a model of the Tomb of Seti I, with two of the chambers reproduced in full scale.[77]

Since his return from Felpham in the autumn of 1803, Blake had resided at South Molton Street, within easy walking distance of the site in Piccadilly opposite the end of Bond Street where the Egyptian Hall was erected in 1812. Belzoni's exhibition opened there in May, 1821, and was on view for a full year. In the course of that same year, Blake removed to Fountain Court, Strand. However, he must certainly have been aware of Belzoni's exhibition, and may very well have visited it. It is also tempting to speculate as to whether he might not have met Belzoni, but of this there is no evidence.

It will, therefore, be apparent that during his entire lifetime Blake had ample opportunity, such as no previous generation could have afforded, to become familiar with Egyptian antiquities from descriptions and engravings, and that he indeed might well have seen a very considerable number of important original objects. However, in spite of the numerous designs executed by him which relate either directly or symbolically to Egypt, there are few indications that he made use of such knowledge. Let us examine briefly the rare instances in Blake's work in which actual comparison suggests itself.

There is only one work by Blake which seeks to give a direct representation of an Egyptian monument. This is an engraving of "A Colossal Statue at Thebes" which appears, accompanied on the same sheet by five other ancient and Oriental objects, upon one of the four plates which Blake executed to illustrate the article on sculpture by John Flaxman in Abraham Rees's *Cyclopaedia*. The plate in question (PLATE XXI) is dated March 1, 1816. The project had been undertaken quite a few years before, for in a letter dated January 2, 1804, Flaxman had written to Hayley concerning another article in the same work, for which Blake also engraved a plate. "I have troubled You, by Mr. Blake, with a Short tract written for Dr. Rees's Cyclopedia, on Basso Relievo, with one of the prints referred to at the end of the article, the rest are not yet engraven." This letter is of interest, for it links Blake not only with the project as engraver, but also with Flaxman's text.[78] Flaxman and Blake had, of course, been friends for many years; undoubtedly Blake must have read his encyclopedia articles and discussed them with him. That on sculpture contains an excellent section on Egypt, especially when one considers the limitations imposed by the nature of the article and the early date at which it was written. It also cites sources, thus providing us with important evidence as to the works on the subject to which Blake's attention would most probably have been directed. After listing various ancient authorities, Flaxman continues: "The best modern books on this subject are Pococke's Voyages, Savary's Travels in Egypt, Norden's Egypt, Denon's Egypt; to which may be added, the most magnificent work of ancient and modern Egypt, now publishing in Paris." In addition, in the course of his text Flaxman refers to the descriptions of various modern travelers, including Bruce and "M. Ripaud."

As we would expect, all the best illustrated works on Egypt are included, from Pococke to the *Description de l'Egypte*. "Savary's Travels" refers to *Letters on Egypt* of Claude Etienne Savary, the English edition of which was published in 1787. This work is not illustrated, nor is the *Report of the Commission of Arts to the First Consul Bonaparte, on the Antiquities of Upper Egypt* by Louis Madeleine Ripault, issued in London in 1800. Blake's engraving for Flaxman's article, based most probably on a drawing provided by Flaxman himself, poses something of a puzzle, for it agrees with none of the plates which the artist or engraver could have known.[79] Pococke and the *Description* show frontal views, which indicate the figure between the legs as being much smaller than those at the sides, whereas here they are all of equal height.[80] Norden and Denon show the figure only from the sides, and the central figure thus cannot be seen. All the versions differ in various details, more particularly with regard to the face and headdress. It is evident, however, that the figures were so badly damaged as to make many details largely conjectural, and to a greater or lesser extent the illustrators interpreted freely and had few inhibitions about supplying features which had been obliterated, as indeed Pococke frankly acknowledges. The best explanation of the version engraved by Blake seems to be that it is based upon the pose of Pococke's figure, with details of the headdress and side figures modified in accord with the representation of them in Norden, and with the small central figure increased to correspond in size with those which flank the base. There is nothing to indicate dependence upon the more recent sources of Denon or the *Description*, although even the latter had been issued by the time the plate was published.

While one would normally not expect Blake to copy details literally in his own designs, it might be thought that perhaps he might do so under exceptional circumstances, as for instance when intending to represent hieroglyphic writing. There are in fact two examples which we can cite. The first is very brief and is to be found on the cover of the book which appears in the lower left of the Visionary Head, "The Man Who Built the Pyramids." While hieroglyphic in appearance, it clearly signifies "15 Degrees of Cancer ascending," which is inscribed in pencil at the lower right.[81] More extensive is the band which separates the two halves of the enigmatic relief etching which has been discussed at length earlier (PLATE XVI). While clearly intended to simulate hieroglyphs, it is of course not copied from any ancient inscription, but is made up of elements suggestive of Blake's own symbolism. The pyramid and square of the Fallen World, the segmented disk of the Urizenic rational sun which has replaced the Divine Likeness, the worm (or serpent) of Vegetated existence, and the moon of Beulah can all be recognized. The two horizontally striped figures may represent the "coverings of Earth," which when shaken off reveal at the exact center of the design the Divine Sun of Imagination, flanked by the birds of Inspiration. Thus we are reminded that even at the nadir of the Fall of the "divided Albion" the redeeming power of God's love remains and from "within that Center Eternity expands" (*Mil* 31:48, *K* 520), emblematic of the promise of Divine Pity. "Pity must join together those whom wrath has torn in sunder" (*J* 7:62, *K* 626).

The above discussion will make it clear—as indeed one would expect—that Blake, although undoubtedly familiar with Egyptian art through personal contacts, published sources, and original objects, never rendered it in a direct manner. It is typical of him that, from the time of his early reading of Jacob Bryant onward, he adopted Egypt as a concept of his symbolic vocabulary, both verbal and pictorial, in a completely imaginative sense. The same may be said of the vast body of hermetic and other mystical writings which had for centuries woven a spell of the fabulous around Egypt and things Egyptian. It is well known that Blake was familiar with a number of these, and yet again he adapted them exclusively to his own ends. Out of fable, as well as out of the fruits of scholarship, he forged his personal vocabulary of vision. And why, we may ask, should one expect that he would look outside himself for any knowledge of the monuments of Egypt when he had direct experience of them? For he tells us "The Artist having been taken *in vision* into the ancient republics, monarchies, and patriarchates of Asia, *has seen* those wonderful originals called in the Sacred Scriptures the Cherubim, which were sculptured and painted on walls of Temples, Towers, Cities, Palaces, and erected in the highly cultivated states of *Egypt*, Moab, Edom, Aram, among the Rivers of Paradise" (*DesC*, No. 2; *K* 565). With respect to Egypt he could indeed say, as on another occasion he did concerning the Last Judgment, "I have represented it as I saw it" (*LJ* 68, *K* 605).

# Philosophical and Religious Transmutations

ASLOOB AHMAD ANSARI

# Blake and the Kabbalah

As in regard to Christianity, so in the case of Judaism, Blake's attitude is marked by a high degree of ambivalence. He is unsparing
in his denunciation of what he conceives to be the ethical de-
cisiveness and rigor of the Jewish law; he is no less insistent and
unequivocal in his assertion that "The Return of Israel is a Return
to Mental Sacrifice & War" (*J* 27, "To the Jews"; *K* 652), and
"The Hebrew Bible & the Gospel of Jesus are not Allegory, but
Eternal Vision or Imagination of All that Exists" (*LJ* 68, *K* 604).
But whatever the adequacy of the Blakean stance regarding the
value of comparative religions and however incontrovertible the
fact that Blake's genius is radically Christian rather than Jewish
in inspiration, Blake, like Milton, did owe something to the Hebraic
sources.

Blake's is a highly complex and original mind and it is considerably intrigued by the act of transvaluation of the established
norms and patterns. This is manifest, more than anywhere else,
in his interpretation of the personality of Christ. Being an anti-
nomian, Blake could not feel enthusiastic about the Decalogue,
which he might very well have called the "Abomination of Desolation." But he must have been attracted by the mythic content
of the kabbalah which expressed itself as a vengeful conquest of
its upholders against the custodians of the rabbinic wisdom. The
esoteric tradition known as the kabbalah, embodying mainly the
*Zohar* and later reinterpreted and refined upon with irrefragable
logic and ingenuity by such persons as Isaac Luria and Moses
Cordovero, has a mythic structure and a romantic appeal. Blake's
interest in this tradition may have been stimulated by his reading
of Swedenborg and the mystical doctrines of Jacob Böhme and
the innumerable translations of the *Zohar* that were in vogue in

the eighteenth century. He had also started learning Hebrew, as is evident from a letter he wrote to James Blake (30 Jan. 1803, K 821). To uncover a few strata of significances common to this bold body of speculation and the cosmic drama enacted in Blake's major epics, therefore, promises to be a rewarding enterprise.

The fundamental basis of being in the *Zohar* is the ineffable, hidden Deity who begins as Ain, or the Negative Existence, and moves on to become Ain Soph—the Positive or the Unbounded and the Illimitable One. When He proceeds from the latent to the active mode and emerges from the state of repose and passivity to one of awakening, He is apprehended as Man and appears in his creative totality as the First Man. This primary, ontological being, called Adam Kadmon, bears a close resemblance to Blake's Universal Man who is constantly designated as Albion. Albion represents the original, unsundered unity of Manhood in the eternal world:

> Four Mighty Ones are in every Man; a Perfect Unity
> Cannot Exist but from the Universal Brotherhood of Eden,
> The Universal Man, to whom be Glory Evermore.   Amen.
>
> (*FZ* i:9-11, *K* 264)

Adam Kadmon is presented in the kabbalah in purely anthropomorphic terms. The central plan of creation is visualized as occurring in the various configurations of light emanating from the different bodily organs of the Deity. The first glimpse of a "tribal Deity of personal characteristics," glorying in his power of oppressing other nations and posturing hypocritically as benevolent, we come across fairly early in the figure of "the Father of the ancient men" ("Earth's Answer," *K* 211), who is obviously modeled upon Blake's concept of the Jehovah. This is elaborated in the Prophetic Books in the figure of Albion, and all the traits of the Jehovah are projected into him. The tendency towards anthropomorphism, latent in Blake from the very beginning, becomes more and more pronounced as he comes to create his shadowy, gigantic, archetypal beings. Blake was strongly averse to harboring the conception of the abstract and transcendent God of the deist construction. God was not to be sought according to him "in the distant skies" but in "a pulsation of the artery." The progress from the notion of a personalized God to that of the protoplastic man, moved by human passions and desires and having a recognizable physiognomy, is a perfectly logical one.

In the prefatory note to *Jerusalem*, chapter ii, entitled "To The Jews," Blake makes an important statement: "You have a tradition, that Man anciently contain'd in his mighty limbs all things in Heaven & Earth: this you recieved from the Druids." And this is followed by: "But now the Starry Heavens are fled from the mighty limbs of Albion" (*K* 649)—an observation also made in *Milton*, Book the First. The tradition referred to here is obviously the kabbalistic tradition, and the flight of the "Starry Heavens" implies the fallen condition of the archetypal man. The belief that man comprehended within himself all that belongs to heaven and earth meant of necessity that the primordial man was possessed of enormous proportions, and there was little difference between what was within and what was without, for all was one. This notion came to be inverted later, and the Elizabethan opposition between macrocosm and microcosm was a form of this inversion. According to the Aggadah the fall of the all-embracing man brings about the fall of the entire universe and the latter henceforth enters the "stage of diminution." The process of the physical shrinkage of man is underlined by Blake thus:

> The Eye of Man, a little narrow orb, clos'd up & dark,
> Scarcely beholding the Great Light, conversing with the ground:
> The Ear, a little shell, in small volutions shutting out
> True Harmonies & comprehending great as very small:
> The Nostrils, bent down to the earth & clos'd with senseless flesh
> That odours cannot them expand, nor joy on them exult:
> The Tongue, a little moisture fills, a little food it cloys,
> A little sound it utters, & its cries are faintly heard.
>
> (*J* 49:34-41, *K* 680)

Little by little, according to Blake, the entire being of Albion suffers contraction, and the four senses, corresponding to the four Zoas, decline in point of receptivity and sharpness so that he is reduced to the mere effigy of what he was in Eternity. The picture of Albion undergoing disfigurement and left derelict in the surrounding universe is etched in with complete vividness at two places in the Prophetic Books:

> The Eternal Man sleeps in the Earth, nor feels the vig'rous sun
> Nor silent moon, nor all the hosts of heaven move in his body.
> His fiery halls are dark, & round his limbs the Serpent Orc
> Fold without fold encompasses him . . .
>
> (*FZ* viii:507–10, *K* 354)

> In a dark & unknown Night:
> Outstretch'd his Giant beauty on the ground in pain & tears:
> His Children exil'd from his breast pass to and fro before him,
> His birds are silent on his hills, flocks die beneath his branches,
> His tents are fall'n; his trumpets and the sweet sound of his harp
> Are silent on his clouded hills that belch forth storms & fire.
>
> (*J* 18:45–19:4, *K* 641)

This clearly underscores the point that the primeval man is now a homeless creature, out of tune with the entire object-world he once assimilated within his cosmic framework.

The idea was earlier mentioned that the Deity moves from the state of undifferentiated oneness to that of multifariousness and that this transformation is effected through the agency of the Sephiroth. In other words the Sephiroth are the bond of connection between the abyss of the Godhead and the world of matter. The intellectual ancestry of this idea has been traced back to Proclus and the Neo-Platonic thesis in general, according to which the One has emanated downwards through an ordered hierarchy. Contrary to the Christian view of creation, which makes inevitable the notion of a supreme God who fashioned the universe for reasons of His own, the Neo-Platonists affirm that the visible universe is an immanent offspring and image of the Divine.

According to the kabbalah the dynamic totality of God has been projected into ten Sephiroth which together subsume its entire potential. The Ain Soph, referred to earlier, throws out a ray of its light which assumes the form of the first Sephirah, known as Kether (Crown). Kether, which is equivalent more or less to the First Cause, contains within itself two hypostases; the male one is called Chokmah (Productive Reason), and the female is called Binah (Discerning Intellect). Kether thus functions as the uniting intelligence for these two. At a lower point in the scale of emanation are to be found Chesed (Mercy) and Geburah (Rigor), and both these find their point of convergence in Tiphereth (Beauty). Still another pair of entities, male and female, are designated as Netzach (Firmness) and Hod (Splendor), and these are brought together by Yesod (Regenerative Power), which has an explicit phallic signification. The tenth and last Sephirah at the bottom is Malkuth (Kingdom), also known as Shekhinah, or the Bride, and she receives the influx of all the other Sephiroth. Thus it is apparent that the nine Sephiroth, excluding the Shekhinah, form a trinity of triads as against the one Neo-Platonic triad constituted of the One, the Nous (Mind), and the Soul. Each one of the kabbalistic triads has within it a duad of opposite sexes which are brought into contact by the uniting intelligence. Furthermore each triad, like the components of the Neo-Platonic triad, is active in relation to the one below it and passive in relation to the one above it. Moreover, parallel to the horizontal division of the Sephiroth, there is a vertical one also which is constituted of Kether, Tiphereth, Yesod, and Shekhinah. These Sephiroth or hypostases are not to be treated as the fixed and frozen attributes of God but as the channels through which God steps out of His jealously guarded seclusion. They may as well be regarded as stages in the actualization of the intradivine life, and the Sephirotic tree, which, according to Mathers,[1] has much in common with the tree *Yggdrasill* of the Scandinavians, may be accepted as an emblem of the theogonic process. Putting it differently, one may also uphold that the ten Sephiroth, with male and female counterparts, constitute in their totality and unity the archetypal man, and the Sephirotic tree, corresponding to various bodily organs, is an image both of the human organism and of the entire cosmos.

It may not be a wild surmise to suggest that combining the Neo-Platonic idea of emanation and the notion of the kabbalistic Sephiroth, Blake evolved a highly exciting structure of psychology. Thus Albion, the Universal Man, is visualized as made up of four essential powers or faculties which, taking the cue from the four beasts Ezekiel saw by Chebar's flood, Blake calls Zoas. These four primal components of the human psyche are Urthona which is equivalent to Intuition, Urizen which stands for Reason, Luvah which is synonymous with Passion, and Tharmas which represents the energy of the Instincts. Each of these basic impulsions has a corresponding Emanation—a female counterpart—and these have been designated as Enitharmon, Ahania, Vala, and Enion respectively. Generally speaking, the Emanation represents the principle of repose and stability as related to the exuberant and tempestuous life of the Zoas. The complete integration and understanding between a particular Zoa and its Emanation is a prerequisite of the achievement of psychic wholeness and well-being. Rejecting this essential and happy communion, the Zoa is turned into a Spectre—a sterile, truncated, monstrous being who preys upon the vitals of the living and is condemned to nourish its own isolated, solipsistic existence:

> These spectres have no [Counterparts], therefore they ravin
> Without the food of life. Let us Create them Coun[terparts;]
> For without a Created body the Spectre is Eternal Death.
> (*FZ* vii:408–10, *K* 330)

Moreover, each Zoa must develop an attitude of sympathy and affectionate commingling towards its Emanation rather than behave in a superior or disdainful way because the Emanation in fact represents the totality of loving relationships. Similarly, if the Emanation fails in reciprocity and tries to exert its baneful influence over the male, she is turned into the Female Will. The latter, very much like the Spectre, is a dark, frustrating, nihilistic force which blocks completely all channels of living dialogue and fruitful commerce between the two.

The relationship of God with Shekhinah in the kabbalistic doctrine offers a close parallel to that of Albion with Jerusalem in Blake's myth. Shekhinah may more or less be equated with the Soul in the final reference to the Deity, and Jerusalem, too, has the status of the genuine Emanation—as opposed to the spurious one, Vala—in relation to Albion. She has been variously interpreted as Liberty, Imagination, Brittannia, "the daughters of inspiration in the aggregate," and the "Indwelling Glory." But broadly speaking she might be treated as Soul, and the symbol of eternal womanhood. Soul in Neo-Platonic philosophy has been looked upon as feminine in character whereas Intellect is frequently referred to as the male principle. And there is a feminine trait both in the kabbalistic Shekhinah and in Blake's Jerusalem. Since Malkuth, or Shekhinah, is conceived of as having an intimate, organic relationship with God—and Jerusalem has been alienated from Albion only as the result of a major crisis—this argues for the presence of a feminine element in God Himself. Furthermore, light as an emblem of the soul may be traced back to many and earlier systems of thought. Light imagery is the recurrent imagery in both the *Bahir* and the *Zohar*. In the original condition, that is, before man was tainted with sin and thus suffered disfigurement, his body or "vestment" was still of the nature of light, and the Divine countenance shone brightly in it. Conforming to the same tradition, Blake makes it abundantly clear, firstly, that Jerusalem, as an essential substratum of personality, finds its habitation in every man's bosom and, secondly, that being the finest invisible substance that permeates every fiber of man's make-up, it can be apprehended only as light:

In Great Eternity every particular Form gives forth or Emanates
Its own peculiar Light, & the Form is the Divine Vision
And the Light is his Garment. This is Jerusalem in every Man,
A Tent & Tabernacle of Mutual Forgiveness, Male & Female Clothings.
(*J* 54:1–4, *K* 684)

Human souls, kabbalistically speaking, are the sparks of light which fly forth and scintillate from the beard of Macroprosopus—the dense, insupportable light of Divinity.

The notion of the true or universal Form is of signal importance in Blake. Man is possessed of both an inner and an outer self, the inner self constituting the ideal to which the outer one should endeavor to approximate. The outer self is a mere husk or covering which has to be sloughed if the inner one is to come into its own. It is also the repository in which must be sought the genesis of all spiritual and ethical values. In the context of the fallen conditions of life this self lies submerged under the debris of materialism, and salvation in the Blakean universe is bound up with uncovering and resuscitating it. Like the Platonic Soul, and even more emphatically and insistently, this inner self has the Wordsworthian aura of grace or consecration about it. Broadly speaking, the "Form" of anything is its true image or archetype, and it should be preserved in its state of pristine wholeness and integrity. In a passage of surprising audacity and breath-taking excitement, Blake identifies this truly human Form with the most important segment of personality:

> Thus Milton stood forming bright Urizen, while his Mortal part
> Sat frozen in the rock of Horeb, and his Redeemed portion
> Thus form'd the Clay of Urizen; but within that portion
> His real Human walk'd above in power and majesty,
> Tho' darken'd, and the Seven Angels of the Presence attended him.
>
> (*Mil* 20:10–14, *K* 502)

Later in *Jerusalem* Blake highlights how this inmost essence of personality remains unchanged because it has an element of incorruptibility about it:

> Learn therefore, O Sisters, to distinguish the Eternal Human
> That walks about among the stones of fire in bliss & woe
> Alternate . . .                              (*J* 49:72–74, *K* 680)

The same truth is seen differently thus: "In Eternity one Thing never Changes into another Thing. Each Identity is Eternal" (*LJ* 79, *K* 607). There is a striking parallelism between this approach to the quintessential self and what is designated in the *Zohar* as the "interior shape":

Those lights are formative agents in the lower world to perfect the shape of all those who are included in the name of man. This is the name given to every interior shape; and thus every shape which is comprised in this extension is called man, which properly indicates man's spirit, emanating from the realm of holiness, to which his body is a vestment, as we read, Thou clothest me in skin and flesh of man implying that the real man is within and the flesh which is his body is only a vestment.[2]

Thus the "real" or "eternal" Human or "Eternal Identity" in Blake and the "interior shape" of the kabbalistic conception both place emphasis on the potential self at the center which is circumscribed by the spurious one lying at the periphery. And the real spiritual quest of man, therefore, is tantamount to rediscovering this archetype and preserving it untarnished by the incrustation of materiality.

The kabbalistic version of the Christian Fall is to be found in the inharmonious functioning of the different triads on the Sephirotic tree which have been named earlier. The doctrine of equilibrium and balance is fundamental to the kabbalah. At the very beginning of *The Book of Concealed Mystery*, a good deal is implied by the pregnant phrase—the lack of "equilibrium of balance." I am inclined to believe that this is what partly constitutes and explains the fact of evil as a metaphysical reality in the universe. Isaac Luria conceives of the Sephiroth as vessels and not as attributes, and these are unable to endure the inrush of the Divine Substance. He, therefore, upholds that chaos and evil necessarily follow the breaking of the shells.

In his view of the Fall Blake follows the kabbalah rather than the Bible. He rejects outright the familiar, orthodox pattern of crime and punishment and provides us with a psychological myth of the Fall. The Fall for Blake involves both maladjustment and coercion in the primal relationships of the Zoas. It is tantamount to the internecine and utterly self-destructive series of struggles in which the Zoas are engaged in order to bring about one another's downfall. Urizen's attempt to dislodge Urthona from his northern kingdom, Luvah's possession of the Horses of Light which of right belonged to Urizen, Albion's effort to appropriate Vala to himself—all these are clear instances of mythic displacement. In fact, the Prophetic Books are a dramatic enactment of the calculated moves and countermoves, the discords and rivalries, the renewed conflicts and intrigues hatched by the Zoas, and the consequent tension and anarchy which reign supreme in their universe. Another interesting facet of this upheaval is the estrangement which occurs between the Zoas and their Emanations. As remarked earlier, every Emanation is the reservoir of the restorative potential of its corresponding Zoa, and whenever a particular Zoa, in sheer wilfulness or apathy, throws out his creative counterpart, he unwittingly brings upon himself incalculable disaster. The Prophetic Books are replete with bickerings, skirmishes, and loud threatenings of one Zoa against the other as well as with the heart-rending lamentations of the passive Emanations against their aggressive and egocentric male partners. Implicit in the lamentations is the longing to call for a truce and to be reunited in blissful co-operation and reciprocal understanding and harmony, in the absence of which the Zoas are turned into hermaphroditic entities—indefinite, monstrous, and completely dehumanized. The Fall has, therefore, been visualized in terms of a twofold process.

Though the exact reasons for the Fall are by and large shrouded in mystery in Blake as well as in the kabbalah, yet there is one particular of it which finds explicit mention in both. We are told in the *Zohar* that this catastrophe ensued when Adam contemplated only the later Sephirah-Shekhinah—and mistook it for the whole of the Godhead. Thus instead of penetrating the totality, he isolated a part of it and equated it with the whole, favoring it therefore above the other components. This situation finds an exact parallel in Blake in the incestuous involvement of Albion with Vala, who is anyway not his genuine counterpart. Broadly speaking Vala is a Negation and not a Contrary as far as Albion is concerned, and she also symbolizes the material aspect of sex as opposed to the spiritual one which is represented by Jerusalem. By this reckless adventuring Albion concentrates on the idea of sex in isolation from an implicit sexuality.[3] Vala is the natural counterpart of Luvah, and by his infatuation with her and consequent rejection of his own proper Emanation, Albion is guilty of a double crime which comes as a rude shock to the denizens of Eternity:

> Among the Flowers of Beulah walk'd the Eternal Man & saw
> Vala, the lilly of the desart melting in high noon;
> Upon her bosom in sweet bliss he fainted. Wonder siez'd
> All heaven; they saw him dark; they built a golden wall

Round Beulah. There he revel'd in delight among the Flowers.
. . . . . . . . . . . . . . . . . . . . . . .
Many sons

And many daughters flourish'd round the holy Tent of Man
Till he forgot Eternity . . .          (*FZ* vii:239–43, 251–53; *K* 326)

As a consequence of this unaccountable usurpation of an emanative principle other than one's own and of mistaking a part of reality for its entire corpus, Albion implicates himself in the imbalance into which the pattern of things in the eternal world is thrown.

The processes of materialization and externalization follow quickly in the wake of the Fall. "What is within" is "now seen without" (*FZ* ii:55, *K* 281); the knower and the known are visible as distinct and separate from each other; and the upward and the downward, whose identity[4] is insisted on so repeatedly by all mystical doctrines, now stand unrelated. Blake speaks time and time again about the rocky substances of the material world as well as of the process of hardening of what was so malleable in the world of Eternity. Both according to the kabbalah and according to Blake, everything in the unfallen world was enmeshed and intertwined with everything else, and all levels of being formed links in a consecutive chain. Hence what was spontaneous and flexible becomes hard and rigid, what was inward becomes exteriorized, and what was unified and coherent becomes discrete and inharmonious. The living dialogue between creatures of the earth, the cementing force which held together the different strata of being, man's sense of interrelatedness with the cosmic environment—all these suffer disruption.

A Rock, a Cloud, a Mountain,

Were now not Vocal as in Climes of happy Eternity
Where the lamb replies to the infant voice, & the lion to the man of years
Giving them sweet instructions; where the Cloud, the River & the Field
Talk with the husbandman & shepherd.          (*FZ* vi:134–38, *K* 315)

With the Fall God also ceases to be immanent and becomes remote and transcendent.

Vala, who in Blake represents the limitations of the feminine perceptions, is also emblematical of the phenomenal world. This is brought out in Albion's forthright colloquy with her:

> Is not that Sun thy husband & that Moon thy glimmering Veil?
> Are not the Stars of Heaven thy children? Art thou not Babylon?
> Art thou Nature, Mother of all? (*J* 34:7-9, *K* 660)

Blake is fully sensitive to the dangerously seductive appeal of Nature, and on that account he perhaps regards her as an illusion. She has only a quasi reality and a shadowy existence. The fact that she is not possessed of a self-subsistent being but depends on something exterior to her is communicated thus:

> Vala is but thy Shadow, O thou loveliest among women!
> A shadow animated by thy tears, O mournful Jerusalem!
> Why wilt thou give to her a Body whose life is but a Shade?
> Her joy annd love, a shade, a shade of sweet repose.
>
> (*J* 11:24-12:2, *K* 631)

According to the kabbalistic doctrine Nature was a spiritual substance in the eternal world but became materialized and degraded in the context of the fallen conditions. Furthermore, though, philosophically speaking, the phenomenal world is brushed aside by Blake as the mere fabric of a dream, yet in moments of rare lucidity and perceptiveness he concedes it some degree of existential reality. It is also significant that at the very end of *Milton*, Book the First, Blake calls Nature a "Vision of the Science of the Elohim." Scholem defines *Elohim* as "the union of the hidden subject *Mi* and the hidden object *Eleh*" and continues that "Elohim is the name given to God after the disjunction of subject and object has taken place, but in which this gap is continuously bridged or closed." [5] This paradoxical view of nature, namely, that nature is something which is only an illusion, and also something which partakes of the semblance of reality if the gaze of the false Vegetated Eye is dispensed with, is implied, I think, in the forementioned *Milton* quotation and the reference to the Elohim. This finds striking confirmation in the following lines from the *Zohar:*

"Therefore He carved out (*that is, hollowed out a space by which He might flow in*) and instituted proportions in Himself (*in as many ways as the Lights of His Understanding could be received, whence arose the paths of the worlds*), and spread out before Him a certain veil (*that is, produced a certain nature, by which His infinite light could be modified, which was the first Adam*)." [6]

Speculation regarding the emergence of the physical world is generally found at the center of all religious and mystical systems of thought. The orthodox Christian view is that God created the world out of chaos, and hence the divine act of creation is an act of benevolence and love. The rabbinical theology makes a slight but subtle variation upon it and upholds the notion of *creatio ex nihilo*. Ibn Gabirol also subscribes to the same view and seeks to explain grades of angelic and planetary worlds with assistance from Aristotelian concepts of matter and form. The kabbalistic mystical doctrine makes a clean sweep of the traditional verbiage and insists upon the notion of creation out of "Nothing" which, one may hasten to add, is not so much a "creationist" as an "emanationist" theory. For the mystics "Nothing" does not connote nonexistence but the inmost Divine Being or Reality itself. It is the undifferentiated point of origin of all phases of living or the spectrum in which the isolated units of light are constellated. Hence creation out of "Nothing" involves for all intents and purposes either creation out of the Divine Being or refraction of the divine radiance into prismatic glasses or vessels which may contain it. Isaac Luria, among the Safed kabbalists, offered a unique and radical modification of this doctrine by propounding the notion of *Tsmitsum*. He starts with the assumption that if God is everywhere and encompasses everything, then a created universe is unthinkable. An act of creation postulates, therefore, God's withdrawal into Himself, and He thus engenders, out of His own plenitude or vacuum, something which is known as pleroma or primordial space. Into this space God sends out a ray of His infinite light, and this ray is the seed which quickens and fertilizes the eternal womb and gives rise to the appearance of phenomena as we know them. This gesture of contraction is an act of judgment and limitation, which has to be posited before we concede the existence of anything other than the Deity Himself. It is, therefore, obvious that this highly speculative doctrine involves effort and conflict on the part of the Supreme Being and presupposes the notion of something which, like a cistern, is emptied of part of its supernal content and then is filled up again with whatever it is made to contain later.

Blake will have none of this—neither the Christian nor the kabbalistic interpretation squares well with his distinctive metaphysics. In *A Vision of the Last Judgment* he declares unequivocally:

Many suppose that before the Creation All was Solitude & Chaos. This is the most pernicious Idea that can enter the Mind, as it takes away all sublimity from the Bible & Limits All Existence to Creation & to Chaos, To the Time & Space fixed by the Corporeal Vegetative Eye . . . Eternity Exists, and All things in Eternity, Independent of Creation which was an act of Mercy. (*LJ* 91–92, *K* 614)

Blake does not lend credence to the hypothesis of a state of chaos and solitude because he is convinced that life in the Eternal World or the Garden of Eden was one of perfection and ideal serenity, and it was characterized primarily by the pursuit of intellectual warfare. Life in the phenomenal world, on the contrary, is symptomatic of the Fall, but the act of creation is, nevertheless, governed by a providential purpose. The Fall started the process of petrifaction of the expansive energies which flowed uninhibited in the Eternal World as well as the process of gradual decrease in translucence. God in His infinite mercy set bounds beyond which this precipitate descent could not go, and thus the created world provides a bulwark against it. The Limit of Contraction came to be represented by Adam and that of Opacity by Satan; and thus Adam and Satan, coexistent within the larger cosmic pattern, exercise an equally beneficent function:

And first he found the Limit of Opacity, & nam'd it Satan,
*In Albion's bosom, for in every human bosom these limits stand.*
And next he found the Limit of Contraction, & nam'd it Adam,
While yet those beings were not born, nor knew of good or Evil.
(*FZ* iv:271–74, *K* 304)

The Divine hand found the Two Limits, first of Opacity, then of Contraction.
Opacity was named Satan, Contraction was named Adam.

(Mil 13:20–21, K 494)

Thus whereas in the later kabbalistic speculation the Deity imposes a limitation on His own Self, in Blake's scheme of things He devises these two Limits in order to ensure man's continued existence in the face of utter annihilation which would otherwise have been his irrevocable destiny.

Another important concept which is crucial to Blake's proposed solution of the human predicament is that of the Seven Eyes. It may have been derived from the Bible (cf. Zechariah and Revelation) where the Seven Eyes of the Lord are mentioned, but it occurs in the *Zohar*, too. "This is that which is written, Zech. iv. 10: 'Those Seven are the eyes of Tetragrammaton going forth throughout the whole earth.'" [7] Also: "Like as it is written, Job xxxiv. 21: 'Because His eyes are upon the ways of man'. And when they are illuminated with that whiteness, then they behold all the lords of truth, in order to do good unto the world because of them; and every glance (*of those eyes*) is benevolent towards Israel." [8] The Seven Eyes are equivalent to the sequence of "states" along the track of Experience, and by living through them man may hope to emerge out of the tangle of error and reach up to the ideal of Truth. The track of Experience has been established by divine mercy with the purpose of enabling man to overcome spiritual darkness which encompasses his sojourn in the terrestrial world, and this is also the implied meaning of the *Zohar* quotation: "and every glance (*of those eyes*) is benevolent towards Israel." The ultimate beneficent purpose of this divinely instituted machinery as well as the nature of the Eyes themselves is defined by Blake thus:

> Then they Elected Seven, called the Seven
> Eyes of God & the Seven Lamps of the Almighty.
> The Seven are one within the other; the Seventh is named Jesus,
> The Lamb of God, blessed for ever, & he follow'd the Man,

Who wander'd in mount Ephraim seeking a Sepulcher,
His inward eyes closing from the Divine Vision . . .

(*FZ* i:553-58, *K* 279)

And those in Eden sent Lucifer for their Guard.
Lucifer refus'd to die for Satan & in pride he forsook his charge.
Then they sent Molech. Molech was impatient. They Sent
Molech impatient. They Sent Elohim, who created Adam
To die for Satan. Adam refus'd, but was compell'd to die
By Satan's arts. Then the Eternals sent Shaddai.
Shaddai was angry. Pachad descended. Pachad was terrified.
And then they sent Jehovah, who leprous stretch'd his hand to Eternity.
Then Jesus came & Died willing beneath Tirzah & Rahab.

(*FZ* viii:398-406, *K* 351)

The Seven Eyes may as well be regarded as successive stages
in the history of man's evolution, starting from the beginning and
leading up to the Christian dispensation. Lucifer is the angel who
fell because of pride; he is ignorant and uneducated, and is the
symbol of solipsistic consciousness. Molech is the one to whom
the first-born were sacrificed; he, therefore, is the Executioner—
the blind force that will brush aside anything that impedes its
movement. Elohim are the judges who define guilt and give error
an outward and tangible form. Shaddai—the all-powerful—still im-
putes guilt to others; he is domineering and yet is overcome by
anger and weariness. Pachad represents bewilderment at the horrors
of injustice as well as the nadir of human apathy and hostility.
Jehovah is the Jewish God who formulates the moral system and
enforces it with rigor; he is leprous because this system seeks its
sanction from the gruesome image of the doomed man. The cycle
of vegetative existence is climaxed by the epiphany of Jesus who
abrogates the law of guilt and punishment, proclaims the Everlasting Gospel of Forgiveness of Sin, and opens the radiant path
towards Eternity. It is also worth noticing that three of the terms
employed by Blake, namely, Elohim, Shaddai, and Pachad, may
have been taken directly from the kabbalah.

It was pointed out in the preceding pages that the relation of
God or Adam to Shekhinah finds its parallel in the relation Albion

bears to Jerusalem. Perhaps it would not be straining the implications of the Lurianic concept of *Tsmitsum* too far if one were to maintain that the exile of Shekhinah is modeled upon God's exile from His own Self. When Jerusalem is separated from Albion in Blake, she falls into ruins. This is emblematic of the fact that the firmest bond of unity in the primeval world has snapped and consequently utter chaos finds its way into the structure of the universe:

> Jerusalem, his Emanation, *is* become a ruin,
> Her little ones *are* slain on the top of every street,
> And she herself led captive & scatter'd into the indefinite.
> (*FZ* i:545-47, *K* 279)

One of the most dramatic moments in Blake's poetry is Tharmas' realization of his estrangement from his Emanation—Enion—for this turns him into a "dark Spectre." This shattering of instinctual unity unleashes the forces of anarchy, and the blundering, stalking, dehumanized figure strikes us with a sense of primitive horror. This skeletal being is urged on to reachieve his human lineaments, but his efforts are frustrated:

> But from the Dolorous Groan one like a shadow of smoke appear'd
> And human bones rattling together in the smoke & stamping
> The nether Abyss, & gnashing in fierce despair, panting in sobs,
> Thick, short, incessant, bursting, sobbing, deep despairing, stamping, struggling,
> Struggling to utter the voice of Man, struggling to take the features of Man, Struggling
> To take the limbs of Man . . .                    (*FZ* iii:153-58, *K* 296)

No less pathetic is the lamentation of the "ever-weeping melancholy Shadow" (*J* 53:26, *K* 684)—Jerusalem—when she loses all vital and cohesive contact with Albion:

> My brother & my father are no more! God hath forsaken me!
> The arrows of the Almighty pour upon me & my Children!
> I have sinned and am an outcast from the Divine Presence!
> My tents are fall'n! my pillars are in ruins! my children dash'd
> Upon Egypt's iron floors & the marble pavements of Assyria!

I melt my soul in reasonings among the towers of Heshbon.

(J 78:31-79:3, K 719)

My fires are corrupt, my incense is a cloudy pestilence
Of seven diseases! Once a continual cloud of salvation rose
From all my myriads, once the Four-fold World rejoic'd among
The pillars of Jerusalem between my winged Cherubim.

(J 79:56-59, K 721)

I walk in affliction. I am a worm, and no living soul!
A worm going to eternal torment, rais'd up in a night
To an eternal night of pain, lost! lost! lost! for ever!

(J 80:3-5, K 721)

This nostalgic note forcefully reminds us of what has been said in later kabbalism about Shekhinah weeping in exile, namely, that she is "the beauty who no longer has eyes." Similarly, one may conclude that the reunion of God and Shekhinah constitutes the meaning of redemption in the kabbalah just as the reuniting of Albion and Jerusalem is one of the surest signals of the attainment of paradisal bliss in the Blakean universe.

Since the Fall in the sense of dispersion or dislocation is the ineluctable fact of experience, the way back to an integrated functioning of the Zoas, each with the other, and the reciprocal interrelationship between these and their corresponding Emanations, is the ideal of psychic wholeness which is well worth achievement. The internecine conflicts among the Zoas may be resolved once the value of synthesis in the economy of the human organism is firmly grasped. It may be stressed that Blake's view of the Fall, unlike that of Milton, is psychological rather than moral or theological. At the moment both the macrocosm and the human psyche are in a broken state, and the sundered unity of manhood can be repaired by an act of accommodation and understanding. This ideal is set forth by Blake with impassioned eloquence as the one which is well worth trying and struggling for:

If Gods combine against Man, Setting their dominion above
The Human form Divine, Thrown down from their high Station

In the Eternal heavens of Human Imagination, buried beneath
In dark Oblivion, with incessant pangs, ages on ages,
In enmity & war first weaken'd, then in stern repentance
They must renew their brightness, & their disorganiz'd functions
Again reorganize, till they resume the image of the human,
Co-operating in the bliss of Man, obeying his Will,
Servants to the infinite & Eternal of the Human Form.

(*FZ* ix:366–74, *K* 366)

The kabbalistic idea of *Tikkun* comes very near to this effort at reconstitution: "all things of which this world consists, spirit as well as body, will return to their principle, and the root from which they proceeded." [9] The scattered lights of Ain Soph have to be gathered together in order that the primeval unity may be re-achieved and the soul return to its pristine state of nobility and felicity. It is also possible that these lights, during the process of dispersion, got mixed up with *Kellipoth*, or "shells"—equivalent to the forces of evil—and have to be winnowed and purged of all filth and dross.

Attention was drawn earlier to the close resemblance between the kabbalistic Adam Kadmon and Blake's Albion. This resemblance rests, among other things, on the fact that both are androgynous—combining the male and the female within themselves. Blake was firmly convinced that the androgynous protoplast was sexless and the differentiation of sex was one of the clearest symptoms of the Fall: "Humanity knows not of Sex: wherefore are Sexes in Beulah?" (*J* 30:33, *K* 656). When souls were incarnated they came to be distinguished by their different sexes. And it is the same in the *Zohar:* "And therefore, is it written: 'ATH HADM, *Ath Ha-Adam*, the substance of man,' because it comprehendeth equally the Male and the Female, for to the word ADM, ATH is subjoined, so as to extend and exaggerate the species which is here produced. Most assuredly here therefore is it as Male and as Female." [10] Also: "Thus in this Adam androgyneity hath commenced to be disposed when it hath been formed in its disposition. It hath commenced from His back." [11] Since all souls pre-existing in the world of emanations were androgynous in the original state, sex as a potent factor contributing to division was not yet in evidence. The sense of shame and the enforcement of the moral taboos—symptoms of a masochistic approach to life and experience —are the inevitable consequences of the loss of innocence and the acceptance of a naturalistic mode of existence as an ultimate. "The Sexes sprung from Shame & Pride, / Blow'd in the morn; in evening died" ("To Tirzah," K 220). According to the *Zohar* also separation, in terms of sex, designates death and disintegration. The birth of a separate will and of selfhood and an insistent and clamorous assertion of individuality followed logically in its wake. In Eternity nothing of this sort was permissible, and hence the institution of marriage did not exist either. "In Eternity Woman is the Emanation of Man; She has No Will of her own. There is no such thing in Eternity as a Female Will . . ." (*LJ* 85, K 613). It also follows as a corollary that, in the restored order of things, sex as a mode of self-assertion and separated wills shall cease to exist, and man will be a truly unified being again.

Geographical spaces, which have partly a local and partly an esoteric and personal significance, are a function of meaning in Blake, as is also the sense of direction. Of special importance in this connection is the idea of quaternity (the four points of the compass, the four universes, the four Zoas, and the four modes of perception) and the symbolism of right and left. In the *Zohar* we read: "There is no left in that Ancient Concealed One, but all is right." [12] The principle of evil is thus located in the left side and that of good in the right side, and this is corroborated by a later entry: "and Benignity is from those on the right, but Severity from those on the left." [13] Blake retains this implication of the two directions:

> Terrified at Non Existence,
> For such they deem'd the death of the body, Los his vegetable hands
> Outstretch'd; his right hand, branching out in fibrous strength,
> Siez'd the Sun; His left hand, like dark roots, cover'd the Moon,
> And tore them down . . .                                          (*FZ* ix:5-9, K 357)

It has, however, been pointed out by Mueller[14] that the left side does not itself represent evil before it puts itself in the place of the right. Its function is to supplement the absolute good of the right side, and only when it presents an antithesis to it does it turn into "the other side"—something which is inimical to existence. It may be of some interest to remind ourselves here that St. Augustine propounded a similar doctrine when he identified evil with the act of hindering the good, and thus deprived it of any positive status.

Corresponding to the four modes of life, Blake outlines in his poetry the existence of the four universes, Eden, Beulah, Generation, and Ulro. Eden is the supreme world in which life is all perfection and harmony and in which the distinction between the Creator and the created is meaningless. It is also the world in which the Zoas lived a life of complete integration, and there was here no room for either striking an attitude of superiority or employing any coercion against one another. Immediately below Eden is the region, called Beulah, in which "Contrarieties are equally True" and where these are united in an unforced wedlock. It is also the region which is watered by kindly and pitiful impulses, and in which those incapable of the creative fury of eternal strife in Eden find a resting-place and a moment of sustainment. Next to it comes Generation in which the disjunction between the Subject and the Object is a patent fact. Though the world of Generation represents a steep decline from the ideality of Eden, yet it is governed by a providential purpose and is designated as the "Image of Regeneration." At the very lowest rung of the ladder is Ulro, in which the Contraries exist in a warlike embrace; it represents the phase of complete petrifaction in which everything wears a rocky appearance and the life-giving fountains of energy stand frozen. Whatever enters here becomes sexual and vegetative. These four universes of the Blakean cosmology find a near equivalent in the four kabbalistic worlds which are designated as Atzilouth, Beriah, Yetzirah, and Asiah. The first one, like Eden, is Archetypal—perfect and immutable; the second one, like Beulah, is Creative and is an emanation of the preceding one; the third one, like Generation, is Formative, where intelligent and uncorporeal beings exist; and the fourth one, like Ulro, is purely Material. These four universes represent successive stages of the emanation of the Ain Soph. They are all inhabited by the Sephiroth who represent degrees of Spirituality and refinement in a descending order of purity. Hence the last one, the Asiatic world, is the world of "shells," or evil spirits, and unlike Generation, or Yetzirah, is incapable of being redeemed. The archetypal and the material worlds—Atzilouth and Asiah— like Blake's Eden and Ulro, represent the polar opposites. Whereas the former is the direct emanation of the Deity and is full of angels of the purest substance, the latter, on account of its imponderable heaviness and materiality, represents the nadir of existence.

Following the Neo-Platonic tradition, Blake believes that the archetypal world contains images of things and events which are created and unfolded in the nether regions of the world. Though he does not subscribe to the idea of the Supersoul, of which the individual souls are only fragmented or atomic substructures, he does believe firmly that the transcendental world contains semblances of things existing here below:

All things acted on Earth are seen in the bright Sculptures of
Los's Halls, & every Age renews its powers from these Works
With every pathetic story possible to happen from Hate or
Wayward Love; & every sorrow & distress is carved here,
Every Affinity of Parents, Marriages & Friendships are here
In all their various combinations wrought with wondrous Art,
All that can happen to Man in his pilgrimage of seventy years.
(J 16:61–65, K 638)

One finds an interesting analogue to this in the idea of the cosmic "curtain," described in the *Book of Enoch*, on which is inscribed the pre-existing reality of forms and images of every event and passion which is to be unfolded and actualized in the world of here and now. Blake also remarks on another occasion: "There Exist in that Eternal World the Permanent Realities of Every Thing which we see reflected in this Vegetable Glass of Nature" (*LJ* 69–70, K 605). And this finds an exact echo in the kabbalah: "The lower world is made after the pattern of the upper world: everything which exists in the upper world is to be found as it were in a copy upon earth: still the whole is one." [15]

NORTHROP FRYE

# Blake's Reading of the Book of Job

Blake's Job engravings and paintings have often been commented on, and never more lucidly than by the subject of this *Festschrift*. But one aspect of Blake's great work could perhaps be discussed a little more fully. Everyone realizes that Blake re-created the Book of Job in his engravings and was not simply illustrating it. At the same time he appears to be following the book with some fidelity, and his attitude toward it, in striking contrast to his attitude toward Dante's *Commedia*, seems to be on the whole an attitude of critical acceptance. He remarked, apropos of Homer, that "Every Poem must necessarily be a perfect Unity," but the rest of the sentence suggests that the *Iliad* is not "peculiarly so": in other words, the perfect unity is only potential in the poem itself, and is really achieved by the reader. The extraordinary sense of unity that one feels about the Job engravings, considered as a series, indicates that Blake succeeded in creating this unity out of his reading of the Book of Job. Hence it may be worth attempting some conjectural reconstruction of the reader's "vision" of Job that preceded the final re-creation in the engravings.

In the first place, the Bible as a whole was to Blake an epic of the fall and redemption of man: man loses his paradisal garden with its trees and water of life early in Genesis and gets it back at the end of Revelation. One thing that Blake clearly saw in the story of Job was a microcosm of the whole biblical story. This was the chief reason for the relatively few definite changes that he makes from what is in the text, the most obvious of which is his altering of the character of Job's wife. In the Book of Job the wife is a Delilah figure, a temptress who suggests that Job renounce his integrity, and this is how Blake depicted her in earlier illustrations of the book. But when the Book of Job is thought of as a miniature Bible, Job occupies the place of Adam or Israel or Blake's own Albion, the symbolic figure of humanity, and Job's wife thus becomes the Eve or Rachel who must form a part of his redemption. In *Jerusalem* Albion's wife, Brittannia, is a very shadowy character: the main theme is the restoration to Albion of his daughter Jerusalem. This emphasis on the restored daughter (apart from the link with *King Lear*, whose three daughters are among the daughters of Albion) was doubtless derived from a parallel emphasis in the Book of Job, as illustrated in Blake's twentieth plate. Similarly, the three friends are almost wholly demonic in Blake's illustrations, assimilated to the threefold accuser figure who runs through all Blake's work from the "Accusers of Theft, Adultery and Murder" to Hand in *Jerusalem*, and who is identified with the three accusers of Socrates (*J* 93) and, probably, the three witnesses against Faithful in *The Pilgrim's Progress*. It is said of the friends, in a verse quoted on Blake's Plate 8, that "they sat down with him upon the ground seven days and seven nights, and none spake a word unto him: for they saw that his grief was very great" (Job 2:13). Seven days of silent sympathy from friends who are at least not fair-weather friends, and have nothing to gain from visiting Job in his destitution, are surely on the credit side of any moral ledger. But when we think of Job as continuously martyred humanity, it is hardly possible to see in the friends anything but representatives of the continuous social anxiety, the Theotormon complex, so to speak, that makes human misery constant by trying to rationalize and explain it away in every crisis.

The Book of Job has a formidable literary reputation, but it is not easy to make sense of it as it stands. It begins with the astonishing scenes of Satan in the court of God, where Satan has the role, always central to his nature, of the accuser of mankind. He suggests that God has set things up in such a way that he can't lose: if he rewards obedience, he gives man so powerful a motive for being obedient that service of God becomes merely a conditioned reflex. What Satan is really raising is the issue of man's free will.

Under the conventional view of the law, as accepted by Job's friends, in which God sends rain and sunshine on the just and storms and drought on the unjust, man has no real power of moral choice, and God has not yet succeeded in creating anything more than an automaton. The friends' view of providence is easily refuted by experience, but there are two equally easy ways of countering this. One is to say that God's ways are inscrutable when they appear to be merely insane on such premises; the other is to assume that this providence will manifest itself in another world, from which no evidence ever leaks out. Hence for Blake the religion of Job's friends is socially as strongly established as it ever was, except that its basis has tended to shift somewhat from "Honesty is the best policy" to "Maybe it doesn't seem so now, but you just wait." Satan may be the accuser of mankind, but if he had not stated his case so sharply in the opening of the Book of Job it is a question how either Judaism or Christianity could ever have developed. The latter is centered on a martyred God and the former on a chosen people which is also a homeless and frequently persecuted people, hence both are radically opposed to the kind of wish-thinking that Job's friends represent, however much of it they accept or compromise with in practice.

Job's friends are better poets, and have more flexible minds, than one would imagine from Blake's pictures, but it is true that they keep revolving around the central point in their whole system of values: somehow or other it must be a crime to be unfortunate, otherwise God is not a just God. The suppressed premise here is that God administers both the human moral law and the physical natural law, but it never occurs to them to doubt this. Hence in all their gropings after some explanation for Job's plight that will make imaginative, if not rational, sense in their terms, the one explanation that they are too pious even to speculate about is the one that has already been given to the reader. The account of God's having left Job to fight alone in order to win a wager with Satan hangs sardonically over all their debate.

The three friends, we are told, ceased to answer Job "because he was righteous in his own eyes" (Job 32:1). But Job is not really righteous in his own eyes: he is merely convinced that there is far too great a disproportion between what has happened to him and anything he could conceivably have done, when considered as a crime and punishment situation. Better a God wholly indifferent to moral values than so insufferably stupid a God as the one the friends are forced to appeal to. Job's friends cannot shake his convictions without beginning to disturb their own, so the discussion comes to a deadlock. Elihu then breaks in impatiently to overwhelm Job with the eloquence of what he has to say "on God's behalf" (36:2), but although his powers of eloquence are considerable, he succeeds only in restating the earlier arguments. Then God himself answers Job out of the whirlwind and asks: "Who is this that darkeneth counsel by words without knowledge?" (38:2), meaning apparently Elihu, and we wait for the definitive revelation to which the whole drama seems to have been leading up.

God is also quite a good poet, if not as good as Elihu, whom he paraphrases extensively, but nonetheless we feel uncomfortable about the way in which he triumphantly displays a number of trump cards that seem to belong to a different game. He begins by asking Job a long series of rhetorical questions which have a hectoring and bullying sound to them. The general theme is: Were you around when I made the world, or do you understand all about how it was made? No? Well, then, why are you raising doubts about my administrative competence? This is followed by poems on two beasts, Behemoth and Leviathan, which appear to be hyperbolic descriptions of a hippopotamus and a crocodile. They are remarkable poems, but we wonder about their relevance to Job's boils and murdered children. Job replies meekly that he has "uttered that I understood not; things too wonderful for me, which I knew not. . . . Wherefore I abhor myself, and repent in dust and ashes" (42:3, 6). God then appears to say, in effect, "Well, that's better," and forthwith restores him to prosperity. Nothing further is said about Satan, so that Job, unlike us, learns nothing about the original compact. No wonder that Bernard Shaw should speak of the ignoble and impertinent retort of God at the end of the Book of Job, or that Shaw's black girl, on her way to seek

God, should find the God of Job one of the lowest possible forms of religious experience.

The Book of Job starts with much the same problem as that of Plato's *Republic*. In Plato also justice is related to the extreme case of one who suffers nothing but misery and humiliation by persisting in justice. Like Plato, too, the author of Job uses the dramatic form of dialogue. Socrates builds up dialectically, step by step, a picture of a just human community, asks whether such a community does or is likely to exist, is told probably not, and then remarks that the wise man will live according to the laws of this ideal human community regardless of the kind of world he actually does live in. His superb and brilliant performance is, in the broadest sense, a comedy: this is the comic vision of human life, where we are led up to, and by implication inspired by, a glimpse of a community in which everyone lives happily ever after, even if we do not leave the theater in exactly the same condition. The myth of the Christian Bible, ending as it does in apocalyptic vision, is comic in the same sense. In the Book of Job we recognize at first a tragic and existential counterpart to Plato, a discussion following out the irony of the human situation until it reaches the point that we now call the metaphysical absurd. The Book of Job is technically a comedy by virtue of Job's restoration in the last few verses, but the comic conclusion seems so wrenched and arbitrary that it is hard to think of it as anything but a wantonly spoiled tragedy.

The simplest answer is to suppose that the Book of Job, begun by a colossal poetic genius, then fell into the hands of a superstitious editor whose own attitude was a cruder version of that of Job's friends, and who twisted one of the world's profoundest poems into an obscurantist tirade against the use of the questioning intelligence in matters of religion. Something like this could have happened: there are signs of nervous editing, as in so many parts of the Bible, and it is impossible to say how far they have gone. But such a hypothesis is of little practical use to anyone, least of all Blake. The version we have is the only one that exists, and the only one that has influenced later literature and religion. Even Blake could hardly have reconstructed an Ur-Job, and anyone faced with Blake's task clearly has to make more sense of the total structure of the poem as we have it than this account of it has so far made.

In the first place, of course, the comic conclusion, the restoration of Job to prosperity, would not seem arbitrary to Blake, or for that matter to anyone who was thinking of the story of Job as an epitome of the story of the Bible as a whole. In the total story Adam loses his garden and is led back to a restored garden which is also a city: this means, according to Milton, that he loses paradise as a physical environment and regains it as an inner state of mind, the latter being "happier far." Similarly Job, as Blake sees him, begins in the state of Beulah, the pastoral repose of Plate 1, and ends in the apocalyptic Eden of Plate 21, where the musical instruments have been taken down from the trees and the sheep are waking up. Through suffering Job passes from obedience to law to the service of freedom. The former is symbolized by the sacrificial altar in front of Plates 1 and 21, with its significant inscriptions about the importance of outgrowing the moral and ritual aspect of religion which sacrifice represents. The genuine form of sacrifice, called in Blake the annihilation of the Selfhood, is the real subject of Plate 18. But for the Christian myth that Blake, like Milton, is using, Job's restoration is possible only as a result of a redemptive act, the Incarnation of God as Man. Clearly there must have been, for Blake, something in the final revelation to Job that we have missed, something with an effective redemptive force.

We said earlier that the assumption underlying the religion of the three friends was that moral and natural laws are administered by the same God. For Blake, of course, this was "natural religion," and nonsense. Nature to him was the state of experience, indifferent to human values and exhibiting no sense of design or purpose beyond an automatic and mechanical one. Anyone who associates human and natural law is trying to make the latter the model of the former, eliminating everything unpredictable from human behavior and with it everything that makes for a free and creative human community. Persistently through history man has projected his gods, thrown shadows of himself into the objective, which in this context means the alienated, world. He continually tries to invent a God who is a philosophical first cause, a personal guarantor of the mindless order of nature, who will be some variant of the old man with the compasses lowering over *Europe* as the idol of all the eighteen centuries of "Christian" tyranny. As long as an obedient moral life is associated with a comfortable physical one, this deity may look providential and benignant. But when the crunch comes he turns into Satan, the sense of littleness and futility that makes us accept any kind of misery as somehow ultimately just, or, at least, inevitable. Thus for Blake Satan and the God he consults with at the opening of the book are two aspects of the same God. Satan is clearly younger than God, and they seem to be related much as Father and Son are in *Paradise Lost,* God being the weak, sick *dieu fainéant* of Plates 2 and 5 resigning his power to his own demonic Messiah. Many years earlier Blake had remarked in *The Marriage of Heaven and Hell* that "in the Book of Job, Milton's Messiah is call'd Satan" (Pl. 5, *K* 150). Blake here was thinking partly of the Son's activity in spoiling his own creation in Book X of *Paradise Lost* (technically Sin and Death spoil it, but the Creator cannot abdicate responsibility so easily), and then destroying it altogether in the Flood.

This pattern of age followed by youth is repeated later when Elihu takes over from his three elders. By turning dialogue into monologue he is trying to consolidate their confused and variable notions of natural religion into a single closed system of fatalism. This of course is why he is shown pointing to twelve stars, representing the cycle of the zodiac, with his left or sinister hand in Plate 12. Elihu here has much the same role as that of Newton in *Europe:* he is a spokesman of natural religion so fully articulate that he overreaches himself and blows his whole system, in more than one sense, sky-high.

If this analysis is so far sound, it throws a very different light on God's speech to Job at the end. Perhaps all the rhetorical questions about the creation are designed, not to bully Job into an uncritical submission, but to warn him off from looking in the wrong direction for his redeeming power. Job's instinctive tendency is to search for the *cause* of his calamities. There may be something in his previous history, or in that of his family (cf. Job 1:5), which was a fatal but unconscious sin, like the sin of Oedipus. As Job refuses to believe in any such cause, the friends give up and Elihu takes over. Under Elihu's influence Job is carried back to the conception of a transcendent power from which everything good or bad proceeds. Elihu is of course also preoccupied with the perennial theological chess problem of how to account for evil without involving God in it. But still the argument runs: If God does seem to be the author of evil, his power is too great to be questioned; which, if true, is still the impotent and unredeeming truth that does not satisfy Job. Two opposed attitudes, however, have been developing through the drama. Elihu, pointing to the stars in Plate 12, insists: "Look upon the heavens & behold the clouds which are higher than thou" (cf. Job 35:5). But in the hymn to wisdom which forms part of Job's speech in chapter 28, it is said: "Neither is [wisdom] found in the land of the living. The depth saith, It is not in me: and the sea saith, It is not with me." God comes down on the side of Job and not Elihu. The implication of what he says is, in effect: Don't look into the objective world to find me: I'm not there. Even if you carried your search to the mainsprings of creation, you would find no help there. The answer to the question of how you can get out of your calamities is not concealed in the question of how you got into them. This last point brings the Book of Job closer to Blake's view of the Fall than even the story of Adam in Eden, where the Fall results from a breach of contract, reassuring to theological lawyers but something of an obstacle to poets, including even Milton. We notice that Blake's later accounts of the Fall, notably the one in *Jerusalem* 29, echo Job rather than Genesis.

If we are right, it looks as though Blake's vision of Job was a pretty drastic overhaul of the original, for this seems to imply that the God of the opening scenes with Satan and the God who answers Job out of the whirlwind are opposed principles, whereas the text clearly regards them as the same God. And yet in Blake they are really the same God too. The true God for Blake is the creative imagination of man, the eternal Jesus whose religion is the Everlasting Gospel, and all false gods are the shadows projected by this imagination into the outer world. Job's progress, as Blake sees it, is from a God projected into the sky, an amiable Providence who cannot survive the first disasters of experience, to the recovery or resurrection of this God in Job's own mind. The metaphor of a lawsuit hangs over the entire book: Job keeps trying to identify his prosecutor and to call on his advocate (the word translated "redeemer" in 19:25). He eventually finds that the former is the ghost of the latter.

For Blake the God who is man's mind and the narcissistic reflection of this God in nature have faced each other in every age of history. The tendencies in man to be "idolatrous to his own shadow" and yet continually to recover his own creative powers alternate like the pillar of cloud and the pillar of fire in the Exodus story. In *A Vision of the Last Judgment* Blake speaks of "That Angel of the Divine Presence mention'd in Exodus, xiv c., 19 v. & in other Places; this Angel is frequently call'd by the Name of Jehovah Elohim, The 'I am' of the Oaks of Albion" (80–81, *K* 610). The Angel of the Divine Presence is the existential reality, or "I am," of God, who when projected into the outer world becomes the deified order of nature. In the latter situation two characters in Blake are identified with this Angel: Laocoön, strangled by the serpents of reasoning, and the God of Job in Plate 2, about to resign in favor of Satan. The verse in Exodus that Blake refers to reads: "And the angel of God, which went before the camp of Israel, removed and went behind them; and the pillar of the cloud went from before their face, and stood behind them." This suggests the Angel coming the other way, from the outer world into the human consciousness, and thereby making possible, for Israel, the great feat of crossing the Red Sea, escaping from Egypt, and achieving its identity as a community.

The "whirlwind" out of which God answers Job is thus, for Blake, closely akin to, perhaps identical with, the "vortex" in *Milton* which takes Milton from "Heaven" to earth, earth being of course the only place where "Heaven" can be actualized. Milton enters Blake's left foot, but ordinarily, when the projected God becomes the real one, the Word of human imagination, what he enters is the ear, which is also a kind of vortex, called "labyrinthine" in *Jerusalem*, and described in *The Book of Thel*, in a very different context, as a "whirlpool fierce to draw creations in" (6:17, *K* 130). In the margin of Plate 12, the lowest point of the series, marking the consolidation of error which is necessary before it can be thrown off, we see the sleeping Albion with his emanations rising into the sky and becoming the withdrawn and alienated universe of Satan. In the margin of Plate 13 we see the "Eyes" of God forming a single gigantic "whirlwind" in which the God speaking to Job is Job's contemporary, so to speak. In Blake's symbolism there are seven Eyes, of whom Jehovah and Jesus are the sixth and seventh, but actually every "Eye" is Jesus, the divine and human Logos, when imaginatively used. In the parallel between the Job engravings and the tarot trumps suggested by Professor Damon (*Blake Dictionary*, s.v. "Job"), the thirteenth occupies the position of Christ the Hanged Man, the archetypal martyr whose ordeal eventually turns into triumph. In Plate 17 the God whom Job finally sees is clearly Christ, and the verses from the Gospel of John quoted at the bottom indicate that the only possible visualized form of God is the Son of Man.

In both the poem itself and in Blake a strong emphasis is thrown on the destroyed and reintegrated *community* of Job. This is essential for that aspect of the symbolism in which Job represents not simply *a* man but mankind as a whole. And yet Job has to be an individual too, for Satan's assault on him is part of a struggle between alienation and identity in which the former carries its conquests up to the very last stronghold of the latter, which is the individual consciousness. Everything Job has, as distinct from what he is, disappears into the illusory satanic world of time. He is alienated from his own body by his boils, and from society by the accusing or "Elect" friends, leaving Job himself in the isolated position of the "Reprobate" prophet, the scapegoat driven like Elijah into the wilderness, with only his wife to represent the "Redeemed." Finally Elihu, pointing to the stars so far above him, alienates him from his earlier view of God, who is now wholly replaced by the accuser. With the turning point of Plate 13 the community starts rebuilding again, extending to a risen God in Plate 16, the friends in Plate 18, and a still larger community in Plate 19.

This ambiguity between Job as individual and Job as social being or patriarch is of a kind central to all mythical structures of this descent-and-return shape. The suffering Job, we said, must be an individual, but when we think of the restored Job as an individual continuous with his previous sufferings, difficulties arise. The origin of the Book of Job appears to have been an ancient folk tale preserved in the prose beginning and ending of the book we now have, and in such a folk tale the restoration of Job as an individual can be accepted without question. But for a work so profound as the existing book, restoration could only be the arbitrary act of a deity quite separate from Job, and a somewhat vulgar act at that. That is, the restored Job would have to lose his memory to feel that three new daughters could "make up for" the murdering of the previous daughters. To give the restoration any point, we must allegorize the individual Job, as all commentary, including this one, is obliged to do to some extent. Otherwise, we appear to be assuming that when Job improves his state of mind or his theology, his misery disappears too, which takes us back to the point at which the book began, and makes the book itself pointless. To say that Job is restored in a different world from the world of his sufferings is more logically consistent, but considerably impoverishes the human significance of the story.

The general critical principle involved here is that in a descent-and-return mythical structure the individual descends; the community returns. Temptation, alienation, despair, decisive choice, death itself, are ordeals that only the individual can carry to their limit. But only a re-created society, like the one that crystallizes in the final scene of a comedy around a hero's marriage, can fully experience the sense of a brave new world. In Plate 20 Job's arms, outspread over his daughters, show that he with his daughters forms part of a larger human body, so that although the objective order from which his calamities came has been annihilated for Job, the calamities being depicted on the walls "In the shadows of Possibility," as Blake says in *Jerusalem* (92:18, *K* 739), Job's renewed state is not a subjective one. This ambiguity of "human body," which may be an individual or a society, is involved in the contrast between the natural body which dies and the spiritual body which rises again. Job has a "vile body" given over to boils, but it is in his "flesh" (Job 19:26) that he sees God, the subject of Plate 17.

The dialectic between the existential and the projected aspects of God which Blake extracts from his text is accompanied by a parallel dialectic between two aspects of Satan. For Blake, Satan does not disappear from the action after the beginning, nor does Job, as we suggested earlier, really fail to learn the truth about the origin of his calamities. Satan returns to the action in the form of the two monsters, Behemoth and Leviathan, whom God points out to Job as the climax of his revelation. The Satan of the opening scenes is the regent of the universe, the prince of the power of the air, the controlling power of nature as nature really is, indifferent to human values, as full of death and disaster as of life, and caring nothing for the individual. Job suffers not because of anything he has done but because he is in this condition, as all of us are. Satan achieved his power through God's permission, or, to come closer to Blake, through the inevitable collapse of all human efforts to unite the vision of innocence, of the world as created and protected, with the "contrary" vision of experience. Such efforts, as we remarked earlier, look plausible only to those who happen to be both moral and prosperous. But this state is purely a matter of temporary luck, and Job's sufferings exemplify a principle often referred to elsewhere in Blake, that if we stay too long in Beulah it turns into Ulro.

Job in his original prosperity is an imaginative child: but his childlike state of innocence turns into experience and his vision of innocence, like the child's, is driven into the depths of his mind, where it becomes a helpless but still defiant part of his "integrity," a bound Orc. Satan's world is a world in which everybody is an object or thing, and the pressure put on Job to make him admit that he is a thing too is very powerful, but not omnipotent. Satan's world, to adapt a phrase of Kierkegaard, *is* but does not *exist*. Job begins to exist, in this sense, when he remains defiant and calls loudly for some explanation of what has happened to him, paying no attention to the frantic expostulations of his friends and Elihu that such an attitude is blasphemous and will only make matters worse. His existence is at first negative: that is, to be a conscious being is to be isolated, separated from everything else.

Hence he feels that the satanic order is not simply indifferent but is for some reason actively hostile. This attitude becomes positive with God's speech, and Job begins to feel not separated from everything else but identified, or, as Blake would say, outlined. The turning point comes when Job realizes that the satanic state of experience is not something inevitable or ultimately mysterious but something to be fought, and that the dethroned vision of innocence is something he can fight it with.

Just as the crucial turning point of the action is between Plates 12 and 13, so the crucial act of renewed vision is between Plates 14 and 15. Plate 14 is the reappearance of the vision of innocence, the Beulah vision, except that it is coming the other way, out of Job's mind and not from his circumstances. There are three levels in this plate: Job and his friends are on earth; above them is a Demiurge or creator-God controlling the order of nature, and above that is the infinite human universe, in which the morning stars and the sons of God are the same thing. The next step is to realize that Satan is the enemy of God, that his rule is not inevitable but is to be fought by God's creative power, and that this creative power exists nowhere at present except in man's creative power. At that point we pass into Plate 15, where there are only two levels, God and Job united on top, and below them the cycle of nature inhabited by Behemoth and Leviathan.

These monsters are identical with Satan, except that, being Satan revealed instead of Satan mysterious and disguised as God, they represent, not so much the natural miseries of drought and famine and pestilence, as the social and political miseries symbolized mainly, in the Bible, by Egypt and Babylon, and in the Book of Job itself by the Sabean raiders. Ezekiel (chap. 29) identifies the Leviathan with the Pharaoh of Egypt, and Daniel (chap. 4) tells how Nebuchadnezzar of Babylon turned into Behemoth, the subject of several of Blake's pictures. This political aspect of the monsters is brought out in the phrases emphasized by Blake on Plate 15: Behemoth is "chief of the ways of God" and Leviathan is "King over all the Children of Pride." As the power in man that makes for tyranny rather than civilization, they can be, if not destroyed, at least brought under some measure of control, like the Blatant Beast in

Spenser. At the same time the root of tyranny, for Blake, is still natural religion, the establishing of the order of nature, whether theistically or atheistically regarded, as the circumference of human effort (the original meaning of "Urizen"). Hence we are all born inside the belly of Leviathan, the world of stars and its indefinite space, but those who can see Leviathan for what he is have been placed outside him, like Jonah, and like Job in Plate 15. After Job has attained this enlightenment, the prophecy of Jesus is fulfilled and Satan falls from heaven (Pl. 16).

Blake's Vision of the Book of Job was certainly a work of the creative imagination, but what made it possible was a powerful critical analysis of the book. This criticism performed what we are slowly beginning to realize is the essential critical act: it put the Book of Job into its literary context. That context, the Christian Bible as a whole, lay of course ready to hand. Yet to comprehend the story of Job as a microcosm or epitome of the whole Bible, and to comprehend it as intensely as Blake did, and as the quotations on the engravings show that he did, took a critical mind of first-rate quality. We often tend to associate Blake's criticism with what he rejected, and to find him in consequence somewhat erratic. But when we examine his attitude to what he accepted, and see that he was a great critic too, we can understand how he himself can be sympathetic to his own critics, in the sense of being, however difficult, uniquely rewarding to those who are willing to make an adequate effort. Professor Damon was one of the first of those who made such an effort, and his success, the chief reason for the present book, points up its own moral.

GEORGE MILLS HARPER

# The Divine Tetrad in
# Blake's *Jerusalem*

Now I a fourfold vision see,
And a fourfold vision is given to me;
'Tis fourfold in my supreme delight
And threefold in soft Beulah's night
And twofold Always. May God us keep
From Single vision & Newton's sleep!
(To Thomas Butts, 22 Nov. 1802, *K* 818)

In the note "To the Public" which introduces *Jerusalem*, Blake declared that "The Primeval State of Man was Wisdom, Art and Science" (*K* 621). In one sense his entire artistic production represents a search for the return to this "Primeval State" by achieving wisdom through experience: "my Work . . . is an Endeavour to Restore what the Ancients call'd the Golden Age" (*LJ* 71–72, *K* 605). As his most "consolidated & extended Work" in which "Every word and every letter is studied and put into its fit place" (*K* 620, 621), *Jerusalem* deserves a careful study as a stage in Blake's quest. I propose to consider briefly an almost completely neglected aspect of his endeavor: the function of the "divine numbers," the tetrad in particular.

It may seem surprising to students of Blake that numbers should play an important role in the quest for Paradise. We are likely to recall such strongly antagonistic statements as "God is not a Mathematical Diagram" (Annotations to Berkeley, *K* 774), or "The Gods of Greece & Egypt were Mathematical Diagrams" (*Laoc, K* 776), or "God forbid that Truth should be Confined to Mathematical Demonstration!" (Annotations to Reynolds 201, *K* 474). Even in these, of course, we must always be conscious of the qualifiers:

in the first two statements the loaded word is *diagram*, and in the last it is *demonstration*. But the verb is also important: by insisting that truth should not be *confined* to mathematical demonstration, Blake may be insisting—certainly is not denying—that mathematics has a proper function in the visionary quest. Otherwise, we must credit Blake with an irony so involuted as to make the Prophetic Books beyond comprehension, and he surely intended no such deterrent: "I also hope the Reader will be with me" (*J* 3, *K* 621), he wrote, as he introduced his last great poetic vision "Of the Sleep of Ulro" (*J* 4: 1, *K* 622).

No reader of Blake can fail to be conscious of the importance of numbers to the accomplishment of the "great task" which would not let him rest, and no student of Blake's symbolic system can fail to recognize traditional meanings and patterns in the numerology of *Jerusalem*. Although numbers function symbolically in the Prophetic Books almost from the beginning, they are not consistently important until *Milton*, and they bear a much heavier burden in *Jerusalem*. This increased reliance upon the symbolic properties of numbers poses difficult questions for the serious student of Blake. Did some new source of information excite him to extend the function of the divine numbers? Did the significance or meaning of the numbers shift or change from poem to poem? Did he add or drop numbers as his system developed? Was he clearly borrowing from traditional sources, or merely mystifying his overliteral readers? Although I cannot resolve all these problems here, I hope to allay once and for all the lingering suspicion that Blake was playing a whimsical game and to demonstrate that the divine numbers are intended to be a key to "the gates of Paradise."

To Blake, as to Jacob Böhme, who is an important source of his numerology, the word *gate* signifies a kind of exegetical tool for the uninitiated reader. To both men, also, the divine numbers became a concrete symbolic device for the dual function of focusing the rays of their visionary imagination and fixing the falsehood of generated existence until the error of creation can be corrected. The significance of "mathematic power" is emphasized by Los, Blake's prophetic spokesman, in a passage clearly indebted to Böhme:

## The Divine Tetrad in Jerusalem

> I saw the finger of God go forth
> Upon my Furnaces from within the Wheels of Albion's Sons,
> Fixing their Systems permanent, by mathematic power
> Giving a body to Falsehood that it may be cast off for ever,
> With Demonstrative Science piercing Apollyon with his own bow.
>
> (*J* 12:10–14, *K* 631)[1]

Blake was, of course, aware that he was utilizing the tool of Newton, his mighty adversary, in the task of proving that Man, not Nature, "is the great Mystery of God, *the microcosmos*, . . . a living Emblem and Hieroglyphic of Eternity and Time." [2] But the ironic Blake was making a distinction between "theological arithmetic" and "vulgar arithmetic," to borrow the phrases of Thomas Taylor the Platonist, another of his sources. By the time of *Jerusalem*, at any rate, Blake had decided that the divine numbers could "prepare us for the intellectual apprehensions of theology." [3] In the tradition of Plato and the Neo-Platonists (all students of Pythagorean numerology) Blake utilizes the "mathematical forms" as veils for the concealment of divine dogmas, though he was always careful to deny any attempt to hide the truth. Like the Neo-Pythagoreans, as well as many biblical commentators,[4] he had apparently concluded that "the mathematical science . . . discovers numbers adapted to all generated natures, and to their periods and restitutions to their pristine state," and that "it contributes much and in an admirable manner, to the philosophy which is called political, by measuring the times of actions, the various periods of the universe, and the numbers adapted to generations." [5] Thus, in fact, do numbers function in *Jerusalem*. After all, as Blake asked rhetorically, "Are not Religion & Politics the Same Thing?" (*J* 57:10, *K* 689).

Whether or not Blake needed the authority of the Neo-Pythagoreans or Böhme for the divinity of number I am not prepared to argue here, but it is clear that he was acquainted with the classical tradition and that he did not utilize the numbers with the kind of elaborate and rational ingenuity of many biblical explicators, including Böhme. For Blake, the numbers frequently seem to be the equivalent of the Divine Forms, and the function of both is to keep man from falling into Non-Entity. According to Thomas Taylor, in a book Blake probably knew, the Pythagoreans believed that "every form is a number." [6]

Like Plato, I think, Blake recognized the "mathematical forms" as a useful symbolic device by which he could detach himself from, and at the same time project by contrast, "the flux and inconstancy of matter" because the numbers "participate of a certain, exact, sure, and exquisite condition." [7] He needed a system which would convey his faith in the eternal existence of "Definite Form" ("The Infinite alone resides in Definite & Determinate Identity") as well as his conviction that Satan could be "reveal'd in his System" (J 55:44; 29[43]:10. K 687, 653). This he found in number, a system supported by traditional wisdom and practice. Like Eudoxus the Pythagorean, Blake perceived that "number is definite multitude, . . . the first paradigm of the fabrication of the world." [8] Whether or not he believed in the metaphysical reality of the ideal numbers, he certainly believed in their aesthetic validity; and he would not have quarreled with Plotinus' assumption that "Number exists before objects which are described by number," and "the variety of sense-objects merely recalls to the soul the notion of number." [9] Since divine number usually functions as a cosmological symbol in *Jerusalem*, Blake might have said with Proclus that it "pervades from on high, as far as to the last of things, adorning all things, and connecting them by appropriate forms." [10] But Blake was preoccupied with the descent into generation and therefore chiefly concerned with number as a symbolic means of staying the Fall and restoring man to prelapsarian perfection. Hence, Pythagoras and Socrates along with Adam and Noah were among the archetypal figures created by Los "to preserve" Satan and Cain and "all the Kings & Nobles" "from Eternal Death" (J 73:34-42, K 713-14).[11]

Throughout *Jerusalem* Blake clearly differentiates between two conceptions or functions of mathematical science: one, the bad, is experimental and demonstrative; the other, the good, is the "sweet science" of intellectual warfare (FZ ix:853-55, K 379). Like Thomas Taylor and his Neo-Platonic teachers, Blake believed that "science is not the business of sense, since that which is universal is the object of perception in particulars themselves." [12] Translated into Blake's prophetic rhetoric, that might read: "For Art & Science cannot exist but in minutely organized Particulars / And not in generalizing Demonstrations of the Rational Power" (*J* 55:62–63, *K* 687). That is, "Rational Philosophy and Mathematic Demonstration" (*J* 58:13, *K* 690) are one and the same. From the rocks "of Reasonings, of unhewn Demonstrations" is constructed "an awful form": the building of Natural Religion with its altars of Natural Morality (*J* 66:3, 8; *K* 702). Blake and the idealists of his day sought to oppose the deism and rationalism of "Satan's Mathematic Holiness, Length, Bredth & Highth" (*Mil* 32:18, *K* 521) by returning to "The Primeval State of Man": "Wisdom, Art and Science" (*J* 3, *K* 621). This ideological debate is depicted near the end of *Jerusalem* in a great struggle between Los and his Spectre, who express the viewpoints of Blake and Newton. Los insists that "General Forms have their vitality in Particulars" (*J* 91:30, *K* 738) but

> The Spectre builded stupendous Works, taking the Starry Heavens
> Like to a curtain & folding them according to his will,
> Repeating the Smaragdine Table of Hermes to draw Los down
> Into the Indefinite, refusing to believe without demonstration.
> Los reads the Stars of Albion, the Spectre reads the Voids
> Between the Stars among the arches of Albion's Tomb sublime . . .
>                                       (*J* 91:33–38, *K* 738)

This passage is particularly interesting in denying the validity of two false sciences: that of Hermes and that of Newton, with whom the "Voids between the Substances of Creation" (*Mil* 37:46, *K* 528) are invariably associated in the Prophetic Books.

We may ask what Newtonian physics has to do with the prophetic vision embodied in Blake's numerology. Primarily, it represents "the crucifying cruelties of Demonstration" (*J* 24:55, *K* 648) as a step in cosmic dissolution. "To Converse concerning Weight & Distance in the Wilds of Newton & Locke" (*J* 34[30]:39–40, *K* 661) was in itself a symbolic manifestation of the Female Will in suggesting *division* and *separation* (key words in *Jerusalem*), a falling off from divine unity.

Although well acquainted with the numerological lore of Böhme and the Bible, Blake was a metaphysical unitarian and strongly opposed to the Christian doctrine of the Trinity and, by extension perhaps, to threeness in general. His symbolic logic is strikingly illustrated in a line from *Milton:* "The Sexual is Threefold: the Human is Fourfold" (*Mil* 4:5, *K* 483). It is, I think, hard to overestimate the importance of that line to the understanding of both *Milton* and *Jerusalem*. As a symbolic representation of fragmentation (Blake's favorite metaphor for the Fall),[13] the female 3 and all numbers in which it is an organic part (especially 7, 12, and 27) are anathema, whereas the male 4 and its functional kinsmen (especially 16 and 32) invariably project prelapsarian perfection or mark the way back.

In this respect, Blake sides with the Pythagoreans.[14] Like them, he "believed that *the one* is the formal principle and cause of all things," and that "the dissolution of *the one* into the many, is the cause of destruction." [15] Of course, Blake's poetic conception of "Visionary forms dramatic" walking "To & fro in Eternity as One Man" (*J* 98:28, 39; *K* 746) is not Pythagorean. As an artist, he invariably projects his version of the One and the Many in concrete images. Although his ideal state is oneness and his regeneration is truly reunion, his universe is always vital, his Eternity never without Man. Blake's vision of the one great Man who "contain'd in his mighty limbs all things in Heaven & Earth" (*J* 27, *K* 649) is closer to Böhme's microcosmic man than to Plato's one great animal, for Blake's divinity is always anthropomorphic: "Thou art a Man, God is no more" (*EG* d:75, *K* 752). But in a conception more important to this study, Blake rejected Christian doctrine for Pythagorean: his divinity is tetradic rather than trinitarian. Like the Pythagoreans, he conceived of "divine number proceed[ing] from the immortal retreats of unity, until it arrives at the divine tetrad." [16] But Blake emphasized that the fourfold nature of fallen Man is prefigured in the fourfold essentiality of divine unity. A symbolic artist, he saw through the image of fallen Man to eternal reality. Although he projected the Fall in Plotinian terms as a series of emanations, from another angle of vision he conceived fallen Albion and his divine prototype as a fourfold unity.

Although 4 is the number of generation, then, it is also eternal.

As such, it is the only number of significance before the Fall: even in Eternity the Divine Man is conceived as a fourfold unity containing "the Four Zoas, who are the Four Eternal Senses of Man" (*J* 36[32]:31, *K* 663). Although Blake emphasizes oneness and unity, his conception of the Man-God is consistently tetradic. Since, however, there is little that need be said of unfallen Humanity, Blake is chiefly concerned with the "Four Eternal Senses" after they "Became Four Elements separating from the Limbs of Albion" (l. 32). In the process of division and descent, they degenerate into "Four ravening deathlike Forms" (l. 36). Nevertheless, the "Forms Eternal Exist For-ever" (*Mil* 32:38, *K* 522), and the Form of the tetrad is eternal. Blake agreed with Pythagoras that "the soul contains in itself and is the quaternary, the tetraktys, the perfect cube." [17]

Although Blake's choice of the word "Zoa" as a name and definition for the "Four Eternal Senses" may have been suggested by Plato's one great animal of the *Timaeus,* Blake was obviously thinking of the four beasts of Revelation or the four creatures of Ezekiel when he conceived the Zoas as "Four Living Creatures." [18] But his conception of original sin as a kind of cosmic disjunction of the Eternal Senses owes no direct debt to Ezekiel's or St. John's apocalyptic vision.

Indeed, Blake followed no charted route. Although he is obviously aware of traditional symbolic values, it is difficult to point to any single source as the stimulus for his system of divine analogies based upon the number 4. But he does seem close to the Neo-Pythagoreans. In the words of their famous oath, he might have insisted that "all our wisdom springs" from the divine tetractys, "which contains Perennial Nature's fountain, cause, and root," [19] for he surely believed that "the quaternary number belongs to the soul so far as she is connected with matter, which is tempered with four qualities, and four elements; and she is endued with four principal faculties, nutrition, sensation, local motion, and intellection." [20] It is not hard to imagine that Blake's conception of the four Zoas might be directly indebted to this explanation of what happens to the quaternary number of the soul when "she is connected with matter." Although all the long Prophetic Books make use of this Pythagorean doctrine, Blake's most sustained effort to follow the fate of the fallen four as they seek reunion in Paradise is *Jerusalem.*

As the poem opens, the "perturbed Man," already sunk in "the Sleep of Ulro," recognizes the manifestation of the cosmic error: in a canceled line, which Blake may have thought too obvious, Albion declares that "We are not One: we are Many" (*J* 4:23, *K* 622).[21] The poet himself describes the dispersion of the Divine Body in terms of the body politic: "Jerusalem is scatter'd abroad like a cloud of smoke thro' non-entity" (*J* 5:13, *K* 623). And we learn almost at once that the poet's "great task" is essentially twofold: to describe the descent into generation and the building of Golgonooza, the holy city of art which will effect regeneration. The process of descent is conceived in terms of Plato's doctrine of the One and the Many as the terrible Sons of Albion are "Divided into Male and Female forms time after time" (*J* 5:32, *K* 623). The Sons are twelve in number; and 12 itself, as the number of the Tribes of Israel, signifies an advanced stage of the scattering of the Divine Body. Because in Western symbology and myth 12 is almost invariably an efficacious number, we may be surprised at Blake's seeming capriciousness until we observe that it is the product of the female 3 and the male 4. The entire poem may be conceived as a dramatic description of the cosmic struggle of the forces of unity versus the forces of multitude, and these mighty opposites are projected symbolically by male and female numbers and by two correlative symbols, the furnace and the loom. As a male symbol, the furnace is associated with 1, 4, 16, 32, and 64, which function symbolically to enable the poet to fulfill one half of his "great task": building Golgonooza. As a female symbol, the loom is associated with 2, 3, 7, 12, and 27, which enable the poet to fulfill the other half of his task: projecting dispersion "thro' unbounded space" (*J* 5:2, *K* 623).

It is necessary for the poet to recognize these warring symbolic contraries if he is to awaken "the Four-fold Man, The Humanity," from his "deadly sleep" (*J* 15:6, *K* 635). As the key to the positive side of Blake's vision, the number 4 and its extensions are the very foundation of the holy city which Los will create in his furnace to halt Man's Fall "into the deeps of Entuthon Benython"

(*J* 5:56, *K* 624), a region of indefinite abstraction symbolized by looms and starry wheels. At the sociological level the good and the bad are here conceived as the art of handicraft versus the science of the machine: the "Loom of Locke . . . [is] Wash'd by the Water-wheels of Newton" (*J* 15:15–16, *K* 636). The following lines from Plates 12 and 13 summarize Blake's visionary conception and are central to an understanding of the poem:

Fourfold the Sons of Los in their divisions, and fourfold
The great City of Golgonooza: fourfold toward the north,
And toward the south fourfold, & fourfold toward the east & west,
Each within other toward the four points: that toward
Eden, and that toward the World of Generation,
And that toward Beulah, and that toward Ulro.
Ulro is the space of the terrible starry wheels of Albion's sons,
But that toward Eden is walled up till time of renovation,
Yet it is perfect in its building, ornaments & perfection.

And the Four Points are thus beheld in Great Eternity:
West, the Circumference: South, the Zenith: North,
The Nadir: East, the Center, unapproachable for ever.
These are the four Faces towards the Four Worlds of Humanity
In every Man. Ezekiel saw them by Chebar's flood.
And the Eyes are the South, and the Nostrils are the East,
And the Tongue is the West, and the Ear is the North.

And the North Gate of Golgonooza, toward Generation
Has four sculptur'd Bulls, terrible, before the Gate of iron,
And iron the Bulls; and that which looks toward Ulro,
Clay bak'd & enamel'd, eternal glowing as four furnaces,
Turning upon the Wheels of Albion's sons with enormous power:
And that toward Beulah four, gold, silver, brass & iron;
And that toward Eden, four, form'd of gold, silver, brass & iron.

The South, a golden Gate, has four Lions terrible, living:
That toward Generation, four, of iron carv'd wondrous:
That toward Ulro, four, clay bak'd, laborious workmanship:
That toward Eden, four, immortal gold, silver, brass & iron.

The Western Gate fourfold is clos'd, having four Cherubim
Its guards, living, the work of elemental hands, laborious task,
Like Men hermaphroditic, each winged with eight wings.
That towards Generation, iron: that toward Beulah, stone:

That toward Ulro, clay: that toward Eden, metals:
But all clos'd up till the last day, when the graves shall yield their dead.

($J$ 12:45–13:11, $K$ 632–33)

Most of these quaternaries will, I suppose, explain themselves, but several points need emphasis. In juxtaposing Ulro, as "the space of the terrible starry wheels of Albion's sons," with Eden, which is "walled up till time of renovation," Blake is clearly reminding us of the two parts of his great task: to describe the Fall and the restoration. In assigning four senses to the four gates, Blake omitted touch by design because it is the most powerful of the senses and by it man can transcend the limitations of the other four. The four metals of the gate toward Eden suggest the four ages of man, a theory which has a significant place in the message of all the long Prophetic Books as well as Romantic theory in general. By implying that the world is now in the iron age of wheels within wheels, Blake is reminding us that the "time of renovation" is fast approaching.

This passage is followed by a description of the "Wheels of Albion's sons" and the "seven diseases of the earth," after which Blake carries the description of his fourfold city even further:

And every part of the City is fourfold; & every inhabitant, fourfold.
And every pot & vessel & garment & utensil of the houses,
And every house, fourfold; but the third Gate in every one
Is clos'd as with a threefold curtain of ivory & fine linen & ermine.
And Luban stands in middle of the City; a moat of fire
Surrounds Luban, Los's Palace & the golden Looms of Cathedron.

And sixty-four thousand Genii guard the Eastern Gate,
And sixty-four thousand Gnomes guard the Northern Gate,
And sixty-four thousand Nymphs guard the Western Gate,
And sixty-four thousand Fairies guard the Southern Gate.

($J$ 13:20–29, $K$ 633)

Since "the third Gate in every one / Is clos'd as with a threefold curtain," and only three gates are therefore accessible, we are to understand that the building of Golgonooza is not yet complete. In this passage also Blake opposes once more the symbols of eternal versus temporal in "Los's Palace & the golden Looms of Cathedron."

The 64,000 guardians of each gate are interesting only in suggesting the function of the four elements "till time of renovation," and, of course, in extending 4 to the third power. Blake made no further use of 64.

The "four points of heaven" (*J* 17:11, *K* 638) are reflected in four points on earth; for Los's heavenly city has a counterpart in "Babylon the City of Vala, the Goddess Virgin-Mother" (*J* 18:29, *K* 640). Hence the "Four Regions of Human Majesty" (*J* 18:1, *K* 640) must be traced in their fallen state: "All things acted on Earth are seen in the bright Sculptures of / Los's Halls" (*J* 16:61– 62, *K* 638). The task of charting this heavenly geography on earth was formidable indeed. Although Blake did not always succeed in making the analogies clear, he attempted to do so on several levels. In addition to such obvious and traditional quaternaries as the four elements and the four compass points, Blake sought both to picture the Fall and to stay the Fall in more concrete and perhaps more readily understandable geographical analogues. Beginning with the four continents (Asia, Africa, America, and Europe) representing the four directions and the four Zoas, he next charted the four kingdoms of the British Isles (Scotland, England, Wales, and Ireland), the four kingdoms of Ireland (Munster, Ulster, "Connaut," and Leinster), and finally the four cities ("Verulam," London, York, and Edinburgh). He envisioned numerological significance in the political divisions of Great Britain (forty counties of England, twelve counties of Wales, thirty-six counties of Scotland, and thirty-two counties of Ireland), breaking them up into groups and assigning them to the Sons of Israel. The twelve counties of Wales and the thirty-six of Scotland were ideal for Blake's purpose of equal division among the twelve Sons; the forty of England was more difficult, though he must have been pleased to find a significant division—three each for eight of the Sons and four for the other four, to make the total of forty (*J* 16:28–58, *K* 637–38). Blake's symbolic purpose is suggested in the lines which precede the naming and assigning of all the counties except Ireland's:

Here Los fix'd down the Fifty-two Counties of England & Wales,

The Thirty-six of Scotland & the Thirty-four of Ireland,
With mighty power, when they fled out at Jerusalem's Gates
Away from the Conflict of Luvah & Urizen, fixing the Gates
In the Twelve Counties of Wales, & thence Gates looking every way
To the Four Points conduct to England & Scotland & Ireland,
And thence to all the Kingdoms & Nations & Families of the Earth.

(*J* 16:28–34, *K* 637)

For Ireland's thirty-two counties (the thirty-four in the passage above is a slip he subsequently corrected) Blake had a special function reserved, and they are not named until near the end of chapter iii. Plate 71 begins with a metaphysical description of the relationship of earth to heaven:

And above Albion's Land was seen the Heavenly Canaan
As the Substance is to the Shadow, and above Albion's Twelve Sons
Were seen Jerusalem's Sons and all the Twelve Tribes spreading
Over Albion. As the Soul is to the Body, so Jerusalem's Sons
Are to the Sons of Albion.                    (*J* 71:1–5, *K* 709)

Since Jerusalem's Sons are sixteen in number and Albion's Sons are twelve, it is clear that Blake meant for us to recognize the male 16 as the number of the soul and the female 12 as the number of the body. Blake continues by assigning the Isle of Man and the counties of England, Scotland, and Wales to Albion's twelve Sons and twelve Daughters.

Ireland was reserved for a special function based upon numerological properties. Her political division into four kingdoms and thirty-two counties suggested divine analogies out of the ordinary, and Blake's imagination was equal to the task. Since both 4 and 32 were male numbers, Ireland could not be assigned to the twelve Sons, who represent a numerological union of the female 3 and the male 4 and are therefore symbolic of generation. But "Four Sons of Jerusalem" (Rintrah, Palamabron, Theotormon, and Bromion) "never were Generated," and they "Dwell over the Four Provinces of Ireland in heavenly light" (*J* 71:50–52, *K* 710). It turns out, moreover, that the four provinces are assigned to the four chosen Sons of Israel, to each of whom Blake had reserved four rather than three of England's counties: "Munster South in

Reuben's Gate, Connaut West in Joseph's Gate, / Ulster North in Dan's Gate, Leinster East in Judah's Gate" (*J* 72:3–4, *K* 711). Blake's explanation suggests, if it does not make quite clear, why "the Land of Erin" had a peculiarly appropriate function. As twice 16 the thirty-two counties perhaps represented the fourfold gates, both within and without, of the four points:

> And the Four Gates of Los surround the Universe Within and
> Without; & whatever is visible in the Vegetable Earth, the same
> Is visible in the Mundane Shell revers'd, in mountain & vale.
> (*J* 72:45–47, *K* 712)

It is clear at any rate that "the Thirty-two Counties of the Four Provinces of Ireland" (*J* 72:1, *K* 711) had a special place in Blake's affection chiefly because they belong in the tetradic series and are therefore reminiscent of prelapsarian perfection:

> For Albion in Eternity has Sixteen Gates among his Pillars,
> But the Four towards the West were Walled up, & the Twelve
> That front the Four other Points were turned Four Square
> By Los for Jerusalem's sake & called the Gates of Jerusalem,
> Because Twelve Sons of Jerusalem fled successive thro' the Gates.
> But the Four Sons of Jerusalem who fled not but remain'd,
> Are Rintrah & Palamabron & Theotormon & Bromion,
> The Four that remain with Los to guard the Western Wall;
> And these Four remain to guard the Four Walls of Jerusalem
> Whose foundations remain in the Thirty-two Counties of Ireland
> And in Twelve Counties of Wales & in the Forty Counties
> Of England & in the Thirty-six Counties of Scotland. (*J* 72:5–16, *K* 711)

Since Ireland is the kingdom of the West towards which the four walled-up gates are turned, the thirty-two counties of its four political divisions seemed ideally suited to reflect the sixteen gates of Albion in Eternity, whereas the counties of the other three kingdoms of the British Isles clearly belong to a tripartite series of 3's and 12's. As usual Blake was careful to make absolutely clear the important distinction between the triadic and tetradic series:

> The Sons of Albion are Twelve, the Sons of Jerusalem Sixteen.

> I tell how Albion's Sons, by Harmonies of Concords & Discords
> Opposed to Melody, and by Lights & Shades opposed to Outline,
> And by Abstraction opposed to the Visions of Imagination,
> By cruel Laws, divided Sixteen into Twelve Divisions.
>
> *(J* 74:23–27, *K* 715)

The poet, it should be noted, is speaking in his own voice, explaining the properties inherent in these opposing series: the female 12 symbolizing abstract laws and "Rational Morality," the male 16 "Visions of Imagination." One of the annotations to Sir Joshua Reynolds' *Discourses* illuminates these lines and links 12 to reason and 16 to intuition: beside Sir Joshua's discussion of the "taste which relishes a demonstration in geometry," Blake observed that "Demonstration, Similitude & Harmony are Objects of Reasoning. Invention, Identity & Melody are Objects of Intuition" (200, *K* 474). By the logic of intuition 16 really represents no division, standing as it does for the fourfold gates of the fourfold City of God.

The number 16 functions twice more in *Jerusalem*, both times to signify the number of pillars in "Albion's House of Eternity" (*J* 40[36]:5, 7; *K* 666). These "Sixteen pillars" represent the sixteen inspired books of "Spiritual Verse" in the Bible:

> The Five books of the Decalogue: the books of Joshua & Judges,
> Samuel, a double book, & Kings, a double book, the Psalms & Prophets,
> The Four-fold Gospel, and the Revelations everlasting. (*J* 48:9–11, *K* 677)

By pointing out that "Albion in Eternity has Sixteen Gates among his Pillars" (*J* 72:5, *K* 711) in contrast to the twelve gates of the fallen Man, Blake symbolizes the difference between the fourfold human and the threefold sexual, essentially a distinction between the eternal and the temporal. Like St. John's heavenly city, Blake's Golgonooza will be fourfold when the Circle of Destiny is complete and the four "Walled up" gates "towards the West" are reopened. By surrounding Albion in Eternity with sixteen pillars standing for the inspired books of the Bible, Blake is equating the four closed gates with the four closed or misunderstood books of the Bible. And he is no doubt recalling that *gates* is Böhme's favorite term to signify an insight into or revelation of the arcane mystery of God's holy Word. In declaring that these four gates or pillars will be walled up "till time of renovation" (*J* 12:52, *K* 632), Blake seems to suggest that fallen Man has misunderstood the fourfold Gospel. If that is Blake's intention, it is important that the twelve pillars or gates remaining to fallen Man are all in the Old Testament except Revelation. Since at one level *Jerusalem* —like others of the Prophetic Books—is a consistent indictment of Old Testament ethics and a religion founded upon law, Blake probably meant for us to see that the New Testament doctrines of love and mercy revealed in the fourfold Gospel are closed gates to the fallen Albion. If so, "Rintrah & Palamabron & Theotormon & Bromion," "the Four Sons of Jerusalem who fled not but re-main'd," are the symbolic archetypes of Matthew, Mark, Luke, and John. This, of course, leads us to the next step of conjecturing whether or not Blake intended for each of the four Sons to represent a particular one of the four Gospels or its writer. Although this idea might well have appealed to Blake, I am not prepared to defend it: he perhaps would have felt that forcing such a one-for-one identification would distort the fourfold spiritual meaning of the four Sons, though he might have conceived the four Gospels as the perfect instrument for projecting the ideal combination of wrath, pity, desire, and reason which the four Sons embody and which make up the fourfold Man.

Several things about the list of sixteen inspired books are suggestive. First, it is perhaps a little surprising to find only five (the Gospels and Revelation) from the New Testament until we recall that the one is the most popular source book in the Bible for the numerologist and the other is "Four-fold." Like Irenaeus and many another biblical commentator, Blake probably believed that "it is not possible that the gospels can be either more or fewer than they are." [22] Secondly, the method of listing two books as one (Samuel and Kings) or several as one (Prophets) seems capricious until we observe that Blake is concerned with including all his favorites in a total which must add up to exactly 16.[23] Thirdly, it should be pointed out that next to Revelation the "Five books of the Decalogue" are the most exciting labyrinths for the numerologist. Blake may have found in Deuteronomy, as did Thomas Taylor, the justification for numbering the nations of the world according to the number of the angels rather than the children of Israel. "In the first place," Taylor wrote, "it appears from the 32nd chapter of Deuteronomy, v. 8 in the Septuagint version, that *'the division of the nations was made according to the number of the angels of God,'* and not according to the number of the children of Israel, as the present Hebrew text asserts." [24] If Blake chanced upon that passage before the completion of *Jerusalem*, Taylor's reference to the thirty-second chapter might have influenced the choice of 32 as the number of "Nations to dwell in Jerusalem's Gates" (*J* 72:32, *K* 712).

But he had a more obvious numerological analogy in the thirty-two counties of Ireland. After listing them in groups according to their location in the four provinces of Ireland, Blake declared that

> All these Center in London & in Golgonooza, from whence
> They are Created continually, East & West & North & South,
> And from them are Created all the Nations of the Earth,
> Europe & Asia & Africa & America, in fury Fourfold.
>
> And Thirty-two the Nations to dwell in Jerusalem's Gates.
> . . . . . . . . . . . . . . . . . .
> Thirty-two Nations,
> And under these Thirty-two Classes of Islands in the Ocean
> All the Nations, Peoples & Tongues throughout all the Earth.
>
> And the Four Gates of Los surround the Universe Within and
> Without; & whatever is visible in the Vegetable Earth, the same
> Is visible in the Mundane Shell revers'd, in mountain & vale.
> (*J* 72:28–32, 42–47; *K* 712)

So it was that fourfold Ireland became the fourfold image in the "Vegetable Earth" of "the four points of heaven" (*J* 17:11, *K* 638). Although its four gates "toward Eden" are "walled up till time of renovation" (*J* 12:52, *K* 632), Ireland is Jerusalem's "holy place" (*J* 29 [43]:20, *K* 653). No wonder William Butler Yeats was readily convinced that Blake's father was an Irish O'Neil and that his very manner of writing had an "Irish flavour." [25]

As a prophet rather than a mystic, Blake is primarily concerned with commenting upon the problems of this world and the means of returning to the other. Although we are told that the Divine Man was fourfold in Eternity, we see him chiefly as he appears in his fallen but still fourfold state. A passage in *Jerusalem*, repeated almost verbatim from *Milton*, explains symbolically what happened to the Four Zoas after they are drawn "down / Into the Indefinite, refusing to believe without demonstration" (*J* 91:35–36, *K* 738):

> For Four Universes round the Mundane Egg remain Chaotic:
> One to the North, Urthona: One to the South, Urizen:
> One to the East, Luvah: One to the West, Tharmas.
> They are the Four Zoas that stood around the Throne Divine,
> Verulam, London, York & Edinburgh, their English names.
> But when Luvah assumed the World of Urizen Southward
> And Albion was slain upon his Mountains & in his Tent,
> All fell towards the Center, sinking downwards in dire ruin.
>
> (*J* 59:10–17, *K* 691)

Here, as elsewhere in Blake, the Mundane Egg is a term for the Vegetable Earth, and the disorder and chaos surrounding it signify the destruction of the perfect union of the tetradic divinity. Blake is, of course, referring ironically to Milton's cosmological suggestion that the creation of the earth represents an imposition of order upon chaotic and formless matter. For Blake, in contrast, the creation of the world is a descent into the indefinite and therefore a cause of chaos; and almost all physical objects which are indefinite or shifting in outline are symbolic of evil, as this passage describing the wilderness of the world after the Flood suggests:

> The inhabitants are sick to death: they labour to divide into Days
> And Nights the uncertain Periods, and into Weeks & Months. In vain
> They send the Dove & Raven & in vain the Serpent over the mountains
> And in vain the Eagle & Lion over the four-fold wilderness:
> They return not, but generate in rocky places desolate:
> They return not, but build a habitation separate from Man.
> The Sun forgets his course like a drunken man; he hesitates

Upon the Cheselden hills, thinking to sleep on the Severn.
In vain: he is hurried afar into an unknown Night. (*J* 66:68–76, *K* 703) [26]

One of Blake's most pessimistic pictures of the descent into chaos, this passage nevertheless emphasizes that the wilderness is fourfold and therefore reclaimable. Elsewhere he describes the Fall into chaos as the "Four-fold Desart of Albion" (*J* 73:33, *K* 713) and the "Four Forests of Albion" (*J* 80:43, *K* 722). But the identity of the Four Zoas remains determinate even though they are disordered and guilty of the cosmic sin of Selfhood as one seeks to usurp the function of another.

This, of course, is the stated theme of *The Four Zoas,* a comprehension of which is assumed of the readers of *Milton* and *Jerusalem,* where Blake uses his own work as a ready reference. But the nature of the cosmic disorder can best be seen in reorder and reunion. In the apocalyptic conclusion to *Jerusalem,* when "Time was Finished" and "The Breath Divine Breathed over Albion" (*J* 94:18, *K* 742), he "rose in anger" (*J* 95:5–6, *K* 742)

> speaking the Words of Eternity in Human Forms, in direful Revolutions of Action & Passion, thro' the Four Elements on all sides Surrounding his awful Members. . . .        (*J* 95:9–11, *K* 742)

And he compelled "Urizen to his Furrow & Tharmas to his Sheepfold / And Luvah to his Loom," Urthona being at work already at his Anvil (*J* 95:16–18, *K* 742). Throwing "himself into the Furnaces of affliction" by which the divisive Selfhood is destroyed, Albion awoke from the "Dream" of death-in-life, the Four Zoas "arose into Albion's Bosom," and he "stood before Jesus in the Clouds / Of Heaven, Fourfold among the Visions of God in Eternity" (*J* 96:35–36, 41–43; *K* 744). "The Four Eternal Senses of Man" have resumed their proper place in tetradic union, and it is now possible to destroy "Vegetative Generation" (*J* 36 [32]:31, 33; *K* 663). Stretching "his hand into Infinitude," Albion seizes the fourfold bow and arms it with "Arrows of Intellect." The female "Bacon & Newton & Locke" are united with the male "Milton & Shakespear & Chaucer," "And every Man stood Fourfold" (*J* 97:6; 98:7, 9, 12. *K* 744–45). How important the divine tetrad was to Blake's vision of the return to Paradise in the holy city foursquare is strikingly projected in the apocalyptic description of the "Fourfold Annihilation" without which regeneration is not possible:

> Circumscribing & Circumcising the excrementitious
> Husk & Covering, into Vacuum evaporating, revealing the lineaments
>   of Man,
> Driving outward the Body of Death in an Eternal Death & Resurrection,
> Awaking it to Life among the Flowers of Beulah, rejoicing in Unity
> In the Four Senses, in the Outline, the Circumference & Form, for ever
> In Forgiveness of Sins which is Self Annihilation; it is the Covenant of
>   Jehovah.
>
> The Four Living Creatures, Chariots of Humanity Divine Incompre-
>   hensible,
> In beautiful Paradises expand. These are the Four Rivers of Paradise
> And the Four Faces of Humanity, fronting the Four Cardinal Points
> Of Heaven, going forward, forward irresistible from Eternity to Eternity.
>
> (J 98:18–27, K 745)

If Blake's "Dream" of these "Visionary forms dramatic" "walk[ing] / To & fro in Eternity as One Man" (*J* 98:28, 38–39; *K* 746) is, as he suggests, beyond the comprehension of mere mortals, it is nevertheless the most "glorious" symbolic vision in English literature of Man's "awaking to Eternal Life" (*J* 4:2, *K* 622).

Although Blake often seems fearful "Lest the Sexual Generation swallow up Regeneration" (*J* 90:37, *K* 737), the tone of *Jerusalem* is optimistic in that he envisions the reunion of the "Human Four-fold Forms" (*J* 88:7, *K* 733) in the one great Man, the Divine Jesus. "Israel scatter'd abroad / In martyrdoms & slavery" (*J* 89:39–40, *K* 735) will be reassembled. When "the little lovely Allegoric Night of Albion's Daughters" (*J* 88:31, *K* 733) breaks and Albion awakens from his "deadly Sleep of Six Thousand Years" (*J* 96:11, *K* 743), Los and Enitharmon will be as they were "in times of old" and no longer suffer the sorrows of "Two Wills" and "Two Intellects" (*J* 86:61, *K* 732). As the supreme romantic, Blake always expected the "Resurrection to Unity," but his task as cosmic historian was to record the "fall into Division" (*FZ* i:21, *K* 264) and by recording to create the visionary artifact to stay

the Fall. All his life perhaps he had dreamed of "the New Jerusalem descending out of Heaven" (*J* 86:19, *K* 731) on that great
Sabbath which was to terminate the six thousand years of Generation. But that apocalyptic vision was "incomprehensible by Mortal Man" (*J* 98:11, *K* 745), and the poet as creator must therefore
be primarily concerned with fixing the error and pointing the way
to casting it out. In "acting against Albion's melancholy," "Los
built the stubborn structure of the Language" (*J* 40[36]:59–60,
*K* 668), a necessary stage in restoring the ruins of time. But the
language of fact and allegory could open no windows into Eden
nor provide material for rebuilding the "immortal Golgonooza."
Hence Blake sought for a language of symbolic levels. In the light
of his early and continued aversion to mathematics, one of the
most curious of his multidimensional linguistic devices was the
science of numbers. Operating chiefly in the Neo-Pythagorean
tradition but obviously well versed in other numerological lore,
Blake managed to utilize the divine numbers in an amazingly complex system which combined symbol and myth at several levels.
At one level, it is clear, the numbers serve "To bind the Body of
Man to heaven" by projecting concretely the relationship of the
World of Eternity to the World of Generation. Although the symbolic values of the various numbers were not yet precisely established in Blake's mind when he composed *The Four Zoas*, one of
its splendid and frequently misunderstood passages suggests the
cosmic function which the divine numbers were to play thereafter:

Thus were the stars of heaven created like a golden chain
To bind the Body of Man to heaven from falling into the Abyss.
Each took his station & his course began with sorrow & care.

In sevens & tens & fifties, hundreds, thousands, number'd all
According to their various powers, subordinate to Urizen
And to his sons in their degrees & to his beauteous daughters,
Travelling in silent majesty along their order'd ways
In right lined paths outmeasur'd by proportions of number, weight
And measure, mathematic motion wondrous along the deep,
In fiery pyramid, or Cube, or unornamented pillar square
Of fire, far shining, travelling along even to its destin'd end;
Then falling down a terrible space, recovering in winter dire

Its wasted strength, it back returns upon a nether course,
Till fir'd with ardour fresh recruited in its humble season,
It rises up on high all summer, till its wearied course
Turns into autumn. Such the period of many worlds.

(*FZ* ii:266–81, *K* 287)

By the time of *Jerusalem* the generality of "sevens & tens & fifties" had been rejected for the minute particularity of 3's and 4's and 12's, but the role was essentially the same. Blake had created a system for the ordering of his vision. By his Divine Analogy, "all things are assimilated to number." [27] If he had explained his system, he might have "called number the judicial instrument of the maker of the universe, and the first paradigm of mundane fabrication." [28] Like Plato and Pythagoras, he conceived his visionary mathematics as a bridge by which he and those who understood him might "pass over the obscurity of a material nature, as over some dark sea to the luminous regions of perfect reality." [29] As the symbolic instrument for "Overwhelming . . . Bad Art & Science" (*LJ* 92–95, *K* 617), the divine tetrad will awaken Man from his "three years slumber on the banks of the Ocean" (*J* 3, *K* 620) and lead him "in at Heaven's gate / Built in Jerusalem's wall" (*J* 77, *K* 716).

PAUL MINER

# Visions in the Darksom Air: Aspects of Blake's Biblical Symbolism

Obtuse Angle answer'd, "The heathen in the old ages us'd to have Gods that they worship'd, & they us'd to sacrifice to them. You have read about that in the bible."

"Ah," said Aradobo, "I thought I had read of Phebus in the Bible."

"Aradobo, you should always think before you speak," said Obtuse Angle.

"Ha! Ha! Ha! He means Pharaoh," said Tilly Lally.

"I am asham'd of you,—making use of the names in the Bible," said M^rs. Sistagatist.

"I'll tell you what, Mrs. Sinagain. I don't think there's any harm in it," said Tilly Lally.

These lines occur in an early manuscript satire (*IslM* 47, *ca.* 1784) by William Blake and have legitimate application to his later symbolic books, for indeed Satan becomes Phoebus' son, Phaeton, who "in pride of heart / Drove the fierce Harrow [the chariot of the sun] among the constellations of Jehovah . . ." (*Mil* 493:24–25).[1] From his earliest poetry, the Bible was a source that Blake would make peculiarly his own, and in the poet's words of later years, this writing "upon the rock of ages" was a theme which called him "night after night" (*J* 623:23, 622:3)[2]—so much that Blake envisioned building up "Jerusalem / In England's green & pleasant Land."

"Mild Zion's hill's most ancient promontory" was "near mournful / Ever weeping Paddington" (*J* 632:27–28), the "ever weeping" accounted for by the fact that at this time St. George's Burying Ground occupied a large portion of the Paddington area near the intersection of Edgware, Bayswater, and Oxford roads. This also was the location of the Tyburn gallows, Blake's fatal rood tree (*J* 650:25–29), while "Calvary's foot" was just off South Molton Street, where Blake lived (*Mil* 484:21). "Jerusalem's Inner Court, Lambeth" (*Mil* 511:48) was where Jerusalem's foundations began (*J* 729:4). Here also were the looms of Tirzah, a daughter of Zelophehad. To the corporeal eye this was the Asylum for female orphans. The inmates "labour in Tirzah's Looms for bread," and set "Pleasure against Duty" and "make Learning a burden . . ." Blake's language is not purely fanciful, for contemporary accounts observe that the children at the Asylum were "properly employed," were "attentive to their learning," and were "regularly employed . . . in *reading and knitting*." [3]

Frequent allusions demonstrate the pervasive influence that the "Jewish & Christian Testaments" exercised on Blake's imagination. When one of Blake's symbolic characters states, "I am nothing, and vanity" (*Mil* 502:18), Blake's source, ultimately, is Isaiah 40:17. When Blake mentions the "floodgates of the heavens" in *The Four Zoas* (282:90) he alludes to "the windows of heaven" (Gen. 7:11), for these *windows* are glossed in the biblical text as *floodgates*. The "ships of the sea [that] . . . sing the songs of Zion" in Blake's text are an echo of Ezekiel. "The Sun [that] forgets his course like a drunken man" may recall the earth that reels "to and fro like a drunkard" in Isaiah, while the "Looking Glass of Enitharmon" possibly is the "molten looking glass" in Job. Those who gnaw "their tongues / For pain" and sit "beneath the Vine and Fig-tree" also have their prototypes in the Bible. [4]

Hundreds of biblical allusions and references are found in Blake's poetry. The following phrases are biblical in derivation, and they assist in documenting that Blake "found the Word [the Bible] Golden": "The God of This World," "fatness of the earth," "Baptism of Repentance," "image of the Invisible God," "Watcher & a Holy-One," "fear & trembling," "Enemy & Avenger," "a dry & thirsty land," "land of briars & thorns," "Lover and my Friend," "appointed season," "Cry of the Poor Man," "nursing Mothers," "Children of whoredoms," "a Place prepar'd," "blaspheme thy holy name," "confusion of Face," "Moab our bath," "night season," "long season," "howling wilderness." [5] The heavens of brass and the earth of iron in *The Four Zoas* (290:395) find their sources in Deuteronomy 28:23. In *Jerusalem* (659:13) the "place [that] shall not be found as the wind passes over" parallels "For the wind passeth over it, and it is gone; and the place thereof shall know it no more" (Ps. 103:16). It is Romans 8:21–22 that inspired "the whole Creation . . . groans to be deliver'd" (*J* 637:26), and when Albion discovers the "secret places" of Jerusalem (*J* 644:19) a prophecy in Isaiah 3:17 is recapitulated. In *Milton* (511:44–45) reapers who "sowed in tears" go forth with "rejoicing" because the time of their "refreshing cometh," and the language is from Psalm 126:5 and Acts 3:19. Also the five senses or gates smitten with "blasting fancies and with mildews . . ." (*Am* 203:18–20) and the "walls of salvation / And praise" (*Mil* 486:21–22) find their inspiration in the Old Testament.[6]

Some of Blake's loveliest poetry is taken from the Bible, and in the "Introduction" of *Songs of Experience* the lines "O Earth, O Earth, return! / Arise from out the dewy grass" may recall Deuteronomy, ". . . hear, O earth, the words of my mouth," for "speech shall distill as the dew, . . . as the showers upon the grass" (32:1–2).[7] "The wat'ry shore" that is given to Earth "till the break of day" in this poem of *Experience* also may allude to Job, where the power of God "hath compassed the waters with bounds, until the day and night come to an end" (26:10). In *Jerusalem* the following lines are based upon Isaiah and the Canticles:

> Awake, Awake, Jerusalem! O lovely Emanation of Albion,
> Awake and overspread all Nations as in Ancient Time;
> For lo! the Night of Death is past and the Eternal Day
> Appears upon our Hills.                      (*J* 744:1–4) [8]

"I am made to sow the thistle for wheat, the nettle for a nourishing dainty" (*FZ* 290:387) comes from Job: "Let thistles grow instead of wheat, and cockle [weeds] instead of barley" (31:40). The Divine Hand bears Humanity back to safety, "as doves to their windows" (*J* 655:13), an overtone of Isaiah 60:8, while "My robe is turned to confusion, & my bright gold to stone" (*FZ* 360:106) realigns imagery of Psalms and Lamentations.[9]

It is well known that the Bible, that "Poem of probable impossibilities" (Annotations to Watson 390:10–11) motivated much of Blake's thought, but no proper assessment has been given many of the minute particulars which accrue from this source. This neglect has occurred primarily because Blake read the Bible in its "diabolical sense"; and, like his own Satan, we cannot behold him "till he be reveal'd in his System" (*J* 653:10).

Blake's early books are punctuated frequently with biblical imagery. "To Spring" in *Poetical Sketches,* Blake's first published work, is biblical in context.

> O thou with dewy locks, who lookest down
> Thro' the clear windows of the morning, turn
> Thine angel eyes upon our western isle,
> Which in full choir hails thy approach, O Spring!     (*K* 1)

In the Song of Solomon we read of the beloved whose "head is filled with dew," and his locks are wet with "drops of the night" (5:2). Elsewhere the beloved "looketh forth at the windows" (2:9), and the bride also "looketh forth as the morning" (6:10). [10] Blake's "choir" is defined further by the following lines from the Song:

> For, lo, the winter is past, the rain is over and gone;
> The flowers appear on the earth; the time of the singing of birds is come, and the voice of the turtle is heard in our land.     (2:11–12)

It is pertinent here that years later in *The Four Zoas* (373:600–601; cf. *FZ* 355:538–39) Blake used the same imagery,

> For Lo, the winter melted away upon the distant hills,
> And all the black mould sings,

and in *Milton* (520:28–31) the theme is presented again:

Thou hearest the Nightingale begin the Song of Spring.
The Lark sitting upon his earthy bed, just as the morn
Appears, listens silent; then springing from the waving Cornfield, loud
He leads the *Choir of Day:* trill, trill, trill, trill . . .

In the third stanza of "To Spring" Blake implores Spring to allow English winds to kiss Spring's "perfumed garments," possibly a restatement of "Awake, O north wind; and come, thou south; blow upon my garden, that the spices thereof may flow out" (Song of Sol. 4:16). The imagery also recalls the perfumed garments of the bride in the Song of Solomon (4:11). In Blake's poem the "morn and evening breath" of Spring is referred to and possibly has relevance to the "day break" of the Canticles, for these words are glossed as the *breath of day or morning* (4:6).[11] The reference to the "love-sick" land in this same stanza recalls the bride in the Canticles, who is "sick of [unrequited] love" (2:5; 5:8),[12] and in the last stanza of "To Spring" Blake refers to the fair fingers of Spring, presumably an allusion to the bride whose hands and "fingers [drop] with sweet smelling myrrh" (5:5). Spring, which pours kisses on the bosom of the earth, may find its source in the beloved who kisses the bride (1:2) and feeds "among the lillies" (2:16; 6:2–3), the breasts of the bride (4:5; 1:13). The penultimate and final lines of "To Spring" refer to the "golden crown" of Spring and to England's "modest tresses" which are bound up, and the imagery may recall the beloved's head of "most fine gold" and his *curled* hair (as glossed, 5:11).

The "blood of the grape" in "To Autumn," although now a cliché, is an echo of Deuteronomy 32:14. In "Gwin, King of Norway" comets "shake the stars of light / Which drop like fruit unto the earth / Thro' the fierce burning night," and this language is closely paralleled in Revelation, in which "the stars of heaven fell unto the earth, even as a fig tree casteth her untimely figs, when she is shaken of a mighty wind" (6:13).[13]

It is in "Samson" that a "white-robed Angel" guides a "timorous hand to write as on a lofty rock with iron pens the words of truth . . ." (K 37; cf. Am 205:10), an allusion to Job, where words "were graven with an iron pen and lead in the rock for ever!" (19:24; cf. Jer. 17:1).

In "Then she bore Pale desire" (K 41) the sun sheds "Sweet Influence" over the earth, a recall of Job 38:31 (cf. FZ 280:23), and also in this poem Blake records (and then deletes) that ". . . Death is in the Pot." This may recall II Kings 4:40 in which a great pottage is prepared for the "sons of the prophets"—but "there is death in the pot." [14]

In "Holy Thursday" of *Songs of Innocence* (K 121–22) Blake expands on a biblical theme:

> . . . into the high dome of Paul's they like Thames' waters flow.
>
> O what a multitude they seem'd, these flowers of London town!
> Seated in companies they sit with radiance all their own.
> The hum of multitudes was there, but multitudes of lambs,
> Thousands of little boys & girls raising their innocent hands.
>
> Now like a mighty wind they raise to heaven the voice of song,
> Or like harmonious thunderings the seats of Heaven among.[15]

Benjamin Malkin, Blake's friend, specifically notes that Revelation may have influenced "Holy Thursday," and the suggestion may have come from Blake himself (see *A Father's Memoirs of His Child* [London, 1806], p. xxx). And the comparison with Revelation is sufficient to make the point, "And I heard as it were the voice of a great multitude, and as the voice of many waters, and as the voice of mighty thunderings, saying, Alleluia . . ." (19:6; cf. 14:2–3).

In *Tiriel* (100:46–50) Blake refers to "The stink of . . . dead carcases annoying man & beast," and

> . . . your remembrance shall perish; for, when your carcases
> Lie stinking on the earth, the buriers shall arise from the east,
> And not a bone of all the sons of Tiriel remain.

It is in Job that "His remembrance shall perish from the earth . . ." occurs (18:17), but the buriers of the east refer to Ezekiel where it is said that the "graves in Israel" shall "stop the noses of the passengers" (39:11–15). These graves lie in the valley of the "passengers on the east . . ." And "when any seeth a man's bone, then shall he set up a sign by it, till the buriers [of the east] have buried it in the valley . . ." Elsewhere in this poem, the old "father" of Tiriel is told: "thou smellest like the fig-tree . . . like ripe figs" (101:41–42); in Hosea the "fathers [are] as the firstripe in the fig tree . . ." (9:10). The sons and daughters of Tiriel are "Chain'd in thick darkness" (107:28, cf. *Ahan* 255:43), and probably Blake has II Peter 2:4 in mind, because God cast the sinning Angels down "and delivered them into chains of darkness . . ."

In *The Book of Thel* (1789) Blake refers (127:23–24) to the "morning manna" which the "summer's heat melts," a theme in Exodus 16:21.

In *The French Revolution* it is observed that "Our flesh is corrupted, and we wear away" (137:76), language recapitulated in Genesis 6:12 and Exodus 18:18. The "kingdoms of earth [which are] bound in sheaves" (138:92) are a reminiscence of Micah 4:11–12, while the "sorrows which flee at the morning" (142:180) recall the shadows that flee at the arising of the sun in the Song of Solomon (2:17; 4:6).[16] When Blake asks "where, O Sun, is thy dwelling?" (144:219), the biblical correlate is to be found in Job, "Where is the way where light dwelleth?" (38:19).[17]

In *The Marriage of Heaven and Hell* (1793), Blake finds himself on a "bank beside a river . . . , hearing a harper, who sung to the harp" (*K* 156), and probably, again, this is a reminiscence of the "voice of many waters" and the "voice of harpers harping with their harps" in Revelation 14:2. In the *Marriage*, underneath a design depicting Nebuchadnezzar taken from Daniel 4:33, Blake notes that "One Law for the Lion & Ox is Oppression" (also in *Tiriel* and *Visions of the Daughters of Albion*). The line is an echo of Isaiah, where "the lion shall eat straw like the ox" (11:7).[18] Blake also speaks of honoring the gifts of men, "each according to his genius" (*K* 158; cf. *J* 738:9–10), and his source is Matthew 25:15, in which awards are given "to every man according to his several ability . . ." The fiery demon who stamps the stony law or stars to dust in the *Marriage* (*K* 160) has his counterpart in the great little horn in Daniel, by which the "host of heaven" and the "stars" are cast to the ground and "stamped" (8:10), and Blake repeats this imagery in *America* (198:4–5; cf. *J* 687:59, and elsewhere). This also is related to II Kings 23:4–6, 15, where the vessels of Baal and of "all the host of heaven" are burned, and the high place of sacrifice is "stamped . . . small to powder."

It is the aged and the sick, the impotent and sexually perverse in Blake's context, who "silent rob / The vineyards in the night" in a Note-Book poem (*K* 172), and possibly Blake alludes to the "grapegatherers" and the "thieves . . . [and] robbers by night" in Obadiah 5. In "The Garden of Love" in *Songs of Experience*

(*K* 215) " 'Thou shalt not' [is] writ over the door" of the senses, and this garden is "filled with graves," and "Priests in black gowns" are seen "binding with briars my joys & desires." Blake may have remembered here the pastors in Jeremiah who destroy the vineyards and who make the *portion of desire* a "desolate wilderness," for these "spoilers" shall reap "thorns" (12:10–13). And in Numbers he may have noted the *graves of lust* (as glossed in 11:34) or in Isaiah the *fields of desire* and the "thorns and briers" that grow "upon all the houses of joy" (32:12–13).

In *The Book of Urizen* (231:2–9) Blake refers to a "Tent with strong curtains" which binds in the void, and these curtains are erected upon pillars round the Void and fastened with "golden hooks." (Later in *The Four Zoas*, "woven draperies" are hung in the dark deep on "golden hooks" [284:152–54].) In Isaiah we read that "he that sitteth upon the circle of the earth" also "stretcheth out the heavens as a curtain, and spreadeth them out as a tent to dwell in" (40:32); and the golden hooks relate to the Tabernacle in which curtains shall hang upon "four pillars of shittim wood overlaid with gold: [and] their hooks shall be of gold . . ." (Exod. 26:31–33; cf. *J* 692:55).

In "The Human Abstract" of *Experience* (*K* 217) "the fruit of Deceit, / [is] Ruddy and sweet to eat," lines based upon "Bread of deceit is sweet to a man . . ." (Prov. 20:17; cf. *VDA* 191:17, Job 24:20). In *Europe* (1794) ". . . stolen joys are sweet & bread eaten in secret pleasant" (237:6), a clear recall of "Stolen waters are sweet, and bread eaten in secret is pleasant" (Prov. 9:17). It also is in *Europe* (243:2–6) that Newton "blow'd the enormous blast" of "The Trump of the last doom," and the passage becomes significant when we note in Zechariah that "the Lord GOD shall blow the trumpet . . ." (9:14).[19] Blake's meaning is bitterly ironic, for "The last trump" (I Cor. 15:52) concerns resurrection, but Newton's action causes the "Angelic hosts" to fall.

The "fiery beam of Fuzon / [which] Was a pillar of fire to Egypt . . ." in *The Book of Ahania* (250:44–45) recalls the pillar of fire which was a "cloud and darkness" to the Egyptians, though it gave "light by night" to the Israelites (Exod. 13:21; 14:20). *The Book of Ahania* also records that "Mount Sinai [is] in Arabia" (251:46), and in Galatians, Agar (Hagar) appears as "mount Sinai in Arabia" (4:25). In this same text of Blake, the "Eggs of unnatural production" hatch into a serpent (250:7–15; cf. *FZ* 325:166–68), probably the cockatrice, reputed to be hatched by a serpent from a cock's egg, and in Isaiah the Israelites "hatch cockatrice' eggs, . . . and that which is crushed breaketh out into a viper" (59:5).

In the Small Book of Designs one of Blake's illustrations carries the subscript "The Book of my Remembrance" (*K* 262; cf. *LJ* 612), a phrase from Malachi 3:16. In another design of this series a female is seen in the heavens with an infant, with the legend "Teach these Souls to Fly." This imagery may relate to a passage in Ezekiel which Blake uses years later, where it is said that the Lord "will let the souls go, even the souls that ye hunt to make them fly" (13:20).

Blake utilized the biblical text with considerable imaginative latitude. As an example, Los is simply understood to be an anagram for *sol*, "sun" (cf. To Thomas Butts, 22 Nov. 1802, 818:58, and *Mil* 505:6), and as such he sits "clothed in sackcloth of hair" (*J* 719:11), an echo of Revelation 6:12. But Los is not a linear equation in Blake's myth. He, like Urizen, is associated with the Ancient of Days, and Los is seen "planting his right foot firm / Upon the Iron crag of Urizen," springing "Into the heavens" and turning "in a mighty circle" (*FZ* 332:464–66).[20] Elsewhere it is the "Space of Love" that Los divides with "brazen Compasses" (*J* 734:46–47), for he is a generative god. The space of "Canaan" (one of Blake's designations for the womb) closes Los from Eternity (*Mil* 491:10; cf. *J* 656:18–19). Los is "possessor of the moon" (*Eur* 239:7) and "inspir'd by the holy Spirit" (*FZ* 343:108). He is "Lord of the Furnaces" (*J* 627:26), which are located in the "Valley of the Son of Hinnom" (*J* 636:34).[21] Los calls with the Voice of Thunder (cf. Ps. 104:7) and in the form of the constellation Orion stamps starry rocks, reminiscent of the "host of heaven" stamped to powder in Daniel.[22] With his "mace of iron" (Orion's club) he is the symbolic Potter who "breaks the potsherds" (*J* 718–19:3–6) into "shivers" (*J* 640:61), imagery reflected from Revelation 2:27 and Psalm 2:9. Los in various metamorphoses is Blake, Time, Joseph of Arimathea, Jacob, Elias, Elijah, Adam, Jehovah, and Elohim.[23] Los keeps "the Divine Vision in time of trouble" (*J* 655:15), possibly an echo of Jeremiah 14:8, and he particularly is associated with Jesus (*J* 743:3–7). The "Sweat & blood [that] stood on the limbs of Los in globes" in *The Four Zoas* (307:67) recall Christ's agony in Gethsemane, for ". . . his sweat was as it were great drops of blood falling down to the ground" (Luke 22:44; cf. *FZ* 350:349). Los is the "Spirit of Prophecy" (*J* 674:31), and in Revelation the "testimony of Jesus is the spirit of prophecy" (19:10), and Blake mentions the "Testimony of Jesus" in a later passage (*J* 714:14).

The relatively concise symbolic ramifications of Los represent only a fragmented portion of the complex and arcane idiom which concerns Blake's indebtedness to the Bible. Blake has the Whore of Babylon create one of the eminent philosophers of Europe (*Mil* 506:41) and converts two soldiers of his Majesty's dragoons into Adam and Noah (*J* 625:23, 25), and they, "Skofeld" and "Kox," labor "mightily / In the Wars of Babel & Shinar" (*J* 628:41–42).[24] Blake begins a sardonic genealogy of Christ, "annotating" a symbolic passage in the New Testament, but when the biblical text here fails to follow accurate sequence he corrects it (*J* 696:8–13; cf. *FZ* 350:365). Blake gives Noah's wife a name and makes a son his own father.[25] He combines biblical imagery with an English nursery rhyme (*J* 673:45–48) and places the incestuous first son of Jacob on an antiquarian stone secreted by St. Swithin's church (*J* 715:33–34). Blake has the tigers of wrath beat swords into plowshares and the "Devil" quotes Solomon.[26] A glow-worm becomes the Watchman of Isaiah 21:11, and the Last Judgment takes place in the loins (*J* 656:38). A river bordering Moab becomes the generative canals of the female (*Mil* 524:24–31), and Blake takes the fabric of the last four books of the Pentateuch and forms it into an amazing sexual thema.[27] Blake could paraphrase an innocuous passage from the Song of Solomon, associate it with a line from *Comus*, and reduce it all to a highly cerebral eroticism.[28] A man who was learned enough to invalidate the chronology of the Bishop of Llandaff with condescending

exactness but who constructed Stonehenge with stones of Eden
(J 701:1–2) possesses, to say the least, a knowledge and an imagination that have fearful proportions.[29]

For purposes of exposition, we can best acquaint ourselves with
the rudiments of Blake's cryptic grammar by examining random
aspects of its multiplicity and variation. When, for instance, Blake
states that "In the Vale of Surrey . . . Horeb terminates in Rephaim" (Mil 517:57), the context is elusive, for Horeb in the Wilderness has nothing to do with the shades of the dead near Jerusalem.
In prosaic translation Blake means that the negative laws of the
Decalogue,[30] proclaimed on Horeb and invading "England's pleasant pastures," lead inevitably to the sacrifice and destruction of
the spirit.[31] The "Rock of Odours," an enigmatic phrase mentioned in Milton, has biblical significance when we find it relates
to Christ's sepulcher of hewn stone, where spices were brought.[32]
"Billows & waves pass over" Blake's Eternal Man (FZ 301:133),
and the fallen man is "Wash'd with the tides" (FZ 341:5). He
"lays upon the shores, leaning his faded head / Upon the Oozy
rock inwrapped with weeds of death" (FZ 354:513–14).[33] This
imagery, in part, is illuminated when we recall Jonah: "For thou
hadst cast me into the deep, in the midst of the seas; and the floods
compassed me about: all thy billows and thy waves passed over
me. . . . The waters compassed me about, even to the soul: the
depth closed me round about, the weeds were wrapped about
my head" (2:3, 5). In The Four Zoas (362:199–200) when Ahania
is "buried . . . in a silent cave. / [And] Urizen dropped a tear,"
the biblical counterpart appears to be Sarah's death (Abraham
did "weep for her") and her burial in the cave of Machpelah.[34]
A daughter of Albion nails her consort's hands to Bath-Rabbim
(daughter of multitudes), a gate of the wall of Heshbon (reasoning); and, although "Bath-Rabbim" specifically stems from the
Song of Solomon (7:4), Blake is speaking of woman as the creature
who forms the "dark Satanic body" of death, condemning man to
the generative world.[35]

In The Four Zoas (352:438–50) the King of Light, who has
"eyelids like the Sun" and scales like the "windows of the morning," arises in "pride" upon the "petrific hardness" of the deeps.

For it is in Job that the "face of the deep is frozen" (38:30), and Leviathan's "scales are his pride" (41:15) and his eyes are like the "eyelids of the morning" (41:18). In this passage Blake confines his imagery to a relatively compact biblical sequence, but elsewhere disparate lines in his symbolism also frequently emanate from a central source. In Psalm 104:2–5 occurs the following imagery:

Who coverest thyself with light as with a garment: who stretchest out the heavens like a curtain:
. . . who maketh the clouds his chariot: who walketh upon the wings of the wind:
Who maketh his angels spirits; his ministers a flaming fire:
Who laid the foundations of the earth, that it should not be removed for ever.

Blake used this sequence in different texts. In *Jerusalem* (684:2–3) the Divine Vision appears, and "the Light is his Garment," and in *The Four Zoas* (294:107; cf. *J* 738:33–34, *FZ* 333:6) occurs the passage, "Do I not stretch the heavens abroad, or fold them up like a garment?" Luvah is seen "walking on the winds" in a different passage of *The Four Zoas* (272:300), and elsewhere in this poem we read of the "Spirits of Flaming fire" (274:384; cf. Heb. 1:7), while in *Milton* (500:50) Blake refers to the "fast foundations of the Earth." [36]

Another example is seen in *Milton* (493:26) where Satan draws "a third part in the fires as stubble"; and in *America* Orc "serpent-form'd / Stands at the gate of Enitharmon to devour her children" (198:3–4), while later Enitharmon produces "a man Child to the light" in *The Book of Urizen* (232:39–40). These various lines are pertinent to Revelation,

And his tail drew the third part of the stars of heaven, . . . and the dragon stood before the woman which was ready to be delivered, for to devour her child as soon as it was born.
And she brought forth a man child . . .[37]

Blake reorients and amends biblical imagery to suit his purposes. In *Milton* (485:41) "the night of prosperity and wantonness" is reminiscent of "days in prosperity, and . . . years in pleasures" (Job 36:11). In *The Four Zoas* (353:493) it is asked, "Will you keep a flock of wolves & lead them?" and Blake appears to be "revising" a passage from Isaiah in which the wolf and the lamb, among other beasts, are enumerated, "and a little child shall lead them" (11:6). In one sequence in *The Four Zoas* (378:790–806) Luvah is "put for dung on the ground" and the "heavens [are formed] of sweetest woods." The "winter is over & gone" and the "Sea . . . / Vomited out & gave up all," while the "Corn" is taken from the stores of Urizen. All of this imagery has relevance to the Bible, for in Jeremiah the slain "shall be put for dung upon the face of the earth" (8:2; 25:33). Blake frequently speaks of the Tabernacle as a paradigm of the universe, the "sweetest woods" recalling the Temple which was covered "with beams and boards of cedar" (I Kings 6:9). In the Song of Songs the "winter is past, the rain is over and gone" (2:11), while in Revelation the "sea gave up the dead which were in it; . . . and they were judged every man according to their works" (20:13; cf. *J* 687:57–58). The corn of Urizen is reminiscent of the "corn of Heaven" of Psalm 78:24 (and in *FZ* 374:650–53 Urizen's stars are "thresh'd").

In *The French Revolution* the "heavens were seal'd with a stone" and "each star appointed for watchers of night" (143:211–12). In Job 9:7 the Lord "sealeth up the stars," but it is in Matthew 27:66 that the crucifiers of Christ "made the sepulchre sure, sealing the stone, and setting a watch" for the night. The passage in which terrors are "bred from the blood of revenge and [the] breath of desire / In beastial forms" (*FR* 144:215–16) may be germane to the biblical text, for it is in Numbers 35:19 that we read of the "revenger of blood" (as elsewhere), and in Jeremiah 2:24 a bestial form, a wild ass in oestrum, "snuffeth up the wind at her pleasure," or *desire* (as glossed; cf. *FZ* 338:202, *J* 700:48). In *The Four Zoas* (294:103), "All is Confusion. All is tumult, & we alone are escaped." Probably Blake had I Corinthians 14:33 in mind, for here "confusion" is glossed as *tumult,* and it is in chapter 1 of Job that "I only am escaped alone" occurs (cf. *J* 655:82). Later in this text (*FZ* 354:527–31) Blake recalls the "Lion dead, & in his belly [are] worms / [which] Feast on his death . . ." A pale horse seeks for a pool to "lie him down & die," for "his bright eyes decay." The lion, of course, is the animal of Samson's riddle (Judg. 14:8, 14), wherein "Out of the eater came forth meat" (14:14), and the imagery about the horse may relate to Zechariah 12:4, where the Lord "will smite every horse of the people with blindness."

Blake's adaptation of the Bible can be translucent or opaque. In *The Four Zoas* (304:253–55, 270) Blake quotes almost verbatim sequential verses from John (11:21–23), but later in this poem only the slightest isthmus connects a phrase and its biblical source, a tenuous allusion to II Kings 4:35 where Man "sneezed seven times" (341:17).

Blake's approach, however, often is direct. When Blake refers to the "Gates of Thanksgiving, [and] . . . Windows of Praise" (*J* 647:20) he borrows from Psalm 100:4, "Enter into his gates with thanksgiving, and into his courts with praise. . . ." The Daughters of Beulah (*Beulah* being the Hebrew word for *married* as found in Isa. 62:4) anoint Christ's "feet with ointment" and wipe them with "the hair of their head" (*FZ* 347:237–38), lines which pertain to Jesus in Luke 7:37–38 and John 12:3. Blake's passage about "a habitation & a place / In which we may be hidden under the shadow of wings" (*Mil* 519:24–25; cf. *FZ* 304:260) is similar to imagery in Psalms in which the Lord is implored "Hide me under the shadow of thy wings" (17:8), and in a later psalm the Lord looks down from "the place of his habitation" (33:14). In *Jerusalem* (625:12) "thy Daughters are trodden in his vintage," and probably this is a remembrance of Lamentations 1:15 where "the Lord hath trodden the virgin . . . as in a winepress." In another passage of *The Four Zoas* (275:398–99) "My sons are Mad / With wine of cruelty," presumably an allusion to Jeremiah 51:7 in which the nations have drunk of the wine of Babylon, and "therefore the nations are mad." Again in *The Four Zoas* "A portion of my Life / That in Eternal fields in comfort wander'd with my flocks / At noon . . ." (301:137–39) parallels the Canticles: "Tell me, O thou whom my soul loveth, where thou feedest, where thou makest thy flock to rest at noon . . ." (1:7). "I walk by the footsteps of his flocks" (*FZ* 368:427; cf. *FZ* 370:508) also is similar to "go thy way forth by the footsteps of the flock . . ." (Song of Sol. 1:8).

Blake's passage about "Becoming obedient to death" and the "Witnesses" dead in the "Street of the Great City" (*Mil* 506:58–59) utilizes the language of Philippians 2:7–8 and Revelation 11:3, 8. Recollections of Matthew 13:27 and 6:25 occur in the "wild flowers [planted] among our wheat" (*J* 716; cf. *J* 667:20) and the "Body [being] more than Raiment" (*J* 717). When Jerusalem asks Christ if he has been "pierced in the House of thy Friends" (*J* 693:52–53) Zechariah 13:6 is Blake's source, while Isaiah 55:1 and 66:11–12 are noted when Blake mentions salvation "without Money & without Price" (*J* 694:21–22) and the "children [put] to my breasts . . . [and] sons & daughters to my knees" (*J* 720:26). The imagery of II Samuel 14:13–15 and Luke 12:32 is combined when Blake speaks of the "banished ones" and enjoins the "little Flock" to fear not (*J* 653:25–26). The songs which are "turned into cries of Lamentation" (*FZ* 310:206) come from Amos 8:10, while the "Odors" that arise singing a song (*FZ* 376:726–27) are reminiscent of Revelation 5:8–9, in which the "odours . . . are the prayers of saints," and they sing a "new song" (cf. *FZ* 375:683). At times Blake also quotes the formulalike salutations or benedictions that occur in the Bible.[38]

Sometimes Blake's lines carry with them an unstated irony, often a reading of black for white. The "harp, the flute, [and] the mellow horn," the "instruments of music" of "Jerusalem's joy" in *Jerusalem* (721:48–49), are possibly the "flute, harp, [and] sackbut" and "all kinds of musick" that in Daniel signal the worship of the "golden image" of Nebuchadnezzar (3:5 ff.).[39] In *Jerusalem* (628:23–25) the "liquid ruby, / The crysolite, the topaz, the jacinth & every precious stone" are found in Los's furnaces. These stones allude to the jewels in "Eden the garden of God" (Ezek. 28:13), and later in *Jerusalem* the "chaste" rejection of Enitharmon takes on tragic significance, when she demands of Los that he cast away this symbolic semen: "Cast thou in Jerusalem's shadows thy Loves, silk of liquid / Rubies, Jacinths, Crysolites, issuing from thy Furnaces" (*J* 732:17–20).[40]

The following obviously is biblical in content: "O Virgin of terrible eyes who dwellest by Valleys of springs / Beneath the Mountains of Lebanon in the City of Rehob in Hamath . . ." (*J*

706:54–55), but the passage concerns the "undefiled" virgin of the Song of Solomon (6:9), whose eyes "overcome" (6:5) and ravish her beloved (4:9), for "she that looketh forth" is "terrible as an army with banners" (6:10). The bride is implored to come from Lebanon and look from Mount Hermon, adjacent to Beth-rehob (4:8). The valley of this city was near one of the sources of the Jordan, presumably the valleys of the springs.[41] In *Jerusalem* (717–18:2–6, 22, 32–33) "a flame of fire, even as a Wheel / Of fire" devours "all things in its . . . course," while Jesus, who creates "Nature from this fiery Law," demands that "no curse / Go forth out of thy mouth . . ." And these lines are amplified when we turn to James 3:6, 10: "And the tongue is a fire, a world of iniquity: so is the tongue among our members, that it defileth the whole body, and setteth on fire the course [*wheel*, as glossed] of nature; . . . Out of the same mouth proceedeth blessing and cursing. My Brethren, these things ought not so to be."

Blake refers to

The Monstrous Churches of Beulah, [and] the Gods of Ulro dark,
Twelve monstrous dishumaniz'd terrors, Synagogues of Satan,
A Double Twelve & Thrice Nine: such their divisions. (*Mil* 528:16–18)

Although the language is ambiguous, Blake may be alluding in part to the Old and New Testaments, for the Hebrews divided their canon into twenty-four books, or a double twelve, and the New Testament books total to a "Thrice Nine."

With the specific imagery of the Bible—that Double Twelve and Thrice Nine—in mind and the cognizance of its depth, scope, and significance in Blake's symbolism, we can now examine the more convoluted aspects of this "system." These aspects will emphasize how thoroughly Blake was committed to this source for inspiration.

Blake weaves a single theme from unrelated biblical sources in the following, and his imagery represents one of his most concentrated and sustained efforts. To simplify explication the passage will be discussed in two segments. The first segment follows:

My tents are fall'n! my pillars are in ruins! my children dash'd
Upon Egypt's iron floors & the marble pavements of Assyria!
I melt my soul in reasonings among the towers of Heshbon.
Mount Zion is become a cruel rock, & no more dew
Nor rain, no more the spring of the rock appears, but cold
Hard & obdurate are the furrows of the mountain of wine & oil . . .
                                                            (J 719:1-6)

In Jeremiah 10:20 (also note 4:20) the "tabernacle is spoiled, and
all . . . cords are broken," while in II Kings 25:13 Jerusalem is
besieged, and the "pillars of brass that were in the house of the
Lord" are shattered. Egypt is an iron furnace in *Jerusalem* (735:18–
19; cf. Deut. 4:20), and the "marble pavements of Assyria" probably allude to the children "dashed in pieces at the top of all the
streets" of No, which is associated with Nineveh (Nah. 3:10),
capital of the Assyrian kingdom, and noted by Blake in an earlier
passage (*FZ* 279:546–47). *Reasoning* is the Hebraic etymology of
*Heshbon*, and the soul is melted in Psalms 107 and 119 (cf. *FZ*
315:142, *J* 645:4). Mount Zion is "desolate" in Lamentations 5:18,
while dew is upon this mount in Psalm 133:3. But Blake's imagery
also is comparable to that of Haggai 1:10–11: "Therefore the heaven
over you is stayed from dew, and the earth is stayed from her fruit.
And I called for a drought upon the land, and upon the mountains,
and upon the corn, and upon the new wine, and upon the oil, and
upon that which the ground [furrows] bringeth forth . . ." Although
rocks sometimes gush forth with water in the Bible, Blake's imagery
relates to the "clear spring of the rock" mentioned elsewhere (*FZ*
366:346), and this alludes to the crystal spring of the River of Life
in Revelation 22:1 and Ezekiel 47:9, what Blake calls the "Fountain
in a rock / Of Crystal" (*Mil* 526:49–50).

The second segment of Blake's passage refers to

The mountain of blessing [which] is itself a curse & an astonishment.
The hills of Judea are fallen with me into the deepest hell.
Away from the Nations of the Earth & from the Cities of the Nations
I walk to Ephraim. I seek for Shiloh. I walk like a lost sheep
Among precipices of despair; in Goshen I seek for light
In vain, and in Gilead for a physician and a comforter.

Goshen hath follow'd Philistea. Gilead hath join'd with Og.
They are become narrow places in a little and dark land . . .

(*J* 720:7–14)

The mountain of blessing is an allusion to Gerizim, the mount
of blessing which opposed Ebal, the mountain of curses (Deut.
11:29), while "a curse & an astonishment" is a phrase found in
Jeremiah (29:18). It was at the high places of Topheth (a hill
of Judea) in the valley of Hinnom that parents made their children
pass through the fires of Molech, and this valley became known
as the "valley of slaughter," or *hell*, the vale of Gehenna (Jer.
7:31–32). "Nations of the earth" parallels Jeremiah 33:9 and 26:6,
while "Cities of the Nations" is reminiscent of Revelation 16:19,
and Jesus "walked no more . . . among the Jews" but went into
a "city called Ephraim, and there continued with his disciples" in
John 11:54. Shiloh, also located in Ephraim, is identified with the
Messiah, but it was the *place* which the Lord forsook in Psalm
78:60.

In Jeremiah the Israelites have become "lost sheep," which are
"astray" on "the mountains: they have gone from mountain to hill,
. . . [and] have forgotten their restingplace" (50:6). While at Goshen
the "children of Israel had light in their dwellings" when the land of
Egypt was cast into "thick darkness" (Exod. 8:22; 10:21–23). And
following this allusion Blake uses additional imagery from Jeremiah:
"Is there no balm in Gilead; is there no physician there?" (8:22).
The word "comforter" is an allusion to John 14:16, to which Blake
refers in *The Marriage of Heaven and Hell* (*K* 150) and later in Plate
17 of his *Illustrations of the Book of Job*. Goshen has followed
Philistea, for the lost children of light have been perverted to the
foreign religions of "Baalim, and Ashtaroth . . . and the gods of the
Philistines" (Judg. 10:6). It was Sihon, the Amorite king of Gilead,
who allied himself with Og, ruler of Bashan, in attempting to expel
the Israelites in their expeditions east of Jordan, and the "little and
dark land" is "the dark land of Cabul" (*J* 721:63), the area awarded
Hiram for his assistance in construction of the Temple.[42]

The Temple, or Tabernacle, contained the Tables of Law which were "written on both their sides" (Exod. 32:15), and "Moses' Law" represents "The Ancient Heavens, . . . / Writ with Curses from Pole to Pole . . ." (*EG* 754:11–13; cf. Isa. 34:4). The "infernal scroll / Of Moral laws and cruel punishments" is drawn out upon "the clouds of Jehovah" (*Mil* 489:21–22; cf. Zech. 5:1–4), and Blake expands this imagery in a slightly different context when he speaks of Vala's "Veil of Moral Virtue, woven for Cruel Laws," for this whole Veil is a "Law . . . & a Curse" (*J* 646:20–32; cf. *J* 666:10).

In *Milton* "The Clouds of Ololon [are] folded [around Christ] as a Garment [of War] dipped in blood, / Written within & without in woven letters . . ." (534:12–15). These lines, in part, may recall the "vesture dipped in blood [of Christ's enemies]" (cf. Isa. 63:3), a garment on which is "written" the Word of God (Rev. 19:13, 16). In an earlier passage in *Milton* a woven Garment has "writings written all over it in Human Words" (499:6–25), an allusion to the priestly habiliments of Aaron, garments of "curious" embroidery or needle-work (Exod. 28:8; 39:29). In this same sequence "The misery of unhappy Families shall be drawn out into its border," and this garment's border or hem is wrought with the needle and may allude to Numbers 15:38–39, in which the Israelites are bidden to "make them fringes in the borders of their garments . . . ," a fringe which will serve as a reminder of the negative "commandments" of the Lord. "Pestilence shall be its fringe, & the War its girdle," says Blake (cf. *Mil* 528:23–24, 529:26; *J* 625:20), and he speaks of the Clothing of Cruelty and of "Holiness as a breastplate & . . . a helmet," possibly recalling "For he put on righteousness as a breastplate, and an helmet of salvation upon his head; and he put on the *garments of vengeance* for clothing, and was clad with zeal as a cloke" (Isa. 59:17). This "Clothing of Cruelty," which in Blake's text belongs to the Shadowy Female, is "woven of sighs & . . . lamentations" and is "Wrought with the needle" in "pain & woe," and its weavings must be learned by "rote" (cf. *J* 632:38–39). These lines seem to have direct relevance to Ezekiel 2:9–10 where a "roll of a book" (scroll) was "written within and without: and there was written therein *lamentations,* and mourning, and *woe.*" Such imagery is given further definition in Psalm 139:13–16 in which the Lord "covered" (knit together) the embryo in "my mother's womb," for "in thy book all my members were written." This organism is "curiously wrought," and the Hebraic meaning of this phrase is *as embroidered with threads of many colors.*[43] Blake develops this idiom when he speaks of

> Joseph, an infant,
> Stolen from his nurse's cradle, wrap'd in needle-work
> Of emblematic texture, . . . sold to the Amalekite
> Who carried him down into Egypt . . .     (*Mil* 508:17–20)

Joseph, undergoing generation, is stolen from his eternal homeland (Gen. 40:15) and cast into a pit (the womb), and his coat of many or divers colors, the "embroidered" flesh of emblematic and priestly texture,[44] is a vesture dipped in "blood of battle" or War (*J* 704:23, Gen. 37:31). The Amalekites descended from Esau, who sold his birthright for a mess of red pottage,[45] and Egypt is the land of Rahab, the Whore of Babylon and the goddess of generation (cf. Ps. 89:10).

In *Jerusalem*

> The Heavens are cut like a mantle [of skin][46] around from the Cliffs of
>     Albion
> Across Europe, across Africa: in howlings & deadly War,
> A sheet & veil & curtain of blood is let down from Heaven
> Across the hills of Ephraim & down Mount Olivet to
> The Valley of the Jebusite. Molech rejoices in heaven . . .     (706:19–23)

This passage, partially, recounts Peter's vision in Acts 10:11–12,

> And [he] saw heaven opened, and a certain vessel[47] descending unto him, as it had been a great sheet knit at the four corners, and let down to earth:
> Wherein were all manner of fourfooted beasts of the earth, and wild beasts, and creeping things, and fowls of the air.

This mantle is related to the generative "bloody Veil" (*J* 704:16), the "knitted . . . Veil of Vala" (*J* 645:5), a "garment woven / Of War & Religion" (*Mil* 507:16–17). Elsewhere it becomes the "enormous warp & woof [that] rage[s] in the affrighted deep" (*FZ* 284:149) and a "Bloody Shrine of War / Pinn'd around from Star to

Star" (*EG* 757:23–24), an ironic allusion to the Veil of Cherubim, cunningly wrought and hanging in the Tent, or Tabernacle (cf. *J* 698:1–3). The world of generation is symbolized by a "Curtain & Veil & fleshy Tabernacle" (*J* 688:39–40). Although Blake's reference to Ephraim is fraught with overtones,[48] he may allude to the removal of the Ark from Ephraim, where it long remained, to the place where Uzzah was struck and thence to Jerusalem (cf. *J* 706:51, II Sam. 6:1–12). Whatever Blake's symbolic intention, the knitted, bloody sheet of generation unfolds across Ephraim in the north to the Mount of Olives on the eastern suburbs of Jerusalem.[49] Olivet was the mountain of Corruption or Offense, where Solomon built idolatrous shrines to Molech for his heathen wives, and at its foot was the traditional site of Gethsemane. From here, southward, the terrible mantle lets down to Gehenna and the Valley of Hinnom, the *valley of the Jebusite* where Molech rejoiced in the sacrifice of children (Josh. 15:8, Jer. 7:31–32). Also in or near this valley was located the Potter's Field, or *field of blood*, to which Blake refers in *Jerusalem* (640:32). In *Jerusalem* (739:2–5) Blake mentions the English

> taking refuge
> In the Loins of Albion. The Canaanite united with the fugitive
> Hebrew, whom she divided into Twelve & sold into Egypt,
> Then scatter'd the Egyptian & Hebrew to the four Winds.[50]

Here Blake probably is alluding to Jacob's fleeing (a fugitive Hebrew) from Laban in the Genesis account: "So he fled with all that he had" to the "land of Canaan" (31:18–22; 37:1). Jacob is counseled by God to "fear not to go down into Egypt," and he takes "all his seed . . . with him into Egypt" (46:3–7), Joseph already being there. "All the souls that came with Jacob into Egypt . . . came out of his loins" (46:26), and they become a "multitude of people" (48:4). Among Jacob's group is Simeon, who cohabited with a "Canaanitish woman" (Exod. 6:15), and Judah also had offspring from the "daughter of a certain Canaanite whose name was Shuah" (and to whom Blake calls attention in his maternal genealogy of Christ; see Gen. 38:3, I Chron. 2:3). Blake's reference to the "Egyptian" may allude to Manasseh and Ephraim, sons of Joseph who were to represent two of the twelve Hebrew tribes, for their mother, Asenath, was the daughter of the Egyptian priest of On. "Sold into Egypt" is an elaboration of the Joseph theme in which the "Midianites sold him into Egypt" (Gen. 37:36). There also are overtones of Exodus (13:17) in which the Hebrews, again as fugitives, flee out of Egypt and eventually scatter into the region of the Holy Land. The female, here divider of the Twelve Tribes, is similar to Blake's "Daughters of Canaan" who have "divided Simeon," for he "roll'd apart in blood / Over the Nations . . ." (*J* 715:41–51).[51] In another passage Blake notes that the fleshy "Veil which Satan puts between Eve & Adam" is an attempt to enslave the

> Sons of Jerusalem & plant them in One Man's Loins,
> To make One Family of Contraries, that Joseph may be sold
> Into Egypt for Negation, A Veil the Saviour born & dying rends.
> (*J* 686:11–16) [52]

This veil is the generative veil of the female, the womb or the shell of matter.

Because "The laws of the Jews were (both ceremonial & real) the basest & most oppressive of human codes . . ." (Annotations to Watson 393:25), Blake was fascinated as well as horrified by their ritual. With this in mind we can turn to a fragmentary poem in the Note-Book, probably written about 1793.

> I saw a chapel all of gold
> That none did dare to enter in,
> And many weeping stood without,
> Weeping, mourning, worshipping.
>
> I saw a serpent rise between
> The white pillars of the door,
> And he forc'd & forc'd & forc'd,
> [Till he broke the pearly door—*deleted*]
> Down the golden hinges tore.
>
> And along the pavement sweet,
> Set with pearls & rubies bright,[53]
> All his slimy length he drew,
> Till upon the altar white

> Vomiting his poison out
> On the bread & on the wine.
> So I turn'd into a sty
> And laid me down among the swine.　　　　(K 163)

The "chapel of gold" with its pillars of the door, swinging on golden hinges, finds its archetype in the Tabernacle, or Temple, for this structure was overlaid with gold (I Kings 6:21). Brazen pillars were at its entrance (I Kings 7:21), and the doors of the "most holy place" and the Temple itself were mounted on "hinges of gold" (I Kings 7:50). In "The Garden of Love" (K 215) "the gates of this Chapel [also] were shut," and the chapel of gold echoes Numbers 25:6 in which the Israelites are seen "weeping before [without] the door of the tabernacle of the congregation" (cf. Joel 2:17). This chapel is the "Feminine Tabernacle," and the "Vomiting" of the phallic serpent upon the altar is analogous to the High Priest's entrance into the Holy of Holies once a year to sprinkle sacrificial blood upon the Mercy Seat.[54] Blake frequently identifies the priesthood with the serpent, and the Prester Serpent is the "Priest of God," his "Cowl" of flesh probably symbolizing Uncircumcision.[55] The entry of the High Priest into the Most Holy Place with blood was traditionally interpreted as foreshadowing the entrance of Jesus into the heavens (Heb. 9:7, 21, 24–28),[56] and Blake reappraises this symbolism when he speaks of Christ born of the womb, ". . . when compulsory cruel Sacrifices had brought Humanity into a Feminine Tabernacle . . . the Lamb of God . . . became apparent on Earth" (J 652).[57]

Blake continues the theme of the Tabernacle and its offerings (FZ 284–85:166–200) when he refers to Urizen's temple and its "wondrous scaffold rear'd all round the infinite" and to the "Multitudes without number [who] work . . . the hewn stone . . ." Here Urizen leaves this "Golden Hall" and seeks the "Labyrinthine porches" of his heaven:

> 　　　　　　　toward the West, Urizen form'd
> A recess in the wall for fires to glow upon the pale
> Female's limbs in his absence, & her Daughters oft upon
> A Golden Altar burnt perfumes: with Art Celestial form'd

Foursquare, sculptur'd & sweetly Engrav'd to please their shadowy
mother.
. . . . . . . . . . . . . . . . . . . .
                                                    Also her sons,
With lives of Victims sacrificed upon an altar of brass
On the East side, Reviv'd her soul with lives of beasts & birds
Slain on the Altar, up ascending into her cloudy bosom.
Of terrible workmanship the Altar, labour of ten thousand Slaves,
One thousand Men of wondrous power spent their lives in its formation.
It stood on twelve steps nam'd after the names of her twelve sons,
And was Erected at the chief entrance of Urizen's hall.

Blake in this passage compounds the imagery of Solomon's Temple
with that of the Tabernacle of the wilderness. The scaffold to which
he calls attention is possibly the "brasen scaffold" on which Solomon
consecrated his Temple (II Chron. 6:13), a temple made of *hewn*
stone, fashioned before being transported to the temple site in order
that no sound of "any tool of iron" should be heard at the temple
location (I Kings 5:17–18; 6:7). In relays of "ten thousand," men
were sent to Lebanon to gather material for the golden Temple (I
Kings 5:14). The thousand men of wondrous power may allude
to "all the men of might" and to the "craftsmen and smiths" of
Jerusalem, the latter of which numbered a thousand (II Kings
24:16),[58] while the "Labyrinthine porches" are reminiscent of the
great "porch before the temple" and the "chambers round about"
with "winding stairs" (I Kings 6:3–8).

The fires toward the West which "glow" upon the female in
Urizen's absence (for he is a sun god), possibly allude to the golden
candlestick, the light of which glowed from evening to morning
(Exod. 27:21). Though the Bible notes that it was placed "southward" in the sanctuary (Exod. 25:31, 37; 40:24), the candlestick was
*west* of the altar of burnt offerings; Blake's placement, hence, is minor
poetic (or symbolic) license. And Flavius Josephus describes these
"seven lamps" as being "in imitation of the number of planets"
(*Antiquities of the Jews* III. vi. 7).

This imagery receives greater focus when we realize that Blake
is referring to the *golden altar* or altar of incense which stood in the
Tabernacle. This altar of "perfumes" was exactly a cubit *foursquare*, overlaid with gold, and we may assume "*sweetly Engrav'd.*"

It was located toward the *western* part of the Tabernacle, and incense was burned on it morning and evening. The *brazen altar* or altar of burnt offering stood *east* in the tabernacle and directly at the threshold *(chief entrance)*. On this altar of brass, bullocks and doves were sacrificed, but the altar had no steps (Exod. 20:26) but only a ledge around it on which the priests stood. Blake may have recalled the Temple of Herod, in which twelve steps descended from the vestibule to the Court of the Priests. This court surrounded the Holy of Holies and contained the altar of brass. (Also Josephus [*Wars* V. v. 4] notes that the "holy house" in the inmost court, the most sacred part of the Temple, was ascended to by twelve steps; cf. *J* 721:52.)

It is in Exodus (24:4) that Moses "builded an altar" of stones, an altar of burnt offerings, which had "twelve pillars, according to the twelve tribes [or Sons] of Israel." In *Europe* (241:7–9) Blake mentions "oak-surrounded pillars, form'd of massy stones, *uncut* / With tool, stones precious . . . / Of colours twelve . . . ," [59] and he is developing a devious but logical allusion to the Bible and to the unhewn stones of the "twelve pillars" erected by Moses in the wilderness. In Exodus (20:25) the Lord commands: "And if thou wilt make me an altar of stone, thou shalt not build it of hewn stone: for if thou lift up thy tool upon it, thou hast polluted it." In Blake's symbolic text "Albion began to erect twelve Altars / Of rough *unhewn* rocks . . ." (*J* 653:21–22), and Stonehenge, a crucial symbol in Blake's poetry, is built with the "precious unhewn stones of Eden" (*J* 701–2:1–3) called "unhewn / Demonstrations." The "Twelve rocky *unshap'd* forms, terrific forms of torture and woe," are the unhewn demonstrations of the fallen world.[60] The altar of "Ebal, Mount of cursing" (*J* 705:3), had *unhewn stones*, untouched of "iron tool" (cf. Deut. 27:1–8, Josh. 8:30–32), and Ebal and Stonehenge clearly are connected in Blake's symbolism.

The imagery of the tabernacle, or temple, is never far from Blake's mind:

Urizen wrathful strode above, directing the awful Building
As a Mighty Temple, delivering Form out of confusion.[61]
Jordan sprang beneath its threshold, bubbling from beneath
Its pillars: Euphrates ran under its arches: white sails
And silver oars reflect on its pillars & sound on its ecchoing

Pavements, where walk the Sons of Jerusalem who remain Ungenerate.[62]
But the revolving Sun and Moon pass thro' its porticoes:
. . . . . . . . . . . . . . . . . .
Egypt is the eight steps within. Ethiopia supports his pillars.
Lybia & the Lands unknown are the ascent without . . .     (*J* 690:21–36)

Blake here combines various elements related to the temples of Solomon and Herod and to Ezekiel's vision, for the Lord shows Ezekiel the *"form* of the house," or tabernacle (43:11).[63] Arches (40:22) and pillars (42:6) are found in Ezekiel's view of Jerusalem's mighty temple, as are the living "waters [which] issued out from under the threshold" of the East Gate (47:1; cf. *J* 690:43). Many chambers (40:17) and galleries (42:3) were constructed on and about the pavements of the temple, and such an arrangement would presuppose echoes. The reflections upon *shining pillars* may find their hint from Flavius Josephus, whose works Blake helped to engrave in 1785, for Josephus notes of Herod's Temple: "The middle [sanctuary] was much higher than the rest, and the wall of the front was adorned with beams, resting upon pillars, that were interwoven into it, and that front was all of polished stone, insomuch that its fineness, to such as had not seen it, was incredible, and to such as had seen it, was greatly amazing." [64] The sun which passes through the porticoes of the temple probably relates to the East Gate of the Temple at Jerusalem, which was so constructed that on the days of the spring and fall equinoxes the first rays of the rising sun could penetrate into the Holy of Holies. The *eight steps within* are the "eight steps" leading to the inner court (Ezek. 40:31, etc.). The ascent without may be "the gate of the outward court that looked toward the north" which "went up . . . by seven steps" (Ezek. 40:20, 22).[65] In Daniel 11:43 it is said that the Lord shall have power over "the precious things of Egypt: and *the Libyans and the Ethiopians shall be at his steps.*"

In a slightly later but related sequence Blake notes that "in the North Gate, in the West of the North, toward Beulah [the West], Cathedron's Looms are builded" in a wondrous "golden Building" (*J* 691:22–24). These lines may be an echo of the "entry . . . which looked toward the north . . . a place on the two sides westward" (Ezek. 46:19–20). In Ezekiel it is in the inner gate of the north that the "image of jealousy" is found (8:3), and it is also here that the women sat "weeping for Tammuz" (8:14). If this parallel is pertinent to Ezekiel, then Blake possibly alludes to the chambers where the priestly sacrifices were prepared, and Blake clearly considered the corporeal body a "sin offering" (cf. *Mil* 525:6). In this North Gate the Daughters of Los "Weave on the Cushion & Pillow Network fine / That Rahab & Tirzah may exist & live & breathe & love," and they weave "in bitter tears / The Veil of Goats-hair & Purple & Scarlet & fine twined Linen" (*J* 692:42–55), the curtains of the tabernacle (Exod. 36:8–14; 26:1–7). In Ezekiel 13:18–22 the Lord rejects the symbolic pillows and the weavers "promising . . . life": "Woe to the women that sew pillows [magic arm bands] . . . and make kerchiefs [veils] upon the head of every stature to hunt souls! Will ye hunt the souls of my people, and will ye save the souls alive that come unto you?"

In Ezekiel's temple the "west side" had a "wall round about . . . to make a separation between the sanctuary and the profane place" (42:19–20), and in Blake's poetry the "Western Gate fourfold is clos'd" (*J* 633:6), the gate of the tongue "Having a wall builded against it . . ." (*J* 635:26–27). Not only is the West Gate closed but so also is the "East, the Center, unapproachable for ever" (*J* 632:56), imagery accounted for by Ezekiel: "This [east] gate shall be shut, it shall not be opened, and no man shall enter in by it; because the Lord . . . hath entered in by it . . ." (44:1–2). Blake also has the starry "Wheels of Albion's sons," who are constellations in the heavens, form the ornaments (cherubim, palm trees, and flowers [I Kings 6:32]) of the East Gate in *Jerusalem* (633:12–14), and in Ezekiel "the cherubims [with their wheels] . . . stood at the door of the east gate of the Lord's house" (10:19).

Blake mentions a "Tabernacle / Of threefold workmanship" (*J* 735:44–45) and "A triple Female Tabernacle for Moral Law" (*J* 733:19), possibly recalling Herod's Temple which was enclosed by triple or threefold walls, according to Josephus (*Antiquities* XV. xi. 5). These threefold walls were pierced by several gates, and the great "threshold" gate of the East, leading into the Tabernacle, or Temple, was called the Beautiful Gate. Blake may have this imagery partially in mind when he speaks of the "Inner gates" of Enitharmon's bosom, brain, and bowels—before which the Daughters of Beulah weep. For "The East is Inwards" (*J* 635:30), and these gates are "Glorious & bright" and open into Eternity or Beulah (the West) from the female's "inward parts." But Enitharmon refuses to open these "bright gates." [66] They are "clos'd and barr'd . . . fast, / Lest Los should enter into Beulah thro' her beautiful gates" (*FZ* 279–80: 560–68; cf. *J* 635:19–20), and the Emanation which stands "before the Gates of Enitharmon, / Weeping" is reminiscent of the devout before the door of the "chapel of gold." [67] Here also the Daughters of Beulah are "silent in the Porches," possibly recalling the admonition in I Corinthians 14:34 in which the women are commanded to "keep silence in the churches." The East Gate is shut in both Blake's and Ezekiel's visions, the gate where the faithful worship without (Ezek. 46:3).[68]

In another context the walls which separate the sacred from the profane place become a barrier against the Male and Female. Between the "Oak of Weeping" (a gloss of Gen. 35:8) and the "Palm of Suffering" a "mighty Wall," or Veil, is formed (*J* 691:2–9), and "no more the Masculine mingles / With the Feminine, but the Sublime [male] is shut out from the Pathos [female] . . ." (*J* 736:10–11). The Veil of Vala begins to "Vegetate & Petrify" (*J* 691:3) around the earth, and Los forms this into a wall between these two trees, and in time this veil, or wall, becomes the "Mundane Shell" (*J* 691:7). Elsewhere this shell freezes around Canaan, the female space (*Mil* 490:1–7), which is on the vast expanse, where the Daughters of Albion weave the "Web / Of Ages & Generations." This Web is a "Veil of Cherubim" (*J* 698:1–4), the veil of the Temple which has cherubim of cunning work or embroidery (Exod. 26:1). This veil *separates* the Oak and Palm, and in a similar context it is asked, "Why [is] a little curtain of flesh on the bed of our desire?" (*Thel* 130:20). When the "stone walls of separation" are built, the Pathos, or suffering female, weaves "curtains of hiding secrecy," the veil of cherubim which hides the Mercy Seat of the Tabernacle (*J* 736:1–13; cf. *FZ* 332:488–89 and Exod. 25:4, gloss). Satan puts this veil "between Eve & Adam, / By which the Princes of the Dead enslave their Votaries . . ." (*J* 686:11–12), and if the language here applies, the *Oak of Weeping* and the *Palm of Suffering* (cf. Judg. 4:5) possibly are appellations for Adam and Eve, who are divided asunder by the veil of flesh in the corporeal world and stand on the edge of Beulah (*FZ* 277:464–65, *J* 646:20–26).

Blake in referring to Urizen's temple notes that "Quadrangular the building rose, [and] the heavens [are] squared by a line (*FZ* 284:168). Such imagery is similar to the foursquare architecture of Ezekiel's temple (48:16) and the "line of flax" (40:3; cf. Amos 7:7) which is used to measure the dimensions of the temple. Blake elaborates on this symbolism in *The Four Zoas*, where

> . . . Urizen laid the first Stone, & all his myriads
> Builded a temple in the image of the human heart,
> And in the inner part of the Temple, wondrous workmanship,
> They form'd the Secret place, reversing all the order of delight,
> That whosoever enter'd into the temple might not behold
> The hidden wonders, allegoric of the Generations
> Of secret lust, when hid in chambers dark the nightly harlot
> Plays in Disguise in whisper'd hymn & mumbling prayer. The priests
> He [Urizen] ordain'd & Priestesses, cloth'd in disguises bestial,
> Inspiring secrecy; & lamps they bore: intoxicating fumes
> Roll round the Temple; & they took the Sun that . . .
> . . . . . . . . . . . . . . . . . . . .
> Descended to the sound of instruments that drown'd the noise
> Of the hoarse wheels & the terrific howlings of wild beasts
> That drag'd the wheels of the Sun's chariot; & they put the Sun
> Into the temple of Urizen to give light to the Abyss,
> To light the War by day, to hide his secret beams by night,
> For he divided day & night in different order'd portions . . .
>
> (333–34:19–37)

Urizen is here the Lord who "laid the corner stone" of the foundations of the earth and "stretched [squared] the line upon it" (Job 38:4–6). It is in Psalm 40:8 that the "law is within my heart," glossed as *bowels*, and in Jeremiah 31:33 the Lord puts the "law [of the tables] in their inward parts, and write[s] it in their hearts . . ." (cf. II Cor. 3:3, Ezek. 11:19, and Heb. 8:10). In *The Four Zoas* the bosom of the female weaves "A tabernacle of delight for Jerusalem" (266:69–70), and elsewhere the "ark & veil" are hidden in the bosom or heart of Satan (*FZ* 348:291–93; cf. *FR* 139:113–15). In this temple-heart is the Secret Place, where the laws of the testimony are closed beneath the Mercy Seat.

Eventually, the walls (cf. Eph. 2:14) and the veil of separation of this temple Christ will break and rend, opening the way to the Mercy Seat. In *Jerusalem* (656:39–40) Luvah, or Love, draws "the Curtains around Albion in Vala's bosom," but the Lord will "rend the Veil," and Blake may have remembered II Corinthians 3:14–15 where the "vail is done away in Christ" and where "the vail is upon their heart." But in the fallen world the allegoric or phallic wonders of generation are hidden in dark chambers surrounded by intoxicating fumes. And Blake's imagery echoes Ezekiel in which "idols . . . [are] portrayed upon the wall," worshiped by a priest and his votaries, who hold censers in their hands, "and a thick cloud of incense went up." Ezekiel laments what is done "in the dark, [by] every man in the chambers of his imagery" (8:10–12; cf. *VDA* 194:3–7). In this same chapter we see the women "weeping for Tammuz" (8:14) and the fallen worship "the sun toward the east" (8:16). The priestly clothing of beasts is reminiscent of the "Clothing of Cruelty," the raiment of emblematic needlework of Aaron's priesthood (*Mil* 499:6–25), and the loud instruments of Blake's temple recall "the priests [who] praised the Lord day by day, singing with loud instruments . . . ," presumably the trumpets and cymbals of the Tabernacle (II Chron. 30:21; cf. Num. 29:1). Urizen's palace is the "temple of the Sun" (*FZ* 344:140), the "tabernacle for the sun" in Psalm 19:4 which Blake recalls in *Jerusalem* (731:21), and "chariots of the sun" are burned with fire in II Kings 23:11. The Sun, which lights the war by day, is the light which is to "rule the day" in Genesis 1:16 (cf. Ps. 136:8), for the sun and the moon "divide the light from the darkness" (1:18).

Blake frequently alludes to the Tabernacle and its sacrifices, and Stonehenge becomes transposed into a tabernacle of the Hebrew rites:

Bring your Offerings, your first begotten, pamper'd with milk & blood,
Your first born of seven years old, be they Males or Females,
To the beautiful Daughters of Albion! they sport before the Kings
Clothed in the skin of the Victim! blood, human blood is the life
And delightful food of the Warrior; the well fed Warrior's flesh
Of him who is slain in War fills the Valleys of Ephraim [double fruitful-
    ness] with
Breeding Women walking in pride & bringing forth under green trees

With Pleasure, without pain, for their food is blood of the Captive.
Molech rejoices thro' the Land . . .                    (J 706:30–38)

The animal offerings of the Tabernacle were to be the first-born of
both male and female, free of blemish, and at least eight days old.
In Judges 6:25–26 a bullock of seven years is sacrificed to the Lord,
but Blake's allusion, in part, is to the slaying of children. The flesh
of the sacrificed beast (peace offerings) was eaten by the devout at
the place of the sanctuary, and in the Canticles the beloved is raised
"up under the apple tree: there thy mother brought thee forth" (8:5).
Zion, personified as a woman, travailed and "brought forth" a man
child before "pain came" in Isaiah 66:7. "Blood of the Captive" probably is an echo of Deuteronomy 32:42, and Blake appears to allude
to the imagery of Isaiah (57:3–5) in which the "sons of the sorceress"
are seen "Enflaming yourselves with idols under every green tree,
slaying the children in the valleys . . ." And in Jeremiah, Israel, again
represented as a woman, transgresses "upon every high hill and
under every green tree . . . playing the harlot" (2:20).[69]
    In *Jerusalem* Blake continues to agglutinate Celtic and biblical
myth, and the Daughters of Albion (who are in alternate guise the
daughters of Amalek, Canaan, and Moab) sacrifice their victims
with a knife of flint on the Stone of Trial, the sacrificial stone of
the "Druid" temple, Stonehenge.[70] This ancient British monument is
also a tabernacle, and

> The Daughters of Albion clothed in garments of needle work
> Strip them off from their shoulders and bosoms, they lay aside
> Their garments, they sit naked upon the Stone of Trial.
> The Knife of flint passes over the howling Victim: his blood
> Gushes & stains the fair side of the fair Daughters of Albion.
> They put aside his curls, they divide his seven locks upon
> His forehead, they bind his forehead with thorns of iron,
> They put into his hand a reed, they mock, Saying: "Behold
> The King of Canaan whose are seven hundred chariots of iron!"
> They take off his vesture whole with their Knives of flint,
> But they cut asunder his inner garments, searching with
> Their cruel fingers for his heart, & there they enter in pomp,
> In many tears, & there they erect a temple & an altar.
> They pour cold water on his brain in front . . .     (J 702:17–30) [71]

The stripping off of the vestments of the Daughters of Albion parallels the High Priest's laying aside his official garb on the Day of Atonement, when he enters the sanctum sanctorum. The garments of the priest are also sprinkled with blood in the rites of the Tabernacle (Exod. 29:21; cf. *J* 706:48–50), and the daughters who divide the "seven locks" of the sacrificial victim are a composite of Delilah, who in revenge, seeking dominion, had "the seven locks of his head" shorn (Judg. 16:19), an act which leads to Samson's imprisonment by the Philistines.[72] Most of the next three lines are a paraphrase of Matthew 27:28–31:

> And they stripped him, and put on him a scarlet robe.
> And when they had platted a crown of thorns, they put it upon his head, and a reed in his right hand: and they bowed the knee before him, and mocked him, saying, Hail, King of the Jews!
> . . . . . . . . . . . . . . . . . . . . . . . .
> And after that they had mocked him, they took the robe off from him, and put his own raiment on him, and led him away to crucify him.

In the middle of the preceding lines from *Jerusalem* Blake recalls Judges 4:3 in which Jabin, the King of Canaan, had "nine hundred chariots of iron." [73] The "vesture whole" is an allusion to Christ's garment woven "without seam" (John 19:23, glossed as *wrought*).[74] In pomp the daughters enter (cf. *J* 708:44) the temple in the form of a human heart, and the water poured on the head of the victim is the "baptism" of generation (cf. *Mil* 500:9), possibly analogous to the washing of the "inwards" of the sacrificial animal which has its body laid "in order" on the altar, the eyes, nostrils, tongue and ears of Blake's "generated" sacrifice (see Levit. 1:12–13, Exod. 29:17).[75]

Blake had an extreme interest in the significance of language, and at times he treats biblical matters pedantically. He states that "Basileia, βασιλεια, is not Kingdom but Kingship" (Annotations to Thornton 789), alluding to the Greek as it appears in Matthew 6:13 or Luke 11:2. The Four Zoas are "Lifes" (*FZ* 364:283, ζῶα), and Blake's references to Satan as the "Sick-one" and the "Evil One" (*Mil* 493:4, 496:30) presuppose some knowledge of the original Greek and Hebrew texts.[76] "Triple Elohim" (*Mil* 494:22) is the triune god of Genesis, and "Nephilim & Gibborim" (*J* 735:47) are plural forms of the Hebrew words for *giant*. Blake refers to Satan as "the Accuser" (*LJ* 615:86, 90, as elsewhere), the frequent meaning of the word in the Old Testament, while a Greek word for accuser in the New Testament is διάβολος. Bethlehem (*J* 657:25–26) is the "house of bread," the Hebraic meaning of the word. In *The Four Zoas* "all Nations" are "threshed out" (374:653), for in Joel 3:2, 14, the Lord "will also gather all nations" and bring them into the valley of *threshing* (gloss). In *Milton* (508:6) Blake writes, "We call'd him *Menassheh* because of the Generations of Tirzah," and later the vegetated forms become a "Generation of death & resurrection to forgetfulness" (*J* 638:9). Possibly Blake alludes to the glossed meaning of Manasseh's name in Genesis 41:51, *forgetting*.

Blake combines Jacob's wrestling with the Angel, the baptismal waters of the Jordan, the ground of Succoth, and the Valley of Beth Peor:

Urizen rose
And met him [Milton] on the shores of Arnon & by the streams of the brooks.
Silent they met and silent strove among the streams of Arnon
Even to Mahanaim, when with cold hand Urizen stoop'd down
And took up water from the river Jordan, pouring on
To Milton's brain the icy fluid from his broad cold palm.
But Milton took the red clay of Succoth, moulding it with care
Between his palms and filling up the furrows of many years,
Beginning at the feet of Urizen, and on the bones
Creating new flesh on the Demon cold and building him
As with new clay, a Human form in the Valley of Beth Peor.
(*Mil* 500:4–14)

It was on the Jabbok, not the Arnon, that Jacob wrestled with the Angel (Gen. 32:22), though in Numbers 21:15 the Arnon is "at the stream of the brooks." [77] Mahanaim was the place Jacob had his vision of divine favor (Gen. 32:1), while Urizen's baptism of Milton is a parody of John's baptism of Christ (the second Adam) at the waters of Jordan (Mark 1:9). Jacob journeyed to Succoth (Gen. 32:22), but Blake here is initiating an entirely different allusion to the *red clay of Succoth*.

Blake was absorbed with the creation of the first man (Gen. 2:7), in which "Elohim . . . created Adam" (*FZ* 351:401). Adam was made from *adamah*, "red clay," and Blake notes in *The Marriage of Heaven and Hell* that "Red clay brought forth" (148:13), and later, with ironic meaning, Adam "Lay bleach'd on the garden of Eden" (*SoL* 248:20–21; cf. *VDA* 191:19). The word "Adamah" also is mentioned in the *Laocoön* plate (*ca.* 1820), and eight times when Blake was working on his pictorial version of Genesis, he changed the word "ground," meaning earth ("And the Lord God formed man of the dust of the *ground*"), to the Hebraic form, *adamah*, the red clay of Adam. Also in I Kings 7:46 (cf. II Chron. 4:17) it was in the plain of Jordan that Hiram cast the holy vessels of the temple in the "clay *ground* [adamah] between Succoth and Zarthan," a point Blake was to borrow for his own use.[78] What in essence Blake is saying is that the corpus of the Covenant, the Law of Moses, must be re-evaluated because it is a philosophy of "Creeping Jesus" (*EG* 750:25; cf. Rom. 1:23), the Antichrist of the Nay-Sayers.[79] The body of Moses, the vehicular body of the Decalogue, was buried in Beth-peor (Deut. 34:6) and must be regenerated. Milton, who has come to redeem man from these errors, "form'd the Clay" of Urizen-Moses (*Mil* 502:10–12), "building" him with new clay.[80] This clay is the *adamah* of the Lord, the *red clay of Succoth* where holy vessels of the temple are cast, for when redemption comes man will "take off his filthy garments," and he will be clothed with "Imagination" (*Mil* 533:6), the allusion here coming from Zechariah 3:4.

Blake inclined his ear to parable, but it was, to use his own allusion to Jeremiah 6:10, an ear that circumcised the excrementitious (*J* 745:18). Blake's symbolic intent basically was one of revolt against the precepts of the eighteenth century. Although he closed his dark saying upon the harp with a note of affirmation, his reins instructed him in the night seasons that man uninspired by Divine Humanity would lead "youth to slaughter houses" and buy "beauty for a bit of bread" ("The human Image," 174).

Blake rejects the God of Is, who seeks a solid without fluctuation, persecuting Man in the Land of Uz, for this god puts (in the words of Joyce) "All space in a Notshall." Blake abhorred the religion of warped prurience which caused the "youth shut up" to generate "an amorous image." [81] The corporeal world to Blake vacillated between inverted Priapism, what he derisively calls "Religion," and its extroverted terminus, "War." War "is energy Enslav'd," but "religion / [is] The first author of this war . . ." (*FZ* 361:152–53). The "Christian" Philistines, as Blake says in another context, "spoil'd the hasty pudding" (Annotations to Watson 390:9). And Blake would draw a cloven hoof on an ecclesiastic in an illustration for Young's *Night Thoughts*. Compounded with this morality came the technological displacement caused by new inventions, implements which Blake knew would build Satanic Mills against the Divine Imagination in England's pleasant bowers:

> . . . & the water wheel
> That raises water into cisterns, broken & burn'd with fire
> Because its workmanship was like the workmanship of the shepherd;
> And in their stead, intricate wheels invented, wheel without wheel,
> To perplex youth in their outgoings & to bind to labours in Albion . . .
> (*J* 700:18–22)[82]

Blake knew that Horeb would always terminate in Rephaim, that the starry wheels of war would reject the wings of cherubim. But Blake also knew that the Wheels of Abstinence would be defeated, ultimately, by the lovely "Wings of Cherubim" (cf. *J* 645:34–35), and the *touching* of cherubim wings carries with it the Hebraic connotation of *to kiss* (Ezek. 3:13, gloss).

*Jerusalem* must serve as Blake's final textual "philosophy," and it is a hosanna of affirmation. But Blake's journey to organized innocence carried with it a shudder of experience, and, as it has been observed, one need not be a house to be haunted. Graphically, this stratum of experience can be seen in "The Infant Jesus Riding a Lamb" (Figgis, Pl. 41), for to the right of this idyll is a vine that recalls the serpent of Eden. Though virginal Spring looks down through the windows of the morning in *Poetical Sketches*, it is through these same windows that the harlot of Jericho stretches her cord of blood (*FZ* 361:159–60; see Josh. 2:18). The vision of Innocence can portray a figure of joy (?) inside the letter *o* of *Songs* on the title page of *Songs of Innocence*, but its demoniac counterpart of Experience is seen in *The Book of Los*, in which the same letter in *Los* contains within it the fetal Patriarch, tied down by the lacteals and sinews of generation. But despite the fact that London occasionally was the "City of Assassinations," Blake's ideas built Jerusalem in England's bowers.

As in I Corinthians 12:25, Blake hoped "That there should be no schism in the body; but that the members should have the same care one for another." Failure to achieve this mutual unity precipitated man's original fall from grace. Blake could write of those who conquered the classical humors, which ruled man's destiny, as "4 most holy men" (Annotations to Lavater 86:609).

It is highly appropriate that while an apprentice at Basire's workshop Blake executed an engraving of Joseph of Arimathea and a drawing of "Moses and the Tables of Stone" and that at the time of his death he was finishing a tempera version of the "Last Judgment," his most concentrated attempt at biblical iconography, said to contain upwards of one thousand figures. The first poem of *Poetical Sketches* is heavily indebted to the imagery of the Song of Songs, and more than forty years later in *The Ghost of Abel* (1822) Blake terminates his last significant literary effort with an allusion to the redaction of the "E" and "J" texts of the Pentateuch.[83] These works, both graphic and poetic, document the germinal and lasting influence the Bible exerted upon the ethos of Blake's philosophy.[84] A Fairy, the Eternals, and the sexual Daughters of Beulah dictate several of Blake's books, but it is particularly fitting that in the first song of *Innocence* a symbolic child implores the poet to "Pipe a song about a Lamb" and that it is the Saviour who dictates the words of the "mild song" of *Jerusalem.*

Biblical imagery became almost a *sine qua non* through which Blake's later poetry structured itself, a medium through which his poetry functioned. At times this inspiration degenerates into an oblique preciousness, a game of recognition of sources rather than the achievement of imaginative meaningfulness. Ultimately, however, Blake avoids allowing this imagery to become merely a mnemonic exercise for a closed and esoteric school of poetry. He gives a new radius of context to the Judeo-Christian tradition. If Blake spoke in parables to the blind, he also spoke through a hard and perceptive symbology, for he was incapable of writing "Verse as soft as Bartolloze" ("Blake's apology for his Catalogue," 555:2).

In the fallen world, poetry was the truly religious expression (*Mil*

514:60), and "Ideas" were "The Divine Members" (*Mil* 525:5–6). It is "Human Imagination" that is "the Divine Body of the Lord Jesus, blessed for ever" (*Mil* 482:3–4; cf. II Cor. 11:31). It is significant that Blake referred to his own symbolic poetry as *secret furniture* and *beautiful labyrinths,* allusions to the Bible and words exceptionally well put.[85] While Blake ran his "Order'd Race" (*J* 649) his "Talent" (an allusion to Matt. 25:25; see To Thomas Butts, 16 Aug. 1803, 829:8) lay hidden in the earth, but despite this he did as much as any poet of his time in the "Building up of Jerusalem" (*J* 717), and he knew those who calumniated his industry also mocked "the giver of every Mental Gift" (*J* 717). Blake probably is the greatest myth-maker in the language before Joyce, and it must be recognized that the Bible is inextricably woven into Blake's own eschatological tapestry. Unless the full extent of this influence is realized, much of his finest imagery must remain ambiguous to, or truncated from, the tradition with which Blake himself was so pervasively imbued. His system demands that we "admire his minutest powers (*J* 673:58).

PILOO NANAVUTTY

# Materia Prima in a Page of Blake's Vala

The influence of alchemy on Blake's work has not, so far, been thoroughly investigated. Nearly thirty years ago, Milton O. Percival, in *William Blake's Circle of Destiny*, wrote an illuminating chapter on the alchemical symbolism in the Prophetic Books. Yet he stressed only the general aspects of the subject: the fire imagery, the use of the contraries, and the emphasis on transmutation.[1] Attention is drawn to one design, the Mundane Egg in *Milton* 38, which is compared with the Philosopher's Egg of the alchemists.[2]

There are, however, other such hidden emblems in Blake. For instance, the winged globe in *Jerusalem* 37 is the recognized symbol among the alchemists for Primeval Chaos. The wings signify the volatile principle, Mercury. In an eighteenth-century alchemical manuscript, *Figurarum aegyptiorum secretarum*, the god, Mercury, is actually standing on the winged globe.[3] In an earlier work, the *Viridarium chymicum* of Stolcius (1624), the winged dragon of Primal Matter lies across the winged globe of Primeval Chaos.[4]

Turning back to the illustration in *Jerusalem* 37, it will be seen how apt is Blake's use of this image. Man (Albion) rests his right foot on the symbol of Primeval Chaos, and would be in imminent danger of falling into the Abyss if the loving arms of Jesus did not hold him up. In front of him stands the Oak of Weeping, behind him the Palm of Suffering. Human life is chaotic, and our two most constant companions grief and tears. The Divine Mercy enfolds Man and prevents him from sinking into the Primeval Chaos from which, according to alchemical theory, he arose, and to which he will eventually return. Christ's tender yearning and compassion, and his promise to redeem every single individual from total extinction, become all the more poignant in the light of the alchemical symbol used.

The most striking introduction of such imagery, both in the drawings and in the text which they illustrate, is found in folio 13v (12b in Keynes's *Bibliography*) of the *Vala* manuscript, Blake's first major Prophetic Book, which is a study of sexual love and jealousy in terms of creative myth (see PLATE XXII).

Several critics have been intrigued by the unsavory sketches on this page. Foster Damon gives a detailed description of them but declines to relate them specifically to the verse on the page.[5] H. M. Margoliouth also describes this page. He refers to my views, but takes up a slightly different standpoint from mine.[6] Bentley, in his magnificent facsimile edition of the entire *Vala* manuscript, describes the pencil sketches in detail and draws attention to the similarity between a sketch by Blake on this page and a drawing by Dürer in his illustrations to Maximilian's Prayer Book.[7] Bentley does not, however, relate the pencil sketches to the text which they encircle. Yet this page lends itself to alchemical analysis without which it is not fully comprehensible.

At the bottom of folio 13v of the *Vala* manuscript is a winged dragon, triple breasted, with a woman's head, strands of floating hair, and a long, swanlike neck. She holds out a pair of delicate, fan-shaped, webbed hands before her face as if admiring her winsome features in a mirror.[8] Her arms are braided, as it were, with "cords of twisted self-conceit," to borrow Blake's own vivid phrase. Her dragon's tail winds in coils on the right. Instead of legs, Blake has given her the fins of a fish. She is half siren, half dragon, and from the loins at her back is giving birth to a child whose minute face is faintly visible. The child's head is firmly held in the mouth of a dove seated between the fins of the dragon woman.

Above her hovers a fantastic bird with long neck and pointed beak, bat's wings, voluptuous bust, female genitals, and a woman's thighs covered with fish scales which taper into stray wisps at the extremities.

On the left margin are two cherubs. The lower one is a male, and has the outspread wings of a moth. He ascends clasping an erect phallus, partly erased. The other is a female cherub with a mop of curly hair, butterfly wings, exaggerated mammae with swollen nipples, a distended vulva, partially erased, and tubelike structures in the wings which seem to hint at the Fallopian tubes of a woman's generative system.

The dragon woman is Vala, or Nature, the veil which hides the Eternal from man, in Blake's system. She is also the *Materia prima* of the alchemists. John Read, in *Prelude to Chemistry* (p. 107), writes:

> In alchemy, the dragon, or serpent, is often used as a generative or sexual symbol. Sometimes male and female serpents or dragons are pictured as devouring or destroying each other, thereby giving rise to a glorified dragon, typifying the Philosopher's Stone, or transmutation; the same symbol may also denote putrefaction.
>
> Winged and wingless serpents or dragons symbolise the volatile and fixed principles (mercury and sulphur) respectively: three serpents the three principles (mercury, sulphur and salt); and a serpent nailed to a cross, the fixation of the volatile.

The *Materia prima* was always looked upon as poisonous and evil. The idea of a universal matter originated in early Greek philosophy with the Ionian School, whose members postulated a First Matter from which all things were molded. The Gnostics, however, turned matter into a wholly evil principle. Hence the poisonous nature of the *Materia prima*, and the peculiar combination of Ionian and Gnostic ideas which percolated into alchemy.[9]

Although denoting corruption and putrefaction, the *Materia prima* was also a symbol of all nature and regeneration. Berthelot, quoting from a Greek papyrus at Leyden, depicting the serpent Ouroboros with its tail in its mouth, says,

> L'Un fournit a l'Autre son sang; et l'Un engendre l'Autre. La nature réjouit la Nature; la nature charme la nature; la nature triomphe de la nature; et la nature maîtrise la nature; et cela non pas pour telle (nature) opposée a telle autre, mais pour une seule et même nature, (procédant) d'elle-même par le procédé (chimique), avec peine et grand effort.[10]

The *Materia prima* was, therefore, a symbol of "unceasing natural renewal," and of the imagined reversible transformation of matter which it was held that the alchemist should strive to imitate.[11]

Blake was also familiar with this view. Earlier in the *Vala* manuscript he describes the imagined reversible transformation of matter taking place in Nature:

> then high she soar'd
> Above the ocean; a bright wonder, Nature,
> Half Woman and half Spectre; all his lovely changing colours mix
> With her fair crystal clearness; in her lips & cheeks his poisons rose
> In blushes like the morning, and his scaly armour softening,
> A monster lovely in the heavens or wandering on the earth,
> With spectre voice incessant wailing, in incessant thirst,
> Beauty all blushing with desire, mocking her fell despair.
>
> (*FZ* i: 183–89, *K* 269)[12]

The "lovely changing colours" refer not only to the infinite variety of Nature, but also to a late stage of the transmutation process symbolized by the peacock's tail and its rainbow hues.[13] Nature herself becomes the alembic of "fair crystal clearness" in which all the complex richness of life is generated, though the Spectre, embodying the cruel and vindictive side of the physical universe, poisons all. Blake leaves us in no doubt of his meaning, for a remnant of the Spectre's scaly armor can be seen encrusting the buttocks of the *Materia prima* in the pictorial presentation of her on folio 13v of the *Vala* manuscript.

In keeping with alchemical theory, Blake's dragon woman is giving birth to a child, "the glorious Son" of the King and Queen. It was believed that through the marriage of sophic sulphur symbolized by the King, and sophic mercury symbolized by the Queen, would be born a child or the Philosopher's Stone.

The various alchemical processes were divided into seven stages, each with its distinctive color. The first stage was to convert the black, earthy matter, depicted as a toad, black crow, or raven, into a white sublimate typified by the white dove or swan. It was only after the process named *"conjunctio"* or *"solutio"* showing the union of the King and Queen, sophic sulphur and sophic mercury, respectively, had taken place, that the white dove or sublimate emerged, followed by the birth of the child. The swan and dove were, therefore, symbols intimately connected with the self-engenderings of Nature.

In an English alchemical manuscript, George Ripley's *Scrowle*, the seven processes are depicted in circular medallions, each containing the alembic within which the particular stage of the great work is taking place. In the alembic labeled *"solutio,"* the King and Queen are joined in union. Above them flies the white dove. Below this medallion the next stage is shown. A child, in a rayed glory, flies out from the mouth of the retort while a white dove touches the child's head with its outspread wing. The dove had issued from the alembic first, then the child.[14]

In the approved alchemical manner, Blake's dragon woman on page 13v of the *Vala* manuscript also gives birth to a child whose head is held firmly in the mouth of the dove that had proceeded from the womb first.

Whereas the swan represented the poisonous sublimate from the solution of sophic sulphur and sophic mercury, the white dove was particularly associated with the regeneration which followed. In another well-known alchemical treatise, the *Splendor solis* of Solomon Trismosin, the rejuvenated King is shown holding in his hand a golden apple on which stands a white dove.[15] The apple was another acknowledged emblem of generation. Again, in the same work, there is a full-page illustration of the "Bath of the King." The naked King is seated in an iron vessel or copper boiler filled with water and resting upon a circular furnace. On the King's head is a white dove, symbolizing not only the sublimate but also the new birth of the King in the process.[16]

Turning to folio 13v of the *Vala* manuscript, it will be seen that Blake's version of the alchemical swan is the bird which hovers over the dragon woman. Basil Valentine, in a brief appendix to his treatise "Of the Great Stone of the Ancients," has a section headed "Of Arsenick" which explains the full significance of the swan, described by Libavius as "the arsenic of the philosophers":

However, take you notice that I am a poysonous volatile bird, have forsaken my dearest, and most confiding friend, and separated myself as a Leper, which must live aloof off from other men. Cure me first from my infirmity, then I shall be able to heal those which have need of me, that my praise may be confirmed by poyson, and my name for an ever-lasting remembrance to the honour of my Country . . .[17]

The "dearest, and most confiding friend" refers to the King who is sacrificed to the unquenchable thirst of the *Materia prima*, and in the union is himself regenerated and regenerates her as well.

The drawing of Blake's swan seems indebted to a plate in Andreas Libavius' *Commentariorum alchymiae* (1606). The long neck and pointed beak, the voluptuous breasts and outspread wings, are present in the Libavius plate and also in Blake's swan.[18] The bat wings and fish scales are elements borrowed from medieval Christian iconography, and denote satanic corruption and degeneracy. The poisonous nature of the white sublimate is doubly emphasized by Blake, who leaves one in no doubt that he had fully grasped current alchemical theory. The lower half of his swan resembles the fish tail of the siren representing the *Anima mercurii* in an eighteenth-century alchemical manuscript already mentioned, the *Figurarum aegyptiorum secretarum*.[19]

The two cherubs on the left margin of folio 13v of the *Vala* manuscript symbolize the masculine and feminine aspects respectively of the alchemical regenerative process. There is an obvious meaning in the moth and butterfly wings of the cherubs. Just as the moth flies round a candle and is burnt to death, even so the male is sacrificed to the sexual hunger of the female, and in the process he fecundates her so that she rises a regenerated being. This resurrection is indicated by the butterfly wings of the female cherub, and her fecundation by the enlarged mammae and Fallopian-like tubes in her wings.

Enlarged breasts are also depicted in the triple-breasted dragon woman drawn at the bottom of the page under discussion. In his drawing of this creature Blake may have been influenced by a political cartoon dated 1789, depicting the Hydra of the French Revolution as a dragon woman with a long fish tail, multiple breasts, a hag's face, and outspread wings.[20]

The long, turned-up tail, the multiple breasts, and the wings are elements found also in the dragon woman of folio 13v of the *Vala* manuscript.

On the symbolism of the breasts, G. J. Witkowski writes,

Les anciens donnaient aux Sphinx et aux Chimères des seins très pro-
noncés, emblèmes, dans l'idée païenne, de la duplicité féminine. C'est
ainsi que l'on a représenté l'hydre révolutionaire avec des mamelles mul-
tiples et pendantes.

Au moyen âge, les seins désignent, par leur exagération, la *Lubricité*,
et les *Passions charnelles*.

Dans l'iconographie chrétienne . . . le sein découvert a une double
signification: il symbolise, à la Renaissance, l'Innocence et l'Amour de
Dieu; puis, à toutes les époques, la *Procréation* (XVIe siècle), la *Luxure*
et *l'Impudeur*.[21]

Feminine duplicity, sexual hunger, and procreation are evidently
the ideas which Blake wishes to convey by the triple breasts he
has bestowed upon the dragon woman, who, as the *Materia prima*
of the alchemists, "slays her husband and offspring, and revives
them by means of her breasts."

Alchemical ideas are embedded not only in the sketches on this
page, but also in the lines which they illustrate. In Blake's system,
Luvah (Lover), is Passion, Vala's consort, or unregenerate Nature.
Keeping up the alchemical imagery, Blake speaks of Luvah's being
"cast into the Furnaces of Affliction & sealed," while Urizen, the cold,
dominating, rational intellect, and Vala look on. It is characteristic of
Urizen to tyrannize over both physical nature and the passions of
man. The voice of Luvah is heard from "the furnaces of Urizen" in
tortured frenzy:

If I indeed am Vala's King, & ye, O sons of Men,
The workmanship of Luvah's hands in times of Everlasting,
When I call'd forth the Earth-worm from the cold & dark obscure
I nurtur'd her, I fed her with my rains & dews; she grew
A scaled Serpent, yet I fed her tho' she hated me;
Day after day she fed upon the mountains in Luvah's sight,
I brought her thro' the Wilderness, a dry & thirsty land,
And I commanded springs to rise for her in the black desart,
Till she became a Dragon, winged, bright & poisonous.
I open'd all the floodgates of the heavens to quench her thirst,
. . . . . . . . . . . . . . . . . . . . . . .
I carried her in my bosom as a man carries a lamb,

I loved her, I gave her all my soul & my delight,
. . . . . . . . . . . . . . . .
             . . . She bore me sons & daughters,
                       (*FZ* ii:81–97, *K* 282)[22]

The above passage contains several alchemical allusions which require explanation. According to the Eighth Key of Basil Valentine, on Putrefaction:

Many insects and worms receive life, so that by meer putrefaction they attain a vivifying power and motion; which ought to be deservedly esteemed, as a wonder above all wonders: This Nature hath granted, for the same vivifying increase and inspiration of life is very much found in the Earth, and by the same reason is excited in its spiritual Seed by the other Elements.[23]

The Earthworm, would, therefore, be the first of generated things, and naturally be called forth "from the cold & dark obscure," for, according to Basil Valentine, "*materia prima* belongs only to God, and is coagulated in the entrails of Earth."[24] Again, he speaks of "the Dragon's spirit which dwelleth in stony places," and of the "cold Dragon who had his dwelling a long time in Rocky Cliffs, and crept in and out in Subterranean Concaves and Hollow places."[25]

The *Philosophorum praeclara monita*, an eighteenth-century alchemical manuscript in St. Andrew's University Library, Aberdeen, Scotland, has a vivid drawing showing the dragons and griffins of the North wandering in and out of subterranean concaves and hollow places.[26]

Blake's references to the wilderness, the dry and thirsty land, and the black desert can now be understood. The adjective "black" refers to the first stage of the alchemical process, the transformation of the black, earthy matter into the white sublimate.

The hatred of Vala for Luvah can also be explained in the light of the *Materia prima*'s hatred for her King. It was a commonplace of alchemical theory that the *Materia prima* had a longing to devour her husband, the King. This appetite of hers was symbolized by the "grey wolf," a biting agent or acid, usually antimony.[27]

Martin Ruland, in his *Lexicon alchemiae Rulandi* (1612), has

over fifty picturesque synonyms as definitions of the *Materia prima*.
She is the serpent or dragon, for she devours and destroys: "Venom,
Poison, Chamber, because it kills and destroys the King, and there
is no greater poison in the world . . . Bride, Spouse, Mother, Eve
. . . from her royal children are born to the King." She is the

pure and Uncontaminated Virgin—for she remains pure and unimpreg-
nated notwithstanding that she bears children. She is a most extraordinary
mother who slays her husband and offspring, and revives them by means
of her breasts. *Assiduous* says: the Mother of our Stone, which is now
perfected, is still a Virgin, never having reclined in a nuptial couch, because this hermaphrodite and universal matter of the Sun and Moon has
intercourse only with itself, and is not yet impregnated in any special
manner, such as the golden, silver, or mercurial process, etc. Consequently,
it is a pure virginal birth.[28]

Again, Ruland describes her as "A Spiritual Blood—for it is like
blood and so remains: it reddens, vivifies and has the spirit therein."
In another eighteenth-century manuscript, *La Sagesse des anciens*,
there is a picture showing the sick King wearing the heart of the
*Materia prima* in his bosom. Streams of blood pour out from the
heart and feed the children of the planets who stand in a semi-
circle round the King.[29]

Similarly, Luvah nurtures Vala in his bosom and feeds her with
his "rains & dews" till she absorbs him into herself and thereafter
bears him sons and daughters.

The exact significance of the sketches and the text which they
illustrate on folio 13v of the *Vala* manuscript now becomes apparent. According to Blake, the passionate impulses in man, personified as Luvah, find their legitimate satisfaction in Nature and
her abundant variety. Yet both Luvah and Vala must be wedded
in innocence if the union is to be a happy one. The Rational
Intellect, Urizen, however, interferes with man's inner harmony,
isolating the passions and oppressing them, so that Nature, unful-
filled, grows corrupt and heartless: "In joy she heard his howlings
& forgot he was her Luvah / With whom she walk'd in bliss in
times of innocence & youth" (*FZ* ii:78–79, *K* 282).[30]

Vala thus becomes a "soft delusion," and, as her name implies,
a veil drawn over the face of the Spirit. Hence, unregenerate Nature

can but produce a "vegetable" birth, "only fit for burning," to use Blake's own phrase, devoid of the eternal and therefore doomed to decay. It is this inordinate sexual hunger and "incessant thirst" of the *Materia prima* as well as her poisonous self-engenderings that are portrayed on folio 13v, where the text and the drawings are complementary parts of the meaning. The alchemical background alone gives the necessary clue to that meaning, and is dead to the point in driving home Blake's moral.

MARTIN K. NURMI

# Negative Sources in Blake

William Blake is sometimes illuminated but rarely explained by his sources, because his fierce intellectual independence allows nothing to pass into his work unchanged. It is therefore hazardous to accept prior analogues to his ideas as sources, especially on the basis of mere conceptual analogy, and even more hazardous to practice the kind of algebraic substitution in which Blake is made to mean what a supposed source meant.

Blake has suffered more than his share at the hands of source hunters, some of whom would all but explain him away altogether, transmuting him into the baser metal of sources less imaginative than he but bearing a general resemblance to him. Underlying the substitutive use of sources seems to be the assumption that an effect must have a like cause—perhaps a distortion of the second of Newton's "Rules of Reasoning in Philosophy": ". . . to the same natural effects we must, as far as possible, assign the same causes." [1] Visionary ideas, it is assumed, must have visionary sources, or better yet occult ones. In Blake it is always worth considering whether another Newtonian law might not be operating: "To every action there is always an opposed and equal reaction. . . ." (I, 20). In searching for the original of something in Blake, it is often possible that the "source," if it is not the Bible or Milton, is a negative one, a philosophical enemy rather than a friend, and one close at hand rather than an obscure one.

In this essay I will try to show how Blake formed certain of his visionary ideas partly in reaction against philosophical enemies, or at least how the particular form in which he cast these ideas arises out of an attempt to expose the errors of these enemies by his taking some of their central concepts and reconceiving them in a visionary context. According to Blake, "you cannot behold

. . . [Satan] till he be reveald in his System" (*J* 43[29]:10, *E* 189) [2] and one of his main purposes was to display various aspects of systems of satanic thought in such a way that what was satanic about them would be recognizable. But if he was to have any hope of success, the identity of the systems being exposed would also have to be recognizable: the satanic parts of Newton's system must be known to be Newton's or there is no point to the exposure.

Because Blake had to wait almost forty years for a biographer and much longer for serious interpreters, there has not been the kind of continuity of interest that would keep fresh the identities of some of the elliptical allusions in his work which would have been recognized by his contemporaries. By the time Blake study really began, with the publication of Professor Damon's *William Blake, His Philosophy and Symbols* in 1924, the particular significance of a term like "single vision," for instance, had been all but forgotten. When Blake wrote Butts in November, 1802, "May God us keep / From Single vision & Newton's sleep!" [3] he used the term to mean the lowest form of vision, physical seeing, and we can easily catch his general meaning. But he also would have had a rather more particular meaning in mind, more specifically connecting it with physical perception and, very likely, with Newton. At the end of the eighteenth century, most people hearing the term "single vision" would have connected it with the optical phenomenon of seeing one image with two eyes, an idea widely discussed by many philosophers and scientists of the seventeenth and eighteenth centuries, among them Kepler, Descartes, Molyneux, Gassendi, Baptista Porta, Berkeley, Porterfield, Reid, and of course Newton. Blake had read the *Opticks* and would have known Newton's thoughts on it.[4] Some of the scornful force which Blake intended to convey by "Single vision" is restored, I think, if we look at Newton's crabbedly neurological query concerning the physical phenomenon of single vision from *The Opticks:*

Qu. 15. Are not the Species of Objects seen with both Eyes united where the optick Nerves meet before they come into the Brain, the Fibres on the right side of both Nerves uniting there, and after union going thence into the Brain in the Nerve which is on the right side of the Head, and the Fibres on the left side of both Nerves uniting in the same place, and after union going into the Brain in the Nerve which is on the left side of the head . . .[5]

This is certainly seeing with the "vegetable eye." Though Newton's discussion of "single vision" surely did not stimulate Blake to formulate his idea of manifold vision in direct opposition to it, single vision of the physiological kind as conceived in Newton's query, which was the only kind of vision acceptable in a world whose reality resided in external physical objects, would have been quite specifically in Blake's mind as a contrast when he described the various levels of imaginative perception to Butts, and he would have expected Butts to catch the allusion.

To turn to the first of my examples of how a feature of Blake's visionary cosmos might have been formed in reaction to an unvisionary enemy: a concept which Blake very likely did formulate partly as an explicit response to Newton, or at least gave a particular form to in order to reveal the satanic implications of a part of Newton's system, is the idea of "limits." The word has a general meaning that is clear enough of course, but again a very wide public in the eighteenth century would readily have associated it specifically with the calculus, or, as Newton called it, "the doctrine of fluxions." Newton had already used the idea of limits frequently in the *Principia*, where he employed computations derived secretly from the calculus without revealing the method of the calculus itself, but, after the publication of his essay on curves in the first edition of the *Opticks* in 1704 and the publication of the method of fluxions itself in Colson's translation in 1736, the idea of limits became a matter of great general public interest.[6] The idea of limits assumed importance because it was central to the doctrine of fluxions. Essentially, Newton's fluxions involved reducing quantities to infinitesimals, until they are so small that they have no quantity as they approach the "limit" of zero. To many, including Berkeley, this notion was an absurdity, for to deal with quantities that are no quantities was nonsense, and Berkeley satirically called the fluxions "ghosts of departed quantities." In the controversy that grew after Berkeley's criticism in *The Analyst* in

1734, the idea of limits assumed crucial importance, and the debate really centered on the meaning of the concept.

Blake was familiar enough with the doctrine of fluxions to refer to them very knowledgeably in a letter to George Cumberland: "I know too well that a great majority of Englishmen are fond of The Indefinite which they Measure by Newton's Doctrine of Fluxions of an Atom, a Thing that does not Exist." [7] Though this letter was written in the last year of his life, the remark seems to refer more to the issues that had been debated the century before than to the attitudes toward the calculus in 1827. Blake, who had at least skimmed the *Principia* and the *Opticks* and had made Newton one of the heads of the philosophical Cerberus of the epics, would hardly have ignored the debate on the fluxions and limits when they were a matter of public interest.

And the response to this doctrine by a symbolic critic of philosophical systems to whom one criterion of reality was definiteness is not hard to imagine. Newton's doctrine, from this point of view, not only commits itself in a systematic way to indefiniteness but pursues a course of philosophical brinkmanship with existence itself, the brink being the limit beyond which is nonexistence. Blake's own idea of limits certainly suggests such a response. In formulating the twin limits of "opakeness" and "contraction," or Satan and Adam, Blake takes the notion of the brink of existence suggested by Newton's limit and adapts it to his visionary myth, in part at least to show the symbolic implications of systems of thought like Newton's. Though the allusion to the mathematical idea of limits in this conception is suggested by the term itself and by the fact that in one place the limits are said to be formed by "Los's Mathematic Power" (*Mil* 29:38, *E* 126), the meaning of Blake's limits has little to do directly with mathematics, only with the notion of a point beyond which existence ceases. Blake's limits of Satan (as the point at which the satanic is knowable and beyond which it is not) and Adam (as the point at which man is still redeemable) draw on the root conception of the mathematical limit, which, by using zero as a point in a process of progressive contraction, dramatizes the abstract idea of a point of no return.

In the calculus there are not only, as it were, "limits of contraction" at zero but also "limits of expansion" at infinity. Blake, whose limits function in a qualitative rather than a quantitative continuum, explicitly rejects any upper limits, because at the upper end of the continuum is Humanity and man has no limits. Therefore, "there is no Limit of Expansion! there is no Limit of Translucence" (*J* 42:35, *E* 187). Again Blake seems to be setting the concept of limits in a visionary system against the implications of a parallel idea in mathematics.

Certain other terms in Blake's work also probably allude to Newton's mathematics. Blake himself suggested the connection between "the indefinite" and Newton in his letter to Cumberland. When, therefore, Enion in *The Four Zoas* "wanders in Eternal fear of falling into the indefinite / For her bright eyes behold the Abyss" (*FZ* iii, *E* 324), a Newtonian echo, if only a faint one, should probably be heard. And when Vala, also in *The Four Zoas*, is described as an "evanescent shadow," Newton's "evanescent limits" of the method of "rectifying" curvilinear figures by infinitesimal "evanescent parallelograms"[8] is somewhere in Blake's mind. Blake's philosophers who would "rectify every thing in Nature" (Annotations to Lavater 532, *E* 585) would not correct nature but reduce her to mathematically manipulable parallelograms.

If Newton's limits triggered reactions in Blake, Descartes's vortices probably did so too. Professor Damon has noted, in his *Blake Dictionary*,[9] that the "vortexes" may well be related to those of Descartes; it seems to me almost certain that they are, and related to them in much the same way as the limits are related to Newton. In making the "vortexes" such a prominent feature of his cosmology (and ontology), Blake was developing a conception that would— again *in part*—serve as a counteridea to the materialistic, essentially autonomous and godless, whirling cosmic process described by Descartes.

According to Descartes, a particle of matter, in a universe full of matter, can move only if another particle has moved and left a space for it. Actually, this motion must occur simultaneously, since there are no empty spaces in the universe. And, because the figure and division of particles varies at all points in the universe, the overall motion of particles becomes a circular one, with vortices of different kinds of particles. As God has moved the particles "variously at the first, . . . we must not think that they [the particles] would all agree in revolving about a common single center but, about many different ones," so that the different vortices form many different whirling systems in the universe.[10] The functional units in one vortex come into being as follows: the particles of matter rub against each other and friction produces two different kinds of particles: round ones which tend to fly toward the circumference centrifugally and finer ones which lose some of their velocity and move centripetally toward the center of the vortex to occupy portions of space vacated by the fast flying round particles. A third form of matter evolves in the process: when the finer centripetally moving particles move through the spaces between the centrifugally moving round particles, they become distorted, lose their velocity, and sink to form a crust around the nucleus of the vortex, conglomerating into a star or a sun spot or dissolving into ether. When a star is formed, it is subject to the effects of other motions in the system, since its own velocity is diminished, and it can be caught up in the part of the vortex which has a velocity equal to its own and thereby becomes a planet. If its velocity is greater than that of any part of the vortex which it has entered, it moves to another part, as a comet, and continues from one heaven to another. The vortex of the sun is not only a grand vortex itself but contains other vortices revolving about their own centers.

Descartes's theory of vortices was generally accepted on the continent and in England soon after publication in 1644 and continued to hold such sway in England until well into the eighteenth century that twenty-six years after the publication of Newton's *Principia*, with its rival theory, Roger Cotes felt obliged to include a preface in the second edition of the *Principia* specifically attacking Descartes.[11] Cotes, recognizing that the vortices were easier to visualize than Newton's abstract mathematical law, attempted to give a brief popular description of gravitation.

Among the learned in England, the theory of vortices lost out to the law of gravitation fairly early in the century, though in France it continued to be dominant until around 1750.[12] But Descartes by no means dropped out of sight, and we can certainly expect Blake to have known about the vortices of Descartes. So celebrated had the Cartesian vortices been that any use of the term would immediately have suggested Descartes even at the end of the century.

Though the Cartesian theory had been opposed to that of Newton, it is unlikely that Blake relished it any more than he did Newton's, for the vortexes (to adopt Blake's form of the word) derive their operation from the motion of Democritean matter in swirling particles. "Give me matter and motion," says Descartes, "and I will make a world" (p. vi). Though Blake's most elaborate exposition of his own idea of vortexes, in *Milton* (Pl. 15, *E* 108), represents a highly imaginative development in which nothing seems to whirl very much, his earlier use of them in Night VI of *The Four Zoas* connects them with Urizen's exploring his dens. In this passage, the vortexes which "operate" appear to be much closer to those of Descartes.

> For when he came to where a Vortex ceasd to operate
> Nor down nor up remaind then if he turnd & lookd back
> From whence he came twas upward all. & if he turnd and viewd
> The unpassd void upward was still his mighty wandring
> The midst between an Equilibrium grey of air serene
> Where he might live in peace & where his life might meet repose
>
> But Urizen said Can I not leave this world of Cumbrous wheels
> Circle oer Circle nor on high attain a void
> Where self sustaining I may view all things beneath my feet
> Or sinking thro these Elemental wonders swift to fall
> I thought perhaps to find an End a world beneath of voidness
> Whence I might travel round the outside of this Dark confusion
> When I bend downward bending my head downward into the deep
> Tis upward all which way soever I my course begin
> But when A Vortex formd on high by labour & sorrow & care
> And weariness begins on all my limbs then sleep revives
> My wearied spirits waking then tis downward all which way
> So ever I my spirits turn no end I find of all [.]          (*E* 342)

Where a vortex has "ceased to operate," that is, has ceased to whirl about a nucleus, relative ideas like "up" and "down" are impossible because there is no longer any reference point, except the psychological one of the journey's seeming to be constantly upward. A vortex that has ceased to operate is a decayed universe, a sort of ghost of a universe. Between such a ghostly universe and an unpassed void exists a grey equilibrium, where no forces of any kind operate, the only kind of condition in which Urizen in his present state could possibly find peace and repose. But Urizen wants more than this. As a self-appointed deity, he wants to get outside of being so as to get a synoptic view of it and possess it from the outside, either by mounting above the whirling vortexes or by dropping down to find an end below and "travel round the outside of this Dark confusion" there. But he is frustrated in this latter attempt, for when, like the Ancient of Days, he bends into the Abyss in the direction that he thinks is downward, the direction again turns out to be upward, because upward and downward are meaningless ideas without a vortex with a center and circumference. When a vortex is begun, he is able to rest and sleep. Then his journey becomes easier, downward, but even so he finds "no end of all," for matter, as in Descartes's *Principia* (Part I, Principle xxvi), is indefinitely extended.

Urizen himself, as described in the passage just preceding the one quoted, had made vortexes to stem "his downward fall labouring up against futurity." But vortexes are also made providentially "on high by labour & sorrow & care" to give form to chaos.

Blake's description of vortexes in *Milton* represents a refinement of the idea, and, though the vortexes do not "operate," the connection with Descartes is still there. This passage describes the nature of infinity as shown by the passage of a Mental Traveller through infinity, which has the appearance of being organized into vortexes. Of course the word *vortex* itself implies circular motion, as in a whirlpool.

> The nature of infinity is this: That every thing has its
> Own Vortex; and when once a traveller thro' Eternity
> Has passd that Vortex, he percieves it roll backward behind
> His path, into a globe itself infolding; like a sun:
> Or like a moon, or like a universe of starry majesty,

While he keeps onwards in his wondrous journey on the earth
Or like a human form, a friend with whom he livd benevolent.
As the eye of man views both the east & west encompassing
Its vortex; and the north & south, with all their starry host;
Also the rising sun & setting moon he views surrounding
His corn-fields and his valleys of five hundred acres square.
Thus is the earth one infinite plane, and not as apparent
To the weak traveller confin'd beneath the moony shade.
Thus is the heaven a vortex passd already, and the earth
A vortex not yet pass'd by the traveller thro' Eternity.

*(Mil* 15:21–35, *E* 108–9)

As in "The Mental Traveller," a distinction must be drawn
here between the "weak traveller confin'd beneath the moony
shade" and the "traveller thro' Eternity." To the sublunary traveller, being seems globular, but to the traveller through Eternity
being is an infinite plane. He knows that east and west and north
and south are merely relative, existing inside a vortex and deriving
their meaning from the reference point established by the nucleus.
The earth and its universe have been given the form of a vortex
as a kind of order which sublunary man can understand, but the
Mental Traveller needs no such order and knows that this kind
of order is a providentially instrumental one. To him the earth
is "one infinite plane." [13]

This passage makes better sense, it seems to me, if one keeps
Descartes's vortexes in mind, as whirling particles and bodies formed
of smaller conglomerated particles. If Descartes is a source for
the vortexes, therefore, he is a negative one. Descartes conceived
the vortexes as accounting for the creation of the universe and,
though the explanation of cosmic process rather leaves God out
of the details after it begins, Descartes gives Him credit for the
motion which makes the vortexes operate. Blake makes the vortexes into functional features of a fallen world, props for the mental
infirmity of fallen man, who must have his world organized in a
way that he can understand. The objectives prompting Descartes
to conceive the vortexes, therefore, are reversed in Blake.

Though the vortexes *are* a feature of the fallen world, they are
valuable to human life by giving form to chaos. Religion is inimical
to them, as is suggested in *The Four Zoas*, Night VIII, when

Urizen's "Direful Web of Religion . . . fell / From heaven to heavn thro all its meshes altering the Vortexes / Misplacing every Center" (*E* 361). Sometimes the vortexes work, by organizing spectral life, to draw away a spectre, as in Night VIII of *The Four Zoas* (*E* 370). But a vortex also threatens to confuse and perplex by drawing one in—as Descartes's wandering stars are drawn in. An example is the "nameless shadowy Vortex" that tries unsuccessfully to draw in Orc in Night VII b of *The Four Zoas* (*E* 395). And a vortex also organizes error, as in *Jerusalem*, chapter ii, when Albion becomes "the Vortex of the Dead," the "Place, of Murder, & Unforgiving" (*J* 48:54, 56–57; *E* 195). Perhaps also related to the idea of vortexes is Blake's orbital churning of Klopstock's bowels in "When Klopstock England Defied" (*E* 491–92), though this may be more Newtonian than Cartesian.

I should now like to take up an important recurring image in Blake's work, that of material creation as the Mundane Egg, and consider whether this might not be traceable partly to his reaction against a writer who used Newtonian principles to account for the creation: Thomas Burnet. Burnet's cosmology as set forth in *The Sacred Theory of the Earth* (1690–91) is not the only place where Blake could have encountered the image of the world as egg, which is the traditional Orphic egg popularized in Greece by Proclus and appearing in a great many cosmological writers in the Western tradition. In Blake's own time he could have found the idea specifically in Young's *Night Thoughts*, in Bryant's *New System*, in Richard Paine Knight's *Priapus*, in Thomas Taylor's editions of Plato, and a number of other places.[14] But Burnet would surely have come to the attention of anyone in the eighteenth century who was at all interested in the mundane egg, for not only was Burnet's work celebrated and admired—and attacked —but the idea gets more development in his work than in any other contemporary account. Blake may have found some support for his idea of the Mundane Egg in the introductions and notes of Thomas Taylor, but it would have been almost impossible for him to deal with the idea and ignore Burnet. It may be that Thomas Taylor, as George Harper contends, showed Blake how to conceive the mundane egg symbolically, but Blake even without

Taylor would have found enough in Burnet's *Sacred Theory* to set him off toward showing in his own cosmology the satanic elements of Burnet's system, whose symbolic implications were only too clear. And the implications were clear not only to Blake: "Many in the early eighteenth century," says Marjorie Nicolson, "considered Burnet the father of English Deism," and his theory was supported by such eminent Newtonians as Edmund Halley and William Whiston, successor to Newton at Cambridge, who even wrote a *New Theory of the Earth* himself, following Halley, who in turn was stimulated by Burnet.[15] The controversy over Burnet's *Sacred Theory* involved the age's leading men, including members of the Martinus Scriblerus Club, Swift, Pope, and Gay. If Blake, taking over the mundane egg from *Sacred Theory*, was attacking Burnet, he was only doing what many others were.[16]

There are two aspects to Blake's reactive response to Burnet's cosmogony which I should like to discuss briefly before looking at particular evidence for a connection. And the two aspects involve the two stages of the world in Burnet's account: first, the smooth, ovoid prelapsarian form of the world as the mundane egg and, second, the postdiluvian world as a collapsed ruin of gaping seas, veinous caverns, and burning pits. Blake's accounts of the world make references to both stages.

In his account of the creation, Burnet sought to reconcile theology and the new science by explaining the creation on Newtonian principles, especially gravitation. The world was created, says Burnet, by the gravitational deposit of particles of matter out of the chaos surrounding a globe of waters, or liquors, until at first an oozy scum formed, by lighter materials rising like cream, which finally hardened into the surface shell of the prelapsarian world, the great mundane egg. The interior of the egg was formed of four regions: in the center was fire, outside of this a membrane, then water, then the earth shell. Outside of the shell, surrounding it, was air. Thus the creation not only gave ovoid form to the world but separated the four elements. The prelapsarian world had on the outside four regions, with two temperate zones at each end separated by a torrid zone, but had no seasons, and therefore no rainbow (Book I, p. 244). "As to the form of it, 'twas all one smooth Continent, one continued surface of earth, without any Sea, any Mountains, or Rocks; any Holes, Dens or Caverns: And the situation of it to the Sun was such as made a perpetual Æquinox." [17] Burnet is not much interested in the symbolic implications of the Orphic egg. Rather, he wants to explain it on a physical basis: ". . . the inward Form of it was a Frame of four Regions, encompassing one another, where that of Fire lay in the Middle like the Yolk, and a Shell of Earth inclos'd them all. This gives a Solution so easy and natural, and shows such an Aptness and Elegancy in the Representation, that one cannot doubt upon a View, and Compare the Circumstances, but that we have truly found out the Riddle of the Mundane Egg" (Book II, chap. viii, p. 193).

Blake surely reacted against Burnet's reductive materialism and his attempts to prove the existence of God by matter and motion.[18] He would have found in Burnet ironic support for his own conception of the Mundane Shell (wherever he originally got it), because Burnet's egg, from Blake's point of view, was an unwitting confession that the creation was that of a fallen, materialistic world, and that, therefore, in Burnet's account the error of natural religion stands revealed in great detail. Since men like Dr. Johnson could recommend Burnet's *Sacred Theory* as a book which "the critick ought to read for its elegance, the philosopher for its arguments, and the saint for its piety," [19] some public correction of Burnet was necessary, and Blake's giving it such a prominent place in the scheme of his myth was motivated in part by a desire to show the real nature of Burnet's radically mistaken piety.

In his mythic countersystem, Blake shows the Mundane Egg as the image of a fallen world, but he goes one step farther, to make of it a providential creation that gives *some* form to the world in order to stop the falling cosmic process, described by Burnet as the creative work of God, from pursuing its inherent course to the end and leading to complete non-entity or eternal death. "We form the Mundane Egg," says Los, "that Spectres coming by fury or amity, / All is the same, & every one remains in his own energy" (*Mil* 25:42–43, E 121).

To be sure, Blake's Mundane Shell contains some features not to be found in Burnet. The shell proper in Blake is not the surface of the earth but the shell of the sky, which lies outside and resembles a mold from which the earth was cast, since "whatever is visible in the Vegetable Earth, the same / Is visible in the Mundane Shell; reversd in mountain & vale" (*J* 72:46–47, *E* 225). But Blake's shell, like Burnet's, is a "Mighty Incrustation" (*Mil* 17:54, *E* 137), and, where Burnet's world and its surrounding air were separated out of chaos (Book I, chap. v), Blake's Mundane Egg (and Shell) are usually mentioned as being surrounded by chaos (e.g., in *Milton, E* 133, 110, 117, 137).

The most distinctive feature of Burnet's cosmogony is his account of the Deluge and the form the world took after it. Burnet was most dissatisfied with the biblical explanation of the Deluge as having occurred through rain, even torrential rains, and he showed by computations that it simply could not rain hard enough for a deluge. The only likely place where enough water could be found was in the interior of the earth, whose shell exploded when the rains preliminary to the main deluge stopped up holes that released the pressure of internal vapors. He suggests that the mundane egg cracked like an ordinary egg that is boiled too hard:

I do not know but those Rains, so covering up and enclosing the Earth on every side, might providentially contribute to the disruption of it . . . especially by stopping on a sudden all the pores of the Earth, and all evaporation, which would make the Vapours within struggle more violently, . . . and it may be in that struggle, the Doors and the Bars were broke, and the great Abyss gusht out, as out of a womb.

(Book I, chap. viii, p. 83)

The flood persisted for a while and eventually, through the action of winds drying pieces of the broken crust that began to stick up through the water as gravitation pulled the water into low places, the waters were confined into channels and the earth as we know it took form. Burnet's celebrated "portraicture of our Earth, drawn without flattery," describes it as a "great Ruine . . . lying in its rubbish" the inside of which is "generally broken and hollow," full of "Holes and Caverns, and strange Subterranean passages" (Book I, chap. ix, p. 91).

Blake draws very directly on Burnet for the deluge which occurs when the "bounds of Destiny were broken," in Night III of *The Four Zoas:*

The bounds of Destiny were broken

The bounds of Destiny crashd direful & the swelling Sea
Burst from its bonds in whirlpools fierce roaring with Human voice
Triumphing even to the Stars at bright Ahanias fall.          (*E* 322)

And the watery Tharmas, the "parent power," finds himself fallen, divided into earthly bodies of water:

Fury in my limbs. destruction in my bones & marrow
My skull riven into filaments. my eyes into sea jellies
Floating upon the tide wander bubbling & bubbling
Uttering my lamentations & begetting little monsters
Who sit mocking upon the little pebbles of the tide
In all my rivers . . .          (*E* 323)

And the deluge imagery is reinforced in Night IV, when Tharmas conceives himself to be God controlling the deluge:

My Son   O Los thou art Urthona & Tharmas
Is God. The Eternal Man is seald never to be deliverd
I roll my floods over his body my billows & waves pass over him
The Sea encompasses him & monsters of the deep are his companions.
(*E* 327)

The parallels with Burnet are clearest in the crucial passage in Night VI when Urizen is exploring his world.

O thou poor ruind world

Thou horrible ruin once like me thou wast all glorious
And now like me partaking desolate thy masters lot
Art thou O ruin the once glorious heaven are these thy rocks
Where joy sang in the trees & pleasure sported on the rivers
And laughter sat beneath the Oaks & innocence sported round
Upon the green plains & sweet friendship met in palaces
And books & instruments of song & pictures of delight
Where are they whelmd beneath these ruins in horrible destruction
And if Eternal falling I repose on the dark bosom
Of winds & waters or thence fall into a Void where air

Is not down falling thro immensity ever & ever
I lose my powers weakend every revolution till a death
Shuts up my powers then a seed in the vast womb of darkness
I dwell in dim oblivion. (*E* 342–43)

In what seems quite obvious borrowing of imagery from Burnet's world ruined through the Deluge and the Deluge itself ("I repose on the dark bosom of . . . waters"), Blake may seem to be following Burnet, especially since he appears to use Burnet's antediluvian world as the antecedent "climes of bliss" to contrast with the ruined postdiluvian one. There seems to be some inconsistency between this and his use of the Mundane Shell elsewhere. Actually, as Milton O. Percival has pointed out (pp. 150–51), Blake shares with Burnet a common source for the idea of two blissful climates rather than four, and what he is doing in this passage is using, selectively, the Edenic aspect of the antediluvian earth without necessarily swallowing Burnet's version of its origin. In any event, the biblical story provides the main structure of the narrative, Burnet supplying some attractive imagery, and if one is to utilize the Deluge to produce a ruined world, that world must be preceded by an unruined one. For Blake the "climes of bliss" referred to by Urizen are to be found in Eden, as they are for Burnet. The difference is that Burnet would locate Eden on the surface of the corporeal mundane shell, and Blake would not.

It may well be, incidentally, that there is an echo of Burnet in the important matter of Blake's connecting the fallen Zoas with the four elements as he does. Tharmas as water and the parent power might allude to the primeval globe of waters in Burnet; the fiery Orc (whose abode is characteristically inside the earth), to the fire in the yolk of the mundane egg; and Los with his mountains, to Burnet's earthy shell. That leaves the air for Urizen, the sky-god. A distinctive feature of Burnet's creation of the mundane egg is that the elements were divided out of chaos and given places roughly corresponding to those given the Zoas in Blake (Book I, chap. v); in *Jerusalem* (32[36]:31–32, *E* 177) the Four Zoas "who are the Four Eternal Senses of Man / Became Four Elements separating from the Limbs of Albion."

The three main ideas considered in this paper, limits, vortexes, and the mundane shell, are of course related. Both the vortexes and the mundane shell, even in ruins, serve to limit the Fall and to give form to chaos, making the "indefinite" definite. In *The Four Zoas*, where Blake may show a fresher, less fully assimilated use of his sources than in later work, these ideas seem to be especially closely related. In Night IV (*E* 331) Jesus founds the limits of opacity and of contraction in a crucial act of divine intervention in the falling world, and not much later, in Night VI, when Urizen is exploring his dens, the vortexes are associated with the ruined world in a passage quoted above. Though the first part of the eighteenth century set Newton and Descartes in opposition, and though Burnet was regarded by many as a pious and imaginative writer, the ideas of all these men would have seemed to Blake as merely variations on a common materialistic theme and as persuasive materialistic systems whose error had to be revealed in their systems. Blake had to meet his opponents where he found them. And the fact that aspects of the three systems we have considered became major issues in the philosophical debates of Blake's age might suggest that Blake could in one sense be thought of as joining the controversy. What he is really doing is rejecting the bases on which the controversies were conducted and showing that, though real errors were being touched on, the issues as debated were false ones because carried on within false systems, which threaten to enslave. Therefore he cries, through Los, "I Must Create a System, or be enslav'd by another Mans" (*J* 10:20, *E* 151). He creates a countersystem which would establish its freedom in part by specifically opposing and correcting certain features of the systems that would enslave him.

# The Poet

## ROBERT F. GLECKNER
# Blake's Verbal Technique

In his address entitled "To the Public," which serves as a Preface
to *Jerusalem*, Blake wrote: "Every word and every letter is studied
and put into its fit place; the terrific numbers are reserved for the
terrific parts, the mild & gentle for the mild & gentle parts, and
the prosaic for inferior parts; all are necessary to each other"
(*K* 621). Although Blake is speaking here only about *Jerusalem*,
I think it clear that the point refers to his other works as well.[1]
It is an extraordinary claim; but Blake critics have been, as we all
know, at great pains to demonstrate that the substance of the claim
is true, and that largely because of this, what emerges from the
study of Blake's work is an impressively coherent canon. So busy
have we been at the task of elucidating, explicating, and explaining
the "system" and myths contained in that canon, however, that
we have made little progress toward establishing the peculiar ap-
propriateness of Blake's verse, language, use of poetic forms, prosody
—in short, his poetry.[2] As, I hope, a step in this direction, I propose to examine some of the poetry to see to what extent "Every
word" seems to have been "studied and put into its fit place," and
to what extent and how (and perhaps even why) "all are necessary
to each other."

I think that, except for Josephine Miles, it has not generally
been recognized that Blake's poetry is to a remarkable degree a
poetry of adjectives. That is, much of its texture, force, and,
perhaps paradoxically, its substantiality, is achieved through Blake's
fine handling of that much-abused part of speech so often overlooked in poetry, especially by the seekers of images, myths,
allusions, metaphors, symbols, paradoxes, and ambiguities. In *Songs
of Innocence*, for example, we are all aware of the child figure
(as what I have called elsewhere a "major" symbol[3]), of the mother,

the lamb, the divine image, and so on. Each of these figures is related to the others in such a way as to create a particular kind of poetic world, a myth of innocence. More properly in Blake's terms, they conspire to create the "state of the human soul" he called innocence. Further, these relationships constitute a major portion of the tight coherence of the *Songs of Innocence* as not merely a collection of poems but as, in a sense, one poem. I should like to suggest that the major adjectives of the poems convey also that same sense of coherence—and a similar cumulative richness of texture and meaning. The adjectives are *happy, cheerful, glee*[ful], *merry, pleasant, sweet, innocent, tender, soft, wooly, moony, meek, mild, little, small, white, pretty, naked, warm, green, dovelike, clean,* and *human.* Except for perhaps *moony* and *dovelike,* what immediately strikes one about this list is its ordinariness. Yet inherent in the very ordinariness and simplicity of the adjectives are the nouns that they modify—the child and the lamb particularly —and that constitute the major symbol of innocence. Miss Miles maintains that a major portion of Blake's language "he got from the eighteenth century, definable as physical, descriptive, onomato-poetic, invocative, and declarative, fond of participles." Thus she sees his poetry, and in particular the *Songs,* as mainly descriptive in its emphasis, with "stress on descriptive adjectives," as having a "poetic sound" that is "also descriptive. . . . His structure too is descriptive, his sentences heavy with adjectives and substantives, his verbs turned to participial constructions" (*Eras & Modes,* p. 85). While I cannot quarrel with her marshaling of the evidence, I should like to suggest that Miss Miles's interpretation of that evidence may be in error (or is at best partial), that Blake's de-liberate use of eighteenth-century descriptive technique and vocab-ulary toward ends quite foreign to eighteenth-century thinking and poetry is a measure of his antipathy to and distance from the poetic tradition he inherited.

Thus, just as the nouns emerge, as it were, from the adjectives ostensibly "modifying" them, so too do the adjectives emerge from the nouns—a kind of indissoluble grammatical and dictional unity that not only conveys the essentials of the state of innocence but dramatizes the condition of being that state represents. Further, inherent in the adjectives are the major points of view represented in the *Songs of Innocence*—that of the child toward his own state and toward his mother (or nurse or shepherd or whatever form the protector of innocence takes), that of the mother toward the child, and that of the singer of the songs toward the state of the soul of which he sings. In a very real sense, the child, say, as object is considerably less important than the complex of qualities that constitute his existence; for what Blake is presenting after all is not a series of vignettes about childhood but a symbolic painting of a state of the human soul. The adjectives are discrete only in that they operate independent of each other in any given poem: if in "Holy Thursday" the children are described as "innocent," after we read the entire *Songs of Innocence* we know that the children in "Holy Thursday" are also happy, cheerful, merry, pleasant, sweet, tender, soft, wooly, bright, meek, mild, little, small, white, pretty, naked, warm, green, dovelike, and clean. More important, we know that "they" are not real, finally, but only the symbolic frames upon which to hang the richly textured garments of innocence as a "state of the human soul." Had Blake been as eager an experimenter with language as an E. E. Cummings or a James Joyce, we might very well have had a poetry which read as follows (simply taking the adjectives in the random order listed above):

> The happy cheerfuls the merry pleasant,
> And sweet tenders soft on wooly brights.

That is, the adjectives carry the weight of nouns and verbs. They are real; they exist; they act—and are acted upon. And as such they obviously cannot be casually chosen, but must be studied and put into their fit place. They are all necessary to each other.

Still, the fact remains that they are ordinary. In no urgent sense do they "need" each other. If one might worry some about *green* needing *white* to complete its meaning, we do not balk at all about the relationship among *bright, white, clean,* and perhaps even *dovelike.* They are discrete, independent, yet mergeable without much effort or indeed much imagination. And that, of course, is precisely Blake's point. Innocence is a state in which it is simply not extraordinary to see a child on a cloud, to hear a two-day-old infant speak, or to believe a glow-worm can guide an emmet back to her home and children—or indeed to believe that green is white. It is a world where all things are equal to each other and equal to the same thing—quite obviously and uncomplicatedly; and the reader's vision is forced by Blake's language to be as unclouded as the poet's—and the child's. We all see all as one.

Blake consistently maintained, in his poetry and prose alike, that eternity or Eden, the imaginative state of fourfold unity in which all things exist "Really & Unchangeably," (*LJ* 68, *K* 604) was in the form of "One Man" (Letter to Thomas Butts, 2 Oct. 1800, *K* 805), the human form divine. To the senses, however, that unity is unperceivable (and hence inconceivable), and everything is seen only in its separateness, as "grain[s] of Sand," "Stone[s] on the Land," rocks and hills, fountains and rills, herbs and trees, and so on (*K* 804–5). In their separateness these things are indeed describable, but there is no intrinsic relationship between object and quality. The *Songs of Innocence* are also susceptible to these different kinds of perception: that is, seen only by the senses (or sensibly, if you will) they exist only as disparate particulars with no necessary relationship to each other beyond their physical proximity on the page. Seen imaginatively, on the other hand, the several songs tend to merge as one poem, all the parts of which are organically related to, and identifiable with, all the other parts. As Blake wrote in his October 2, 1800, letter to Thomas Butts:

> My Eyes more & more
> Like a Sea without shore
> Continue Expanding,
> The Heavens commanding,
> Till the Jewels of Light,
> Heavenly Men beaming bright,
> Appear'd as One Man.

In innocence that one man is the child.

Such a principle, I suggest, is equally applicable to Blake's language in the *Songs*. The adjectives are only adjectives and the nouns nouns, both discrete and particular, to the unimaginative reader; and the basic principle of description merely accentuates that discreteness and particularity, however much it presupposes and hopes to illustrate some conceptual or rational idea of unity. In the same letter to Butts, his eyes "Expanding" through sense to imaginative vision, Blake sees

> The Light of the Morning
> Heaven's Mountains Adorning:
> In particles bright
> The jewels of Light
> Distinct shone & clear.
> Amaz'd & in fear
> I each particle gazed,
> Astonish'd, Amazed;
> For each was a Man
> Human-form'd. . . .                    (*K* 804)

Essentially, or perhaps I should say imaginatively, each particle (or word) of the *Songs* is "Human-form'd" in this sense, and all are united in the mutuality of innocence, the "equality" of noun, verb, and adjective, the identity of landscape and person, the symbolic figure of the child.

The particulars of this verbal strategy are perhaps seen most clearly in each individual song. One of Blake's best is "A Cradle Song" in *Songs of Innocence*, not the least impressive aspect of which is its manipulation of the relationship between nouns and adjectives:

> Sweet dreams, form a shade
> O'er my lovely infant's head;
> Sweet dreams of pleasant streams
> By happy, silent, moony beams.
>
> Sweet sleep, with soft down
> Weave thy brows an infant crown;
> Sweet sleep, Angel mild,
> Hover o'er my happy child.
>
> Sweet smiles, in the night
> Hover over my delight;

Sweet smiles, Mother's smiles,
All the livelong night beguiles.

Sweet moans, dovelike sighs,
Chase not slumber from thy eyes.
Sweet moans, sweeter smiles,
All the dovelike moans beguiles.

Sleep, sleep, happy child,
All creation slept and smil'd;
Sleep, sleep, happy sleep,
While o'er thee thy mother weep.

Sweet babe, in thy face
Holy image I can trace.
Sweet babe, once like thee,
Thy maker lay and wept for me,

Wept for me, for thee, for all,
When he was an infant small.
Thou his image ever see,
Heavenly face that smiles on thee,

Smiles on thee, on me, on all;
Who became an infant small.
Infant smiles are his own smiles,
Heaven & earth to peace beguiles.          (*K* 120)

Aside from the interconnectedness of the various adjectives, we should note also that many, if not all, of them have the force of nouns definitive of the state of innocence, just as the nouns (*dreams, infant, streams, beams, down, crown, angel, delight, dove,* etc.) all have the force of adjectives descriptive of the state they symbolize. So too the nouns tend to combine by way of their similar characteristics or the fundamental sameness of their imaginative (i.e., true) identities: dreams = sleep = smiles = moans = babe via "sweet"; beams (as well as silence and the moon) = child = sleep via "happy"; and so on. The net result is a complex of equations the total product of which is the unity of quality and thing, of mother-child-Christ and landscape, of action and state of being, of earth and heaven. The verbal technique, then, is as much a symbol of the world it presents as the images, actions, and characters for which it is the vehicle.

In *Songs of Experience* we enter another world, one in which the unitive interrelatedness of innocence has become fragmented and in a very real sense has become anotherness. The child is still there, and the mother, and the green fields—but now all is starry, fallen, dewy, worn, slumberous, watery, dread, drear, stony, grey, cold, selfish, cruel, jealous, heavy, holy, trembling, bleak, bare, frowning, pathless, weak, black, pale, sick, howling, secret, dark, fearful, deadly, modest, humble, chartered, hapless, dismal, dangerous, bound, weary, deceitful, weeping. These adjectives are not, in the same sense as those in *Songs of Innocence,* extensions of their nouns; they do not have inherent in them the fundamental, imaginative essentials of humanity. They are descriptive of the conditions of a world in which the nouns have, as it were, surrendered to the adjectives that describe those conditions. Thus, the child becomes his new adjectives of experience only in the sense that the limited vision of fallen humanity (that is, the humanity of experience) can no longer equate him with the imaginative truth of *happy, cheerful, merry, pleasant, white,* and so forth. In "Infant Sorrow" it is the adultlike, sense-bound child, a parodic and fallen version of the child of innocence, who sees himself as helpless, naked, hidden, bound, and weary, not the poet. Only through imagination can he still be seen as he was in innocence, as he eternally is really and unchangeably; and by means of Blake's technique the reader can see him as both.

Inherent in the adjectives of experience, then, are the adjectives of innocence—warped, perverted, turned upside down and inside out. They are in their own way representatives of the mind-forged manacles by which man perpetuates his separation from true, imaginative existence—that state of being in which adjectives do not modify but extend, in which, indeed, language is unnecessary because imagination is total, unsubordinated communication and communion.[4]

And because imagination or Eden or the New Jerusalem is unsubordinated unity, Blake never really wrote a poem about it—for language, as Shelley also came to know, is insufficient to describe it:

> Woe is me!
> The wingèd words on which my soul would pierce
> Into the height of Love's rare Universe,
> Are chains of lead around its flight of fire.
> (*Epipsychidion*, ll. 587–90)

I am suggesting, of course, that the fall (as Blake interpreted it) from innocence to experience, from oneness to division and disintegration, is also symbolized by him in the disintegration of adjective and noun—and even to some extent the disintegration of adjective and adjective. The relationship that exists easily, truly, essentially, in the state of innocence between *tender* and *white*, say, or *wooly* and *naked* simply does not exist in the state of experience between *starry* and *black*, or *stony* and *watery*, or *holy* and *dangerous*. By an imaginative effort, comparable to that inherent in the poet's invention, the reader can come to see that holiness is dangerous and bleak and bare and so on—the very imaginative effort the man of experience cannot or will not summon up. The latter's world is coherent to him only through his own blind and unimaginative attempts to make it, forcibly, coherent. Thus, in "The Little Vagabond" of *Songs of Experience* the church is cold to the child; and he is right. But to the parents it is healthy and pleasant and warm because their blinded senses see it as such, and their rational minds say that it must be such because that's what churches are supposed to be—or that's what they have been taught churches are. To see the church as starry, fallen, dewy, worn, slumberous, and watery is to see it for what it is imaginatively and thus to deny its false sensuous reality—or, better still, it is to see it as merely an extension of that self created by the senses and the reason, not by the imagination of the human form divine.

The disjunctive nature of experience, as well as the imaginative coherence of its disjunctiveness, is brilliantly exploited verbally in a poem like "Earth's Answer" in *Songs of Experience*. Although some of the adjectives have an immediate relationship to each other (*dread, drear, grey, cold, hoar, heavy*), the rest are ostensibly incompatible: *stony, wat'ry, starry, ancient, selfish, cruel, jealous, vain.* That incompatibility or dissociation Blake intensifies further by means of the deliberate inappropriateness of the adjectives he assigns to the nouns: jealousy is starry, fear is jealous and selfish, delight is chained, Earth's light is dark (or fled), and so on. (One might also point out in passing that the verb linkages are also perverted, paradoxical, and illogical: Earth is prisoned on the open expanse of a watery shore; jealousy keeps a den cold and hoar; delight is chained in and by night; and chains freeze around the bone.) Controlling all of these is the basic disjunctive idea at the center of the poem. It is, strangely enough, a love poem, a fact that we do not fully recognize until the last stanza, in which the word "Love" forces us back upon the whole poem to reread its horrors in new terms. What emerges from this is a portrait of both what love is imaginatively and what love has become because of the degeneration of imagination to sense and the senses.

At the same time the imaginative thrust of the poem is to unite these disjunctives into a coherent picture of disintegration and separateness—by essentially the same basic techniques used in *Songs of Innocence,* now made more complex because of the greater imaginative power necessary to put back together what the senses and reason have torn asunder. Thus, in the first stanza of "Earth's Answer" the earth emerges less clearly as an image than do the conditions of her state, which is dark, dread, drear, lightless, hard, cold, blind, covered, closed or locked-in, grey, despairing, old. What in innocence is easily seen in its wholeness and imaginative integrity, in experience can only be conceptualized, for identity has fragmented to idea. Thus love in the poem takes on all of the adjectival attributes of earth and the landscape, extended into the realm of human relationships: despairing, jealous, animal-like (from "den"), cold, weeping, selfish, cruel, secret, hidden, joyless, vain, ultimately dead. The forcible equations in the poem, then—of noun with noun, noun with adjective, and adjective with adjective—nullify any meaningful unity in the state of experience which the poem dramatizes, while at the same time they mockingly emulate the interchangeability of noun and adjective, adjective and adjective, by which Blake verbally symbolizes the unity of the state of innocence.

But Blake will put even greater burdens upon his adjectival forms. For as the state of experience, the world of the senses, the world of fallen, unimaginative man is extended beyond the confines of that very human life we all know (the world of the *Songs of Experience*), extended to encompass the cosmos, all of nature, and all of history and prehistory, Blake's imaginative vision of it takes on all the attributes of the world of eternity, imagination, oneness. That is, his language itself will assume the condition of oneness and interchangeability, the loss of which it ostensibly describes. This is another way of saying, of course, that the imaginative coherence of Blake's poetic world mocks the unimaginative incoherence it presents, and provides, as it were, a measure of the degree of that incoherence. Much of that mockery depends heavily upon his varied verbal manipulations, which include puns or plays on words; contradictory yoking of two unlike words; complex equations of prefixes; merging of place, point of view, and state of existence; ambiguity of modification; adjectival nouns or nounlike adjectives, which have inherent in them symbolic gestures; verbal irony; and ultimately a vast, seemingly endless equation of nouns and adjectives.

In *The Book of Urizen* we can see the beginnings of this. The first stanza of the Preludium is as follows:

> Of the primeval Priest's assum'd power,
> When Eternals spurn'd back his religion
> And gave him a place in the north,
> Obscure, shadowy, void, solitary. (*K* 222)

The pun on "primeval" helps to link together the assumption of power and the nature of priests, while the last line comments upon the total condition as seen by the imaginative poet. While in the fallen world's terms the priest has a "place," to the eyes of the poet that place is nonexistent, "void." Further, while the adjectives in the last line ostensibly describe that "place," they also describe "him," thus linking together the mutual imaginative unreality of character and landscape. If the place is "obscure," so too the priest's vision is obscuring and obscured; if the place is shadowy, the priest also is unsubstantial, a delusion; and if the place is separated from the Eternals' unity, so the priest is solitary. Space as well as individual identity is thus asserted (from Urizen's point of view) and denied (from the poet's point of view). The first chapter of the poem (*K* 222–23) expands on this. Urizen is "a shadow of horror," not an identity; and he is "Unknown, unprolific, / Self-clos'd, all-repelling," a "form'd" void or vacuum. That is, he cannot be known imaginatively (since he is void and a shadow of an abstraction), but can be seen by the senses (or by himself).[5] Closing himself in and repelling all so that he may be identifiable as separate, Urizen exemplifies all the illusory opposites of unity and eternity, in which all is known, prolific, unclosed, and self-repelling (or all-conjoining). His very unreality, then, becomes through Blake's technique the symbol of all that he is not; and, conversely, his emergence as a palpable reality is constantly undercut by the voidness of his realization. He is, for example, a "self-contemplating shadow," a phrase that comments upon his imaginative blindness as well as his imaginative nonexistence. Again, Blake describes him as "In enormous labours occupied," thus allocating him the spatial dimension and physical energy which Urizen sees in himself, and denying the viability of such space, action, and energy by characterizing the activity as "unknown," "dark," and "silent." Further, that activity is revolving, turning in and on itself to no end, negating creativity and accentuating Urizen's self-closed and unprolific nature.[6] Similarly, the "petrific, abominable chaos" that is his landscape defines the imaginative unreality of himself and his world: it is solid yet void, formed yet chaotic, closed yet open, seen yet unknown, deep yet dimensionless. Urizen himself is thus an abstraction that exists only for him, an unprolific non-entity who breeds other non-entities, a power assumed, not inherent.

What is perhaps unusual about all of this is that while we can more obviously make the strange Blakean ground more familiar and workable by charting his symbolic system, we can do very much the same thing by studying his adjectives—almost aside from the nouns they modify. Just as an object or character or gesture or action accumulates a dense texture of associations as it appears in successive contexts in Blake's poetry, so too do the adjectives in precisely the same way. As each noun appears modified in similar contexts by a succession of adjectives, so too does each recurrence of an adjective, in similar context, recall both its equivalent adjectives and the succession of nouns it has modified.

In another place, I discussed an aspect of Blake's technique by which he can allude to the two contrary states of the human soul at once.[7] The infant in "Infant Sorrow" is a good example. He is simultaneously the infant of innocence and, more importantly, not that infant at all. That we are forced by Blake to read both infants at once is the source of the poem's peculiar power and effect. The point I wish to make here is that that ambiguity is also inherent in his use of adjectives. The force of the adjective, that is, can be in two directions at once, can contain within itself innocence and experience and thus both measure the distance between its present context (usually experience) and eternity, and intensify the present context by alluding to another that is its opposite.

Language, we must all admit, is relatively unmalleable. But we must also admit that all great poets have stretched its limits and often hammered it into incredible shapes. That we have scarcely given Blake credit for such stretching and hammering is unfortunate in view of our mushrooming efforts to elucidate his mythological world. I would hope, then, that the faint clues and indirections of this essay may serve, in a way quite different from the work of Josephine Miles and Alicia Ostriker, to stimulate that sort of concentrated study and analysis Blake's poetic technique requires to establish it as commensurate with, and necessary to, his total poetic achievement.

JOHN E. GRANT

# Two Flowers in the Garden of Experience

The Rose and the Lily have been the favorite floral symbols in European poetry at least since the Middle Ages. In this essay I wish to present a detailed interpretation of Blake's illuminated lyrics, "My Pretty Rose Tree" and "The Lilly," which occur together on the same page of *Songs of Experience* (see PLATE XXIII). Then I shall study other important concurrences of this flower imagery throughout Blake's literary and pictorial work. In order to do so with some thoroughness I shall have to pay scant attention to the great lyric "The Sick Rose," which is only obliquely related to any of Blake's lilies, and can hardly consider "Ah! Sun-flower," though it is the greatest poem on the three-flower page in the *Songs*.

I particularly regret not being able to discuss "Ah! Sun-flower" in this essay because Blake placed it between the two poems in question and surely did not do so simply to fill up a page with brief poems about flowers. As a group the poems evidently present a threefold definition of love. Wicksteed points to the schematic shift in point of view of narration in the three lyrics from first, to second, to third person. But Wicksteed's attempt to adduce a code of color symbolism—according to which the red, yellow, and white flowers equal "earthly love, poetic love, and Human love," respectively—is not persuasive for several reasons, notably because Blake actually painted the Lilly a number of different colors. And Wicksteed's association of the three poems with "Innocence, Vision, and Experience" is altogether too arbitrary to be acceptable. On the other hand, the connection he makes between these poems and Dante's three states of the afterlife—"transgression and pain," "holy and purifying aspiration," and "beatitude"—has greater plausibility.[1]

To these suggestions one can add that the basic tense of each poem differs so that the three contain visions of the past, present, and future, respectively. In thus presenting the three dimensions of time on a single page the artist is like the "Bard" in the "Introduction" to *Experience*, "who Present, Past, & Future sees." The use of flower imagery in the three poems is also quite different: the first employs a flower allegory, the second a flower symbol based on a myth, and the third a flower emblem. As Wicksteed indicates, flowers in Blake represent love; consequently such synoptic variation suggests a conspectus of love relationships. Briefly, the first poem tells how two ostensible lovers fail to achieve regeneration, the second poem how at least the Youth and the Virgin escape the bondage of death,[2] and the third poem how the Lilly can be tenderly invulnerable to the dangers of Experience. And the imaginative range of each poem is notably expanded by its accompanying illustration.

However desirable it might be to take up "Ah! Sun-flower" in its proper place on the page, the work is too complicated, the symbol too resonant in Blake's symbolism, and the scholarship too extensive to consider here. The two poems in question and the ramifications of their key symbols constitute a sufficiently complex subject. Let us first look at the texts as they appear with Blake's punctuation:[3]

### My Pretty ROSE TREE

A flower was offerd to me;
Such a flower as May never bore.
But I said I've a Pretty Rose-tree.
And I passed the sweet flower o'er.

Then I went to my Pretty Rose-tree:
To tend her by day and by night.
But my Rose turnd away with jealousy:
And her thorns were my only delight.

### THE LILLY

The modest Rose puts forth a thorn:
The humble Sheep. a threatning horn:
While the Lilly white. shall in Love delight.
Nor a thorn nor a threat stain her beauty bright

*Two Flowers*

### · THE LACERATIONS OF "MY PRETTY ROSE TREE" ·

The general meaning of this fine poem is clear to every reader, though the interpreter must be alert not to make the dramatic situation implied seem either too occasional or too specific. Many readers have supposed that the poem had as its inspiration some incident in the married life of William and Catherine Blake. While this is quite conceivable, it does not follow that the speaker in the *poem* need necessarily be imagined as married to the woman. Nevertheless, with very little distortion the moral of the poem could be called "the wages of uxoriousness." [4]

The speaker, a man in Experience, tells allegorically that an exceptionally beautiful woman, one above what Nature could produce ("such . . . as May never bore"), offered herself to him. But the speaker, who seems not to have sought the offer, primly rejected it and returned to his beloved in order to "tend her by day and by night." The allegory suggests the cultivation of a gardener, but his service at "night" exceeds what vegetable nature requires. Nevertheless, his continual solicitousness did not satisfy his "Rose," who was jealous anyway, and his only reward was to suffer from her "thorns," doubtless her barbed remarks, etc., rather than to enjoy her love.

A number of symbols require particular comment because they help to clarify the speaker's pitiable and contemptible plight. He has rejected a supernatural woman for a mere May Rose, albeit he imagines her as a Rose-tree—"a whole tree of flowers, which may be legally enjoyed." [5] Furthermore, he admits repeatedly to preferring this flower, which is merely "pretty," rather than beautiful as the supernatural flower undoubtedly was. But since the speaker is also aware that the first woman was above nature (an admission he makes in the somewhat awkward figure of speech) there can be no doubt that he had to repress his impulses in order to reject her. Thus while the jealousy of the Rose is certainly not imagined to be a virtue, the reader is meant to feel that the speaker's misery is good enough for him. The standard of judgment is stated unmistakably in many of Blake's manuscript poems, for example:

Eternity

He who binds to himself a joy
Does the winged life destroy;
But he who kisses the joy as it flies
Lives in eternity's sun rise.             (K 179)[6]

The result of this conflict between desire and duty, impulse and rules, is that the speaker's cowardice receives a reward that is a punishment, a grotesque result which the reader gathers is actually enjoyed by this Rose lover. To be sure, there is an enigmatic quality in the last line of the poem and it is possible to read it in various ways so as to imply different tones or attitudes on the part of the speaker. Another kind of man might be outraged or bitter or ironic at having received such a reward for such a renunciation, but the Rose lover is probably too enervate to be capable of such specific or conscious reactions. Apparently referring to the speaker, rather than the Rose, Price suggestively speaks of his "resentment." [7] This description does seem to fit the speaker's character, especially if he is also imagined to be petulant, rather than bitter. Much hangs on how the reader interprets the last line. The prosaic reading would be that "delight" in this context means "reward," i.e., "I didn't get any." But attention to the exact word, *delight*, reveals that a deeper level of characterization is built into this monologue. Supposing, as one must, that the poet did not stumble into a rhyme, the Rose lover must be saying that he received at least a single "delight," thorns. And it is entirely consistent with Blake's critical attitude toward conventional behavior and symbolism thus to criticize the venerable cult of Rose idolatry because it degrades and fetters both poetry and the human race. In his choice of the conventional love rose, the speaker has preferred a flower on which it is easy to wound himself. Such a predilection implies that he was perversely inclined to suffer in the state of Experience, rather than attempt to make contact with Eternity. Since he concludes by describing his painful fate as his "only *delight*," he must be diagnosed as a masochist. Such a clinical term seems fitting for the case of a man who would prefer a Rose to a nonpareil.

Thus while the standard of behavior may be found in others of Blake's poems, such as "Eternity" (or "The Lilly"), this poem is completed as soon as the Rose lover presents his painful case. The reader is then left to meditate on the fate of this kind of person before an ethical standard is introduced later on the page.

The narrative art of "My Pretty Rose Tree" also deserves some attention. The same pattern occurs in both stanzas. In the first line of each an offer is made and in the second it is more fully described, though in the first stanza the offer is an object while in the second stanza it is an action. In the second half of each stanza negative responses are made to the offers, in lines beginning "But/And." The pattern is varied, however: in the first stanza the speaker first tells what he said and then what he did, while in the second stanza he first tells what she did and then what he felt. Moreover, two lines in these alternately rhymed anapestic quatrains tend to be noticeably irregular, lines 4 and 7. Both of these describe deeds of rejection that were so painful that the speaker's rhythm stumbles.[8] By such devices a neat but intricate balance of repetition and variation is produced that is a technical correlative to the idea of the poem. When the reader observes these structures in the light of Blake's work as a whole, he recognizes in "My Pretty Rose Tree" that the law of retribution is shown to operate in human relationships as it does in hell. He who rejects is himself rejected.

## · THE ILLUSTRATION ·

The picture that accompanies this poem is the largest of the three on this page, but presumably because of its obvious correspondence to the situation described in the poem it has received no careful consideration. Under the text are the two human figures and in the right margin is the lumpish trunk with a spreading rooty base of a leafless tree. Various other details become apparent as the reader looks closely. Across the base of the tree is a twisted bush or vine with three branches, the first of which bears two ostensible leaves, the second, three probable rose blossoms, and the third evidently disappears behind the tree trunk.[9] At the left margin is a clump of long grasses. With his back to them, kneeling on the ground and bent over, hiding his face behind his left fore-arm, is an ostensive man with long hair, in right profile. Lying on the ground, facing the reader, with her left cheek resting on her left hand and her right arm bent in front of her, is a woman whose eyes are averted from the man as she leans on the base of the tree. These human figures evidently depict the plight indicated at the end of the allegorical poem. The Rose lover is in despair, doubtless from pain and also regret, while Rose is bored and cold. And the Rose-tree appears in its vegetable form, as well as its human form, though it is noteworthy that it shows no thorns.

But there are other details in the picture that have no verbal sanction. Behind the humans, appearing above the woman's right leg, is a flight of ten birds, one of which appears much larger, presumably because it is nearer. The tree, which varies in shape somewhat from copy to copy, has two main branches, both of which fork; in all copies the lower branch extends over at least to beneath the middle of the third word in the title. Under the second letter of the first word in the title two tiny birds fly to the left and under the first letter of the second word a larger or closer bird flies in the same direction. Three of the initial letters in the text are also elaborately decorated with loop motifs. In the title the initial letter $M$ has seven (five distinct) loops extending down from it and up to the top of the page. The top of the letter $S$ in "ROSE" ordinarily has a distinct but not unusual serif; the bottom of the letter, however, has a remarkably long thorn, or claw, serif. $T$ in "TREE" has about four regularly diminishing loops across the top of the page. The initial $A$ in "And" in line 8 has fourteen distinct loops that rise and then fall in the left margin. Less im-posing flourishes appear on three other letters. The initial $A$ in line 1 has a curly bump; the initial $S$ in line 2 has a tall slash tail that crosses over the flourish on the $A$; and the $y$ of "my" in the last line has an exceptionally long two-phase tail.[10]

A few variations that result from the coloring of the final two copies may also be noted. In copy $Z$[11] a line appears out of the clump of grass at the bottom left. It goes off the page but evi-dently appears again at the top left, where touches of green suggest the possibility of another tree, though this hint is not developed. The text area is painted a strong blue at the top, but this fades down to a light blue wash in the second stanza. Then there is a distinct area of strong yellow in the area of the woman and the base of the tree. The grass at the left is colored in gold, the man is dressed in blue leotards and has a substantial area of gold on his long orange-brown hair that falls over his face. The woman wears a violet dress with a thin white collar on her square décolleté neckline. The tree, painted dull blue and gray, is outlined in (unpainted) white along its inner edge. Its main branch is connected by a thin line to the tail of the letter *y* in the word "Pretty" of the title. The rosebush, as well as its leaves and blossoms, has been given no color of its own and is thus subordinated. In copy AA both the line in the left margin and the line from the tree to the title (which do not appear in earlier copies I have studied) have been eliminated. The chief difference in coloring is that the whole sky area at the bottom, near the people, is painted a strong orange.

Interpretation of the picture begins as usual with the hypothesis that the iconic function of the details is maximal and the decorative function is minimal. It is obvious that the artist has chosen to subordinate the flower allegory, which constitutes the literal level of the poem, and to focus the reader's attention on the hopelessly separated man and woman. But though the rosebush is scarcely visible, the leafless tree adds an imposing and sinister presence not mentioned in the poem.

The following motif analogies which appear elsewhere in *Songs* are noteworthy. The posture of the mourning Rose lover resembles that of the superstitious parents in "A Little Boy Lost" and also that of the redeemed boy in "The Little Vagabond," as well as the position of the mourning Theotormon in the frontispiece to *Visions of the Daughters of Albion,* another poem concerned with sexual despair. The Rose is stretched out in a position similar to that of the girl in "The Angel," except that her head is at the right side of the page, and both of them also recall the recumbent Venus position of Earth in the "Introduction" to *Experience* and of the mature Lyca in the last page of "The Little Girl Found." The latter two girls have their backs turned to the reader, however. The tree closely resembles the tree of death depicted in "A Poison Tree" and, more distantly, those in "A Little Girl Lost," "The Human Abstract," "The Fly," "The Tyger," "Holy Thursday," and page two of "The Little Girl Lost [and] Found." Looped tendrils, such as the ones that decorate the letters in "Rose Tree," are to be found in "Nurses Song" and "The Angel" and, as letter decorations, they appear in "A Little Girl Lost," "The Little Vagabond," and "The School Boy." The loop motif is also emphasized elsewhere on the flower page for it appears in the tail of the worm or serpent at the lower right and as the roots in the left margin of "Ah! Sun-flower." And it is also present in the loose curls on the initial letter of the title of "The Lilly" as well as the single loop in the decoration at the bottom. Similar curves and loops are to be found in the textual serpents and the briar patch at the bottom of "The Garden of Love." Such cross referencing indicates how these motifs modulate into one another, giving a suggestive rather than a rigid character to the pictorial imagery in the *Songs*. Blake undoubtedly wished the reader to recognize both the sameness and difference in any particular example of his symbolism. As a consequence, when one has recognized a few analogies for any particular motif, he must use them judiciously, rather than as skeleton keys.

The fact that Rose resembles Earth in certain respects, for example, indicates that the interpreter should be wary of condemning her, in spite of her transgressions against the Blakean ethic. On the other hand, her closer resemblance to the girl in "The Angel," who is more stringently considered, cannot be disregarded either. Though the man and the woman are undoubtedly unhappy, a primary question is whether they will continue to be so. Since the poem is in the past tense, it seems probable that the plight of the people is unrelieved, but what is the reader to make of the very bright horizons in the last two copies? Is it possible that Rose will relent from her cruelty and that a new day is dawning? Are the birds winged joys, visions of the possibilities of redemption which may return in the proper season? The presence of a similar bird on the general title page of *Songs* suggests as much: there Adam and Eve are blasted by the flames of wrath, but the bird is on the wing and Eve (in several copies) is at least trying to look out at the reader, much as the "Rose" does in the Song of Experience. Indeed, these joys have not yet departed, in spite of the rejections, and could be seen if the people would raise their eyes. Since the Rose-tree actually depicted has no thorns, perhaps the Rose lover will get over his pains. Such possibilities are conceivable and Blake was free to vary his effects so that even unmistakably sinister symbols, such as the barren tree and the loops, can seem less oppressive and the general prospect more hopeful.

Since Blake's *Songs* are episodes in a larger drama which is never fully set forth in any single exposition but which has a determinate character nevertheless, speculation about the past and future of the characters is by no means irrelevant or absurd. Evidently the basic function of the picture is to indicate that what was true at the time of the poem is still true now and that the desperation is as yet unrelieved. Even the bright sky is probably that of sunset, the twenty-six loops are like snakes and snares, the thirteen birds symbols of missed opportunities that are now going elsewhere, the two large birds suggestions of the (separately) departing spirits of the two people, the blades of sword grass like thorns transposed from the rosebush tormenting the Rose lover, and the Rose itself a mere adjunct to the Tree of Death. Though the Rose-tree looks to the reader like the one in Eternity that has no thorns, its thorns seem real enough to its devotee, who is immersed in the world of Experience. When darkness falls all will be hell indeed, for the vegetation will wither and the man and woman will go to "Eternal Death," as the state of despair is called in the prophecies.[12]

### · THE CHARITY OF "THE LILLY" ·

A number of the implications of this exquisite little poem seem to have escaped comment and deserve to be spelled out. Though it is the briefest of the Songs of Experience, "The Lilly" is not a fragile poem and is invulnerable to charges of naïveté or disabling sentimentality. It quietly declares that even in Experience invincible innocence continues to be the standard of the good and

is always attainable in spite of the challenges to which it is subjected. Indeed the use of the future tense in line 3 constitutes a
prediction that this flower's higher innocence will outlast the state
of Experience and attain to those delights of Eternity that are in-
accessible to the Rose lover and his Rose. The moral allegory of
this flower emblem is extensively set forth in St. Paul's encomium
on Charity in I Corinthians 13:4–8, where Blake undoubtedly
noticed that Charity is personified as "her" in the fifth verse. But
in "The Lilly" Blake shifts Paul's emphasis from a love that is
long-suffering to a love that finds its own "delight," though without
doing so at the expense of others.

In this respect Blake carefully distinguishes the Lilly from the
Clod of Clay in "The Clod & the Pebble," which does appear to
be simply a long-suffering victim.[13] A glance at the more extended treatment of the relationship between serviceability and
love in *The Book of Thel* (*K* 127–30) shows that while the Lilly
of the valley serves as food for "the innocent lamb" (2:5), she
is also able to "Rejoice" (1:21) because she can enjoy the prospect
of flourishing "in eternal vales" (1:25) and is effectively imagined
in her essential being as she "smil'd in tears" amidst her "silver
shrine" (2:2). Later she can even cradle with impunity the destructive Worm (4:2–3) and does so without the sort of admirable
abjectness that characterizes the matron Clay. A more thorough
discussion of Blake's ideological and poetic tactics in handling the
symbolism of the Clod of Clay in *The Book of Thel* would however be necessary before one could proceed to make a satisfactory
interpretation of "The Clod & the Pebble."

In "The Lilly" the Bard, who is hardly distinguishable from
Blake the poet, wishes to declare the fundamental imperviousness
of the Lilly, first in contrast to the other traditional love flower,
the Rose, and second in contrast to the Sheep, which had been
the most innocent of beasts, the Lamb. As Damon[14] and others
have pointed out, in the manuscript draft the "modest Rose" was
first called both "envious" and "lustful," while the "humble Sheep"
was described as a "coward," and Gardner correctly adds that the
modesty of the blushing Rose "is never Innocent in Blake," as
Oothoon declares explicitly in *Visions of the Daughters of Albion*

(6:7–13, *K* 193–94).¹⁵ To this one can add that not only are the thorns of a Rose symbolic of a vicious kind of love, as in "My Pretty Rose Tree," but they are also shown to be ineffectual as a means of protecting a flower from what seems to threaten it. Thus the flower in "The Sick Rose" is depicted as being heavily equipped with thorns, yet not only is its blossom attacked directly by a worm, but its leaves are being eaten away by a caterpillar, which was unhindered by the thorns on the stalk. As Blake explained in "The Human Abstract" (*K* 217) deterrence strategy, according to which "mutual fear brings peace," is simply not validated in Experience.

A whole philosophy of life that can be called, without anachronism, "nonviolence," begins to emerge when the reader connects Blake's various related pictorial and verbal ideas in the *Songs.* True innocence is not based on a timid moral position but is shown to be more realistic than tough or subtle belligerency. Yet Blake rarely limits himself to a simple formula for the Good because the close connection between the good and the desirable makes it difficult to arrive at any concise statement which is both precise and comprehensive. For example, the intent of Auden's declaration "we must love one another or die" ¹⁶ is admirable, but love does not really grant immunity from some kinds of death and there is also an implicit threat in this injunction that tends to make the formula self-defeating. But through a series of cogent epiphanies Blake achieves a full definition of the enemies of peace in "The Lilly." Notice how the posture of "the humble Sheep" with "a threatning horn" anticipates the imperialistic policy of walking softly while carrying a big stick. In revision it occurred to the poet that it is not necessary to call the Sheep a "coward" because his incongruous demeanor reveals him to be both coward and hypocrite. If there is any doubt that Blake intended a primary thrust against militarism in "The Lilly," the reader should notice two ironic and forthright lines deleted from the first draft: "And the lion increase freedom & peace / The priest loves war & the soldier peace" (*K* 171). But Blake finally subordinated these political polemics to arrive at a simpler, more universal, formulation of the truth.

The meter shifts in the second couplet of this quatrain from iambic to anapestic, which constitutes a return to the dominant meter of the other two poems on the page. The transitional word "While" (rather than "But") in the third line helps both to change from the present to the future tense and to increase the *i* assonance of the line; moreover, it further suggests a transition to a different level of being rather than an alternative within the same level. The metrical and musical dexterity in the last line is likewise remarkable, though as with all other aspects of this simple-seeming poem, the art does not obtrude itself into the reader's consciousness. The implication of the first three lines is that the Rose, the Sheep, and the Lilly all have their own styles of existence, but this poetic enumeration of their essential contrasts implies that they are to be evaluated, not merely described. The primary sense of the last line is that "the Lilly *white*" (characterized by her candid color, rather than by demeanor as in the cases of the Sheep and Rose) will display neither the stain of a thorn nor that of a threat on her bright beauty. But there is a second sense to the line that neither thorns nor threats, which are directed against her by jealousy, can actually besmirch her beauty.

If the reader proceeds from the literal level of the poem to an interpretation of this emblematic flower, he can distinguish allegorical and anagogical levels of meaning as well as the moral level already described in connection with Blake's pacificism. The allegorical level has to do with types of women. The human form of the Lilly is Oothoon in *Visions of the Daughters of Albion,* Blake's example of a woman whose free bright beauty cannot really be damaged by encroachments. As Orc declares in *America,* "the soul of sweet delight can never be defil'd" (8:14, *K* 199). In "The Lilly" Blake unostentatiously replaces the conventional image of the Virgin Mary meek and mild, traditionally symbolized by the lily, with the more joyous and liberated woman he calls Oothoon in the prophecies. Later, in *Jerusalem* and *The Everlasting Gospel,* Blake characterizes Mary herself as a woman inviolable and free such as perhaps no other Christian writer ever imagined.

The anagogical level depends on the association in the Sermon on the Mount between "lilies of the field" and clothing. In Matthew 6:30 Christ shifts his imagery from lilies to "grass of the field" and behind this symbolism is Isaiah's declaration (40:6) that "all flesh is grass." [17] In *The Book of Thel* God, "he that smiles on all," addresses the Lilly of the Valley as "thou humble grass" (1:21, *K* 127) and later Thel refers to the vegetable nature of the Lilly as "thy milky garments" (2:5, *K* 128) fed on by the Lamb. And in the symbolism of the later prophecies the female often represents space, matter, or the body, while the male represents time, spirit, or the soul. The implication of such associated images is that the Lilly corresponds to the body, the traditional garment of the soul, which has been much reviled by Platonistic thinkers in the Christian Establishment because it is the vehicle of delight and particularly of sexual pleasure. In the design for the last poem added to *Songs of Experience*, "To Tirzah," Blake alludes to the theological distinction between the physical body and the spiritual body. The Lilly, of course, corresponds to the latter. Blake was confident that however subject the natural body might be to force and threats, man's spiritual body, like the Lilly, could never be essentially debased.

I have attempted to show, with a minimum of counterstatement, how the poem is intelligible and justified without recourse to a theory of radical irony. That "The Lilly" is susceptible to an ironic reading is indicated by the following sentences from Gillham's interpretation: "Where Rose and sheep ask for the delights of 'Love' by showing their readiness to repel it, the lily invites it by appearing ignorant of what is intended. She is far from being innocent in 'Love' but she knows (or senses) that it is enticing to appear to be so, and assumes the appearance of a 'white' unknowing virginity. Plainly 'Love' is regarded as something fascinating but indecent by all the creatures in the poem and they all show they have nothing to do with indecencies. All three are insincere, but the lily shows a refinement of insincerity . . ." [18]

Though these ingenious thoughts are not obviously motivated by the sly sense of fun that seems to lie behind those entertaining misreadings of English poetry in which Robert Graves has specialized, they do tend to invert the plain sense of the poem in a comparable manner. Gillham claims for himself the license conferred by a slight acquaintance with the range of Blake's writings, an indifference to Blake's illustrations, and a casual acquaintance with Blake scholarship and on these "most conservative and orthodox principles" tells the reader what Blake's poem means to him. Structurally what is wrong is that Gillham's own tenuous premises are presented with all the force of elements in a rigorous syllogism. Substantially, the Lilly might be suspected of the stratagem, but no evidence is presented to support this allegation. Yet who can allay moral suspicion once it has been aroused? "If the Rose and the Sheep are hypocrites, what must the Lilly be?" We have all heard that the traditional bordello stocked a "virgin" and some have read about the female wiles of Enitharmon, etc., and so we find ourselves saying "Does she or doesn't she? Maybe she isn't what she appears after all." But Blake is not trying to sell a virgin lily, nor yet to encourage innuendo about her. On the contrary, the point of the poem is not that the Lilly secretly *does*, but that she really "shall" fulfill her nature and delight in doing so.

Well, it may be questioned, if the Lilly really is what she seems to be what is this poem doing in *Songs of Experience?* There is a way of misreading this anthology that assumes the inhabitants of this state must all be sinners, fools, and dissemblers, or at best helpless victims who don't know any better. The notion that Innocence must inevitably fall victim to Experience is neither wise nor justified and some evidence to the contrary can be found in almost every design. Having discovered that Blake, of whom it used to be alleged that "he foundered on sweet cake," was capable of black humor from very early in his career, some readers now seek to find irony pervading every line Blake wrote. There is irony in "The Lilly," in the unveiling of the hypocrisy of the Rose and the Sheep, but the poem is impoverished if it is read as a cynical exposure of the Lilly. As a way of life irony is a defensive posture, more subtle but not different from the hidden thorn and the curly horn. It too must be disarmed before there will be anything better than fitful delight in the world.

## · THE ILLUSTRATION ·

The design for "The Lilly" is the simplest of the three on this page, but like Blake's other subtle designs its significance cannot be understood at a glance.[19] The chief detail is the flower itself, depicted in the lower right margin with its blossom bent down in a lowly manner. Despite line 3 of the poem the blossom of the Lilly was variously colored by Blake. For this tiny design a fairly extensive collation of the coloring in several copies is practicable. In copy A the leaves are yellow-green and the blossom is dull blue; in copy B the leaves are painted with gray-brown washes but the blossom did not print—accidentally, no doubt; in copy C the leaves are green and the blossom uncolored white; in copy E the vaguely indicated blossom is uncolored white; in copy G the leaves are blue-green and the blossom a similar blue; in copy N the blossom is uncolored white; in copy O the leaves are green and the blossom is white; in copy R the leaves are green and the blossom is white; in copy T (a color print) the leaves are green and the blossom is also green, but it is not really distinguishable as a blossom; in copy Y the leaves are green and the blossom is uncolored white; in copy Z a light black has been applied over the brown printed leaves and the blossom is green; in copy AA the leaves are printed brown and the blossom is white. To summarize, in these eleven copies that show a blossom it is either painted various shades of blue or green (four times) or is left white and thus corresponds with the text of the poem. Since the color of the printing and other details such as the leaves also vary from copy to copy, Blake's problem in deciding on the proper color for any particular version of the blossom might be considered merely in relation to what is required to achieve harmonious decoration. On the other hand, white could never have been out of place. Thus one can infer that in those copies in which the coloring does not correspond with the text—these seem to occur at all periods, early and late, of Blake's production—the very discrepancy may have significance. Evidently the ideas of the poem apply equally well to this kind of flower of whatever color, "white" being proverbial for lilies and conventionally exalted but not imaginatively necessitated or endorsed. The "Black Boy" whose soul is said to be "white" comes to mind at this point. Since every color has negative as well as positive associations, the artist can expect a fit audience to make the necessary adjustments of its perspective to recognize the context depicted. Blake had the advantage of using an art form that could be duplicated and yet he was able to vary his colors so as to remind the reader who knows the range of his work to distinguish the essential from the accidental.

It is noteworthy, however, that in this design the Lilly is apparently never colored in vivid reds, oranges, or yellows and is depicted as being so lowly as to be almost "modest" or "humble." This flower bows down into the world of Experience and is presumably subjected to vicissitudes more distressing than those suffered by the Lilly of the Vales of Har in *Thel*, though it is also in prospect of attaining the higher state of blessedness mentioned in the poem. In versions of this design containing a yellow area of dawn, such as copy AA, it is suggestive that the dawn area surrounds the title rather than the blossom. And in copy Z the blue wash background for the whole design is merely lightened in the upper and right areas without any blending of dawn colors. The only touch of pink in this version occurs inside the small loop of the worm that obtrudes into the top of this picture from "Ah! Sun-flower." The fact that both the color and the worm spill over into this design suggests that the Lilly in Experience is not exempted from mundane challenges and that, as in the poem, her invincible innocence will not remain untried. The pink bounded by the worm must therefore be that of sunset, rather than sunrise. But this worm of Night will not cause the Lilly to faint, as it does her pathetic sister, the Sick Rose.[20]

The decorations in the design tell the same story as the representational symbolism. Especially noteworthy is the sinister large vermiculate shape that starts on the first letter of the text and goes down the left margin before undulating under most of the text and ending in a loop. This is painted gold in copy Z, as is an ostensible twisted twig and leaf that branches inward over the text from the initial letter of the poem. The reader thus has the option of interpreting this gold "leaf" as a congener either of the true golden bough in Virgil's *Aeneid* or of the meretricious foliage in Spenser's Bower of Bliss. Another decorative detail occurs on the first letter of the title. There are four distinct loops attached to it, in addition to several irregular "unwound" ones and an extra hump-flourish in the upper left corner that is connected with the loops in some copies. These unmistakably serve an artistic function of balancing the Lilly leaves at the right of the design, but this reiteration of the root-serpent loop motifs from "Ah! Sun-flower" and "My Pretty Rose Tree" also serves to intensify the sense of the presence of indefinite sinister things that are hostile to the Lilly.

One other detail in the design calls attention to itself. Because of the long anapestic fourth line, Blake had no room to place the final word in its natural position; therefore, he demoted the word "bright" to the catchword position in the lower right corner. This has the fortunate result of placing both the words "beauty" and "bright" in a descriptive position next to the depicted blossom and also of making the poem seem momentarily to end with the word "beauty." The habit of disregarding ostensible catchwords is particularly apt to operate when the words look so much alike.[21] The tail on the final *y* in "beauty" is given a very broad curve that fans out off the page and further tends to set off the word "bright." Such separation gives the word an extra force in a second reading and makes the fact that it is a transposed adjective, like the one in the third line, with which it rhymes, more noticeable. The story of the Lilly is summed up in the rhymes of "white," "delight," and "bright." Perhaps the extravagant tail has the further function of cutting off the vermiculate line under the text, making it recoil in a loop before it can "stain" the word "bright." Whether or not the reader will admit to the presence of this particular drama in the decoration and orthography, he should recognize that much significant iconography is contained in this tiny design.

## · BLAKE'S SYMBOLISM OF ROSES AND LILIES ·

Though the flowers of the first and third poems on the flower page frequently occur together in Blake's poetry and painting, they are used to symbolize a wide range of ideas and attitudes. In what is perhaps Blake's earliest extant poem, "How sweet I roam'd," the girl who is speaking meets "the prince of love," who begins his tyrannical courtship in a conventional way: "He shew'd me lilies for my hair, / And blushing roses for my brow" (*K* 6). Then he leads her to his golden pleasure gardens where he traps and imprisons her in a golden cage. In this early poem the lily cannot be distinguished from the rose as bait for a trap.

With the exception of the flower page in *Songs*, the two flowers were not used together again in Blake's poetry until he made his first attempt to write a major epic, *The Four Zoas*. There roses are introduced in the crowns of Los and Enitharmon (i:435, *K* 276) at their sad momentous marriage feast where they are explicitly accompanied by the forlorn Urizen who longs for his bride, Ahania. These relationships become very involved in Night the Second where Los and Enitharmon are "drawn down by their desires . . . / To plant divisions in the Soul of Urizen & Ahania . . ." (287, 289; *K* 287). The imagery employed to evaluate their relationship is complexly antithetical with a quick succession of positive and negative implications. No sooner has their purpose of planting divisions been declared than they are seen, evidently in the eternal past, "Contracting or expanding their all flexible senses" (296), which is always an activity of exuberance in Blake; yet they are also "delighting in sunny beams" (300), a more equivocal indulgence in view of what happens to the girl in "How sweet I roam'd," line 4. The tormented emotions that are displayed immediately thereafter confirm this unpropitious echo:

Los said: "Lo, the Lilly pale & the rose redd'ning fierce
Reproach thee, & the beamy gardens sicken at thy beauty;
I grasp thy vest in my strong hands in vain, like water springs
In the bright sands of Los evading my embrace; then I alone
Wander among the virgins of the summer. Look, they cry,
The poor forsaken Los . . . they laugh & mock at Los."

Enitharmon answer'd: "Secure now from the smitings of thy Power,
     demon of fury,
If the God enraptur'd me infold,

In clouds of sweet obscurity my beauteous form dissolving,
Howl thou over the body of death; 'tis thine. But if among the virgins
Of summer I have seen thee sleep & turn thy cheek delighted
Upon the rose or lily pale, or on a bank where sleep
The beamy daughters of the light, starting, they rise, they flee
From thy fierce love, for tho' I am dissolv'd in the bright God,
My spirit still pursues thy false love over rocks & valleys."

(*FZ* ii:302–17, K 288)

After the relationship further decays and it is revealed that Enitharmon has taken on the alluring forms of Ahania & Enion, "She fled, vanishing on the wind, And left a dead cold corse / in Los's arms" (334–35) and Los vows to "infuse" jealousy while taking revenge before collapsing himself. Their unsatisfaction stimulates Enion to make her great lament on "the price of Experience" (397) and is communicated to Ahania and Urizen.

The central point to be made about this prelapsarian condition is that the wife, who has become idolator, temptress, and shrew, no longer is a garden of delight. She no longer possesses either of the contrary innocent charms of the Lilly or the Rose; they reproach Enitharmon because she eludes the approaches of Los, thus leading him to look for solace elsewhere. Her answer, which is quite in the spirit of Mrs. Rose-tree, essentially confirms the allegations. The burden of her defiance can be expressed in this mundane Strindbergian translation: "You are too radical for me so I've given my soul to the church for security. I'll keep up married appearances with my body, though. You've been chasing the girls, but they run away from you. Even though I belong to the church, you're still my husband, and you're not going to get away from me." A few extra metaphysical elements in the original exchange justify Blake's sublime manner, but it does not falsify the main thrust of the passage to stress its mundane basis.

The two flowers occur again in later episodes of retrospection. Urizen tells of his attack on Luvah, who is "faded like a flower / And like a lilly is thy wife Vala wither'd by winds" (v:226–27, K 311).[22] Shortly thereafter Urizen laments the fact that he has driven his own daughters from him and recalls a happier time when "I gave sweet lillies to their breasts & roses to their hair" (vi:29, *K* 312). This echo of "How sweet I roam'd" is even more noticeable than the one in ii:300, already mentioned, which served as a prelude to the falling out of Los and Enitharmon. Later Los again experiences difficulties with the elusive Enitharmon that are expressed in the same flower imagery. Los complains, in a curious simile, that he cannot enjoy her beauty because: "thy lips decay like roses in the spring" (vii:189). Then he shifts from simile to metaphor as he enumerates her deprivations:

Thy roses that expanded in the face of glowing morn,
Hid in a little silken veil scarce breathe and faintly shine.
Thy lillies that gave light what time the morning looked forth,
Hid in the Vales, faintly lament, & no one hears their voice.

(vii:194–97, *K* 325)

Soon afterward Enitharmon tells the Spectre of Urthona a version of the fall of Albion according to which the Eternal Man spied "Vala, the lilly of the desart melting in high noon" (vii:240, *K* 326) and coupled with her, thus giving birth to Urizen. This deed also leads to the appearance of "a double form Vala . . . a Male / And female" (246–47), the differentiation of Luvah from Vala. Thus in *The Four Zoas* the Lily is frequently subject to blight or violation, especially when it appears in conjunction with the Rose. To be sure, Urizen has paradisal memories about these flowers when he describes his unfallen relations with his daughters. But this reminiscence is tainted by the specific echo of "How sweet I roam'd," which suggests that "the prince of love" was Urizen disguised who used these flowers to bring about the bondage of his own daughters. Blake was profoundly aware of the weakness for making unnatural unions of reason and passion which bedevils all human relationships. It must also be said that fond memories can be pernicious in that they often act as surrogates for redemptive action.

The new *Concordance to the Writings of William Blake*[23] duly lists other concurrences of these flowers in which they are used in merely proverbial contexts, but one in *Milton* is especially arresting. After a remarkable catalogue of birds and at the end of a subsequent catalogue of flowers, the morning emergence of the flowers in question is described as follows:

> the Rose still sleeps
> None dare to wake her. soon she bursts her crimson curtain'd bed
> And comes forth in the majesty of beauty: every Flower:
> The Pink, the Jessamine, the Wall-flower, the Carnation,
> The Jonquil, the mild Lilly opes her heavens! . . .
> (*Mil* 31:56–60, *K* 520–21)

And yet Blake adds that "such is a Vision of the lamentation of Beulah over Ololon" (31:63). I will not pause to explain how this scene of joy can also be envisioned as a "lamentation," a point which is already sufficiently understood. But it is noteworthy that the emergent Rose is undoing her fall which resulted when the "invisible worm" entered her "bed / Of crimson joy" and set about destroying her life. In some versions of the design of "The Sick Rose" it appears that the Rose is able at least to save her soul as the worm enters, but in others the girl's escape is arrested by coils of the worm. Something comparable happens to the Lilly as well, which is depicted in *Songs of Experience* as being bowed down but unbroken. In her regeneration in *Milton* (more exuberantly celebrated by Erdman's exclamation point than by Keynes's semicolon) her mildness can flourish in Beulah.

One extraordinary quality of Blake's later work is the sense in which it is built onto his earlier work and consists, in significant measure, of variations on it or sequels to it. This applies to his designs no less than to his writings. The glorification of the Lily, which is promised in *Experience* and much advanced in the text of *Milton*, is depicted discreetly at the beginning of the second chapter of *Jerusalem*. The address "To the Jews" on Plate 27 contains a fine poem about an English Beulah, "The fields from Islington to Marybone," printed in two columns divided by a vine-stemmed plant which has five distinct blossoms and the suggestion of two others. It might almost be identified as a morning-glory or convolvulus except that the points on the blossoms are too twisted and open to correspond to the funnel-shaped ones of that flower. Probably the five-plus blossoms correspond to what Blake elsewhere refers to as the "enlarged and numerous senses" (*MHH* 11, *K* 153) of prelapsarian man, a vision that animates both the address and the poem on this plate. For these reasons this Blakean hybrid flower can be identified as a glorified Lilly of Paradise.

On the next page is a design of exceptional complexity (see PLATE XXIV) which depicts two figures embracing as they sit on a huge lily having six petals and two leaves that floats above an unbounded expanse of water. While the sex of these two figures is not easy to determine, this design is evidently related to an earlier text descriptive of prelapsarian Beulah as seen by the falling Albion:

> He found Jerusalem upon the River of his City, soft repos'd
> In the arms of Vala, assimilating in one with Vala,
> The Lilly of Havilah; and they sang soft thro' Lambeth's vales
> In a sweet moony night & silence they had created
> With a blue sky spread over with wings and a mild moon,
> Dividing & uniting into many female forms, Jerusalem
> Trembling; then in one comingling in eternal tears,
> Sighing to melt his Giant beauty on the moony river.
>
> (*J* 19:40–47, *K* 642)

Later, however, Jerusalem gives her version of what happened at this moment and begs Vala to reject all notion of sin:

> When Albion rent thy beautiful net of gold and silver twine,
> Thou hadst woven it with art, thou hadst caught me in the bands
> Of love, thou refusedst to let me go . . .
> The Veil shone with thy brightness in the eyes of Albion
> Because it inclos'd pity & love, because we lov'd one-another.
> Albion loved thee: he rent thy Veil: he embrac'd thee: he lov'd thee!
> Astonish'd at his beauty & perfection, thou forgavest his furious love.
> I redounded from Albion's bosom in my virgin loveliness:
> The Lamb of God reciev'd me in his arms, he smil'd upon us:
> He made me his Bride & Wife: he gave thee to Albion.
> That was a time of love. O why is it passed away!
>
> (*J* 20:30–32, 34–41; *K* 643)

These passages contain a remarkable amount of ambiguity. If one emphasizes the evidences of pleasure, it appears that the various love relationships are desirable and are finally sanctioned by the Lamb of God. On the other hand, if one emphasizes the images of bondage and violation what seems to be involved is compulsory spiritual Lesbianism initiated by Vala—such as that in *Christabel* —followed by a rape initiated by Albion, which brings about his own fall. If one also takes into consideration Blake's other accounts of the event, which contain further details and variations, he is confronted with the radical dubiety in this myth that makes it unusually difficult to arrive at any unified interpretation. As in the "phoenix culprit" episode in *Finnegans Wake*, which may well have been influenced by Blake, the chances of understanding a single element in the story (like the Lilly of Havilah) are very slight.

There has been little agreement among the critics as to what is depicted on Plate 28. Frye's remarks are interesting, but not specific about crucial matters. He follows Binyon in identifying the design as "Jerusalem and Vala assimilating into one in the Lilly of Havilah. [And he adds] The ambiguous vision of Beulah, 'where no dispute can come' because the mental reality and the physical appearance both exist, is part of the contrast of form and reflection, vision and analogy (suggested here also by the watery background), that runs all through *Jerusalem* but is particularly important in Part Two, which deals with the ordinary Adamic man who is the focus of both eternal and temporal vision." [24] While this is a suggestive explanation for the ambiguity of the picture and the text, it is not helpful in interpreting a number of specific details in the design, such as the object that is draped over the two figures and painted yellow in the colored version of the work, or even the Lilly itself.

Keynes and Wolf attempt to describe the alterations in the various states of the plate, but their account is inaccurate in important particulars, as Erdman has explained. Their identification of the two figures as "perhaps Albion and Jerusalem," [25] moreover, is altogether improbable at this stage in the epic and contradicts both the quoted passages that relate to the picture.

Wicksteed also fails to describe the various states of the plate accurately and, as is often the case, he gives the reader a number of suggestive cross references but neglects to say exactly what is depicted in the design. His summary statement that the plate shows "the undifferentiated character of Sex in Infancy" is irrelevant and misleading. On the other hand, his argument that the two characters are so fully assimilated into one another, particularly in the colored version of the page, that they approach the hermaphroditic state Blake once called "Seth," would seem to add something to the Binyon-Frye position.[26] But, as Erdman shows, the careful reader will not discover much that can properly be called "assimilation" in any state of the page, in spite of what the text implies.[27]

Before there can be any further progress toward understanding this design, there must be an agreement as to what is actually depicted. A short article by Paden and Zuther, which purports to correct Erdman's errors, is astonishingly confused and does not deserve refutation.[28] The one important correction of Erdman that these authors might have made, identifying the more remote figure as a male and the nearer figure as a female, they did not attempt. Fortunately this has been briskly and convincingly done by Damon. His explanation of the meaning of the picture, however, is less persuasive. For Damon it symbolizes "the ecstasy of newly-married love" and the flower uplifts the couple "temporarily above the cares of material life. The young husband with Apollonian locks sits in the rear, his strong right arm passed around his wife's waist, while his left hand rests on her head. She faces him; their lips meet. Her delicate right hand rests on his right hip, the other hand on his head. Her hair, however, is shorter than his. Neither of them notes the Golden Net (marriage) draped over him. In a trial proof, a caterpillar prophesies the woes of gestation and childbirth." [29] It is not clear, however, what this interpretation has to do with *Jerusalem*, but now that an accurate description of the action and the roles being played has been formulated, a comprehensive interpretation becomes possible.

The first place to look for assistance in deciphering an elusive piece of iconography is elsewhere in the same work. The enormous lily of *Jerusalem*, Plate 28 (PLATE XXIV), is unmistakably related to and contrasted with the huge sunflower of Plate 53

(PLATE XXV). In the latter, on the first page of the third chapter, a solitary winged female figure is shown seated on a sunflower, which is likewise elevated above unbounded waters. In the dark and somber black and white copies this scene of isolation is as different as possible from what appears to be an ecstatic union on Plate 28, but in the colored copy the effect is considerably modified by quite bright coloring. This figure has been variously identified. Damon describes her as follows: "Beulah, mercifully veiling the Sun of Eternity from our eyes. She is crowned with the threefold crown of the three states which she commands; her outer wings contain the Moon and the Stars. . . . She is throned high above the Sea of Time and Space upon the Sunflower of the Desire for Immortality. The Sun glows behind her, but we can see only its rays." This identification is repeated by Blunt who calls attention to an unquestionable source of the triple crown motif on a Hindu goddess also seated on a sunflower. Unfortunately this iconographic source tends to distract the reader from recognizing that a triple crown in Protestant Blake always recalls the sinister papal tiara, as in *Europe*, Plate 11. That the figure on the sunflower is actually the pernicious threefold Rahab has been briefly but convincingly shown by Frye. It is reassuring that Damon has changed his mind and now identifies this strange woman as Vala.[30] Indeed his earlier description of her unlimited authority, which notably includes the earth, is evidence enough that she is the antithesis of freedom. What is entirely unwanted is someone to obscure the light of Eternity. The darker colors employed in this plate of the colored copy of *Jerusalem* indicate how different this page is from the eternal day of Plate 28.

The ultimate form of the abomination presented in Plate 53, as explained by Roe,[31] is Blake's ninety-ninth illustration to Dante (PLATE XI). This picture is of exceptional interest to this paper because it combines rose, sunflower, and lily imagery in a single design for what is probably the only other time in Blake's work than the page of *Songs* that is my point of departure. The fact that all these flowers appear in a context of tyranny, however, does not necessitate a dim view of them in other contexts, early or late.

Though the union on Plate 28 appears to take place in the light of Eternity, not all symbols in the picture are so reassuring. The curious yellow net (which might also be taken to be a stylized stamen) is covering at least the man, as Damon says. Such a device has been related to matrimony in Blake's symbolism since the "prince of love" employed a "silken net" and "golden cage" to catch the girl in "How sweet I roam'd" (K 6; see K 56). One can hardly avoid the further association of this object with the Veil of Vala referred to in Jerusalem's account of the encounter of Albion and Vala, quoted above.

In the early state of this plate preserved in the Morgan copy (see PLATE XXIV) a huge caterpillar appears on the nearest petal of the Lilly of Havilah. Wicksteed draws attention to the text in "The Keys" to the frontispiece of The Gates of Paradise: "The Catterpiller on the Leaf / Reminds thee of thy Mother's Grief" (K 770). Even more relevant are the caterpillars on the stem and the worm in the blossom depicted in the design for "The Sick Rose." The phallic caterpillar appears only in the version of Plate 28 in which the two figures are unmistakably copulating, whereas it is erased in the later version. As we shall see, it may be that Blake produced some unintended ambiguity when he censored this original form of the design so that the two figures confront one another from a chaste if passionate sidesaddle position.

If we look for analogues for the design outside of Jerusalem, we shall discover several that exist in a sequence of significant relationships. As Damon has pointed out,[32] the full-page illustration on Plate 5 of The Song of Los depicts a similar subject. There Blake shows two lily blossoms with a woman lying asleep on both of them and a man with a dark beard and a long stick sitting awake on the blossom to the right. This design in turn, as Keynes points out, is related to the drawing by Robert Blake on page 13 of Blake's Notebook, as well as to two water-color drawings entitled "Oberon and Titania."[33] In Robert's drawing a man and a woman lie side by side on a rose. Above them two bell-shaped lilies hang down, the nearer one with a circle of little figures dancing beneath it. But in spite of Blake's titles for the water-color drawings, it is not safe to assume, as Damon does, that the enigmatic figures in *The Song of Los* should be identified as "The King and Queen of the Fairies," and such an identification is even less likely for the figures on Plate 28 of *Jerusalem*. Shakespeare's little people were treated by Blake merely as intimations of the "giant forms" who enact his myths.

A very important occurrence of the motif of embracing lovers is to be found in the lower left corner of "The Day of Judgment," the final engraved plate in the *Blair's Grave* series.[34] There depicted among the Blessed who are rejoicing in their resurrection is a female seen from the rear kissing and embracing a male who is facing the reader. The fact that these figures neglected to put on their clothing must have seemed offensive to some of Blake's contemporaries and the boldness of the male whose hands are on the woman's thigh and buttocks doubtless seemed positively indecent. Interestingly enough, however, these figures attempt to embrace in an awkward mutual sidesaddle position, like that shown in the later version of the *Jerusalem* page, with the result that the male body is quite out of drawing. Schiavonetti managed this gymnastic reunion without breaking the girl's back, as Blake was forced to do in his *Jerusalem* design, but the male figure was sacrificed as a result. One could speculate that in Blake's original drawing an attempt may have been made to show a more intimate union such as that depicted in the first state of the *Jerusalem* page (which is on paper watermarked 1802), but that Cromek and Schiavonetti thought so erotic a posture would be commercially impractical and thus they toned down the embrace. Even if they did so, however, Blake must have decided independently to make his own gesture toward respectability represented by the alteration of the *Jerusalem* plate. It is notable, in this connection, that in the other surviving designs for the Last Judgment no major figures embrace in so erotic a posture as those in the *Grave* version.[35]

The figures in the *Grave* picture do not establish beyond all doubt the identity of the sexes nor do they reveal the meaning of the figures in *Jerusalem* 28, though they should prove to be decisive for the former question. One difference between the groups is that the figure in the foreground is to the *left* of the one in the background in the *Grave*, whereas in *Jerusalem* this relationship is reversed. It might be argued that Blake's possible symbolism of right=benign, left=sinister is involved here and that he intended the reader to recognize the similar figures in the two designs as being ethically contrary to one another. While I am not convinced by this argument, it is prudent to consider other relevant examples of Blake's pictorial symbolism as well for the light they may cast on the group in *Jerusalem*.

On page 124 of *The Four Zoas* a scene is depicted in which a naked young woman is seated on an extraordinary thirteen-pointed flower. She reaches up with her right hand and touches the head of a man, dressed in a tunic, who bends down to her while holding his staff (or crutch) erect, evidently in his left hand. Though this picture occurs in Night the Ninth, it probably depicts an early stage in the aforementioned relationship between Albion and Vala: "Among the Flowers of Beulah walk'd the Eternal Man & saw / Vala, the lilly of the desert melting in high noon" (vii:239–40, *K* 326). Behind and to the right of Vala on the Lilly of Havilah is a sketchy drawing of a figure in a long robe with an exceptionally full right sleeve, surrounded by flames. This may be Vala after the Fall, the veiled mother of the dissidents Urizen and Luvah.[36]

In all these cases, in Robert's drawing and in the illustrations to *The Song of Los*, *The Grave*, and *The Four Zoas*, the fact that one of the figures is indubitably a man should make one wary of thinking that the figures on Plate 28 of *Jerusalem* could be Vala and Jerusalem. And because the figure who faces the reader in the early version of the plate is performing a masculine function, and has a masculine face, the evidence is decisive that Blake wished to depict the union of Albion with Vala which is described by Jerusalem and both depicted by the artist and described by Enitharmon in *The Four Zoas*. Further pictorial perspective on this encounter is provided by the other two designs. In Robert's drawing, the man and woman must both awake on the rose of mundane love and arise through the magic ring dance into the state of higher delight symbolized by the lilies. But in *The Song of Los* the two figures have not achieved ultimate fulfillment in spite of their having attained to the lilies. The woman sleeps while the man keeps a solitary vigil under a starry sky. Depending on the phase of Blake's symbolism one wishes to employ, the man and woman may be identified as Luvah and Jerusalem or, since Luvah is closely related to Jesus and the man has a pointed beard like Jesus, Jesus and "Earth," the girl depicted in a similar recumbent posture (though from the rear) in the "Introduction" to *Experience* and elsewhere. In any case, though they appear to be at peace in Beulah, their heavens are filled with stars, which by their remoteness signify the Fall of Man from the eternal world of light. In *Jerusalem* the Veil of Vala is said to turn into "the Mundane Shell" (see 59:2–9, *K* 691), an alternative symbol for "the starry heavens." Once this connection has been made the group of two can be understood to be enduring bondage under the starry night. Though their lily beds promise ultimate satisfaction, they must wear out the consequences of the primal coupling under the Veil of Vala. Not until the starry heavens become a starry floor can regeneration be consummated.

This raises the difficult question of why, since Blake undoubtedly believed in untrammeled sexuality, Albion's coupling with Vala was chosen as one of the symbols for the Fall. In an admirably concise attempt to deal with this episode in *Jerusalem*, Bloom shows what is wrong with the sinister combination of Vala and Jerusalem that had attracted Albion. But he makes too comprehensive a condemnation of Albion's deed and even finds fault with his having rent the Veil of Vala, forgetting that this had as its prototype Christ's exemplary rending of the veil to the Temple, which is often alluded to as a decisive act of liberation.[37] At least in *Jerusalem* what was wrong with Albion's behavior was not, as Bloom contends, that he reduced himself to Luvah, the Zoa of passion, but that he felt guilty after having done so and then became obsessed with dividing things up, with analyzing them in order to be able to put his finger on the culprit. The encounter itself was actually pleasurable for all concerned and had received the sanction of the Lamb of God, as Jerusalem unmistakably declares, but Albion made the mistake of repudiating his positive action and, as the text on the problematic page declares, fell, to become "the punisher and judge" of "every labour of love / In all the Garden of Eden" (28:4, 1-2; K 652). Like his insane prototype, Bromion, in *Visions of the Daughters of Albion*, he first had intercourse with a woman closely associated with flowers and then became obsessed with condemning and extirpating every manifestation of love. So far as the picture of Albion and Vala on the Lilly of Havilah is concerned, they are shown together because he had performed the admirable deed of rending the Veil, but the fact that it is still draped over their heads anticipates the moment described in the text on Plate 21 when Vala will trap Albion in her Veil (21:50, K 644), an episode in which he fulfills his own cowardice. Because the love of Albion for Vala need not have produced the Fall, their relationship is allowed to look most attractive, especially in the colored copy of the page where the sinister yellow Veil looks almost like glorious yellow hair.[38] As is often the case, it was not the act but the reaction that was disastrous.

There is another design in *Jerusalem* that also features lilies and roses and is thus closely related to Plate 28. In the text on Plate 18 is a design in which two winged humans, crowned respectively with lilies and roses, fall away from one another, though their right toes still touch (see PLATE XXVI). The lily figure, who is probably male, projects out an indubitable female with his right hand, whereas the rose figure, who is certainly female, projects out an unmistakable male. These projected figures meet in an embrace and kiss. Above each of the main figures is a crescent moon with a sail, presumably "little moony arks." Damon makes the following interpretation and identifications: "Jerusalem and Vala, each beneath a Moon of Beulah, sleep in harmony, one crowned with the lilies of spiritual beauty, the other crowned with the roses of material beauty. . . . Their emanations rush forth to embrace between them." [39] Evidently because the Lily is "higher" than the Rose, Wicksteed also identifies Jerusalem with lilies and Vala with roses.[40] But the fact that in all the crucial texts, it is Vala who is associated with lilies indicates that the lily figure on this page must be related to Vala—though it cannot be Vala herself, since the depicted figure is probably male. This difference cannot be disregarded, in spite of the fact that in a parenthetical text four lines above the picture Blake himself explained: "Vala produc'd the Bodies. Jerusalem gave the Souls" of the children of Jerusalem.

It is a difficult problem to decide on the exact identity of this male figure with a crown of lilies, but it is necessary to make at least a functional identification in order to interpret the design. The question may be formulated: "Since the male figure is not Vala, who is he?" The most general answer is probably Luvah, the Zoa of passion particularly associated with Christ and, politically, with France. More narrowly he is perhaps identical with Shiloh, "the Masculine Emanation among the Flowers of Beulah" (*J* 49:47, *K* 680), who has the same associations as Luvah and moreover is especially associated with providential generation, regeneration, and Freedom. Since the equivocal Vala is said merely to have "*produc'd* the Bodies," whereas the indubitably beneficent Jerusalem "*gave* the Souls," Blake allowed himself the artistic license to depict a somewhat different relationship. Furthermore, this complication is justified in several ways by the fact that the symbolism was becoming particularly intricate on Plates 18 and 19. First, almost all of the former plate is taken up with a description of the lamentable idolatry of Vala as Babylon and "Mother! Nature!" (18:30, *K* 640) so that it would be confusing to depict her in her beneficent aspect. Second, by depicting Shiloh instead of Vala, Blake employed a masculine figure to produce the feminine Emanation and thus balance off the masculine Emanation produced by Jerusalem. Third, at the bottom of the next plate is the text describing the sinister vision seen by the about-to-fall Albion of Jerusalem "assimilating in one with Vala" (19:41, *K* 642); thus it was important not to make the blessed union depicted on Plate 18 seem to illustrate this malign combination. This way of expressing Blake's problem is merely schematic, of course, since the manuscript material is not available that would indicate the order of conception of text and pictures in the plates of *Jerusalem*.

I doubt whether Blake himself was delighted by such a convoluted solution to the various problems that arose at this point in his story, but he did give some other clues in the design of that page that the basic relationship depicted is creative and provi-dential.[41] The most important of these is the union of the Emana-tions of Shiloh and Jerusalem which is depicted by the same figures (though their sexes have been reversed in left-right orien-tation) as those shown at the bottom of the title page of *The Marriage of Heaven and Hell*. And the two "Moony arks" above them indicate that this union of Body and Soul will succeed in floating over the Sea of Time and Space just as the larger ark does in Plate 24 of *Jerusalem*. Therefore, the falling figures in the margin are simply understood as the Children of Albion who be-lieve only in the Body, which is all that Mother Nature can produce. The attempt to live exclusively by this half-truth results in the greatest of disasters.

The motif of two figures either uniting or separating is vari-ously modulated on the succeeding pages.[42] At the top of Plate 20 two draped women approach one another, while in the inter-textual designs two draped women suffer diverse fates. Then at the top of Plate 22 a winged or muffled figure parts again from a naked woman who has no wings. Wicksteed identifies most of these figures as Albion and Vala, but they are probably Vala and Jerusalem. This leads to the plight of Jerusalem depicted on Plate 23 where she is shown suffering a grotesque fate as a result of her rejection by Albion. The only detail that requires notice here is the fact that Jerusalem has fallen between two flowers. According to Wicksteed, "at her feet we see the little Star of Bethlehem and at her head the lily of Calvary." [43] Presumably the presence even here of the Flowers of Beulah is to reassure the reader that beneficent influences are at work in the very depths of despair and that regeneration is always possible.

It is a striking fact that Blake found no place for the lily in the general redemption that concludes this epic. Evidently the apocalypse is so strenuous an event that to employ the symbolism of flowers of any kind would tend to weaken the effect of power that is essential to the final explosion of creation. Blake was ap-parently content with the hybrid flower depicted on Plate 27 accompanying the text which looks forward to the conversion of the Jews in the time of the end. In this context there is room for a design which is discreetly illustrated by such a Lily as May never bore.

But Blake did not forget the origins of his Lily and the Rose among the Flowers of Beulah. In the great Boston Museum series of illustrations for *Paradise Lost*, the bower of Adam and Eve has a floor of roses and adornments of lilies in both "Satan Watching Adam and Eve" and "Adam and Eve Sleeping"—and in the former picture she holds a rose while he holds a double lily. And in "The Archangel Raphael with Adam and Eve" lilies appear above their table and roses beneath it, while at the lower left of the picture is a group of lilies and at the lower right is a group of roses.

Later in Blake's final design for Milton's *Il Penseroso*, "Milton, in his Old Age," is seen prophesying in his mossy cell "surrounded by the Spirits of the Herbs & Flowers" (*K* 619). Here the only flowers given significant attention are the lily and the rose. Under the outspread right arm of Milton rise two small rosebushes between which a man and woman kiss and embrace as they engage in a swirling dance together under an arch made up of three *putti* with pipes, who must represent the amatory songs of threefold Beulah. Under the right hand of Milton rises a lily that has four blossoms, two white and two pink. This must be a fourfold Lily of Eden, in front of which a man rises from the ground and draws with him a woman as they begin the resurrection into eternity.

The Lily and the Rose also appear in Blake's last completed major project, the engravings for the Book of Job. In the marginal design for Plate XIX, "Every one also gave him a piece of Money," these two flowers appear at the bottom beneath the twin palm trees that rise in either margin. Here three rose blossoms lie on the ground at the left and three lilies are bent to the ground at the right. Each is on a stalk that has the fat bud of a fourth at its tip and one of the converging spirits[44] above them carries at least one rose. Since Job has come through the darkness to the edge of Eternity, these Flowers of Beulah now appear in front of the "palms of suffering" (see *J* 59:6, *K* 691).[45] In the designs for Job they no longer bait the trap of generation as they had done in "How sweet I roam'd," but announce the freedom of regeneration.

### · APPENDIX: REGENERATION IN ·
### · *THE MARRIAGE OF HEAVEN AND HELL* ·

The best evidence that the plight of the Rose lover and his Rose need not be eternal is to be found on the second page of *The Marriage of Heaven and Hell,* in the picture that accompanies "The Argument" (see PLATE XXVII). This complex page has never been properly interpreted but only the relevant features need be considered here. The secret of the page is that it depicts how the Fall into sexual division can be overcome. The orthodox reading would be that the girl receiving the gift from the man in the tree is Eve being seduced and that at the bottom left one sees Adam and Eve after their falling out. On Plates 3 and 14 of *The Marriage,* however, we are told that "Now is . . . the return of Adam into Paradise" (*K* 149) and "the cherub with his flaming sword is hereby commanded to leave his guard at tree of life . . ." (*K* 154). It follows that in Plate 2 we are to start with the fact of Fall, in which the man and woman are even more antithetical than in "My Pretty Rose Tree," and then go to the picture in the border, which shows how their undoing is to be undone by reversing the primal transgression. Their mistake was to have eaten of the Tree of Death, called the Knowledge of Good and Evil, here depicted as the stunted, twisted, and enlooped bush standing between the two events depicted. In the major design, though the position of the woman indicates that all is not yet well, they are sharing the fruit of the Tree of Life, which is lightly foliaged in the spring of renewal and delicately entwined at the top, as is proper to its loving nature. The bush and tree in this design are, of course, the same two, reversed in stature, as in the design for the Song of Experience. If there is any doubt that the episode depicted in the border is basically redemptive rather than lapsarian, this is dispelled when one recalls two closely related pictures, the second of "The Ecchoing Green" and the fifth of Blake's illustrations to Gray's "Ode on a Distant Prospect of Eton College." In both, what the boy hands down from a tree to the girl is a joy, which is fleeting in the world of Experience, but real in the world of Innocence. All these gestures prefigure the gift of Christ to Man that is depicted on the title pages of the Genesis manuscript now in the Huntington Library.[46] But all these related clues only confirm what the picture itself shows: in the Song of Experience thirteen birds depart; in *The Marriage of Heaven and Hell* five birds, corresponding to the five senses, disport.

One further caution and an observation should help to support this quite intricate and compressed series of interpretations. In discussing such designs as "Ah! Sun-flower" and *Jerusalem* 78 I have simply asserted that the sun is setting (at the right) in the former and that it is rising (at the left) in the latter. On the contrary, it has been strenuously maintained, notably by Edward J. Rose ("Visionary Forms Dramatic: Grammatical and Iconographical Movement in Blake's Verse and Designs," *Criticism*, VIII [Spring, 1966], 111–25), that east and west are invariably represented at the left and right sides respectively of Blake's pictures, as is the case with ordinary maps. If this were in fact the case some of my interpretations would have to be drastically modified. In a forthcoming article entitled "Envisioning the First *Night Thoughts*" to be included in *Blake's Visionary Forms Dramatic*, edited by David V. Erdman and John E. Grant (Princeton, 1969), I shall outline a new rationale for understanding the significance of direction in Blake's pictures which should be applicable to the designs in question.

The reclining antithetical posture of the man and woman in Plate 2 of the *Marriage* remains one of Blake's key symbols from this its first introduction in his work. The prototype for this motif occurs in Botticelli's great painting "Venus and Mars" which is in the National Gallery, London. I do not know whether Blake could have seen it either in the original or in a reproduction or whether he might have seen an earlier or later version of the picture done by another artist. But I am sure that Blake was aware of it as a traditional motif and that he found it as expressive as the others which he borrowed from Renaissance and eighteenth–century artists. If it could be shown that Blake's borrowing in this case was directly from Botticelli one could be certain that he did not remain indifferent to the rest of the symbolism in this profound and enigmatic picture.

# "The Fly"

The text of Blake's "The Fly" is, like the "Introduction" to the *Songs of Experience*, printed against a cloud at the top of the page (see PLATE XXVIII).[1] The design that interprets it is printed below. The first three stanzas appear on the left, surrounded by lines formed by the branches and extensions of an only partially visible border tree—branches that are leafless and, like the cloud, suggest Experience. These lines appear over the head of a girl who has struck or is about to strike a shuttlecock, one of the two representations of the fly in the design.

> Little Fly
> Thy summers play
> My thoughtless hand
> Has brush'd away.
>
> Am not I
> A fly like thee?
> Or art not thou
> A man like me?
>
> For I dance
> And drink & sing:
> Till some blind hand
> Shall brush my wing.

These stanzas, clearly addressed to the fly, relate the incident that has produced a sobering reflection and establish, in its simplest terms, the man-fly equation.

The last two stanzas, a kind of Part II of this short poem, appear enclosed in a space created by the branches of the other border tree, which is more fully shown but which, like its sister to the left, is also bare and therefore a symbol of Experience. These stanzas provide a conceptual basis for the feeling of identity with the fly, which the poet has expressed. That understanding is profound and effectual, and leads to the upsurge of joy and confidence with which the poem closes.

> If thought is life
> And strength & breath:
> And the want
> Of thought is death;
>
> Then am I
> A happy fly,
> ˙If I live
> Or if I die.

Close to the last stanza appears the second visual representation of the fly, a bird or insect hard to classify who flies upward away from the tree and away also from the group below it. Just as the branches of the tree on the right border enclose the stanzas, they also partially enclose the scene of a sad mother teaching a boy to walk.

The speaker of these simple-seeming lines is a lyrical "I." [2] That is, he is Everyman or, more precisely, Everyboy, and his character should not therefore be too minutely delineated. Blake is not satirizing him or even dramatizing him but making him the mouthpiece of an experience available to all. Yet though the speakers of short lyrics should not be made as subtle as actors in long dramas, Blake's recurring habits as a designer of his own lyrics permit us to visualize his speaker. He is perhaps one of Blake's many young Poet-types, a boy about the same age as the girl in the design—an adolescent on the verge of manhood, someone who still laughs, dances, plays, and sings and who—typically—calls himself a man. It is fanciful, though perhaps not excessively so, to suggest that the invisible speaker hovers somewhere in the text which he utters, above the head of the girl, and that he may be conceived of as the other participant in the game of battledore and shuttlecock in which she is engaged. If so, Blake has most delicately enforced the clear sexual implications already present in both word and design. Blake has elsewhere provided a visual analogue to the speaker of this poem: for example, when he illustrates the "I" of Gray's poetry or the abstractions "Mind" or "Thought" in Young's *Night Thoughts* (see PLATES XXIX, XXX). But perhaps the closest equivalent comes, appropriately, from the frontispiece to the *Songs of Experience*, where a boy carries a winged child on his head as he advances from his sheep toward the spectator. Blake has provided a gallery of portraits for his lyrical "I" in his many and only slightly varying visual personifications of shepherds, poets, travelers, and pilgrims.

In a thoughtless but not a guilty moment, the speaker has, by a stroke of his hand, wounded or killed a butterfly, a bird, or some species of common fly. The deed done, he at once recognizes a sobering affinity between his pleasures and the fly's, between the fate of the fly and what could be his. But are boy and fly, alike in their innocent joys, necessarily doomed to be the victims of an accidental or malignant force? They are not! For the very meaning and power of life—in fact, life itself—is love, or imaginative sympathy. And that is a force powerful enough to frustrate the death of the spirit, which can be defined precisely as a lack of just such imaginative sympathy. The philosophy is essentially optimistic, for man is free to avoid the death of the spirit, and once that lesson has been learned, man has passed through a kind of Last Judgment and achieved a happiness that will survive any kind of accident whatever.

The words alone, taken literally, could be interpreted to refer to death and immortality.[3] But the design, which must be allowed to control the reading of the verse, emphasizes human life and society, human joy and sorrow, and suggests that life and death in the text refer metaphorically to the life and death of the spirit in a society of human institutions like the family. The meaning of the poem is, as we shall see, almost infinitely extended; but the design enables us to see what it is extended from and therefore gives the event that is verbally described a firm rooting in everyday reality. The landscape, with its bare trees forming a roof over the scene and with its curving lines repeated in the human bodies, is the familiar landscape of Experience. But two of the figures are still in Innocence, the girl who is playing on its frontier and the boy who is taking his first steps toward it. The mother has crossed the border and is now a sad and resigned victim of Experience. She bends over the child as though in the process of smothering him with her legacy of thwarted desire. We could in fact read the design as a graph of the inescapable cycle of frustration: little boy, to adolescent girl in play, to saddened and resigned mother. But word and picture must be allowed to interact, and the words call for a more optimistic reading: boy to mother (one possible but not inevitable destiny) to girl, whom the world has not yet wounded and who can remain, whatever happens in Experience, the "happy fly" of the text.

The general and preliminary interpretation just given will be expanded, refined, and also defended in the remainder of the essay, which will attempt to answer the following questions:

(1) What does the fly represent in this particular context?

(2) Whose is the blind hand that wounds or destroys it?

(3) What is "thought"?

## · THE "LITTLE FLY" ·

In the first version of his poem Blake wrote about a splendid butterfly:

> Woe alas my guilty hand
> Brushd across thy summer joy
> All thy gilded painted pride
> Shatterd fled.                    (Notebook, *E* 716)

But in the final version Blake chooses to remain more ambiguous about his title-character, who is only a "little fly" and who is not endowed with "gilded painted" wings. In Blake's day "fly" could mean "any winged insect; as the bee, gnat, locust, moth, etc." (*OED*), and in Blake himself "fly" could refer to all of these and also to bird or butterfly. If Blake had wanted us to think of any specific winged creature, he could easily have drawn it in the design, even after he, for unknown reasons, had suppressed it in the text. But instead he gives us only two representations of his fly: metaphorically in the shuttlecock which is being struck and literally but still indeterminately in the small winged creature that flies up between the text and the branches to the right. Blake's intention was obviously to be no more specific than that. Why? Perhaps because his full meaning requires multiple and maybe even contradictory associations. Butterfly or bird would invoke beauty, aspiration, and resurrection but not tiny, insignificant, and nasty life. A common housefly would eliminate the associations of butterfly and bird, which apparently Blake also wishes to keep. Blake is of course not interested in the bemused contemplation of particular animals—the kind that his contemporaries loved: the fluttering breast of Burns's humanized mouse or Cowper's squirrel, "flippant, pert, and full of play"

> With all the prettiness of feign'd alarm
> And anger insignificantly fierce.[4]

The venerable tradition, which a clearly specified and splendid butterfly or bird would not have recalled but which an ambiguously conceived fly can invoke, sees flies as unpleasant creatures. Flies in the Bible swarm nastily and dangerously, as in the Egyptian plague. For Swift flies are "odious insects" who deposit "viscous matter" or who, "driven from a *Honey-pot* will immediately, with very good Appetite alight, and finish [their] Meal on an *Excrement*." Flies are also insignificant and ephemeral. Burke sees men without tradition as "little better than the flies of a summer," and James Hervey says the "highest character" of the bee is "to be insignificantly pretty." The flies of the evening in Ossian move on feeble wings, and the motley winged fly in Cowper stands for the flitting millions of idle dreamers gone astray in their own delusions. The central tradition has asserted flatly with Pope that "Man is not a Fly." [5]

It would be impossible to prove that Blake had all these associations firmly in mind when he engraved the word "fly" on his plate. But as an emblematist springing from the tradition of the English emblem and, more importantly, as a reformer and cleanser of perception, Blake wants his reader to feel strongly how he has subverted a venerable habit of seeing and thinking and symbolizing. And of course Blake's fly in this poem and his winged creatures everywhere else reverse completely the tradition of the nasty, transient, and harmful fly. Blake's fly is a "winged joy," a "minute particular" [6] that is the microcosm of all life, a tiny atomic center that opens upon the world of imaginative vision,[7] a window to Eden, a gateway to the forgiveness of sins and to life in a redeemed society. All this because man *does* possess the microscopic eye that Pope had denied to him[8]—a point that can be most effectively made if "fly" means any small winged creature and not only butterfly or bird.

Though "fly" in this poem can and finally must be extended to mean imaginative vision, we must never lose sight of the precise associations provided by what we have called Part I of the poem, its first three stanzas. There the fly exemplifies dancing, drinking, singing, play—that is, the joys of natural life: the "Ha Ha He" of "Laughing Song"; the young tossing their heads in a merry ring; innocent, frank, open, daylight sexuality. In these stanzas the fly stands for what winged life had always stood for in Blake and will continue to stand for: in the *Poetical Sketches* joys with "pinions light" sing in the trees ("To Autumn") and in *Milton* "gorgeous clothed Flies" wind the intricate mazes of the delightful dance, each sounding his own instrument, each touching the other, receding, caressing, returning in a love ballet by the children of imaginative vision (*Mil* 26).[9] But the flies closest in time and meaning to the fly of this poem are of course those winged creatures of indeterminate kind that appear often in the designs to *Innocence* and *Experience*. In general they describe the curve of aspiration, the line that can break the circle of Experiential destiny; but more specifically they refer to "Love! sweet Love!" which has been made a crime in the world of Experience ("A Little Girl Lost," *E* 29).[10]

The fly of this poem, then, stands primarily for the loving, uninhibited joys of Innocence that "play," "dance," "drink," and "sing." By the noble extension of meaning provided in the concluding two stanzas of the poem these joys can be made permanent and profound by vision. The most fundamental imaginative act required by the poem is to see that a great salvation is wrought: the humble are exalted and the tiny become sublime through the contemplation of a small fly of ambiguous genre, a creature much scorned in the central Western tradition.

## · THE "BLIND HAND" ·

Blake's Innocence is frail, and his fly—and also man—can be bruised and crushed by the hand of rough mischance. But although Blake likens the fate of man to the fate of the fly, he emphatically does not assimilate the two hands that perform the harmful acts. In the first stanza a boy kills or catches a fly in a thoughtless, not a guilty, act—an act we are all capable of performing. But it does not follow that the blind hand that bruises or brushes man in the third stanza is also only careless and accidental. In fact, the evidence points the other way.

But before we consider the blind hand, let us consider more fully the careless hand. Blake, as the Notebook shows, has very precisely transformed the action of the speaker from a guilty one that scatters the beauty of a destroyed butterfly to a thoughtless one that bruises or destroys a creature of unspecified kind. That change is purposeful, and cannot be ignored. Its reason is made obvious by the final context. A *thoughtless* act, to be repented of, calls for *thought*, and *thought* follows the act in the final version of the poem. A thoughtless act, however deleterious its results, can be the act of a good man, a man of sensibility, who quickly repents of what he has done and whose sympathy is deepened by his reflection. Blake does not want us to reject his speaker as guilty; he wants us to identify ourselves with him and with him to think precisely on this and similar events.

It is with Blake's intended and precise change from "guilty" to "thoughtless" in mind that we should consider what is in some respects a close parallel to the harmful action of this poem: the seventh engraving in *The Gates of Paradise*. A boy in tights, ready to catch with his hat another human "fly," stands before his victim, apparently a female child who lies on the ground, arms outstretched, in the position of the dead person under the

"Poison Tree," a pose typical of the victims of Experience. The other child—also a girl, apparently—looks back at the boy as she flies away. Blake wrote: "One is slain & One is fled," and calls the slain girl a "Female Martyr," asking a question to which the answer must be affirmative: "Is She also the Divine Image?" (*E* 260, 266).[11] Blake has here portrayed the lethal effect of love in the dispensation of Urizenic Experience.

Does this tragic situation provide parallels to "The Fly"? Only in part. The boy in the design of *The Gates of Paradise* is very much like the speaker of "The Fly," and the sexual implications of living and dead joy are present in both works. But in the design of *The Gates* the boy impresses one as guilty, as he stares at his next victim. At least he has been made to feel guilty and criminal. But in the design to "The Fly" the young look up, and the speaker is made to feel thoughtless, not guilty, and is finally judged to be worthy of salvation and safety.

Blake has thus carefully adjusted our perspective on the action that harms the fly, but he has not mitigated the guilt of the blind hand (st. 3) that destroys or bruises man and puts an end to his joy. It is in truth the act of Urizen, who literally appears on other pages of the *Songs of Experience* as the Censor-God of the legalistic moral Establishment. The trained reader of Blake's total form (a form that unites word and design) inevitably visualizes words, even abstract words, to say nothing of concrete words like "blind" and "hand." And here he sees the hoary head, the sinister expression, the heavily lidded and closed eyes of Urizen—and also his destructive hand.

Let us consider three visual parallels, one of them extremely close, all of which portray hands that are potentially destructive. In illustrating a line in Gray's "Ode to Spring," "Brush'd by the hand of rough Mischance," Blake created a grisly, bearded, staring, snub-nosed, nude man, who in rising or climbing crushes winged creatures in both his powerful hands.[12] Here are blind hands destroying winged life; but the man, although Urizenic, is not Urizen himself. In illustrating the "Ode on a Distant Prospect of Eton College," a reflective poem on innocence and experience by an admired predecessor, Blake illustrates Gray's personified Father

Thames by portraying Urizen.[13] Like the traditional river god
he rests his left hand on his urn in the usual posture. But if his
left hand is conventional, his right is not: it is a hand that could
be thought of as brushing the wings of young life. Trailing in
the water, it seems ready to catch the young swimmers and destroy
them. But the closest parallel to the blind hand of "The Fly"
appears in Blake's illustration to the title page of the first book of
Young's *Night Thoughts* (PLATE XXXI).[14] Young's Death becomes
Blake's Urizen, his eyes shut under heavy lids, a giant with a white
beard, his left foot forward. The instrument of his destructive
action is his right hand, which sweeps four boys or young men
(all Blake's artist types, all full of hope, all like our putative speaker
in "The Fly") into his beard, a beard that, however paradoxically,
suggests a fiery furnace or a hell-mouth.

In this design for Young, Blake has himself provided a visual
gloss on the blind hand of "The Fly." If the hand belongs to
Urizen, as the context suggests most strongly, we must remember
that it is the Urizen of the earliest prophetic period—the social
oppressor, the god of repression, the kill-joy deity of the moral
law. This suggested parallel is therefore intended to reinforce the
implications of the design to the poem—that its action takes place
in time and within institutionalized society and that the death
referred to is primarily the death of the joyful, youthful spirit in
Experience.

## · "THOUGHT" ·

In spite of the destructive action of Urizen's right hand, the
design for Young is optimistic. For from his open left hand two
figures rise to newness of life and are met in the air by two
angels who receive them. These resurrected bodies represent either
those who attain eternal life beyond the grave in a somewhat
literal rendition of Young's meaning, or—more probably, since
Blake tends to illustrate his own meaning more often than Young's
—those who achieve the Eternal Now of imaginative vision and
so frustrate the death of the spirit. "The Fly" is similarly optimistic, for by its last stanza the speaker has himself attained a

deepened version of the joy that he had harmed in the first stanzas, and he cries out exultingly: "Then am I / A happy fly." The word "Then," which opens that ejaculation, follows a stanza devoted to "thought," which is in fact the instrument of the speaker's salvation.[15] At this point we arrive at the poem's burning center; if we penetrate to Blake's full meaning here, we not only possess the poem but the poem possesses us. We mount the fiery chariot of inspiration, and meet the Lord—and our speaker—in the air.

But first the mind must be disabused. "Thought" does not mean philosophical thought or ratiocination; the term should not be allowed to invoke deism, the mechanistic and materialist philosophy of the eighteenth century; nor is there the remotest relation between the "thought" of this stanza and what Blake derides in *An Island in the Moon.*[16] Except, indeed, that such thought and Blake's are at polar opposites. At the touch of Blake's "thought" all charm is intended to flow *into* the poem, for thought means sensibility or sympathy—in its richest later eighteenth-century meaning; or, in the more technical language of Blake's latest vision, love, the affections, intellect, mind, art; indeed, vision itself. It is thought which can restore the destroyed or threatened summer's play, the dancing, singing, drinking. It is thought which can undo the mischief wrought by the mistaken hand and the crime wrought by the blind hand. It is thought which transforms a thoughtless boy into a visionary; and it is thought which can—as Milton does in *Milton* (Pl. 20)—remake Urizen himself.

Blake's special sense of *thought* is original and profound but not eccentric, for it is related to that of the "Age of Sensibility" [17] and to an even older tradition. Two meanings in the *OED* (1.b and 4.c) are relevant: thought (a) as "a function or attribute of a living being" and (b) as "conception, imagination, fancy." The first is illustrated in the *OED* by a clear association of heart and thought made around 1400: "Alle hys hert & alle his thought, He to love was yn brought." The second meaning is illustrated from Collins, in 1742, where thought and pathos are related: "thought creates unnumber'd scenes of woe." [18]

Thus Blake's conception of *thought* has its roots deep in his age, the age that transformed sentiment as a moral utterance (ethical sentence) to sentiment as sympathetic feeling. Blake's thoughtless-thoughtful speaker addressing his fly is a cousin of My Uncle Toby apostrophizing his. But here as elsewhere Blake contributes a new *Gestalt* to what he borrows, and that must be clearly understood if the fourth stanza of "The Fly" is to achieve its full meaning.

Blake early in his career began defining *thought*.[19] The first task was to make a separation, the next to make an indissoluble connection. The separation involved distinguishing "Science" from "intellect" and elevating the latter; and also distinguishing between "intellect" and "affection" and giving the priority of power to the latter. So it is that love as the very life of man, without which every thing else is passive, must animate and control mind or thought or intellect. If the understanding is to rise, it must rise with love, for they are elevated together. But then, once animated by the affections, the intellect itself becomes a principle of redemption. But good thought is necessarily impelled by love.

Out of that matrix sprang Blake's conception of *thought*. Thought animated by affection must perforce issue in deeds of love, and so Blake cries out against Bacon's separation of mind and action: "Thought is Act." Thought, being affection and act, cannot escape being art—visionary art, of course, for art is the loving imagination at work—the "Human Eternal Body in Every Man," "The All in Man." Blake's formula is that thought equals art equals love equals the forgiveness of sins equals "The Divine Vision." Thought is virtually everything for Blake—his whole mission as an artist and a reformer of man, society, and nature. It should not be surprising that the words "life" and "strength" and "breath" accompany "thought" in "The Fly." [20]

It is essential to sense the full weight of the Blakean term *thought*, but it is also essential to order and give emphasis to those meanings that are the most closely relevant to the fourth stanza of "The Fly." These are three in number: (a) thought as the source of loving joy, primarily the love of individual men and women, boys and girls, (b) thought as the source of social sympathy, primarily a collective emotion that begins in individual feeling, and (c) thought as an instrument of redemption.

(a) Thought is intimately related to the summer's play of the fly and the boy, who dance, drink, and sing. In other words, thought creates innocent sexual joy, the joy of the young and the free, the delight that society and fallen nature would not let Thel even begin to enjoy or Oothoon continue to enjoy. Fallen thought leads to fallen love: "When *Thought* is closed in Caves. Then *love* shall shew its root in deepest Hell" (*FZ* v, *E* 337).[21] But when the thought of man operates as it should, then it creates "Realities of *Intellect,* from which All the *Passions* Emanate" (*LJ* 87, *E* 554). The profoundest sacrament is one that allows man to break "The Bread of sweet *Thought* & the Wine of *Delight"* ("To my dear Friend Mrs. Anna Flaxman," *E* 681).

(b) Social sympathy is also intimately associated with thought. One is impressed again and again with how indissolubly Blake has bound the intellect to the "Tear of Love & forgiveness sweet."

> For a Tear is an Intellectual thing . . .

> The Tear shall melt the sword of steel
> And every wound it has made shall heal.[22]

(c) Thought is also the peculiar agency of both individual and social salvation. It is, as it were, the Holy Spirit that effectuates the presence and message of Christ. Thought is therefore associated with Blake's agents of redemption, revolutionary or artistic. The fires of Orc are "thought-creating" (*SoL* 6:6, *E* 67), and when Los appears to the poet he endows him with "the bows of my Mind & the Arrows of Thought" (To Thomas Butts, 22 Nov. 1802, l. 78; *E* 693).

Blake has provided in the Young illustrations[23] two stunning visual analogues of the quality we have been discussing: one a personification of the very word we are discussing, Thought; the other of virtually the same, Mind. Both figures are young nudes, usually Blake's agents of salvation, although "Thought" in the design has been destructive. "Mind" is peculiarly relevant to this poem: in the drawing for Young a nude youth springs across a landscape away from a tomb and a graveyard to the common joys of life—kite-flying, cricket-playing, and reading. In both this design and "The Fly" Blake is saying that thought (or mind or intellect) can preserve the individual and social joys of Innocence and carry them safely through Experience into Eden.

## · CONCLUSION ·

If the reader has accepted the interpretations of "little fly," "blind hand," and "thought" given in this essay, he will clothe the following bare summary with Blake's deepest meaning and, in addition, perceive the extremely tight coherence of the entire poem:

A thoughtless boy puts an end to the innocent joys of a fly—an act that recalls the similar destruction by society of human love and play. He perceives that the sympathy he has felt is the very breath of life and that it can be renewed in the mind and therefore in art. That awareness constitutes a conversion, not from villainy or crime but from thoughtless insensitivity. That conversion, which in reality provides the conditions under which joy can be preserved, leads to the lyrical lines of assurance and hope with which the poem ends.

Those lines, which comprise the last stanza, have proved baffling.[24] Why? Partly because Urizen has not been perceived in the third stanza and "thought" not properly understood in the fourth, with the result that the polarities of the poem have been obscured. Partly because the character of the speaker has been misconceived, or at the very least his triumph at the end has not been discerned. And partly because the last two lines, "If I live / Or if I die," have been overinterpreted. "Fly," "hand," "thought," "death," "want of thought" are all expressions of weight and significance. The last word of the poem, "die," is not. If it is made a word of weight, Blake becomes guilty of a distressingly circular bit of reasoning, or one needs the concept of an erroneous and confused speaker, whose meaning Blake ridicules or undercuts in one way or another. For Blake is then made to say: I know that thought is the essence of life and the lack of it is death; but in either case I'm happy—as happy, in fact, as the fly I have just killed. But we need lay no such crime of confused meaning to the charge

of Blake or of his lyrical "I." For the last luminous word of the
poem is "happy." The final two lines come as a denouement. "If
I live or if I die" means simply, "Whatever befalls me." The
singer of a Sunday-school hymn[25] or the person familiar with the
simple childlike mottoes of the emblem books ought not miss the
meaning or the tone. A closely parallel phrase comes from *Auguries
of Innocence:*

> Man was made for Joy & Woe
> And when this we rightly know
> Thro the World we safely go.     (ll. 56–58, E 482)

Adapted to "The Fly," the tone and meaning go something like
this: Man was made for thought, or imaginative vision; when we
rightly know this, we go safely through the world, come what
may. "If I live or if I die," then, is not a phrase of semantic
weight; but it is not unimportant. It breathes a simple assurance
of salvation.

The *Auguries of Innocence,* which attunes us to the nuances
of the last lines of "The Fly," also provides a perspective on the
whole poem. That perspective is that we should consider Blake's
speaker to have undergone a Last Judgment.

Last Judgment in Blake means something special, as do almost
all terms of the Christian and Hebrew Scriptures. Let us observe
how this concept emerges from the *Auguries.* That fine poem,
like "The Fly," is concerned with small life and small objects—
the grain of sand, the wild flower, the skylark, the moth; and also
with a wanton boy that kills a fly. Whenever a minute particular,
a small living being, is harmed or destroyed, persecuted or op-
pressed, the whole sensorium trembles in sympathy. And the Last
Judgment is invoked: "Kill not the Moth nor Butterfly / For the
Last Judgment draweth nigh" (*Aug* 39–40). The association of
Judgment and treatment of the small and insignificant and weak
is of course traditional: Christ on the Last Day will separate the
sheep from the goats on the basis of what they have done to the
humble: "Inasmuch as ye have done it unto one of the least of
these my brethren, ye have done it unto me" (Matt. 25:40).

So the Gospel; and so too, in its own way, Blake's Everlasting Gospel. But since Blake is never simple or conventional, the "least of these my brethren" comes to include the tiniest atom of life, even the "unhappie happie Flie." [26] When the fly is harmed, the speaker, himself a part of the world that is bound together in bonds of love, trembles in sympathetic pain. That pain leads to reflective thought and the casting out of error and insensibility and, finally, to an enduring happiness. That, in Blake's special idiom, is a Last Judgment: "whenever any Individual Rejects Error & Embraces Truth a Last Judgment passes upon that Individual" (LJ 84, E 551).

Perhaps the best gloss on the central action embodied in "The Fly" is a comment made by Blake about the response he expected to one of his own paintings. In that comment some of the most important words or concepts of "The Fly" reappear: "thought," "happy," small "Particulars." But even more important is the similarity between our speaker's ascent to meaning and happiness and the resurrection into immortality of Blake's ideal spectator.

If the Spectator could Enter into these Images in his Imagination, approaching them on the Fiery Chariot of his Contemplative *Thought* if he could Enter into Noahs Rainbow or into his bosom or could make a Friend & Companion of one of these Images of wonder which always intreats him to leave mortal things as he must know then would he arise from his Grave then would he meet the Lord in the Air & then he would be *happy* General Knowledge is Remote Knowledge it is in *Particulars* that Wisdom consists & *Happiness* too.        (LJ 82, E 550) [27]

KATHLEEN RAINE

# A Note on Blake's "Unfettered Verse"

In his preface to Book I of *Jerusalem*, Blake defines his own practice as a writer of verse.

When this Verse was first dictated to me, I consider'd a Monotonous Cadence, like that used by Milton & Shakespeare & all writers of English Blank Verse, derived from the modern bondage of Rhyming, to be a necessary and indispensible part of Verse. But I soon found that in the mouth of a true Orator such monotony was not only awkward, but as much a bondage as rhyme itself. I therefore have produced a variety in every line, both of cadence & number of syllables. Every word and every letter is studied and put into its fit place; the terrific numbers are reserved for the terrific parts, the mild and gentle for the mild & gentle parts, and the prosaic for inferior parts; all are necessary to each other. Poetry Fetter'd Fetters the Human Race.          (*J* 3, *K* 621) [1]

The first thing to note is that Blake wrote his verse from "dictation"; in other words, its growth in his mind was spontaneous and organic. He did not first decide upon a verse form, and then write to that form. No technical analysis of his verse, therefore, is more than a clumsy method of examining the result of a process that owed nothing to a deliberate aiming at certain metrical forms. The verse form is born with the poem, with the mood and the meaning; in some of the *Songs*, it almost *is* the poem—as in "Infant Joy," or "The Sick Rose." The verse is the informing idea itself, the poem is its music. Yet Blake claims that "every word and letter" is studied and put into its fit place; for inspiration is concerned with "minute particulars."

How far is Blake's claim for his verse justified? His lyrics have always been valued for their spontaneity of formal beauty; but

it should also be said that in his use of the long line he is un-
equalled among English poets.

Already in *Poetical Sketches* Blake was experimenting in free
rhythms. The pieces of poetic prose published in this volume bear
witness to two influences, the Psalms and *Ossian*. The cadence
of the English Bible and the parallelisms of Hebrew poetry can
be heard in

My hand is feeble, how should I stretch it out? My ways are sinful, how
should I raise mine eyes? My voice hath used deceit, how should I
call on Him who is Truth? My breath is loathsome, how should he not
be offended? If I lay my face in the dust, the grave opens its mouth for
me; if I lift up my head, Sin covers me as a cloak.

("The Couch of Death," *K* 36)

But in other passages, the rhythm approximates to the epic hexameter
or heptameter:

In former times, on such an evening, when the cold clay breathed with
life,
and our ancestors, who now sleep in their graves, walked on the steadfast
globe . . .                                      ("The Couch of Death," *K* 35)

This is the echo of *Ossian*, whose underlying cadence is that of
the classical epic meters, as can be seen by rearranging the prose of
the opening of Cath-loda as verse:

Why thou wanderer unseen! Thou bender of the thistle of Lora;
Why thou breeze of the valley, hast thou left mine ear?
I hear no distant roar of streams! No sound of the harp from the rock!
Come, thou huntress of Lutha, Malvina, call back his soul to the bard.
I look forward to Lochlin of lakes to the dark billowy bay of U-Thorno.

As an experimenter in prosody, Macpherson is not without interest; in an uncritical mood, it is not difficult to become drunk
with the Ossianic incantation; but apart from his own success or
failure as a poet, Macpherson suggested to Blake the possibilities
of what is now called "sprung" rhythm; and as late as 1826, long
after the decline of *Ossian*'s fame, Blake was honest enough to
confess his continued admiration for a poet who had influenced

him profoundly in his youth: "I own myself an admirer of Ossian equally with any other Poet whatever" (Annotations to Wordsworth, *K* 783).

Blake could scarcely have said less of a poet who had not only influenced his style by example, but who had also expressed views on verse that broke with the tradition of the eighteenth century. In his preface to the second edition of *Ossian*, Macpherson wrote:

The novelty of cadence in what is called a prose version, though not destitute of harmony, will not to common readers supply the absence of frequent returns of rhime. This was the opinion of the Writer himself, though he yielded to the judgement of others, in a mode, which presented freedom and dignity of expression, instead of fetters, which cramp the thought; whilst the harmony of language is preserved.

Blake's preface to the first book of *Jerusalem* is an impassioned restatement of this view, even to the borrowing of the word "fetters."

Blake found in Macpherson a view of verse that was, in his application of it, productive of a variety of verse forms that are appropriate to the many moods of the personae of his myth. After *Poetical Sketches* Blake seldom used an iambic pentametric line.

Blake's hexameters are among the best that have been written in English; the passage (*Mil* 41, *K* 533) that begins

To bathe in the Waters of life: to wash off the Not Human
I come in Self-annihilation & the grandeur of Inspiration

is based upon the dactylic hexameter of "heroic" verse, but varied by the use of "sprung" rhythm, and an occasional heptameter line:

He smiles with condescension: he talks of Benevolence & Virtue
And those who act with Benevolence & Virtue, they murder time on time
(*Mil* 41:19–20, *K* 533)

There are some fine hexameter passages also in *Jerusalem*, exceedingly free, vigorous, and virile:

He who envies or calumniates: which is murder & cruelty,

Murders the Holy-one: Go tell them this & overthrow their cup,
Their bread, their altar-table, their incense & their oath:
Their marriage & their baptism, their burial & consecration:
I have tried to make friends by corporeal gifts but have only
Made enemies: I never made friends but by spiritual gifts:
By severe contentions of friendship & the burning fire of thought.

(*J* 91:12–18, *K* 738)

These lines have the apparent naturalness of spoken English, its
cadences matched to the hexameter with an ease that we tend to
assume belongs by right only to blank verse. This is the verse
of a master, wielding the language with complete control of its
resources.

It is remarkable to find an English poet whose ear was as little
attuned to the iambic pentameter line as was Blake's.

We have only to compare with *Ossian* such a passage as Enion's
famous lament, to see that Blake is the master, where Macpherson
was the slave, of his sound pattern; there is, in *Ossian*, no wedding
of meaning to meter, no enhancement of significant words by
the cadence: but in Blake this is always so.

What is the price of Experience do men buy it for a song
Or wisdom for a dance in the street? No it is bought with the price
Of all that a man hath his wife his children
Wisdom is sold in the desolate market where none come to buy,
And in the witherd field where the farmer plows for bread in vain

(*FZ* ii:397–401, *K* 290)

Here Blake has made six- and seven-stressed lines as sensitively
responsive to the rhythms of spoken English as ever Wordsworth
made his blank verse, and here we see him, characteristically,
modulating from a hexameter to a heptameter, using the longer
line for enhancement as Dryden and Pope use an occasional alex-
andrine to give greater weight and roundness to the close of a
paragraph. Like Wordsworth he was aware of the natural texture
and resistance of the medium in which he worked:

I call them by their English names: English, the rough basement.
Los built the stubborn structure of the Language, acting against
Albion's melancholy . . .                          (*J* 40:58–60, *K* 668)

Blake's most characteristic line, that in which he shows his greatest mastery and his natural bent, is a heptameter. Of this line we find every variety. His "mild and gentle" line is an iambic heptameter, with pyrrhic feet (two short syllables) and no caesura, as we find in *The Book of Thel:*

> But Thel is like a faint cloud kindled at the rising sun:
> I vanish from my pearly Throne, and who shall find my place.
> (2:11-12, K 128)

Blake's habit of writing his verse with a minimum of punctuation seems to reflect the unbroken musical cadence of the verse as it sang itself to his inward ear.

The same line shows every kind of variation of tempo and energy:

> Each has its Guard, each Moment Minute Hour Day Month & Year
> (Mil 28:59, K 516)

It may be varied by the introduction of a spondee:

> And every Space that a Man views around his dwelling-place
> (Mil 29:5, K 516)

or by choriambic feet, as in the Memorable Fancy:

> How do you know but ev'ry Bird that cuts the airy way,
> Is an immense world of delight, clos'd by your senses five?
> (MHH 7, K 150)

The line that can be so mildly feminine in *Thel* can resound in the masculine majesty of

But now the Starry Heavens are fled from the mighty limbs of Albion.
(J 75:27, K 716)

Blake possessed a copy of Chapman's Homer, and there are echoes of the verse of Chapman in *The Four Zoas,* often in passages that also reveal the influence of the substance of Homer.

The uninhibited conflicts of the Homeric gods form the pattern of conduct of the Zoas in their caerulean houses—far more Homeric than Miltonic; and in the rough and dynamic heptameters that form the characteristic narrative style in this poem there are unmistakable echoes of Chapman's vigorous and virile tongue; such passages as this from Chapman:

His sister therefore chid him much, the Goddess that commands
In games of hunting, and thus Spake; Fliest thou, and leav'st the field
To Neptune's glory, and no blows? O fool, why dost thou wield
Thy idle bow? No more my ears shall hear thee vaunt in skies
Dares to meet Neptune, but I'll tell thy coward's tongue it lies

are echoed in the "prosaic" verse of Blake's "inferior parts."

This seven-stressed line is close to the English "ballad meter" of iambic lines alternating four and three feet; and is thus as native to the language as the iambic pentameter of blank verse. Blake in adopting this meter is, consciously or unconsciously, reviving a "gothic" music.

Enitharmon answerd "Wherefore didst thou throw thine arms around
Ahania's Image I decievd thee & will still decieve.
Urizen saw thy sin & hid his beams in darkning Clouds
I still keep watch altho I tremble & wither across the heavens
In strong vibrations of fierce jealousy for thou art mine
Created for my will my slave tho strong tho I am weak.
Farewell the God calls me away. I depart in my sweet bliss
(FZ ii:327–33, K 288)

This is surely Chapman, freed from the "bondage" of rhyming.

This guess becomes a certainty when we find, in passages whose imagery points directly to Chapman's *Homer*, Blake, his mind running on a poem he knew and loved, falling into Chapman's cadences. The casting-out of Ahania by Urizen suggests the severe punishment meted out to his consort Hera by Zeus, when she was hung suspended in the sky, though the image is in fact taken from the casting-out of another goddess, Ate:

. . . by her bright hair he caught,
Held downe her head, and over her made this infallible vow:

That never to the cope of starres, should reascend that brow,
Being so unfortunate to all. Thus, swinging her about,
He cast her from the fiery heaven. . . .

And Urizen casts out Ahania in the same meter:

Then thunders rolld around & lightnings darted to & fro
His visage changd to darkness & his strong right hand came forth
To cast Ahania to the Earth he siezd her by the hair
And threw her from the steps of ice that froze around his throne
(*FZ* iii: 110–13, *K* 294)

In both Chapman and Blake, the "stubborn" quality of spoken English is tensed against the verse meter, producing an effect that is the exact opposite of the gentle flow of the voice of *Thel,* in which there is a deliberate avoidance of this kind of contrapuntal stress of sentence against line.

Blake excels in cumulative repetition, often a reiterated rhetorical question. Here again we see the influence of the Old Testament poets; one may cite Thel's lament, which closes her poem, or its more elaborate version in *Milton:*

Can such an Eye judge of the stars? & looking thro its tubes
Measure the sunny rays that point their spears on Udanadan
Can such an Ear filld with the vapours of the yawning pit,
Judge of the pure melodious harp struck by a hand divine:
(*Mil* 5:28–31, *K* 485)

This is Blake the "true orator"; and we cannot doubt that this is poetry to be declaimed aloud. *Visions of the Daughters of Albion* contains fine examples of the repetition of a question. But Blake's cumulative repetition is not always in the form of a question; the description of the building of the edifice of Time by the Sons of Ozoth (*Mil* 28:44–61, *K* 516) employs a repetition whose pleasure is always enhanced by a new cadence in each line:

And every Month a silver paved Terrace builded high:
And every Year, invulnerable Barriers with high Towers
And every Age is Moated deep with Bridges of silver & gold
(ll. 54–56)

When we read such passages as this, we are almost ready to admit Blake's claim that every syllable and letter of his verse is in its right place.

The spirits of Revolution have a taste for crude violence; and if these "dictated" *The French Revolution*, it seems that history is to blame. I read this poem once, with difficulty, and I have never been able to bring myself to repeat the experience. Let no poet be judged by his worst, or we shall be hard put to it to decide between the authors of *A Monody on the Death of Chatterton, Queen Mab, Sleep and Poetry*, and *The French Revolution*. But a poet's worst is always revealing; and the "wind and splutter" (Swinburne's phrase) of this early attempt by Blake in the "terrific" manner could never have been written but by a poet whose genius was possessed by the creative vigor of "hell or energy." It is violent, noisy, and excessive, and moves in thumping time:

The millions of spirits immortal were bound in the ruins of sulphur heaven
To wander enslav'd; black, deprest in dark ignorance, kept in awe with the whip
To worship terrors, bred from the blood of revenge and breath of desire
In bestial forms, or more terrible men; till the dawn of our peaceful morning.                    (*FR* 213-16, *K* 143)

This dactylic heptameter, which frequently overflows into an eight-stressed line, is surely a "shape superimposed." The words burst out of feet strained beyond the resources of any "sprung" rhythm; the meter is not counterpointed against the natural cadence of the sentences, it is mere violation; and there is no modulation of mood; crude and factitious excitement swallows up alike pathos and beauty, and obscures narrative:

Like the morning star arising above the black waves, when a shipwreck'd soul sighs for morning,
Thro' the ranks, silent, walk'd the Ambassador back to the Nation's Assembly, and told
The unwelcome message; silent they heard; then a thunder roll'd round loud and louder

is scarcely a lucid account even of a "visionary" event, and there is no attempt to match meter to meaning (*FR* 255–57, *K* 145). When Blake later wished to raise the din of Pandemonium, he could do so with artistry:

Thousands & thousands labour, thousands play on instruments
Stringed or fluted to ameliorate the sorrows of slavery
Loud sport the dancers in the dance of death, rejoicing in carnage
The hard dentant Hammers are lulld by the flutes lula lula
The bellowing Furnaces blare by the long sounding clarion
The double drum drowns howls & groans, the shrill fife shrieks & cries:
The crooked horn mellows the hoarse raving serpent, terrible but
    harmonious.                   (*Mil* 24:60–66, *K* 509)

The alliteration of "hard dentant Hammers," "bellowing . . . blare," "double drum drowns howls," "shrill fife shrieks," and "lulld . . . flutes lula lula" contributes to the sound pattern; the meter is full of drumlike choriambic overtones: "ameliorate the sorrows," "double drum drowns," and especially in the last line, "The crooked horn mellows the hoarse raving serpent." The result is indeed "terrible but harmonious"; and Blake's "terrific numbers" are not unbearable in passages of this kind, in which they are not continued for too long.

Blake evidently felt that the last pages of *Jerusalem* demanded his "terrific numbers," and he uses a line of eight feet:

Murmuring the Bowstring breathes with ardor. Clouds roll round the
    horns
Of the wide Bow, loud sounding Winds sport on the Mountains brows:
The Druid Spectre was Annihilate loud thundring rejoicing terrific
    vanishing
Fourfold Annihilation & at the clangor of the Arrows of Intellect
The innumerable Chariots of the Almighty appeard in Heaven.
                      (*J* 98:4–8, *K* 745)

This is terrific, certainly; but neither Blake nor his readers can keep it up for very long. The first two lines, with their fine spondees, have certainly a grandeur. The rest of the passage has to be stretched like elastic to fit the meter, and the last line relapses into a crowded hexameter. One is reminded, in the stress falling on "and" in the fourth line, of Hopkins' *The Windhover:*

> Buckle! *and* the fire that breaks from thee then, a billion . . .

We are also reminded, in this context, that Hopkins succeeded where Blake failed, in the use of the eight-stressed line in long passages. *That Nature Is a Heraclitean Fire* and *The Golden Echo* are written in eight-stressed lines:

> Of us, the wimpled-water-dimpled, not-by-morning-matchèd face,
> The flower of beauty, fleece of beauty, too too apt to, ah! to fleet

Hopkins' flowing lines without caesura remind us of the music of

Ah Thel is like a watry bow and like a parting cloud.   (*Thel* 1:8, K 127)

Whatever the length of line that Blake is using, we find that there is a continual pressure to make it longer. In *The French Revolution* seven feet are not enough, he tends towards a line of eight feet; when he writes hexameters, he tends towards lines of seven feet. Nearly always we find that passages are varied by lines longer, not shorter, than the norm. Is this the result of that "overflowing and bursting of the mind" that Yeats found in Blake? He tends towards the unbounded, but never, it must be said, to the formless, only to the longer phrases of ever more comprehensive form.

# Texts and Facsimiles

DAVID V. ERDMAN

# A Temporary Report on Texts of Blake

*". . . they . . . took the forms of books"*

Are they all alike? as widely different in text as in format? What is the inside story of the many new editions of Blake, out recently or promised soon—not to mention the long promised and now finally published *Concordance*?[1] Competition may be the life of publication, but what is it doing to the words of Blake? Can editorial friends be commercial rivals—or who writes those promotional releases? It would make a merry tale, the inside interpersonal stories of these several concorders, collators, transcribers, editors, publishers, reviewers: Dragon-Men "clearing away the rubbish" in one chamber, Vipers adorning with precious stones, Eagles building in the cliffs, Lions melting the punctuation, Unnam'd forms (the unsung heroes of keyboard and pressroom) casting the metal words into the expanse to take the forms of books and be "arranged in libraries."[2] No. For the present occasion a most impersonal report is called for, concerned not with persons or packages or incidentals but with substantive text. This requires some comparison of the current and forthcoming editions and some account of their tangled influences upon each other. (Happily I can offer a simple recipe—it may be the most useful thing in this parcel—for making one's own collation of any present or future edition, without recourse to electronic equipment. So it will be unnecessary to go into any more detail here than needed to make a point.) But the questions to be considered are How far we have come toward a definitive text of Blake's writings, and What particular passages remain incompletely transcribed or not certainly established.

A preliminary answer is that no passages still in doubt are as central and significant as the Plate 3 deletions in *Jerusalem* (now restored), though fascinating puzzles of palimpsest still challenge ingenuity and patience in the manuscript pages of *The Four Zoas*. In the wholly legible writings that come to us in the medium of printing—from type or from etched plates—there are many scribal or typographical errors, more or less manifest; most of these are trivial and have been definitively repaired; very few call for substantive emendation, but of these some certain errors cannot be certainly corrected while some plausible corrections are not certainly required. As we rest from the labors of transcribing and collating, we may be increasingly attracted to the pleasures of emendation—especially when enlarged perception of the text shows it to be our duty. But to the tale.

The base of all the recent texts of Blake is Geoffrey Keynes's Nonesuch Press edition of *The Complete Writings of William Blake with All the Variant Readings* (1957), the culmination of progressive improvements upon Keynes's *Writings* of 1925—though it must be noted that Sir Geoffrey has disclaimed responsibility for the word "all" in that title. Immediately upon its appearance, a concordance of poems, prose, and variants was begun by Richard J. Wolfe and myself, with a team of helpers, including Palmer Brown, who had made an independent transcript of *An Island in the Moon*, from photostats, and Gerald E. Bentley, Jr., who was completing a fresh transcript of the manuscript of *Vala, or the Four Zoas*. Fortunate delays held the *Concordance* text open for revision throughout the following decade. Bentley published his *Vala* text (Clarendon Press, 1963) with halftone plates of the manuscript pages. My own eyes, with a window of magnifying glass, went about examining all the original sources (though not every copy of each Illuminated Work) and pored over photographic blowups of their curious parts. A web of mutual communication of reports and queries and photostats expanded from Brinkley to South Pasadena, from Riverside to Chapel Hill, and steadily the *Concordance* "Appendix" of corrections and additions thickened upon the Nonesuch base.

Toward the end of 1964 a list of these went to Sir Geoffrey for as much use as could be made of them in a new (offset) edition of the *Complete Writings*, which was published, a bit tardily, in 1966 in the Oxford Standard Authors series, going into second and third impressions in 1967. I had meanwhile prepared a full text (barring some letters) of *The Poetry and Prose of William Blake*, which was published by Doubleday in September, 1965, with commentary by Harold Bloom. This went into a "second printing" (really a second edition) with much further revision in early 1966.[3] For convenience we may cite these editions as *K* and *E*, distinguishing printings (when necessary) as $K^1$, $K^2$, $K^3$ and $E^1$, $E^2$; both are approaching further, revised printings, and both editors welcome further *errata corrigenda* in text and notes. In the wings is an edition of the *Poems* in the series of Longmans Annotated Classics, being prepared by myself and William H. Stevenson, who is annotating the poetry but also proposing some improvements in text; these in turn are being noted for subsequent printings of *K* and *E*. (This Longmans edition will be cited as *E-S*.)

All these revisions are also being supplied to Gerald Bentley, Jr., for use in the edition he is preparing for a later date, to be published by the Clarendon Press. Important features, I understand, will be thorough bibliographic description and a collation of all copies of the Illuminated Works, including reports on differences in the printing and coloring of the plates. (The Longmans edition will contain brief comments on the illustrations as such.) Bentley has also prepared (and published, August, 1967) a separate edition of *Tiriel*, with facsimile and transcript of the manuscript and reproduction of the "Tiriel" drawings. And I am preparing a typographic and facsimile edition of Blake's *Notebook* (the "Rossetti Manuscript"), with infrared photography to bring out the rubbed or erased pencil text and drawings. Both of these facsimile volumes are Clarendon publications. Palmer Brown ought now to be urged to do a facsimile of the manuscript of *An Island in the Moon*, with its page of lion and lamb and horse, and Blake, profiles.

We all want of course to see in facsimile the recently rediscovered Blake-Varley *Sketchbook,* being readied by Martin Butlin
for publication by Heinemann (though this does not directly
concern text).[4] It is also to be hoped that the Blake Trust and
the Trianon Press, having resolved to surmount the difficulties
involved in a facsimile reproduction of *Europe* (by making up
an eclectic edition), will be able to go on to the slighter but
precious *Ahania, Book of Los,* and (difficult as the task now
seems) *Song of Los.* By the end of the second decade after Keynes
1957, the libraries of the world should be copiously supplied with
the writings of William Blake both (visually) as he wrote them
and (editorially) as we read them: facsimiles of the manuscripts
and colored etchings; Blake's own punctuation and non-punctua-
tion transcribed in the Doubleday and the several Clarendon books,
as well as his capitalization and spelling; modern punctuation, of
one sort in the Longmans, of another in Keynes (Bentley expects
to employ throughout the ingenious system used in his *Tiriel*
transcript—simultaneously recording and emending Blake's punctuation); thoroughgoing "modern spelling" and decapitalization,
in the Longmans. In the substance of the text, all these editions
as successively revised will approach concordant harmony. But
how will the user easily locate the passages where they do not?
By use of the *Concordance to the Poetry and Prose of William
Blake,* now at last out of the computer and off the press of Cornell
University.

The text used for this "index" consists of the Nonesuch 1957
edition stripped of punctuation (except for apostrophes inserted
to help the machine do its sorting) and, in effect, of capitalization,
since all letters have been punched as capitals. Lines containing
corrections or additions are marked by asterisks, and in an Appendix these lines are given in text order, with an indication and
explanation of the revision. Such changes were continually made
until May, 1966; so the Appendix constitutes a virtual collation
of the Nonesuch text of 1957 with that of the Doubleday second
printing of 1966 ($E^2$); it also makes possible a rapid collation
(since it constitutes a tabulation of all recognized cruxes as of
1966) of any printing of $K$ with any printing of $E$ and with the

Nonesuch. For the scholar working with any edition of $K$ or with $E^1$ (once acquired, not soon replaced) will need some such collation. It will also serve as a guide to future editions,[5] if future editors will in some way call attention to their further improvements and discoveries. For there is still in sight no end to the discovery of "slight" misreadings—involving near homographs of equal semantic validity—that may be more than slight in significance.[6]

The *Concordance* Appendix, however, and any hasty, quantitative computation of the differences between $E$ and $K$ could produce a false impression that much of the Blake text remains in obscurity or dispute. Hundreds of asterisked lines that remain unchanged in $K$ are mere spelling "corrections" such as the revision of the Nonesuch "falsehood" to Blake's "falshood." It must be borne in mind that Keynes in editing the new edition was severely limited by the conditions of offset printing and had to make a fairly Spartan choice among the typographical and even the substantive corrections accumulated. But for this consideration, and the further accumulation of corrections after his cut-off date of late 1964, the readings of $K^1$ and $E^1$ would be much more frequently in unison. $K^2$ dealt only with a few plain printer's errors, on pages 621–22; $K^1$ and $K^2$ are otherwise identical. But $K^3$, it is a pleasure to note, has been brought into almost complete agreement with $E^2$ for the whole Illuminated canon.[7] In other areas of the text they remain far apart; yet the grounds for the disparity have largely disappeared. It would be irresponsibly dramatic to overread Sir Geoffrey's observation in his new Preface ($K^2$, $K^3$ [viii]): "Apart from technical limitations, it seemed reasonable to be selective, because the readings of so many of the deleted or altered words are, to say the least, dubious and some 'corrections' remain a matter of opinion." As I have suggested, the real cruxes that remain—even among the deletions and alterations (when they can be read at all)—are few.

To indicate the nature and the limited extent of uncertainties that still need attention, it seems advisable to survey the different categories of textual sources, with their different levels of authenticity and varying problems of transcription and emendation.

## · WORKS IN ILLUMINATED PRINTING ·

In the canon of Blake's own hand-printed works, etched from his own script, there remain a mere handful of deletions undeciphered. Only the three gouged-out lines following *Jerusalem* 84:16 will remain so forever. Deletions partly visible and susceptible of some combination of positive and conjectural restoration are *Milton* 7:5 (7:3 in *E*) and 10:7 f. and *Jerusalem* 1:7, 29[43]:83 (numbered the other way round in *E*), 36 [32]:34 (where the partial restoration in *E* is a dubiety quite wisely excluded from *K*), and, a very hopeful line, 91:1. (For these passages, see either the textual notes in *E* or *Concordance* Appendix B.)

A Blakean revision, verified in time for the *Concordance* and *E*, not in *K*[2] but now happily adopted in *K*[3], is Foster Damon's discovery[8] of a "Devil" in *The Marriage of Heaven and Hell*, Plate 6. Other mendings and deletions reported in *E* and the *Concordance* but not in *K* are "sung" mended to "sang" in a late copy of "The Clod & the Pebble"; one revision in Plate 3 and five in Plate 5 of *The Book of Urizen* ("they" to "he" or "He"); one rather significant mending in three of the four copies of *Milton* (2:21, "That cause" to "What cause") and one of no significance, 6:35; and in *Jerusalem* three trivia, 7:65, 56:37, 98:11, and an interesting double revision in 69:1, from "combined" to "conjoined" in the copper plate, then by pen in the Mellon copy back to "combined." A similar reversal in 98:45, from "thy Covenant Jehovah" to "the Coven[an]t of Jehovah" (on the plate) and back to the first reading, by ink, in the Morgan copy, is in the *Concordance* but surprisingly unreported in *E*![9]

Emendations called for by small and obvious scribal errors present no difficulty, but half a dozen emendations that have *seemed* necessary are certainly subject to dispute. Two that ease the flow of the text are Margoliouth's suggestion that *Milton* 25:53 should read "To Thor" instead of "The Thor" and Keynes's that *Jerusalem* 60:55 should have "Nought" for "Not" (though a case can be made for retaining "Not"). There can hardly be a reasonable doubt that one of the "hands" in *J* 82:43 is a mistake for "feet": "I have naild his hands on Beth Rabbim & his hands on Heshbons Wall"—but should it be hands and feet or feet and hands? Since more than two hands are out of the question, we can at least be certain that the text is in error.[10] More debatable is the need to emend *Jerusalem* 49:35, "conversing with the ground," to "conversing with the [Void]"—the reading given in *E*, rather cavalierly without annotation, though the bracketing does give warning of emendation. Context shows that "ground" is an impossible word, echoed from two lines earlier; the proper word, Void, is supplied from *Milton* 5:22, part of a long passage copied here almost verbatim; yet a case, if a poor one, *could* be made for "ground" as an intentional variant. Standing *only* on the evidence of context, but standing very firmly, is Stevenson's suggestion that *Jerusalem* 55:20 should read "The Universal Conclave" (not "Concave"): the erroneous phrase, regarded out of context, may have a certain plausibility, but Blake in *Jerusalem* 55 is writing about "an Assembly" of Mountains, Forests, Rivers, Winds, Cities & Nations, Seas, Stars, all loudly "Contending"; it is this universal Conclave that line 20 describes as raging "thunderous sounds"; concavity is not the topic.[11]

### · TEXTS FROM PRINTED SOURCES ·

Small printer's errors sprinkle the texts of *Poetical Sketches* (corrected by Blake in some copies), *The French Revolution*, and *A Descriptive Catalogue*. Perfect transcription of these works and indicated correction of the small errors are attainable in the next printings of *K* and *E*. Among the editors' emendations (mostly bracketed in *K*, all bracketed or noted in *E*) only two seem to remain in dispute. *K* emends line 41 in "An Imitation of Spencer"; *E* disputes the need to emend. *E* emends "clarions of cloud breathing war" to "clarions of loud breathing war" in *The French Revolution* 101; *K* does not.

The detection of errors can be expected to continue, however, as ever closer study reveals textual anomalies. Even as I write, William F. Halloran of Wisconsin is proposing a rearrangement of five lines of *The French Revolution* which, on close analysis, do seem an "inadvertent misplacement . . . in the manuscript or during the printing process."[12] And a California student, Joanne Witke, in a polite postcard asks whether the "darkning locks" of

Albion in *J* 43[29]:28 could be a scribal error for "darkning rocks," the image established in line 2 of the same plate; from the full context there can be little doubt she is right. Emendation is a valuable by-product of interpretation, dangerous only when incorporated in editorial silence.

## · TEXTS FROM MANUSCRIPT SOURCES ·

Turning to the works that survive in manuscript, we step at once into "the crooked roads without Improvement"—or with improvements by Blake that are sometimes more crooked still. And in this area, both in the reading of final drafts and in the pursuit of erasures and deletions, the disparity between editions is large and difficult to describe summarily. Here there is less accommodation in *K* of the corrections and additions listed in the *Concordance*. *E* also here becomes somewhat selective: "annotation of inessentials" (i.e., the reporting of minor variants) "is somewhat less exhaustive for the manuscript poems than for the Illuminated canon—and is largely omitted for the prose texts." In transcribing the prose, *E* omits or summarizes "mended letters, slips of the pen, and trivial, passing revisions and deletions" (p. 711). Ultimately the Bentley edition can be expected to retrieve these omissions; meanwhile, in its cumbersome way, the *Concordance* does call attention to all noticed illegible deletions (except mended letters) by a system of triple *X*'s, translated into approximations of length of deletion in the Appendix. This takes care of all substantive changes—except of capitalization, which can bear meaningful revisions, e.g., from "man" to "Man" or from "Devil" to "devil."

By and large, nevertheless, it can be said with fair confidence that even in the manuscript texts the readings of deletions and alterations that remain "dubious" or "a matter of opinion" do not (*pace* Sir Geoffrey) add up to very many. With some important exceptions in *The Four Zoas*, the Notebook, and the marginalia, which I shall come to, the still illegible passages are few and small. Most of the partially read words or groups of words have been reduced to a very slight and insignificant dubiety, and few real surprises seem still possible.

An unselective illustration will make the point—even by its tediousness. Let us see what has happened to all the deletions in *An Island in the Moon* that were reported illegible in 1957 or that have been questioned since. In the list that follows, the Nonesuch reading is separated by a colon from the *Concordance* or *E* reading; parentheses enclose the location in *K* and my present observations:

[tipsy *del.*]:[? *tipsy*]  (*K* 44B)

3 Philosophers—:3 Philosophers [⟨*the*⟩?*older*]  (*K* 44C. Fact of deletion here not previously noted.)

[*words del.*]:[*here the*]  (*K* 45A)

[replied]:⟨said⟩ (*K* 45D. Here "replied" had been editorially supplied; the word "said" is Blake's insertion, written in the margin and smudged while the ink was wet.)

[& the three Philosophers . . .]:[& the three Philosophers com[in]g]  (*K* 46B. The three dots meant "illegible scribble.")

[*word del.*]:[*Conjunctives*]  (*K* 46D)

[*Several words del.*]:[*Why ?I ?know that*]  (*K* 48D. The words following this deletion are "why I know that"; the remaining uncertainty in the reading scarcely leaves room for a dramatic discovery.)

[what is this . . . used for *del.*]:[*what is this gim crank for*]  (*K* 49B)

[*word del.*]:[*?Phi*]  (*K* 49C. The next word is "Fissic.")

[*word del.*]:[*twen*[ty]]  (*K* 49D)

[*several words del.*]:[*This is unfair* . . . (one or two more words)]  (*K* 52A. This report is tantalizing, since the remnant of about six letters is *almost* legible.)

[*word del.*]:[*?talk*]  (*K* 52B. The next word is "Talk.")

An Easy of Huming Understanding, by John Lookye [pantryman *altered to*] Gent.:An Easy of [*Human*] ⟨Huming⟩ Understanding by John Lookye Gent  (*K* 52D. *E* textual note: " 'Gent' is written over a deletion, possibly 'pantryman.' ")

[*several words del.*]:[*xxxxx xxx ?about*] (*K* 52D)

The last passage presents a small mystery unsolved. But it happens that this deletion lies precisely below the conjectured "pantryman" of the preceding line. Now examining the photostat once more, I see that the slant line that seemed to be the $y$ of "pantryman" is an ascender from the word preceding "?about"; it makes, in fact, the $b$ of "book"— and the whole deleted interruption reads "its a book about" (parts of these letters were all visible beneath deleting squiggles; it was a matter of finding a clue). And so down goes "pantryman"—and since the $G$ of "Gent" seems written over an almost identical letter, a very good guess is that "Gent" is written over "Gentleman" (a change made while the ink was wet; Blake smudged the long word horizontally, then heavily wrote the short one on top).

The few tiny remaining deletions in this manuscript are good, firm ink words, hidden by loops or lines, or smears, but waiting to be made out.

Has this sort of piecemeal puttering any justification? Yes, when finished we see that Blake at first gave Scopprell his line with only two puns: "An Easy of Human Understanding by John Lookye Gentleman"; that he quickly mended the last word to the saucier "Gent"; then later with different ink and pen changed the "Human" to "Huming" (half the pun of which we hide by emending to "Hum[m]ing"—for it is fairly safe to suspect Blake of seeing Locke's *humming* as Hume-ing too). Whether in this kind of playful creativity or with much sterner stuff on his anvil, the bard's final product is appreciated through our watching him shape it.

"Tiriel" is a similar but neater manuscript. The only difficult deletions are brief false starts or repetitions. Perhaps only one of the few differences between $K$ and $E$ represents a debatable point. In 4:3, $K$ emends "come down" to "came down"; $E$ accepts the textual reading as grammatically defensible, "come" serving as participle not verb: Ijim, come down from his woods, met Tiriel at their entrance. The transcript in Gerald Bentley's new *Tiriel* agrees on this point, suggests two new readings (that the first spelling of Hela may have been Hala instead of Hili, and that the deletion in 4:85 [4:74 in $E$] may be "tormented" rather than "torn like"), but bears also its quota of new errors.[13]

Blake's Notebook, the Rossetti Manuscript, is a much more complex document: fair copies and drafts of lyrics in all stages of construction; squibs plain and fancy; drafts of essays and various memoranda. Here *K* and *E* stand rather far apart, largely because much of the total transcript consists of revisions and deletions, just the area Keynes was required to scant in *K*² to save room for the correction of final readings. Far too many advances had been made in the reading and sorting out of the heavily worked lyrics and epigrams to be accommodated without setting fresh type and renumbering lines.[14] By the same token, there will be few surprises in the typographic transcript being made for the Clarendon facsimile edition of the Notebook; its virtues, textually, will be those of a diagrammatic guide to the manuscript pages.

Notebook passages still undeciphered are few enough to tally here.[15] On page 3 there are traces of erased black ink lines under lines 1, 2, and the beginning of 3, of stanza "2." On page 18 a breaking-off of an edge of the paper before the present binding makes a small, irrecoverable lacuna. On page 22 the heavy pencil shading might be suspected of concealing earlier writing, but photography shows this is not the case. On page 35 lines 4 and 6 of "On H___ys Friendship" have illegible erasures beneath them, and another buried attack on Hayley on page 50 also has thus far defied detection: Hayley is in the first four lines of the "Epitaph for William Cowper Esqre" on top of which Blake wrote his declaration that his only tolerable friend was Fuseli. The four lines are *there*, awaiting engineering refinements that will make them legible. A missing quarter of the leaf comprising pages 71–72, cut out by Rossetti to send a sample of Blake's writing to Horace Scudder, an American friend, may still turn up in an autograph collection: on page 71 it will have most of the fifth paragraph of Blake's essay on The Last Judgment; on page 72 it will have the top of a small drawing—and one cannot tell what else.

The other puzzles are insignificant. Three erased words beneath "ever Existent Images" on page 69 might prove interesting. The exact wording of items 1, 2, and 3 in the list of subjects from Exodus 7 on page 116 matters little; so does the discarded adjective under the last part of "cautious *& refind*" on page 106.

Sharp eyes will continue, of course, to discover small mistakes in the editorial tradition (even though each editor makes his own "independent" transcript of original documents, his familiarity with the previously received text will influence his reading, especially where there is difficulty or unfamiliarity in what presents itself to the eye), sometimes of large import. A current instance is Stevenson's querying the epigram headed "From Cratelos." Is it possible to read "Cratetos" (with an uncrossed *t*), he asks, because "the epigram is in fact a translation from the Greek of Crates, not Cratylus: it is found in an anthology by the world-famous Stobaeus, who attributes it κράτητος (i.e., 'of Crates')." [16] Another look at the manuscript reveals that in fact both *t*'s *are* crossed. Here precise annotation becomes a path to correct transcription.

In Blake's manuscript marginalia in various books there remain several rubbed or erased or palimpsest passages that have defied confident transcription. The rubbed flyleaf of Swedenborg's *Divine Love and Divine Wisdom* is brought into considerable visibility by infrared photography and enlargement; the text in *K* represents an interim reading; that in *E* is the result of further application, but still considerably short of a definitive text. Even photographic refinements will be insufficient to recover and bring order into the chaos of rapid revisions and insertions on the third page of Blake's annotations to Thornton's new Lord's Prayer. But his notes in Malone's edition of Reynolds, now to a great extent recovered from the obscurity of erasure and palimpsest, still contain much matter to be restored or removed from conjecture to certainty, matter doubtless crackling as the transcribed comments are with sarcasm and opposition. Photography has been most disappointing with these Reynolds marginalia; some of the penciled lines have been so thoroughly erased that on a dark day they seem quite invisible, only to return to visibility and even partial legibility with sunshine (reflected from a white sheet, not direct) and a clean lens. (These remarks will explain the uncertainty of my intention to prepare a separate volume of Blake on Reynolds, with more extensive simulation of habitat—i.e., of the Malone and Reynolds text that gives rise to Blake's commentary.)

In the Watson marginalia one tantalizing puzzle remains, on page 9: ". . . the plan of Providence . . . was not restored till [*we in*] Christ [xxx xxxxxxx]"—two words in dark ink, heavily deleted by loops of ink.

That many substantive disparities exist between *K* and *E* in the transcripts of marginalia is true, but the reason is evidently that Keynes had exhausted his options for correction in the major works. In the third printing (*K*³) one finds the important correction of *K* 387 "Why did Christ . . . Was not Christ marter'd" to "Wherefore did Christ . . . Was not Christ murderd"; perhaps the next impression will contain the correction of *K* 388 "Paine [the Devil *del*.] says" to "[the Deists say *del*.] Paine says" and of *K* 401 "Innocence" to "Innocents" (see *E* 604).

The text of *Vala, or the Four Zoas* remains to be touched upon, if only touched upon. Palimpsest pages still only partially deciphered amount to a full score: 3–7, 9, 10, 12, 23, 25, 27, 33, 34, 42, 56, 58, 80, 117. Some of the erased and over-written lines seem hopelessly lost; at the other extreme, hovering on the verge of legibility, are such passages as the erased line beneath 10:15. For some of these the Bentley facsimile edition, even though the halftones are not of the finest screen, is practically as useful as immediate photography; for most of them it is not. Bentley's transcript of the whole manuscript, collated with Margoliouth's partial one,[17] supplied the *Concordance* text with numerous corrections and additions to the Nonesuch. Further study of the manuscript, and some photographic work, yielded a few changes and additions before the *Concordance* deadline; still more appear in *E*².[18] The Oxford Press, on the dust jacket of *K*, claiming for it "almost all Blake's substantive variants," excepts "some in the exceptionally complex manuscript of *Vala*" and refers readers to the facsimile text. This is very well for actual variants, i.e., deleted or over-written words and passages; the Keynes edition even in the original format of 1957 was able to supply only an imperfect impression of "exactly what Blake was doing" (see Preface, p.

xii) in the more complicated revisions. Yet it seems an undue hardship that the user be left to discover and correct by collation with other editions the numerous mistakes that stand in the variants *K* does give and also in the undeleted passages. We must urge Sir Geoffrey to resume the editorial chair and his publishers to open the next impression to substantive corrections in both the undeleted part of the text and in the variants given—and even to make some room for additional variants of indubitable legibility (an unhappy omission in the fourth line of the *title* could be remedied by resetting the line "of the Ancient Man" to read "of the [Eternal *del.*] Ancient Man").

Let me submit some samples of substantive corrections in the undeleted portions of *Vala* that will explain the urgency of this appeal. (An appeal, not a complaint: several of these readings were not available in 1964, for they had not been detected.) In Night I (giving page and then line number in *K*), 268:144, "vailing clouds" should be "trailing clouds"; 166, "these" should read "them"; 271:244, "drave the Males" should be "drave all the Males"; 273:317, "murder'd the Man" should read "murder'd the other"; 277:487, "they" should be "thus"; 279:563, "These gates" should read "Three gates." In Night III, 292:37, "field" should read "fields" (otherwise the series, fields, halls, dens, is marred); 296:175, "rendered me" is a misprint for "rended me." In Night IV, 298:31, "these" should read "thou"; punctuated, the reading should be "Renew thou; I will destroy." In Night V, in 306:59 and 308:142 the spirits act "in" not "on" the deep; 311:233, "bow'd" should read "bound," and the caves in 239 are "caverns" not "cavern"; in VII, in 325:199 the animals should be called "to their delights" not "delight"; the iron in 327:283 is "for spades & plowshares" not "spade"; the fires in 331:445 are "ascending" not "assembling"; in the next line Enitharmon's locks are "beaming" not "beamy." In VII (b) in 335:85 and 87 it is a "tower" not a "bower" that Los builds for her upon a rock. In Night VIII, "repelld" instead of "expell'd" will make sense of 343:100; in 350:346 "feminine powers" should be "feminine pomp"; the world in 350:373 and 351:396 is not "Crested with snow" or "crush'd with Snow" but in both places "Crusted"; Rintrah in 389 acts in fury and "fire" not "fear"; the "Larma" in 352:446 is a "Lamia"; in 353:476 change "in" to "on" and "breathing" to "trembling"; in Night IX, 371:540, Tharmas fades not "as" but "like a water lilly"; in 373:613 correction of "forms" to "form" will transform the image. The lion in 376:707 should be "couching" not "crouching at their side."

A self-sobering note is in order at this point. While pursuing these corrections of a word here and there in K, I left out of E an important long line of the exordium of *The Four Zoas* (Night I: K 264:22–23) and failed to restore it even in the second printing. This ink insertion after line 4 of manuscript page 4

His fall into the Generation of decay & death & his
Regeneration by the Resurrection from the dead

is in all other editions[19] and in the *Concordance*—without asterisk, an indication that the omission was not deliberate—and will have to be fitted into the next printing of E. The mistake can be traced back to the typist, I find, but the typist was myself.

As for the *Four Zoas* variants which are now offered in K and the correction of which would require minimal resetting, let me make a small list of those that seriously need mending. The correction of "living wheels" to "turning wheels" in 317:236 having been made, the "living spheres" in 271:247 should be changed to "turning spheres" to permit Blake the consistency of his text (and at the same time "of Beulah" could be moved to follow "spheres" from its false position at the end of the line). In 272:276 "(Los *del.*) Beulah" should be changed to read "(Vala *del.*) Luvah"; in 286:245 "[*words erased and illegible*]" might well be replaced by "[Cubed *del.*] in [window square *del.*]" as the final reading, if there is not room to give in full: "[(Circled) Cubed] in [(infinite orb) window square]"; in 295:141 "[*word del.*]" could be filled in: "[darkning *del.*]"; a similar gap in 308:117 could be written "[rejoice *del.*]"; "[dismal *del.*]" in 315:148 should be "[eternal *del.*]"; in 333:1 "the [Rock *del.*] tree of Mystery" needs revising to "the [tree *del.*] Roots of Mystery"; in 333:11 "O . . . Prince" can read "O Urizen Prince"; in 336:144 "his [*word erased*] fury" can be changed to "his [triumphant *del.*] fury"; in 340:287 "anger" should read "anguish"; in 341:11 the wings, already called "Silvery," should shine "upon the dark blue sky in silence," not "in silver"; in 346:215 "[*name del.*]" can be replaced by "[the Moon *del.*]"; Rahab in 350:345 can be "[above *del.*]" instead of "[alone *del.*]"; in 352:415 "[was . . . *del.*]" can become "[was darkend *del.*]" (not to bother with the doubtful earlier reading "was ?tormented"). In 356:585 "Rahab hew'd(?)" may as well be corrected to "Rahab (built *del.*) hewd"; the deleted word in 361:175 is "plow"; and in the Additional Fragments (*K* 380–82) several substantive amendments can now be made. In the first fragment: "Aloud" (l. 4) should read "O Luvah"; the unread half-line 10 is "[After their sin *del.*]"; line 20 needs "high rocks" in place of "rock." In the fifth fragment, line 4, "desart" should read "beast"; in the sixth the half-line unread at 18 is a whole line: "In which is Tirzah untranslucent an opake covering"; in 29 "merciful" should read "mournful." But perhaps if the Press is to be urged to allow revision of *The Four Zoas* in *K*, another fifty or so minor corrections ought to be asked for, really to tidy up the *K* version.

These comparisons may sound competitive after all, and I may seem to be making in public suggestions that should be made only to the persons concerned. Yet many considerations come into play, and the persons ultimately concerned are as many as read Blake. Of the making of new editions there may be no end, but those of us who find new words are driven by a strong wind to disseminate them for adoption in as many editions as may be, and in the margins of old editions in the hands of frugal scholars, that the unison of right readings may extend "into the expanse" and thence into the minds of men.

### · POSTSCRIPT: THE CAVE IN THE CHAMBERS ·

The symbolism of Blake's "Printing house" has been dealt with by many explicators (for a convenient collection of symbolic and allegorical readings, see Clark Emery's booklet on *The Marriage of Heaven and Hell* in University of Miami Critical Studies, No. 1, 1963). But I do not know that anyone has satisfactorily come to grips with the primary terms, the rough basement, of this all too infinitely suggestive "Memorable Fancy." In what follows I am concerned only with the primary terms or counters, as derivable from Blake's actual process of illuminated printing, and with unriddling their apparently scrambled sequence; this is not to deny, indeed it is to insist, that Blake intended us to read larger meanings here, whether Foster Damon's symbolism of the body and the five senses, or Martin Nurmi's dual allegory of the liberation of man and the interaction of the contraries, or even Clark Emery's rather free-wheeling translation of these into a medieval sequence of "internal" senses plus "a dash of Hobbes on Wit and a soupçon of Coleridge and Wordsworth on Fancy and the Imagination." I suggest that it was precisely because he wanted to cause the inside of his allegory of a printing house "to be infinite" that Blake not only sublimated his description of the work processes but departed from their natural order.

The idea has been generally accepted that on Plate 5 Blake's vision of a Devil hovering on the sides of a rock with corroding fires is a vision of himself at work on a copper plate with aqua fortis, the result a sentence opening "an immense world of delight." It has probably been observed that the bird "that cuts the airy way" is a feathered metamorphosis of the engraver that cuts the "sides of the rock."

In the printing house the Viper "folding round the rock & the cave" is at the center of similar activity. Our first clue is the inference that rock and cave are two aspects of the same thing, a copper plate. Viewed as a rock it is "a flat sided steep" (Pl. 5); viewed as the three-dimensional stereotype inscribed with text and adorned with illuminations and in the interstices hollowed to infinity, it is a metal cave. Metonymously the flat sheet of paper upon which these inscriptions and adornments and infinities are reproduced by impression is also that cave; we refer variously to copper or paper as a plate. In the printing-house passage Blake, except in the phrase quoted, keeps to the term cave and directs attention to the end rather than the beginning of the process.

Each "chamber" is, of course, a room or working area in the shop. There have to be six to match the six days of creation, though an actual six-room shop was not to be had by William

Blake except in a "Fancy." One stumbling block to interpretation is removed when we see the "cave" as a plate being moved from place to place and stop trying to visualize a literal cave in a house and one that somehow "runs through the first chamber into the second" (Emery, p. 71). Now let us follow the process.

In the first chamber the Dragon-Man "clearing away the rubbish from a caves mouth" is the engraver, the "number of Dragons . . . hollowing the cave" the various engraving tools, or his fingers using them. In the second chamber the Viper and his helpers are *illuminating* the plate—and, when it is the sheet of paper, "adorning it" with inks and paints of the colors of "gold silver and precious stones." In the third chamber the Eagle or poetic genius is applying ideas, visions ("with wings and feathers of air"; compare the bird that cut the airy way); his helpers building "palaces in the immense cliffs" are, again, his hands and tools getting the *text* onto the plate (and thence the paper). The fourth process described is etching, "melting the metals into living fluids": Blake's mind jumps from the fluids that cut the surface of the metal into organized words and pictures to the vital mental fluidity of their content of ideas and images.

"In the fifth chamber were Unnam'd forms, which cast the metals into the expanse." How did we get *here?* The casting of the copper plates should be the first process, not the penultimate one—or are these the used plates being sent off to the copper-smith for renewal? Blake almost surely did not cast his own plates (hence "Unnam'd"?). Or is "forms" the operative term and "cast" a metaphor? We are now in the pressroom, from which the finished work is "cast into the expanse," i.e., "now published and on Sale at Mr. Blake's, No. 13, Hercules Buildings," to quote his almost contemporaneous Prospectus. The "metals" are now the *plates* of "the most beautiful wove paper"; in the sixth stage (here "chamber" is a sliding term) the plates are collated into "the forms of books" (still in Blake's chamber) and are received by customers ("Men"—no arch language here) into their chambers or "libraries."

Even while trying to keep the terms primary I have got tangled in their elliptical and multiple functioning. To insist once more on a primary focus is to recognize that we have not been shown through the printing house progressively from composing room to bindery. For such a tour we ought first to watch the casting of metal in chamber 5, then the application of text to the plate (chamber 3), then its pictorial adornment (2a: adornment of the rock), then its etching (4), then its supplementary engraving and burnishing (1). We are not shown the preparation of paper and ink and paint (water colors); nor the printing (in one color) and complementary coloring (in others). But we may return to 2b: adornment of the paper "plate"; and then go to the fifth chamber as pressroom and the sixth as bindery. We can say that there is a conflation of processes throughout the account, most elliptical perhaps in chambers 2 and 5.

A Stony Brook student, Thomas D. Rowland, suggests that the fourth chamber describes the inking process: the "Lions of flaming fire" (flaming colors) who rage around and melt the "metals [plates] into living fluids" are inking their surfaces; and that the fifth chamber describes the printing from inked plates onto the white expanse of paper: they are locked into "forms, which cast the metals [i.e., their fluid surfaces] into the expanse." [20]

As I promised, I shall refrain from entering the immense worlds of delight opened to the minds of men by Blake's arrangement and creative use of his printing-house images, and conclude with the simple observation that one effect of the conflation of casting and publishing is to make the poet more blacksmith than scribe, a creator of books of rare metals and precious stones rather than perishable paper and ink. We all surely agree on that evaluation.

GEOFFREY KEYNES

# The William Blake Trust

As an editor of Blake texts at intervals since 1925, when the first Nonesuch edition appeared in three handsome illustrated volumes, I have often been assailed by dissatisfied readers. "Why," they complain, "can't we have nice cheap editions of the *Songs of Innocence* and other books including the decorations as well as the text? That is the way Blake meant us to see them." I have always been full of sympathy, but could only reply that any inexpensive reproduction in black and white or in color would be so unlike the original colored prints that no one would be satisfied. The result would be a travesty of Blake's intention and would be unfair to both him and his admirers. In fact the only answer I have been able to find has been in the series of books published by the William Blake Trust of London during the last seventeen years. These are true *facsimiles* of Blake's books, the term facsimile being used in contrast to *reproduction* to imply that the result can be placed beside the original book without any fear that the one will suffer seriously by comparison with the other.

My interest in the possibility of achieving this end goes a long way back in time. In 1920, when I was working on the production of my *Blake Bibliography* published by the Grolier Club of New York in 1921, I had prevailed on General Archibald Stirling of Keir to allow his unique colored copy of *Jerusalem* to be sent to London so that a close copy of one plate in color might be made by the firm of Charles Whittingham and Griggs. This was successfully done, but the result was a reproduction rather than a facsimile, being made by fallible human hands through lithography at rather high cost. The effect was good, but the cost of reproducing the 100 pages of *Jerusalem* by this method would have been prohibitive. Yet nothing short of this would have contented me.

I was forever tormented by the thought that some catastrophe might happen to this unique book and the world be deprived of one of the finest works of art and intellect that it had ever seen.

The problem remained unsolved until 1947, when in Boston I chanced to be shown a facsimile of a series of water colors by Cézanne made, I was told, by a firm called the Trianon Press in Paris. The effect was that of a *facsimile* rather than *reproduction,* and the cost was said to be moderate. Back in London, I made contact with the proprietors of the Trianon Press, two young men named Arnold Fawcus and Patrick Macleod, and arranged with the owner of *Jerusalem* for them to make a close examination of the book. I had previously obtained estimates from Sir Emery Walker and the Oxford University Press for reproducing the book by color collotype. Their independent estimates were identical—each said £10,000, whereas the Trianon Press assured me that their superior process of coloring through stencils over a collotype base could be done for £4,000. The owner of the book, now Colonel William Stirling of Keir, son of Sir Archibald, wished to feel assured that the value of his book would not be depreciated by the publication of a facsimile, and that it would not suffer by being disbound into its separate leaves and sojourning for two years in Paris in the nominal charge of the Bibliothèque Nationale. Colonel Stirling accepted my assurance that the publicity afforded by a facsimile would enhance rather than reduce the value; I am glad to say that his generosity in loaning the book was amply rewarded when some years later it became the property of Mr. Paul Mellon.

At this point I rather rashly decided to raise the money required by enlisting the help of ten guarantors of £500 each. I had found only five of these when I still more rashly handed the book over to the two young men for its immediate transport to Paris, so that the work might begin. The book was insured for £10,000 and my slight acquaintance with the proprietors of the Trianon Press hardly justified the lighthearted way in which I entrusted the book to their hands. I suffered real anxiety when after a week I had no news of its safe arrival in Paris. This was increased when in- quiries at their London flat met with the reply that they had gone away without leaving any address. What seemed a very long fortnight elapsed before it occurred to the Trianon Press to let me know that the book was safely lodged at the Bibliothèque Nationale. I am glad to say that never again has there been any anxiety—except when Macleod was on his way back to England with *Jerusalem* in the trunk of his car. At the Belgian frontier it was discovered by a zealous customs officer, who very intelligently guessed that the book was worth £10,000 and then impounded it because no import license had been obtained when it entered France. Explanations were unavailing and the book was released only after intervention by the French cultural attaché in London and much international argument. Ultimately it reached London unharmed, and was rebound by Gray and Son of Cambridge better than before, the leaves being guarded instead of sewn by overcasting, so that it opened more fully and was pleasanter to handle.

This, however, is anticipating details of the book's later history. The work had started in the Parisian workshops employed by the Trianon Press early in 1948, but the financial basis was still precarious, only £2,500 having been guaranteed. It had not proceeded very far when my act of faith was justified by a wholly unexpected event. The great Blake collector, Walford Graham Robertson, had been seriously ill for some time and his death in September, 1948, could not cause surprise, but soon afterwards it was announced that he had left a very large fortune, almost the whole of which was to be devoted to charitable causes at the discretion of the executors. It soon occurred to me that endowment of a trust formed expressly to finance the *Jerusalem* project might commend itself to the executors as a worthy cause. The suggestion was put to Mr. Kerrison Preston, the senior executor, who was himself deeply interested in Blake, and he immediately offered to provide £10,000 as an endowment for such a trust if a suitable constitution could be framed. I took counsel with my friend, Mr. George Goyder, a man experienced in business affairs, and we decided that this was a practicable plan. We each subscribed £10 as a founding endowment fund and with the help of expert legal advice the William Blake Trust was duly formed. The terms were

carefully devised to qualify the Trust as a legally constituted
non-profit-making educational charity to be administered by a
board of eight trustees with myself as chairman. When this had
been completed the Graham Robertson executors added their
£10,000 to the endowment fund, thereby removing all further
difficulty in financing the *Jerusalem* project even if the cost of the
facsimile should exceed the original estimate of £4,000, as indeed
it inevitably did. The Trustees had no financial interest in the
success or failure of the Trust, but were responsible for the ad-
ministration of the fund in furthering its objects. The constitution
was so worded that we were empowered to make facsimiles of
Blake's *Jerusalem* and of his other Illuminated Books as funds permitted and to include other projects connected with Blake if we
wished. We were thus able to add to the facsimile of *Jerusalem*
a volume of commentary by Joseph Wicksteed and a reproduction
made from another copy printed in black with a version of the
text in ordinary typography.

Two years after the formation of the Trust the facsimile of
*Jerusalem* was published in an edition of five hundred copies with
the imprint of the Trianon Press, Messrs. Faber and Faber acting
as distributors. The quality of this facsimile was seen to be equal
to our expectations and the selling price could be kept low since
the Trust was not formed to make profits and had very small
administrative expenses. Meanwhile the Graham Robertson executors had determined to sell, with certain reservations, the whole
of the Blake collection at auction except for a few pictures be-
queathed by their late owner to the Tate Gallery. When the sale
at Christie's was fixed for July 29, 1949, the Blake Trustees decided
rather hurriedly to embark on having a series of biblical subjects
reproduced in full-size color collotype before the pictures were
distributed at auction. Six of these were undertaken by the firm
of Sir Emery Walker and two by the workshops in Paris. Later
one more subject, the "Black Virgin and Child," now in the Paul
Mellon Collection, was added, this being done by lithography.

The process of making facsimiles as developed in the Parisian
workshops was essentially a combination of a printed collotype
base with coloring applied by hand through stencils. The crucial

stage in the process is the use of expert judgment needed for "breaking down" the colors into their constituent parts as used by Blake and for the cutting of the stencils through which the colors can be painted on the prints. This painting does not consist in the application of flat water-color washes; every stroke of the brush is used to make the correct gradations. The paper has been made specially to resemble that used by Blake, with a watermark of the artist's monogram in every leaf to prevent the facsimiles' being mistaken for originals.

It was soon apparent that sales of the *Jerusalem* facsimile would refund the money spent by the Trustees, so that they would be justified in forming a policy for the publication of further volumes as time and funds permitted. It was assumed that the sale of each succeeding volume would ultimately cover the cost of its production, though there might be some difficulty by reason of accumulation of stock not easily convertible into cash. This was eased by a generous loan from Mr. Lessing J. Rosenwald, whose continuous support in lending copies of the Illuminated Books from his collection has been a very important factor in maintaining the steady succession of facsimile volumes, which have now reached a total of eight published over sixteen years. A slight handicap in fulfilling the aims of the Trust has been the fact that only those copies painted with water colors can be successfully copied in facsimile. The books executed by Blake in his peculiar color-printing technique cannot be used, the effect of the thick opaque pigments being impossible to imitate. Three books—*The Song of Los, The Book of Ahania*, and *The Book of Los*—are thereby excluded. Of the others, the Blake Trust has published facsimiles of *Songs of Innocence* (a copy with very simple coloring in Blake's early style), *Songs of Innocence and of Experience* (an example of the later more elaborate style), *The Book of Urizen, The Marriage of Heaven and Hell, Visions of the Daughters of Albion, America, The Book of Thel*, and *Milton*. All these books are in the Rosenwald Collection, now a part of the Library of Congress, except *America*, which is in the Paul Mellon Collection. Only *Europe* remains to be done, but this presents great difficulties.

No available copy is executed entirely in water colors and its production may prove to be impracticable.

Since the constitution of the Trust was not made too rigid, the Trustees have been able sometimes to go outside the range of the Illuminated Books. Thus an illustrated Catalogue of Blake's entire output of biblical subjects has been published, the nine full-size reproductions of pictures being added. These had not been easy to sell separately, owing to the purchase tax exacted in Great Britain; as part of a book they did not attract this tax. Every picture in the Catalogue is reproduced as a small print in collotype, so that a visual list of the pictures is provided, an invaluable feature for use in galleries and libraries of art. The Trustees have also published a reproduction of Samuel Palmer's sketchbook of 1824, by good fortune recovered through my agency from Vancouver, B.C., and recently purchased from the owners (members of the Linnell family) for the Department of Prints and Drawings at the British Museum.

The point has now been reached when the Trustees can envisage the winding up of the Trust, since its original aims have been accomplished. Because of their quality the books published have not been cheap; but they have been brought within the means of most libraries and galleries interested in Blake, where they can be seen by far more people than can have access to the few existing originals. In order to use up such funds as remain Mr. Martin Butlin of the Tate Gallery has been commissioned to compile a *Catalogue Raisonné* of Blake's entire output of paintings and drawings. The work is already well advanced but will take some time to complete.

Lastly it should be recorded that the Trustees have sponsored without financial responsibility an exhibition of the facsimiles with some of the originals. This was successfully organized by Mr. Arnold Fawcus, who designed it to show the intricate method of production. The exhibition was first staged at the Tate Gallery, London, and was afterwards shown under the aegis of the Smithsonian Institution at the National Gallery, Washington, D.C., and in other cities in the United States and Canada. It will presently be seen also in various centers in Great Britain, the Arts Council having undertaken to organize the tour. The generous help towards the aims of the Trust and for this exhibition given by Mr. Lessing J. Rosenwald and Mr. Paul Mellon has been recognized by their appointment with two others as Associate Trustees in the United States; the terms of the foundation prevented their being made full Trustees. Bernard Quaritch, Ltd., of London has for some time been the sole distributor of the Blake Trust books.

The activities of the Trust will have extended over more than twenty years by the time its planned demise has taken place. Any success it may have had could not have been achieved without the devoted work done by Mr. Arnold Fawcus and his staff at the Trianon Press; he has for some years been the sole Director. The resulting volumes have been up to the present time the only possible answer to the complaints recorded at the beginning of this statement.

The constitution and aims of the William Blake Trust are, it is hoped, made plain by this account written for the volume published in honor of Professor S. Foster Damon, whose contribution to Blake scholarship has been so important a feature in the progressive understanding of Blake's art and message during the last forty years.

# Abbreviations
# and Notes

# List of Abbreviations

In citations to works by Blake, an abbreviation of the title is followed by the plate, subdivision, or page number in the original edition; the line number (if numbered); the edition cited (*K* or *E*); and, finally, the page number in *K* or *E* (line 31 on Plate 42 of *Jerusalem*, found on page 187 of David V. Erdman's *The Poetry and Prose of William Blake*, is cited as *J* 42:31, *E* 187). A somewhat different system is used in Paul Miner's "Visions in the Darksom Air" (pp. 256–92). This system is explained in note 1, page 461.

| | |
|---|---|
| *Ahan* | *The Book of Ahania* |
| *Am* | *America* |
| *Aug* | *Auguries of Innocence* |
| *BoL* | *The Book of Los* |
| *DesC* | *A Descriptive Catalogue* |
| *E* | *The Poetry and Prose of William Blake*, ed. David V. Erdman, commentary by Harold Bloom (Garden City, N.Y., 1965) |
| *E-S* | Blake's Poems, ed. David V. Erdman and William H. Stevenson; to be published by Longmans, London |
| *EG* | *The Everlasting Gospel* |
| *Eur* | *Europe, a Prophecy* |
| *FR* | *The French Revolution* |
| *FZ* | *The Four Zoas* |
| *GoP* | *The Gates of Paradise* |
| *IslM* | *An Island in the Moon* |
| *J* | *Jerusalem* |
| *K* | *The Complete Writings of William Blake*, ed. Geoffrey Keynes (London, 1966) |
| *Laoc* | Laocoön plate |
| *LJ* | *A Vision of the Last Judgment* |
| *MHH* | *The Marriage of Heaven and Hell* |

# ABBREVIATIONS

| | |
|---|---|
| *Mil* | *Milton, a Poem* |
| *PS* | *Poetical Sketches* |
| *SoI* | *Songs of Innocence* |
| *SoL* | *The Song of Los* |
| *Thel* | *The Book of Thel* |
| *Ur* | *The Book of Urizen* |
| *VDA* | *Visions of the Daughters of Albion* |

# Notes

## · S. FOSTER DAMON: THE NEW ENGLAND VOICE ·

1. As a sequel to his studies with Professor Anesaki at Harvard, Foster once wrote a Japanese Noh drama, *Kiri no Meijiyama,* but that was pastiche, not parody. Indeed, it was so faithful to the Japanese spirit that after it was printed in *The Dial* (February, 1920) Arthur Waley wrote from England asking Foster where in the world he had found the Japanese original, which he assigned to the sixteenth century.

## · BLAKE AND THE POSTMODERN ·

1. Denis Saurat, *Blake and Modern Thought* (New York, 1929), pp. ix–xii, 198.

2. "William Blake," *Selected Essays, 1917–1932* (London and New York, 1932), p. 275.

3. Letter to Charles Augustus Tulk, 1818.

4. I have dealt with some of these matters in *Blake and Yeats: The Contrary Vision* (Ithaca, 1955). See also Northrop Frye, "Yeats and the Language of Symbolism," *Fables of Identity* (New York, 1963), pp. 218–37.

5. "Quest and Cycle in *Finnegans Wake*," *Fables of Identity,* pp. 256–64.

6. *Blake: A Psychological Study* (London, 1946).

7. *Northrop Frye in Modern Criticism,* ed. Murray Krieger (New York, 1966).

8. "Horses of Wrath: Recent Critical Lessons," *Hateful Contraries* (Lexington, Ky., 1965), pp. 3–48.

9. Against these movements Wimsatt sees three other strands related generally to emphasis upon moral and social power. Here we find the prophetic tendencies of Shelley and Carlyle, the humanism of Matthew Arnold, and finally Irving Babbitt and Paul Elmer More

and the sociological emphasis from its Hegelian roots through Tolstoy to the muckrakers and the Marxists of the thirties. These movements are not germane to my interest here, although there is a political and prophetic tendency in several critics influenced by Blake and Frye.

10. "Myth as Information," *Hudson Review*, Summer, 1954, pp. 228–35.

11. See Philip Wheelwright, *The Burning Fountain* (Bloomington, Ind., 1954).

12. "Horses of Wrath," pp. 20–21.

13. *Ibid.*, p. 25.

14. *Blake's Marriage of Heaven and Hell: A Critical Study* (Kent, Ohio, 1957), *passim*.

15. "Horses of Wrath," p. 21.

16. Princeton, 1964.


· THE VISIONARY CINEMA OF ROMANTIC POETRY ·

1. *The Collected Poems of Wallace Stevens* (New York, 1961), p. 311.

2. *The Poetical Works of William Wordsworth*, ed. E. de Selincourt and Helen Darbishire (Oxford, 1949), V, 396, ll. 580–96.

3. *Ibid.*, p. 398, ll. 662–76.

4. *Ibid.*, p. 399, ll. 726–42.

5. Geoffrey H. Hartman, *Wordsworth's Poetry, 1787–1814* (New Haven, 1964), p. 363, n. 28.

6. Frederick A. Pottle, "The Eye and the Object," in *Wordsworth: Centenary Studies*, ed. Gilbert T. Dunklin (Princeton, 1951), p. 39.

7. *The Complete Poetical Works of Percy Bysshe Shelley*, ed. Thomas Hutchinson (London, 1961), p. 414, ll. 91–110.

8. *Opus Posthumous*, ed. Samuel French Morse (New York, 1957), p. 47.

9. *Letters of Wallace Stevens*, ed. Holly Stevens (New York, 1966), p. 367.

## · BLAKE'S MILTONIC MOMENT ·

1. Harold Bloom, *The Visionary Company* (New York, 1963), p. 3. See further, D. Saurat, *Blake and Milton* (London, 1935), *passim*; S. Foster Damon,*William Blake, His Philosophy and Symbols* (Boston, 1924), chap. xxvi.

2. On Wordsworth's affinities with Milton, see H. J. C. Grierson, *Milton and Wordsworth* (Cambridge, 1937), *passim*.

3. Herbert Read, *Wordsworth* (London, 1958), Introduction, p. 25.

4. *The Prelude*, Book I, 464–68. Quotations from this poem are from *Wordsworth's Prelude*, ed. E. de Selincourt, 2nd ed. (Oxford, 1959).

5. Book VI, 155–57.

6. "That by labour and intent study... I might perhaps leave something so written to aftertimes, as they should not willingly let it die" (*Works* [New York, 1931], III, 236).

7. *Ibid.*, III, 230; IV, 340.

8. Book VI, 396; Book X, 502 (see de Selincourt *ad loc.*).

9. Book X, 452–53.

10. I am indebted at this point to an unpublished essay by D. H. Hirsch analyzing "A Slumber Did My Spirit Seal."

11. *Samson Agonistes*, l. 85.

12. David V. Erdman, *Blake: Prophet Against Empire* (Princeton, 1954), pp. 8 f.

13. Milton's supposed debt to the kabbalah has been much exaggerated. He was primarily interested in and influenced by the nonoccult branches of Hebraism. See, by the present author, "Hebraic Style and Motifs in Paradise Lost," in *Language and Style in Milton*, ed. T. H. Shawcross and R. Emma (New York, 1967).

14. Blake's knowledge of the kabbalah was derived from such intermediate and inaccurate sources as Jakob Böhme, Emanuel Swedenborg, and Richard Clarke. The influence of the earlier writers Robert Fludd, Thomas Vaughan, and Knorr von Rosenroth is more doubtful, but Blake may well have got hold of their ideas at second hand through the occult circles in which he moved.

On the kabbalistic side of Blake, see D. Saurat, *Blake and Modern Thought* (London, 1929), pp. 98–106; and Désirée Hirst, *Hidden Riches* (London, 1964), *passim*. The former study is insufficiently critical; it attempts to relate everything interesting in Blake to the kabbalah; the latter, while well-informed on eighteenth-century occultism, fails to keep attention focused on the main nerve of Blake's poetry. I think Blake's chief kabbalistic positions may be set out as follows:

(a) He adopted the dialectical philosophy of the kabbalah, especially its doctrine of evil as part of the interior divine realm and necessary for the emergence of the good. In this sense, *The Marriage of Heaven and Hell* is Blake's most kabbalistic book. Blake applied this notion to history (cf. Erdman, p. 11).

(b) He adopted the notion of a primordial catastrophe, a pre-Adamic Fall, from which God, Man, and Nature still suffer. Here the *Zohar* links up with the teachings of the Gnostics. (Cf. G. Scholem, *Major Trends in Jewish Mysticism* [New York, 1941], pp. 236–38.)

(c) The notion of the exile of the *Shekhinah*, or female part of the divinity, from its male partner gives us the germ of Blake's system of Spectres and Emanations.

(d) The later kabbalah stresses the responsibility and power of the adept who could through his acts and prayers repair the metaphysical breaches in the universe. For Blake this task was performed by inspired poetry (see below).

(e) The doctrine of *Adam Kadmon* (see Scholem, p. 215) or the primordial Adam who "anciently contain'd in his mighty limbs all things in Heaven & Earth" is referred to by Blake in his address "To the Jews" (*J* 27, *K* 649). Here is the origin of Blake's image of the Giant Albion. This important kabbalistic doctrine is considerably distorted by Blake in the interests of his more radical humanism. The kabbalah is ultimately interested in God: Blake, in Man.

15. See Kathleen Raine, "Who Made the Tyger?" *Encounter*, II, No. 6 (June, 1954), 43–50.

16. See note 14 (d) above.

17. Cf. Hirst, pp. 158, 274.

18. Cf. Erdman, p. 291.

19. Northrop Frye, *Fearful Symmetry: A Study of William Blake* (Princeton, 1947), p. 159.

20. *Works*, IV, 340. Italics added: "*that . . . Sion.*"

21. Cf. Blake's letter to Hayley of 28 May 1804 (*K* 845).

22. Damon, p. 172.

23. Cf., by the present author, *Jerusalem and Albion: The Hebraic Factor in Seventeenth Century Literature* (London and New York, 1964), pp. 12–14.

24. *Works*, IV, 339.

25. Damon interestingly suggests an affinity with the symbolism of Thomas Vaughan (*op. cit.*, p. 417).

26. "Little Gidding," Sec. I.

27. *Ibid.*, Sec. V.

28. See Harold Bloom, *Blake's Apocalypse* (Garden City, N.Y., 1965), pp. 334 ff.

29. *Ibid.*, p. 402; cf. also *The Visionary Company*, p. 102. Bloom does in both books recognize the differences between Milton's God and the Divine Humanity posited by Blake, but he does not recognize that these differences are what render a theodicy impossible for Blake.

30. On this aspect of Blake, see, for instance, M. Roston, *Prophet and Poet* (London, Boston, and Evanston, Ill., 1965), p. 160.

31. Cf. *Blake's Apocalypse*, p. 390, and *The Visionary Company*, p. 129, where he speaks of "the dialogical image of mutual confrontation" of Los and Albion in *Jerusalem*.

32. *Op. cit.*, p. 401.

33. *Blake's Apocalypse*, pp. 378–80.

34. Cf. *Paradise Lost*, III, 5: "Bright effluence of bright essence increate."

35. Book XIV, 377–78; 379–84.


· BLAKE AND THE "PROGRESS OF POESY" ·


1. See, especially, Harold Bloom, *Blake's Apocalypse* (Garden

City, N.Y., 1963), pp. 3–8, and Robert Gleckner, "Blake's Seasons," *Studies in English Literature*, V (Summer, 1965), 533–51. Gleckner refines M. Lowery's *Windows of the Morning* (New Haven, 1940) and approaches the complexity of Blake's season poems mainly through "his deliberate warping, reshaping, or inverting of poetic traditions . . . a technique which became more and more characteristic of him." His remarks on the parodistic element in "To Winter" (pp. 547–51) anticipate my own.

2. In Akenside's "Inscriptions," apparently the only series of blank verse lyrics before Blake, the measure clearly points to the classical source. Thomson's blank verse is not especially unconventional, *The Seasons* being a didactic (*Georgics*-inspired) poem.

3. See Milton's note on "The Verse" prefacing *Paradise Lost*. In a prefatory note to *Jerusalem* concerning the measure in which the poem is written, Blake rejects even blank verse as not unfettered enough. But this is some twenty-five years later.

4. For these remarks on the Progress poem and on the Progress of Poesy, cf. René Wellek, *The Rise of English Literary History* (Chapel Hill, N.C., 1941), and R. H. Griffith, "The Progress Pieces of the Eighteenth Century," *Texas Review*, V (1920), 218–29. A second Progress theory, discussed below, emphasized a North-South movement. See also Northrop Frye, *Fearful Symmetry* (1947), pp. 179–82.

5. Wellek, p. 193.

6. For "western isle," cf. Collins, "Ode to Peace," st. 4. It is significant that Hölderlin, who inherited the same mythology of history (see, e.g., his description of the flight of the eagle in "Germania," which is a Progress of Poesy from East to West), will also become involved, as prophetic poet, in a so-called *abendländische Wendung* which exactly parallels the *turn* ("Look homeward . . . ") attempted by Milton and then by Blake. The remarks made throughout this essay on the problem of mediation can provide a link between German and English Romanticism that is relatively comprehensive. That Hölderlin considered Homer rather than Virgil the first literary "mediator" is a significant but slight difference in the context of this larger unity of concern.

7. Erwin Panofsky, "Et in Arcadia Ego," *Meaning in the Visual Arts* (New York, 1955), pp. 300 ff. It was Dante, of course, who

already understood, and transformed, this mediating function of Virgil's.

8. Blake's Summer is asked to sit "beside our springs," to "throw thy / Silk draperies off" and "rush into the stream"; while Autumn, "stained / With the blood of the grape," is invited to "pass not, but sit / Beneath my shady roof." By "parody" I mean a translation of the "translation" motif that subverts its original meaning: the motif is made to remind us of the free, or "bacchic," nature of the poetical spirit.

9. "To Morning" (*Poetical Sketches*) is an especially strong mingling of classical and Hebraic, in favor of the latter.

10. This also has traditional support in the conception of Hesperus as evening *and* morning star *and* Venus.

11. I.e., Ossian, the Eddas, "Northern Antiquities." The contents of *Poetical Sketches* are pretty evenly divided between homage to the Elizabethans (particularly Shakespeare) and to the North in the form of ballads and Ossianic paraphrases.

12. Thomson is by no means a pure apologist for the North. See Alan D. McKillop's account of his treatment, throughout *The Seasons*, of the conflict between primitivism and progress: *The Background of Thomson's Seasons* (Minneapolis, 1942), pp. 106 ff. The theme of progress is a major concern of the poem.

13. See Thor J. Beck, *Northern Antiquities in French Learning and Literature* (New York, 1934), and McKillop, pp. 109 ff.

14. Another striking instance of parody in *Poetical Sketches*, which directly involves the Progress of Liberty from Troy to England, is the Minstrel's song at the end of "King Edward the Third." See David V. Erdman's interpretation in *Blake: Prophet Against Empire* (Princeton, 1954), pp. 69–70.

## · BLAKE AND SHELLEY ·

1. So identified by Gilchrist. See Alexander Gilchrist, *The Life of William Blake, with Selections from His Poems and Other Writings: A New and Enlarged Edition Illustrated from Blake's Own Works, with Additional Letters and a Memoir of the Author* (London, 1880), I, 202–3.

2. S. Foster Damon in *A Blake Dictionary* (Providence, 1965), *s.v.* "Oxford, Bard of."

3. See Geoffrey H. Hartman, *Wordsworth's Poetry, 1787–1814* (New Haven & London, 1964), p. 233.

4. See David V. Erdman, *Blake: Prophet Against Empire* (Princeton, 1954), p. 196; John Middleton Murry, *William Blake* (New York and London, 1933), pp. 99–100; Harold Bloom, *Blake's Apocalypse* (Garden City, N.Y., 1963), pp. 155–56.

5. Bloom, p. 156.

6. Northrop Frye, *Fearful Symmetry: A Study of William Blake* (Princeton, 1947), p. 135.

7. See James A. Notopoulous, *The Platonism of Shelley* (Durham, N.C., 1949), pp. 186–88; and Neville Rogers, *Shelley at Work* (Oxford, 1956), pp. 68–70.

8. D. H. Lawrence, *Reflections on the Death of a Porcupine*, "Him with His Tail in His Mouth" (Bloomington, Ind., 1963), p. 127.

9. See Damon, *Blake Dictionary, s.v.* "Jehovah."

10. See Frye, p. 138.

11. *Unpublished Letters of Samuel Taylor Coleridge, Including Certain Letters Republished from Original Sources*, ed. by Earl Leslie Griggs (New Haven, 1933), II, 128–29.

12. Erich Neumann, *The Origins and History of Consciousness* (New York, 1962), p. 37.

13. Neumann, p. 105.

· WILLIAM BLAKE AND D. H. LAWRENCE ·

1. F. R. Leavis, quoted in *The Letters of D. H. Lawrence*, ed. A. Huxley (London, 1932), p. x.

2. *Ibid.*, p. xviii.

3. Constantine N. Stavrou, "William Blake and D. H. Lawrence," *University of Kansas City Review*, XXII (1956), 235–40.

4. Eugene Goodheart, *The Utopian Vision of D. H. Lawrence* (Chicago, 1963), p. 168.

5. E. T. (Jessie Chambers), *D. H. Lawrence, a Personal Record*, 2nd ed. (London, 1965), pp. 62–63, 101.

6. D. H. Lawrence, *Studies in Classic American Literature* (New York, 1963), pp. 79, 82.

7. *The Collected Letters of D. H. Lawrence*, ed. H. T. Moore (London, 1962), p. 872.

8. *Phoenix: The Posthumous Papers of D. H. Lawrence* (London, 1936), p. 560.

9. *Ibid.*, p. 137.

10. See *Women in Love* (London, 1921), chap. viii.

11. *Collected Letters*, p. 702.

12. *Phoenix*, p. 480.

13. D. H. Lawrence, *Selected Essays* (London, 1950), p. 69.

14. *Lady Chatterley's Lover* (New York, 1957), pp. 180–81.

15. D. H. Lawrence, *Assorted Articles* (London, 1930), p. 23.

16. *Ibid.*, pp. 99, 100, 104.

17. *A D. H. Lawrence Miscellany*, ed. H. T. Moore (Carbondale, Ill., 1959), p. 86.

18. *Collected Letters*, p. 282.

19. D. H. Lawrence, *Fantasia of the Unconscious* (London, 1933), pp. 10, 11.

20. H. M. Daleski, *The Forked Flame: A Study of D. H. Lawrence* (London, 1965), p. 18.

21. E. Cassirer, *An Essay on Man* (New Haven, 1925), p. 77.

22. *Phoenix*, p. 295.

23. "The Crown," in *Reflections on the Death of a Porcupine* (Philadelphia, 1925), p. 3.

24. *The Complete Poems of D. H. Lawrence*, ed. V. de S. Pinto and Warren Roberts (London and New York, 1964), p. 348.

25. Middleton Murry, *William Blake* (London, 1933), pp. 165–71.

26. See *Women in Love*, pp. 15, 222, 267, 286.

27. *Ibid.*, pp. 238–39.

28. *Ibid.*, p. 493.

29. *Ibid.*, p. 243.

30. *Ibid.*, p. 217.

31. *Ibid.*, p. 506.

32. See *FZ* iii, *E* 319–23.

33. *Women in Love*, p. 225.

34. *Ibid.*, p. 452.

35. *Ibid.*, p. 481.

36. *Ibid.* The actual title of the picture by Blake to which Lawrence refers here is "The Ghost of a Flea." There are two pictures by Blake with this title. One of them, a pencil drawing of the head of the monster, was among the "Visionary Heads" which Blake drew for John Varley about 1819 (see *The Pencil Drawings of William Blake,* ed. G. Keynes [London, 1927], No. 49). This drawing is now in the Tate Gallery, London. Blake also made a tempera painting of a full length figure of the creature, which was in the Graham Robertson collection and was acquired by the Tate Gallery in 1948. It was exhibited at the Tate in 1913 when Lawrence could have seen it. I think, however, that it is much more probable that it was the drawing which he had in mind when he wrote this passage. There is an engraving of it in Alexander Gilchrist's *Life of William Blake* (London, 1880), I, 255. A copy of this book is in the Nottingham Public Library. It was acquired by the Library in 1893, and would, therefore, have been available for Lawrence when he was a student at the old Nottingham University College in 1906–8. The library was in the same building as the college and was used by the students, who had no library of their own at that date. The engraving in Gilchrist's book with its curved proboscis and savage, sneering mouth, looks rather like a caricature of a very sinister Prussian or Central European type and may well have played a part in suggesting to Lawrence the character of Loerke.

37. *The Plumed Serpent* (London, 1926), p. 83.

38. *Complete Poems*, p. 637.

39. *Phoenix*, p. 703.

40. *Collected Letters*, p. 1045.

41. *Ibid.*, p. 1046.

42. *The Tales of D. H. Lawrence* (London, 1934), p. 614.

43. *Women in Love*, p. 217.


· THE EVOLUTION OF BLAKE'S
LARGE COLOR PRINTS OF 1795 ·


1. The following prints of the twelve subjects are known to the author. Those in the Tate Gallery are reproduced in Martin Butlin,

*William Blake (1757–1827), A Catalogue of the Works of William Blake in the Tate Gallery* (London, 1957), Pls. 9–13. Reproductions of the other prints are given in the list below:

"Elohim creating Adam." Tate Gallery, London.

"Satan exulting over Eve." Gregory Bateson (repr. Geoffrey Keynes, *William Blake's Illustrations to the Bible* [London, 1957], Pl. 9a); John Craxton (repr. *Apropos, No. 4: English and French Romantic Painting* [London, n.d. (1946)], p. 1).

"God judging Adam." Tate Gallery; Metropolitan Museum of Art, New York (repr. *The Burlington Magazine*, C, 1958, p. 45, Fig. 4); Mrs. William T. Tonner (repr. *The Burlington Magazine*, C, 1958, p. 45, Fig. 5).

"Lamech and his Two Wives." Tate Gallery; private collection, Great Britain.

"Nebuchadnezzar." Tate Gallery; Minneapolis Institute of Fine Arts (repr. Keynes, *William Blake's Illustrations to the Bible*, Pl. 84c); Museum of Fine Arts, Boston (repr. exhibition catalogue, *The Romantic Movement*, John Herron Museum of Art, Indianapolis, February–April, 1965, No. 23).

"Naomi entreating Ruth and Orpah to return to the Land of Moab." Victoria and Albert Museum, London (repr. Thomas Wright, *The Life of William Blake* [Olney, 1929], Vol. I, Pl. 37); Sir Geoffrey Keynes (repr. Keynes, *William Blake's Illustrations to the Bible*, Pl. 54a ii).

"Christ appearing to the Apostles after the Resurrection." Yale University Art Gallery, New Haven (repr. Keynes, *William Blake's Illustrations to the Bible*, Pl. 151b); National Gallery of Art, Washington (Lessing J. Rosenwald Collection); Tate Gallery.

"The House of Death." Tate Gallery; Fitzwilliam Museum, Cambridge, Eng.; British Museum, London (repr. Laurence Binyon, *The Drawings and Engravings of William Blake* [London, 1922], Pl. 31).

"Pity." Tate Gallery; Metropolitan Museum (repr. exhibition catalogue, *William Blake*, Andrew Dickson White Museum of Art, Cornell University, Ithaca, February–March, 1965, p. 29); private collection, Great Britain.

"Hecate." Tate Gallery; National Gallery of Scotland, Edinburgh (repr. National Gallery of Scotland, *Illustrations* [1952], p. 11); Henry E. Huntington Library, San Marino (repr. C. H. Collins

Baker and R. R. Wark, *Catalogue of William Blake's Drawings and Paintings in the Huntington Library* [San Marino, 1957], Pl. XXXV).

"The Good and Evil Angels." Tate Gallery; Mr. and Mrs. John Hay Whitney (repr. Darrell Figgis, *The Paintings of William Blake* [London, 1925], Pl. 71).

"Newton." Tate Gallery; Mrs. William T. Tonner (repr. sale catalogue, Parke–Bernet, New York, 2 Nov. 1938, Pl. 9).

2. Martin Butlin, "Blake's 'God Judging Adam' Rediscovered," *The Burlington Magazine*, CVII (1965), 86–89.

3. There is a short discussion of this complex relationship in my article "Blake's 'Vala, or the Four Zoas' and a new Water-colour in the Tate Gallery," *The Burlington Magazine*, CVI (1964), 382.

4. The water colors are in the collections of George Goyder (repr. Keynes, *William Blake's Illustrations to the Bible*, Pl. 64) and the Cecil Higgins Museum, Bedford (repr. Anthony Blunt, *The Art of William Blake* [New York, 1959], Pl. 32a) respectively.

5. Both occur in *The Marriage of Heaven and Hell*, Pls. 4 and 24. There is also an anticipation of "Newton" in *There is No Natural Religion*, Pl. 10.

6. For a very tentative summary of the possible significance of the individual prints in the series see my Tate Gallery Little Book, *William Blake* (London, 1966), n.p.

7. The word "fresco" appears with Blake's signature on five of the prints: "God judging Adam," Metropolitan Museum; "Naomi entreating Ruth," Victoria and Albert Museum; "Christ appearing to the Apostles," National Gallery of Art, Washington (Lessing J. Rosenwald Collection); "Hecate," National Gallery of Scotland; "Newton," Mrs. William T. Tonner. For Blake's use of the word for his temperas see below.

For the technique of the color prints see Frederick Tatham's account as amended by W. Graham Robertson in his edition of Alexander Gilchrist's *Life of William Blake* (London and New York, 1907), pp. 405–6; also Ruthven Todd, "The Techniques of William Blake's Illuminated Printing," *Print Collector's Quarterly*, XXIX (November, 1948), 25–36.

8. The idea that one application of color sufficed for more than

one print was first suggested by a comparison of the three versions of "God judging Adam"; see Martin Butlin, "The Bicentenary of William Blake," *The Burlington Magazine*, C (1958), 42.

9. The technique of these tiny books deserves a study in itself, standing apart from the general development examined in this article. It seems to have involved an alternative form of color printing, by a single impression from plates inked in up to three colors.

10. Geoffrey Keynes and Edwin Wolf 2nd, *William Blake's Illuminated Books, A Census* (New York, 1953), Copy O. See my review of the Blake Trust's facsimile of Copy C in *The Burlington Magazine*, CII (1960), 546.

11. Keynes and Wolf, Copies A, B, and C.

12. Keynes and Wolf, p. 35.

13. Keynes and Wolf, Copy G, reproduced in facsimile by the Trianon Press for the Blake Trust (London, 1958).

14. Keynes and Wolf suggest that Pls. ii and 1 of Copy A were painted rather than printed in opaque pigments, but inspection of the book, now in the collection of Mr. and Mrs. Paul Mellon, is not altogether conclusive: the frontispiece seems definitely to have been color-printed.

15. Keynes and Wolf, Copy A.

16. *The Marriage of Heaven and Hell*, Keynes and Wolf, Copy D, and, perhaps, *Europe*, Copy A.

17. Keynes and Wolf, Copy D. See also the plates from *Urizen* in the British Museum's copy of the so-called *Small Book of Designs*, Keynes and Wolf, Copy A.

18. The Huntington Library color print is reproduced in Geoffrey Keynes, *Engravings by William Blake: The Separate Plates* (Dublin, 1956), Pl. 22, and in Collins Baker and Wark, Pl. XXXIV. The British Museum print, acquired in 1966, is slightly smaller, $7\frac{3}{16}$ x $9\frac{11}{16}$ inches as against $7\frac{15}{16}$ x $10\frac{3}{4}$, showing that Blake expanded his design when he color-printed it.

19. Repr. Keynes, *Engravings by William Blake: The Separate Plates*, Pl. 17.

20. See Keynes and Wolf, p. 85.

21. These include the designs from *Urizen*, Pl. 5, in the Miriam Stark Lutcher Library, University of Texas, Austin, and *Urizen*,

Pl. 9, at Wellesley College, Wellesley, Mass. In addition the Tate Gallery owns a copy of the design from *Urizen*, Pl. 3, but this seems to have been colored by hand in water color, not color-printed (see Butlin, *William Blake (1757–1827), A Catalogue of the Works of William Blake in the Tate Gallery*, p. 38, No. 10, repr. Pl. 6).

22. Keynes and Wolf, Copies A (ex collection Messrs. Evans) and D (ex collections Thomas Butts and F. T. Palgrave).

23. William Blake, *A Descriptive Catalogue* (London, 1809); see especially pp. 6–7 (reprinted *K* 566).

## · BLAKE'S 1795 COLOR PRINTS: AN INTERPRETATION ·

1. Robert Rosenblum, "The International Style of 1800: A Study in Linear Abstraction" (unpublished doctoral dissertation, New York University, April, 1956), pp. 100–105 and *passim.*

2. See Sir Anthony Blunt, "Blake's 'Ancient of Days'—The Symbolism of the Compasses," *Warburg Journal*, II (1938–39), 53–63; Jean H. Hagstrum, *William Blake, Poet and Painter* (Chicago, 1964), pp. 23–75; Piloo Nanavutty, "Blake and Emblem Literature," *Warburg Journal*, XV (1952), 258–61.

3. Karl Popper, *The Open Society and Its Enemies* (London, 1945), Vol. I, chap. ix and *passim.*

4. These images are presented, respectively, in (1) *Urizen*, Pl. 27; *Visions of the Daughters of Albion*, frontispiece; "The Garden of Love"; *Europe*, Pl. 15; (2) *Songs of Experience*, title page; *Urizen*, Pl. 26; *Marriage*, Pl. 21; "Infant Sorrow"; (3) *Europe*, Preludium; *Visions*, Pl. 4; *Europe*, Pl. 10; *Urizen*, Pl. 17; *Europe*, frontispiece; (4) *Urizen*, Pls. 10 and 13; Pls. 22 and 23; (5) *Visions*, frontispiece, title page, Pls. 4, 8; *Urizen*, Pl. 6; (6) *America*, Pls. 1, 5, 14; *Visions*, Pl. 3; *America*, Pl. 4; *Europe*, Preludium; (7) *Europe*, frontispiece; *Urizen*, title page; *America*, Pls. 4, 14.

5. These images are presented, respectively, in (1) "The Divine Image"; *Thel*, title page; *Visions*, Pl. 4; (2) "The Ecchoing Green," Pl. 2; *America*, Pl. 15; (3) *Songs of Innocence and of Experience*, title page; *America*, Pl. 11; (4) *America*, Pl. 2; *Visions*, title page.

6. *The Letters of William Blake,* ed. Geoffrey Keynes (London, 1956).

7. Blunt, *The Art of William Blake* (New York, 1959), p. 58.

8. Martin Butlin, "Blake's 'God Judging Adam' Rediscovered," *The Burlington Magazine,* CVII (February, 1965), 86–89.

9. Joseph H. Wicksteed, *Blake's Vision of the Book of Job* (London, 1910), Pl. 2 and *passim.*

· BLAKE'S *NIGHT THOUGHTS* ·

1. The opportunity to study the original water colors for *Night Thoughts* was given me in the form of a Summer Faculty Fellowship from the University of California, Berkeley. The work was made possible by the cooperation of the British Museum Print Room, its curator and staff. I have received points of information from Mr. Edward Rose, Mr. Martin Butlin, Miss Amy Tsuji, and Sir John Summerson. To all these, my thanks. Unless otherwise indicated, quotations from Young are from the pages inlaid on Blake's water colors; these pages are from the first editions of the individual Nights, published for R. Dodsley from 1742 to 1745. These editions will be cited according to Night and page number (e.g., i, 16). Arabic numbers in my text refer to the number of the water color in the series, which is abbreviated as *NT.* The engraved designs in the edition published by Richard Edwards in 1797 are indicated by the abbreviation *Edw* followed by the page number. Thus the title page to Night Three, for example, is designated 78, *Edw* 43. In referring to *Vala* or *The Four Zoas,* I use either title without distinction.

2. Prefixed to *The Dramatic Works of Shakespeare,* ed. George Steevens (London, 1803), I, n.p. Blake himself engraved one of these illustrations (after Opie) in 1799: see G. E. Bentley and M. K. Nurmi, *A Blake Bibliography* (Minneapolis, 1964), p. 152.

3. See David V. Erdman, *Blake: Prophet Against Empire* (Princeton, 1954), pp. 405–6.

4. As reprinted by Sir Geoffrey Keynes in "Blake's Illustrations to Young's 'Night Thoughts,' " *Blake Studies* (London, 1949), p. 62.

5. William T. Whitely, *Artists and Their Friends in England, 1700–1799* (London and Boston, 1928), II, 71–72; *DNB*, *s.v.* "Boydell."

6. T. W. Hanson, "Edwards of Halifax," *Papers, Reports, &c., Read Before the Halifax Antiquarian Society* (Halifax, 1912), p. 171.

7. J. Comyns Carr, while observing that "The whole poem is here passed under the artist's strange process of interpretation," does not say anything about what that interpretation was ("William Blake," *The Cornhill*, XXXI [1875], 729). Frederic Shields, in his sensitive and enthusiastic "Descriptive Notes of the Designs to Young's 'Night Thoughts,'" does not make any use of what was known even in his time about the symbolism of the Prophetic Books. (His essay was published as an appendix to the second edition of Alexander Gilchrist's *Life of William Blake* [London, 1880], II, 289–307.) There are a few remarks on the subject in Keynes's notes on the thirty pictures published in *Illustrations to Young's Night Thoughts* (Cambridge, Mass., 1927); in H. M. Margoliouth, "Blake's Drawings for Young's *Night Thoughts*," *Review of English Studies*, V (1954), 47–54; and in Jean H. Hagstrum, *William Blake, Poet and Painter* (Chicago, 1964), pp. 121–23.

8. "Worldliness and Other-Worldliness; the Poet Young," *Essays and Leaves from a Notebook* (Edinburgh and London, 1874), p. 67.

9. As noted by Gerald E. Bentley, Jr., "Blake and Young," *Notes and Queries*, CXCIX (1954), 529–30.

10. S. Foster Damon, *William Blake: His Philosophy and Symbols* (Boston and New York, 1924), p. 86, n. 4; *A Blake Dictionary* (Providence, 1965), *s.v.* "Young."

11. Keynes, "Blake's Library," *The Times Literary Supplement*, 6 Nov. 1959, p. 648.

12. See Bentley, "Additions to Blake's Library," *Bulletin of the New York Public Library*, LXIV (1960), 601, n. 7.

13. Michael J. Tolley ("*The Book of Thel* and *Night Thoughts*," *Bulletin of the New York Public Library*, LXIX [1965], 375–85) argues that Blake's lines are actually closer in wording to a passage in James Hervey's *Meditations Among the Tombs*, which in turn echoes Young.

14. *Blake Dictionary*, *s.v.* "Young."

15. (London, 1759), pp. 60, 84–85.

16. *William Blake,* p. 121.

17. *The Farington Diary,* ed. James Greig (London, n.d.), I, 151.

18. K. A. Esdaile, "An Early Appreciation of William Blake" (translation with comments of Robinson's "William Blake, Kunstler, Dichter und religiöser Schwärmer," published in the *Vaterlandisches Museum,* Hamburg, 1811), *The Library,* 3rd Ser., V (1914), 248–49.

19. (London), p. 734; see also Dibdin's *Reminiscences of a Literary Life* (London, 1836), II, 788.

20. Edward Bulwer-Lytton, "Conversations with an Ambitious Student in Ill Health," *New Monthly Magazine,* XXIX (1830), 518–19.

21. Matthew Pilkington, *A General Dictionary of Painters,* 2nd ed. (London, 1840), p. 52, col. 2.

22. *William Blake,* 2nd ed. (London, 1868), p. 28; later, writing to R. H. Horne in 1882, Swinburne described them more favorably as "a most lovely and wonderful set of coloured designs...some of them in his best style, alternating the flower-like beauty of the Songs of Innocence with the sublime imagination of that Marriage of Heaven and Hell which I venture to think the greatest thing produced by the eighteenth century—at least in England" (*The Swinburne Letters,* ed. Cecil Y. Lang [New Haven, 1960], IV, 285).

23. *William Blake,* trans. J. Lewis May (London, 1928), p. 36.

24. "William Blake and His Illustrations to *The Divine Comedy,*" *Essays* (New York, 1924), p. 147. Of the *NT* illustrations themselves, Yeats wrote (p. 153), "... the great sprawling figures, a little wearisome even with the luminous colours of the original water-colour, became nearly intolerable in plain black and white."

25. This is also the scene in the frontispiece to *The Book of Urizen.*

26. *Op. cit.,* p. 56.

27. In *K* the third word of l. 18 is "where," but I have found this to be incorrect; see my note *"Europe* iii:18," *Blake Newsletter,* No. 3 (15 Dec. 1967), pp. 16, 18.

28. The "Explanation" is on a single leaf following the numbered pages of Edw. Keynes (*Blake Studies,* p. 63) thinks Fuseli may have been the author. Bentley and Nurmi's *Blake Bibliography* assigns it

to Benjamin Heath Malkin on p. 4, but says "perhaps by Fuseli" on p. 167.

29. *Fearful Symmetry* (Princeton, 1947), p. 124.

30. See Erdman, *Blake*, pp. 288-89; and my "Method and Meaning in Blake's *Book of Ahania*," *Bulletin of the New York Public Library*, LXX (1966), 27-33.

31. "Blake's Drawings," p. 53.

32. *Blake Dictionary, s.v.* "Vala."

33. *William Blake's Designs for Gray's Poems*, ed. H. J. C. Grierson (London, 1922).

34. As identified by Shields, "Descriptive Notes," p. 294.

35. Bulwer-Lytton, "Conversations," p. 519.

36. From Francis Quarles' *Emblems, Divine and Moral* (London, 1718), p. 118; *OED, s.v.* "span." (Curiously Blakean is an example from Jeremy Taylor: "So must we take the measures of eternity by the span of a mans hand.")

37. This picture, engraved as *Edw* 70, much resembles Dante illustration 25, as Albert S. Roe has noted (*Blake's Illustrations to the Divine Comedy* [Princeton, 1953], p. 81), showing hell-hounds hunting destroyers of their own goods. Nimrod himself is the subject of Dante illustration 61. Roe discusses the Fallen World theme in the Dante series, particularly with respect to the *Inferno*, both extensively and persuasively.

38. Bulwer-Lytton, "Conversations," p. 519.

39. Alexander Pope, *An Essay on Man*, ed. Maynard Mack (New Haven and London, 1950), p. 17 (Epistle I, l. 33). See Arthur O. Lovejoy, *The Great Chain of Being* (Cambridge, Mass., 1936), pp. 204-7.

40. Another massy black chain is shown in *NT* 245; "Truth's ballance" is suspended from it. It weighs the materials imparted by Sense and Fancy, "*Underlings*" which Blake represents by a black and a golden disc at either end of the balance. Although the chain is much nearer to the radiant golden disc than it is to the black one, it is the former that Blake shows as sinking down.

41. *Paradise Lost*, VII, 225-27 (*The Works of John Milton*, ed. Frank Allen Patterson [New York, 1931], Vol. II, Part I, p. 219).

42. See *Blake Dictionary, s.v.* "Eyes of God."

43. *Illustrations to Young's Night Thoughts*, No. 19. The picture is also reproduced in Hagstrum, Pl. lxv.

44. *Blake Dictionary, s.v.* "Rahab."

45. See Jacob Bronowski, *William Blake: A Man Without a Mask* (London, 1944), pp. 51–52; and Erdman, *Blake,* pp. 193–207 and Plate VI.

46. Cf. Mic. 3:12; Jer. 26:18; see *Blake Dictionary, s.v.* "Plow."

47. Rev. 6:14; *FZ* ix: 14, 33 (*K* 357, 358).

48. *The Drawings and Engravings of William Blake* (London, 1922), p. 8.

· "THE THUNDER OF EGYPT" ·

1. *Laoc, K* 776.
For bibliographical details concerning works of Blake etched and published by himself, see Geoffrey Keynes and Edwin Wolf 2nd, *William Blake's Illuminated Books: A Census* (New York, 1953; hereinafter "Keynes and Wolf"); all references to the Prophetic Books, other than quotations of text, will be to the plates as numbered and described in this work.

2. For a detailed discussion of this drawing, see Albert S. Roe, *Blake's Illustrations to the Divine Comedy* (Princeton, 1953), pp. 193–96.

3. *Paradiso,* cantos xxxi–xxxiii. The substitution of the sunflower for the rose, as well as the nakedness of the figure, indicates that Blake here sees confusion on Dante's part between Divine Love and the selfish, possessive, and carnal aspects of love in the Fallen World.

4. Henry Crabb Robinson, *Reminiscences,* as reprinted in Arthur Symons, *William Blake* (London, 1907), p. 290.

5. This annotation is found on the drawing entitled "Homer, Bearing the Sword, and his Companions" (Roe, pp. 56–60). The penciled notes on this and other drawings of the Dante series are given in *K* 785–86.

6. S. Foster Damon, *William Blake, His Philosophy and Symbols* (Boston and New York, 1924), pp. 219–20.

7. The most complete and recent description of the various edi-

tions of this work, and of the plates engraved by Blake, will be found in G. E. Bentley, Jr., and Martin K. Nurmi, *A Blake Bibliography* (Minneapolis, 1964), pp. 106-8. See also Archibald G. B. Russell, *The Engravings of William Blake* (London, Boston, and New York, 1912), pp. 158-59, and Geoffrey Keynes, *A Bibliography of William Blake* (New York, 1921), pp. 234-35, 239, 245-46.

8. A further discussion of "Fertilization of Egypt" will be found in Geoffrey Keynes, *Blake Studies* (London, 1949), pp. 67-68, Pl. 21. Fuseli's and Blake's sketches of the design are reproduced in Anthony Blunt, *The Art of William Blake* (New York, 1959), Pl. 21 a and b. Keynes is, however, in error in stating that the figure with outstretched arms does not appear in Fuseli's drawing, and this error has unfortunately been perpetuated by Bentley and Nurmi (*op. cit.*, p. 108). Although the reproduction in Blunt is very faint, the figure can be discerned; the present author has definitely confirmed its presence by an examination of the original drawing at the British Museum.

9. It should be noted that the inscription on the Fuseli drawing is in Frederick Tatham's handwriting, and must therefore have been made many years after the drawing (Tatham was born in 1805 and became acquainted with Blake about 1825, the year of Fuseli's death). Its ascription to Fuseli by Tatham should, therefore, be regarded with caution; it could conceivably have been begun by Fuseli with later additions made by Blake, or even be entirely by Blake regardless of the caption. While the drawing is so sketchy as to make any stylistic judgment highly speculative, the present author's opinion would lean toward attributing the drawing to Blake in spite of Tatham's inscription; certainly the more lightly penciled portions are very characteristic of Blake. Such speculations aside, however, the critical point is that the finished design, as evolved in Blake's drawing and published in the engraving, can be interpreted in a manner wholly consistent with Blake's personal symbolic vocabulary, as the following discussion will demonstrate.

10. The nearest prototype in Fuseli's work for the principal figure of "Fertilization of Egypt" is the diminutive form which stands on the hand of the ass-headed Bottom in the painting of "Titania and Bottom," now in the Tate Gallery, London. This figure, raising its

arms as if performing an act of reverence, is closely linked, in both form and symbolism, with the illustration to Darwin's poem. The painting was commmissioned by Alderman John Boydell and was first exhibited when his Shakespeare Gallery opened in Pall Mall in May, 1789, two years before the publication of *The Economy of Vegetation*. Blake, whose friendship with Fuseli dated from 1780, must certainly have known this painting well. For a reproduction, see Arnold Federmann, *Johann Heinrich Füssli, Dichter und Maler* (Zurich and Leipzig, 1927), Tafel 4. The detail of the figure under discussion may be more clearly seen in reproductions of engravings of the subject: T. S. R. Boase, "Illustrations of Shakespeare's Plays in the Seventeenth and Eighteenth Centuries," *Journal of the Warburg and Courtauld Institutes*, X (1947), Pl. 30a, facing p. 103; Gert Schiff, *Johann Heinrich Füssli, Ein Sommernachtstraum* (Stuttgart, 1961), Pl. 4.

The pose of the principal figure is also reminiscent of that in the drawing of an executioner by Fuseli in the Staatliche Kunstsammlung, Weimar (repr. Frederick Antal, *Fuseli Studies* [London, 1956], Pl. 15a), but it will be observed that in the latter the elongated proportions are very characteristic of Fuseli, while the Anubis of the engraving is more compact. The same pose is used by Blake with tremendous impact in the water color from Revelation, "The Red Dragon and the Woman Clothed with the Sun," now in the Brooklyn Museum (repr. Blunt, Pl. 38a; also Geoffrey Keynes, *William Blake's Illustrations to the Bible: A Catalogue* [London, 1957], Pl. 163b).

11. The entire passage, which commences with l. 24 of Pl. 12 and continues to the top of Pl. 14, is of the greatest significance, and should be consulted. Here and in subsequent quotations I have italicized words pertinent to the theme of Egypt.

12. *Jerusalem* 98:51, 91:44 (K 746, 738); also letter to Thomas Butts, 6 July 1803 (K 824), and one of the supplementary passages to *The Everlasting Gospel* (K 757).

13. The instrument appears in only the more sketchy of the two preparatory drawings in the British Museum, where it is faintly indicated in much larger scale than in the engraving. A sistrum appears beneath the paw of a sphinx, a creature associated by Blake

with the Female Will, in the handsome device designed and engraved by Gravelot on the title page of the first volume of Richard Pococke, *A Description of the East* (London, 1743). As will be discussed hereafter, Blake when an apprentice of Basire almost certainly knew this work. For Gravelot and Basire, see Blake's *Public Address* (*K* 594).

The President of the Aegyptian Society, founded in 1741 with Pococke as a member, had a sistrum laid before him to serve the purpose of a gavel. See letter of William Stukeley to Roger Gale, reprinted in *Publications of the Surtees Society*, LXXIII (1880), 325–26.

14. It is, of course, usual for Blake to have multiple meanings to his symbolism, so that the sistrum, as suggested here, is to be considered both as representative of the "arts degraded" and of their redeeming power.

15. *FZ* ii:389–90, *K* 290; letter to Thomas Butts, 6 July 1803 (*K* 823). For Blake's particular connotation of "states," see Roe, p. 23 n. An important passage in this connection is *Mil* 32:10–38.

16. *The Book of Urizen* is dated 1794. All of chap. ix, from which these lines are quoted (*K* 235–37), is of great interest in this context.

17. James Greig, ed., *The Farington Diary* (London, 1923), II, 103, entry for 28 May 1803 (italics mine). Fuseli had contacts with Darwin through the literary circle of Joseph Johnson, the bookseller and for a time an employer of Blake (Antal, pp. 78, 105 n.). David V. Erdman, *Blake, Prophet Against Empire* (Princeton, 1954), p. 141, postulates on the basis of a letter of 1791 from Johnson to Darwin (quoted in Keynes, *Blake Studies*, pp. 68–69) that Blake was personally known to Darwin; while the letter does not so state explicitly, the inference is certainly highly probable. Through Johnson Blake must certainly have known of the Lunar Society, of which Darwin was the organizer. For the suggestion that it is satirized in Blake's *An Island in the Moon,* see Bernard Blackstone, *English Blake* (Cambridge, 1949), pp. 18–27. Erdman (pp. 86–95) does not accept this view.

18. Canto iii, 56–58.

19. In a letter to Richard Phillips, publisher of *The Monthly*

*Magazine,* in which it appeared on 1 July 1806; the letter was pro-
voked by a criticism of Fuseli's "Ugolino" in *Bell's Weekly Mes-
senger* for 25 May (*K* 863–64).

20. Darwin's poem has been described as dealing with everything
from "the electric eel to the Apollo Belvedere" (James Venable
Logan, *The Poetry and Aesthetics of Erasmus Darwin* [Princeton,
1936], p. 116). The footnote quoted occurs in connection with a
remarkable passage, *Economy of Vegetation,* i, 345–58, which introduces the simile of the "electric kiss," of which Logan (p. 117 n.)
remarks, "a greater gaucherie would be difficult to find in all English
poetry." Darwin's previous footnote discusses the principle of "the
very sensible electrometer improved by Mr. Bennet," and "the
holy Halo" has reference to a second and equally inept simile in these
extraordinary lines.

21. The work referred to is Sir Joshua Reynolds' "Death of
Cardinal Beaufort," painted in 1789 for Boydell's Shakespeare Gallery. The original, now much darkened and repainted, is at Petworth
Castle (C. H. Collins Baker, *Catalogue of the Petworth Collection
of Pictures in the Possession of Lord Leconfield* [London, 1920],
No. 309, p. 106). The demon mentioned by Darwin is now invisible, but is clearly apparent in an engraving by Caroline Watson
published 25 Mar. 1790. In a later version of the engraving, dated
1 Aug. 1792, the demon has been obliterated, on the basis, we may
infer, of such criticisms as those cited by Darwin. The painting
was amusingly caricatured by James Gillray in a political satire of
1792, *Tom Paine's Nightly Pest* (repr. in *Hogarth and English
Caricature,* ed. F. D. Klingender [London and New York, 1944],
Pl. 31; see M. Dorothy George, *Catalogue of Political and Personal
Satires in the British Museum* [1935], Vol. VI, Nos. 8132 and 8137).

22. In view of this and of numerous other connections established
in the present essay with *The Botanic Garden,* as well as of the fact
that Blake engraved illustrations for it, it is highly probable that
the book was in his personal library and should be added to those
works already identified. The most recent listing of these will be
found in Bentley and Nurmi, pp. 195–212.

For an interesting discussion of the background which for a brief
period led to the enthusiastic reception of Darwin's poem, "with its

fantastic mingling of technical description and classical allegory," see Francis D. Klingender, *Art and the Industrial Revolution* (London, 1947), pp. 30–38.

23. In a letter of 14 May 1792, to Thomas Barrett, Horace Walpole wrote of this passage: "The twelve verses that by miracle describe and comprehend the creation of the universe out of chaos, are in my mind the most sublime passage in any author, or in any of the few languages with which I am acquainted" (*Letters*, ed. Mrs. Paget Toynbee [Oxford, 1905], XV, 110). Joseph Farington records that Walpole spoke of the same lines with similar enthusiasm at Strawberry Hill several years later (*Diary* I, 153, entry for 24 July 1796). Farington, however, heard a very different reaction from a younger generation a few years afterwards. The diary entry for 25 Mar. 1804 (II, 209), describes an evening at Sir George Beaumont's: "Coleridge said Dr. Darwin was a great *plagiarist*. 'He was like a pigeon picking up peas, and afterwards voiding them with excrementitious additions.'! " The verses do indeed put one strongly in mind of Joseph Addison's well-known hymn, "The spacious firmament on high," written in 1712.

24. Note the connotation in which Blake adopts Darwin's "salamanders."

25. Jacob Bryant, *A New System, or, an Analysis of Ancient Mythology: Wherein an Attempt is made to divest Tradition of Fable; and to reduce the Truth to its Original Purity*, 3 vols. (London, 1774–76).

26. See Bentley and Nurmi, pp. 103–4. The connection of the tailpiece of Bryant's work with Blake was first suggested by Russell, *Engravings*, p. 191, and developed by Ruthven Todd, *Tracks in the Snow* (New York, 1947), pp. 37–38, Pl. 12. Keynes, *Blake Studies*, pp. 42–45 and Pls. 10–12, took up the theme again and suggested that several other plates in this work also reveal connections with Blake.

27. Todd (pp. 29–56) establishes this connection in his article on "Blake and the Mythologists," but does not trace in detail the close relationship between Bryant's text and certain of Blake's major symbols, particularly with reference to Egypt, as is attempted here.

28. III, 291–367.

29. II, 321.

30. In the original edition the plate is inserted facing p. 242. It is reproduced in Keynes, *Blake Studies*, Pl. 10.

While considering the plates of this second volume of Bryant's *New System*, it is of interest to speculate that Blake's antipathy to the popular "dot & lozenge" manner of engraving may well have been aroused at this time. One of the few plates in Bryant's work not engraved by the Basire studio is a representation of a cameo, "finely engraved by Bartolozzi from a drawing of Cipriani" (p. v and Pl. XI, facing p. 394). With its simpering *putti* and "soft" technique, this plate is a perfect example of a style of art that was to be anathema to Blake for the rest of his life. After one of his most frustrating artistic disappointments, when the task of engraving his own designs to Robert Blair's *The Grave* was turned over to Luigi Schiavonetti after having been promised to him, Blake gave vent to his opinions in his notebook (see *Public Address, K* 591–94): "[Engraving] is drawing on copper, as Painting ought to be drawing on canvas or any other surface, & nothing Else....Engraving, by Losing drawing, has Lost all the character & all Expression, without which The Art is Lost....I do not Pretend to Engrave finer than Alb. Durer, Goltzius, Sadeler or Edelinck, but I do pretend to Engrave finer than Strange, Woolett, Hall or *Bartolozzi*, & all because I understand drawing which They understood not" (italics mine).

31. Reproduced in Todd, Pl. 12, and in Keynes, *Blake Studies*, Pl. 11.

32. Roe, pp. 139–41, and Pl. 72. Another striking example of the moon-shaped boat is to be found in the design at the top of *J* 24.

33. *New System*, II, 331.

34. II, 327.

35. II, 322, 323, 333–34.

36. Richard Pococke, L.L.D., F.R.S., *A Description of the East, and Some other Countries. Volume the First. Observations on Egypt* (London, 1743). The plate re-engraved in Basire's shop for Bryant's work is Pl. XLII, facing p. 108, "Hieroglyphical representations in The Mausoleum of Osymanduas." This plate depicts three sacred boats arranged one above another. The upper two are reproduced as

Pl. IV of Vol. I of Bryant's *New System*, facing p. 252. The upper section has the caption "The Ship of Isis Biprora with an Ark," and the lower is inscribed "The Ship of Isis and Image. From Pocock's Account of Egypt. Plate XLII." The plate is signed "Basire Sc." The third boat, which is found at the bottom of the Pococke plate, appears with the caption, "*Baris, sive Navis sacra Agyptiaca*," as Pl. III of Vol. II of Bryant's work, facing p. 230. It occupies the bottom portion of the page, beneath representations of two Hellenistic coins.

37. "*Juno Samia Selenitis cum peplo sacro*," Vol. II, Pl. VII, facing p. 344.

38. On the basis of the foregoing discussion, it would appear highly likely that a copy of Bryant's *New System* was in Blake's personal library and might well be a tentative addition to the list given by Bentley and Nurmi, pp. 195-212.

39. Geoffrey Keynes, *Pencil Drawings by William Blake* (London, 1927), Pl. 41; Martin Butlin, *A Catalogue of the Works of William Blake in the Tate Gallery* (London, 1957), p. 56 (No. 43) and Pl. 27; Kerrison Preston, ed., *The Blake Collection of W. Graham Robertson* (London, 1952), p. 223 (No. 112a).

40. For a full discussion (including an interpretation by Joseph Wicksteed) and reproductions of both known impressions, see Geoffrey Keynes, *Engravings by William Blake: the Separate Plates* (Dublin, 1956), pp. 38-39, Pls. 23 and 24. See also the catalogue of the exhibition of Blake's work held at the Philadelphia Museum of Art in 1939, repr. facing p. 159 and No. 24, p. 160.

41. Russell, pp. 89-90 (No. 22). For *America*, see the color reproduction published by the Trianon Press for the William Blake Trust in 1963.

42. Keynes and Wolf, pp. 34 and 37 (Copy D). This is the copy reproduced in color by the Trianon Press for the William Blake Trust in 1960, where the pyramids may be noted.

43. Russell (*loc. cit.*) pointed out the stylistic relation with *Jerusalem*. There are also some interesting relationships of detail; compare for instance the buried heads with the design at the bottom of Pl. 54 of *Jerusalem*, or the pose of the main figure with that on Pl. 95, which has distinct similarities, although in *Jerusalem* the figure is shown in rear view.

44. Russell, of course, knew only the version engraved for publication by Luigi Schiavonetti. While he did, in fact, suspect the existence of an impression from a plate engraved by Blake himself (*op. cit.*, pp. 88–89, No. 21), its existence was not in fact verified until it was exhibited in 1926. See *Catalogue of an Exhibition of Drawings, Etchings, and Woodcuts by Samuel Palmer and other Disciples of William Blake* (London: Victoria and Albert Museum, 1926), No. 27, repr. Pl. II. It was also exhibited at the Philadelphia Museum of Art in 1939 (catalogue, p. 162, No. 228). For a full discussion, see Keynes, *Separate Plates*, pp. 40–42, Pl. 25.

45. See *K* 775–81. The relief etching here considered is comparable in dimensions to *The Ghost of Abel;* the plates of the other two works are larger.

46. Symons, *William Blake*, p. 260. For a description of the mathematical form of Urizen's universe, see *FZ* ii:266—86.

47. Preston, pp. 122–23, Pl. 41; Keynes, *William Blake's . . . Bible*, No. 28.

48. Neither "Famine" nor "Plague," both also in the collection of the Museum of Fine Arts, Boston, has details indicative of an Egyptian setting; the latter is quite clearly suggested by the Great Plague of London. See Darrell Figgis, *The Paintings of William Blake* (London, 1925), Pls. 63 and 64. There are four versions of "Plague" listed by Keynes (*William Blake's . . . Bible*, Nos. 38 a–d; the first of these seems doubtful). "Fire," formerly in the collection of W. Graham Robertson, likewise has no details suggestive of Egypt (Figgis, Pl. 65; Preston, pp. 124–25, Pl. 42).

49. See n. 58 below.

Nimrod and his tower once more lead us back to Jacob Bryant, to whom Blake, as we have seen, was indebted for so much of his imagery. In Vol. I of *A New System*, pp. 8–11 are devoted to him as one of the original archetypes of a giant race. Pp. 399–471 contain a long section embracing several chapters on the significance of towers and high places, and their wide geographic dissemination; included is an engraving executed by the Basire shop (Pl. VI, facing p. 410) with representations of "The ancient Tower at Torone," and "Tower of Cronus in Sicily." In this section the connection of Nimrod and his tower is developed (pp. 413–16). More than twenty years after his letter to Butts, Blake treated the Nimrod theme again in a highly imaginative way in an illustration to canto xxxi of Dante's *Inferno* (Roe, pp. 120–22, Pl. 61).

50. This figure is, of course, to be associated also with the angel of the Passover. The latter is, however, first mentioned in Exod. 14:19; while there is no specific reference to an angelic presence in the episode which Blake is illustrating (Exod. 12:29–30), it seemed fitting to Blake, for the reason just stated, to introduce the figure into his design.

This work recalls forcefully the episode of Tiriel's curse (*Tiriel*, chap. v, K 106); in fact, save for the Egyptian details, it could well serve as an illustration for this passage from Blake's earliest prophecy (*ca.* 1789). Blake certainly had it in mind when designing the water color under discussion some sixteen years later.

51. C. H. Collins Baker, *Catalogue of William Blake's Drawings and Paintings in the Huntington Library* (San Marino, 1938), pp. 28–29, Pl. 21; 2nd ed., enlarged and revised by R. R. Wark (1957), pp. 37–38; Pl. XXVIII.

Blake made an engraving of this subject on a greatly reduced scale, which was published facing p. 32 in *Remember Me! A New Years Gift or Christmas Present* (London: I. Poole, 1825). See Russell, p. 102, No. 32; Keynes, *Bibliography*, p. 215, No. 78 (with reproduction of the water color here discussed); Laurence Binyon, *The Engraved Designs of William Blake* (London, 1926), p. 65, No. 104, and Pl. 15; Bentley and Nurmi, p. 148. Keynes, *Blake Studies*, pp. 186–90, Pl. 47, gives an account of *Remember Me!* and reproduces a unique impression of the plate, now in the Rosenwald Collection of the National Gallery of Art; as published the design was cropped somewhat at the left and at the top.

In the engraved version the form of the sleeping child in the ark is carefully detailed; in the water color it is only lightly indicated in pencil and is, in fact, reminiscent of the babe in the cocoon of the frontispiece of *The Gates of Paradise* (repr. K 760). Otherwise the engraving follows the drawing closely, save for slight variations of detail in the background.

52. In a sense, in spite of vast differences in format, medium, iconographic and artistic sources, treatment of archaeological detail, etc., one can draw a comparison between Blake and Poussin in their

renditions of biblical themes in Egyptian settings. For both Egypt provides a theme suggestive of the ruins of the material world which is yet endlessly renewed by the redeeming power of the spirit; in both the moment of time becomes eternal, and the subject quietly suggests interpretation on many levels. (See Charles G. Dempsey, "Poussin and Egypt," *Art Bulletin* XLV [1963], 109-19.)

53. The course of the Nile as depicted here should be compared with the well-known water color, "The River of Life," which is related in its imagery. See Preston, pp. 70-71, Pl. 18; also Butlin, p. 51 (No. 37), Pl. 22. The latter summarizes somewhat more clearly Joseph Wicksteed's interpretation, as set forth in a booklet on the drawing (Bentley and Nurmi, No. 2134, p. 354).

54. "Fourfold vision" is the subject of the important poem included in Blake's letter of 22 Nov. 1802 to Thomas Butts (*K* 816-19; note especially the concluding lines). The significance of the steps in the water color under discussion is comparable to the designs of Pls. 29 and 33 of *Milton*. In the former the figure of Blake falls backward toward a flight of *three* steps, representative of the peril of William's soul in the World of Generation. In the second plate, his soul is saved at the moment of the Fall into Ulro by the vision of the name of his brother, Robert, which appears above the falling form, as a blazing star descends toward the right (spiritual) foot of the figure; the number of steps shown has become *four*.

55. The engraved version of this design (n. 51, above) makes clear, as the water color does not, that the buildings to the left, between the river and the pyramids, represent brick kilns. Blake thus suggests a link between the servitude of the Israelites and that of the industrial laborers of his own day. Blackstone, *English Blake*, pp. 3-4n, and Erdman, *Blake: Prophet Against Empire*, refer to the fact that in Blake's youth brick kilns were already casting a blight upon the outskirts of London. They take their place in the imagery of his Fallen World; note the very specific description of the lot of the toilers in the brick yards in *FZ* ii:211-28 (*K* 285-86).

56. Preston, pp. 92-93, Pl. 26. It is finely reproduced in color on the scale of the original in Keynes, *William Blake's...Bible*, Pl. II.

57. Compare such other of the *Songs of Innocence* as "Infant Joy," "The Little Boy lost," "The Little Boy found," etc.

58. Blake refers twice to a version of this theme in letters to Thomas Butts dated 25 Apr. 1803 (*K* 822) and 6 July 1803 (*K* 823–24). The latter begins: "I send you the Riposo, which I hope you will think my best Picture in many respects. It represents the Holy Family in Egypt, Guarded in their Repose from those Fiends, the Egyptian Gods, and tho' not directly taken from a Poem of Milton's (for till I had design'd it Milton's Poem did not come into my Thoughts), Yet it is very similar to his Hymn on the Nativity, which you will find among his smaller Poems, & will read with great delight. I have given, in the background, a building which may be supposed the ruin of a Part of Nimrod's tower . . ." (see n. 49, above).

As the Metropolitan water color is dated 1806, it cannot be the version referred to; although distant pyramids are visible, the Egyptian Gods are present only by implication. On the other hand, the tempera now in the collection of George Goyder, Esq. (PLATE xx), bears a date considerably earlier than that of the letters, which state that the work sent to Butts is just completed. It is also not properly a Riposo. The escorting figures provide a guard from the Egyptian gods, but there is no evidence of Nimrod's tower. As noted by Geoffrey Keynes (*The Letters of William Blake* [New York, 1956], p. 84n), there is a possibility that the work referred to was a tempera described in Rossetti's catalogue, but not since traced and presumably destroyed.

In 1809 Blake did a series of designs based upon Milton's hymn, to which he refers in the letter quoted. In these the poses of the Holy Family are very reminiscent of those of the Metropolitan water color and also of the Huntington "Finding of Moses." In keeping with the text of the poem, an abundance of Egyptian and other pagan deities is introduced. See Geoffrey Keynes, "*On the Morning of Christ's Nativity*": *Milton's Hymn with Illustrations by William Blake* (Cambridge, 1923).

59. Inscribed "Fresco by Wm. Blake 1810." See *The Tempera Paintings of William Blake* (London: Arts Council of Great Britain, 1951), pp. 26–27 (No. 24); Keynes, *William Blake's . . . Bible*, No. 97 (repr.).

The poses of the Virgin and Child in this work are almost identical, save for reversal, with those of the magnificently colored tempera of the Virgin and Child, inscribed "Fresco 1825 Blake," which is now in the remarkable collection formed by Mr. and Mrs. Paul Mellon, and recently presented to Yale University. See *Painting in England, 1700–1850, Collection of Mr. & Mrs. Paul Mellon* (Richmond, Va.: Virginia Museum of Fine Arts, 1963), I, 199, No. 380; II, Pl. 14. It is splendidly reproduced in color as the frontispiece to Keynes, *William Blake's ... Bible.*

60. Keynes, *William Blake's ... Bible*, No. 174 (repr.). The work is signed with Blake's monogram and dated 1806. While William Michael Rossetti included it in his list of Blake's works appended to the second volume of Gilchrist's *Life* (1880 ed., p. 244, No. 220), it is clear that he had not seen the work, but knew of it only from the description in the catalogue of the Butts sale of 29 June 1853 (Bentley and Nurmi, No. 453, p. 180).

61. From the viewpoint of Fallen Man, eternal verities are seen in reverse. "The Modern Church Crucifies Christ with the Head Downwards" (*LJ, K* 615). At the moment of release from the World of Generation, the soul perceives the material aspect of that world in its true perspective. Hence the symbol of that materialism, the pyramid, is now shown in its least stable aspect.

62. The painting is now in the collection of George Goyder, Esq. I am much indebted to Mr. Goyder for providing me with an excellent photograph and giving me permission to reproduce it. It was formerly in the collections of Thomas Butts and W. Graham Robertson, among others. See Preston, pp. 146–47, Pl. 49; also Keynes, *William Blake's ... Bible*, No. 95.

Rossetti (p. 208, No. 10) read the date inscribed on the work as 1790. However, as Blake and Butts first met in 1793 or 1794 (G. E. Bentley, Jr., "Thomas Butts, White Collar Maecenas," *PMLA*, LXXI [1956], 1054–55), this would seem most unlikely. The last numeral in the date was probably damaged and incorrectly restored. Butlin (pp. 45–47) has examined the work and reached this conclusion. In addition, Butlin points out that another tempera dated 1790 by Rossetti, "Christ Blessing Little Children," (p. 208, No. 11) now in the Tate Gallery, can definitely be dated in 1799 on the basis of recent restoration. Butlin also calls attention to the fact that the first positive evidence that Butts had commissioned works from Blake is to be found in a letter from Blake to George Cumberland dated 26 Aug. 1799 (*K* 794–96).

63. For a full discussion, see Roe, pp. 164–71.

64. See the extensive study by Erik Iversen, *The Myth of Egypt and its Hieroglyphs in European Tradition* (Copenhagen, 1961). Valuable background material and references will also be found in Nikolaus Pevsner and S. Lang, "The Egyptian Revival," *Architectural Review*, CXIX (1956), 242–54. Further information on topics referred to below without specific bibliographical citation can be found by consulting these sources.

Leslie Greener's recent book, *The Discovery of Egypt* (London, 1966), had not been published when this article was written. Its appearance has not necessitated modification of the original text.

65. The most important sections of this work for our purposes are those devoted to "La Religion des Egyptiens," in the second part of the second volume (1719) and to "Les Dieux Egyptiens," which comprises the sixth book of the supplement to the second volume (1724).

66. See n. 36 above.

67. Earlier editions, in French, were published in Copenhagen in 1751 and 1755.

68. See pp. 2 and 9–10 of Piranesi's text. The quotations are taken directly from the original edition, which contains parallel texts in Italian, French, and English.

69. Keynes, *Letters*, pp. 29, 211. For Reveley see H. M. Colvin, *A Biographical Dictionary of English Architects, 1660–1840* (London, 1954), pp. 492–93.

70. *Museum Worsleyanum or a Collection of Antique Basso Relievos Bustos Statues and Gems with Views of Places in the Levant taken on the Spot in the Years MDCCLXXV VI and VII* (London, 1794; a second edition was issued by Septimus Prowett in 1824). The reference to Reveley occurs on p. 2 of Vol. I; the plate will be found facing p. 89 of Vol. II. Other plates in the work are from

drawings by William Pars. For Sir Richard Worsley, Bt. (1751–1805) see *DNB*. Reveley's knowledge of the Pyramids is also referred to in the text of the publication of Luigi Myer's *Views in Egypt, from the Original Drawings in the possession of Sir Robert Ainslie* (London, 1801), pp. 16–17.

71. The scale of the work did not impress the critic who reviewed it for the *Edinburgh Review*, I (1802–3), 330–45. "We cannot take leave of these *colossal* volumes without entering our protest against such a form of publication. M. Denon's taste has been formed perhaps upon the gigantic monuments of the Thebaid, and will relish no book that is not as large as a pannel [*sic*] charged with hieroglyphics; but in this quarter of the world, we believe there are few readers who will think themselves indemnified for the great price of this work by the satisfaction of turning over four square feet of pasteboard in every leaf, and having their eyes dazzled by characters like those on a tombstone" (pp. 344–45).

72. Keynes, *Letters*, pp. 101, 112, 114, 127, 142. Another brother of Richard and James Edwards was Thomas Edwards of Halifax, Yorkshire, who succeeded the father William in the family business, which enjoyed a reputation particularly for fine bookbinding. Thomas was also a prominent dealer and collector. The original water-color designs by Blake for Young's *Night Thoughts* eventually came into his hands, as did a number of Blake's illuminated books (see Keynes, *Blake Studies*, pp. 64-65; Keynes and Wolf, pp. 13, 63). For the Edwards family, see especially two articles by T. W. Hanson: "Richard Edwards, Publisher," *Times Literary Supplement*, 8 Aug. 1942, p. 396; "Edwards of Halifax, Bookbinders," *Book Handbook*, Vol. I (1948), No. 6, pp. 329-38. For bibliographical description of the catalogue of the Thomas Edwards sale, which was held in Manchester and included the drawings for *Night Thoughts*, see Bentley and Nurmi, No. 438, p. 176.

73. Morchard Bishop, *Blake's Hayley* (London, 1951), pp. 124–25, 140, etc. Hayley made only one trip abroad, to Paris for three weeks in 1790; in the following year he composed a comedy in French, but it was refused performance.

74. Also in Keynes, *Letters*, p. 122. Other references to Phillips in

Blake's correspondence will be found by consulting the index of this edition.

75. *Synopsis of the Contents of the British Museum, Fifteenth Edition* (London: Printed by Richard and Arthur Taylor, Shoe-Lane, 1819).

76. For a fascinating and well-documented account of Belzoni, see Stanley Mayes, *The Great Belzoni* (London, 1959). A useful bibliography of works on Egyptian travel and antiquities will be found on pp. 323–26.

77. A view of the exterior of the Egyptian Hall and of the interior with Belzoni's exhibition *in situ* will be found in Mayes, facing p. 257. A small pamphlet with a description of the tomb and of the model was published for sale to visitors (*Description of the Egyptian Tomb, Discovered by G. Belzoni* [London: John Murray, Albemarle-Street, 1821]). See also Hugh Honour, "Curiosities of the Egyptian Hall," *Country Life*, 7 Jan. 1954, pp. 38–39.

78. The complex problem of the publication of Rees's *Cyclopaedia*, which appeared in seventy-nine fascicles from 1802 to 1820, is considered at length in Bentley and Nurmi, No. 399, pp. 145–48. The original of the Flaxman letter to Hayley is in the Pierpont Morgan Library.

79. Of the three plates of Egyptian monuments which are included in Flaxman's *Lectures on Sculpture*, 2nd ed. (London, 1838), two are signed by Maria Denman, Flaxman's sister-in-law; the list of plates in the volume, however, states that they were based upon drawings by Flaxman. It seems, therefore, a virtual certainty that Flaxman provided Blake with a drawing which served as the basis of the engraving published in the *Cyclopaedia*. That reproduced here is from an unbound impression in the Lessing J. Rosenwald Collection of the National Gallery of Art, Washington.

80. The work shown in Blake's engraving is one of the Colossi of Memnon. As recent good photographs reveal, the central figure is now completely obliterated. See, for example, K. Lange and M. Hirmer, *Egypt* (London, 1956), Pl. 162 and note on pp. 328–29.

81. Keynes, *Pencil Drawings*, Pl. 41; Butlin, p. 56 (No. 43) and Pl. 27. The drawing is dated "Octr. 18. 1819."

## · BLAKE AND THE KABBALAH ·

1. *The Kabbalah Unveiled*, ed. S. L. MacGregor Mathers (London, 1887), p. 28. This work is based on Knorr von Rosenroth, *Kabala denudata* (1677–84).

2. *Zohar*, ed. Harry Sperling and Maurice Simon (London, 1931), I, 86.

3. Harold Bloom, *Blake's Apocalypse* (Garden City, N.Y., 1963), p. 202.

4. "That which is below is like that which is above, and that which is above is like that which is below, for the performance of the miracles of the one substance" (Smaragdine Tablet of Hermes Trismegistus).

5. Gershom G. Scholem, *Major Trends in Jewish Mysticism* (New York, 1954), p. 221.

6. "The Greater Holy Assembly," Art. 31 (in *The Kabbalah Unveiled*, p. 114).

7. *Ibid.*, Art. 625, p. 188.

8. *Ibid.*, Art. 627, p. 188.

9. *Zohar*, II, 21 b 30.

10. "The Greater Holy Assembly," Art. 936, p. 226.

11. *Ibid.*, Art. 945, p. 227.

12. *Ibid.*, Art. 81, p. 121.

13. *Ibid.*, Art. 980, p. 233.

14. Ernst Mueller, *The History of Jewish Mysticism* (Oxford, 1946), p. 99.

15. *Zohar*, III, 61 b.

## · THE DIVINE TETRAD IN BLAKE'S *JERUSALEM* ·

1. Wheels and furnaces are central symbols in Böhme's system; less important is the "finger of God," though the exact phrase appears in the Law edition.

2. *The Works of Jacob Behmen, the Teutonic Philosopher*, ed. William Law (London, 1764–81), IV, 3. This quotation is from

*Signatura Rerum.* Since the pagination begins at p. 1 with each new work, it is sometimes confusing.

3. Thomas Taylor, Introduction to *The Theoretic Arithmetic of the Pythagoreans* (Los Angeles, 1934), p. xiv. First published in 1816.

4. See Vincent F. Hopper, *Medieval Number Symbolism* (New York, 1938). As Hopper points out, the medieval Church "recognized that number was at least one key, and an important one, to cosmic secrets" (p. 89). In the words of St. Augustine, "We must not despise the science of numbers, which in many passages of Scripture, is found to be of eminent service to the careful interpreter. Neither has it been without reason numbered among God's praises, 'thou hast ordered all things in number, and measure and weight'" (p. 78). Of course, Blake could not agree with this extremity: "Bring out number, weight & measure in a year of dearth" (*MHH* 7:14, *K* 151).

5. Taylor, *Theoretic Arithmetic*, p. xv.

6. *The Philosophical and Mathematical Commentaries of Proclus . . . on the First Book of Euclid's Elements* (London, 1788–89), I, ix. Reissued in 1792, this book was apparently widely known among English writers and scholars.

7. *Ibid.*, I, xciv.

8. Quoted by Taylor, *Theoretic Arithmetic*, p. 3.

9. Quoted by Hopper, p. 46.

10. *The Six Books of Proclus . . . on the Theology of Plato*, trans. Thomas Taylor (London, 1816), I, 287.

11. Pythagoras and Socrates appear in an erased line recovered by David V. Erdman. See *E* 226.

12. *Philosophical and Mathematical Commentaries*, I, lxxix.

13. See especially *Ur* 23, *K* 234.

14. At least four of Thomas Taylor's books which deal at length with the science of numbers had been published and were well known in London before the writing of *Jerusalem*. They were: *The Philosophical and Mathematical Commentaries* (1788–89, 1792), *The Cratylus, Phaedo, Parmenides and Timaeus of Plato* (1793), *The Metaphysics of Aristotle* (1801), and *The Works of Plato* (1804). Several others appeared before *Jerusalem* was completed.

15. *The Metaphysics of Aristotle*, trans. Thomas Taylor (London, 1801), p. 30 *n*. This book has an extended discussion, number by number, of the Pythagorean system.

16. Quoted by Taylor, *Philosophical and Mathematical Commentaries*, I, xxiii.

17. Leonard Bosman, *The Meaning and Philosophy of Numbers* (London, 1932), p. xx.

18. See *A Vision of the Last Judgment*, K 612.

19. *Iamblichus' Life of Pythagoras*, trans. Thomas Taylor (London, 1818), p. 109.

20. Taylor, *Philosophical and Mathematical Commentaries*, I, xcvi.

21. Erdman restored this line.

22. Hopper, p. 84.

23. It is very likely that a similar motive led Blake to expand *Jerusalem* to 4 books and 100 plates. See Damon, *A Blake Dictionary* (Providence, 1965), *s.v.* "Jerusalem," pp. 208–10, for an account of its gradual expansion.

24. *Six Books of Proclus*, I, xii.

25. *The Works of William Blake*, ed. E. J. Ellis and W. B. Yeats (London, 1893), I, 2–4.

26. See Damon, *s.v.* "Chaos," for an excellent discussion of Blake's cosmic conception.

27. Taylor, *Theoretic Arithmetic*, p. 162.

28. *Ibid.*, p. 163.

29. *Ibid.*, p. iv.

## · VISIONS IN THE DARKSOM AIR ·

1. References to Blake's poetry and prose consist of an abbreviation of the title followed by the page number in *K* and a line reference. Italics have been supplied for emphasis in many quotations.

A special note of recognition should be given Michael J. Tolley, of the University of Adelaide, Australia, for his suggestions have proved invaluable in the preparation of this study. Tolley at present is writing a book on Blake and the Bible. Also Morton Paley, of the University of California, was kind enough to check several of Blake's illustrations to *Night Thoughts* in the British Museum, thus permitting confirmation to several conclusions reached in this study.

2. In Isa. 26:4 "everlasting strength" is glossed as *the rock of ages*. All references to the Bible are from the King James, or Authorized, Version.

3. *London and its Environs Described*, printed for R. and J. Dodsley (London, 1761), I, 219-20; cf. also B. Lambert, *The History and Survey of London* (London, 1806), IV, 157.

Two bits of speculative evidence should here be elaborated upon. In *J* 653:1-4 the sun sets behind the Gardens of Kensington, where Zion's Hill was located on Tyburn's River (the Westbourne stream). Blake may have had in mind Buckden Hill. Lambert's *History* (III, 536) notes: "At the north-west corner of this park [Hyde Park] is a very beautiful inclosed eminence, called Buckdenhill, which being only separated from Kensington-gardens by a haha, appears, at a distance, to be a part of it." There was a foot path across this hill to Kensington Gardens.

In another passage Jerusalem, personified as a female, is seen in Westminster and "Marybone," among the "ruins of the Temple" (*J* 657:40-41), and (though this is conjectural) Blake may allude to the Temple, or Pantheon, for this temple of entertainment, located near Blake's boyhood home, fell into disrepute around 1812-14 (at one time even its nails were auctioned off). This suggestion gets indirect support from the fact that many other topographical features of London are mentioned by Blake in this context, and Blake specifically mentions the stones for the new construction of Bethlehem Hospital (also about 1812).

4. In their order: *J* 720:38, Ezek. 27:25. *J* 703:74, Isa. 24:20, 23; cf. also *FZ* 306:28-29 and 357:15. *J* 697:21, Job 37:18; cf. the Mundane Shell, *J* 691:7-8, *LJ* 605 (last line), and *Mil* 498:21-22. *J* 662:8-9, Rev. 16:10; cf. also *FZ* 306:58, *J* 667:38, Matt. 8:12 and elsewhere. *J* 640:19, I Kings 4:25 and elsewhere.

5. *J* 741:24, as elsewhere, II Cor. 4:4; cf. John 12:31. *Am* 199:5, Gen. 27:28, 39. *J* 697:28, Acts 19:4, as elsewhere; cf. Mark 1:4. *Mil* 481:12, Col. 1:15. *J* 718:12, Dan. 4:13, 17, 23. *J* 692:51, II Cor. 7:15, as elsewhere. *J* 682, Ps. 8:2, as elsewhere. *FZ* 282:87, Ps. 63:1, Ezek. 19:13. *FZ* 354:534, Isa. 7:24. "The Birds," 423:16, Ps. 88:18.

*Mil* 517:46, Num. 9:2, 7, 13. *Mil* 535:34, Ps. 34:6. *J* 637:23 (cf. *LJ* 613), Isa. 49:23. *J* 658:64, Hos. 1:2 and elsewhere. *J* 653:11, Rev. 12:6. *J* 693:62, Jas. 2:7. *J* 639:53–54, Ezra 9:7; cf. Dan. 9:7–8. *J* 725:31, Ps. 60:8, 108:9. *FZ* 340:285, Job 30:17. *J* 696:27, II Chron. 15:3. *J* 696:27, Deut. 32:10.

6. See Deut. 28:22, Amos 4:9, as elsewhere, and Isa. 60:18. Pl. 9 of *Europe* illustrates horns which drop with "blasting" mildew.

7. Note *FZ* 370:500, "Where is the voice of God that call'd me from the silent dew?" Also see *FZ* 367:388–89, "Come forth, O Vala, from the grass & from the silent dew, / Rise from the dews of death . . . " Cf. Jer. 22:29.

8. See Isa. 51:9, 17; 52:1; Gen. 9:19; Song of Sol. 2:11–12. Also note *FZ* 373:600–601 and 378:798.

9. Ps. 109:29 and Lam. 4:1. Illustration 381 of Blake's illustrations to *Night Thoughts* portrays a devil scattering tares through wheat (?), and probably Blake had Matt. 13:25 in mind. See the reference to tares in *IslM* 52.

10. Note *FZ* 352:441 and 361:160.

11. Blake may allude to this imagery in *J* 675:13 when he refers to the "morning's breath"; also in *FZ* 367:387 the "breath of morning" is mentioned (note also the following lines, 388–97, in this context). Cf. *FZ* 349:303.

12. Cf. *J* 707:62; also *FZ* 371:538, Mil 521:62. For other allusions to the Song of Solomon note 2:13, 15; 7:12 and *Am* 202:26; also 1:8, 5:9, 6:1, and *J* 631:24; 7:4 and *J* 735:26. In *The Four Zoas* (371:533–49) Blake refers to the "steps" of Enion in the gardens of fruits, and Tharmas laments that he is *sick* of "this garden of Pleasure." Enion is "like the ruddy morn / When infant spring appears in swelling buds & opening flowers . . . " This imagery, again parallels that of the Canticles, where the beloved is found "in the secret places of the stairs" (2:14), and he is "come into his garden" (4:16; 5:1; 6:2) of "pleasant fruits" (4:13). Tharmas' sickness also is relevant to 5:8 of the Song of Songs (see *Mil* 521:62). The motif of spring is seen in the winter that is over and in the "flowers [that] appear on the earth" (2:11–12), though it is the beloved rather than the bride who is "ruddy" (5:10). See also *FZ* 370:508 and 1:8. Note also Blake's reference to Enion's "modest

head," which recalls the "modest tresses" in "To Spring" (last line).

13. Later Blake was to use the verse just preceding in Revelation: see *FZ* 337:169.

14. In a scurrilous poem years later Blake repeats the imagery ("And his legs carried it...," 537:29), but in the later context it is Blake who is "Death."

15. Cf. Jer. 10:13. "Beneath them [the multitudes] sit the aged men..." (l. 11), and Joseph Wicksteed (*Blake's Innocence and Experience* [London, 1928], p. 103) notes that the word *beneath* in Blake's poem needs explanation, since "there is no seated gallery at St. Paul's." He concludes that "The simplest answer is that the old men were sitting down while the children stood up to sing...." This, however, negates the imagery which places the multitudes in the high dome of Paul's; and special tiers of benches actually were constructed beneath the dome. The "wise guardians of the poor" (l. 11) sat in chairs *beneath* the tiers. See G. L. Prestige, *St. Paul's in Its Glory* (London, 1955), pp. 102–3. The library of St. Paul's has in its collection of prints and engravings an illustration showing the arrangement of tiers, I am advised by A. R. B. Fuller of the library.

16. Cf. *Am* 198:2, "shadows pass, the morning 'gins to break."

17. There are frequent overtones from Job in Blake's poetry; see: Job 1:21, *FZ* 355:574–75 and To Thomas Butts, 10 Jan. 1802, 813; 4:18, *J* 679:31; 7:5, *J* 741:17; 14:17, *J* 643:13; 17:14, *GoP* 209: No. 16; 19:19, *J* 667:14; 19:26, *J* 696:16; 31:6, *J* 708:34–35; 41:24, *FZ* 323:112.

18. Recall the different context of the lion who will graze after the lamb and weep in "Night" of *Songs of Innocence*.

19. The angelic hosts fall "Yellow as leaves of Autumn"; Blake's allusion is to the fallen angels who lay "Thick as Autumnal Leaves" on the inflamed sea in *Paradise Lost*, I, 302; cf. *FZ* 363:238. Note also *FZ* 358:42–43. Satan is "Newton's Pantocrator" in *Mil* 483:9–11. "Pantocrator" is from the Greek and frequently used in Revelation, where it is translated as "Lord Almighty." But the word, insofar as Blake is concerned, may have been suggested by Newton himself, for it appears in his *Principia*. See Miner, "Newton's Pantocrator," *Notes and Queries*, January, 1961, pp. 15–16.

20. Cf. also *FZ* 267:101–2. Blake's imagery, though ultimately alluding to Prov. 8:27, applies more directly here to *Paradise Lost*, VII, 224–29: "One foot centred, and the other turn'd / Round through the vast profundity obscure. . . . "

21. As in Jer. 7:31. Topheth (*fireplace*), where the children were forced to pass through fires of Molech, was located in this valley, southwest of Jerusalem; note II Kings 23:10, II Chron. 33:6, and Jer. 32:35. Rephaim, the valley of dead giants, also is associated with the valley of Hinnom, which leads "unto the south side of the Jebusite." Note Josh. 15:8, 18:16; *J* 706:23.

22. *FZ* 319:297–309 and note *BoL* 257:20; cf. Dan. 8:10, II Kings 23:4–6, 10, 15. Also note parallel imagery in "A Song of Liberty," *K* 160, and *Am* 198:5.

Orion is followed across the heavens by Canis major and Canis minor, and in *J* 729:80–83 Los, a constellation, "all night watches / The stars"; with him "went down the Dogs of Leutha," probably Orion's dogs. In *FZ* 288:315–16 "beamy daughters of light" flee from Los, certainly an allusion to the Pleiades which precede Orion across the sky. Note also *FZ* 336:132. Blake executed a magnificent illustration of Orion for *Night Thoughts* (ix:1735–36); this constellation also is depicted in Pl. 25 of *Jerusalem* and in "The Peaceful Hermitage" to Milton's *Il Penseroso*. S. Foster Damon in *Blake's "Job": William Blake's "Illustrations of The Book of Job"* (Providence, 1966), p. 38, calls attention to Blake's Illustration XIV of this series, in which Orion's belt and the Pleiades (Job 38:31) are shown in the upper corners.

23. The list is not exhaustive; in their order: *Mil* 505:8–14, *Mil* 509:68, *FZ* 349:338–40 (cf. Matt. 27:57–60), *FZ* 350:377, *Mil* 510:71, *J* 674:31, *FZ* 330:395, *J* 627:18, *J* 713:24. Los also utters "Ambiguous words" (*FZ* 302:205), possibly a recall of *Paradise Lost*, V, 703, and VI, 568.

24. A search has been made in the *Muster Books and Pay Lists* (W. O. 12/454 to 465), and they reveal that John Scholfield (Schofield, Schoffield, Scholefield) enlisted with the 1st Dragoons on 19 Mar. 1793 at Sarum, Wiltshire; he was promoted to corporal on 18 Dec. 1794 and to sergeant on 3 Sept. 1797. On 30 Dec. 1798, Scholfield was reduced from sergeant to private (reason not given)

and remained in this rank up to his death at Canterbury on 31 Jan. 1812. (Could Blake have known this? See *J* 640:59, "Go thou to Skofield: ask him if he is Bath or if he is Canterbury.") Scholfield served in the Peninsular War at Belem in Portugal from early September, 1809, until 24 Nov. 1811, when he was sent back from Belem to the Depot in England.

According to the *Casualty Returns* (W. O. 25/1392) of the 1st Dragoons, John Scholfield was born in Manchester and was a fustian cutter by trade.

The *Muster Books and Pay Lists* (W. O. 12/457 to 464) mention a Trooper John Cook (Cock), who served in the same company as Scholfield in the 1st Dragoons. Cook joined the regiment on 21 Mar. 1800, having previously been in the Berkshire Fencibles, a militia unit. During 1803 he was stationed with John Scholfield in Truro, county Cornwall, until May, the company then marching to Dorchester, county Dorset, then to Chichester, Sussex, where it remained from June to February, 1804. Cook was discharged in Ireland on 24 Sept. 1808 after which time no trace of him can be found.

A search also made in the *Soldiers Documents* for the period in question (W. O. 97/33 and W. O. 97/118) has not brought to light any papers referring to either Scholfield or Cock.

I am indebted to John Taylor, Public Record Office, Chancery Lane, London, for this information.

A minor point should here also be cleared up. At the time of Blake's argument with Scholfield, he accused the soldier of being "sent by his Captain [Leathes] *or* Esquire Hayley to hear what he [Blake] had to say and [then Scholfield was] to go tell *them*. . . ." See West Sussex Record Office QR/W643 f. 78. This is misprinted in Mona Wilson's *The Life of William Blake* (London, 1948), p. 155, as "sent by his Captain *to* Esquire Hayley," and this has led to the incorrect conclusion that *them* would refer to Blake and his wife. But it would rather refer to Captain Leathes and Hayley as the original document clarifies.

A debt of gratitude should here be expressed to Francis W. Steer, County Archivist of the West Sussex County Council, Chichester, for his valuable commentary on the extant judicial documents relating to Blake's trial.

25. Blake initially derives Christ's ancestresses from the race of Cain (returning to the correct line at the mention of Noah). Blake selects Naamah, daughter of Lamech of Cain's line, as Noah's wife, unnamed in the Bible. Alexander Pope also associates Naamah as being the wife of Noah in *The Rape of the Lock* (canto i, 145). Note also Damon's *Blake Dictionary* (Providence, 1965), *s.v.* "Naamah." Blake also mentions in this passage "Shuah's daughter," the Canaanite wife or concubine of Judah; it was through Tamar, however, that Judah became ancestor to Christ.

Blake diverts the deliberately incomplete and symbolic chronology of Matthew by his reference to Zibeah. In Matt. 1:8 Joram begets Ozias, but in II Kings 8:24 and I Chron. 3:11 Joram is the father of Ahazia, who in turn is husband of Zibeah. Concerning the loins of Abraham and David, see *J* 652 and Matt. 1:1. Abraham was the first from whose family it was predicted that the Messiah would spring (Gen. 22:18), and David was the one king of all the line from whom the throne the Messiah was to occupy took its name, "the throne of David."

Nimrod is the son of Cush (Gen. 10:8), but see *J* 625:19, 644:3–4. In *J* 625:19 "Cush is adjoin'd to Aram," but it is Canaan which is adjacent to Aram in biblical geography. Also in *J* 692:18–19 Canaan, rather than Cush (Ethiopia), is associated with Mizraim (Egypt).

26. Concerning the tigers, note *FZ* 365:301–7; cf. 300:90–91 and 327:282. Attention should be called to the illustration of the tiger by Blake (No. 246) for *Night Thoughts*. About Solomon see *MHH* 158 and Prov. 27:22.

27. See Miner, "William Blake's 'Divine Analogy,'" *Criticism*, Winter, 1961, pp. 46–61.

28. See *FZ* 301:138–39; cf. Song of Sol. 1:7, *FZ* 295:120–24, and *Comus* 428–29; note also *FZ* 369:455–57, *FZ* 469–70, and *J* 660:10–12. See also the *roof* which is womblike in *Ur* 225:28–29 and the "shaggy wild" or rooflike skull in *Ur* 228:33–34, which encloses the Immortal. Blake possibly pursues this theme graphically in the frontispiece to *America* (1793), where the head of the winged creature apparently has transformed itself into the genitals of the female (reproduced in Laurence Binyon, *The Engraved Designs of William Blake* [London, 1926], Pl. 50). The winged pudendum appears later in *Jerusalem* (Pl. 58; cf. also Pl. 25, figure at the top). Pertinent to

the period of 1793, however, Blake frequently utilized sexual imagery in his designs. See Pl. 3 in *MHH* (bottom); compare the Note-Book sketch of a bearded creature in the womb and the winged patriarch on the title page of *VDA*; note the skeleton-embryo in *Ur*, and in this same work see the design of the female who is being created by a globe of blood (cf. *Ur* 235:18 in which "the Web is a Female in embrio"). The bat-winged figure at the bottom of the design for the "Preludium" to *Europe* (1794), I interpret as a fetus (cf. Note-Book sketches, p. 74); also note the iconography of the winged female and the englobed embryo (?) in "A Prophecy" of *Europe*.

29. Bishop Watson, in his public letters to Paine, states that the *Apology* of Justin Martyr was written "not fifty years after the death of St. John" (i.e., A.D. 79); Blake notes in the margin of Watson's text "A:D:150" (*K* 395), which is essentially correct.

30. Horeb and Sinai are interchangeable words because of textual variations in source documents. Note *J* 638:68.

31. The "Sea of Rephaim" (*J* 704:39–40) is not mentioned in the Bible, but Blake associates it, in part, with the Dead Sea, as the allusion to Sodom and Gomorrah, cities flooded over, confirms; cf. *J* 735:51 and Deut. 29:23.

The Vale of Rephaim also is the Vale of the Atlantic (*J* 678:32–33), where Vala's Veil or Net is "cast into the Atlantic Deep / To catch the Souls of the Dead..." (*J* 691:2–3; cf. *J* 671:77–81). This probably is an ironic allusion to Christ's disciples who are seen "casting a net into the sea: for they were fishers [of men]" (Matt. 4:17–19, Mark 1:16–18). In Illustration 488 of *Night Thoughts* fishermen are seen casting a net into the sea, and Blake almost certainly had these verses in mind, as the net contains human bodies and Christ is seen at the top of the illustration. In this vale the "Human Harvest waves" (*J* 678:34; cf. *FZ* 270:209–10), and in Isa. 17:5 the ears of corn are gathered during harvest time in the valley of Rephaim.

32. See *Mil* 526:57–60, *FZ* 349:336–37, and *J* 722:27–28. Note also *J* 700:38–39 and Mark 16:1–2, as elsewhere.

33. Cf. *FZ* 359:95–96; *FZ* 370:488, 495; *Mil* 497:36–40; and *FR* 138:96–97.

34. See Gen. 23:2, 19; Blake refers to this cave in *J* 699:38.

35. *J* 726:43; also see 662:9–10 and 719:3.

36. Cf. *FZ* 357:17 and Ps. 18:7, 15.

37. Rev. 12:4–5. See *FZ* 352:447–48, Rev. 8:12, Isa. 5:24, and Joel 2:5. Note also Blake's illustrations to Milton's "On the Morning of Christ's Nativity," where the dragon's tail is seen among the stars (C. H. Collins Baker and R. R. Wark, *Catalogue of William Blake's Drawings and Paintings in the Huntington Library* [San Marino, 1957], Pl. XVI).

38. See *Mil* 495:3, Jude 25, and note *Mil* 519:16; *Mil* 519:31, Rom. 1:25; *J* 667:47, II Cor. 11:31.

39. Cf. *FZ* 366:336; note marginal gloss in Dan. 3:5 and *Mil* 484:28. "Tabret, pipe & harp" of *J* 736:59 recounts I Sam. 10:5.

40. Note *FZ* 308:135 and *J* 657:17–18, 623:34, and 731:14–18. These gems also symbolize the Twelve Tribes of Aaron's breastplate: i.e., ruby (sardius), jacinth (ligure), chrysolite (beryl). See Exod. 28:17 ff. Concerning the furnaces, note *J* 713:24–26.

Later Orc, a "Serpent wondrous among the Constellations," buds with these gems, the "fruit" of the Tree of Mystery (*FZ* 342–43:65–76); cf. Ezek. 28:13–14.

41. Note Judg. 18:28. In Num. 13:21 the Israelites send spies from the Wilderness of Zin "unto Rehob, as men come to Hamath"; cf. *J* 707:60–61.

42. Hiram rejected "the land of Cabul" (I Kings 9:12–13), a hard, dry, unproductive land; the name may be a pun upon the Hebrew word "nothing" or "worthless" *(kebal).* Possibly it represents the voids of space for Blake; cf. *J* 715:56–57.

43. See *The Abingdon Bible Commentary*, ed. Frederick C. Eiselen (New York, 1929), p. 595. Blake, in a letter to Thomas Butts, 25 Apr. 1803, stated he had been reading Ps. 139, and he quotes vs. 14 ("I am fearfully & wonderfully made"); it is vs. 15 which carries the imagery of the body being "curiously wrought." In addition to the denotation of weaving, the language also describes the variegated color of the viscera; note *The Expositor's Bible*, ed. W. R. Nicoll (Grand Rapids, 1956), III, 326.

In this same text the Shadowy Female states, "I will have Kings inwoven upon it [the garment] & Councellors & Mighty Men..." (*Mil* 499:15; cf. *FZ* 374:659), and in Job 12:17, 18, and 19 *counsellors, kings,* and *the mighty* are mentioned, and possibly Blake recalled the biblical sequence. Note the Daughters of Enitharmon who "weave the ovarium & the integument" from their bowels in *FZ* 346:210–11; also see *FZ* 266:84, 90. Note in *J* 688:13–14 "the moth-labour'd Woof, / [which is] A Garment and Cradle weaving for the infantine Terror..." Recall the spectres who are "caught into the flax" of Vala's distaff, *J* 722:33–34 (cf. *J* 699:32–34). Also note *FZ* 356:607 and Josh. 2:6. In *J* 693:33–34 "a peculiar Tabernacle...cuts the integuments of beauty..." See *J* 652, 651:53–55, 707–8:28–29.

44. In *J* 724:11 "Joseph's beautiful integument" is stripped off. The coats of the priests of Aaron were gathered about their loins with a symbolically ornamented girdle of needlework; see Exod. 28:39, 39:29, and *FZ* 281:57. Note also *J* 688:34–36 and 665:51–54. Blake may have recognized that Joseph's name is sometimes associated with a verb form meaning "he taketh away," and the Hebrew writer in Gen. 30:23, 24 plays upon this etymology. See *The Westminster Dictionary of the Bible*, ed. John D. Davis, rev. Henry S. Gehman (Philadelphia, 1944), p. 328.

In "The Angel Appearing to Zacharias" (cf. Luke 1:8–13), a tempera painting on canvas believed to have been executed about 1800, Blake delineates with considerable accuracy the priestly clothing of Aaron, showing the golden mitre and its gold plate, the breastplate and ephod. The robe of the ephod, or jacket, is correctly colored (blue) and at its hem tinkle the alternate golden bells and pomegranates (note *J* 731:29). This painting is reproduced in Darrell Figgis, *The Paintings of William Blake* (London, 1925), Pl. 38.

Also note the priest, holding a censer, with garments inscribed with symbolic emblems in one of Blake's designs for Dante (Albert S. Roe, *Blake's Illustrations to the Divine Comedy* [Princeton, 1953], pp. 51–52 and Pl. 3). Note the garment-body in *FZ* 266:83–93.

45. *Amalekite* is Blake's interpolation; because of textual differences Gen. 37:25, 28 refer to Ishmaelites or Midianites.

46. Scholfield is woven into "the same mantle of skin" with Joseph; note *J* 705:1–2, also 704:22–23, 736:31; cf. *FZ* 318:245–46 and *Ur* 235:17–18.

47. The Greek word here is general, meaning utensil, instrument, or object, but this same word is used in I Pet. 3:7 and in I Thess.

4:4 to signify the human body. Blake alludes to I Pet. 3:7 in *An Island in the Moon* (K 53). See *The Interpreter's Bible*, IX (New York, 1954), 136. Note also the woven "dark Woof" which is "let down" over "the whole Earth" to the "Four Quarters of the World" (*Mil* 525:11-17). In Illustration 463 of *Night Thoughts* there is a scroll amid flaming stars, and human bodies are enmeshed in it. Also seen are various animals (ox, sheep, lion) and various "fetal" sketches, similar to those in Blake's Note-book. This scroll appears to be similar to the sheet let down over the world in Peter's vision. See the Web of Religion that swags from heaven to heaven in *FZ* 345:176-77; also note *FZ* 322:104-5, *FZ* 372:563-64, and Isa. 34:4. Recall the female who "lets down her Tabernacle" which the male enters in *J* 656:34-35 and the "wide woof" that flows down in *FZ* 378:784; cf. *J* 728:73-74. Also note Isa. 25:7 where a veil is over the nations of the earth.

48. Blake refers to the wood of Ephraim (*J* 653:17-18; cf. Ps. 132:6), and on this mountain the Palm of Suffering was located (Judg. 4:5) and Dinah was ravished in Ephraim (*J* 715:54, Gen. 34:2).

49. See *Paradise Lost*, I, 399-405. Note the Web of Generation which hangs from "globe to globe" (*FZ* 319-20:318-19). In *J* 704:31-33 starry spears (knitting needles) weave "the deaths of the Mighty into a Tabernacle..." In *J* 635:4-5 the "Polypus [of generation is seen] growing / From Albion over the whole Earth..."

50. See Ezek. 5:10, "and I will execute judgments in thee, and the whole remnant of thee will I scatter into all the winds." Cf. *FZ* 357:13, "...Judgment from the four winds!"

51. In *J* 661:52-54 Gwendolen divides into "Rahab & Tirza in Twelve Portions," and Los sends Reuben "Over Jordan" to Canaan; this theme may recall Judg. 19:29 in which a concubine was "divided ...together with her bones, into twelve pieces, and sent...to all the coasts of Israel." Cf. *FZ* 350:341-44.

52. See Matt. 27:50-51; also note Mark 15:38 and Luke 23:45.

53. In *Mil* 529:6 (cf. 531:24-25), Blake notes "a Paved work of all kinds of precious stones"; see Exod. 24:10 in which "a paved work of a sapphire stone" is seen under the feet of God. Also note Ezek. 1:26, 10:1; Rev. 4:3. Note *Mil* 532:17-18 and *J* 647:17-19.

54. See Exod. 29:16. Note *FZ* 354:509–11 in which the "corrupting members" of the Serpent Orc "Vomit out the scaly monsters of the restless deep." The Bread and Wine are given sexual connotations in *FZ* 274:355 and 361:164–65. In *Am* 198:6–7 the spectre-serpent stains "the temple long / With beams of blood"; also note *Eur* 241:2–3. Cf. *Am* 199:14–19 in which the "Eternal Viper" "rent the ancient Heavens," and the "harlot womb" heaves in "enormous circles." The Mundane Shell functions as Blake's matrix.

55. See *FZ* 335–36:113–15, *FR* 139–40:126–27, and cf. *Am* 202:16–22. Note also *J* 708:38–44 and *FZ* 328:323–25. In *J* 674:24–25 the "Spectrous Uncircumcised Vegetation" forms a "Sexual Machine, an Aged Virgin Form."

The narrator in Blake's poem about the golden chapel ultimately turns into a sty (becomes generated); cf. *EG* 756:5–6, 757:27. Note also the "Cabinet . . . form'd of Gold" ("The Crystal Cabinet," 429:21–24).

56. See Heb. 9:11–12, where Christ as a "high priest" enters a "more perfect tabernacle" and "holy place."

57. The tabernacle in Heb. 9:11 is "not made with hands," and in *Mil* 529:15–16 Satan's heart also is a "building . . . not made with hands," and Blake frequently associates the heart with the Tabernacle and its furnishings.

58. Note Flavius Josephus *Antiquities of the Jews* XV. xi. 2, in which ten thousand "skilful workmen" constructed the Temple of Herod, and "a thousand" priests were "taught the arts of stonecutters . . . and carpenters." Josephus in *Wars of the Jews* (V. v. 4–5) notes that the veil which hung before the Temple's gates was a "Babylonian curtain," embroidered with blue, and fine linen, and scarlet and purple, and that these colors had a mystical interpretation, symbolizing "a kind of image of the universe" (the four elements). "This curtain [says Josephus] had also embroidered upon it all that was mystical in the heavens, excepting that of the [twelve] signs, representing living creatures." Josephus also notes that the seven lamps signified the "circle of the zodiac." Possibly Blake was familiar with this imagery, for in *The Four Zoas* (284:151–55; cf. *J* 692:54–55) the "universal curtains" of the temple, hanging on golden hooks, serve as "Atmospheres" and "spread out from Sun to

Sun / The vehicles of light." The stars are lamps in *FZ* 272:304 and 379:829.

59. Blake here alludes to Aaron's breastplate; cf. *FZ* 312:27–28, *Mil* 484:23–24, *Mil* 490:30–33, *J* 635:21–22, and *J* 731:14–18.

60. See *J* 687:56, *FZ* 348:276, *FZ* 382:9.

61. The "Spectres of Albion / Rear their *dark Rocks* among the Stars of God" (*J* 690:48–49; cf. 737:49–50), and the tower of *burnt* bricks "whose top may reach unto heaven" is Babel, or *Confusion* (gloss, Gen. 11:3–4; cf. "Then she bore Pale desire" in *PS, K* 41). Babel was built on the "plain in the land of Shinar" (Gen. 11:2), and Blake equates it with Stonehenge on the "Plain of Salisbury" (*J* 701–2:1–7). The Stonehenge trilithons appear in Blake's *Illustrations of the Book of Job,* and for Blake's association of the Temple, or Tabernacle, with Stonehenge, see Miner, "William Blake's 'Divine Analogy,' " *Criticism,* Winter, 1961, pp. 46–61.

62. Babylon was the major city on the Euphrates, and in Blake's water color "By the Waters of Babylon" (*ca.* 1806; cf. Ps. 137:1–3) ships with sails are seen upon this river, surrounded by pillars. See Darrell Figgis, *The Paintings of William Blake,* Pl. 84. Note *J* 729:8 and 735:38. Note also *J* 647:30, 35 and I Kings 6:33 (gloss).

63. Solomon's Temple preceded Herod's; both built in Jerusalem, they were dedicated to Jehovah and contained the holy objects of the Tabernacle. In Herod's Temple the Holy of Holies was empty, the Ark having disappeared.

64. We are indebted to Josephus for many of the particulars of Herod's Temple; see *Antiquities of the Jews* XV. xi. 5. Cf. Isa. 33:20–21.

65. It is difficult to determine precisely Blake's meaning here. The *ascent without* (Ezek. 40:40), for example, could apply to the ascent of the North Gate *outside* of the *outer* court or to the ascent *within* the *outer* walls—but leading to the inner court!

66. Jerusalem's Gates of the "West were Walled up" (*J* 711:5, 8), and a "Wall & Curtain" are built against America's shore (to the west) in *J* 680:49. Cf. *J* 691:18–19, 632:52.

67. Cf. *FZ* 329:378–82. The "Couch" becomes a Tabernacle in *Mil* 502–3:46–48, probably the Death Couch which is the womb (*Mil* 534:1).

68. Note the "Religion of Chastity" which "clos'd up in Moral Pride" the "Head & Heart & Loins" in *J* 693:48-49. Although Blake is not consistent concerning the symbolic East Gate, it is related to the rivers of bliss (*J* 745:16) and the "Center," or temple and tabernacle (*FZ* 333:18, *J* 734:52). It is associated with Los (*Mil* 526:66-67), and his furnaces are located before this Gate (*J* 623:28). Luvah, or Love, has his region in the East Gate of Jerusalem (*J* 657:23-25) and the Female Womb also is Eastward (*J* 734:52).

The harlot-sisters of the Bible are Aholibah and Aholah, the cities of Jerusalem and Samaria, respectively, and Blake may utilize the glossing of their names in Ezek. 23:4 (*My tabernacle in her* and *His tent or tabernacle*), for the Spectre becomes the female's "Priest & she his Tabernacle" (*J* 701:60); Albion pleads for Vala to "hide me in thy Scarlet Tabernacle" (*J* 645:30; cf. Ps. 27:5 and *EG* 755:65). Note also *J* 640:30-32 and Ezek. 23:13, 17.

See *J* 635:17-20 in which there is "a beautiful golden gate" located in the loins (cf. also *Ur* 224:14-17). Blake sketched a tabernacle (?) over the pubis of a female in a sketch of *The Four Zoas*. This appears to be some kind of triptych, comparable to the illustration of a Gothic church in *Jerusalem* (Pl. 57). Blake placed a city over the female generative organs in "The Sunshine Holiday," and the connection of the tabernacle and the loins is not foreign to Blake. Note the connection of the "Reins" (technically, *kidneys*, but in Blake's context the loins) and the Veil of Seraphim in *J* 731:22-24. The tabernacle frequently is associated with the loins, as in *J* 656:34-35.

69. See Ezek. 6:13, Deut. 12:2, I Kings 14:23, II Kings 17:10, and II Chron. 28:4.

70. London Stone is a stone of sacrifice (cf. *J* 670:50, 689:5-7, 742:23-24), probably the altar stone of Stonehenge in view of *J* 650:33, 701:56-57, 701-2:2-3, and 703:57.

71. It is the womb in Blake's imagery which *shrinks* the Divine Form of eternity to a generated mortal; cf. *Ur* 230:56 (note *Ur* 224:16-17), *Ur* 236:29-30, *Mil* 490:6. Note also *J* 702:40, 679:17-18, 717:10-11. In *J* 703:83 the "Senses of Men shrink . . . under the Knife of flint / In the hands of Albion's Daughters among the Druid Temples . . ." Cf. also *J* 697:20-22, 698:38-41. Regarding the females

who search the heart, in *J* 662:3 Los rages in the "Divisions of Reuben"; in Judg. 5:15–16 "the divisions of Reuben" cause "great searchings of heart."

72. An early theme in Blake: "Samson, the strongest of the children of men, I sing; how he was foiled by woman's arts, by a false wife brought to the gates of death!" ("Samson," *PS*, *K* 37).

73. Rahab and Tirzah circumscribe the brain "& pierced it thro' the midst with a golden pin" (*J* 705:41–42). These lines allude to Jael, the woman who "smote the nail into his [Sisera's] temples"; see Judg. 4:21, 5:26; also *FZ* 278:512–13, *Mil* 482:1–2, *Mil* 500:20, and *J* 691:16. Note Judg. 5:20 and *J* 686:27. Sisera's "prey" (spoils of War) is a garment "of divers colours of needlework on both sides" (Judg. 5:30).

Rahab is redeemed in "blood & fury & jealousy" (*FZ* 361:159), probably an allusion to Ezek. 16:38 in which Jerusalem, described as a harlot, is punished in "blood in fury and jealousy."

74. Christ's "robes of blood" (see *FZ* 287:261–65) relate to incarnation. In Matt. 27:28 Christ's crucifiers "put on him a scarlet robe" and in *J* 736:4–5 "a scarlet robe" becomes a "Veil & Net / Of Veins of red Blood ... " Elsewhere, the Looms of generation (*J* 699:36–38) "drop with crimson gore" along the "Valley of Rephaim," the valley of death, and here also is located the sacrificial "Snake / Of the Druid," or Stonehenge (*J* 740:25–26). Blake often connects the act of birth with the crucifixion; cf. *J* 703:83–84, *J* 698:38–41, *FZ* 347:233–36.

75. Recall "To Tirzah" of *Experience*, "Thou, Mother of my Mortal part, / With cruelty didst mould my Heart, / ... Didst bind my Nostrils, Eyes, & Ears ..." (*K* 220).

76. See *The Interpreter's Dictionary of the Bible* (New York, 1962), II, 183.

77. Blake transposes these rivers; in *J* 735:26 "The Rocks of Rabbath [are] on the Arnon," but Rabbah-ammon was located at the headwaters of the Jabbok. In the above context the Arnon is probably the river of generation; see *FZ* 346:215 and *Mil* 532:4–5. The Arnon is the river of parental love (*Mil* 524:30); this river bordered Moab (possibly, *seed of a father*) and flowed west into the Dead Sea (of materialism to Blake; cf. *J* 745:17).

78. See *J* 630:3-5 in which Los "ladles the Ore / . . . pouring it into the *clay ground* prepar'd with art . . . "

Reuben sleeps "Between Succoth & Zaretan" on the Stone of Bohan (*J* 661:43-45, 51), a stone which helped to demarcate tribal boundaries. Bohan probably is associated with London Stone because this landmark also was believed to be used for measuring distances; see *J* 715:33-34.

Reuben sleeps in the "Cave of Adam" (*J* 662:5-6), a city of the clay valley of Jordan near Zaretan (Josh. 3:16), and he is encompassed in "mire & clay."

79. Note also the associations with Satan and Michael, who fight over the body of Moses, as in Jude 9; see Rev. 12:7 and note *Mil* 488:32.

80. See gloss of Gen. 2:22 in which Eve is *builded* from the rib of man; note also *J* 662:3-4.

81. *VDA* 194:5-7. Preformationism, the theory that the ovum or sperm contained a completely formed organism (a homunculus), was still a formidable question in both biology and theology in the eighteenth century, and onanism for the male carried with it inherent aspects of literal and symbolic homicide. Does Blake refer to this animaculist-ovist controversy in *J* 698:12-13? See Joseph Needham, *A History of Embryology* (Cambridge, Eng., 1934), p. 193 n.

82. Cf. Eccles. 12:6, ". . . or the pitcher be broken at the fountain, or the wheel broken at the cistern." Also note Ezek. 1:16, and elsewhere. See Erasmus Darwin's *The Botanic Garden* (Pt. I, canto i, 254): "Savery applied it [steam power] to the raising of water to supply houses and gardens. . . . A few years ago Mr. Watt . . . much improved this machine, and with Mr. Boulton . . . has applied it to a variety of purposes, such as raising water from mines. . . ." The draining of mines, allowing them to continue in operation, did *perplex youth in their outgoings.*

83. Scholars of Blake's time were well acquainted with the *Elohim* and *Jehovah* documents, their integration combining the words Elohim-Jehovah.

84. There is in the Tate Gallery a rough sketch attributed to Robert, Blake's brother, with the words "The preaching of warn-

ing" on the recto side, phrasing attributed to William Blake by Frederick Tatham. The phrase may recall Paul's preaching of a warning in Col. 1:28.

85. See *J* 632:38–41 and 727:25–27; also note *J* 677:6–12, 711:5–9, and 666:7.

## · *MATERIA PRIMA* IN A PAGE OF BLAKE'S *VALA* ·

1. M. O. Percival, *William Blake's Circle of Destiny* (New York, 1938), pp. 197–215.

2. *Ibid.*, p. 204.

3. C. G. Jung, *Psychologie und Alchemie* (Zurich, 1944), p. 443, Fig. 164.

4. John Read, *Prelude to Chemistry* (London, 1936), Pl. 60 (i); cf. p. 270. See also Désirée Hirst, *Hidden Riches* (London, 1964), pp. 124, 134–35.

5. S. Foster Damon, *William Blake, His Philosophy and Symbols*, 3rd ed. (Gloucester, Mass., 1958), p. 400.

6. *William Blake's Vala: Blake's Numbered Text*, ed. H. M. Margoliouth (Oxford, 1956), p. 107.

7. William Blake, *Vala, or the Four Zoas*, ed. G. E. Bentley, Jr. (Oxford, 1963), p. 27.

8. Cf. the webbed feet of the siren in the Bodleian Bestiary, Bodl. MS 602, fol. 10r. Reproduced by M. R. James, *The Bestiary* (Oxford: Roxburghe Club, 1928), Supplementary Plates.

9. P. E. M. Berthelot, *Les Origines de l'alchimie* (Paris, 1885), pp. 247–78; and Lynn Thorndike, *History of Magic and Experimental Science* (London, 1923), I, 305.

10. Berthelot, *Collection des anciens alchimistes grecs* (Paris, 1883), III, 23.

11. Read, p. 241.

12. Blake, *Vala*, ed. Bentley, p. 7.

13. Read, frontispiece.

14. British Museum MS Sloane 5025, fol. 2. Dr. Jung twice misnames this MS, describing it as Additional 10302, which is actually Norton's *Ordinall*. See Jung, p. 442, n. 7; p. 560, Fig. 228.

15. British Museum MS Harley 3469, fol. 16v. See J. K., *Splendor solis* (London, 1921), Pl. VII.

16. MS Harley 3469, fol. 21v. See J. K., Pl. XI.

17. *The Last Will and Testament of Basil Valentine* (London, 1671), p. 304.

18. Read, Pl. 40. Cf. p. 219, and Blake's *Jerusalem* 71.

19. Jung, p. 415, Fig. 157.

20. G. J. Witkowski, *Tetoniana, Curiosités médicales, littéraires et artistiques sur les seins et l'allaitement* (Paris, 1898), p. 111, Fig. 70.

21. *Ibid.*, p. 112–13.

22. Blake, *Vala*, ed. Bentley, pp. 26, 27.

23. *The Last Will and Testament*, p. 257.

24. *Ibid.*, p. 346. Cf. p. 344.

25. *Ibid.*, pp. 284, 343.

26. Read, Pl. 5.

27. *Ibid.*, pp. 200–201.

28. Martin Ruland, *Lexicon of Alchemy*, Eng. trans. 1892, p. 221–22.

29. Jung, p. 403, Fig. 149.

30. Blake, *Vala*, ed. Bentley, p. 26.


· NEGATIVE SOURCES IN BLAKE ·


1. Isaac Newton, *Sir Isaac Newton's Mathematical Principles* . . . (Berkeley, Calif., 1962), II, 398.

2. I am, of course, following the lead of Northrop Frye in his chapter "The Case Against Locke," in *Fearful Symmetry* (Princeton, 1947), and accordingly leave Locke out of the discussion.

3. *The Letters of William Blake*, ed. Sir Geoffrey Keynes (New York, 1956), p. 79.

4. See Marjorie Nicolson, *Newton Demands the Muse* (Princeton, 1946), pp. 166–67, and Jacob Bronowski, *William Blake 1757–1827: A Man Without a Mask* (Harmondsworth, 1954), p. 181.

5. Newton, *Opticks*, 4th ed. (London, 1730), Book III, pp. 320–21.

6. See Florian Cajori, *A History of the Conceptions of Limits and*

*Fluxions in Great Britain from Newton to Woodhouse* (Chicago and London, 1919).

7. 12 Apr. 1827, *Letters*, pp. 202–3.

8. *Mathematical Principles*, p. 30.

9. S. Foster Damon, *A Blake Dictionary* (Providence, 1965), *s.v.* "Vortex." Bronowski, p. 213, seems certain that Blake had read about vortexes in Descartes.

10. René Descartes, "The World; or Essay on Light," in *Descartes, Selections*, ed. Ralph M. Eaton (New York, 1927), p. 330. The theory of vortexes is developed in detail in *Principia philosophiae*, Part III, in Vol. VIII of *Oeuvres de Descartes* (Paris, 1905).

11. See *Mathematical Principles*, "An Historical and Explanatory Appendix," pp. 629–32.

12. *Ibid.*

13. M. H. A. Newman is quoted in Bronowski, p. 212, in a reading of this passage which makes the description that of "solid analogue of the surface of a sphere," which may well be correct, in which case Blake's geometrical imagination is miraculous. Northrop Frye describes passing a vortex as consisting of going through an apex of a cone of existence, which, once passed, takes on the appearance of a globe (*Fearful Symmetry*, p. 350).

14. Frye, p. 168, suggests Young; see also Richard Payne Knight, *An Account of the Remains of the Worship of Priapus* (London, 1786), pp. 20–21; the case for Thomas Taylor is made by George M. Harper, *The Neoplatonism of William Blake* (Chapel Hill, N.C., 1961), pp. 129–33.

15. Marjorie Hope Nicolson, *Mountain Gloom and Mountain Glory* (New York, 1959), pp. 238, 242–45. Miss Nicolson's chapter on "The Burnet Controversy," pp. 225–70, gives an exhaustive but lively account of the matter. Though Burnet's theory appealed to some Newtonians, Newton himself objected to parts of it (Nicolson, p. 235 n).

16. Milton O. Percival, in *William Blake's Circle of Destiny* (New York, 1938), pp. 64–65, 72, 150, 181, has called attention to a possible connection with Burnet, though Percival does not consider Blake to be critical of Burnet.

17. Thomas Burnet, *The Sacred Theory of the Earth* (Carbon-

dale, Ill., 1965), Book II, chap. iv, p. 175. A reprint of the 1690–91 edition.

18. See, for instance, Book II, chap. x, p. 212.

19. Samuel Johnson, *Lives of the English Poets* (London, 1779, 1781), I, 303.

## · BLAKE'S VERBAL TECHNIQUE ·

1. See also, e.g., *A Vision of the Last Judgment:* "As Poetry admits not a Letter that is Insignificant, so Painting admits not a Grain of Sand or a Blade of Grass Insignificant—much less an Insignificant Blur or Mark" (*K* 611).

2. The two principal attempts to date have been the work of Josephine Miles ("The Sublimity of William Blake," in *Eras & Modes in English Poetry* [Berkeley and Los Angeles, 1957], pp. 78–99, and *Renaissance, Eighteenth-Century, and Modern Language in English Poetry: A Tabular View* [Berkeley and Los Angeles, 1960]) and of Alicia Ostriker (*Vision and Verse in William Blake* [Madison and Milwaukee, 1965]).

3. *The Piper and the Bard: A Study of William Blake* (Detroit, 1959), especially chap. iii.

4. We should recall here that among the various implications and manifestations of Urizen's archetypal fall from eternity is his initial utterance of "Words articulate," which precedes all other forms of separation and division (*Ur* 4:4, *K* 223).

5. A further sense of "unknown," then, is "self-known" and of "unprolific" is "self-prolific." Urizen knows only himself and can only reproduce himself, while to the imaginative eye he is unknowable because nonexistent, and sterile because "all-repelling" and "void."

6. The virtually untranslatable imaginative density of the verse here can be illustrated by the first line of chap. i, st. 4: "Dark, revolving in silent activity." It also means: "Silent, revolving in dark activity" and "Dark, silent, in revolving activity" and "Active, in dark, silent revolutions." Yet the activity is, as the next line but one tells us, "unknown and horrible," and we have already been told

that Urizen is a "shadow of horror." The permutations of the adjectives, verbs, and phrasal and clausal constructions create a graphic grammatical conflict that tends to raise the words to the level of characters who play out the ramifications of innocence and experience, imagination and the senses, unity and division in ways parallel to the struggles of the major controlling symbol of the poem, Urizen himself.

7. *The Piper and the Bard*, pp. 76–78.

## · TWO FLOWERS IN THE GARDEN OF EXPERIENCE ·

1. Joseph H. Wicksteed, *Blake's Innocence and Experience* (London, 1928), pp. 149–51.

I wish to thank David V. Erdman, E. J. Rose, and Michael J. Tolley for reading drafts of this essay. While all may continue to disagree with some of my contentions, each has helped to free me from avoidable errors. I am especially grateful to Mr. Tolley for a number of leads and amplifications, several of which I have duly passed on to the reader.

2. I am aware that this interpretation is not self-evident and that it is antithetical to those of Harold Bloom, *Blake's Apocalypse* (Garden City, N.Y., 1963), p. 140, and D. G. Gillham, *Blake's Contrary States* (Cambridge, Eng., 1966), pp. 210–11. The crucial line, number seven, is "Arise from their graves and aspire": any ironic interpretation according to which the second verb is taken to mean "long for (without achieving)" must devise a theory to explain away the resurrection described by the first verb. I do not believe this can be done.

3. Transcribing Blake's punctuation is wearisome and thankless work. The most thorough attempt to do so occurs in *E*. Erdman, p. 25, punctuates ll. 3 and 5 of the former poem and ll. 2 and 3 of the latter differently than I do. It is questionable whether Erdman's normalizations really improve Blake's own pointing. If any attempt is to be made to "correct" Blake's punctuation it should be by substituting a colon for the semicolon at the end of the first line of the

former poem. The tail of Blake's comma is often not prominent and could here be construed as a slip of the pen. Moreover Blake freely employed colons in every other possible place whereas Erdman has converted some of these to semicolons. Wicksteed felt free to retain the original colon but, like Erdman after him, he could not abide Blake's probable medial periods and thus substituted commas within the second and third lines of the latter poem. Some copies seem to indicate a period at the end of "The Lilly," but it is not clear enough to include in this transcription.

4. This view of the poem was first put forward by Thomas Wright, *The Life of William Blake* (Olney, 1929), I, 70. Hazard Adams, *William Blake: A Reading of the Shorter Poems* (Seattle, 1963), pp. 244–45, discusses the poem as an example of the moral dilemmas of Experience. He also conveniently lists other interpretations on p. 323. E. D. Hirsch, *Innocence and Experience: An Introduction to Blake* (New Haven, 1964), pp. 253–55, continues to follow the autobiographical interpretation. This leads him, despite his generally sensible interpretation, to make such a meaningless statement as "the author does satirize himself."

5. S. Foster Damon, *William Blake, His Philosophy and Symbols* (Boston, 1924), p. 281. Stanley Gardner, *Infinity on the Anvil* (Oxford, 1954), p. 111, asserts that roses are always domesticated flowers in Blake. A rose *tree*, in any case, is invariably domesticated and thus contains suggestions of unfreedom. To be sure, in his "rose tree, rose tree" E. E. Cummings, who was much influenced by Blake, could use a rose tree as a symbol of natural joy, but only by envisioning it in relation to bees, which are uninjured by the thorns, rather than to humans who can never be. Yeats's "The Rose Tree," on the other hand, is nothing less than the Tree of Life in the Garden of Ireland, though it has been withered by disspirited words and foreign oppression and can only be rejuvenated by sacrifice. The archetypal image of the rose also includes a thornless variety which is a paradisal symbol in religious contexts. Evidently a naturally thornless species was commonly cultivated in Elizabethan gardens, but in Blake's poem the speaker feels the pricks of his Rose.

6. Textual references for location are to *K*. Manuscript variants that are inessential, as in the case of this poem, are not given, but

Keynes's punctuation, where harmless, is followed. As a matter of course quotations have been checked against *E* and I have sometimes used Erdman's readings (see n. 3).

7. Martin Price, *To the Palace of Wisdom: Studies in Order and Energy from Dryden to Blake* (Garden City, N.Y., 1964), p. 398. Gillham, *Blake's Contrary States*, p. 170, makes a shrewd comment on the interpersonal relationship implied in the poem: "In passing over the [nonpareil] the speaker gives such a smug reason that his wife... would have grounds for jealousy, even if she had no knowledge of the other woman. She would sense that the interest her husband showed in her was a proprietary one. He is not really capable of being attracted to anyone, and so the likelihood of his being impelled to love his wife is as remote as his being impelled into the arms of a mistress."

8. L. 4 may be read in different ways: the fact that Blake elides the *e* in "offerd," l. 1, and "turnd," l. 7, suggests that the fourth line may be more regular as verse than it would be as prose.

And I passed the sweet flower o'er.

This scansion tends to imply a routine rejection, whereas if "passed" is read as a monosyllable the rejection is more vigorous.

9. In general shape this odd bush bears some resemblance to the upside down bush in the text on the sinister first page of the "Preludium" to *Europe* and also to one on *Jerusalem* 78, which will be mentioned again in my final note. That the bush depicted in the Song is indeed the Rose-tree is harder to prove than one might expect. Blake generally did not color the ostensible blossoms but in at least one case, copy O (here reproduced), he colored them green likes the leaves on the first branch. In the Benn facsimile of 1927, said to have been "reproduced from a copy in the British Museum," both the blossoms and the leaves are colored yellow. But exactly which copy was reproduced cannot easily be determined. The pages do not correspond exactly to copies A, B, or T, the only three copies in the British Museum according to the standard guide, Geoffrey Keynes and Edwin Wolf 2nd, *William Blake's Illuminated Books: A Census* (New York, 1953), pp. 50–69. It is interesting that these authorities were also unable to say which copy was reproduced (see p. 69).

10. If the reader were to assign an iconographic significance to this last detail, he might observe that the strong flourish in effect italicizes the possessive "my" (and also points to the despondent Rose lover). This contradicts the meter but heightens the sense. The tail on the *y* of "only," while lighter than the other *y*, also underlines the word in which it occurs.

11. The Blake Trust facsimile of copy Z, the immediate basis for my description, has been carefully collated with the Rosenwald original. The Micro-Methods filmstrip of copy AA has not been so collated with the Fitzwilliam Museum original, though I have also made a thorough study of that copy.

12. In his comment on the design Hirsch confuses the picture and the text, thus conflating what Blake carefully put asunder: "The thorns of the pretty rose tree are graphically associated with self-regard and Urizenic hypocrisy" (*Innocence and Experience*, pp. 254–55). In Blake's picture, on the contrary, Rose doesn't show her thorns, the Rose-tree has no thorns (and sometimes has colored blossoms), and the Tree of Death is blunt if contorted. The only points in sight are the blades of spear grass, which are evidently the Rose lover's gold in copy Z. For a fuller perspective on this picture see the Appendix at the end of this essay, "Regeneration in *The Marriage of Heaven and Hell*."

13. The word "delight" in this poem echoes the final word in "My Pretty Rose Tree." This, in turn, as Mr. Tolley reminds me, recalls "The Clod & the Pebble": the selfish love of the Pebble seeks nothing more than "to bind another to Its delight" and "builds a Hell in Heaven's despite" (*K* 211). This program is enacted by the modest Rose on her lover in spite of his good intentions: she gives her thorns instead of her blossoms (if she still has any) to her devotee, who is in Hell.

14. Damon, *William Blake*, p. 282.

15. William Blake, *Selected Poems*, ed. Stanley Gardner (London, 1962), p. 181. Hirsch, who interprets the poem correctly, nevertheless misunderstands Blake's principle of symbolism. He declares that "Both the Rose and the Sheep have the divine, vital force, but in their external obedience to the Urizenic system they have repressed and perverted it" (*Innocence and Experience*, pp. 256–57). One may, with perfect justification, ask what a "repressed" or "perverted"

rose or sheep might be. These creatures are only significant in that they stand for kinds of men or styles of human action, as explained in "Auguries of Innocence" (*K* 431–34).

16. The source is of no importance to the structure of my argument, but it is of some interest that this is the last line of the penultimate stanza of "September 1, 1939," a stanza which W. H. Auden has suppressed in recent editions of his poems. It was, however, printed in a number of places including *A Little Treasury of Modern Poetry: English and American*, ed. Oscar Williams, rev. ed. (New York, 1950), p. 460.

17. Mr. Tolley calls my attention to clusters of lily imagery in Song of Sol. 2:1–2, 16; 4:5; 6:2–3. In the first of these verses the girl identifies herself as both "the rose of Sharon, and the lily of the valleys." One line of thought suggested by this text is that Blake must have been prompted to discriminate the contradictory implications of this twofold floral identity in his *Songs of Experience*.

18. Gillham, *Blake's Contrary States*, p. 174.

19. There is no excuse for Hirsch's assertion that the poem has no illustration whatever: see *Innocence and Experience*, pp. 254 and 258.

20. Several points in these two paragraphs are maintained with a greater certainty than it is necessary to feel. As is often the case, however, interpretation may be obscured by too much tentativeness. What is required is an awareness that though certain basic premises can only be established with probability, not with certainty, these premises have consequences that follow perforce from them. For example, some copies of the *Songs* are unattractively colored while others are brilliantly executed. But what can be done with this datum? The coloring of inferior copies may be attributed to somebody else, Mrs. Blake being a favorite scapegoat, or one may imagine that Blake himself did the work in haste or when he was uninspired. Probably if one had color photographs of every copy of the *Songs* and had carefully studied the originals he could achieve somewhat greater certainty about these matters than anybody has done to date. But unless many more hard facts, such as might be contained in an account book, are uncovered, some kinds of authoritative pronouncements are going to remain informed guesses. Nevertheless, all authentic copies of the *Songs* I have seen, whether they are

successful works of art or not, seem to me to have been deliberately done. For this reason (and because the argument from accident usually leads to a more revealing portrait of the critic's mind than of the artist's) I pursue a rigorous argument from design.

My interpretation for the posture of the Lilly may seem to have a tenuous basis but some theory seems to be necessitated to account for the fact that the flower is depicted as being so extraordinarily bent over. Undoubtedly there is a compositional factor involved: the Lilly is shown to bend and yet will make it, whereas diagonally across the page, the girl in the Sun-flower stretches but is stuck. The descending sun in the clouds at the right (usually obscured with paint) and worm in the middle picture are also part of this overall pattern of declension on the page. I am not satisfied that such formalistic explanations are ever sufficient, however; Blake always strove to address the intellect, though he employed devices of the imaginative eye to do so.

Finally, the creature I call a worm may also be called a snake, and the difference would be of some significance for complete interpretation. The coloring of this tiny creature seems never to be decisive: in copy Z it is liberally painted with gold, which suggests that it may be imagined as pursuing the work of Providence, but this does not help to define its species. I call it a worm chiefly because of the affinities between this page and "The Sick Rose" and *Thel* where the creature in question is a worm rather than a snake.

21. It must be admitted, however, that no other such catchwords occur in the original designs for *Songs of Experience*. The only analogy is to "A Little Girl Lost."

22. Mr. Tolley recalls the biblical imagery of Isa. 40:6–8 and Ps. 103:15–16.

23. *A Concordance to the Writings of William Blake*, ed. David V. Erdman *et al.*, 2 vols. (Ithaca, N.Y., 1967).

24. Northrop Frye, *Fearful Symmetry* (Princeton, 1947), pp. 433–34.

25. Keynes and Wolf, *William Blake's Illuminated Books*, p. 106. See n. 27.

26. Joseph Wicksteed, [*A Commentary on*] *William Blake's Jerusalem* (London, 1953), pp. 95 and 160. But see Albert S. Roe, "A Drawing of the Last Judgment," *Huntington Library Quarterly*,

XXI (1957), 51, on the depiction of "Seth," who does not resemble either of those in question.

27. David V. Erdman, "Suppressed and Altered Passages in William Blake's *Jerusalem*," *Studies in Bibliography*, XVII (1964), 18–20. The evolution and details of the various states of the plate appear to have been accurately described for the first time in this remarkable work of scholarship. It is difficult to distinguish objective scholarship from interpretation of pictorial images, however, and perhaps one should identify the flower depicted on this page as a lotus, following the lead of George Wingfield Digby, *Symbol and Image in William Blake* (Oxford, 1957), p. 79. Digby himself does not explain that the sacred lotus of India is a water lily, though Blake may have known this fact and conceivably may have also known some Hindu myth that corresponds to other details in his symbolism. In any case, it would be pleasant to discover that Blake's "Lilly of Havilah" anticipated Eliot's lotus in the pool in *Burnt Norton* as an Occidentalization of this Oriental symbol. Indeed, the fact that the lotus is literally mentioned in the sixth line of *The Book of Thel* (K 127) indicates that one should be less tentative about this matter. After I wrote this I was happy to see that S. Foster Damon, *A Blake Dictionary: The Ideas and Symbols of William Blake* (Providence, 1965), *s.v.* "Lilly," also suspects the flower is a lotus.

28. W. D. Paden and Gerhard H. W. Zuther, "Blake's 'Jerusalem', Plate 28: A Further Correction," *Notes and Queries*, XII (1965), 182–83.

29. *A Blake Dictionary, s.v.* "Lilly."

30. Damon, *William Blake*, p. 472; Anthony Blunt, *The Art of William Blake* (New York, 1959), p. 38 and Pls. 50 C and D; Frye, *Fearful Symmetry*, pp. 434, 234, 389; Damon, *A Blake Dictionary*, *s.v.* "Sunflower."

31. Albert S. Roe, *Blake's Illustrations to the Divine Comedy* (Princeton, 1953), pp. 193–96 and Pl. 99.

32. Damon, *William Blake*, p. 470.

33. Keynes and Wolf, p. 91. Robert's drawing is reproduced in Geoffrey Keynes, *Blake Studies* (London, 1949), Pl. 4. One of the Oberon and Titania paintings has been reproduced in W. Moelwyn Merchant, "Blake's Shakespeare," *Apollo: The Magazine of the Arts*,

LXXIX, 320 and Pl. 7. See also the same author's *Shakespeare and the Artist* (London, 1959), p. 82 and Pl. 29a. In this version the woman sleeps on one upright lily that touches another on which the bearded king watches. It is a starry night and in the distant background is a strip of water. Insofar as this scene is related to the episode depicted on Pl. 28 of *Jerusalem*, it is a sequel to it.

In Blake's great unpublished series of water colors for Young's *Night Thoughts, ca.* 1795–97, the symbolism of roses and lilies in the same picture occurs four times: Nos. 26, 51, 67, 203; roses only are shown in Nos. 36, 56, 205, 473. Another version of the motif of embracing lovers (without flowers) appears in No. 512.

34. This is conveniently reproduced in *Blake's Grave: A Prophetic Book*, ed. with a commentary, by S. Foster Damon (Providence, 1963), Pl. XII.

35. The most accessible reproductions of the two best known of these are in *E*, Pl. 2, and Damon, *A Blake Dictionary*, Pl. I. See also the article by Roe mentioned in n. 26.

Since this study is necessarily concerned with Blake's theories of sexual ethics and since a full-fledged debate seems to be shaping up between libertarian and desexualizing schools of Blake interpreters, a brief caveat is in order here. While I myself refer to Blake's de-eroticizing of particular designs as being gestures toward respectability, this may be too simple (or partisan) a way of describing Blake's thinking which lay behind these changes. Some of the current accounts of Blake's ideas about sex, whichever school they may belong to, are clouded by partisanship, anachronism, or imprecision. It may be that there is also an element of misplaced concreteness in some expositions of this "problem." While all Blake's ideas on Love cannot be found neatly set forth and explained on a single page, his final thoughts can probably best be seen in his great illustration for Dante's Paolo and Francesca episode. See Roe, *Blake's Illustrations to the Divine Comedy*, Pls. 10 and 10E, and Roe's clear exposition of the ideas, pp. 63–65. The reader of this paper will also recognize that the lovers in the Divine Sun are in a more refined version of the same posture we began tracing in Pl. 28 of *Jerusalem*, though they are unaccompanied by flowers in their profoundly human encounter.

36. The best reproduction of this page occurs in William Blake,

*Vala, or the Four Zoas,* ed. G. E. Bentley, Jr. (Oxford, 1963), Pl. 124. Bentley, p. 133, describes the plant as being "like a lotus." Many details in the drawing are quite indistinct, but if comparison is made between the petals in the front of this flower and those of the flower on Pl. 53 of *Jerusalem* it is clear that this flower is a hybrid of a lily and a sunflower. Beneath the figure in flames (or spear grass) is what may be an area of water.

This drawing is in turn closely related to the tempera painting "David Spying on Bathsheba at the Bath," which has been most clearly reproduced in Martin Butlin, *William Blake* (London, 1966), Pl. 12. The presence of many huge lilies and roses in this picture makes it especially germane to the concerns of this study.

37. Bloom, *Blake's Apocalypse,* pp. 388–89. But see, e.g., *Jerusalem* 30:40; 69:38 ff (*K* 656, 708).

38. Presumably one reason that the golden net becomes a "scarlet Veil" (*J* 21:50) is that this symbol is partially based on the crimson tapestries and purple net employed by Clytemnestra to trap Agamemnon. It would seem also that Cassandra contributed to the characterization of Jerusalem. See also Damon, *A Blake Dictionary,* *s.v.* "Vala's Veil," and the curious (yellow) scroll-like object covering embracing lovers rising from the water in Pl. X, "Milton's Dream."

39. Damon, *William Blake,* p. 469.

40. Wicksteed, *William Blake's Jerusalem,* pp. 94, 147–48. But in *A Blake Dictionary,* *s.v.* "Lilly," Damon identified the *lily*-crowned figure as Vala.

41. As Damon, *A Blake Dictionary,* *s.v.* "Shiloh," explains, "Although at war, the ideal of both nations [England and France] was really peace, as the names of both Jerusalem and Shiloh signify." The political allegory of this picture, then, would be that these nations are falling out when they should be joined in mutual amity. Another figure crowned with lilies is being swallowed by the sea serpent in "The Spiritual Form of Nelson Guiding Leviathan." This tempera is clearly reproduced in David V. Erdman, *Blake: Prophet Against Empire* (Princeton, 1954), Pl. VIII, and the figure is persuasively identified as Christ and related to France by Erdman, p. 417. The criticisms of Anthony Blunt, *The Art of William Blake* (New York, 1959), pp. 102–3, cannot be sustained except that he

correctly points out that the crown on this figure is not of thorns, as Erdman had originally said. I am indebted to Mr. Rose for suggesting that the crown is in fact made of lilies.

42. The same motif of a parting male and female occurs on Pl. 3 of *Milton*, but the man is among wheat and the woman among grapes. Damon, *William Blake*, p. 429, calls them "the sleeping spiritual forms of the bread and the wine."

43. Wicksteed, *William Blake's Jerusalem*, p. 154.

44. There is a distinctively Blakean satisfaction to be had from recognizing that these spirits who fly together—they seem both to be girls—are counterparts of the divergent and flying girls depicted at the bottom of "The Little Boy lost" in *Songs of Innocence*. Such symmetrical rhythms of closure unify Blake's work as a whole, both in word and in picture.

45. S. Foster Damon, *Blake's "Job": William Blake's "Illustrations of the Book of Job"* (Providence, 1966), p. 48, uses a different but not incompatible vocabulary in discussing this design. He speaks of the "palms of victory" and the "roses and lilies of material and spiritual beauty."

46. The second version (dated 1825) is reproduced in Damon, *A Blake Dictionary*, Pl. II. This version, which is noticeably adorned by lilies, roses, and a lotus, is discussed by Piloo Nanavutty, "A Title-Page in Blake's Illustrated Genesis Manuscript" *Journal of the Warburg and Courtauld Institutes*, X (1947), 114–22, esp. 115–19. The reader who looks this article up will also find a bonus in the next article, which contains pictures of the thornless Mary-rose.

The remarkable confluence of flowers in this page and the extraordinary amalgamation of flowers in the ninety-ninth illustration to Dante may alert the reader to find traces of "My Pretty Rose Tree" on the title page to the fourth chapter of *Jerusalem* (Pl. 78) because of the symmetrical arrangement of the lily on *Jerusalem* 28 and the sunflower on *Jerusalem* 53, the title pages of the two preceding chapters. The tightest connection is the object I called, in n. 9 above, an upside down bush, which somewhat resembles the Rose-tree depicted in the Song of Experience. This object has also been identified as the Polypus but its roots and shorter twigs give it a distinctly vegetative quality. It would follow that the eagle-headed watcher was the former Rose lover who had lifted up his head, abandoned his uxorious bondage to Rose and demoted her vegetable form to a position beneath him, and prepared for the new day that is dawning. The fact that the *setting* sun is depicted (though not colored as such) in "Ah! Sun-Flower," and that the serpentine forms in the *Songs* page easily assimilate with the Rose-tree to result in the problematic object in *Jerusalem* 78, is yet another connection. And the two small birds that fly beneath the second verse paragraph may be returning from the flight described in the first design considered. While these connections are tenuous, they are real, and should assist in arriving at a precise interpretation of Blake's enigmatic page.

## · "THE FLY" ·

1. The present article is indebted to the following studies of the poem: John E. Grant, "Interpreting Blake's 'The Fly,'" *Bulletin of the New York Public Library*, LXVII (November, 1963), 593–615, reprinted in *Blake: A Collection of Critical Essays*, ed. Northrop Frye ("Twentieth Century Views," 1966); Leo Kirschbaum, "Blake's 'The Fly,'" *Essays in Criticism*, XI (April, 1961), 154–62, with an editorial postscript by F. W. Bateson and a reply by John E. Grant (XI, 481–87); and E. D. Hirsch, Jr., *Innocence and Experience: An Introduction to Blake* (New Haven, 1964), pp. 236–41. Although I have benefited greatly from these analyses, it is my disagreement with their basic points of view that has led me to undertake yet another study. I am also indebted to briefer comments in well-known works by Damon, Wicksteed, and Bloom.

2. It is about the character of the speaker that I am in deepest disagreement with Grant, who considers him an actor in a complex drama. Grant finds him artless, callous, perhaps a nominal Christian, unaware of his own paradoxes, of Blake's respect for all life as holy, of prophetic sympathy. Yet apparently we are not supposed to be wholly unsympathetic to him, even though his first principles are erroneous and he is a poor reasoner.

3. I disagree with the emphasis of Hirsch, who makes immortality the theme of the poem: "thought" is primarily a vital principle;

possessing it, man and fly survive death in happiness. I also disagree with Grant's view that "the central idea in Blake's poem is human mortality" (p. 605) shared by man and fly (p. 607).

4. William Cowper, *The Task*, vi, 315–20.

5. Exod. 8:21, 31; Ps. 78:45; Jonathan Swift, *Gulliver's Travels*, Part II, chap. iii; *A Tale of a Tub*, conclusion; Edmund Burke, *Reflections on the Revolution in France*; Hervey, *Theron and Aspasia*, I, 304; James Macpherson, *The Songs of Selma*; Cowper, *The Task*, iii, 133–36; Alexander Pope, *Essay on Man*, i, 194. Cf. Burns, "O Philly": "I care na wealth a single flie," and Gay's sneer even at the butterfly: "And what's a Butterfly? At best He's but a catterpillar, drest" (*Fables*, I, xxiv, 41).

6. This highly Blakean phrase is also used by Boswell—but how differently: "I remain firm . . . in my opinion, that minute particulars are frequently characteristick, and always amusing, when they relate to a distinguished man" (*Life of Johnson*, ed. G. B. Hill and L. F. Powell, I, 33).

7. See E. J. Rose, "The Symbolism of the Opened Center and Poetic Theory in Blake's *Jerusalem*," *Studies in English Literature 1500–1900*, V (Autumn, 1965), 587–606.

8. *Essay on Man*, i, 193.

9. See also the song in *Poetical Sketches*, "Love and harmony combine": "Joys upon our branches sit / Chirping loud, and singing sweet."

10. See the title pages to the *Songs of Innocence, Experience*, and *Innocence and Experience*; "The Little Girl Lost" under "Girl," "The Shepherd" (below the text and above the landscape), and especially "A Little Girl Lost," where there are two flying creatures to the left below "A" and four to the right below "Lost." It is here that the association with "Love! sweet Love!" (l. 4) is the clearest.

11. The engraving appeared in 1793 in the work entitled *For Children: The Gates of Paradise*, with only this one-word inscription, "Alas!" (*E* 32, 722). The inscriptions I have quoted come from the reissue: *For the Sexes: The Gates of Paradise*, which Erdman dates "a good deal later than 1805" but not as late as 1818 (*E* 734).

12. H. J. C. Grierson, *William Blake's Designs for Gray's Poems* (London, 1922), p. 5 for "Ode to Spring."

13. *Ibid.*, p. 4 for Eton ode.

14. British Museum, Department of Prints and Drawings, C. 107. This is one of 537 original water colors, mostly unpublished. This one, however, was engraved for the edition of Young that appeared in 1797. The woman in the design I take to be Clotho, who spins the thread of life. From left to right Blake's four male youths seem to be (1) a curly-headed poet, (2) a musician with a lyre, (3) a boy with a scroll, and (4) a seated boy writing on a tablet. Blake seems to intend his design to represent the death and resurrection of young artists.

15. Blake altered the simple declarative "Thought is Life" to the "If" clause of the final version (*E* 717). I accept the view of Kirschbaum that *if* is an intensive having the force of *since*.

16. A parallel suggested and rejected by Grant, "Interpreting... 'The Fly,'" p. 601.

17. The phrase is Northrop Frye's, who comments that in this period of "pity" and "imaginative animism," there was a "curiously intense awareness of the animal world." Blake's "The Fly" might well be added to Frye's list of examples ("Towards Defining an Age of Sensibility," *Eighteenth Century English Literature: Modern Essays in Criticism*, ed. James L. Clifford [New York, 1959], p. 316).

18. It may give the reader a notion of the range and complexity of meaning that *thought* possessed if we give three additional examples. Rosalind calls Cupid a "wicked bastard of Venus that was begot of thought" (*As You Like It*, IV, i). In *Spectator* 26 Addison associates *thoughtfulness* with the gloom and melancholy of Westminster Abbey. Wordsworth's bent traveler going to see his dying son possesses "thought" (refined sympathy, settled quiet?): his look, figure, and limb "all bespeak / A man who does not move with pain, but moves / With thought..." ("Animal Tranquillity and Decay").

19. See Annotations to Swedenborg's *Divine Love*, E 591–98.

20. Annotations to Bacon's *Essays* 44, E 612; Annotations to Berkeley's *Siris*, E 652–53.

21. Emphasis added in this and the two following quotations.

22. *J* 52:25, and abandoned MS stanzas, E 732.

One could continue annotating the association of thought and sympathy (or forgiveness). It will suffice to bring the fly into this context. Observe that in *Milton* (20:27–28) the "little winged fly" has "a heart" like a man. Observe that at the climax of *Jerusalem* (98:43–45) the fly, along with other small creatures (dove and worm) and with large creatures (lion, tiger, horse, elephant, eagle), is "humanized" in the forgiveness of sins, in the new covenant of mercy. Blake at his apocalyptic climax cannot forget the man-fly equation.

23. British Museum, Department of Prints and Drawings, 1929–7-13-11 (verso) and 1929-7-13-6 (verso). Though the lines on this page are not, as was customary with Blake, marked for illustration, he is evidently illustrating the following: "O lead my Mind, / (A Mind that fain would wander from its Woe,) / Lead it thro' various scenes of *Life* and *Death* ... "

24. Grant finds that this stanza has loose ends because the speaker's principles and reasoning are erroneous ("Interpreting ... 'The Fly,'" p. 603). Hirsch blames the confusion on Blake's disastrous alteration of the penultimate stanza to the "if-then" syllogism (pp. 240–41).

25. E. M. W. Tillyard has said that Blake's *Songs of Innocence* are related to the newly created Evangelical Sunday School (*Poetry Direct and Oblique* [London, 1934], p. 256).

26. Edmund Spenser, *Muiopotmos*, l. 234.

27. Emphasis added.


· A NOTE ON BLAKE'S "UNFETTERED VERSE" ·

1. References to *K* are given for the location of quotations from Blake's works, but Blake's own punctuation—or nonpunctuation—has been retained.


· A TEMPORARY REPORT ON TEXTS OF BLAKE ·

1. Begun in 1957; copyright 1967; actually published March, 1968. See below.

2. I am improvising on the base of the description of the "Printing house in Hell" where Blake "saw the method in which knowledge is transmitted from generation to generation" (*MHH* 15). For such improvisation Blake himself set the precedent. See Postscript below.

3. To correct the first printing (except for its wretched index) a seven-page list of "Errata Emendata" is available upon request. The more important of these *errata* are given in *Blake Newsletter*, No. 3 (15 Dec. 1967), pp. 11–13. By the time of reading proof of the present essay (February, 1969) both a $K^4$ and an $E^3$ have been published, both containing minor revisions, too late for full reference here.

4. The book contains sketches by Blake and by John Varley and a few remarks attributed to the subjects of Blake's portraits, e.g., the Empress Maud and Hotspur; one is identified as "Spiritual communication to Mr Blake"; none is certainly in Blake's own hand and all seem to be Varley's reporting. They are of some interest, and about twenty lines are (on the impulse of the sudden discovery) given in the Supplement to $K^3$ as "notes in Blake's or Varley's hand," but inclusion in the writings of Blake seems a dubious matter.

5. Here is the recipe for making one's own rapid collation. Beside any edition you are examining, open the *Concordance* at Appendix B ("Corrections and Additions to the Keynes Text"). Check through all substantive queries or corrections listed there; compare any other post-*Concordance* editions at these points.

6. Quite recently Morton Paley discovered that a perfectly legible "when" in l. 18 of the Preface to *Europe* is mistakenly printed "where" in all modern editions—a difference that is momentous, in context. (See *Blake Newsletter*, No. 3 [15 Dec. 1967], pp. 16, 18.) But the case is instructive: the very legibility of this plate and the absence of illustrations, and its relative inaccessibility, have exempted it from close scrutiny.

7. Errors in the Nonesuch text that reappeared in $K^1$ but are eliminated from $K^3$ occur in lines $J$ 29[43]:65 ("Luvah" omitted), $J$ 30[44]:18 ("Bending," corrected to "Rending"), $J$ 70:11 ("birth-pang":"birth-pangs"), $J$ 71:55 ("Mountain":"Mountains"), $K$ 716 prose ("an account":"on account"), $J$ 83:69 ("turned":"turn"), $J$ 90:67 (corrected to "thunder ... thunder's cry"). In the final text there remains only $J$ 66:79 ("on" for "upon").

8. Reported in correspondence and, now that one looks for it, visible in some copies.

9. For details about these and other *Jerusalem* revisions, see

Erdman, "The Suppressed and Altered Passages in Blake's *Jerusalem*," *Studies in Bibliography*, XVII (1964), 1–54. The availability of this treatise led me to condense or eliminate the pertinent textual notes in *E*.

10. A curiously similiar typing or printing error shows up, as a student merrily noted, in *E*, where "Heads deprest... hands work-bruis'd" (*Am* 3:10) appears as "Hands deprest" etc.

11. Not considered here are questions of arrangement, for example, of the plates in chap. ii of *Jerusalem* or of the two Nights VII in *The Four Zoas*. In the first example there is no problem of transcription or of emendation; we have two established texts; the editor's difficulty is simply which of Blake's alternative arrangements to choose. In the other example (and a similar puzzle, the question where to begin Night II) we are more nearly involved in emendation, having to choose one arrangement or another, without unambiguous indications of Blake's intentions. One boon to readers, from the existence of several modern editions, is that in each of the instances just cited there are texts that present each of the choices. The alternative arrangements of chap. ii can be studied in the Blake Trust facsimiles of the Rinder and Mellon copies—and in transcription in *E* and *K* respectively (and here *E-S*, the Longmans edition, follows *E*). The two Nights VII can be read in sequence in *K* or *E-S*, while *E* retires VIIb to the pages following the end of the poem to permit a sequential reading of VIIa–VIII. As for Night II, *K* and *E* begin it at the latest point, *E-S* at the earliest.

Smaller problems of arrangement also occur in *The Four Zoas*, e.g., in the placement of marginal additions not clearly marked, and in a few of the lyrics.

12. The discovery is worth—and has produced—an article, "William Blake's *The French Revolution*: A Note on the Text and a Possible Emendation," published in the *Bulletin of the New York Public Library*, LXXII (January, 1968), 3–18.

13. Substantive misprints that one can correct from the facing photographs are (with the line numbers of this edition) "vales" for "dales" in 180, "heavens" for "heaven" in 359—and "were" for "was" in 154 (though this may be intended as an emendation). In l. 333 where *E* gives "began" written over "begun" the reading is simply "begun" without note of palimpsest.

This illustrated edition is of immense value in its gathering and reproducing of nine Tiriel drawings, with the manuscript. But in the transcript and commentary new—and imaginary—textual difficulties are introduced: by the querying of some quite legible readings (e.g., "flatterer" in l. 374, presumably because of the appearance of extra strokes in the word, though these can be accounted for as the tops of the *t* and *b* of the underlapping "tribe"); by the report of *"word illeg"* or *"words illeg"* (ll. 230 and 273) where Blake has merely extended his deleting loops over blank paper; and by omission of Blake's section numbers from the transcript. Failing to sense the narrative cadences of the sections, Bentley assumes (p. 52) that these numbers (Blake's characteristic Arabic 1–8, not "1–7") were "probably" not written by Blake and are only folio numbers on "the rectos of the leaves." Unhappily two of the eight leaves are not numbered on the rectos (one is not numbered at all), while two of the numbers occur on versos; indeed, as Bentley fails to see, leaf seven is numbered on both recto and verso (7–8). The "misnumbering" that he does see puzzles him. Further on (p. 55) he "can suggest no likely explanation" of the fact that several pages "are left partly blank at the bottom, in mid narrative [sic], for no clear reason." The simple explanation of both phenomena is that the eight sections are of unequal length but are begun (and hence numbered) each on a fresh page. The sectioning *is* functional and the numbers, in Blake's hand, belong to the text.

14. In the Notebook prose there are few important corrections still pending for *K*. It should be worth some resetting to make the following transpositions. In *Public Address* (*K* 599) the clause "they Produce System & Monotony" should be moved from the middle of the third paragraph to where it belongs at the end of the first (after "One is an Epigram only & no Grand Work can have them"). The clause "It is the Fashion" should be replaced by "words illegible" (probably two words, but the paper is broken away; the first possibly "visible" or "invisible"). In *A Vision of the Last Judgment* (*K* 613–14) the phrase "& Queens [of England *del*.]" should be removed from the penultimate paragraph of p. 613 and the dots in the first line of p. 614 should be replaced with "Kings & Queens of England." (These words, squeezed sideways in the margin, are easily read with the wrong sentence.)

15. For a recent recovery, by infrared photography, of the complete Klopstock poem on p. 5, see my note in *Blake Newsletter*, No. 4 (15 Mar. 1968), p. 8—or $E^3$ 492, 791.

16. Stevenson, in correspondence; now printed in *Blake Newsletter*, No. 1 (15 June 1967), p. 7.

17. *William Blake's Vala: Blake's Numbered Text*, ed. H. M. Margoliouth (Oxford, 1956).

18. The *Concordance* Appendix designates which readings differ from Bentley. Emendations account for a few further differences in *E*. One is the conflation of pp. 7 and 143, a logical deduction from Bentley's evidence. Another, suggested by Stevenson, is the exclusion from Ahania's speech (Night III, p. 38:15 through p. 42:17) of changes that Blake penciled in the manuscript not, obviously, for revision of the poem itself but in order to adapt the passage for use in *Jerusalem* 43:33-82.

At the time of publication of the Bentley transcript, I prepared a detailed critique for the 1964 volume of *The Library* (XIX, 112-229, finally published June, 1968) called "The Binding (et cetera) of *Vala*." Revisions were admitted in 1966 to bring the readings abreast of the second printing of *E*, but the argument, intended to stir debate on the nature and dating of the manuscript, now looks cold in print.

19. The insertion was deleted, but faintly; in the preparation of *E* it got lost in a limbo of queries; it is now lodged in the textual notes in $E^3$. In *K* the insertion is treated as two lines of verse, but I believe Blake's indenting of the second line indicates he intended one long line, matching in length the revised l. 3.

20. Blake's later more rapturous and extended account of "the strength of [his] Art" in *Four Zoas* VIIa (*K* 331-32:456-99) began at first with an echo of these metaphors of rock and cave: "So . . . Los his hands divine inspired began / To hew the cavernd rocks . . . into forms of beauty"; but he canceled the second line. Compare his dread, in his November, 1802, poem to Butts, of going back to "A dark black Rock & a gloomy Cave" rather than onward with "Silver Angels" and "Golden Demons."

# Plates

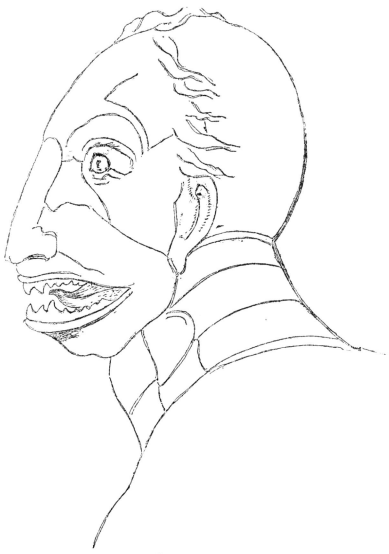

PLATE I. The Ghost of a Flea

PLATE II. Elohim Creating Adam

PLATE III. God Judging Adam

PLATE IV. Pity

PLATE V. The House of Death

12

But rises in demand for her delay;
She makes a scourge of past prosperity
To sting thee more, and double thy distress.
    LORENZO, fortune makes her court to thee;
Thy fond heart dances, while the syren sings:
Dear is thy welfare; think me not unkind,
I would not damp, but to secure thy joys:
Think not that fear is sacred to the storm;
Stand on thy guard against the smiles of fate.
Is heaven tremendous in its frowns? most sure—
And in its favours formidable too:
* Its favours here are trials, not rewards;
A call to duty, not discharge from care;
And should alarm us, full as much as woes;
Awake us to their cause and consequence;
And make us tremble, weigh'd with our desert.
Awe nature's tumults, and chastise her joys,
Lest, while we clasp, we kill them; nay, invert
To worse than simple misery their charms:
Revolted joys, like foes in civil war,
Like bosom friendships to resentment sour'd,
With rage envenom'd rise against our peace.
Beware what earth calls happiness; beware
All joys, but joys that never can expire:
Who builds on less than an immortal base,
Fond as he seems, condemns his joys to death.
    Mine died with thee, PHILANDER! thy last sigh
Dissolved the charm; the disenchanted earth
Lost all her lustre: where her glitt'ring towers?
Her golden mountains where?—all darken'd down

PLATE VI. *Night Thoughts*, Night I, Page 12 (*NT* 26)

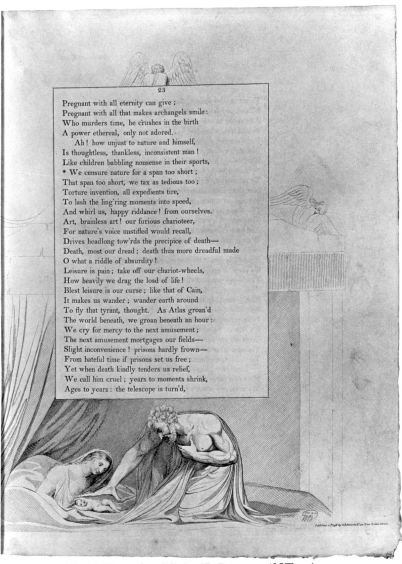

23

Pregnant with all eternity can give ;
Pregnant with all that makes archangels smile :
Who murders time, he crushes in the birth
A power ethereal, only not adored.

    Ah ! how unjust to nature and himself,
Is thoughtless, thankless, inconsistent man !
Like children babbling nonsense in their sports,
\* We censure nature for a span too short ;
That span too short, we tax as tedious too ;
Torture invention, all expedients tire,
To lash the ling'ring moments into speed,
And whirl us, happy riddance ! from ourselves.
Art, brainless art ! our furious charioteer,
For nature's voice unstifled would recall,
Drives headlong tow'rds the precipice of death—
Death, most our dread ; death thus more dreadful made
O what a riddle of absurdity !
Leisure is pain ; take off our chariot-wheels,
How heavily we drag the load of life !
Blest leisure is our curse ; like that of Cain,
It makes us wander ; wander earth around
To fly that tyrant, thought.   As Atlas groan'd
The world beneath, we groan beneath an hour :
We cry for mercy to the next amusement ;
The next amusement mortgages our fields—
Slight inconvenience ! prisons hardly frown—
From hateful time if prisons set us free ;
Yet when death kindly tenders us relief,
We call him cruel ; years to moments shrink,
Ages to years : the telescope is turn'd,

PLATE VII. *Night Thoughts*, Night II, Page 23 (*NT* 44)

( 6 )

Then nearest Thefe, when Others moft Remote ;
And All, ere long, fhall be remote, but Thefe.
How dreadful, *Then*, to meet them all alone,
A Stranger! Unacknowledg'd! Unapprov'd!
*Now* woo them; wed them; bind them to thy breaft;
To win thy Wifh, Creation has no more.
Or if we wifh a *Fourth*, it is a Friend ;
But Friends, how mortal? Dangerous the Defire.

*Alone indeed,* the Banifht from Himfelf,
By Day's Intrufions loud, and rude Affaults,    *20.*
A tide of Tumult, and a Storm of Tongues.
Take *Phœbus* to yourfelves, ye bafking Bards!
Inebriate at fair Fortune's fountain-head ;
And reeling thro' the wildernefs of Joy;
Where *Senfe* runs Savage, broke from *Reafon's* chain,
And fings falfe Peace, till fmother'd by the Pall.
My Fortune is unlike ; unlike, my Song;
Unlike the Deity my Song invokes.
I to *Day's* foft-ey'd Sifter pay my Court,

(*Endy-*

PLATE VIII. *Night Thoughts*, Night III, Page 6 (*NT* 81)

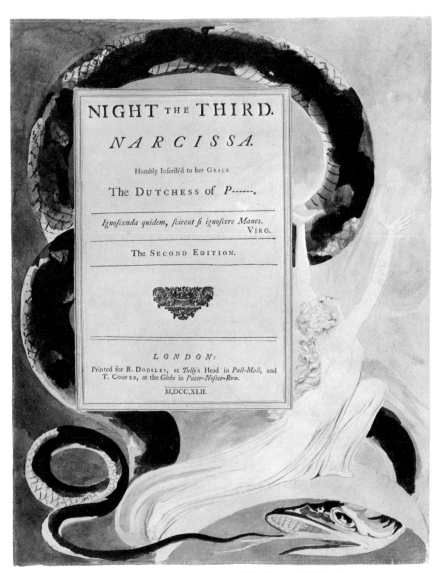

PLATE IX. *Night Thoughts*, Night III, Title Page (*NT* 78)

PLATE X. *Night Thoughts*, Night VIII, Title Page (*NT* 345)

PLATE XI.  The Queen of Heaven in Glory

PLATE XII. The Mission of Virgil

PLATE XIII. Fertilization of Egypt

PLATE XIV. The Angelic Boat Wafting Over the Souls for Purgation

PLATE XV. *Juno Samia Selenitis cum peplo sacro*

PLATE XVI. The Sleep of Albion

PLATE XVII. The Hiding of Moses

PLATE XVIII. The Holy Family in Egypt

PLATE XIX. The Flight into Egypt

PLATE XX. Beatrice Addressing Dante from the Car

Durga Slaying Mahishasura, a Hendoo group.

An Etruscan Patera, in the British Museum.

A Colossal Statue, at Thebes.

Persian Sculpture, at Persepolis.

A Chinese Statue.

Persian Sculpture, at Persepolis.

Blake sculp.

Published as the Act directs, March 1.1816. by Longman,Hurst,Rees,Orme & Brown, Paternoster Row.

PLATE XXI. Sculpture

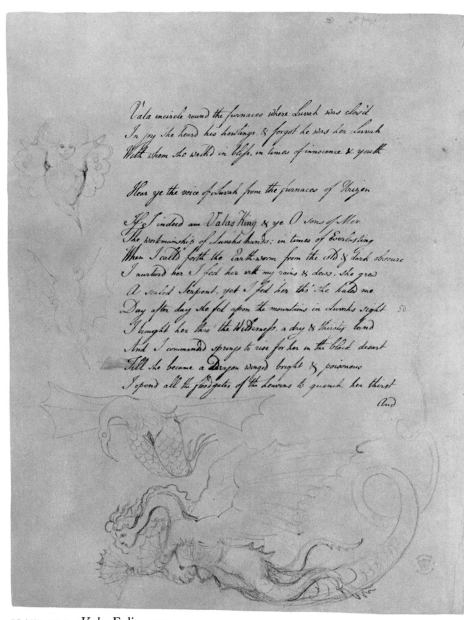

Vala incircle round the furnaces where Luvah was clos'd
In joy she heard his howlings & forgot he was her Luvah
With whom she walkd in bliss, in times of innocence & youth

Hear ye the voice of Luvah from the furnaces of Urizen

If I indeed am Valas King & ye O Sons of Men
The workmanship of Luvahs hands: in times of Everlasting
When I calld forth the Earth-worm from the cold & dark obscure
I nurturd her I fed her with my rains & dews, she grew
A scaled Serpent, yet I fed her tho' she hated me
Day after day she fed upon the mountains in Luvahs sight     50
I brought her thro' the Wilderness, a dry & thirsty land
And I commanded springs to rise for her in the black desart
Till she became a Dragon winged bright & poisonous
I opend all the floodgates of the heavens to quench her thirst

And

PLATE XXII. *Vala*, Folio 13v

**My Pretty ROSE TREE**

A flower was offerd to me;
Such a flower as May never bare.
But I said I've a Pretty Rose-tree.
And I passed the sweet flower oer.

Then I went to my Pretty Rose-tree;
To tend her by day and by night.
But my Rose turnd away with jealousy:
And her thorns were my only delight.

**AH !SUN-FLOWER**

Ah Sun-flower ! weary of time.
Who countest the steps of the Sun:
Seeking after that sweet golden clime
Where the travellers journey is done.

Where the Youth pined away with desire.
And the pale Virgin shrouded in snow:
Arise from their graves and aspire.
Where my Sun-flower wishes to go.

**THE LILLY**

The modest Rose puts forth a thorn:
The humble Sheep. a threatning horn:
While the Lilly white. shall in Love delight,
Nor a thorn nor a threat stain her beauty bright.

PLATE XXIII.

*Songs of Innocence and of Experience*, Plate 43

*Jerusalem*, Plate 28

*Jerusalem*, Plate 28, an Early Proof

PLATE XXIV.

PLATE XXV. *Jerusalem*, Plate 53

PLATE XXVI. *Jerusalem*, Plate 18

# The Argument.

Rintrah roars & shakes his fires in the burdend air;
Hungry clouds swag on the deep

Once meek, and in a perilous path,
The just man kept his course along
The vale of death.
Roses are planted where thorns grow,
And on the barren heath
Sing the honey bees.

Then the perilous path was planted:
And a river, and a spring
On every cliff and tomb;
And on the bleached bones
Red clay brought forth.

Till the villain left the paths of ease,
To walk in perilous paths, and drive
The just man into barren climes.

Now the sneaking serpent walks
In mild humility.
And the just man rages in the wilds
Where lions roam.

Rintrah roars & shakes his fires in the
    burdend air;
Hungry clouds swag on the deep.

PLATE XXVII. *The Marriage of Heaven and Hell*, Plate 2

PLATE XXVIII.

*Songs of Innocence and of Experience*, Plate 40

( 6 )

Thro' this Opaque of *Nature*, and of *Soul*,
This double Night, tranfmit one pitying ray,
To lighten, and to chear: O lead my Mind,
(A Mind that fain would wander from its Woe,)
Lead it thro' various fcenes of *Life* and *Death*,
And from each fcene, the nobleft Truths infpire:
Nor lefs infpire my *Conduct*, than my *Song*;
Teach my beft Reafon, Reafon; my beft Will
Teach Rectitude; and fix my firm Refolve                    50
Wifdom to wed, and pay her long Arrear.
Nor let the vial of thy Vengeance pour'd
On this devoted head, be pour'd in vain.

The Bell ftrikes *One:* We take no note of Time,
But from its Lofs. To give it then a Tongue,
Is wife in man. As if an Angel fpoke,
I feel the folemn Sound. If heard aright,

I₁

PLATE XXIX. *Night Thoughts*, Night I, Page 6

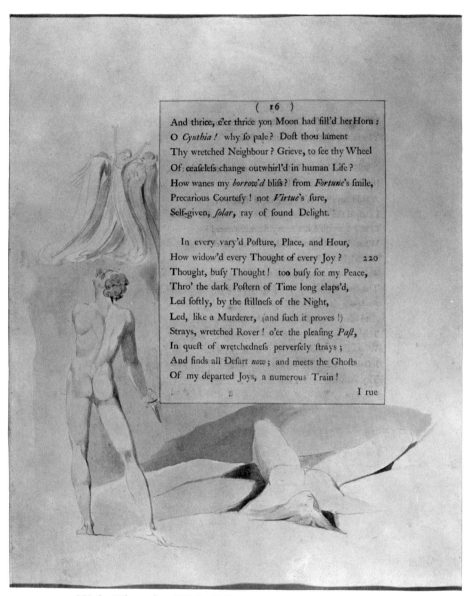

( 16 )

And thrice, e'er thrice yon Moon had fill'd her Horn :
O *Cynthia* ! why so pale ? Dost thou lament
Thy wretched Neighbour ? Grieve, to see thy Wheel
Of ceaseless change outwhirl'd in human Life ?
How wanes my *borrow'd* bliss ? from *Fortune*'s smile,
Precarious Courtesy ! not *Virtue*'s sure,
Self-given, *solar*, ray of sound Delight.

In every vary'd Posture, Place, and Hour,
How widow'd every Thought of every Joy ?        220
Thought, busy Thought ! too busy for my Peace,
Thro' the dark Postern of Time long elaps'd,
Led softly, by the stillness of the Night,
Led, like a Murderer, (and such it proves !)
Strays, wretched Rover ! o'er the pleasing *Past*,
In quest of wretchedness perversely strays ;
And finds all Desart *now* ; and meets the Ghosts
Of my departed Joys, a numerous Train !

I rue

PLATE xxx. *Night Thoughts*, Night I, Page 16

THE

# COMPLAINT:

OR,

## 𝔑𝔦𝔤𝔥𝔱 = 𝔗𝔥𝔬𝔲𝔤𝔥𝔱𝔰

ON

## LIFE, DEATH, & IMMORTALITY.

NIGHT THE FIRST.

HUMBLY INSCRIB'D

To the RIGHT HONOURABLE

## *ARTHUR ONSLOW*, Efq;

SPEAKER of the Houſe of COMMONS.

The SECOND EDITION.

*Sunt lacrymæ rerum, & mentem mortalia tangunt.* VIRG.

*LONDON;*

Printed for R. DODSLEY, at TULLY'S Head in *Pall-Mall.* 1742.

[ Price, One Shilling. ]

PLATE XXXI. *Night Thoughts*, Night I, Title Page